Social Media in Higher Education:

Teaching in Web 2.0

Monica Pătruţ
Vasile Alecsandri University of Bacău, Romania

Bogdan Pătruţ
Vasile Alecsandri University of Bacău, Romania

T0338747

Information Science
REFERENCE

Managing Director:	Lindsay Johnston
Editorial Director:	Joel Gamon
Book Production Manager:	Jennifer Yoder
Publishing Systems Analyst:	Adrienne Freeland
Development Editor:	Myla Merkel
Assistant Acquisitions Editor:	Kayla Wolfe
Typesetter:	Christina Henning
Cover Design:	Jason Mull

Published in the United States of America by
Information Science Reference (an imprint of IGI Global)
701 E. Chocolate Avenue
Hershey PA 17033
Tel: 717-533-8845
Fax: 717-533-8661
E-mail: cust@igi-global.com
Web site: http://www.igi-global.com

Library of Congress Cataloging-in-Publication Data

Social media in higher education : teaching in Web 2.0 / Monica Patrut and Bogdan Patrut, Editors.
     pages cm
 Includes bibliographical references and index.
 Summary: "This book provides research on the pedagogical challenges faced in recent years to improve the understanding of social media in the educational systems"--Provided by publisher.
  ISBN 978-1-4666-2970-7 (hardcover) -- ISBN 978-1-4666-2971-4 (ebook) -- ISBN 978-1-4666-2972-1 (print & perpetual access) 1. Education, Higher--Effect of technological innovations on. 2. Social media. 3. Web-based instruction-- Social aspects. 4. Web 2.0--Social aspects. I. Patrut, Monica, 1972-
  LB2395.7.S635 2013
  378.1'7344678--dc23
                          2012039291

British Cataloguing in Publication Data
A Cataloguing in Publication record for this book is available from the British Library.

All work contributed to this book is new, previously-unpublished material. The views expressed in this book are those of the authors, but not necessarily of the publisher.

Table of Contents

Section 4
Educational and Ethical Issues in Web 2.0 Age

Detailed Table of Contents

Section 1
Teaching 2.0

Chapter 1
Domenico Consoli, University of Urbino, Italy

With the advent of Web 2.0 and with the development of interactive tools that allowed users to express opinions and suggestions on different topics, the way to do business, socialize with other people and also the academic environment, both in terms of teaching and research, is changing. In companies, thanks to interactive tools of Web 2.0, managers are in a close contact with end customers to improve the product/service. In the academic world, this technology can be used exploiting e-learning platforms enriched with interactive virtual channels thus promoting the methodology of learning by doing and the constructivist theory of collective participation of students in the knowledge construction. In this context it is also possible to develop a collaborative research between academics and scientists. The number of websites of the science 2.0, with scientific cooperations and the creation and distribution of quality papers in journals, is growing. Also, the ability to manage complex scientific projects and seek funding sources is increasing. In this chapter, the author analyzes different models of e-learning and designs a University 2.0 framework that supports, by advanced Web 2.0 tools, teaching and research in the university.

Chapter 2
Theodosios Tsiakis, Alexander Technological Educational Institute of Thessaloniki, Greece

Teachers use social media in order to have instant, comfortable and effective way to communicate and transact with students. Online classrooms also are becoming more and more social. So why not use these methods that are already in wide use as a teaching tool? Social media began as an entertainment tool, then became a marketing phenomenon, and now is seen as a new pedagogical tool. The Marketing Information System course aims in offering students (the tomorrow marketers) an in-depth view and understanding of information systems that support an effective way the marketing activities. MIS is the process of connecting people, processes, and technology. The use of ICT has changed the way marketing decisions are made. On the one hand, using information technologies supports achievement of a current marketing strategy while on the other hand these technologies set new marketing rules, and social media is the technology that represents a unique way of transmitting information in all directions. So with one concept (social media), we can achieve multiple benefits. This chapter (1) provides a literature review (overview) of the current use and benefits of Web 2.0 or so-called social media tools in the support of teaching or pedagogical process, (2) offers a systematic way of understanding and conceptualizing online social media as a teaching tool, and (3) suggests the framework in which social media tools can be applied and used in the Marketing Information System (MkIS) course both as part in the course structure and as a mean to teach MkIS.

Chapter 3

Mădălina Manolache, "Transilvania" University of Braşov, Romania
Monica Pătruţ, "Vasile Alecsandri" University of Bacău, Romania

One of the defining traits of our existence as users of the Internet is convergence. This feature is a widespread common good within each level of online participation. Nowadays, we are obliged to perform communicative acts in a more transparent manner than in the Web 1.0. age, and the content itself allows for a higher degree of self-awareness. This is also the case of the learning media. We are offered more intuitive devices which reshape our mindset and forward us towards different mainframes of our innate intelligence, reshaping us into highly educated citizens. Nonetheless, technology is not the only construct with a pervasive character. Gender mainstreaming also claims a front place, either as an explaining factor for policy failures, economic deficits or social fractures. As such, it is our purpose within this chapter to outline the use of new web-based technologies in the new Web 2.0 pedagogical environment, with an emphasis on Web 2.0 teaching strategies in the case of gender studies.

Chapter 4

Swati Jaywant Rao Bute, National Institute of Health and Family Welfare, India

With the advancement of technology, new modes of communication have emerged and are being used in the field of academics. Traditional media played a pivotal role in spreading knowledge in all sections of societies in the world. Traditional media proved to be a powerful tool in the process of making learning and teaching more effective, interesting, and simple to insure everyone benefits to the maximum. Social media are newly-emerged communication networks which are in use not only for sharing information but also for education, knowledge transfer, and for building a global community of academicians. Different tools of social media are in use in different streams of education. Over the years, it has been realized that both traditional and social media have much potential and use in education at all three levels e.g. primary, secondary, and higher education. But, the integration of traditional and social media still has a long way to go in terms of acceptance. This chapter highlights some major points related to changing academic environment, with the use of technology in classes, students vs. teachers' perspectives on learning and teaching, academics, and use of media – Traditional vs. New media in classes and integrating traditional and social media within the academic environment.

Chapter 5

Ioana Boghian, "Vasile Alecsandri" University of Bacău, Romania

Educators have started to turn to social networking sites as they began to recognize the assistance that such sites may provide in information dissemination, creation and cooperation activities, and also in receiving feedback. As promoter of personality, individuality, self-expression, self-assertion, and communication, Facebook responds well to the particularities and requirements of the student-centered approach to teaching and learning. By critically analyzing certain pedagogic approaches to Facebook and by highlighting the common denominator of Facebook and student-centered strategies in terms of didactic benefits, this paper intends to answer the following questions: Can Facebook be regarded and used as an effective and efficient educational tool? If yes, in what way(s)?

Section 2
Student 2.0

Chapter 6

Ilya Levin, Tel Aviv University, Israel
Andrei Kojukhov, Tel Aviv University, Israel

The chapter deals with trends of educational processes and learning environments in post-industrial society. A historicist approach is used for this purpose. This approach is based on two theoretical recourses: analysis of historical forms of acquiring knowledge and analysis of historical forms of educational processes. The authors show that the contemporary educational process is greatly affected by two innovative phenomena: social media and personal identity online (PIO). They consider socialization and personalization as two unique entities having opposite characteristics of the post-industrial educational process. Based on such a dialectic approach to the educational process, they define the concept "Personal Ubiquitous Educational Environment". The authors report the preliminary results of research on a teachers' training course conducted on the basis of such an environment. The research focuses on clarifying both innovative components of contemporary educational processes: social media and PIO.

Chapter 7

Marie-Luise Groß, University of Vienna, Austria

Today's students are tomorrow's knowledge workers. They will be paid to find innovative solutions to organizations' most pressing problems. In times of decreasing training budgets and a dynamic job market, employees have to take over responsibility for their own personal development. Social Media and Social Software both on the WWW and organizations intranets offer a myriad of possibilities to employees and managers to be successful knowledge workers in increasingly virtual organizations and to ensure continuous learning. However, social media also puts new challenges on employees. Particularly young people, who – as the Generation Y'ers – are expected to possess extensive social media skills, need to know how they can use social media in a business context to ensure their personal development and be successful in their jobs. In this chapter, the Personal Knowledge Management model is used to discuss influential factors of successful knowledge work and personal development and to outline what students need to learn to be prepared for Enterprise 2.0.

Chapter 8

This chapter presents the results of EU Kids Online II project about the children's and adolescent's uses of the social network sites. The results showed both the main differences and similarities regarding this issue both at the European and at the country (i.e. Romania) level. Although at the European level one can notice the emergence of different groups of users, in Romania, the use of the Internet is only at the beginning and has no clear pattern. The individual characteristics in the self-efficacy variant positively vary with the using of SNS and, at the same time, none of the negative individual characteristics predicts the possessing of a profile on a social network. The strongest connection exists between having competences regarding the use of the Internet and owning a profile on a social network. Moreover, the results agree with previous researches that highlight a complex influence of the parental mediation on the social behaviors.

Chapter 9

In this chapter it is assumed that students have only limited interest in reading and writing academic texts. After a brief introduction to the problem, the impact of academic reading and writing skills is shown. Furthermore, the authors want to emphasize how these literacies can support students' development, pedagogically speaking, by using action-based projects. The University of Augsburg provides examples for publishing projects in which students can participate. The examples demonstrate the positive effects of students' participation in such projects on the development of media literacies, especially in the areas of text comprehension and writing. Finally, prospects for student-publishing projects at universities are identified as well as the challenges associated with cross-media development, social software and Web 2.0 (Mayrberger, 2012).

Section 3
Tools and Technological Issues in Web 2.0

Chapter 10

As the current focus of education is often on test scores rather than student learning, many public school teachers do not emphasize the development of cross-curricular writing skills in their curriculum. With the inherent pressures of standardized tests and growing class sizes, the burden of assessing writing projects often makes them prohibitive. However, recent research has shown that developing strong cross-curricular writing programs can not only support content knowledge but also raise standardized test scores. Web 2.0 document sharing technology can reduce teacher workload while providing more scaffolding and instruction than traditional writing assignments. Using these programs, instructors can implement collaborative writing projects that will allow students to learn as they write. This chapter uses pedagogical frameworks such as Balanced Literacy, Gradual Release of Responsibility, and Lev Vygotsky's Zone of Proximal Development to support the implementation of cloud software in public schools. It also outlines action research from a middle school classroom using cloud technology and makes practical suggestions for use of free software in secondary curriculum.

Chapter 11

In this chapter, the authors systematically relate to the question: "What are the main ideas that should be considered when elaborating software Systems for the communication's streamlining and diversification (CSD) between the actors of a learning system?" The broader perspective within which these ideas are debated is represented by the context that is created through the inception of what, in the specialized literature, is called social media (as a problematic universe) and Web 2.0 (as a fundamental technological universe). Naturally, the authors will not miss some considerations that highlight the impact of the phenomenon "social media" on the information systems of the near future.

Chapter 12

Twitter as a learning tool offers many possibilities; however, what comes with use of this platform for education purposes is a need for awareness around and establishment of consistent pedagogies that support learning communities, learners, and the educators themselves. This chapter aims to establish what qualitative researchers in this field have found in regards to Twitter as an explicit social networking platform for educational purposes in higher education, including a discussion of literature. Interwoven is a case study of one Australian academic who is using Twitter both as a networked learner and networked teacher in the higher education learning environment. Exploration is shared into Twitter and what it can offer for different levels of engagement for the teacher as a learner who wants to engage with new and innovative ways of accessing information and knowledge. From this stance, Twitter is seen as learning centered on the teacher for the student in teaching courses and workshops in higher education thus learning with and through social media.

Chapter 13

The positive and negative aspects of using Facebook© as a crucial communication tool between Aboriginal academics and their Aboriginal students will be discussed within this chapter. Initially, the authors' use of Facebook © was to provide support for our Australian Aboriginal students within their own communities. The original intention was to supplement existing electronic forums provided by the University to maintain contact with students between study blocks, encourage reluctant technology users to interact online, and build links to the students' own communities and families. In 2009, the authors' students were involved in a research project (Milton, Gruppetta, Vozzo & Mason, 2009) and their use of Facebook © to interact with students was recognised as innovative and the authors were encouraged to investigate the potential within another research project (Vozzo, et al., 2011). From a peripheral practice conducted by two Australian Aboriginal academics, the importance of utilizing Facebook © to build social capital and support an Indigenous Academic community has become crucial to the success and retention of our Aboriginal tertiary students. The authors' most recent research project relies heavily on Facebook © as the main communication tool due to the vast distances between Aboriginal communities in Australia and the variety of technology provided by each state/territory.

Section 4
Educational and Ethical Issues in Web 2.0 Age

Chapter 14

Matthew J. Kruger-Ross, Simon Fraser University, Canada
Tricia M. Farwell, Middle Tennessee State University, USA

This chapter seeks to critically examine and question common assumptions underpinning educators' use and incorporation of technology in the classroom. Drawing upon transformative learning theory, the authors argue that incorporating technology in education cannot and should not be done without first questioning assumptions regarding power, teaching, and assessment. Technology is transforming education in expected ways, but can also transform education in unexpected, unexplored ways. Educators need to move beyond the quick fix of bulleted lists to explore the implications of technology in the classroom more fully.

Chapter 15

David Mathew, Centre for Learning Excellence, University of Bedfordshire, UK

This chapter argues that as educators moving into a Web 2.0 world, we are likely to experience anxiety, which is an important part of the educational process (as it is for our learners). It is also a response to a perception of an older and worn out version of the internet. Anxiety has implications for the design of Web 2.0 educational materials. Web 2.0 is more than a tool for the beginnings of the future of education: it is also, in and of itself, the beginnings of the future of education. Web 2.0 is about learning from the learner, and this chapter asks: What role does the educator play in his/her own developmental learning of the tools of the trade? How does this inform his/her preparations for the learners' experiences? The chapter also argues that in addition to online educational environments owning their own systems of localized logic and systems of internal rules, they are also sentient systems.

Chapter 16

Osman Tolga Arıcak, Fatih University, Turkey
Taşkın Tanrıkulu, Fatih University, Turkey
Sinem Siyahhan, Arizona State University, USA
Hüseyin Kınay, Fatih University, Turkey

Twenty years ago, who would have thought that children as young as twelve would own a cell phone, or people would check their e-mails and Facebook several times in a given day? Things have changed a lot over the last several years. The information and communication technologies made access to information easier and allowed people to communicate with long-distant family and friends instantly. Despite these positive changes, the advances in information and communication technologies also introduced problems that are unique to information age. In this paper, the authors review one of these problems, namely cyberbullying, which affects school age children. Many studies reported significant number of children late elementary through high school experiencing cyberbullying—the use of electronic means to harass others—through cell phones and the Internet. The authors discuss the nature of cyberbullying and why it became a problem among youth. They conclude this chapter with suggestions for parents and future research.

Chapter 17

Ana Adi, Bournemouth University, UK
Christina Gasser Scotte, Lancaster University, UK

With technological innovation and social media infiltrating every field of activity, it was only a matter of time until universities and faculty would need to embrace the technological challenge. This chapter offers three case studies of social media training delivery in universities and researcher centres in the UK, USA, and Bahrain. These case studies cover the use of emerging technologies in higher education research, teaching and policy, and associated first- and second-order barriers to their implementation. Results and impact of the training sessions, including questions asked and feedback provided by participants are also discussed. The chapter emphasizes the increasing interest in training in emerging technologies for educators and affiliated university staff, but also highlights the challenges faced when promoting tools and platforms not supported by either the IT infrastructure of the universities or the policies in place.

Chapter 18

Mar Camacho, Universitat Rovira i Virgili, Spain

Mobility and networking are two important emerging issues that affect educational practices nowadays. Learners and teachers are continuously involved in ubiquitous relationships with other people on the Internet, swapping information and sharing knowledge and skills. However, in the Mobile Learning area, a great deal of emphasis has been placed on mobile technologies and the transfer of content, whereas the potential to support community building processes and collaboration through their integration within social networks has tended to be underemphasized. With the advent of Mobile Learning, a certain growth in its practice and research has been activated by technological innovation and progress. Mobile technologies offer potentiality for the exploitation of contextual learning and have unbound learners and technologies out of the limitation of classrooms at the time that enhance collaborative processes in informal contexts. The emergence of mobile gadgets has democratized the access to technology, changed the concept of user-generated content, and allowed learners and technologies to experiment with technologies outside the classroom, although it has posed challenges to educational stakeholders on how to match the nature of their practice for both life and learning with those traits that educators would like to heighten.

Chapter 19

Georgeta Drulă, University of Bucharest, Romania

It is already a fact that social media are engaged in research activities. Social media may make the object of research studies or an important data source. This chapter addresses issues related to social media research in media and communication studies. The pursued objective is to capture how researchers consider and analyze social media through scientific methods, in their work with academic purposes, in order to present the discussed theories. The ideas addressed by this chapter are case studies arising from the articles in the academic publications, topics related to social media and media and communication fields, outputs of researches, and appropriate methods for studying social media. The conclusions of this chapter show that social media research in media and communication studies, theories, and methods must be transformed or must be used more appropriate to social media. New and social media are faced with other practices and types of communication related to users' participation and social actions and are based on network studies.

Foreword

With the emergence/increased use of social media tools, a large number of higher education institutions are embracing this new ecology of information offered by social media. More and more colleges and universities from all over the world are transitioning from traditional teaching/learning towards *social media teaching/learning*, widening their curriculum landscape beyond technology by integrating different forms of social media, like social networks, microblogs, or cloud computing. However, in this era of fundamental changes in education brought by virtual worlds and augmented reality, dominated by mobile devices and applications, it is necessary to rethink the academic work environments based on social media tools and applications like Facebook, Twitter or YouTube, in accordance with the learning needs, skills, and competencies of students.

Thus, as the title suggests, this book provides a framework in which diverse scholars explore different issues of using social media in education, in general, with a focus on the academic environments, both from the perspectives of educational actors and institutions.

The 19 chapters of the book document the many distinct aspects in which higher education actors perceive and use social media, trying to find out the answers to questions such as:

- How do faculty members use social media like Facebook, Twitter, or document sharing tools as reflective and collaborative teaching and learning tools, also for research and professional development? (See Chapters 5, 10, 12)
- Could social media be a main communication/collaboration/sharing channel in the Aula? Or, regarding power, teaching, and assessment, does it rank low among other online applications? (See Chapters 4, 14)
- Do we know which social media tools/applications are the most used by our students as learning media? Can Twitter or Facebook be regarded and used as effective and efficient educational tools? If yes, in what way(s)? (Chapters 5,12,13)
- Which are the most popular social media tools within teachers' communities? (Chapters 8, 19). And how are they used (with an emphasis on Web 2.0 teaching strategies in the case of gender studies)? (Chapter 3)
- What are the main ideas that should be considered when elaborating software systems for the communication's streamlining and diversification between the actors of a learning system? (Chapter 11)

- Today's students are tomorrow's knowledge workers. More importantly, employees have to take over responsibility for their own personal development. Such as: What skills and competencies are needed for students' future careers, to become highly educated citizens? (Chapters 2,6,7,8,9) What are the trends in the development of cross-curricular writing skills in their curriculum? (Chapter 10)
- It is well known that young people, particularly the Generation Y'ers, are expected to possess extensive social media skills, need to know how they can use social media in a business context to ensure their personal development and be successful in their jobs. Thus: What role does the educator play in his own developmental learning of the tools of the trade? How does this inform his preparations for the learners' experiences? (Chapters 2, 7)
- Which are the potential benefits, challenges, and disadvantages in using social media in universities? Are there special policies? (Chapters 13, 17)
- How can social networks provide access to remote students, in a country with very long distances between rural and urban zones? (Chapter 13)
- Which is the bad and the ugly side of information age? Which is the role of the parental education? (Chapter 16), etc.

The international perspective of 31 contributing authors focues on conceptual and on practical issues as well as, presenting a diverse set of viewpoints on the trends and issues of social media theory, research and practice in HE (like publishing projects in which students can participate from the University of Augsburg or examples that demonstrate the positive effects of students' participation in such projects on the development of media literacies from Romania, Germany, Australia, or Spain).

Social media have evolved from an entertainment tool to a marketing tool, and nowadays they have become a widespread pedagogical tool. The case studies presented in the book cover the use of emerging such technologies in higher education research, teaching, and policy, emphasizing the increasing interest in training, in emerging technologies for educators and affiliated university staff. It is also shown that the contemporary educational process is greatly affected by two innovative phenomena: social media and personal identity online (PIO) (Chapter 6). More importantly, different models of e-learning are analyzed, such as University 2.0 (Chapter 1) - a framework that supports, by advanced Web 2.0 tools, the teaching and the research in the university.

The broader perspective within which these ideas are debated is represented by the context that is created through the inception of what in the specialized literature is called mobile social media (as a problematic universe) and mobile Web 2.0 (as a fundamental technological ubiquitous universe). In Chapter 18, the most relevant theoretical frameworks in the field of Mobile Learning are provided, especially when linked to social learning and the nature of the 21st century learners. An overview is offered of the most outstanding features concerning the pedagogical challenges that social media may imply for the Higher Education stakeholders, and the chapter poses some questions on the challenges that educational institutions have to face.

Although social media redefine the relation between technology and education, using it in academic courses does not represent an easy teaching/training/researching and learning method. It implies a sum of efforts, and especially knowledge of these technologies, with both advantages and limits. As such, in this volume, one can find not only highlights of rigorous and critical theories and paradigms but also best practices and findings of researches, carried out by scholars engaged in teaching with social media in higher education from all over the world. However, the authors herein stressed and underlined just a small landscape/picture of what social media represent for academia.

More importantly, this book can serve as a(n) (in)valuable/reliable pedagogical (re)source for academic actors: students, teachers, researchers, and practitioners.

Gabriela Grosseck
West University of Timisoara, Romania

Gabriela Grosseck *is Associate Professor in the Department of Psychology at the West University of Timisoara, Romania. She received her PhD in 2006 with a thesis on marketing on Internet. She has particular expertise in ICT in education (teaching, learning and researching), a solid experience in students'/teachers' training both f2f and online environments. Her research interests cover main aspects of Web 2.0 tools and technologies in education, collaborative aspects and proper use of social media (by teachers, students, researchers, policy makers and other educational actors). She is also an editor-in-chief of Romanian Journal of Social Informatics, an author of many articles in the field of e-learning 2.0, a speaker at different international events, a workshop organizer and a member of editorial committees (journals and conferences).*

Preface

In today's business world and society, social media continue to play a vital role in the transformation of communication into an interactive dialogue. The success of social media has encouraged the integration of these aspects in higher education teaching practices.

Besides commercial and entertainment applications, the social-media services and technologies have entered nowadays in educational areas as well. In recent years, social media have become *scholar media*, new means by which scholars communicate, collaborate, and teach. There are a lot of research studies that reveal the importance of using social networks, wikis, and virtual communities in teaching and learning.

"Social Media in Higher Education: Teaching in Web 2.0" provides research on the pedagogical challenges faced in recent years in order to improve the understanding of social media in the educational systems. It highlights the role of the social media at different levels:

- Learning centered on student
- Teaching courses and seminars/labs
- Research activity of the academic staff
- Academic management
- Collaboration between students and the academic organizations
- Teams and work groups
- Information systems
- Individuals as actors in the postmodern educational process.

The book "Social Media and the New Academic Environment: Pedagogical Challenges" addresses all those who want to know, to continue and enrich the research on the implications of social media in higher education. Based on the idea that social media radically transform the environment in which university students and professors interact, in the teaching-learning process, but also in the field of scientific research, this book aims at presenting the latest achievements, studies, national practices related to social media use in higher education.

This book provides researchers, teachers, BA and MA students and doctoral candidates, as well as software developers, with working tools and analyses of the impact of the different social media tools upon the nowadays educational environment. Using Web 2.0 technologies, higher education faces unprecedented challenges for teachers and learners.

Are we witnessing today a new academic paradigm? Can we talk about University 2.0? Can Facebook be regarded and used as an effective and efficient educational tool? If yes, in what way(s)? Do social media have real implications in the educational field, or are they just a set of tools meant to entertain the participants? Are there any clear cases of successful use of Twitter in nowadays education? If yes, then what are the results? These are just some of the questions that the authors will answer.

This book is a collection of papers written by a group of researchers, from various parts of the world, belonging to various cultures and educational environments. The general conclusion is that social media can have an impact upon the educational academic environment, and this phenomenon is worthy of further research.

The book is structured into four sections. The first two sections, *Teaching 2.0* and *Student 2.0*, approach pedagogical challenges of social media in higher education. Chapter 1, authored by Domenico Consoli, University of Urbino, Italy deals with the concept of University 2.0. In this chapter, Consoli analyzes different models of e-learning and he designs a University 2.0 framework that supports, by advanced Web 2.0 tools, the teaching and the research in the university. In the second chapter, Theodosios Tsiakis (Thessaloniki, Greece) provides an overview of the current use and benefits of Web 2.0 in the support of teaching or pedagogical process. Also, this chapter offers a systematic way of understanding and conceptualizing online social media as a teaching tool and it suggests the framework in which social media tools can be applied and used in the Marketing Information System course.

Chapter 3, written by Mădălina Manolache and Monica Pătruț (Bacău, Romania) deals with the use of new web-based technologies in strategies of teaching gender studies. Nowadays the Internet users are obliged to perform communicative acts in a more transparent manner than in the Web 1.0. age, and the content itself allows for a higher degree of self-awareness. This is also the case of the learning media. Also, technology is not the only construct with a pervasive character. Gender mainstreaming also claims a front place, either as an explaining factor for policy failures, economic deficits or social fractures. It is the purpose within this chapter to outline the use of new web-based technologies in the new pedagogical environment, with an emphasis on Web 2.0. teaching strategies in the case of gender studies.

Swati Jaywant Rao Bute (New Delhi, India) presents in Chapter 4 the issues of integrating social media and traditional media within the academic environment. This chapter highlights some major points related to changing academic environment with the use of technology in classes, students vs. teachers' perspectives on learning and teaching, academics and use of media – Traditional vs. New media in classes and integrating traditional and social media within the academic environment.

In Chapter 5, "Using Facebook in Teaching," Ioana Boghian (Romania) claims that Facebook responds well to the particularities and requirements of the student-centered approach to teaching and learning, because Facebook promotes the personality, individuality, self-expression, self-assertion, and communication of the student.

Chapter 6 (Ilya Levin and Andrei Kojukhov, School of Education, Tel Aviv University, Israel) uses a historicist approach in order to present the trends of educational processes and learning environments in post-industrial society. The authors analyze the historical forms of acquiring knowledge and the historical forms of educational processes. The contemporary educational process is greatly affected by two innovative phenomena: social media and personal identity online (PIO). The authors consider socialization and personalization as two unique entities having opposite characteristics of the post-industrial educational process. They introduce the concept of "Personal Ubiquitous Educational Environment" and present the preliminary results of research on a teachers' training course conducted on the basis of such an environment.

Chapter 7 is written by Marie-Luise Groß from the University of Vienna. Social software offers a lot of possibilities to employees and managers to be successful knowledge workers in increasingly virtual organizations and to ensure continuous learning. In this chapter, the Personal Knowledge Management model is used to discuss influential factors of successful knowledge work and personal development and to outline what students need to learn to be prepared for Enterprise 2.0.

Chapter 8 (Anca Velicu and Valentina Marinescu, researchers from Bucharest) presents the results of EU Kids Online II project about the children's and adolescent's uses of the social network sites. The results showed both the main differences and similarities regarding this issue both at the European and at the country (i.e. Romania) level.

In Chapter 9 (authored by Sandra Hofhues, Hamburg University of Applied Sciences, Germany and Anna Heudorfer, University of Augsburg, Germany) it is assumed that students have only limited interest in reading and writing academic texts. After a brief introduction to the problem, the impact of academic reading and writing skills will be shown. Furthermore, the authors want to emphasize how these literacies can support students' development, pedagogically speaking, by using action-based projects. The examples from the University of Augsburg demonstrate the positive effects of students' participation in publishing projects on the development of media literacies, especially in the areas of text comprehension and writing.

The third Section, *Tools and Technological Issues in Web 2.0,* presents some technological and philosophical issues of Web 2.0, and also examples of using social media "tools" (like Facebook or Twitter) in education.

Chapter 10 (Katherine Landau Wright, Texas A&M University, United States) uses pedagogical frameworks such as Balanced Literacy, Gradual Release of Responsibility, and Lev Vygotsky's Zone of Proximal Development to support the implementation of cloud software in public schools.

Chapter 11 (authored by Dorin Bocu & Răzvan Bocu, Transilvania University of Brasov, Romania), and Bogdan Pătruț, "Vasile Alecsandri" University of Bacău, Romania) presents the role of the web technologies in connection with the communication's streamlining and diversification between the actors of a learning system. In this chapter, the authors systematically relate to the question: "What are the main ideas that should be considered when elaborating software systems for the communication's streamlining and diversification among the actors of a learning system?" The broader perspective within which these ideas are debated is represented by the context that is created through the inception of social media and Web 2.0. There are some considerations that highlight the impact of the phenomenon "social media" on the information systems of the near future.

Chapter 12 (Narelle Lemon, RMIT University, Melbourne, Australia) deals with aims to establish what qualitative researchers have found in regards to Twitter as an explicit social networking platform for educational purposes in higher education. Twitter is seen as learning centered on the teacher for the student in teaching courses and workshops in higher education thus learning with and through social media.

Chapter 13 is authored by Maree Gruppetta (University of Newcastle, Australia) and Terry Mason (University of Western Sydney, Australia). The chapter discusses the positive and negative aspects of using Facebook as a crucial communication tool between Aboriginal academics and their Aboriginal students will be discussed. This chapter reports on continuing developments in the use of Facebook as the most effective communication tool between Australian Aboriginal academics and their Australian Aboriginal tertiary students within the Bachelor of Education Course at the University of Western Sydney in Australia. Most of Australia is sparsely populated, arid and very poorly serviced compared to the few large and coastal population centres. This poses immense challenge in maintaining a strong relationship between academics and students.

The fourth section deals with some special educational and ethical issues in the Web 2.0 Age. The focus of Chapter 14 is the use of subversive technologies in education. Matthew J. Kruger-Ross, from Simon Fraser University, Canada, and Tricia M. Farwell, from Middle Tennessee State University, USA, critically examine and question common assumptions underpinning educators' use and incorporation of technology in the classroom. Drawing upon transformative learning theory, the authors argue that incorporating technology in education cannot and should not be done without first questioning assumptions regarding power, teaching and assessment. Technology is transforming education in expected ways, but can also transform education in unexpected, unexplored ways.

Chapter 15 (David Mathew, researcher from United Kingdom), focusing on online anxiety, is a provocative one. The author argues that as educators moving into a Web 2.0 world, we are likely to experience anxiety, which is an important part of the educational process (as it is for our learners). Anxiety has implications for the design of Web 2.0 educational materials. Web 2.0 is about learning from the learner, and this chapter asks: What role does the educator play in his own developmental learning of the tools of the trade? How does this inform his preparations for the learners' experiences? The chapter also agrues that every learner who becomes enabled and empowered by a contiguous existence in an online milieu might evolve into a learner who develops anti-social tendencies in the very same environment.

Twenty years ago, who would have thought that children as young as twelve would own a cell phone, or people would check their e-mails and Facebook several times in a given day? Despite the positive changes, the advances in information and communication technologies also introduced problems that are unique to information age, like the cyberbullying, that affects school age children. Many studies reported significant number of children late elementary through high school experiencing cyberbullying—the use of electronic means to harass others—through cell phones and the Internet. The authors of Chapter 16 discuss the nature of cyberbullying and why it became a problem among youth. This chapter is authored by Osman Tolga Arıcak, Taşkın Tanrıkulu, and Hüseyin Kınay (Fatih University, Turkey) and Sinem Siyahhan (Arizona State University, USA).

In Chapter 17, Ana Adi and Christina Gasser Scotte (Bournemouth and Lancaster Universities, UK) offer three case studies of social media training delivery in universities and researcher centres in the UK & USA, Bahrain, and Scotland. These case studies cover the use of emerging technologies in higher education research, teaching and policy, and associated first- and second-order barriers to their implementation. Results and impact of the training sessions, including questions asked and feedback provided by participants are also discussed. The chapter emphasizes the increasing interest in training in emerging technologies for educators and affiliated university staff, but also highlights the challenges faced when promoting tools and platforms not supported by either the IT infrastructure of the universities or the policies in place.

Mobility and networking are two important emerging issues that affect educational practices nowadays. The aim of Chapter 18 (Mar Camacho, Universitat Rovira i Virgili, Spain) is to provide a revision through the most relevant theoretical frameworks in the field of Mobile Learning. An overview is offered of the most outstanding features concerning the pedagogical challenges that it may suppose for Higher Education stakeholders, and poses some questions on the challenges that educational institutions have to face, especially concerning the blurring between formal and informal learning.

Chapter 19, "Media and Communication Research facing Social Media," is authored by Georgeta Drulă, from the University of Bucharest, Romania. This chapter addresses issues related to social media research in media and communication studies. The conclusions of this chapter show that social media research in media and communication studies, theories and methods must be transformed or must be applied more appropriately to social media.

For a more comprehensive image about the changes brought by social media in education, we recommend to read this book together with our previously edited book (co-edited by Camelia Cmeciu), "Social Media and the New Academic Environment: Pedagogical Challenges," also published by IGI Global.

Monica Pătruţ
"Vasile Alecsandri" University of Bacău, Romania

Bogdan Pătruţ
"Vasile Alecsandri" University of Bacău, Romania

September, 16, 2012

Acknowledgment

We wish to personally thank the all authors of this book and, also, the following people for their contributions in reviewing the chapters and other help in creating this book:

Albert Sánchez (Polytechnic University of Catalonia, Barcelona, Spain)

Almudena González del Valle Brena (Bureau Veritas Business School, Spain)

Andrei Gaitanaru (National School of Political Studies and Public Administration, Bucharest, Romania)

Angelica Hobjila ("Alexandru Ioan Cuza" University of Iasi, Romania)

Anita Grigoriu ("Spiru Haret" University, Bucharest, Romania)

Anita Howarth (Kingston University London, United Kingdom)

Antonella Esposito (University of Milan, Italy)

Aránzazu Román San Miguel (University of Seville, Spain)

Aurora-Adina Ignat ("Ştefan cel Mare" University of Suceava, Romania)

Aykut Arikan (Yeditepe University, Istanbul, Turkey)

Bianca Marina Mitu (University of Westminster, London & University of Bucharest)

Bogdan Nadolu (West University of Timisoara, Romania)

Camelia Cmeciu (Danubius University of Galaţi, Romania)

Can Bilgili (Yeditepe University, Istanbul, Turkey)

Carmen Holotescu (Politehnica University of Timisoara/Timsoft, Romania)

Charlotte Holland (Dublin City University, Ireland)

Christina Gasser Scotte (University of Wyoming, USA)

Cosmin Herman (Moodle Romania)

David Fonseca (Ramon Llull University, Barcelona, Spain)

Derek E. Baird (Disney Interactive, Palo Alto, CA, United States of America)

Elizabeth Shaffer (The University of British Columbia, Vancouver, Canada)

Ernest Redondo (Polytechnic University of Catalonia, Barcelona, Spain)

Ersin Erkan (Yeditepe University, Istanbul, Turkey)

Francesc Pumarola (Expert in Internet issues, Spain)

Gabriela Grosseck (West University of Timisoara, Romania)

Gabriela Oana Olaru (Yeditepe University, Turkey)

Gemma Martínez Fernández (The University of the Basque Country, Spain)

Hanna Vuojärvi (University of Lapland, Finland)

Hüseyin Kınay (Fatih University, Turkey)

Ioan Hosu (Babeş-Bolyai University of Cluj-Napoca, Romania)

Ioan-Lucian Popa ("Vasile Alecsandri" University of Bacau, Romania)

Isidro Navarro (Polytechnic University of Catalonia, Barcelona, Spain)

Iulian Furdu ("Vasile Alecsandri" University of Bacau, Romania)

Laura Păuleţ-Crainiceanu ("Alexandru Ion Cuza" University of Iaşi, Romania)

Laurenţiu Şoitu ("Alexandru Ioan Cuza" University of Iaşi, Romania)

Liliana Mata ("Vasile Alecsandri" University of Bacau, Romania)

Lori B. Holcomb (North Carolina State University, United States of America)

Luciana Duranti (University of British Columbia, Canada)

Manuela Epure (Spiru Haret University, Bucharest, Romania)

Maria Lazăr ("Alexandru Ioan Cuza" University of Iasi, Romania)

María-Jesús Díaz-González (University of A-Coruña, Spain)

Marin Vlada (University of Bucharest, Romania)

Martin Ebner (Graz University of Technology, Austria)

Mercedes Fisher (Milwaukee Area Technical College, United States of America)

Mihai Deac (Babeş-Bolyai University of Cluj-Napoca, Romania)

Miikka Eriksson (University of Lapland, Finland)

Miriam Judge (Dublin City University, Ireland)

Mohd Sobhi Ishak (University Utara, Malaysia)

Myla Merkel (IGI Global Publisher, USA)

Nadia Florea (Spiru Haret University, Bucharest, Romania)

Natalia Quintas Froufe (University of A-Coruña, Spain)

Nicoleta Laura Popa ("Alexandru Ioan Cuza" University of Iasi, Romania)

Norsiah Abdul Hamid (University Utara, Malaysia)

Olena Goroshko (The National Technical University: Kharkiv Polytechnic Institute, Ukraine)

Otilia Clipa ("Ştefan cel Mare" University of Suceava, Romania)

Parvaneh Khosravizadeh (Sharif University of Technology, Tehran, Iran)

Pauliina Tuomi (Tampere University of Technology, Finland)

Pavel Zemliansky (University of Central Florida, United States of America)

Raluca Moise (University of Bucharest, Romania)

Rick Kenney (Florida Gulf Coast University, USA)

Rocío Alcántara López (University of Seville, Spain)

Ruxandra Vasilescu (Spiru Haret University, Bucharest, Romania)

Sara Konnerth (Lucian Blaga University of Sibiu, Romania)

Scott Talan (American University, Washington D.C., USA)

Sinem Siyahhan (Arizona State University, United States)

Sónia Pedro Sebastião (Technical University of Lisbon, Portugal)

Taşkın Tanrıkulu (Fatih University, Turkey)

Terry Mason (University of Western Sydney, Australia)

Theresa Renee White (California State University, Northridge, CA, United States of America)

Timea Kabai ("Ioan Slavici" National College, Satu Mare, Romania)

Ufuk Ozgul (Yeditepe University, Istanbul, Turkey)

Violeta Maria Şerbu (The Bucharest Academy of Economic Studies, Romania)

Vladimir-Aurelian Enăchescu (Academy of Economic Studies, Bucharest, Romania)

Section 1
Teaching 2.0

Chapter 1
The Implementation of a University 2.0 Model

Domenico Consoli
University of Urbino, Italy

ABSTRACT

With the advent of Web 2.0 and with the development of interactive tools that allowed users to express opinions and suggestions on different topics, the way to do business, socialize with other people and also the academic environment, both in terms of teaching and research, is changing. In companies, thanks to interactive tools of Web 2.0, managers are in a close contact with end customers to improve the product/ service. In the academic world, this technology can be used exploiting e-learning platforms enriched with interactive virtual channels thus promoting the methodology of learning by doing and the constructivist theory of collective participation of students in the knowledge construction. In this context it is also possible to develop a collaborative research between academics and scientists. The number of websites of the science 2.0, with scientific cooperations and the creation and distribution of quality papers in journals, is growing. Also, the ability to manage complex scientific projects and seek funding sources is increasing. In this chapter, the author analyzes different models of e-learning and designs a University 2.0 framework that supports, by advanced Web 2.0 tools, teaching and research in the university.

INTRODUCTION

Nowadays, we live in a globalized world where, thanks to new technologies, the distances are reduced and contents on a specific topic are transmitted very fast on the network from one country to another one. In Internet, everyone, by web 2.0 tools and social media, at low cost, can participate in the production of contents: text, image, audio and video.

The web technologies, supporting the interactive exchange of information, are revolutionizing the teaching and the research. The electronic learning is changed from the first distance modality

DOI: 10.4018/978-1-4666-2970-7.ch001

(video recording, CD, DVD) until the e-learning (web technology) and the e-learning 2.0 that uses web 2.0 channels.

Exploiting web 2.0 tools it is possible to design a new framework for stimulating the participation and the collaboration in the academic world. So it is possible to experiment a model of University 2.0 where teachers, scientists and students can collaborate for a fruitful work.

The University 2.0 model, supported by social media and web 2.0 tools, finds a large contribute in young students that use these tools in the private life. Young people are born with a technological culture that supports them in the use of new mobile phones or digital devices. They, always, are involved in a participation and discussion on specific topics in virtual communities (VC) and social networks (SN).

In the chapter, we analyze the evolution of the e-elearning platform and we design an original framework for the implementation of a University 2.0 model. At the end, best practices of university 2.0, benefits and limits are discussed.

BACKGROUND

In recent years, web 2.0 tools (chat, blog, forum, wiki and social network) (O'Reilly, 2005, 2007) are developing. By these tools, enterprises interact with all stakeholders (customers, suppliers, sponsors, partners), listening opinions and suggestions to improve the product/service. For an enterprise, customer's opinions are very important both for the improvement of products and also for the reinforcement of the customer loyalty. The customer will be motivated to be loyal if the enterprise shows a strong attention to his/her needs and identity.

A new way of doing business (McAfee, 2006), a participative business where the companies and customers work together (co-operate, co-create, co-produce,...) (Tapscott and Williams, 2006) to improve the final product/service, is affirming.

Therefore we can say that the web 2.0 is invading all areas of our life: work, business, school, university, leisure and holidays.

In the web 2.0, which supports a network of people, we can take in consideration two aspects: technological and social. The technological aspect concerns the hardware and software architecture (computer, network, applications) while the social aspect is relative to people that interact and exchange information. The technology surely is the trigger but the people are the real core of this evolution. Every day, people exchange and share experiences, opinions, photos and video.

The key features of the web 2.0 are: sharing, cooperation, collaboration and interactivity. A collaboration between companies, people, students, teacher and so on, in a context of co-creation and co-production, encourages the realization of the figure of the prosumer (producer and consumer at the same time) (Toffler, 1980). The consumer is becoming a co-creator of value (Witel et al., 2011) while in the past he/she was a passive responder to the market supply.

The Web 2.0 also leads to a revolution in the content generation. Until few years ago, users read only, in a passive manner, information from websites but now they have the opportunity to actively insert information, graphics and multimedia objects. The user can create contents, movies, express opinions and give advices using different web 2.0 tools: digital video, blogs, podcasts, wikis, Flickr, YouTube, Facebook, Wikipedia. He/she becomes User-Generated Content (Strobbe et al., 2010) or Consumer Generated Content (Sumi, 2008). In the web, the contents' production is no longer the prerogative of media centers, press and traditional producers but everyone, by web 2.0 tools, can participate in the discussion and produce interesting contents.

In the era of Web 2.0 there is no clear boundary between who produce and who consume contents; everything is indefinite; "everything is miscellaneous" (Weinberger, 2007).

To emphasize the role of users Grossman (2006) in Time magazine affirmed "Person of the year are you: For seizing the reins of the global media, for founding and framing the new digital democracy, for working for nothing and beating the pros at their own game".

A collaborative model can be easily implemented in the university context in both research (science 2.0) and education activities (teaching 2.0). A learning by doing (step by step) and the logic of constructivism are based on the exchange of information, participation and collaboration in the knowledge building.

Nowadays, every person can learn in different contexts: formal (school, university, professional training), non-formal (workplaces, associations, clubs), informal (personal life) and incidental/experimental learning (Baylor, 2001). For a best training it is important to join all type of educational platforms and learn everywhere at everytime.

The training can be done in presence, online (e-learning) or in blended modality alternating online and in-presence lessons. In recent years the methodology of e-learning by digital tools and mainly by web 2.0 tools, is increasingly adopted. The true value of e-learning emerges in supporting synchronous and asynchronous modalities of interaction, sharing and collaboration among members of the virtual community.

The e-learning concept, over time, was expressed by different terms: online learning, online education (Harasim, 1990), computer mediated distance learning (Paloff and Pratt, 1999, 2001, 2003, 2005), web-based learning or web-based training (WBT) (Kruse and Keil, 1999; Oakes, 2002), distributed learning (Resnick, 1996), computer-assisted learning, on-line resource-based learning (ORBL), networked collaborative learning (NCL), computer-supported collaborative learning (CSCL) (Ally, 2004; Khan, 2004).

Europe, since 2000, has heavily invested in e-learning from the Lisbon European Council (2000) on the knowledge-based economy more competitive and dynamic.

In 2010 the European Commission has shown the guidelines for an Europe 2020 describing the strategy for a smart, sustainable and inclusive growth. The Community Action Programme in Lifelong Learning (Lifelong Learning Programme 2007-2013) (European Commission, 2011) has dedicated a specific action for an education and training opportunities for all. Europe has always shown attention to learn policies in schools and universities and still now in spreading the Web 2.0. By web 2.0 tools it is possible to create and disseminate, in a global context, new and useful knowledge collaborating, cooperating and sharing information.

E-LEARNING 2.0

Learning in a Context of Web 2.0

The Web 2.0 technology has encouraged the evolution of e-learning towards a platform 2.0 more participative and interactive. The e-learning 2.0 (Downes, 2005; Bryan, 2006) improved the integration between formal and informal learning thanks to social software (Shirky, 2003) which facilitates and develops the interactive and collaborative aspect of a digital platform.

The learning 1.0 was highly structured, formal, based on a rigid division of the roles among teachers, students and tutors while in the e-learning 2.0, the web becomes a means that increases the participation and co-operation of all subjects. In this context contents and learning objects can be created, shared, remixed and re-proposed.

In the Figure 1 the impacts of web 2.0 in a learning context are represented.

Figure 1. Impact of web 2.0 tools in a learning context (Source: own)

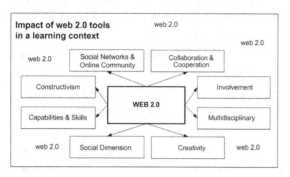

The Web 2.0 improves the communication skills, the creativity of individuals and everyone has the possibility to create web contents, also multidisciplinary, to share with other subjects who interacting among themselves can build new knowledge (constructivism theory) (Jonassen, 1999). Now, it is possible to write in a web platform without skills in programming languages; all people are able to create a blog, a video and a virtual community.

Social networks like Facebook and MySpace allow users to create their own web pages, with a personal profile describing their interests, photos, blogs and a set of other functions that help members to connect in a virtual world. In any workspace, employees, teachers, students can build communities of practice to stay in touch and exchange ideas, documents, audio, video and other materials.

The use of digital technologies, for a network learning, modifies the paradigm of the distance education of the older generation: at the center there is the person who learns and not the training course.

The advent of e-learning and the diffusion of web 2.0 have made the network more interactive and dynamic, replacing the first generation of models and completely revolutionizing models, methodologies and traditional tools of the teaching.

The Web 2.0, participatory and collaborative, can integrate formal, non-formal and informal learning paths eliminating the lines of demarca-tion. Individual participants can choose flexible learning solutions and share a new knowledge using a social software.

The social software (Shirky, 2003) has marked the transition from the model of a typical online community of practice to a horizontal open collaborative group with a great sense of community (Wenger, 1998). The production of new knowledge (Scardamalia and Bereiter, 1992) is a collaborative activity involving all participants who individually are responsible for their learning objectives. The ideas, practices and conventions are developed and shared among the community members.

The main threads are based on participation, growth, communication, co-construction and sharing of knowledge. The model of the collaborative learning, of the last generation, allows the growth of a person within a group that share objectives: it is possible to learn together and the individual learning is the result of a collective process.

The Personal Learning Environment

Over the years, the e-learning system has evolved from a Virtual Learning Environment (VLE) (Piccoli, Ahmad and Ives, 2001; Molka et al., 2009; Burnett, 2011) to the emergent paradigm of Personal Learning Environment (PLE) (Valtonen, 2012; Green, Nacheva-Skopalik and Pearson, 2008; Syvänen, Muukkonen and Sihvonen, 2009).

Personal Learning Environment is centered on the person and integrates formal and informal learning while a VLE or a Learning Management Systems was centered on the specific course.

A comparison between the two systems is represented in Table 1.

The PLE platform supports a learning methodology 2.0, where the role of teachers changes. The teacher becomes an e-tutor, facilitator, a skilled specialist who executes the following functions:

- Moderator of the practice community
- Facilitator of learning processes
- Team-leader of the working group

Table 1. PLE vs VLE

Virtual Learning Environment (VLE) (Traditional paradigm 1.0)	Personal Learning Environment (PLE) (Emergent paradigm 2.0)
• focus on the course • (access control, roles, asymmetry) • student community • separation between the study and other objectives • focus on standards • closed contents, learning objects • technologies that support the learning process	• focus on the person or student • (autonomy, symmetry) • open community (students, friends) • integration of different stages of the life • focus on connectors (mashup services) • open contents • flexible technologies adapting to people needs

- Content Expert (Galliani and De Waal, 2005)
- Cognitive, emotional and technological scaffolding

The creation of media or applications, student-centered, in a sharing and collaborative context (Godwin-Jones, 2006) is important for the learning in an individual or group modality.

Using a PLE platform students gain collaborative and creative skills. They develop practices, critical and conscious thinkings (Bruns and Humphreys, 2005) and are able to transfer the acquired knowledge (Ferdig et al., 2004).

The Pedagogic Aspect of the E-Learning Platform

Technologies are still considered as the enabling factor but, at the base, it is necessary to take in consideration a strategic teaching plan, practice-oriented, that has theoretical foundations in the educational pragmatism of John Dewey (1986) and in the constructivism (Jonassen, 1999). In fact the e-learning methodology relies on constructivist learning theory (Vygotsky, 1978; Chapman, 1988; Bruner, 1991; Resnick 1996; Jonassen, 1999).

In the constructivism theory, the knowledge is built step by step and by doing. Constructivists believe that in learning process the learner takes

a central role while the designer/teacher assumes a marginal role, as a facilitator of the completion of this process. Basing on this approach, the designer of e-learning courses should produce a didactic path focused on the learner. It is important to insert in the learning course practical activities, structured and unstructured simulations that stimulate in the learner the creativity and the formation of new knowledge. The learner will acquire information even from sharing information and observations with colleagues involved in the educational process. All these actions contribute to the construction of a collective knowledge.

The e-learning 2.0 is a type of conversational learning (Jonassen, 1999). The knowledge building is a conversational and relational process.

The e-learning 2.0 platforms have pedagogical implications and in particular favour students to acquire specific skills (capabilities, social and methodological attitudes).

This path leads to some important pedagogical indications:

- Define clearly the knowledge and skills that students need to acquire.
- Explicit personal-social-methodological attitudes to improve and plan strategies for a critical development.
- Propose activities in which students must produce results.

Sometimes the lesson listened in a learning object is more understood than in presence. In this context it is important the experiment of McKinney, Dyck and Luber (2009). To determine the effectiveness of audio lectures, by iTunes U of Apple, authors lead an experiment with undergraduate psychology students in presence and in e-learning modality. Participants listened for 25-min a lecture of the professor using PowerPoint slides. In the other case, participants received a poadcast of the same lecture with the PowerPoint handout. Participants in both conditions were instructed to keep a log of the study time and the activities to prepare the exam. Results indicated that, with the poadcast file, students scored significantly higher than in presence.

During the courses, students often acquire a knowledge that is theoretical and out of date, different and distant from the realistic one problem-based. We must give to students the opportunity to learn updated contents by specific tools and methods. In this way they can exchange and reuse information and documents contributing to the creation of new knowledge.

To improve the learning process it is important to take in consideration other two methodological theories: Dialogic Learning and Cultural Intelligence.

Dialogic Learning (Flecha, 2000) is the result of an egalitarian dialogue, a dialogue among people based on the validity and not on the power of assertions. In fact the learning communities emphasize an egalitarian dialogue among all members, including teaching staff, students, families and other entities regardless of the learners' ages and the type of the workplace, both formal (school or course) or informal (free dialogue).

Students, in a learning context, have a behavior that depends on the own cultural qualification. This phenomenon is studied from the theory of the Cultural Intelligence (Earley and Ang, 2003; Earley and Mosakowski, 2004). It is important that members of a global learning community are available, by sensitivity and adaptability, to understand international people by a cultural intelligence (CI) or cultural quotient (CQ). The Cultural Intelligence methodology outlines the strategies to improve the cultural perception in order to distinguish individual behaviors from those driven by the culture. To this end we can consider three aspects of CI to understand the cultural diversity: *Cognitive* (by head), *Physical* (by body) and *Motivational* (by emotions). All these aspects are important for a learning process.

Digital Natives and Digital Immigrants

The e-learning is strongly felt and attended by young people, the so-called "digital natives" (Prensky, 2001a, 2001b) who intensely use these technologies 2.0 in the private life.

Mark Prensky calls "digital natives" who were born and grown with new technologies: current students are different from those of the past used to the old education system.

Prensky describes digital natives as students who live in a virtual environment, using new technologies that, for many teachers, are revolutionaries. The Net Generation of students is multi-task, used to the use of mobile smart phones, MMS, post, tweet, e-mail while browsing on Internet and watch the television. They are ready for a multimedia learning, more flexible and global, and not tied to the time or to a specific location.

The Digital Immigrants, by contrast, are those who have learned to use the technology, but who do not speak nor fully understand the language of digital natives. In this era, teachers are mostly immigrants and they struggle a lot in the process of adaptation to the new reality.

The cognitive, relational style and the relationship of digital natives can be illustrated with the following features:

- Receive more information in a fast modality.
- Prefer iconography to the text.
- Prefer an open access to resources.
- Love multi-task learning processes.
- Work better through the network.
- Prefer the games to serious work.

The terms more used from digital natives are: embedd, link, clip, bookmark, forward, share, tag, twitter, post, etc…

Digital Immigrants who understand the language of pre-digital era have a difficulty to teach to the population who speaks a completely new language. Therefore in a person-centered learning model it is necessary to review contents and teaching methods: "We need to invent Digital Native Methodologies for all subjects, at all levels, using our students to guide us" (Priensky, 2001a).

Today students have high expectations, equipped with a set of tools that enable an always-on collaboration and sharing of ideas and information.

Now students are used to interact by Facebook, Twitter, Foursquare and create and remix media with YouTube. They are no longer satisfied to passively listen lectures or conferences in three-hour in a traditional top-down modality. Certainly, the generation born with the television is happy to list passively an audio or video transmission.

The ECAR study published in EDUCAUSE (Caruso and Kvavik, 2005) on the use of ICT from teachers showed the followings results:

- 41% prefer that teachers make a moderate use of ICT.
- 27% would like a heavy use.
- 26% would like a limited use.

The younger generation demand to teachers an intensive use of these technologies to better create and disseminate the knowledge.

The current and important question is if teachers will use these new web-based technologies (like blog, wiki, chat, social media) in their professional activities or not.

It is evident that not all teachers are trained on the pedagogical use of ICTs. The new learning model differs from the previous one. In any case, the presence of digital natives (Palfrey and Gasser, 2008; Prensky 2001a, 2001b) to the university could revolutionize this context, probably making easier the introduction of web 2.0 approaches that increase the cultural gap between students and teachers. In this context it is also important to take in consideration the digital divide. Nowadays, there are still several segments of the population without the access to the technology - mostly

elderly, immigrants, disabled and unemployed - and others that use technological tools without having developed an adequate critical conscience. Therefore a new e-learning platform risks to introduce a widen gap, generating new and old forms of social exclusion.

The adoption of a web 2.0 approach in schools and universities is a complex process to overcome technological, managerial and human barriers. For these reasons, the design of strategic goals, accepted and promoted by professors, is absolutely necessary. This first step requires, in many cases, a radical cultural change for people used to operate in a different context. It is also important in activating the change that students promote the new learning system otherwise there is a risk to return back.

UNIVERSITY 2.0 MODEL

In this section we describe a University 2.0 model (Figure 2) that involves all internal resources of the university: teachers, students, and administrative staff.

Every subject has an own space and can exchange information with other ones involved in a high education context. Only an intensive com-

Figure 2. University 2.0 model (Source: own)

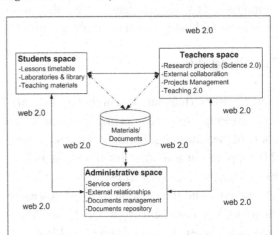

munication can improve the performance of the university system. All internal actors of the model insert and pick up data from an unique materials/documents database.

The university 2.0 model gathers a collective intelligence (Levy, 1997; De Kerchove, 1997), integrates different subjects and promotes a peer-to-peer dialogue.

For Levy the collective intelligence is the product of a collective work in creating new knowledge. De Kerckhove insists in the open nature of the concept of the connective intelligence against the image of a "closed container". The knowledge doesn't reside only in the head of people but also in the network through a digital global interconnection. Internet is like a brain that learns continuously; it is the global conscience and the common public space. Everyone can connect and disconnect from this shared intelligence, a "mind always in use". Each community produces signs, meanings and share values that contribute to collective intelligence. An open platform stimulates the creation and sharing of knowledge, among members of the community.

In the model of Universty 2.0 beyond the Teaching 2.0 it is important also to consider the Science 2.0, a context where, by web 2.0 tools, scientific communities collaborate and the co-operate in the research (Chesbrough, 2003a, 2003b; Weber, 2005; Benkler, 2006; Tapscott and Williams, 2006). Students collaborating together, by interactive tools, can suggest useful solutions to professors and assistants in the problem solving.

Teaching 2.0

Active users (teachers/researchers/assistants/students/employees) have an important role in the chain of the knowledge building. The technology 2.0 supports, in a bi-directional and interactive modality, the creativity (Lessig, 2001, 2004), productivity and the creation of new knowledge changing the paradigm from "push" to "pull" modality. There is a passage from an era 1.0 associ-

ated to the old hierarchical portals and a restricted group of content creators to a paradigm 2.0 open and collaborative that use horizontal and peer-to-peer digital tools. This new open knowledge paradigm is growing with the success of the free software that implicates a low distribution cost (almost zero).

As participant in a learning community, teachers, students and employees can use an advanced personal Desktop 2.0 (Figure 3). The Desktop 2.0 is the collaborative platform that all subjects involved in the University 2.0 model use to communicate among themselves and with external environment and so he/she can contribute in the knowledge building. This desktop is very useful in the new Teaching 2.0 modality where students can better learn.

The Desktop 2.0 includes the following tools:

- **Support:** Shared calendar, planner, surveys, alert systems, virtual classroom, and lesson plans.
- **Simulation:** Virtual reality, games and 3D simulation.
- **Communication and Collaborative:** Mailing lists, instant messaging, chat rooms, forums, bulletin board systems, e-mail, web forums, blogs, video conferencing, wikis, social networks, social bookmarking, collaborative writing, e-voting, and mobile smartphones.

Figure 3. Desktop 2.0 (Source: own)

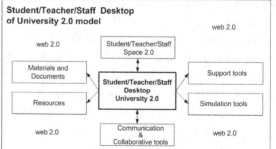

- **Resources:** Search engines, maps, RSS, podcast, mobile devices, learning objects, and assessment tests.
- **Materials and Documents:** Disk space, images, documents, text, audio and video files.

By this platform 2.0, it is possible to follow formal and informal courses. From this environment, we can select the type of course and the lectures. Each course is associated to an e-tutor. All students enrolled in a specific course can interact with each other, express reviews suggestion and create and sharing new knowledge by a wiki space. In the search section it is possible to search, filter and find different topics, courses and contacts. By mobile devices (m-learning) students can everywhere search specific personalized lessons just-in-time and just-for-me.

The Desktop 2.0 can exploits an open source and collaborative platform like ELGG (http://elgg.org) (Ebner, Holzinger and Maurer, 2007; Sharma, 2008; Curry, Kiddle and Simmonds, 2009; Cui, Wang and Cao, 2008). Inside the platform 2.0 it is possible to integrate also private social networks, blogs and other tools to exchange open contents and develop creative operations of mash-up (Baldwin and Clark 2000, Zittrain 2006).

In the Desktop 2.0 also simulators, virtual and augmented reality are important tools to use. Virtual reality can be considered as an experiential interface, in which the perceptual component (visual, tactile) and the interactivity are merged. The augmented reality provides more information added to real or graphic objects. It possible to know the objects and use them to learn, in real time, through a direct experience in a context of action-reaction. The subject can acquire skills and complex motor abilities in flight simulators or in medical and surgical simulations. Shared virtual worlds, like Second Life, can be an effective tool for teaching. The use of virtual reality often requires technical expertises and high development costs but this problem can be overcome by the use of an open source software.

Users can personalize the own space of the Desktop 2.0 adding different RSS feeds and other components 2.0. Activating an account, the user can freely configure the own profile. The private space becomes a multi-functional environment from which it is possible to call different personal contacts, social networks (private and public) and all available resources. The desktop is similar to a web paper where it is possible to simply write anything.

Science 2.0

In a University 2.0 model the research must be collaborative with the exchange and sharing of various scientific contributions (Paulus and Nijstad, 2003; Katsouyanni, 2008; Fitzgerald, Hanks and McCauley, 2010; Feng, Ma and Fan, 2011, Moser et al., 2011). In this context also the digital simulation can be a useful tool for the analysis and the study of real trials. Bibliographies, papers, journals and reports must be diffused in the scientific community. By an appropriate quality criteria it is possible to create a "science citation index" that enable researchers to the selection of most important articles for their research.

An open interdisciplinary and intercultural exchange stimulates a collaborative research. The Princeton University has decided that the academic work of internal researchers will no longer be distributed to editors of scientific journals with the full protection of copyright because these magazines subscriptions require expensive and restrictive practices; no problem for the magazines that do not require these restrictions (Creagh, 2011).

The use of new technologies, Internet and Web 2.0, can facilitate the process of the scientific research and online publications of academic results like emerging theories, claims of discoveries and drafts of articles that anyone can read and comment.

In this section we present a Science 2.0 model (Figure 4) which includes different phases: the research collaboration (Research Teams), the sharing of bibliographic references (References

Figure 4. The Science 2.0 model (Source: own)

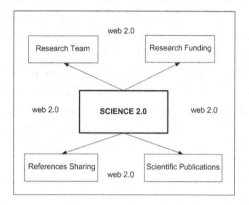

Sharing), the funding research (Research Funding), the organization and publications, including data analysis of scientific materials (Scientific Publications).

For each group we present a list of website to consult. Every teacher, scientist use the best one and the more useful for his/her goal.

Research Teams

As Research Teams we consider the following groups/websites: Openwetware (openwetware. org), Methodspace (methodspace.com), ResearchGate (researchgate.net), Academia.eu (academia. edu), iamResearcher(iamresearcher.com), Cordis (cordis.europa.eu), Sciencestage (sciencestage. com), IndexCopernicus (indexcopernicus.com), myExperiment (myexperiment.org), Current Controlled Trials (controlled-trials.com).

OpenWetWare is a project that includes about 100 research laboratories and aims to promote the exchange of information in the field of engineering and life sciences in order to create a large global laboratory in which researchers collaborate across the world with their contributions, publishing articles, the results of their experiments and research questions.

Methodspace is a community focused on research methods. In this virtual space scientists share researchs, sources and discussions and there is a free access to selected journal papers and book chapters.

ResearchGATE, project designed by a group of scientists at Harvard University, is now a real social network where everyone can define the own profile, describe the professional curriculum, research skills, publications and create a network of contacts to establish partnerships, share resources and materials related to the research field. Thanks to the 'open access journals', it is possible, by a wiki, to contribute in actual scientific publications.

Academia.edu is a platform to share papers, track and monitor analytic indexes around the impact of the research. The website attracts over 3.9 million unique visitors for month.

IamResearcher is an intelligent networking platform that connect researchers from around the world to share and discover updated resources (publication, conferences, news, etc.) and to connect and collaborate with other peers. The website is designed to assist researchers in their daily activities.

Cordis is the service of the European Community where find information on the proposals within the Seventh Framework Program for the technologic development. The goal is to link in a European network researchers and practitioners. In addition, it promotes the development and the dissemination of the knowledge stimulating the acceptance of new technologies and innovations. In the website anyone can propose himself as potential partner to evaluate/monitor projects or as partnership seeker.

ScienceStage is a virtual place in which scientists, teachers, scholars, students and professionals from all sectors have the opportunity to present and share scientific ideas and results through the use of streaming video, audio and text documents.

By Index Copernicus it is possible to join in global projects or propose new ones and consult different sources of information. In this way, financial resources available for the research are best addressed.

In addition, the website improves the opportunities for a methodological research, reducing discrepancies between original trial protocols and published results.

MyExperiment represents a virtual environment for searching public scientific workflows but also to propose, share and develop new ones, in order to create communities and develop relationships. Inside the website, after the registration, it is possible to download software that allows to present the "my experiment".

Current Controlled Trials allows users to search, record and share information on clinical trials. The website manages an international meta-Registrer of Controlled Trials (mRCT), that provides information about ongoing trials and also on details of experiments already completed. The mRCT, thanks to a better dissemination of information, will help to reduce a duplication of efforts, wastage of resources, the bias of publications and to optimize the distribution of funds for the research.

References Sharing

In this topic we consider the followings websites: Zotero (zotero.org), Citeulike (citeulike.org), Mendeley (mendeley.com), Pubmed (ncbi.nlm.nih.gov/pubmed), Connotea (connotea.org), Google Scholar (scholar.google.com) and Google Books (books.google.com).

Zotero (zotero.org) is a easy-to-use tool to collect, organize, cite, and share research sources. Citeulike (citeulike.org) is a service for managing and discovering academic references. Mendeley (mendeley.com) is a reference manager and academic social network to organize research paper and to discover the latest research.

PubMed is a service of the U.S. National Library of Medicine that includes links to full text of articles and million of citations from MEDLINE and other reviews of the biomedical literature. It is based on the NCBI Entrez retrieval system, developed by the National Center for Biotechnology Information (NCBI) to submit citations before publishing the paper.

Connotea is a social bookmarking service addressed to the scientific community, where it is possible to import the bibliography in Research Information Systems (RIS) used for scientific references. It is possible also to comment the Uniform Resource Identifier (URI), create discussions and give advices like in blogs or social networks.

Google Scholar is a search engine to find documents, books, abstracts, articles from academic publishers and professional registers. Google Book, a part of the Library Project, helps users in finding relevant and specialist books, especially those impossible to find, as the books out of print, respecting the copyrights of authors and publishers. The biggest goal is to work with publishers and libraries to create a virtual complete catalog available for the research, that allows users to discover new books and for publishers to find new readers.

Research Funding

In this topic the main websites are: Open Genius (opengenius.org) e Innocentive (innocentive.com).

The goal of Open Genius is to make qualitative research projects facilitating the funding through a global and highly motivated community (Gaggioli and Riva, 2008). The crowdfunding is a powerful channel with engaged communities for obtaining economic resources for science projects and therefore to increase and improve the research and the transparency in funding allocation.

Innocentive is an online community that aims to link companies with technological problems and organizations available to finance scientists and researchers to solve their specific problems.

Scientific Publications

In this field the main websites are: Thomson Reuters Web of Knowledge (thomsonreuters.com), Elsevier (Elsevier.com), ScienceDirect

(sciencedirect.com), DOAJ (doaj.org), Plos One (plosone.org), Scivee (scivee.tv), VassarStats (faculty.vassar.edu/lowry/VassarStats.html) e SOCR (socr.ucla.edu).

Thomson Reuters Web of Knowledge is a research platform that gives the access to contents and tools to search, monitor and measure scientific productions. This intelligent research platform provides access to the world's leading citation databases including powerful cited reference searching.

Elsevier is one of the largest abstract and citation database of peer-reviewed literature and web sources of high quality. ScienceDirect is a large database of scientific full-text with an offer of millions of peer-reviewed journal articles, book chapters and books.

Directory of Open Access Journals (DOAJ) on its website collects information about cultural and quality scientific journals available, online, in the full text format. This initiative, a service of the University of Lund - Sweden, intends to expand its current scope to cover all areas of knowledge and all languages. In March 2008 there were 3,304 magazines whose 1,069 journals. Overall the service allows to find 174,995 articles.

PLoS ONE is an international journal published by PLoS, a non-profit organization of scientists and doctors who work together to make publicly available medical and scientific literature, through the concept of the peer review. PLoS ONE has an open access and in this magazine it is possible to publish articles in any scientific discipline, with the particularity that they may be updated and improved, over time, with contributions of readers who can comment, criticize and correct.

SciVee is a platform for sharing scientific researchs. Designed to help researchers to exchange scientific information and documents through a video presentation. In addition to limitations imposed by copyright, there is also the barrier of too specialized topics. Even the dissemination of video make too incomprehensible the contents.

VassarStats is a website created by Vassar College (Poughkeepsie, New York, USA) that can be considered a valid and useful service, where find materials to perform all statistical calculations by interactive masks in Java language.

Statistics Online Computational Resource (SOCR) is a collection of online calculators useful for the design, validation and the free dissemination of the knowledge of the probability and statistical analysis. Inside the website, which contains many calculation libraries, it is possible to make distributions (calculations and graphics), models (polynomial and spectral), experiments (games and virtual simulators of processes) and analysis (statistical analysis).

BEST PRACTICES OF UNIVERSITIES 2.0

In this section we analyze some of the best practices of universities that use, in an intensive modality, web 2.0 tools in online courses or for administrative goals. The best practices are classified for topic/user: teaching/professor, learning/students and administration/staff.

Teaching/Professors

According to the Open Course Ware Consortium (OCWC), that involves universities in France (Paris Tech), Japan (Japan OpenCourseWare), China (Core Group), America (MIT), in March 2010, 13,000 free university courses are available on the web (ocw.mit.edu/about/next-decade/timeline/). At the first position there is the Massachusetts Institute of Technology (MIT) with 2,000 published courses.

Some academic institutions in the United States, from years, have launched projects to share and review instructional materials. Teachers of different universities contribute to online courses in biology, physics, economics with the

Merlot community, founded by the California State University and supported by the prestigious National Science Foundation.

In the world, some online excellent universities 2.0 are those of MIT Open Course Ware, Stanford on iTunes U, Harvard Law School, University of Arizona, Harvard Open Access Policy, University of Warwick, University of Edinburgh, Universitat Oberta de Catalunya, etc…

The Khan Academy (khanacademy.org) is an educational organization no profit created in 2006 by Salman Khan. The goal is to provide a high quality education to anyone and anywhere. The organization website collected, at the end of 2011, over 2,700 video lessons and 268 practice exercises, uploaded by YouTube's video sharing, on a wide range of disciplines (mathematics, history, finance, physics, chemistry, biology, astronomy, economics). Each lesson takes about ten minutes and are free of charge. The Academy courses have an average of more than 35,000 visits daily. The financing of the project is done from volunteers with donations. In September 2010, Google has announced the plan to donate two million dollars in order to facilitate the creation of new courses and to allow the translation of basic lessons in the main languages of the world.

The focus of eTTCampus 2.0, a project funded with the Lifelong Learning Programme, is the transformation of the European Virtual Campus in a networked learning environment that emphasizes the social aspect. In this space it is possible to develop new tools and methodologies, define quality criteria for the system evaluation.

Social networks (Reinhardt, 2009; Heinze and Reinhardt, 2011), are used in seminars in German universities, where the communication and collaboration has been integrated into the design of a formal learning. During these seminars have been used several digital tools to allow students to engage a collaborative work process.

The Polytechnic University of Catalonia with Isfol, Scienter, University of Greenwich, University of Surrey, Eden and Europen Institute for

e-learning has developed a system for assessing skills of teachers and trainers to include in the personal portfolio of an e-social reputation.

Some universities, like Tor Vergata University in Rome and Milan Polytechnic have online full graduated programs. In Italy, 53 of 77 universities offer training courses in e-learning mainly in the scientific and economic disciplines.

Learning/Students

One of the best examples of pedagogical practices that exploit the Web 2.0 can be found in a graduate program at Columbia University, where students study the capabilities of these new technologies, social bookmarking classification systems and other functions 2.0 in their distributed research projects.

At the University of Florence, students and alumni of the Educational Technology Laboratory will exchange opinions, suggestions and news by the LTEver platform (Bonaiuti, 2006), a social network developed by the open source software Elgg. There is an integration between formal and informal systems, between individual and social experiences: students and workers can become the architects of a new learning system. Even Facebook, MySpace and Ning, can be integrated in the platform and can become fertile ground to combine leisure and education. Some groups have been formed to share lecture notes, calendar of events, links.

The Faculty of Humanities and Philosopy of University of Siena provides sharing resources in online courses to support educational experimentation. It offers a free space for students to meet, talk and create discussion groups. This is an experimental project, funded by the Italian Government to promote technological innovations inside graduated courses and will feed the online platform Marvin to support students and teachers in online activities and to create also a community among employees of the university.

The TagBoLab (tagbolab.it) is a project of the Master Degree in Public Communication and Social Sciences of University of Bologna (Bazzarin and Lalli, 2011). The Lab includes students and two coordinator professors. The goal is to train students to a widest use of web 2.0 tools in the promotion of the territory, like a sort of a driven traineeship to work. The central idea of TagBoLab is to offer to citizens, in an aggregate modality, all events promoted in Bologna. In this sense, the Lab implements a communication campaign collaborating with public and private groups and promoting activities by social media. Everday students monitor all regional blogs, online communities and communication channel. In the first edition of the 2009-2010, the Lab has analyzed and monitored the festivals in the Bologna area by blogger, facebook groups and online communities. In the website all material tagged Bologna was assembled. All data was available for download on a wiki platform and everyone had the opportunity to improve the analysis. In line with the philosophy of open data, everything is downloadable and modifiable.

The working group, like any communications agency, has been involved in managing the flow of information to analyze communication plans, partners, sponsors and accessibility.

Students monitoring regional blogs, analyze the different styles of the approach to the network and create a database classified by sectors (from the kitchen to the politics) and locations (from Piacenza to Rimini). Some participants already gratuated, have decided to continue the project in other topics and territory: CultureTag, TagSardegna and TagCampania.

The TagBoLab laboratory is an aggregator of data independently produced by citizens-users-prosumers to make more easily accessible and visible the information. Nowadays, it is possible to find, primarly, many significant news in relational networks, fed from words of mouth, rather that in magazines.

An other important project is that of iTunes U of Apple (McKinney et al. 2009; Rugg, 2009) dedicated to the m-learning for university courses. By mobile tools like smartphones and tablets, students can have the access to different e-courses, over 350,000 lessons, videos, lectures and free poadcasts from the best academic institutions around the world.

Universities such as Stanford, Yale UC Berkeley, Oxford, Cambridge, MIT, the Open University in Beijing and the University of Tokyo offer free contents on iTunes U. Students can download contents from the storage website and listen them on any device such as Mac, PC, iPod, iPhone or iPad. To see and listen this material it is necessary to install the iTunes player on the device.

Stanford University has decided to use iTunes extensively, devoting contents both to students and public. Everything is directly accessible by the internal website (http://itunes.stanford.edu/).

The project includes two type of websites:

- A public website which includes Stanford courses, interviews, speeches, faculty lectures, events, music, sports, etc...
- A restricted access to the website which includes appropriate materials for the community management. Instructors can create iTunes courseworks visible only to registered users of a specific class.

Administration/Staff

American colleges are also exploiting the Web 2.0 outside the education context. Administrators and law enforcements acquire information from discussions and online posts monitoring any illegal activity in campuses.

Tufts University combines (mashup) Google mapping technology (satellite images and links) with resources of Institutions of Higher Education (IHE) to provide to students, teachers, assistants, campus visitors, the full exploration of the campus and the location of buildings and online services.

At Penn State University, text messages are used to rapidly provide ads to students according to their preferences. Marywood University, Purdue University, Berkeley College adopt web 2.0 tools in web-based kiosks for canteen services where students can use a touch screen and control the balance of meal calories, see the menu of the day or even send a request for a special diet or a feedback to responsibles of the canteen. A login system allows to generate nutritional tables for monitoring daily calories. The Duke University, in 2004, gave iPods to freshmen as part of the multi-years Duke Digital Initiatives to stimulate a creative use of technology in the digital life of the academic campus. The Duke has developed various educational apps for iPods, many of which include interactive elements typical of Web 2.0. Students can record lectures, discussions, interviews, presentations and then upload images and audio of the course. Teachers register interviews, oral examinations, classrooms and download contributions of students directly in their iPod.

In addition, the Duke University is conducting research on how multimedia tools and technologies can be exploited in the academic field, especially in the areas of podcasting, the creation of multimedia materials for teaching, video projects, the use of tablet PCs and digital capture of lectures and class presentations.

The Buffalo State College incorporates web 2.0 tools inside the website making available a RSS feed so that subscribers can receive updated information in their PC. The college also uses poadcasts to promote events. The college allows to students to communicate directly with an admissions officer by AOL Instant Messenger.

The University of Phoenix (UOP), founded in 1976 that has received the first registrations in 1978, now, has more than 250,000 students. It makes online marketing to adults and other non-traditional students, whose needs are often ignored by other IHEs. The campus services, included the lessons of courses, are available online to satisfy people who can not follow the lessons during the day.

Colleges and universities in North America continue to increase the adoption and the use of social media for their marketing and recruiting offices. A recent report (Barnes and Mattson, 2009) shows how these institutions have passed, on the blogging side, both brands of Fortune 500 and Inc 500. These universities plan to extend the use of social media on the teaching and services to students. In the spring of 2008, Ithaca College signed a contract with Apple and began the process of deploying iTunes U on the campus. University identified key contents to provider, establishing a pilot group for developing the support to the infrastructure and the implementation of communication and collaboration projects with the campus community (Rugg, 2009).

BENEFITS AND LIMITS

Benefits

The University 2.0 model has two important benefits: *social and technical disintermediation*. Usually the emphasis is on the socializing aspect, on the large capacity aggregating around the web 2.0 tools. Undoubtedly the web 2.0 stimulates a new and very interesting communication space for the ability to quickly create volumes of information and put together many collaborative people (teachers, researchers, students,…). Certainly this does not always mean quality; in some cases the collaboration does not lead to excellent results.

The second key aspect of Web 2.0 is the disintermediation, which has eliminated the mediation of skilled persons to publish something on the web. Now, with minimal skills, everyone can become creative and write in the web like in a paper sheet but it is important to have some concepts to express.

Other benefits are the *open access,* the *easy use of contents,* the *low cost* and *the increased creatvity*. By low costs in the knowledge building using crowdsourcing (Freire 2008, Howe 2006), the lifecycle of new products/services becomes very short and the creativity in the production of contents increases. New models of licences, as Creative Commons, introduce a flexibility respect to the absolute restriction of uses and the copyright. The use of technological and social standards like tagging systems/folksonomy is relevant to make the information available in search engines and aggregators for other reuses (Weinberger 2007).

Another benefit is that the Web 2.0 provides an environment where it is possible to learn by doing, failing and trying again and therefore learning from previous and on-going experiences. The Web 2.0 context is yet an experimental sector where it is possible a trial-and-error approach. In organizations there are leaders or passionate users (Young 2007, Von Hippel 2005) who are always willing to try and improve their work. For example in developing a learning platform with functionalities defined a priori, universities could let the community (teachers and students) to explore, test and adapt specific tools. The institution should focus in monitoring this activity and integrate the successful experiences and best practices.

Learning by doing applying collaborative methods for an active learning is an important approach to develop in a web 2.0 dynamic context.

Web 2.0 facilitates a change of paradigm; from a top-down system to a networked approach where teachers should change their roles to become coaches and facilitators of the learning process (Anderson, 2007; Brown and Adler 2008; O'Reilly 2005).

In the past, Web 2.0 has already used in some university with a bottom-up logic. Teachers, researchers and students, in most cases without any institutional stimulus, started, some years ago, to use social software tools (Anderson, 2007; OECD, 2007).

Limits

As limits, we can consider the followings restraining factors:

- The refusal of the adoption of these advanced tools from some teachers, administratives and students.
- The absence of a system of incentives.
- The availability of existing technologies previous the Web 2.0.
- The culture of aversion to the innovation and entrepreneurship manifested by universities.
- The lack of security on web 2.0.

Many of users of tools available in the Internet 1.0 are reluctant and fearful to learn new abilities in the use of new software and change their attitudes about education and knowledge.

These behaviours are due to the institution inertia that impedes to develop adequate incentives like recognition of qualifications (skills, technical competences, etc.) and also for the lack of the support to reluctant users.

The existing previous technologies, also open source, do not stimulate the change. It is better to use new technologies for institutions that do not have before made large investments in technology.

In some cases, universities have a culture of the aversion to the innovation and entrepreneurship. The adoption of technology and working methods associated with web 2.0 requires a high dose of experimentation and creativity. Bureaucracy, governance, decision-making and inertia in large institutions are in many cases the worst environment for an internal innovation.

Members of the e-learning 2.0 or science 2.0 communities have afraid of data integrity and security (Davidson and Yoran 2007; Noureddine and Damodaran 2008; Prandini and Ramilli 2011).

The adoption of a learning approach web 2.0-based in universities is a complex process that must overcome technological, managerial and human barriers.

The development of a strategy accepted and encouraged by leaders, responsible of the knowledge management, is absolutely necessary. This first step requires, in many cases, a radical cultural change by people used to work and make decisions in a different context. In universities, the introduction of a learning approach 2.0, must pass through a strategy of adaptation, which can be processed by integrating the previous experiences in education, research and business. Bottom-up adaption is slower and in many cases there are digital divides between universities, some teachers and internal employees.

The report of Forrester Research (Koplowitz and Young, 2007) identifies the risks associated to web 2.0 that an organization perceives: reliability, security, governance, compliance and privacy.

These risks are associated to the growing trend of unsanctioned usage and to some consequences as violations of intellectual property overcoming institutional firewalls.

The response of some universities in implementing web 2.0 policies and specific guidelines, could eliminate the opportunities provided by web 2.0 like the openness, trust and collaboration.

For a best implementation of these policies, it is important a balanced trade-off among following factors:

- Visibility that obligates the openess to the external environment by important efforts in marketing and communication.
- Security and trust that obligates the restriction of some activities inside the organization.
- The implicit criticism to the traditional and closed model of university.
- The centralization of IT departments that in a context 2.0 is considered irrelevant.

A trusted and collaborative learning system for educational, administrative and managerial goals must prevent and solve some riskies (Havenstein 2007).

Probably, new developments in social networks could be a potential useful solution to this compromise providing, in a controlled environment, web 2.0 tools with a system of restrictions to users and contents.

Regarding the Science 2.0 model, the open access modality makes scientific researchs more collaborative and therefore more productive. Instead according other scientists, who preliminary publish online results, there is the risk that someone steal their ideas and gain recognitions or patents. Despite the pros and cons, the number of Science 2.0 websites is growing.

FUTURE RESEARCH DIRECTIONS

The future research directions aim to implement and use a more technological platform for e-learning and e-collaboration in scientific researchs. It is important that the digital platform of the University 2.0 model integrates tools used in the real life and therefore the formal and informal context. Especially young digital natives are facilitated and encouraged in this direction.

In the future it is important the development of a platform 3.0, that provides learning objects to anyone at anytime, anywhere (with mobile learning solutions) and just-for-me (personalized), based on the semantic web (web 3.0) and in particular on distributed computing and artificial intelligence techniques where computers can interpret the meaning of sentences. In this way will be more easier to find educational materials and documents within the platform, by a search engine based not on keywords but on sentences written in natural language. Intelligent agents will enable users of the platform to participate in a smarter and collaborative modality. Thus the platform 3.0 will be more adaptable and responsive to the needs of individual teachers/learners. For the collaborative research will be necessary to ensure that researchers are more stimulated to share scientific results. A platform 3.0 will enable teachers with different skills to manage and execute complex research projects useful to the community.

CONCLUSION

Web 2.0 tools have made the web more participative and have changed social behaviors, the way to do business, teaching and research. The participation of people, users or students, improves the overall quality of processes and the final product/service both tangible and intangible as the acquisition/creation of new knowledge.

How happens in the business sector, also the universities feel the need to innovate the teaching and the research. Mainly in the sector of the knowledge building, the use of interactive and collaborative technologies can bring significant added values. Students, digital natives are willing to adopt a digital platform that integrates formal and informal environments with interactive tools like social networks that they use in the private life. Obstacles may be present in teaching staff where some professors can be contrary to the publication and sharing of materials and especially of scientific results. In addition, older teachers, digital immigrants, do not use a lot these new technologies. This obstacle can be overcome, with an increased awareness and encouragement in the adoption of these tools for the scientific production. In this way will be possible to manage global projects and reach more interesting shared results for the scientific and social community.

REFERENCES

Ally, M. (2004). Foundations of educational theory for online learning. In Anderson, T., & Elloumi, F. (Eds.), *Theory and practice of online learning* (pp. 3–31). Athabasca, Canada: Athabasca University.

Anderson, P. (2007). *What is Web 2.0? Ideas, technologies and implications for education. JISC Technology and Standards Watch, February 2007.* Bristol: JISC.

Baldwin, C. Y., & Clark, K. M. (2000). *Design rules: The power of modularity.* Cambridge, MA: MIT Press.

Barnes, G., & Mattson, E. (2009). *Social media and college admissions: Higher-ed beats business in adoption of new tools for third year.* Report 2009.

Baylor, A. L. (2001). Perceived disorientation and incidental learning in a Web-based environment: internal and external factors. *Journal of Educational Multimedia and Hypermedia, 10*(3), 227–251.

Bazzarin, V., & Lalli, P. (2011). *The medium is the community (?). A pilot laboratorial activity at University of Bologna to tell and promote the city. In 2011 Proceedings of Understanding Media Today* (pp. 323–330). Barcelona.

Benkler, Y. (2006). *The wealth of networks: How social production transforms markets and freedom.* New Haven, CT: Yale University Press.

Bonaiuti, G. (Ed.). (2006). *E-learning 2.0.* Trento, Italy: Erickson.

Brown, J. S., & Adler, R. P. (2008). Minds on fire: Open education, the long tail, and learning 2.0. *EDUCAUSE Review, 43*(1), 16–32.

Bruner, J. (1991). The narrative construction of reality. *Critical Inquiry, 18*(1), 1–21. doi:10.1086/448619

Bruns, A., & Humpreys, S. (2005). Wikis in teaching and assessment: The M/cyclopedia project. [San Diego, CA, USA.]. *WikiSym, 05*(October), 16–18.

Bryan, A. (2006). Web 2.0: A new wave of innovation for teaching and learning. *EDUCAUSE Review, 41*(2), 32–44.

Burnett, C. (2011). Medium for empowerment or a centre for everything: Students' experience of control in virtual learning environments within a university context. *Education and Information Technologies, 16*(3), 245–258. doi:10.1007/s10639-010-9122-z

Caruso, J., & Kvavik, R. B. (2005). *ECAR study of students and information technology, 2005: Convenience, connection, control, and learning.* EDUCASE Report.

Chapman, M. (1988). *Constructive evolution: Origins and development of Piaget's thought.* Cambridge, UK: Cambridge University Press.

Chesbrough, H. W. (2003a). *Open innovation: The New imperative for creating and profiting from technology.* Boston, MA: Harvard Business School Press.

Chesbrough, H. W. (2003b). The era of open innovation. *Sloan Management Review, 44*(3), 35–41.

Creagh, S. (2011). Princeton goes open access to stop staff handing all copyright to journals unless waiver granted. In *Conversation*, September 28, 2011.

Cui, X., Wang, H., & Cao, Z. (2008). An Ajax-based terminology system for e-learning 2.0. In Z. Pan, X. Zhang, A. Rhalibi, W. Woo, & Y. Li (Eds.), *Proceedings of the 3rd International Conference on Technologies for E-Learning and Digital Entertainment* (Edutainment '08), (pp. 135-146). Berlin, Germany: Springer-Verlag.

Curry, R., Kiddle, C., & Simmonds, R. (2009). Social networking and scientific gateways. In *Proceedings of the 5th Grid Computing Environments Workshop* (GCE '09). (p. 10). New York, NY: ACM.

Davidson, M. A., & Yoran, E. (2007). Enterprise security for Web 2.0. *Computer, 40*(11), 117–119. doi:10.1109/MC.2007.383

De Kerchove, D. (1997). *Connected intelligence, the arrival of the web society.* Toronto, Canada: Somerville House.

Dewey, J. (1986). Experience and education. *The Educational Forum, 50*(3), 241–252. doi:10.1080/00131728609335764

Downes, S. (2005) E-learning 2.0. [Quick Edit] *eLearn Magazine, 2005*(10).

Earley, C., & Ang, S. (2003). *Cultural intelligence: Individual interactions across cultures.* Stanford University Press.

Earley, C., & Mosakowski, E. (2004). Cultural intelligence. *Harvard Business Review*, (October): 1–9.

Ebner, M., Holzinger, A., & Maurer, H. (2007). Web 2.0 technology: Future interfaces for technology enhanced learning? In C. Stephanidis (Ed.), *Proceedings of the 4th International Conference on Universal Access in Human-Computer Interaction: Applications and Services* (UAHCI'07), (pp. 559-568). Berlin, Germany: Springer-Verlag.

European Commission. (2010). *EUROPE 2020: A strategy for smart, sustainable and inclusive growth.* April 24, 2011.

European Commission. (2011). Document 78. *The lifelong learning programme: Education and training opportunities for all.* Retrieved from http://ec.europa.eu/education/lifelong-learning-programme/doc78_en.htm

European Council. (2000). *The Lisbon Special European Council: Towards a Europe of Innovation and Knowledge*, March 23-24, Lisbon.

Feng, B., Ma, J., & Fan, Z.-P. (2011). An integrated method for collaborative R and D project selection: Supporting innovative research teams. *Expert Systems with Applications, 38*(5), 5532–5543. doi:10.1016/j.eswa.2010.10.083

Ferdig, R. E., Roehler, L. R., Boling, E. C., Knezek, S., Pearson, P. D., & Yadav, A. (2004). Teaching with video cases on the Web: Lessons learned from the reading classroom explorer. In Brown, A., & Davis, N. E. (Eds.), *Digital technology, communities and education: World yearbook of education 2004* (pp. 164–175). London, UK: Routledge Falmer. doi:10.4324/9780203416174_chapter_10

Fitzgerald, S., Hanks, B., & McCauley, R. (2010). Collaborative research in computer science education: A case study. In *Proceedings of the 41st ACM Technical Symposium on Computer Science Education* (SIGCSE '10), (pp. 305-309). New York, NY: ACM.

Flecha, R. (2000). *Sharing words: Theory and practice of dialogic learning*. US: Rowman and Littlefield Publishers.

Freire, J. (2008). Universities and Web 2.0: Institutional challenges. *eLearning Papers, 8.*

Gaggioli, A., & Riva, G. (2008). Working the crowd. *Science, 321*(5895), 1443. doi:10.1126/science.321.5895.1443a

Galliani, L., & De Waal, P. (2009). Learning face to face, in action and on line: integrated model of lifelong learning. In Bernath, U., Szucs, A., Tait, A., & Vidal, M. (Eds.), *Distance and e-learning in transition: Learning innovation, technology and social challenges*. Budapest, Hungary: ISTE-Wiley.

Godwin-Jones, R. (2006). Emerging technologies tag clouds in the blogosphere: Electronic literacy and social networking. *Language Learning & Technology, 10*(2), 8–15.

Green, S., Nacheva-Skopalik, L., & Pearson, E. (2008). An adaptable personal learning environment for e-learning and e-assessment. In B. Rachev & A. Smrikarov (Eds.), *Proceedings of the 9th International Conference on Computer Systems and Technologies and Workshop for PhD Students in Computing* (CompSysTech '08). New York, NY: ACM.

Grossman, L. (2006, December 13). Time's person of the year: You. *Time Magazine*. Retrieved from http://www.imli.com/imlog/archivi/001051.html

Harasim, L. (1990). Online education: An environment for collaboration and intellectual amplification. In Harasim, L. (Ed.), *Online education: Perspectives on a new environment* (pp. 39–66). New York, NY: Praeger Publishers.

Havenstein, H. (2007, September 7). IT is a key barrier to corporate Web 2.0 adoption, users say. *Computerworld.*

Heinze, N., & Reinhardt, W. (2011). Future social learning networks at universities – An exploratory seminar setting. In Wankel, C. (Ed.), *Educating educators with social media*. Emerald Publishing Group. doi:10.1108/S2044-9968(2011)0000001010

Howe, J. (2006). The rise of crowdsourcing. *Wired,* 14-06.

Jonassen, D. (1999). Designing constructivist learning environments. In Reigeluth, C. (Ed.), *Instructional design theories and models: A new paradigm of instructional theory* (*Vol. II*, pp. 215–239). Mahwah, NJ: Lawrence Erlbaum Associates.

Katsouyanni, K. (2008). Collaborative research: Accomplishments and potential. *Environmental Health, 7*(3).

Khan, B. H. (2004). *Comprehensive approach to program evaluation in open and distributed learning (CAPEODL) model*. George Washington University.

Koplowitz, R., & Young, G. O. (2007, September 14). *Web 2.0 social computing dresses up for business*. Forrester Research.

Kruse, K., & Keil, J. (1999). *Technology-based training*. San Francisco, CA: Jossey-Bass/Pfeiffer.

Lessig, L. (2001). *The future of ideas*. Vintage Books.

Lessig, L. (2004). *Free culture: The nature and future of creativity.* New York, NY: Penguin Press.

Levy, P. (1997). *Collective intelligence: Mankind's emerging world in cyberspace.* Cambridge, UK: Perseus.

McAfee, A. (2006). Enterprise 2.0: The dawn of emergent collaboration. *Sloan Management Review, 47*(3), 21–28.

McKinney, D., Dyck, J. L., & Luber, E. S. (2009). iTunes University and the classroom: Can podcasts replace professors? *Computers & Education, 52*(3), 617–623. doi:10.1016/j.compedu.2008.11.004

Molka, J., Bryan, D., Carter, W., & Creelman, A. (2009). Empathy in virtual learning environments. *International Journal of Networked Virtual Organizations, 6*(2), 123–139. doi:10.1504/IJNVO.2009.022971

Moser, R. P., Hesse, B. W., Shaikh, A. R., Courtney, P., Morgan, G., & Augustson, E. (2011). Grid-enabled measures: Using Science 2.0 to standardize measures and share data. *American Journal of Preventive Medicine, 40*(5Suppl. 2), 134–143. doi:10.1016/j.amepre.2011.01.004

Noureddine, A. A., & Damodaran, M. (2008). Security in web 2.0 application development. In G. Kotsis, D. Taniar, E. Pardede, & I. Khalil (Eds.), *Proceedings of the 10th International Conference on Information Integration and Web-based Applications and Services* (iiWAS '08), (pp. 681-685). New York, NY: ACM.

O'Reilly, T. (2005). *What is Web 2.0: Design patterns and business models for the next generation of software.* O'Reilly Media.

O'Reilly, T. (2007). What is Web 2.0: Design patterns and business models for the next generation of software. *International Journal of Digital Economics, 65*, 17–37.

Oakes, K. (2002). E-learning. *Training & Development, 4*, 68–70.

OECD. (2007). *Participative web and user-created content. Web 2.0, wikis, and social networking.* Paris, France: OECD.

Palfrey, J., & Gasser, U. (2008). *Born digital: Understanding the first generation of digital natives.* Basic Books, Perseus Books Group.

Paloff, R. M., & Pratt, K. (1999). *Building learning communities in cyberspace* (p. 206). San Francisco, CA: Jossey-Bass.

Paloff, R. M., & Pratt, K. (2001). *Lessons from the cyberspace classroom: The realities of online teaching* (p. 204). San Francisco: Jossey-Bass.

Paloff, R. M., & Pratt, K. (2003). *The virtual student: A profile and guide to working with online learners.* San Francisco, CA: Jossey-Bass Publishers.

Paloff, R. M., & Pratt, K. (2005). *Collaborating online: Learning together in community* (p. 112). San Francisco, CA: Jossey-Bass.

Paulus, P. B., & Nijstad, B. A. (Eds.). (2003). *Group creativity: Innovation through collaboration.* Oxford, UK: Oxford University Press.

Piccoli, G., Ahmad, R., & Ives, B. (2001). Web-Based virtual learning environments: A research framework and a preliminary assessment of effectiveness in basic IT skills training. *Management Information Systems Quarterly, 25*(4), 401–426. doi:10.2307/3250989

Prandini, M., & Ramilli, M. (2011). Security considerations about the adoption of web 2.0 technologies in sensitive e-government processes. In E. Estevez & M. Janssen (Eds.), *Proceedings of the 5th International Conference on Theory and Practice of Electronic Governance* (ICEGOV '11), (pp. 285-288). New York, NY: ACM.

Prenksy, M. (2001a). Digital natives, digital immigrants. *Horizon*, *9*(5), 1–6. doi:10.1108/10748120110424816

Prensky, M. (2001b). Digital natives, digital immigrants, part II: Do they really think differently? *Horizon*, *9*(6), 1–9. doi:10.1108/10748120110424843

Reinhardt, W., Moi, M., & Varlemann, T. (2009). Artefact-actor-networks as tie between social networks and artefact networks. In *Proceedings of the 5th International ICST Conference on Collaborative Computing: Networking, Applications and Worksharing*, CollaborateCom 2009.

Resnick, M. (1996). Distributed constructionism, In *Proceeding for International Conference on the Learning Science*, AACE, Northwestern University.

Rugg, B. M. (2009). Getting iTunes U at Ithaca College up and running! In *Proceedings of the 37th Annual ACM SIGUCCS Fall Conference* (SIGUCCS '09), (pp. 275-282). New York, NY: ACM.

Scardamalia, M., & Bereiter, C. (1992). An architecture for collaborative knowledge-building. In Dc Corte, E., Linn, M., Mandl, H., & Verschaffel, L. (Eds.), *Computer-based learning environments and problem solving* [NATO-ASI Series F: Computer and Systems Science]. (pp. 41–46). Berlin, Germany: Springer-Verlag. doi:10.1007/978-3-642-77228-3_3

Sharma, M. (2008). *Elgg social networking: Create and manage your own social network site using this free open-source tool*. Packt Publishing.

Shirky, C. (2003). *Planning for Web services: Obstacles and opportunities*. O'Reilly.

Strobbe, M., Van Laere, O., Dauwe, S., Dhoedt, B., De Turck, F., & Demeester, P. (2010). Interest based selection of user generated content for rich communication services. *Journal of Network and Computer Applications*, *33*(2), 84–97. doi:10.1016/j.jnca.2009.12.008

Sumi, K. (2008). Anime de Blog: Animation CGM for content distribution. In *2nd International Conference on Advances in Computer Entertainment Technology*, Vol. 352, Yokohama, Japan (pp. 187-190).

Syvänen, A., Muukkonen, J., & Sihvonen, M. (2009). Are the open issues of social software-based personal learning environment practices being addressed? In *Proceedings of the 13th International MindTrek Conference: Everyday Life in the Ubiquitous Era* (MindTrek '09) (pp. 142-148). New York, NY: ACM.

Tapscott, D., & Williams, A. D. (2006). *Wikinomics: How mass collaboration changes everything*. New York, NY: Penguin.

Toffler, A. (1980). *The third wave*. Bantam Books.

Valtonen, T., Hacklin, S., Dillon, P., Vesisenaho, M., Kukkonen, J., & Hietanen, A. (2012). Perspectives on personal learning environments held by vocational students. *Computers & Education*, *58*(2), 732–739. doi:10.1016/j.compedu.2011.09.025

Von Hippel, E. (2005). *Democratizing innovation*. MIT Press.

Vygotsky, L. S. (1978). *Mind in society: The development of higher psychological processes* (Cole, M., John-Steiner, V., Scribner, S., & Souberman, E., Eds.). Cambridge, MA: Harvard University Press.

Weber, S. (2005). *The success of open source.* Harvard University Press.

Weinberger, D. (2007). *Everything is miscellaneous: The power of the new digital disorder* (p. 288). Henry Holt.

Wenger, E. (1998). *Communities of practice: Learning, meaning and identity.* Oxford, UK: Oxford University Press.

Witell, L., Kristensson, P., Gustafsson, A., & Lofgren, M. (2011). Idea generation: Customer co-creation versus traditional market research techniques. *Journal of Service Management, 22*(2), 140–159. doi:10.1108/09564231111124190

Young, G. O. (2007, September 7). *Passionate employees: The gateway to enterprise web 2.0 sales.* Forrester Research.

Zittrain, J. (2006). The generative internet. *Harvard Law Review, 119*, 1974–2040.

KEY TERMS AND DEFINITIONS

Consumer Generated Media (CGM): An active consumer who produces and develops media contents.

Enterprise 2.0: An enterprise open towards the external environment that exchanges information using web 2.0 tools (blog, forum, chat, wiki) and social networks.

Personal Learning Environment (PLE): A didactic environment where people use virtual tools to personalize a learning path.

Prosumer: Producer and consumer at the same time. An active consumer who participates in the productive process to improve the final product/service.

User Generated Content (UGC): An active user who produces and generates contents (information, knowledge).

Virtual Learning Environment (VLE): A didactic environment where people use virtual channels to learn contents.

Chapter 2
Using Social Media as a Concept and Tool for Teaching Marketing Information Systems

Theodosios Tsiakis
Alexander Technological Educational Institute of Thessaloniki, Greece

ABSTRACT

Teachers use social media in order to have instant, comfortable and effective way to communicate and transact with students. Online classrooms also are becoming more and more social. So why not use these methods that are already in wide use as a teaching tool? Social media began as an entertainment tool, then became a marketing phenomenon, and now is seen as a new pedagogical tool. The Marketing Information System course aims in offering students (the tomorrow marketers) an in-depth view and understanding of information systems that support an effective way the marketing activities. MIS is the process of connecting people, processes, and technology. The use of ICT has changed the way marketing decisions are made. On the one hand, using information technologies supports achievement of a current marketing strategy while on the other hand these technologies set new marketing rules, and social media is the technology that represents a unique way of transmitting information in all directions. So with one concept (social media), we can achieve multiple benefits. This chapter (1) provides a literature review (overview) of the current use and benefits of Web 2.0 or so-called social media tools in the support of teaching or pedagogical process, (2) offers a systematic way of understanding and conceptualizing online social media as a teaching tool, and (3) suggests the framework in which social media tools can be applied and used in the Marketing Information System (MkIS) course both as part in the course structure and as a mean to teach MkIS.

DOI: 10.4018/978-1-4666-2970-7.ch002

INTRODUCTION

Students today want new, effective and fascinating teaching methods. They dislike and do not tolerate passive learning. A novel approach to solve this problem and motivate the learning process is with the use of Social Media. Students already use social media (in text messaging, chat, Facebook, Twitter etc.). Nowadays, as information (more and more) is available everywhere and mainly on the web, people need the skills and knowledge to find, access and use it effectively and this necessitate the information literacy (Islam and Tsuji, 2010). Marketing professional need information to forecast changes in product demand, increase selling productivity and manage sales and distribution expenses (Proctor, 1991). Coinstantaneously, decisions concerning product development, new markets and response to competitor activity can be improved by good marketing information (Kitchen and Dawes, 1995). As stated above the need for marketing information is not new but in the contemporary extreme antagonistic, complex and dynamic economic environment, the translation of data into information relevant to management decisions is vital to the long-term survival of a business (Romeiro-Serna and Garmendia, 2007). Lin and Hong (2009) consider marketing information being mainly descriptive, based on observation and its goal to provide managers with general enlightenment about an ongoing competitive market situation.

Marketing is a process that requires particular management philosophy and especially accurate, authoritative and timely information. Marketing plays a major role in any organizations. Marketing is "the activity, set of institutions, and processes for creating, communicating, delivering, and exchanging offerings that have value for customers, clients, partners, and society at large" (American Marketing Association, January 2008). In the case of products, the basic of marketing is condensed in the 4 Ps (product, price, place, promotion) and in services the 7 Ps (service product, price, place, promotion, people, process and physical evidence).

The concept and the practice of function-oriented marketing have been fundamentally reshaped and it is still shaped and redefined (Xu, 1999). As Brady et al. (1999) indicate, marketing is and will continue to be heavily influenced and conditioned by Information Technology (IT). But there are certain constraints to what IT can do and of course IT cannot work miracles by itself. And those organizations that are willing and have the ability to fully embrace IT for their marketing applications will be able to compete effectively (Leverick et al., 1997). But in the 1990's, the application appeared to concentrate on functional support, rather than strategic support (Xu, 1999).

The use of Information Systems (IS) in marketing also is maturing and several maps of IT in marketing distinguish systems according to their technical features (Daniel et al., 2003). Leverick et al. (1997) in their paper also refer to Baker (1994) work for the distinction between four broad areas of IT application to marketing activities:

1. IT to enhance operating efficiency - application of IT to marketing activities that were already in practise in the organization, such as making presentations or analysing sales statistics.
2. IT and changed methods - application of IT to enable the department of marketing to complete internal functions that were extreme possible before.
3. IT for enhancing customer service –use of IT for providing better and faster communication with customers and customer market support.
4. IT and marketing innovation – services like on-line databases; direct mail services etc.

Social Media Marketing is one of the fastest expanding digital marketing channels. (Stahlschmidt et al, 2011) define Social Media Marketing (SMM) as "special form of online marketing with the objective of using social media platforms to pursue a customer-oriented marketing campaign". Five constructs of perceived SMM activities for example in a case of luxury fashion brands are (1) entertainment, (2) interaction, (3) trendiness, (4) customization and (5) word of mouth (Kim and Ko, 2011). So, Traditional (ex. one way communication) and New Media Marketing (ex. multi directional communication) result to effective Marketing Mix.

MARKETING INFORMATION SYSTEMS

The exigency of enterprises to handle the increasing external and internal information flow and to improve its quality, created the need to take advantage of the opportunities offered by modern Information Technology (IT) and Information Systems (IS) and managing marketing information by means of IT become nowadays one of the most vital elements of effective marketing (Talvinen, 1995). "It was the use of IT in the customer service transaction that has revolutionised the potential for data collection associated with customers and transactions" (Rowley, 1999). The importance of marketing information is distinctly apparent as the economy continues to emphasise services as a primary source of value and information is becoming a service in its own right (AL-allak, 2010). The importance of marketing information is particularly apparent Harmon (2003) refers aright as the economy continues to emphasize services as a primary source of value. Continuing, Wood (2001) indicates that the majority of marketing information systems utilise mainly internal data simply because they are easy to obtain in antithesis to managers that require external information to base their long-term decisions. Preparative to manipulate the plethora of external and internal information flow and both to improve information quality, organizations have to benefit the opportunities offered by contemporary information technology (IT) and information systems (IS).

The use of IT in the customer service transaction has revolutionised the potential for data collection associated with customers and transactions. Two key tools in this transformation are loyalty cards and electronic or e-shopping over the Internet (Rowley, 1999). A good and well established marketing information system can make the process of decision making more efficient and effective as it can be used to help create a competitive advantage and/or even substitute for expensive assets (Buttery and Tamaschke, 1996). Despite the improvements in the use of tools to gather and handle information, the process continues being the same: Input, Process, Output (Romeiro-Serna and Garmendia 2007). Both input and output modules of a marketing information system must be considered. Input is conditioned by how the information is collected (directly captured from sales or collected externally from market research) (Buttery and Tamaschke, 1996).

Marketing information system (MkIS or/and MIS) lies at the middle part between the environment and the marketer (information user) and is a whole flowing process concerning the transfer and feedback of the information and data. The company obtains the information of the environment as an input of the MIS based on the market research and analysis (stage 1). The company then processes this kind of information in order to acquire its essence and dispose them using the MIS (stage 2). This kind of information is provided to the marketers through the MIS and finally the marketers will frame the reasonable marketing plans and control its performance (stage 3) (Figure 1) (Zhongke, 2010).

Marketing information system has four components (Al-Allak, 2010):

1. **The Internal Recording System:** Including orders received, inventory records and sales invoices.

Figure 1. The flowing process of the information (Adapted from Zhongke, 2010)

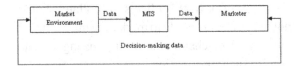

2. **The Marketing Research System:** Taking the form of systematic studies and analysis of data (and information) either ad hoc or continuous for the identification and solution of any problem in the field of marketing.
3. **The Marketing Intelligence System:** Is the one that systematically gathers and processes critical business information obtained from external sources transforming them into actionable management intelligence for marketing decisions.
4. **Marketing Models:** Descriptive vs Predictive vs Normative, Informal vs Formal.

In the early stages, MkIS were seen according to Talvinen and Saarinen (1995) as tools especially for analysing internal and external effectiveness of marketing and for controlling marketing activities and environment. Internal dimensions of MkIS effectiveness embrace improvements in the reporting system and the effective management of the company's internal relationships. External dimensions of MkIS effectiveness include the ability to monitor a company's market environment more effectively (AL-allak, 2010). Talvinen (1995) studied that the purpose of the earliest marketing systems was "to gather, sort, analyse, evaluate and distribute pertinent, timely and accurate information for marketing decision makers to improve their planning, implementation and control". The improvements of MkIS are then classified into three groups:

1. Improvements in Marketing
2. improvements in Sales
3. Overall Organizational Improvements

Marketing information system (MkIS) is simply "a computerized system that provides an organized flow of information to enable and support the marketing activities of an organization and serves collaborative, analytical, and operational needs" according to Harmon (2003). O'Brien et al. (1995) define a MKIS as "an organized set of data that is analyzed through reports and statistical routines and models on an ongoing basis" where data are transformed into information allowing the marketing manager to make better decisions and perform better planning and budgeting" (Figure 2).

Proctor, (1991) classifies marketing information systems under the following headings:

- **Planning Systems:** Providing information on sales, costs and competitive activity, together with any kind of information which is needed to formulate plans.
- **Control Systems:** Providing continuous monitoring of marketing activities and enable marketing executives to identify problems and opportunities in the marketplace.
- **Marketing Research Systems:** Allowing executives to test decision rules and cause/effect hypotheses.
- **Monitoring Systems:** Providing management with information concerning the external environment in which they are operating.

Figure 2. Overview of the marketing information system (Adapted from O'Brien et al., 1995)

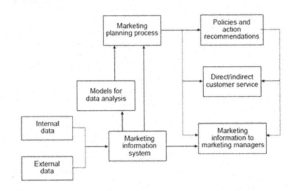

Rowley, (1999) broadly categorise marketing information systems similar to other types of information systems into four kinds where these categories reflect the different levels at which marketing information is collected and analysed:

1. Transaction and Operational Data Processing Systems
2. Management Information Systems
3. Decision Support Systems
4. Executive Information Systems

A marketing information system (MKIS) is an essential tool for translating raw data into useful information and so the emphasis should be placed on the instant conversion of knowledge into customer value which fundamentally depends on the ability to develop, deploy, and manage powerful new marketing information systems (Harmon, 2003), (O'Brien et al., 1995).

Mitchell and Sparks (1988) state that Kotler's (1984) definition "a continuing and interacting structure of people, equipment, and procedures to gather, sort, analyse and distribute, pertinent, timely and accurate information for use by marketing decision makers to improve their marketing planning, implementation and control" is comprehensive but there are two other points. The first is that accurate might be useful for operational management decisions but strategic management decisions require more aggregated data and therefore accuracy is not the prime concern. Secondly the information MkIS collects and collates should not be restricted mainly to marketing management but should be channelled to any managers who require such information.

Hess et al. (2004) considering that both Kotler (1997) and Burns and Bush (2000) present nearly identical models of marketing information systems (relationships between managerial tasks, uses of the MKIS, information development of MKIS and decisions in the marketing environment) reproduce the model for MkIS referenced as the 'K/BB model (Figure 3).

Rowley, (1999) and (1994) in her paper refers to Beaumont, (1991) work, where "marketing information systems (MKIS) must be designed to support the types of decision making in which marketeers need to engage. These decisions derive from the basic questions that marketers need to ask" (Table 1).

The primary benefits of the MkIS impact the areas of functional integration (coordination of activities), market monitoring (identification of emerging market segments and changes in consumer behavior), strategy development (necessary information to develop marketing strategy), and strategy implementation (enablement of decision makers to more effectively manage) (Harmon, 2003). Having in mind the potential benefits that

Figure 3. Model for marketing information system (Adopted from Hess et al., 2004)

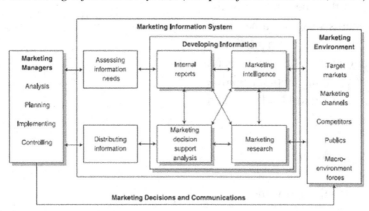

Table 1. Fundamental marketing questions

Who?	Are our customers? Should our customers be? Are our competitors?
What?	New/existing products and services should we develop? New/existing markets should we enter?
Where?	Should we develop? Are our customers? Should we distribute our products and services? Are our competitors?
When?	Should we launch new products and services? Should we enter new/leave existing markets?
How?	Should we promote our products and services? Should we distribute our products and services? Should we handle consumer reactions/expectations? Should we compete? Should we maximize our returns? Should we maintain our performance and evaluate new opportunities?
Why?	Should consumers buy our products and services? Should we develop new products and services? Should we remain in particular markets/businesses?

derived from successful use of an MKIS, certain implementation problems exist due to; i) the managers often are reluctant to utilise information systems that have not been involved in their design and development and also have not training properly to utilize the system; ii) in many firms, marketing planning systems have not transformed from market status reporting to market response predicting; iii) response model specification is quite complex (O'Brien et al., 1995).

A determinative element is the data storage and retrieval due to the fact of getting information into a system is relatively easy but finding it and retrieving it is rather intricate (Buttery and Tamaschke, 1996). In the current competitive contemporary economic environment the link between the enterprise and the market environment is the Marketing Information System (Zhongke, 2010).

SOCIAL MEDIA

From the beginning it should be realized that social computing is about a dialog and thus implies more listening than speaking and the sooner this is identified the sooner there will be business value (Prohaska, 2011). Moreover marketing initiatives such as a website, or social media presence, represent an investment, not an expense. An assemblage of technical factors such as high speed broadband connectivity, wireless connectivity, falling cost of data storage and hardware mobility foster connectivity through social media.

Online social media represent a fundamental shift of how information is being produced, transferred and consumed. Social media provide a connection between our social networks, personal information channels and the mass media (Leskovec, 2011). Social media has exploded as a category of online discourse where people create content, distribute materials, share ideas, express opinions, and use information and knowledge, share bookmark and network at a prodigious rate (Heinrichs et al., 2011) (Asur and Huberman, 2010) (Wen-Huei et al, 2010,). As Singh et al. (2009) suggest in a scenario where individual agents may be interested in maximizing their personal utility gain, the key question is "how can an individual user optimally decide his/her contribution strategy i.e. when (and when not) should he/she undertake the social media task". Solomon et al. (2011) phrase that it is self-motivation to interact, work together and create vast quantities of online content that results in content sharing, timely communication, constant feedback etc. (to work all together with emergent outcomes). Sweetser and Kelleher (2011) refers that psychologists have identified a range of four factors (Intrinsic motivation, Identified regulation, External regulation, Amotivation) to explain what motivates people. This area of social interaction is one of the fastest growing segments on the web as Parra-López et al (2011) found, including social sharing of opinions through blogs and microblogs (i.e. Blogger and Twitter), social photo and video sharing (i.e. Flickr and YouTube), social sharing of knowledge (i.e. Wikipedia), social bookmarking (i.e. Delicious) and many other forms of user-generated content.

Social Networking Site (SNS) is defined as a linked collection of Web pages that allow members to communicate one with another, as well as post personal information including blogs, pictures, and videos (Malesky Jr. and Peters, 2012). Social network sites are defined as web-based services that allow individuals to (1) construct a public or semi-public profile within a bounded system, (2) articulate a list of other users with whom they share a connection, and (3) view and traverse their list of connections and those made by others within the system (Silius et al., 2010).

Blogs (short for "web logs") are web sites, publishing tools, owned, managed and written by a particular identified author (individuals). The blogger writes and publishes an entry, and readers respond in the blog's comments—or even on their own blog and these entries (including text, graphics, video and more) appear in reverse chronological order (Reyneke et al, 2011), (Shepherd, 2011), (Click and Petit, 2010).

Wikis are a kind of web site or collection of web pages designed to support the entries of different users. An entry, in this context, is like an article in an encyclopaedia, but created by a volunteer user, and then modified, corrected and amended in a controlled fashion by other users. Wikis are often used to create collaborative websites and to power community websites. Several websites offer no-cost wiki hosting and Wikipedia is the most well-known initiative (Shepherd, 2011).

Social bookmarking allows users to store, organize, search, manage, and share webpage bookmarks. Delicious (delicious.com) is the most popular social bookmarking site. Media sharing systems are important aspects of Web2.0 and should also be emphasised. These not only allow users to share videos (Youtube), photographs (Flickr), documents (DocStoc) and presentations

(SlideShare), but also let others offer their evaluations and opinions. Picture sharing web sites, the best known of which are Flickr, Yahoo Images, and Google Images (Google I) allow users to store and share images. Video sharing web sites allow users to upload and share videos. Typically, unregistered users can watch the videos, while registered users are permitted to upload an unlimited number of videos. The best known of the video sharing web sites is YouTube.

Social media are internet-based applications that carry consumer generated content which encompasses media impressions created by consumers, typically informed by relevant experience, and archived or shared online for easy access by other impressionable consumers (Haiyan, 2010). Social media are online applications, platforms and media which aim to facilitate interactions, collaborations and the sharing of content. They take a variety of forms, including weblogs, social blogs, microblogging, wikis, podcasts, pictures, video, rating and social bookmarking (Kim and Ko, 2011). Social Media is a group of Internet-based applications that build on the ideological and technological foundations of Web 2.0, and that allow the creation and exchange of User Generated Content (Haenlein and Kaplan 2009). Consumer-generated content (CGC) refers to media content created or produced by general public than by paid professionals and primarily distributed on the internet (Haiyan, 2010). The term requires drawing a line between two related concepts that are frequently named in conjunction with it: Web 2.0 and User Generated Content. The Web 2.0 Web 2.0 is a term to describe a new way in which software developers and end-users started to utilize the World Wide Web (Haenlein and Kaplan 2009). It is necessary to be mentioned also that there is a clear distinction between multimedia and Web 2.0 (Bonsón and Flores, 2011).

Social media are beginning to transform the ways in which individuals and organizations relate to each other. Relationships make social media social (different relationships play different roles)

and social media datasets are especially useful for mapping relationships between people (Hansen, 2011) (Gilbert and Karahalios, 2009).

Content is increasingly being delivered in streams (a series of text documents that arrive over time) and people that publish to the Web mainly use streams in order to share information and their interests, daily activities, and opinions with others (Jonghun et al, 2011). Individuals participating in social media framework can be thought of as information sources that emit units of information in a streaming fashion (Mathioudakis et al., 2010). As enterprises and organizations adopt social media tools like blogs, wikis, friend and contact networks, activity streams and file, photo, and video shares a rich new source of social network data is created (Smith et al, 2009). A simple question that arises is why we are care so much about information in social media? Weerkamp (2010) array three examples:

1. **Viewpoint Research:** Someone wants to take note of the viewpoints on a particular issue.
2. **Answers to Problems:** Many problems that have been encountered before, and people have shared solutions.
3. **Product Development:** Gaining insight into how people use a product and what features they wish for, eases the development of new products.

The access method (ex. through mobile devices desktop computers, and/or notebooks) to reach the social networking sites consist the determinative of success as it have an impact on the usage be-

Figure 4. Spectrum of approaches to using social media (Adapted from Weinberg & Pehlivan, 2011)

Traditional   Emergent

havior in information sharing and content creation of the various social networking sites (Heinrichs et al., 2011). Especially small or medium-sized enterprises (SMEs) can benefit/profit a lot from social media in team collaboration due to ease of use and access (Zeiller and Schauer, 2011). Social media users typically receive contact information from others users (ex. requests to join an online game, uploads of media files). Two important categories of contact information in social media are collaborative activity and social relation (Chi-Lun, 2011).

Weinberg and Pehlivan (2011) identified three general approaches toward using social media that varies in extent to which the approach is traditional or emergent in nature (Figure 4).

The first is traditional in marketing nature, that treats social media channels the same as long-established media channels (e.g., television, radio, print). The second is experimental in involving testing and learning to identify the important factors/critical-ends associated with social media (e.g., conversation, engagement, evangelism). And third, (also) experimentation, 1 searching for factors inherent in or distinct about social media (e.g., communicating with a more 'human' voice than a 'corporate' voice). "Social networks aren't about Web sites. They're about experiences" (Hanna et al., 2011)

The question of what factors influence individual participation in social media conversations highlight that the conversations (around user posted content) are important to understand the nature of the underlying social network sites because conversations can be used to consider a number of issues such as user behaviour and information roles (De Choudhury and Sundaram, 2011).

There is a diverse ecology of social media sites, which vary in terms of their scope and functionality (Kietzmann et al, 2011). Hanna et al. (2011) refers to the divide of social media ecosystem [according to Corcoran (2009) and Li and Bernoff (2008)] into three media types:

1. **Owned Media:** Controlled by the marketer; e.g., Company website.
2. **Paid Media:** Bought by the marketer; e.g., Sponsorships, advertising.
3. **Earned Media:** Not controlled or bought by the marketer; e.g., Word-of-mouth, viral.

And segment active participants in the ecosystem based on five different types of social behaviors:

1. **Creators:** e.g., Publish, maintain, upload
2. **Critics:** e.g., Comment, rate
3. **Collectors:** e.g., Save, share
4. **Joiners:** e.g., Connect, unite
5. **Spectators:** e.g., Read

Traditionally, consumers where simply consuming content (read it, watched it and use it) in order to buy products and services (Kietzmann et al, 2011). Social media transforms the way by which we create and use knowledge. Consumers are now engaged in the active role of co-creating marketing content with companies and their respective brands. They are no longer passive recipients in the marketing exchange process (Hanna et al., 2011). The early adopters of social media have focused on the marketing opportunities as a

Table 2. A timeline for implementing social media

Timeframe	Phase	Description
2011	Innovation	Define "social," identify the business benefits, determine how to measure such benefits, and map out how long it will take to realize them.
2013	Strategy and Implementation	Develop a detailed strategy that integrates with the organization's strategy and operating plan.
2013–2015	Business as usual	Social media becomes a part of everyday business operations, and the public sector and governments invest in social media to obtain citizen feedback.

Figure 5. Social media and corporate dialogue (Adapted from Bonsón & Flores, 2011)

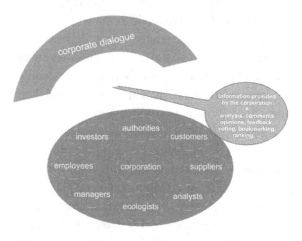

"build it and they will come" strategy but this isn't enough and correct. Creating an engaging dialog with users/customers will require constructing a timeline plan (Table 2) (Prohaska, 2011)

Bonsón and Flores, (2011) indicate that in the context of corporate reporting the main application of the Web 2.0 technologies and the social media is that of corporate dialogue meaning that companies are capable of taking advantage of Web 2.0 potentialities in order to provide information in much greater detail and of more use to users between the stakeholders of any public or private entity (shareholders-owners, managers, employees, customers-users, suppliers, authorities, competitors, local communities, environment) (Figure 5).

There is a plethora of definitions available for the term social media. Social media are defined according to Reyneke et al., (2011) "as media designed to be disseminated through social interaction between individuals and entities such as organizations, that use internet and web-based technologies to transform broadcast media monologues (one to many) into social media dialogues (many to many)". From a sociological perspective, social media can be described as "collective goods produced through computer-mediated collective action" (Smith et al., 2008). For example in the case of Wikipedia, the collective goods are articles and in the case of Digg, the collective goods are news stories. Social media and specifically, social networking sites (SNS) originate from sociology as mentioned but in a business context, refer to two or more connected business relationships, where an 'exchange' exists between business partners (Michaelidou et al., 2011). From an educational perspective, on line social networks consists a learning practice as the learning environment of the university itself is a social system of individuals' interacting within a shared academic context. In this educational context, on line social networks behavior is related to learning and academic success by creating systems of information, contacts and support (Yan Yu et al., 2010).

Because social media are a relatively new (as a concept and media format), include such a diverse collection of tools and services, few have only attempted to formally classify or categorize or distinguish social media. Reyneke et al. (2011) briefly distinguish SM between blogs, micro-blogs, social network sites, picture sharing, video sharing, and social news web sites. Parent et al. (2011) lay out a description based on Fraser and Dutta (2008) work and offer five broad categories:

1. **Egocentric:** Sites for users to build profiles.
2. **Community Sites:** Sites replicating physical world into a virtual world.
3. **Opportunistic Sites:** Facilitating business connections.
4. **Passion-Centric Sites:** Specialized for medley of fans.
5. **Media-Sharing Sites:** Sites for users sharing enriched media content – ex. image, audio, video.

Kietzmann et al. (2011) use a honeycomb of seven functional building blocks that allows to unpack and examine first a specific facet of social media user experience and second its implications for firms (Figure 6):

Figure 6. The honeycomb of social (Adopted from Kietzmann et al., 2011)

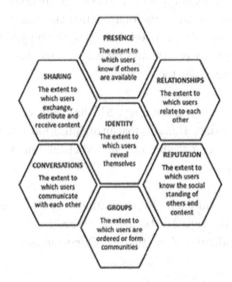

1. **Identity:** (Functional) block represents the extent to which users reveal their identities in a social media setting.
2. **Conversations:** The block that represents the extent to which users communicate with other users in a social media setting.
3. **Sharing:** Represents the extent to which users exchange, distribute, and receive content (evaluating if the object can and should be shared as what objects of sociality their users have in common).
4. **Presence:** (Building) block that represents the extent to which users can know if other users are accessible, where others are (in the virtual world and/or in the real world) and whether they are available.
5. **Relationships:** Represents the extent to which users are related to other users (by 'relate,' it means that two and/or more users have some form of association that leads them to establish a relationship.
6. **Reputation:** The extent to which users can identify the standing of others, including themselves, in a social media setting. Also it have different meanings on social media platforms.

7. **Groups:** (Functional) block that represents the extent to which users can form communities and sub-communities and the more 'social' a network becomes, the bigger the group of friends, followers, and contacts becomes too.

As every technology, SM has both benefits and barriers. Benefits that an organisation obtains using social media, include (Michaelidou et al., 2011):

1. Build Direct Relationships with Customers
2. Increase Traffic to Their Website
3. Identify New Business Opportunities
4. Create Communities
5. Distribute Content
6. Collect Feedback from Customers
7. Generally Support their Brand

On the contrary perceived barriers are:

1. Lack of money, time and training.
2. Ellipsis of perceived ease of use and usefulness.
3. As well as unfamiliarity with the particular technology.
4. Negative usage intention.According to Everett (2010) the security risks posed by all social networking sites are basically the same (anonymity, data leakage and risk - legal implications).

MkIS COURSE STRUCTURE INCLUDING SM

Educational and learning environment has been reformed as a result of the diffusion of Information and Communications Technologies (ICT). Social media now comprise the new variable. On line social networking is penetrating university campuses, influencing multiple aspects of student life and students' learning outcomes (Yan Yu et al., 2010). In this frame we have to examine how social media technology can be used to improve education and the adjustment to college (De Andrea et al., 2012). As Malesky Jr. and Peters (2012) characteristically stete "it is yet to be determined what role this rapidly evolving method of communication will play in an academic setting". In the business field similarly corporate behaviour tends to follow what happens outside work in reference to social media (Shepherd, 2011). In some cases universities seemed to lack a clear understanding of whose responsibility social media is, which by turn leads to confusion, lack of leadership and social media being under resourced (Nicholas et al., 2011).

In the current educational environment we face a new instantiation of the digital divide where students are often more technologically adept than their instructors (Vie, 2008). This generation characterised as "Internet/net generation" (grown up with technology – other names refer to Generation M (media), Generation V (virtual) or Generation C, (connected-click)) in difference with "digital immigrants" (who adopted digital media later or grown up without them). But that does not conclude that all digital natives are digital learners. These learners have different styles of information processing and learning expectations, which creates to the educational institutions the need to reconsider pedagogical approaches (Yan Yu et al., 20103).

Similar to other Information and Communication Technologies (ICT), SNS are targeted as young people widely used them (Pfeil et al., 2009). Social media are so attractive to so many users currently that emerging new media literacies have to be associated with social media, especially when it can be aligned with a course content structure (Mehlenbacher et al., 2010).

Social media impacts educational information in two aspects. Firstly, based on the support of social media, education information (expressed either as text, picture, animation, video, audio etc.) has changed the representation of educational information. Secondly, educational information is no longer personal but social sharing (once information is released, it can be accessed, reproduced, shared, and be commented and so on) (Shipin et al., 2011). Jacobs et al. (2009) consider that the course design, when is developing, should have a few basic tenets in mind, such as a the course should exposed students to a multidisciplinary approach to social media systems, their uses and to structure the course around two different organizational contexts (ex. evaluate social media based upon technology, social capabilities, system usability and to structure materials based upon the literature).

CREATING A CONTEMPORARY MkIS

Traditionally each new medium of communication or information technology invented (ex. printed media – books/multimedia – e-learning) has altered and transformed the educational process. If we want to better understand how our students perceive knowledge and to be informed then we need to reshape our educational methods. There are many ways in which social media can be used to facilitate workplace learning. Teaching and related activities can benefit greatly by using forums to discuss issues and share ideas, blogs as learning journals, wikis as a focus for group collaborative projects, podcasts and videos as a means for sharing research (Shepherd, 2011). Social media services can be divided into six (6) categories (Silius et al., 2011):

1. Content Creation and Publishing
2. Content Sharing
3. Social Network Sites
4. Collaborative Productions
5. Virtual Worlds
6. Add-Ons

Many faculty use Learning Management Systems (LMSs) or course management systems (CMS) to share lecture notes, collect homework assignments, conduct online exams. They are defined as an online web-based tool allowing administration (instructors) and/or students to share materials and interact online (inside and outside the physical classroom). Examples are Scholar360, Moodle and Blackboard. Social media enhanced learning systems allow students among other things to contribute content, exchange opinions and create communities for different needs (Silius et al., 2011. A comparison between typical SNS and a traditional CMS appears is given by (Brady et al, 2010) (Table 3). A little modification has been made, as second indications have been added to file sharing and Wiki in SNS row and media sharing in CMS row. This comparison makes apparent the supremacy of SNS towards educational use.

College students are active users mainly of Facebook and Twitter and similar technologies. Universities in order to support and communicate

Table 3. A timeline for implementing social media

Tools	SNS	Traditional CMS
Forum	✓	✓
Blog	✓	✓
Media Sharing	✓	✓
Messaging	✓	✓
Wiki	✓	
RSS	✓	
Chat	✓	✓
Calendar	✓	✓
Tagging	✓	
Own Brand & Visual Design	✓	
Realtime Activity Stream	✓	
Groups	✓	
Friends	✓	
Profile Pages	✓	
File sharing	✓	✓

well with college students could embrace both as a vehicle, especially Facebook as it integrates static user-designed Webs (personal pages), synchronous (instant messages) and asynchronous chats (wall posts), picture uploading, group formation, event hosting, Web development tools, dynamic searches, RSS feeds (news feeds), blogs (web logs), mass and individual messaging, and e-mail (Heiberger and Harper, 2008). Although there is a paucity of empirical studies examining its use in educational settings (Ryan et al., 2011). On Facebook, individuals establish profiles with detailed personal information. Twitter provides a Web-based service that enables users to send short messages (140 characters) or to engage in microblogging, also known as tweets. On Twitter, people might and also do choose names that may obscure their real identities (Click and Petit, 2010).

Wagner (2011) had discover five ideas for both Facebook and Twitter for teaching and learning.

The ideas for Facebook are:

1. **Use as Learning Management System (LMS):** If there is no access to Blackboard, Moodle, or other LMS, Facebook can be used to share documents, poll/quiz your students, and conduct group discussions.
2. **Reference Citations:** Facebook has hundreds of applications (apps) that can be used for educational purposes. One example is Worldcat.org's CiteMe application that provides formatted citations for books.
3. **Announcements:** Send and post reminders, upcoming, events and schedule changes.
4. **Post Class Notes:** Post documents with descriptions in any file format.
5. **Create Group Discussions:** Creation by splitting class in to smaller study groups for class projects. You can keep track of student's participation, provide guidance, and monitor progress.

The ideas for Twitter are:

1. **Log a Teachable Moment:** Students can tweet about variations of skills they learn during their course – lecture experiences.
2. **Quiz:** Send quiz questions to your class and provide bonus points to students who respond within a given timeframe.
3. **Track a Concept:** Present a concept in class and ask students to tweet about the concept when they read about it in the professional literature.
4. **Track Time:** Students can use Twitter to keep track of their time spent in their marketing construction settings.
5. **Learning Diary:** Students can keep a journal of the things that they learn during their modules.

Wiki could implemented both as to host the curriculum, syllabus, assignments, and lesson plans and to encourage students to work together to create definitions, explore complex issues such as ethics and tease out answers to questions posed by the educators (Carroll et al., 2011). Wikis are rapidly gaining favor among educators because they believe in their ease of use with which this Web 2.0 tool supports collaborative learning process.

Blogs could serve for students as a source of information and as a daily log of activities, especially to be encouraged to reflect on what they were learning and experiencing on the module, through their interactions, reflections and also their actions in the form of the production of artefacts (Carroll et al., 2011), (Kelm, 2011).

Del.icio.us, is a bookmarking tool that use keywords, it can be offered as a way to share bookmark links bibliographies, papers and other resources to assist students in learning process. Google Docs, it may not come to mind as a social media platform, but Google Docs provides a way to share a pack of files like documents, spreadsheets and presentations in a certain environment. Also Youtube could be used as an educational tool to upload tutorial videos inside and outside classroom.

Thus using Social Media Functions for Teaching has:

- **Forums:** Discuss weekly projects and readings.
- **Blogs:** Students reading and responding.
- **On-Line Communication as Office Hours:** Flexibility for me and students.
- **Uploaded Material:** Instant, unlimited with out need to print.

Although a large number of universities require courses in Management Information Systems (also referred as MIS) and Marketing Information Systems for their business majors, •there is little information about what objectives should be included in the course and the course topics vary greatly across institutions (Foltz et al., 2004). A typical MkIS course aims to set students an adequate understanding of the concept, basic theory, structure and application mechanisms of MkIS. The dual nature of the teaching process of the course (theoretical and practical) has divided student to consider MkIS course either as a pure theoretical or to regard it as a computer based course due to the implementation of computing systems. As a consequence to learn it largely by rote or confused by computer based concept (Haihe, 2011). Haihe (2011) also presenting a literature in a similar course of Management Information System (MIS), found that the result of students have a great difference of scores and learning effect (in the same class) and attribute the problems of the current MIS course teaching exist mainly in the following aspects

1. The MIS course has many cross-cutting prerequisites and without relevant knowledge students gradually loose interest in learning.

And here is where the idea of using social media as a teaching medium/process is determinative.

2. How MIS operate in enterprises (practical) can't be fully understood by enrolled students.

3. Since management consist a subject that introduced, students think erroneously that it is a theoretical course and can be learnt by rote (following the route of loosing interest).

4. The students are impediment to connect the knowledge learned in class with practice. They are confused and often don't know how and from where to start.

While academic faculty is evaluated according to the three criteria of teaching, research and services (the former is evaluated by students and the two latter are evaluated by college faculty), industry both evaluate and prefers academic programs that impart higher level of business and leadership knowledge and use more experiential learning models (Simon and Soliman, 2003), (Benamati et al., 2010). Social media is the current trend that market wants and needs to employ. Therefore, it is fundamental to formulate a curriculum in conformity with training goals required by a specialized course in marketing information system, to address current implications - relations with the other courses and foremost to optimize various teaching procedures along with the best teaching tools and materials (Shiju, 2007). Students are now considered as both producers and consumers (i.e., 'prosumers' - neologism) of learning content (Cheng et al., 2010).

A typical marketing information systems course focuses on understanding the role of information technology and systems in supporting enterprises needs, enabling decision making in marketing and providing how information systems enable organizations to achieve their objectives in an efficient and effective way. The main goal of the course is to familiarize students with the development of ICTs and their marketing implications, to explore various ways in which information technology relates to organisational objectives. The course will provide the practical knowledge and insights required to establish the objectives and strategies of marketing information systems. The philosophy behind the course is the following.

Goals and Objectives

- Introduce students to important terms and concepts relative to the use of information technologies for marketing.
- Provide students with a basic understanding of the technologies influencing current marketing practices.
- Understand the use of information systems to gain competitive advantage with marketing/management of information as an organizational resource.
- Identify the importance of the role of IT in the acquisition, production, and distribution of goods and services.
- How to identify, analyze and propose information systems solutions to organizational problems (how data stored and information transformed and handled).
- Describe the current marketing information systems and social media marketing ecosystem.
- Review of the various social media platforms and purposes.
- Understand various forms of social media, determine their uses, benefits barriers and how to integrate social media marketing.
- Understand online presence, website construction and how enterprises and their brands are perpetuate, reformed and damaged online.
- Distinguish and analyze the various stakeholders online and social media best practices.
- Understand current legal, ethical, Information Security & Privacy issues.

- Research and analyze social media marketing process and strategies (including the creation of user-generated content, multimedia channels, mobile marketing and apps).
- Most importantly, provide students with hands-on experience in the construction and maintenance of social media such as blogs and wikis.

Finally a typical week tentative lecture topics could be:

1. Marketing Perspective in the Internet Age
2. **Internet Fundamentals:** Operations, Management
3. **Marketing Information Systems:** Business Driven
4. Information Systems in Global Business Today, Organizations, and Strategy
5. **E-Business:** Value, Digital Markets, Digital Goods
6. Building Information Systems
7. **Enterprise Applications:** Business Communications
8. Marketing Internet Development
9. The Evolution of Social Technology
10. How to Interact with Social Media
11. Contemporary Internet Marketing Mix

CONCLUSION

Marketing is a managerial process, a term given to describe the activities between consumers/customers and businesses/organisations (an exchange process). The classical marketing tasks of identifying, targeting and understanding consumers is changing and evolving. Web 2.0 as a technology and idea is transforming consumers control over marketing functions. We are witnessing a rapid rise of social media. This along with the popularity of social media indicates that can't be ignored. The implementation of social media as a platform of marketing, communication and social interaction is becoming bigger and bigger. These new media have changed the game of marketing. There is an obvious exigency to study the role of social media in the marketing mix and to acknowledge how to manage and exploit the new media for businesses. The MkIS course should aims to equip students with a good overview of the basic principles of social media marketing, how to integrate and align social media strategy marketing into the overall marketing plan, explore appropriate channels, content, tools and techniques and how to measure the success of your social media activity.

Colleges and universities as a wide social communities form their discrete role in shaping skills, knowledge and culture. The social media landscape reflects the link between different social movements and the respective online portals supporting these movements. All that student gain from embranglement with Social Media are important for their social and professional life. Furthermore, social media and constantly connected students are reshaping the pedagogy, learning and teaching process. Today students are using internet to learn what they need to know, for social needs, for sharing opinions and material etc. The discussion about whether social media are having a positive or negative impact on education the only thing that we can say with absolute confidence is neither positive neither negative. It is yet to find out, but the good signs are more that the bad ones and of course the usage is the one that defines the purpose.

REFERENCES

Al-Allak, B. (2010). Evaluating the adoption and use of internet-based marketing information systems to improve marketing intelligence (the case of tourism SMEs in Jordan). *International Journal of Marketing Studies*, 2(2), 87–101.

American Marketing Association. (2008). *Marketing definition*. Retrieved May 1, 2010, from http://www.marketingpower.com/AboutAMA/ Documents/American%20Marketing%20Association%20Releases%20New%20Definition%20 for%20Marketing.pdf

Asur, S., & Huberman, B. (2010). Predicting the future with social media. *IEEE/WIC/ACM International Conference on Web Intelligence and Intelligent Agent Technology* (WI-IAT), (pp. 492–499).

Baker, M. J. (1994). Marketing intelligence for intelligent marketing, In J. Chapman & C. Holtham (Eds.), *IT in marketing*. Henley on Thames, UK: Alfred Waller in association with UNICOM.

Beaumont, J. R. (1991). GIS and market analysis. In Maguire, D. J., Goodchild, M. J., & Rhind, D. W. (Eds.), *Geographical information systems: Principles and applications* (pp. 139–151). London, UK: Longman.

Benamati, J., Ozdemir, Z., & Smith, J. (2010). Aligning undergraduate IS curricula with industry needs. *Communications of the ACM, 53*(3), 152–156. doi:10.1145/1666420.1666458

Bonsón, E., & Flores, F. (2011). Social media and corporate dialogue: The response of global financial institutions. *Online Information Review, 35*(1), 34–49. doi:10.1108/14684521111113579

Brady, K., Holcomb, L., & Smith, B. (2010). The use of alternative social networking sites in higher educational settings: A case study of the e-learning benefits of Ning in education. *Journal of Interactive Online Learning, 9*(2), 151–170.

Brady, M., Saren, M., & Tzokas, N. (1999). The impact of IT on marketing: An evaluation. *Management Decision, 37*(10), 758–767. doi:10.1108/00251749910302854

Burns, A. C., & Bush, R. F. (2000). *Marketing research*. Prentice Hall.

Buttery, A., & Tamaschke, R. (1996). The use and development of marketing information systems in Queensland, Australia. *Marketing Intelligence & Planning*, *14*(3), 29–35. doi:10.1108/02634509610117339

Carroll, F., Jenkins, A., Woodward, C., Kop, R., & Jenkins, E. (2011). Exploring how social media can enhance the teaching of action research. *Action Research*, *9*(4), 1–19.

Cheng, E., Davis, S., Burnett, I., & Ritz, C. (2010). The role of experts in social media - Are the tertiary educated engaged? *IEEE International Symposium on Technology and Society*, (pp. 205-212).

Chi-Lun, L. (2011). Contact information management system architecture for social media. In *Proceedings of 20th International Conference on Computer Communications and Networks (ICCCN)*, (pp. 1–5).

Click, A., & Petit, J. (2010). Social networking and Web 2.0 in information literacy. *The International Information & Library Review*, *42*, 137–142. doi:10.1016/j.iilr.2010.04.007

Corcoran, S. (2009). *Defining owned, earned, and paid media*. Retrieved September 30, 2010, from http://blogs.forrester.com/interactive_marketing/2009/12/defining-earned-owned-and-paid-media.html

Daniel, E., Wilson, H., & McDonald, M. (2003). Towards a map of marketing information systems: An inductive study. *European Journal of Marketing*, *37*(5/6), 821–847. doi:10.1108/03090560310465161

De Choudhury, M., & Sundaram, H. (2011). Why do we converse on social media? An analysis of intrinsic and extrinsic network factors. ACM SIGMM International Workshop on Social Media (WSM '11), (pp. 53-58). New York, NY: ACM.

DeAndrea, D., Ellison, N., LaRose, R., Steinfield, C., & Fiore, A. (2012). Serious social media: On the use of social media for improving students' adjustment. *The Internet and Higher Education*, *15*(1), 15–23. doi:10.1016/j.iheduc.2011.05.009

Everett, C. (2010). Social media: opportunity or risk? *Computer Fraud & Security*, *6*, 8–10. doi:10.1016/S1361-3723(10)70066-X

Foltz, B., O'Hara, M., & Wise, H. (2004). Standardizing the MIS course: Benefits and pitfalls. *Campus-Wide Information Systems*, *21*(4), 163–169. doi:10.1108/10650740410555043

Fraser, M., & Dutta, S. (2008). *Throwing sheep in the boardroom*. Cornwall, UK: Wiley.

Gilbert, E., & Karahalios, K. (2009). Predicting tie strength with social media. Paper presented at the 27th International Conference on Human Factors in Computing Systems (CHI '09), (pp. 211-220). New York, NY: ACM.

Haenlein, M., & Kaplan, A. (2009). Unprofitable customers and their management. *Business Horizons*, *52*(1), 89–97. doi:10.1016/j.bushor.2008.09.001

Haihe, S. (2011). A practical teaching approach to management information system course. *6th International Conference on Computer Science & Education* (ICCSE), (pp. 631–633).

Haiyan, C. (2010). An impact of social media on online travel information search in China. *3rd International Conference on Information Management, Innovation Management and Industrial Engineering*, (pp. 509-512).

Hanna, R., Rohm, A., & Crittenden, V. (2011). We're all connected: The power of the social media ecosystem. *Business Horizons*, *54*(3), 265–273. doi:10.1016/j.bushor.2011.01.007

Hansen, D. (2011). Exploring social media relationships. *Horizon*, *19*(1), 43–51. doi:10.1108/10748121111107726

Harmon, R. (2003). Marketing information systems. In Bidgoli, H. (Ed.), *Encyclopedia of information systems (Vol. 3*, pp. 137–151). Elsevier Science. doi:10.1016/B0-12-227240-4/00110-6

Heiberger, G., & Harper, R. (2008). Have you Facebooked Astin lately? Using technology to increase student involvement. *New Directions for Student Services, 124*, 19–35. doi:10.1002/ss.293

Heinrichs, J., Jeen-Su, L., & Kee-Sook, L. (2011). Influence of social networking site and user access method on social media evaluation. *Journal of Consumer Behaviour, 10*, 347–355. doi:10.1002/cb.377

Hess, R., Rubin, R., & West, R. Jr. (2004). Geographic information systems as a marketing information system technology. *Decision Support Systems, 38*(2), 197–212. doi:10.1016/S0167-9236(03)00102-7

Islam, M., & Tsuji, K. (2010). Assessing information literacy competency of information science and library management graduate students of Dhaka University. *IFLA Journal, 36*, 300–316. doi:10.1177/0340035210388243

Jacobs, S., Egert, C., & Barnes, S. (2009). Social media theory and practice: Lessons learned for a pioneering course. *39th IEEE International Conference on Frontiers in Education Conference* (FIE'09), (pp. 1125-1129). Piscataway, NJ: IEEE Press.

Jonghun, P., Yongwook, S., Kwanho, K., & Beom-Suk, C. (2011). Searching social media streams on the Web. *2011 International Conference on Computational Aspects of Social Networks* (CA-SoN), (pp. 278–283).

Kelm, O. (2011). Social media: It's what students do. *Business Communication Quarterly, 74*(4), 505–520. doi:10.1177/1080569911423960

Kietzmann, J., Hermkens, K., McCarthy, I., & Silvestre, B. (2011). Social media? Get serious! Understanding the functional building blocks of social media. *Business Horizons, 54*(3), 241–251. doi:10.1016/j.bushor.2011.01.005

Kim, A., & Ko, E. (2011). Do social media marketing activities enhance customer equity? An empirical study of luxury fashion brand. *Journal of Business Research, 65*(10).

Kitchen, P., & Dawes, J. (1995). Marketing information systems in smaller building societies. *International Journal of Bank Marketing, 13*(8), 3–9. doi:10.1108/02652329510098864

Kotler, P. (1984). *Marketing management: Analysis, planning, and control*. Prentice-Hall.

Kotler, P. (1997). *Marketing management: Analysis, planning, and control*. Prentice-Hall.

Leskovec, J. (2011). Social media analytics: tracking, modeling and predicting the flow of information through networks. 20th International Conference Companion on World Wide Web *(WWW '11)*, (pp. 277-278). New York, NY: ACM.

Leverick, F., Littler, D., Wilson, D., & Bruce, M. (1997). The role of IT in the reshaping of marketing. *Journal of Marketing Practice: Applied Marketing Science, 3*(2), 87–106. doi:10.1108/EUM0000000004324

Li, C., & Bernoff, J. (2008). *Groundswell: Winning in a world transformed by social technologies*. Boston, MA: Harvard Business Press.

Lin, C., & Hong, C. (2009). Development of a marketing information system for supporting sales in a tea-beverage market. *Expert Systems with Applications, 36*(3), 5393–5401. doi:10.1016/j.eswa.2008.06.056

Malesky, A. Jr, & Peters, C. (2012). Defining appropriate professional behavior for faculty and university students on social networking websites. *Higher Education, 63*, 135–151. doi:10.1007/s10734-011-9451-x

Mathioudakis, M., Koudas, N., & Marbach, P. (2010). Early online identification of attention gathering items in social media. *Third ACM International Conference on Web Search and Data Mining* (WSDM '10), (pp. 301-310). New York, NY: ACM.

Mehlenbacher, B., McKone, S., Grant, C., Bowles, T., Peretti, S., & Martin, P. (2010). Social media for sustainable engineering communication. *28th ACM International Conference on Design of Communication* (SIGDOC '10), (pp. 65-72). New York, NY: ACM.

Michaelidou, N., Siamagka, N. T., & Christodoulides, G. (2011). Usage, barriers and measurement of social media marketing: An exploratory investigation of small and medium B2B brands. *Industrial Marketing Management, 40*(7), 1153–1159. doi:10.1016/j.indmarman.2011.09.009

Mitchell, J., & Sparks, L. (1988). Marketing information systems in the major UK banks. *International Journal of Bank Marketing, 6*(5), 14–28. doi:10.1108/eb010840

Nicholas, D., Watkinson, A., Rowlands, I., & Jubb, M. (2011). Social media, academic research and the role of university libraries. *Journal of Academic Librarianship, 37*(5), 373–375. doi:10.1016/j.acalib.2011.06.023

O'Brien, T., Schoenbachler, D., & Gordon, G. (1995). Marketing information systems for consumer products companies: A management overview. *Journal of Consumer Marketing, 12*(5), 16–36. doi:10.1108/07363769510147777

Parra-López, E., Bulchand-Gidumal, J., Gutiérrez-Taño, D., & Díaz-Armas, R. (2011). Intentions to use social media in organizing and taking vacation trips. *Computers in Human Behavior, 27*(2), 640–654. doi:10.1016/j.chb.2010.05.022

Pfeil, U., Arjan, R., & Zaphiris, P. (2009). Age differences in online social networking - A study of user profiles and the social capital divide among teenagers and older users in MySpace. *Computers in Human Behavior, 25*(3), 643–654. doi:10.1016/j.chb.2008.08.015

Proctor, R. (1991). Marketing information systems. *Management Decision, 29*(4), 55–60. doi:10.1108/00251749110141824

Prohaska, B. (2011). Social media for the collaborative enterprise. *IT Professional, 13*(4), 64–66. doi:10.1109/MITP.2011.67

Reyneke, M., Pitt, L., & Berthon, P. (2011). Luxury wine brand visibility in social media: An exploratory study. *International Journal of Wine Business Research, 23*(1), 21–35. doi:10.1108/17511061111121380

Romeiro-Serna, J., & Garmendia, F. (2007). Marketing information systems - MIS: More than simple technological boxes. *EsicMarket, 128*, 81–93.

Rowley, J. (1994). Marketing information systems. *Aslib Proceedings, 46*(7/8), 185–187. doi:10.1108/eb051364

Rowley, J. (1999). Loyalty, the Internet and the weather: The changing nature of marketing information systems? *Management Decision, 37*(6), 514–519. doi:10.1108/00251749910278032

Ryan, S., Magro, M., & Sharp, J. (2011). Exploring educational and cultural adaptation through social networking sites. *Journal of Information Technology Education: Innovations in Practice, 10.*

Shepherd, C. (2011). Does social media have a place in workplace learning? *Strategic Direction, 27*(2), 3–4. doi:10.1108/02580541111103882

Shiju, Z. (2007). On the curriculum arrangement & teaching procedures in management information system. *International Conference on Wireless Communications, Networking and Mobile Computing, WiCom 2007* (pp. 6281–6284).

Shipin, C., Yongfeng, D., & Jianpin, Z. (2011). Social media: Communication characteristics and application value in distance education. *The 2011 International Conference on Electrical and Control Engineering* (ICECE), (pp. 6774–6777).

Silius, K., Kailanto, M., & Tervakari, A.-M. (2011). Evaluating the quality of the social media in an educational context. *2011 IEEE Global Engineering Education Conference* (EDUCON), 04-06 April 2011, Amman, Jordan, (pp. 505–510).

Silius, K., Miilumki, T., Huhtamki, J., Tebest, T., Merilinen, J., & Pohjolainen, S. (2010). *Social media enhanced studying and learning in higher education. 2010 IEEE Education Engineering* (pp. 137–143). EDUCON.

Simon, J., & Soliman, K. (2003). An alternative method to measure MIS faculty teaching performance. *International Journal of Educational Management*, *17*(5), 195–199. doi:10.1108/09513540310484913

Singh, V., Jain, R., & Kankanhalli, M. (2009). Motivating contributors in social media networks. *Proceedings of the First SIGMM Workshop on Social Media* (WSM '09), (pp. 11-18). New York, NY: ACM.

Smith, M., Barash, V., Getoor, L., & Lauw, H. (2008). Leveraging social context for searching social media. *2008 ACM Workshop on Search in Social Media* (SSM '08), (pp. 91-94). New York, NY: ACM.

Smith, M., Hansen, D., & Gleave, E. (2009). Analyzing enterprise social media networks. *2009 International Conference on Computational Science and Engineering* - Vol. 4 (CSE '09), (pp. 705-710). Washington, DC: IEEE Computer Society.

Solomon, B. S., Duce, D., & Harrison, R. (2011). Methodologies for using social media collaborative work systems. *First International Workshop on Requirements Engineering for Social Computing* (RESC), 2011, (pp. 6–9).

Stahlschmidt, T., Ziemer, L., & Kuhn, N. (2011). Social media in the context of academic marketing - Case study: The Umwelt-Campus blog. *International Conference on Computational Aspects of Social Networks* (CASoN) 2011, (pp. 114-119).

Sweetser, K., & Kelleher, T. (2011). A survey of social media use, motivation and leadership among public relations practitioners. *Public Relations Review*, *37*(4), 425–428. doi:10.1016/j.pubrev.2011.08.010

Talvinen, J. (1995). Information systems in marketing: Identifying opportunities for new applications. *European Journal of Marketing*, *29*(1), 8–26. doi:10.1108/03090569510075307

Vie, S. (2008). Digital divide 2.0: 'Generation M' and online social networking sites in the composition classroom. *Computers and Composition*, *25*(1), 9–23. doi:10.1016/j.compcom.2007.09.004

Wagner, R. (2011). Social media tools for teaching and learning. *Athletic Training Education Journal*, *6*(1), 51–52.

Weerkamp, W. (2010). Finding people and their utterances in social media. *33rd International ACM SIGIR Conference on Research and Development in Information Retrieval* (SIGIR '10), (pp. 918-918). New York, NY: ACM.

Weinberg, B., & Pehlivan, E. (2011). Social spending: Managing the social media mix. *Business Horizons*, *54*(3), 275–282. doi:10.1016/j.bushor.2011.01.008

Wen-Huei, C., Yu-Ting, L., & Kuang-Hsia, L. (2010). Decent digital social media for senior life: A practical design approach. *2010 3rd IEEE International Conference on Computer Science and Information Technology* (IEEE ICCSIT 2010), 9-11, July 2010, Chengdu, China, (pp. 249–253).

Wood, E. (2001). Marketing information systems in tourism and hospitality small- and medium-sized enterprises: A study of Internet use for market intelligence. *International Journal of Tourism Research, 3,* 283–299. doi:10.1002/jtr.315

Xu, X. (1999). The strategic orientation of marketing information systems – An empirical study. *Marketing Intelligence & Planning, 17*(6), 262–272. doi:10.1108/02634509910293070

Yan Yu, A., Wen Tian, S., Vogel, D., & Chi-Wai Kwok, R. (2010). Can learning be virtually boosted? An investigation of online social networking impacts. *Computers & Education, 55*(4), 1494–1503. doi:10.1016/j.compedu.2010.06.015

Zeiller, M., & Schauer, B. (2011). Adoption, motivation and success factors of social media for team collaboration in SMEs. In S. Lindstaedt & M. Granitzer (Eds.), *11th International Conference on Knowledge Management and Knowledge Technologies* (i-KNOW '11). New York, NY: ACM.

Zhongke, Z. (2010). The study on the application of marketing information system. *The 2nd IEEE International Conference on Information Management and Engineering* (ICIME), (pp. 428–431).

KEY TERMS AND DEFINITIONS

Curriculum Design: The process of developing a curricula for students.

Learning Management Systems (LMSs) or Course Management Systems (CMS): An online web-based tool allowing administration (instructors) and/or students to share materials and interact online (inside and outside the physical classroom).

Marketing: The activity, set of institutions, and processes for creating, communicating, delivering, and exchanging offerings that have value for customers, clients, partners, and society at large (American Marketing Association, January 2008).

Marketing Information System (MKIS): An essential tool for translating raw data into useful information and so the emphasis should be placed on the instant conversion of knowledge into customer value which fundamentally depends on the ability to develop, deploy, and manage powerful new marketing information systems.

Web 2.0: A term to describe a new way in which software developers and end-users started to utilize the World Wide Web.

Chapter 3
The Use of New Web–Based Technologies in Strategies of Teaching Gender Studies

Mădălina Manolache
"Transilvania" University of Braşov, Romania

Monica Pătruţ
"Vasile Alecsandri" University of Bacău, Romania

ABSTRACT

One of the defining traits of our existence as users of the Internet is convergence. This feature is a widespread common good within each level of online participation. Nowadays, we are obliged to perform communicative acts in a more transparent manner than in the Web 1.0. age, and the content itself allows for a higher degree of self-awareness. This is also the case of the learning media. We are offered more intuitive devices which reshape our mindset and forward us towards different mainframes of our innate intelligence, reshaping us into highly educated citizens. Nonetheless, technology is not the only construct with a pervasive character. Gender mainstreaming also claims a front place, either as an explaining factor for policy failures, economic deficits or social fractures. As such, it is our purpose within this chapter to outline the use of new web-based technologies in the new Web 2.0 pedagogical environment, with an emphasis on Web 2.0 teaching strategies in the case of gender studies.

INTRODUCTION

As new web-based technologies focus the term social media (Doyle, 2010), especially in relation to the concept of user generated content, the pedagogical environment needs to approach the challenge of generated micro-content starting with the user. The term *user* coins, in our opinion, a post-modern frame of the individual, a frame which merges roles and identities. The term *content* presents no structure due to its pervasive character, whereas the term micro-content stands in for content which conveys one primary idea or concept (Anil, 2002). Furthermore, it allows

DOI: 10.4018/978-1-4666-2970-7.ch003

more and more inputs and travel of concepts but with no structured codes of interpretation or of conduct, which could allow the information to be filtered down, in a higher degree of resonance with the user's needs.

Despite the altered nature of the included interaction within communication, the Web 2.0 is increasingly becoming an almost always present dimension of teaching practices and of academic collaborations, as technology is becoming more transparent, (so the) attention is focused (more) on content (Alexander & Levine, 2008).

Since the 1970s, European universities have witnessed the steady development of a wide variety of MA programmes in gender studies, women's studies and feminist studies.

One outcome of this academic *institutionalization* of gender has been the initiation of a debate on the extent to which the course materials and research approaches of other disciplines incorporate gender as a primary unit of analysis and engage seriously and critically with feminist and gender issues.

A second outcome focuses the challenges of the methodologies used to teach gender studies in order to convey their trans-disciplinary character. Within a shifting learning environment based on a peer (equal)-to-peer (equal) education (UNAIDS, 1999) approach, the teaching strategies themselves underwent a structural and a cultural change, shifting from teaching strategies to strategic teaching (Greenberg & Davila, 2002).

A third outcome refers to the synchronistic character of the Web 2.0 and to where the limits should be defined, according to the learning environment within which the Web 2.0 tools are applied. This also refers to how the scholars should foster the pedagogical discourse within the re-configured learning environments, considering the global equality architecture.

Starting from these outcomes our research objectives are:

1. Determining how gender studies are mainstreamed within the academic syllabus;

2. Pinpointing the transformation of teaching strategies into strategic teaching;

3. Identifying a possible connection between what is perceived as global equality architecture and the global participation architecture, in the case of the Web 2.0 pedagogical setting.

In order to reach our objectives, we shall use the following methods:

1. Content analysis, by means of text analysis (Wordstat 6.1);

2. Visual analysis, by means of chromatic patterns (M.A.K. Halliday functional grammar);

3. Connector analysis to social networks;

4. Connector analysis to the common user.

As objects of study for our objectives we have chosen several universities from Hungary, Sweden, The Netherlands and United Kingdom. These universities[1] are:

*   Hungary
    *   Central European University in Budapest, Department of Gender Studies
*   Sweden
    *   Linköping University in Sweden, The Posthumanities Hub and GenSet
    *   Umeå University, Umeå Centre for Gender Studies (UCGS)
*   The Netherlands
    *   Utrecht University, Research Institute for History and Culture, Gender Studies
    *   University of Amsterdam, Amsterdam Research Centre for Gender and Sexuality
*   United Kingdom
    *   London School of Economics and Political Science, Gender Institute
    *   University of Cambridge Center for Gender Studies
    *   The Women's Library, London Metropolitan University

BACKGROUND

All these academic institutions make use of various Web 2.0 tools such as social media platforms, sharing tools, RSS feeds, newsletter feeds, event feeds, video sharing for education, blog postings and complex software packages, such as lecture capture technologies so as to turn any event (seminar, workshop, conference) into a *hybrid* event (what we perceive as a computer-mediated-communication product). What we are interested in is the inter-relation between the use of Web 2.0 tools and the thematical approach on gender studies of the academic institutions, namely the flow of content's convergence between Web 2.0 tools and the representations of knowledge on gender studies provided by the chosen universities.

Before proceeding with our analysis, we shall outline several micro-literature reviews emerged either from peer reviewed academic literature or from practitioner literature (Doyle, 2010), as most of the operational concepts within our chapter are just starting to benefit from a structured attention, both from the academic community, as well as from the practitioner community.

Micro-Literature Review on Web 2.0

The topics of Web 2.0 and social media phenomena present insufficient coverage within academic literature, but plenty of practitioner oriented background.

Social media, as a term, has often been used instead of Web 2.0, when a clear distinction between the two should have been made (Doyle, 2010).

It was Tim O'Reilly (2006) who coined the term Web 2.0 and defined the web as a network depicted as a platform, spanning all connected devices, which

[...] delivers software as a continually-updated service that gets better the more people use it, consuming and remixing data from multiple sources,

including individual users, while providing their own data and services in a form that allows remixing by others, creating network effects through an architecture of participation, and going beyond the page metaphor of Web 1.0 to deliver rich user experiences (O'Reilly, 2006, p.16).

As we may notice, this definition provides an encompassing frame of what Web 2.0 is perceived to be, "incorporating people, processes and technology [...] all for delivering a richer user experience while on the internet." (O'Reilly, 2006, pp.17-37), thus providing the basis for a clear distinction between Web 2.0 and social media. Kaplan and Haenlein offered another definition for Web 2.0 as

[...] describing a new way in which software developers and end-users started to utilize the World Wide Web; that is, as a platform whereby content and applications are no longer created and published by individuals, but instead are continuously modified by all users in a participatory and collaborative fashion (Kaplan & Haenlein, 2010, pp.60-61).

Web 2.0 encourages a more human approach to interactivity on the Web, better supports group interaction (Sharp, Burns, & Barr, 2005) and fosters a greater sense of community in a potentially *cold* social environment (Wallace, 1997 *apud* Kamel Boulos & Wheeler, 2007). As Abram (2006) has claimed, the social Web [...] is about conversations, interpersonal networking, personalization and individualism. It is the People-centric Web (Robinson, 2005).

When dealing with the main differences between Web 1.0. and Web 2.0, O'Reilly (2006) separates the two, from the point of view of their emerging features (See Table 1).

Greater levels of participation, agency and democracy are possible in the social Web, where users act simultaneously as readers and writers.

Table 1. Web 1.0 and 2.0 differences: Adapted from O'Reilly²

Web 1.0.	Web 2.0
Encyclopedia Britannica http://www.britannica.com/	Wikipedia http://en.wikipedia.org/
Personal Web sites	Blogs (Web logs)
Publishing (Content Management)	Participation
Taxonomies	Folksonomies
Directories	Tagging
'Stickiness'	Syndication

The rigidity of Web 1.0 directory systems (taxonomies) is improved by the facility to formulate 'folksonomies'—fluid and flexible categorizations uniquely created by each interest group to provide quicker, more relevant access to practice-specific knowledge. The notion of 'stickiness' can also be challenged—content in Web 2.0 environments is never permanent but always open to changes, updates, remixing and reuse. Web 2.0 emphasizes the pre-eminence of content creation over content consumption. Information is liberated from corporative control (traditional content owners or their intermediaries), allowing anyone to create, assemble, organize (tag), locate and share content to meet their own needs [...] Web 2.0 is structured around open programming interfaces that allow widespread participation. Increased user contribution leads to the growth of 'collective intelligence', and re-usable dynamic content. Such engagement with content promotes a sense of community, empowerment and ownership for users (Kamel Boulos & Wheeler, 2007).

In an attempt to pinpoint a pattern of key-words, which we shall use in our comparative analysis, there are two occurrences that should draw our attention, namely *participation* and *collaborative*, and in both cases the following relations may be identified:

- **Participation:** Is tagged with people-centric, conversation, architecture of, engagement, practice-specific knowledge;
- **Collaborative:** Is tagged with network(ing), community, platform, remixing (mashing up), personalization, individualism.

Micro-Literature Review on User Generated Content (UGC)

Before providing the inter-relation characteristics towards the user, it is noteworthy to distinguish between user created content (UCC) and user generated content (UGC). In the opinion of the Organisation for Economic Co-operation and Development (*apud* Wunsch-Vincent & Vicker, 2006) UCC is defined as "(1) content made publicly available over the Internet, (2) which reflects a certain amount of creative effort, and (3) which is created outside of professional routines and practices" (p.4). According to Clever, Kirchner, Schray & Schulte (2009) UGC "refers to different kinds of media content created and published by amateurs who have just been at the consuming end in the past" (p.1).

On the other hand, the Interactive Advertising Bureau provides a clear-cut definition of what UGC is, namely:

[...] consumer-generated media (CGM), [which] refers to any material created and uploaded to the Internet by non-media professionals, [...] UGC has been around in one form or another since the earliest days of the Internet itself. But [...] thanks to the growing availability of high-speed Internet access and search technology, it has become one of the dominant forms of global media. It is currently one of the fastest growing forms of content on the Internet (Interactive Advertising Bureau, 2008, p.1).

whereas in a study performed for the European Commission by IDATE, TNO & Institute for Information Law (2008) 'the UCC classification proposed [...] is based on a content and user approach as opposed to a platform or service approach' (pp.23-25) and makes use of criteria such as type of content, social aspect, economic aspect. The first criterion [...] refers to the level of editorialisation/scenarization of content by the creator. This criterion establishes a distinction between a personal content (with no real added value, it is a kind of rough content not specifically created to be shared out) and a content elaborated in a way to tell a story to other people and it covers the two following aspects: personal - refers to content developed without editorial views and story-telling - refers to content developed with editorial views.(IDATE et al., 2008, p.24).

The second criterion refers to the level of sharing of the content wanted by the creator and the third criterion refers to the possibility for the creator to earn money or not thanks to his content. In our analyses we shall use this distinction to support one of the components of the transformation process of teaching strategies into strategic teaching.

Micro-Literature Review on Social Media

When dealing with the task of defining social media, there is a certain degree of difficulty in providing a structure, partly because it can present a definition for each domain in which it is used or applied. There is one definition which portrays social media on the basis of the characteristics, accumulated by reviewing academic and practitioner literature, and also by observing the phenomenon itself, that is to say as:

[...] a low cost form of communication, where participants interact through online conversations and form relationships with each other, where reputation is increased by collaborating and contributing information. This information

is permanently stored online and can be accessed by any participant, and can be freely distributed to any other participant (Doyle, 2010, p.8).

Another definition of social media, belonging to Kaplan & Haenlein (2010) draws the lines on the basis of two concepts, one being "a group of Internet-based applications that build on the ideological and technological foundations of Web 2.0" (p.59), and the second "creation and exchange of User Generated Content."(pp.59-60)

Schaefer (*apud* Cohen, 2011) considers three indicators of social media:

[...] Evolution, Revolution and Contribution. First, it is an evolution of how we communicate, replacing email in many cases. It's a revolution: For the first time in history we have access to free, instantaneous, global communication. Third, social media is distinguished by the ability of everybody to share and contribute as a publisher (Schaefer apud Cohen, 2011).

The definition of Bruns & Bahnisc (2009) of social media encapsulates in a three-fold perspective what we consider to be relevant to our study case: "We define social media as websites which build on Web 2.0 technologies to provide space for in-depth social interaction, community formation, and the tackling of collaborative projects" (p. 5).

Micro-Literature Review on Peer Education and Strategic Teaching

As we have mentioned earlier, our interest focuses on the flow of content's convergence between Web 2.0 tools and the representations of knowledge on gender studies provided by the chosen universities.

The paradigm of participation and of collaboration, from a social media/Web 2.0 perspective bestows upon education, and especially on teaching a pressure to adapt, to transform. But this pressure was envisaged before the Web 2.0

even had a name. In 1996, a UNESCO commission profiled the seven main tensions affecting education, namely:

- The tension between the global and the local; the tension between the universal and the individual;
- The tension between tradition and modernity; the tension between the spiritual and the material;
- The tension between long-term and short-term considerations;
- The tension between competition and equality of opportunity and
- The tension between the extraordinary expansion of knowledge and the capacity of human beings to assimilate it.(Brander et al., 2002, p.346)

They also highlighted what they called "the four pillars of learning" (p.346-347) as a strategy that could help face these challenges, namely: learning to live together, learning to do, learning to know and learning to be. As a consequence, the process of education took in all these aspects and allowed for an evolution against non-formal and informal backgrounds. That is why the peer-to-peer approach from non-formal education became relevant in a higher degree within what is now perceived as the process of education.

Defining peer education, even if a popular concept, suggests a multitude of elements, intertwined in a special manner, that is to say:

[...] an approach, a communication channel, a methodology, a philosophy, and a strategy. Peer education typically involves the use of members of a given group to effect change among other members of the same group. Peer education is often used to effect change at the individual level by attempting to modify a person's knowledge, attitudes, beliefs, or behaviours (UNAIDS, 1999, pp.5-6).

'A [teaching] strategy is goals' directed and a consciously controllable process that facilitates performance.(Reid, 2006), whereas

Strategic teaching is a way of making decisions about a course, an individual class, or even an entire curriculum, beginning with an analysis of key variables in the teaching situation. These variables include the characteristics of the learners, the learning objectives, and the instructional preferences of the teacher (Greenberg & Davila, 2002, p.1).

How are the UNESCO tension/challenge and peer education related between each other and how do they relate to strategic teaching? The key words connecting the two are knowledge and equality architecture.

Traditional pedagogy is being challenged by information age technologies. Opportunities for students to use the internet to acquire, share, and collaboratively develop *learner generated content* shift the locus of control from *teacher as expert* to guide and collaborator in the learning process (Lee & McLoughlin, 2007, p.2).

Synthesizing

The new affordances of Web 2.0 are now making learner-centered education a reality, with tools like web logs (blogs), wikis, media sharing applications, and social networking sites capable of supporting multiple communities of learning. These tools enable and encourage informal conversation, dialogue, collaborative content generation, and the sharing of information, giving learners access to a vast array of ideas and representations of knowledge. The emergence of Web 2.0 technologies and social software tools has created: a new set of dynamics leading to increased user-led content and knowledge production that is transforming higher education curriculum and instruction. It considers the different ways in which social computing applications can be used for teaching and learning, and suggests changes to pedagogy based on greater learner control, agency, and engagement in content creation, as well as peer-to-peer sharing and review of ideas (Lee & McLoughlin, 2007, pp.5-8).

Micro-Literature Review on Gender Mainstreaming in the Web 2.0 Learning Environment

According to the Council of Europe:

Gender mainstreaming is the (re)organization, improvement, development and evaluation of policy processes, so that a gender equality perspective is incorporated in all policies at all levels and at all stages, by the actors normally involved in policy-making. Gender Mainstreaming is a typical example of a strategy that involves multiple levels in governance, but also multiple shifts in governance.[...] Gender Mainstreaming involves individual and institutional actors from inside and outside the state bureaucracy, including fields such as science and economy. The strategy of Gender Mainstreaming aims at a multiplication of the actors, policy areas and policy levels that are involved in working towards gender equality (Council of Europe, 1998, p.12).

In 2001, within a project co-funded by the European Commission (Stevens & Van Lamoen, 2001) a manual was created entitled "Manual on gender mainstreaming at universities" in which an instrumental approach and a process-model approach were developed in relation to gender mainstreaming and academia. According to this report:

The competitiveness that accompanies these processes [organization and culture of Europe-based research] is also perceptible in academic education. A signal of this direction is the 'Anglo-Saxon turn' in the European-wide endorsement of the Bachelor-Master system, promoting flex-ibility and mobility among students. The struggle for students that is fed by the increasing social demand for high educated citizens stimulates a search for attractive educational approaches and teaching methods, electronic learning and international classrooms, flexible and contract courses and, finally, international exchange facilities. Implementing these new approaches demands flexibility and puts the traditional educational systems of universities under pressure (Stevens & Van Lamoen, 2001, p.28).

The authors perceive gender mainstreaming as "an engine for innovation" (p.29), while dealing with the challenges of "specialisation, hybridisation and flexibility" (pp.29-30) at the same time. Nonetheless, in all the 182 pages of the report the word *electronic* appears only one time, and that is in relation to learning environment. In 2001 the inter-relatedness between virtual learning environments and teaching processes was not yet crystalized. It would have to wait until 2004 when the convergence between the level of competitiveness, the gender mainstreaming, the academic environment and the opportunities of the web e-learning environment reached a turning point, due to the article of Stephen Downes (2004) entitled "Beyond learning objectives" in which he emerged a new approach of the teaching/ learning paradigm: "that what makes something a learning object is not what it is, but rather, how it is used", namely the focus shifted from an approach centered on participating in a singular learning environment (similar to the Web 1.0.) towards an approach centered on mainstreaming of a collaborative learning environment (similar to the Web 2.0).

It is our opinion that in the case of gender studies within the academic Web 2.0 learning/teaching setting, the mainstreaming of gender intertwines with the mainstreaming of a collaborative learning environment, thus allowing a potential connection between a global equality architecture and a global participation architecture.

STRATEGIC TEACHING OF GENDER STUDIES AND THE WEB 2.0 LEARNING ENVIRONMENT

In order to pinpoint the inter-relation between the Web 2.0 tools and the thematical approach of the gender studies agenda of the academic institution, we focused on establishing certain patterns between textual elements, visual elements and connector elements. We are of opinion that these elements form a representation of knowledge on the topic of gender studies, representation specific to each academic institution, and it is from these representations that we may observe the mainstreaming paradigm from a twofold perspective:

- One with regards to gender mainstreaming in the academic curriculum.
- The second with regards to participation/collaborative mainstreaming in the learning/teaching setting.

We considered textual elements the following:

- Thematical description of the department (purpose statement).
- Thematical approach within the syllabus of the courses.
- Bibliographies, reports, newsletters, journals, titles.
- Descriptions of events (seminars, conferences, book launches).

The textual elements were depicted by means of text analysis software (QDA Miner and Wordstat 6.1.), through two types of proximity plots (PP) and dendograms of key-words, namely:

- The dendograms provide the broad representation of knowledge (RK) on *gender* per each institution.
- The first type of PP (PP1) provides frequency patterns only for the word *gender*

in relation to the first 30 words occurring within the textual elements (items3, in Word Stat).

- The second type of PP (PP2) provides frequency patterns for the word *gender* in relation to concepts, processes and disciplines, within the items, allowing for an in-depth RK on gender.

We divided the visual elements in two categories:

- **C1:** Logo of the institution, logo of the department.
- **C2:** Logos of specific events (book launches, workshops, conferences, webinars), menu and submenu display, and visual elements available on Facebook and/or Twitter.

We considered connector elements the following:

- Inserted buttons within the main webpage for social networks such as Facebook and Twitter.
- RSS feeds either for events, publications or courses and content patterns, either generated and then shared or generated on both the main website and the Facebook/Twitter page. They were depicted by snapshots.

The visual and connector elements were analyzed using Halliday's functional grammar (See Figure 1 in the Appendix) (Halliday, 2004), according to whom transitivity does not mean a mere grammatical identification of a direct object within the syntax of a sentence. Transitivity is focused on the way in which the individual or an institution positions him/her/itself in relation with the outer and inner world, the underlining concept being experience: external experience with the society and internal experience represented through consciousness and imagination. Starting from these two types of experiences, representation is formed of six processes which are assigned a color (See Table 2).

The C1 visual elements shall be interpreted in relation to the dendograms and the first type of PP, within research objective 1, while the C2 visual elements and the connector elements shall be interpreted in relation to the second type of PP, within research objective 2.

Objective 1: Determining how Gender Studies are Mainstreamed within the Academic Curriculum

Within this objective, it was our intention to map the mainstreaming of gender studies through a three-level analysis:

Level 1: Refers to the dendograms[5], namely to categories that tend to appear together and which are combined at an early stage, so we shall identify the first 4 categories for each approach (Hungarian, Swedish, Dutch and British) (See Table 3), pinpointing the RK (representation of knowledge) on gender studies.

Level 2: Refers to interpreting the proximity plots of the key-word *gender* (PP1) to the first 30 words occurring within the items (See Table 4).

Level 3: Refers to the correlation between level 1, level 2 and C1 visual elements (See Table 10 and Table 11 in the Appendix).

Level 1

In Table 3 the word categories were chosen according to the agglomeration order, indicated by the value of Jaccard's coefficient[6], which may present a value in the interval (0,1). In each case, we took into consideration the combination at the most early stage (the Jaccard's coefficient values tend to 1) within the interval (an example of a segment of a dendogram is presented in

Table 2. The 6 processes of representation, according to M.A.K. Halliday[4]

Process	The way in which the message is built	Non-artistic signifier
Relational (major process)	To have an identity To symbolize	Yellow (primary colour)
Material (major process)	To do To take action To create/change	Red (primary colour)
Mental (major process)	To see To feel To think	Blue (primary colour)
Behavioral (between material & mental processes)	Psychological levels of the individual	Violet (combination of red & blue)
Verbal (between mental & relational processes)	The individual's means of expression	Green (combination of blue & yellow)
Existential (between material & relational processes)	The individual's layers of existence	Orange (combination between red & yellow)

Figure 6.in the Appendix). The representation of knowledge will be outlined through the process of mainstreaming, associated to a certain type (grass-root or multiple) and/or to a domain (social, economic, policy, mentality).

Level 2

As a result of the proximity plots (PP1) for the key-word gender in relation to the first 30 words occurring within the items analyzed (See Figure 2-5 in the Appendix), we have identified three frequency patterns (See Table 4):

1.   Key-words appearing in all four sets of items;
2.   Key-words appearing in three out of four sets;
3.   Key-words appearing in two out of four sets.

As we may observe the words *woman, social* and *work* appear in the case of all four universities, which is normal, considering that gender "refers to the social (as opposed to the biologi-

Table 3. Word categories chosen according to the agglomeration order (dendograms)

Word Categories	Hungary	Sweden	The Netherlands	United Kingdom
Category 1 [0.6 - 1]	Analysis Critical Disciplinary Traditional Field Subject Humanity Science · Construct Process Relation Knowledge Culture Society	Care Domestic Labour Market State Welfare Service Family	Issue Work Woman Study Press Social Sexuality Research Political Knowledge	Adjustment Structural Development World Economic Social Policy Lone Mother National Population
Representation of Knowledge (RK$_{C1}$)	"Grass-root"[7] mainstreaming – focus on teaching strategies (specific goals, controllable process)	Social mainstreaming – focus on strategic teaching, with the key variable "social welfare"	Multiple mainstreaming – focus on strategic teaching, with the key variables "social welfare","sexuality"	Multiple mainstreaming – focus on strategic teaching, with the key variables "economic development","single parenting"
Category 2 [0.45 – 0.6]	Academic Development · Scholarly Develop Focus Integrative Perspective Gender Study · Change Pattern Cultural Social Discourse	Genital Female Ethnic Minority Combat Stigmatization	Development European	Accord Insurgent Biosphere Reserve Failure Governmentality Globalising Vernacular
Representation of knowledge (RK$_{C2}$)	Multiple mainstreaming – focus on strategic teaching, with the key variables "academic development","cultural discourse", "change pattern"	Mentality mainstreaming – focus on strategic teaching, with the key variables "sexual stigmatization", "minority"	Economic mainstreaming – focus on strategic teaching, with the key variables "economic development", "European (Union)"	Policy mainstreaming – focus on strategic teaching, with the key variable "governance"
Category 3 [0.25 – 0.45]	Difference Equality Welfare Work World	Building Capacity · Recruitment Retention	Cultural Europe Culture Feminist	Female Head Household Feminisation Poverty Labour Market
Representation of knowledge (RK$_{C3}$)	Social mainstreaming – focus on strategic teaching, with the key variable "social welfare"	Mentality mainstreaming – focus on strategic teaching, with the key variables "capacity", "retention"	Culture mainstreaming – focus on strategic teaching, with the key variable "feminist"	Social mainstreaming – focus on strategic teaching, with the key variable "social welfare"
Category 4 [0.15 – 0.25]	Mainstream Policy Conflict Question Woman Feminist Theory	Critical Cultural Feminist Theory Nature · Body Feminism	-	Ambivalence Intergenerational Anticipation Solidarity Oppose Commitment Parental Societal
Representation of knowledge (RK$_{C4}$)	Policy mainstreaming – focus on strategic teaching, with the key variable "conflict"	Culture mainstreaming – focus on strategic teaching, with the key variable "feminism"	-	Social mainstreaming – focus on strategic teaching, with the key variables "social welfare","intergenerational"

Table 4. Key-words appearing in PP1 (gender in relation to the first 30 words, chosen by frequency)

Key-words appearing in all four sets of items				
woman	Hungary	Sweden	The Netherlands	United Kingdom
social	Hungary	Sweden	The Netherlands	United Kingdom
work	Hungary	Sweden	The Netherlands	United Kingdom
Key-words appearing in three out of four sets of items				
study	Hungary	Sweden	The Netherlands	
European	Hungary	Sweden	The Netherlands	
issue		Sweden	The Netherlands	United Kingdom
feminist		Sweden	The Netherlands	United Kingdom
man		Sweden	The Netherlands	United Kingdom
women		Sweden	The Netherlands	United Kingdom
Key-words appearing in two out of four sets of items				
research	Hungary		The Netherlands	
relation	Hungary			United Kingdom
knowledge	Hungary		The Netherlands	
focus	Hungary			United Kingdom
development	Hungary			United Kingdom
world	Hungary			United Kingdom
policy		Sweden		United Kingdom
university		Sweden	The Netherlands	
sex/sexuality/sexual		Sweden	The Netherlands	
integrative/include	Hungary	Sweden		
society		Sweden	The Netherlands	
culture/cultural		Sweden	The Netherlands	
change		Sweden		United Kingdom
press			The Netherlands	United Kingdom

cal) characteristics of, and relations between, the two sexes. 'Gender' is not a fixed and immutable feature of humanity, but rather a series of socially ascribed and therefore contingent aspects of social life."(Webster, 2000, pp.1-2)

However, the specifics emerge when we proceed towards the second and third level of frequencies, namely when we start to visualize what are the key variables for gender mainstreaming in the academic setting. As such, we may observe that there is a similarity between Hungarian, Swedish and Dutch approach in connecting *gender* to *European*, and between Swedish, Dutch and British approach in connecting *gender* to *issue*,

feminist, man and *women*. We may interpret that gender mainstreaming for the Hungarian, Swedish and Dutch implies a positioning within the European frame of the gender studies' domain, whereas for the Swedish, Dutch and British, gender mainstreaming implies forwarding the *women/ feminist – man* occurrence to *gender* as an *issue*, namely as either a matter in dispute between two parties or as a final outcome which constitutes a solution (as of a problem) or as a resolution (as of a difficulty). Reaching the binary sets, we may observe that:

- Hungarian and British approaches share four frequency patters, namely:
  ○ *Gender – Relation*
  ○ *Gender – Focus*
  ○ *Gender – Development*
  ○ *Gender – World*
- Swedish and Dutch approaches share four frequency patterns as well, namely:
  ○ *Gender – University*
  ○ *Gender – Sex/Sexuality/Sexual*
  ○ *Gender – Society*
  ○ *Gender – Culture/Cultural*
- Hungarian and Dutch approaches share two frequency patterns:
  ○ *Gender – Research*
  ○ *Gender – Knowledge*
- Swedish and British approaches share two frequency patterns:
  ○ *Gender – Policy*
  ○ *Gender – Change*
- Hungarian and Swedish share one frequency pattern:
  ○ *Gender – Integrative/Include*
- Dutch and British share on frequency pattern:
  ○ *Gender – Press*

Level 3

At this level in our analysis we will correlate the representations of knowledge for the first and second categories with the representational processes (RP) depicted in the logos of the institution and of the department (See Table 5-8).

There is a strong relation between RKC1 and the visual RP, as the singular approach to gender studies reflects the monochromatic pattern, through one colour: red. Furthermore, at the second level, namely RKC2, one of the key variables is the process of change, as one of the verbs used in building the message is to create/to change. There is indeed a connection to the European Union, but the gender mainstreaming in the case of the Hungarian university tends towards a firm, impermeable approach rather than a flexible one, from the point of view of participation/collaborative mainstreaming in the learning/teaching setting.

The choices of non-artistic signifiers clearly support the representations of knowledge emerged from the text analysis, as the social and mentality mainstreaming(s) project themselves in the processes: social welfare – to think, psychological levels of the individual; sexual stigmatization, minority - to have an identity, to feel, psychological levels of the individual. Thus there is a strong correlation between the textual analysis results and the visual analysis results.

In the case of the Dutch, we may observe a different correlation path, as the key variables social welfare, sexuality, economic development correlates with to see, to think, to feel and with the psychological levels of the individual.

Table 5. Representational processes and key variables of gender mainstreaming in the case of Hungarian university

	RK$_{C1}$ (representation of knowledge for category 1)	RK$_{C2}$ (representation of knowledge for category 2)	Key-words appearing in all four sets of items Key-words appearing in three out of four sets	RP (representational processes)
Hungary	"Grass-root" mainstreaming – focus on teaching strategies (specific goals, controllable process)	Multiple mainstreaming – focus on strategic teaching, with the key variables "academic development", "cultural discourse", "change pattern"	Gender-European	Material process The way in which the message is built: To do, To take action, To create/change Non-artistic signifier Red (primary colour)

Table 6. Representational processes and key variables of gender mainstreaming in the case of Swedish universities

	RK$_{C1}$ (representation of knowledge for category 1)	RK$_{C2}$ (representation of knowledge for category 2)	Key-words appearing in all four sets of items Key-words appearing in three out of four sets	RP (representational processes)
Sweden	Social mainstreaming – focus on strategic teaching, with the key variable "social welfare"	Mentality mainstreaming – focus on strategic teaching, with the key variables "sexual stigmatization", "minority"	Gender-European Gender-Issue/Feminist/ Man/Women	Relational process The way in which the message is built: to have an identity, to symbolize Non-artistic signifier Yellow (primary colour) Mental process The way in which the message is built: to see, to feel, to think Non-artistic signifier Blue (primary colour) Behavioral process The way in which the message is built: Psychological levels of the individual Non-artistic signifier Violet (combination of red & blue)

Table 7. Representational processes and key variables of gender mainstreaming in the case of Dutch universities

	RK$_{C1}$ (representation of knowledge for category 1)	RK$_{C2}$ (representation of knowledge for category 2)	Key-words appearing in all four sets of items Key-words appearing in three out of four sets	RP (representational processes)
The Netherlands	Multiple mainstreaming – focus on strategic teaching, with the key variables "social welfare", "sexuality"	Economic mainstreaming – focus on strategic teaching, with the key variables "economic development", "European (Union)"	Gender-European *Gender-Issue/Feminist/ Man/Women*	Mental process The way in which the message is built: to see, to feel, to think Non-artistic signifier Blue (primary colour) Behavioral process The way in which the message is built: Psychological levels of the individual Non-artistic signifier Violet (combination of red & blue)

Table 8. Representational processes and key variables of gender mainstreaming in the case of British universities

	RK$_{C1}$ (representation of knowledge for category 1)	RK$_{C2}$ (representation of knowledge for category 2)	Key-words appearing in all four sets of items Key-words appearing in three out of four sets	RP (representational processes)
United Kingdom	Multiple mainstreaming – focus on strategic teaching, with the key variables "economic development", "single parenting"	Policy mainstreaming – focus on strategic teaching, with the key variable "governance"	*Gender-Issue/Feminist/ Man/Women*	Behavioral process The way in which the message is built: Psychological levels of the individual Non-artistic signifier Violet (combination of red & blue)

The frequency pattern gender-European is common to all three institutions, but we may observe that the Hungarian approach presents a rather inbound-structured mainstreaming in the curriculum, whereas the Swedish and the Dutch prefer a more outbound-structured mainstreaming.

Comparing the processes within the representations, we may observe that Sweden and The Netherlands have in common the mental and the behavioral process, but the Dutch approach does not tend towards an identity construct, focusing more on the unfolding of the mainstreaming rather than on the course of the mainstreaming (Sweden presents the relational process).

In the case of United Kingdom, there is a new element regarding the mainstreaming of gender, namely the policy element. However, all the key variables "economic development", "single parenting" an "governance" correlate to the behavioral process (psychological levels of the individual).

Between Sweden, The Netherlands and United Kingdom there is a common frequency pattern, namely Gender-Issue/Feminist/Man/Women, but we may observe that Sweden focuses on the course of mainstreaming, The Netherlands on the unfolding of the mainstreaming whereas the United Kingdom approach deals only with the individual frame, namely the psychological moods.

Objective 2: Depicting the Transformation of Teaching Strategies into Strategic Teaching

As a result of the changing profile of the university and college student (Windham, 2006), we are witnessing a blurring of the distinctions between learning, work, and leisure activities. As such the syllabus of the courses, the literature used for courses and even the workshops and the conferences organized by the academic institutions present a trans-disciplinary character and a trans-domain perspective.

It is our opinion that the key variables of the strategic teaching, in the case of gender studies learning/teaching setting are: concepts, disciplines and processes, so in *Table 9* we will present the concepts, disciplines and process which emerged from the proximity plots in relation to gender (PP2), outlining only the ones repeating for at least two plots. We shall also correlate these plots to the second category C2 visual elements (See *Table 12 and Table 13*), to connector elements, and to the interpretation results from Objective 1. In order to pinpoint the transformation of teaching strategies into strategic teaching, we shall also include in *Table 9* the key variables of the gender mainstreaming depicted in *Table 5-8* and the tags associated to participation and collaboration in the micro-literature review on Web 2.0.

As we have mentioned in the micro-literature review on peer education and strategic teaching, the key variables in the latter case are:

- The characteristics of the learner;
- The learning objectives;
- The instructional preferences of the teacher.

Regarding the characteristics of the learner, we are of opinion that these are reflected by the words participation and collaborative (associated tags in *Table 9*), whereas the learning objectives, in the case of gender mainstreaming in the academic curriculum, articulate the frequency patterns between gender and concepts, disciplines and processes. The instructional preferences of the teacher(s) are best visualized in the type of events organized (seminars, lectures, conferences, workshops, book launches) and in the collaborative/participatory fashion these events and the content emerged out of them (user created content - UCC) is embodied as UGC (user generated content).

In the case of Hungary, the singular embodiments of the learners are to be found on Facebook and Twitter pages, embodied in visual elements, by means of photos of students. However, these

Table 9. Concepts, processes and disciplines occurring in relation to gender (PP2) and elements depicted from Table 10 and Table 11, pinpointed through associated tags

	Hungary	Sweden	The Netherlands	United Kingdom
CONCEPTS (Key variables of gender mainstreaming in the academic curriculum – PP2)	Equality Feminist Mainstream Represent	Discrimination Equality Family Mainstream Stereotype Participation Representation	Feminist Ethnicity	Discrimination Equality Family Ethnographic/Ethnography Mainstream Stereotype Participation
PROCESSES (Key variables of gender mainstreaming in the academic curriculum – PP2)	Knowledge Labour Policy	Employment (job, profession, labour, recruitment) Policy	Knowledge	Labour
DISCIPLINES (Key variables of gender mainstreaming in the academic curriculum – PP2)	Epistemology History Humanity	Epistemology History Management Philosophy	Literature	Economy
Key variables of gender mainstreaming in the academic curriculum (PP1)	"academic development", "cultural discourse", "change pattern"	"social welfare" "sexual stigmatization", "minority"	"social welfare","sexuality" "economic development", "European (Union)"	"economic development","single parenting" "governance"
Tags for participation people-centric, conversation, architecture of, engagement, practice-specific knowledge	Conversation (Newsletter/Events feeds, not from Home page); Low-level of practice specific knowledge (two book launches, no blogs, no film screening, no lecture-capture technology)	People-centric (Hub); Conversation (Newsletter/ Events feeds from Home page); Medium level of practice-specific knowledge (book launches, film screening, workshops, no blogs, no lecture-capture technology)	People-centric Conversation (Newsletter/ Events feeds from Home page); High level of practice-specific knowledge (lecture-capture technology, book launches, art exhibits, workshops, no blogs)	People-centric Conversation (Newsletter/ Events feeds from Home page); High level of practice-specific knowledge (blogs, podcasts, useful links)
Tags for collaborative network(ing), community, platform, remixing (mashing up), personalization, individualism	Community (Facebook closed group); Medium level of personalization (website, no logo on the website, but on the page of the 8th edition of the Department's Conference); Low level of networking	Community (Facebook page, not so active on collecting feedback); Medium level of personalization (logo of the Hub, no posters for events, no individual website for conferences); Medium level of networking (posts and information available, but no feedback)	Community (share button on Facebook, but no page); High level of personalization (logo of the departments/centers, individual pages for lectures, conferences) Low level of networking (no UGC on social networks, only UCC on the website)	Community (Facebook page, active on collecting feedback, on posts, on events); High level of personalization (logo of the departments/ centers, individual pages for lectures, conferences) High level of networking (active UCC, embodied in UGC)

photos are an element linked to the university, and not the gender studies (GS) department. On Facebook there is only one group of users related to the GS department, which is a closed group, so we cannot observe whether the UCC from the GS department page has the potential of UGC. Also, from the point of view of Newsletter/Events feeds, they are only available should one click the type of event one wants to access, aspect which undermines the accessibility of the learner/user, as it is not a feature available from the home page of the department. Gender mainstreaming in the academic curriculum is articulated by concepts such as *Equality, Feminist, Mainstream, Represent*, by disciplines such as *Epistemology, History, Humanity* and by processes such as *Knowledge, Labour* and *Policy*. As far as the events, they are presented on the website of the institutions, but only under the form of titles. There is no other type of information provided (descriptive details, useful links), as a UCC able to be embodied as UGC. It is the eighth edition of the conference of the department which marks a turning point in both the mainstreaming domains (gender and participation/collaborative), depicted already in the textual analysis (RK_{C1} towards RK_{C2}), as it presents a visual element (a poster with the major color blue) and an individual website (with the main color green).

Synthesizing the information depicted within the Hungarian institution's approach, we may reach the following conclusions:

- From the point of view of gender mainstreaming in the academic curriculum, the representation of knowledge tends towards history and humanity (grass-root mainstreaming) as fundamentals for involving other concepts, such as representation, equality or feminist theory, and in a second level does the mainstreaming involve variables such as cultural discourse or change pattern (multiple mainstreaming);
- From the point of view of participation/ collaborative mainstreaming, the events organized (lectures, conferences, workshops, one book launch) present a strong traditional mainframe and a lack of e-learning/ teaching elements (no forums, no blogs, no projects promoted by means of photo galleries or power-point presentations).

In the case of Sweden, the learner characteristics present a higher tendency towards participation and collaboration, as even the name of the department (Posthumanities Hub) implies a community formation and tackling of collaborative projects. On Facebook there is the same visual element as on the departments' page, so the learners/users grasp the non-artistic identifiers better. As far as the Events/Newsletter feeds, they are available from the home page, right side of the screen, aspect which indicates a relative high level of content accessibility. Furthermore, the events organized by the Hub are presented on the main page and on Facebook as well, so there is a medium transgression from UCC to UGC, as there are also reaction, comments, likes and shares on the Facebook wall. Gender mainstreaming in the academic curriculum is articulated by concepts such as *Discrimination, Equality, Family, Mainstream, Stereotype, Participation* and *Representation*, by disciplines such as *Epistemology, History, Management, Philosophy* and by one process, *Employment*. From the point of view of the type of events, namely the instructional preferences of the teachers, there are several types of events organized, but there is a low-towards-medium level of generated content, namely they present the titles, the speakers, the literature, which stands for the created content, but do not present conclusions, outcomes, videos or any other piece of textual/ visual information which may allow for a generated content to be experienced or re-used by the learners/users. This aspect actually correlates to the interpretation in *Table 5*, where we mentioned the fact that the Swedish approach, even if it does present an outbound-structured mainstreaming, focuses on the course of the mainstreaming, not on its unfolding.

Synthesizing the information depicted within the Swedish institutions' approach, we may reach the following conclusions:

- From the point of view of gender main-streaming in the academic curriculum, the representation of knowledge tends towards history, management (social mainstreaming) and philosophy (mentality mainstreaming) as fundamentals for involving concepts like discrimination, equality, stereotype, participation;
- From the point of view of participation/ collaborative mainstreaming, the events organized present a relative modern frame (complex lectures, workshops, book launches), but a medium openness towards e-learning elements, such as lecture-capture technologies, blogs, notes or events on Facebook.

In the case of The Netherlands, there is one embodiment of learners/users, namely a visual composite element, accessible from the main page of the department. The visual element is not the image of a student or teacher, like in the previous cases, but images depicting an art-work from the exhibition "The Gatewatcher", thus a relative new approach to the learner characteristics. From the point of view of UCC transgression to UGC, there is only the feature of sharing the content on the page of the user, so the department only creates content, without allowing the generating of it as well. However, their gender mainstreaming in the academic curriculum is articulated by concepts such as *Feminist, Ethnicity*, by one discipline-*Literature* and by one process, namely *Knowledge*. From the point of view of the instructional preferences of the teachers, the Dutch are the only ones which present a lecture-capture technology (http://www.sonicfoundry.com/), thus setting themselves apart in terms of typology of events and UGC. This technology actually allows the user/learner state to be a continuum, in the sense that the content created at one time develops the quality of becoming generated content for multiple instances of user/learner state. It is a clear example of what we see as "how the learning object is used", in the mind-frame of Stephen Downes (Downes, 2004).

Synthesizing the information depicted within the Dutch institutions' approach, we may reach the following conclusions:

- From the point of view of gender main-streaming in the academic curriculum, the representation of knowledge tends towards a multiple mainstreaming, filtering down towards an economic one (social welfare, economic development);
- From the point of view of participation/collaborative mainstreaming, they present a high level of user-experience, even though there is no UGC on social networks.

In the case of United Kingdom the embodiments of learner/user are in the form of pictures depicting women (either teachers or associates), embodiment continued on the Facebook page as well. It is also relevant to mention that, out of all the departments analyzed, their Facebook page is the only one using the Timeline application, thus it does show that they are active, so willing to support a transgression from UCC to UGC. From the point of view of News/Events feeds, this is not an available feature, but they do present podcasts, videos and interviews posted on affiliated blogs. Gender mainstreaming is articulated in the academic curriculum by concepts such as *Discrimination, Equality, Family, Stereotype, Participation*, by one discipline *Economy* and by one process *Labour*. From the point of view of learning objectives, the concepts do present a fluency towards the workshops, research seminars and film screenings organized by the department, fluency which is best argued by the generated content on the Facebook page as well. Also, within the typology of events, there is also the element of book exhibitions, covering concepts like stereotype or participation.

Synthesizing the information depicted within the British institutions' approach, we may reach the following conclusions:

- From the point of view of gender main-streaming in the academic curriculum, the representation of knowledge tends towards concepts like discrimination, equality, family, stereotype (multiple mainstream-ing), and only in a secondary level does the mainstreaming involve policy aspects (economy, labour);

- From the point of view of participation/collaborative mainstreaming, the events organized present a high level of e-learning elements (blogs, podcasts, active created content, useful links) and also a high level of user-experience, as there are posts on affiliated blogs and on the Facebook page which support this level.

Objective 3: Mapping a Possible Connection between what we See as a Global Equality Architecture and the Global Participation Architecture, in the Case of the Web 2.0 Learning/Teaching Setting

When O'Reilly coined the term Web 2.0 in 2006 he used the term *architecture of participation* when referring to the network effects created by "consuming and remixing data from multiple sources" (O'Reilly, 2006, p.17). It is these sources which allow the content to become generated, as the process of generating implies a platform – technological and communicative at the same time.

The term *architecture of equality* was used by Borchorst (Borchorst, 2011) in relation to what she names "gender equality machinery" (p.5), in the case of the Nordic countries institutional apparatus and by Cole (Cole, 2008) in relation to institutional mechanisms, to individual experience and to social existence.

In the case of our analysis, we propose the term *equality architecture* as framing the effects of gender mainstreaming within the academic curriculum, namely the convergence of the mainstreaming

process towards disciplines and processes, which are perceived as fundamental for our experience and existence, either as students/teachers and/or users/learners. It is not a surprise that new terms such as learner-generated content or peer-to-peer sharing [of ideas] find themselves in close proximity within the Web 2.0 pedagogical discourse, as the paradigm of equal-to-equal resonates with the re-signification of the teacher's locus, from teacher as expert to guide and collaborator.

We are of opinion that the flow of content's convergence, namely the unfolding of the key variables for both gender mainstreaming (academic development, cultural discourse, change pattern, social welfare, sexual stigmatization, minority, sexuality, economic development, European (Union), single parenting, governance) and participation/collaborative mainstreaming (people-centric, conversation, architecture of, engagement, practice-specific knowledge, network(ing), community, platform, remixing (mashing up), personalization, individualism) represent an effect of the transformation of the "four pillars of learning" (Brander et al., 2002, pp.346-347) highlighted by UNESCO, namely: learning to live together, learning to do, learning to know and learning to be, in the context of the Web 2.0 learning environment. Furthermore, we may observe that this transformation is supported by the common terminology, namely peer-to-peer participation and peer-to-peer education.

As the term architecture of participation implies consuming and remixing data from multiple sources, so does the term architecture of equality imply mainstreaming gender in multiple domains, disciplines. We agree to the definition of architecture coined by Wright (1970), according to whom

Architecture is that great living creative spirit which from generation to generation, from age to age, proceeds, persists, creates, according to the nature of man, and his circumstances as they both change. That really is architecture (Wright,

1970, p.311) and it is this definition we propose in relation to equality and participation, in this chapter, within the new Web 2.0 learning/teaching setting.

CONCLUSION

As new web-based technologies emerge on a daily basis, so do new web-based users/learners and new-web-based content, both created and generated. Also, as the discourse of equality is mainstreamed more and more, not only within the academic curriculum, but within the *daily existence* curriculum, it will be a challenge to observe, analyze and map the evolution of the high(ly) educated citizen, gendered or not.

Our research only focused on some of the gender studies' research centers within the European Union universities, in an endeavor to go beyond the traditional pedagogical fabric, embedded with strategies of teaching, towards the new Web 2.0. learning environment, embedded with strategic teaching. We wanted to highlight the possible correlations between textual, visual and connector elements and to show that there are connections between gender mainstreaming in the academic curriculum and participation/collaborative mainstreaming in the Web 2.0. learning/teaching setting, connections which are supported by different patterns of representation and transitivity.

Our research showed that we are witnessing an expansion of knowledge on gender studies and that indeed the process of mainstreaming unfolds rapidly within the academic curriculum of the universities in the EU. Also, we argued that a mapping of the connection between gender mainstreaming and participation/collaborative mainstreaming is possible by means of textual, visual and connector analyses, within the learning/teaching setting. Furthermore, we brought into discussion the issue of participation and equality architecture, as an intertwined *continuum* which "proceeds, persists, creates"(Wright, 1970, p.311).

REFERENCES

Abram, S. (2006). Web 2.0, library 2.0, and librarian 2.0: Preparing for the 2.0 world. *Sirsi-Dynix OneSource*. Retrieved February 26, 2012, from http://www.imakenews.com/sirsi/e_article000505688.cfm

Alexander, B., & Levine, A. (2008). Web 2.0 storytelling. Emergence of a new genre. *EDUCAUSE Review*. Retrieved February 24, 2012, from http://net.educause.edu/ir/library/pdf/ERM0865.pdf

Anil, D. (2002, November 13). Introducing the micro-content client. *A Blog about Making Culture*. Retrieved February 21, 2012, from http://dashes.com/anil/2002/11/introducing-microcontent-client.html

Borchorst, A. (2011). *Institutionalizing intersectionality: The Danish board of equal treatment as case.* Presented at The Financial Crisis, Welfare State Challenges and New Forms of Risk Management, Aalborg, Denmark.

Brander, P., Gomes, R., Keen, E., Lemineur, M.-L., Oliveira, B., Ondráčková, J., Surian, A., et al. (2002, May). *COMPASS: A manual on human rights education with young people.* Council of Europe Publishing F-67075 Strasbourg Cedex.

Bruns, A., & Bahnisc, M. (2009). *Social media: Tools for user-generated content social drivers behind growing consumer participation in user-led content generation* (State of the Art No. Volume 1) (p. 60). Eveleigh NSW, Australia 201: Smart Services CRC Pty Ltd., Australian Technology Park Locomotive Workshop.

Clever, N., Kirchner, A., Schray, D., & Schulte, M. (2009). *User-generated content.* 453 Research Compile. Retrieved February 14, 2012, from http://453.stilled.net/wp-content/uploads/2010/06/Eessay-user-generated-content.pdf

Cohen, H. (2011, September 5). *30 social media definitions*. HeidiCohen.com. Retrieved February 26, 2012, from http://heidicohen.com/social-media-definition/

Cole, K. (2008). *The Bolivarian alternative for the Americas and the regional political architecture of equality*. Presented at the XXVIII International Congress of the Latin American Studies Association, Rio de Janeiro.

Council of Europe. (1998). *Conceptual framework, methodology and presentation of good practices: Final report of activities of the group of specialists on mainstreaming* (No. [EG-S-MS (98) 2]). Strasbourg, France.

Downes, S. (2004, February 13). Beyond learning objects. *Australian Flexible Learning Framework*. Retrieved March 3, 2012, from http://community.flexiblelearning.net.au/GlobalPerspectives/content/article_5173.htm

Doyle, C. (2010). A literature review on the topic of social media. Retrieved February 21, 2012, from http://cathaldoyle.com/ph-d/

European Commission. (2008). *User-created-content: Supporting a participative information society* (No. SMART 2007/2008).

Greenberg, J., & Davila, M. (2002). *Teaching materials - What is strategic teaching?* MIT Teaching and Learning Laboratory. Retrieved February 21, 2012, from http://web.mit.edu/tll/teaching-materials/teaching-strategically/TLL-Strategic-Teaching-Diagram.pdf

Halliday, M. A. K. (2004). *An introduction to functional grammar* (3rd ed.). London, UK: Arnold.

Interactive Advertising Bureau. (2008). *User generated content, social media, and advertising — An overview*. Interactive Advertising Bureau.

Kamel Boulos, M. N., & Wheeler, S. (2007). The emerging Web 2.0 social software: An enabling suite of sociable technologies in health and health care education1. *Health Information and Libraries Journal*, *24*(1), 2–23. doi:10.1111/j.1471-1842.2007.00701.x

Kaplan, A. M., & Haenlein, M. (2010). Users of the world, unite! The challenges and opportunities of social media. *Business Horizons*, *53*(1), 59–68. doi:10.1016/j.bushor.2009.09.003

Lee, M. J. W., & McLoughlin, C. (2007). Teaching and learning in the Web 2.0 era: Empowering students through learner-generated content. *International Journal of Instructional Technology and Distance Learning*, *4*(10), 21–34.

O'Reilly, T. (2006). Web 2.0 compact definition: Trying again. *Communications & Strategies*, *65*(31), 17–37.

Reid, B. (2006). *Cognitive strategy instruction, teaching strategy*. Retrieved February 26, 2012, from http://cehs.unl.edu/csi/teachingstrategy.shtml#definition

Robinson, D. K. (in press). Web 2.0? Why should we care? *eweek.com*.

Sharp, D., Burns, A., & Barr, T. (2005). *Smart internet 2010—Social networks* (No. 2010, p. 170). Swinburne, Australia: Faculty of Life and Social Sciences, Swinburne University of Technology.

Stevens, I., & Van Lamoen, I. (2001). *Manual on gender mainstreaming at universities: Equal opportunities at universities: towards a gender mainstreaming approach*. The Netherlands: Garant Uitgevers NV.

UNAIDS. (1999). *Peer education and HIV/Aids: Concepts, uses and challenges* (UNAIDS Best Practice Material) (p. 39). Geneva, Switzerland: UN.

Webster, J. (2000). *Gender policy review policy directions report version 1* (No. Version 1). Retrieved February 20, 2012, from ftp://ftp.cordis.europa.eu/pub/citizens/docs/webster_report_en.pdf

Wright, F. L. (1970). *An organic architecture: The architecture of democracy*. Cambridge, MA: MIT Press Classic.

Wunsch-Vincent, S., & Vicker, G. (2006). *Participative Web: User-created content*. Organisation for Economic Co-operation and Development, Directorate for Science, Technology and Industry Committee for Information, Computer and Communications Policy.

ADDITIONAL READING

Blair, J., & Level, A. V. (2008). Creating and evaluating a subject-based blog: planning, implementation, and assessment. *RSR. Reference Services Review, 36*(2), 156–166. doi:10.1108/00907320810873020

Brown, R. (2000). Personal and professional development programmes for women: Paradigm and paradox. *The International Journal for Academic Development, 5*(1), 68–75. doi:10.1080/136014400410123

Cohen, S. F. (2008). Taking 2.0 to the faculty. *College & Research Libraries News, 69*(8), 472–475.

Council of Europe. (1998). *Conceptual framework, methodology and presentation of good practices: Final report of activities of the group of specialists on mainstreaming* (No. [EG-S-MS (98) 2]). Strasbourg, France: Council of Europe.

Dennis, A. R., Fuller, R. M., & Valacich, J. S. (2008). Media, tasks, and communication processes: A theory of media synchronicity. *Management Information Systems Quarterly, 32*(3), 575–600.

Gillin, P. (2007). *The new influencers: A marketer's guide to the new social media*. Sanger, CA: Quill Driver Books.

Graham, P. (2005). *Web 2.0*. Retrieved February 24, 2012, from www.paulgraham.com

Gross, J., & Leslie, L. (2008). Twenty-three steps to learning Web 2.0 technologies in an academic library. *The Electronic Library, 26*(6), 790–802. doi:10.1108/02640470810921583

Gunawardena, C., Kwesiga, J., Lihamba, A., Morley, L., Odejide, A., Shackleton, L., & Sorhaindo, A. (2004). *Gender equity in commonwealth higher education: Emerging themes in Nigeria, South Africa, Sri Lanka, Tanzania, and Uganda*. Funded by the UK Department for International Development, DFID, and the Carnegie Corporation of New York and coordinated by the Center for Higher Education Studies of the University of London Institute of Education.

Hirshbein, L. D., Fitzgerald, K., & Riba, M. (2004). Women and teaching in academic psychiatry. *Academic Psychiatry, 28*(4), 292–298. doi:10.1176/appi.ap.28.4.292

Hourigan, T., & Murray, L. (2010). Using blogs to help Language Students to develop reflective learning strategies: Towards a pedagogical framework. *Australasian Journal of Educational Technology, 26*(2), 209–225.

Jaworski, J., & Senge, P. M. (2011). *Synchronicity: The inner path of leadership*. San Francisco, CA: Berrett-Koehler.

Kwesiga, J. C., & Ssendiwala, E. N. (2006). Gender mainstreaming in the university context: Prospects and challenges at Makerere University, Uganda. *Women's Studies International Forum, 29*, 592–605. doi:10.1016/j.wsif.2006.10.002

Lenhart, A., et al. (2010). *Social media & mobile internet use among teens and young adults.* Pew Internet & American Life Project. Retrieved February 24, 2012, from http://pewresearch.org/pubs/1484/social-media-mobile-internet-use-teens-millennials-fewer-blog

Lenhart, A., Madden, M., Smith, A., & Macgill, A. (2007). *Teens and social media: An overview.* Washington, DC: Pew Research Center.

Leo-Rhynie, E. (1999). *Gender mainstreaming in Education: A reference manual for governments and other stakeholders.* Cape Town, South Africa: Institute of Development and Labour Law.

Mangold, W. G., & Faulds, D. J. (2009). Social media: The new hybrid element of the promotion mix. *Business Horizons, 52*(4), 357–365. doi:10.1016/j.bushor.2009.03.002

Manlow, V., Friedman, H., & Friedman, L. (2010). Inventing the future: Using social media to transform a university from a teaching organization to a learning organization. *Journal of Interactive Learning Research, 21*(1), 18.

Miners, Z. (2009). Twitter goes to college. *U.S. News & World Report.*

Park, J. H. (2010). Differences among university students and faculties in social networking site perception and use: Implications for academic library services. *The Electronic Library, 28*(3), 417–431. doi:10.1108/02640471011051990

Peat, F. D. (1987). *Synchronicity: The bridge between matter and mind.* New York, NY: Bantam Books.

Perrons, D. (2005). Gender mainstreaming and gender equality in the new (market) economy: An analysis of contradictions. *Social Politics International Studies in Gender State & Society, 12*(3), 389–411. doi:10.1093/sp/jxi021

Razavi, S., Miller, C., & Development, U. N. R. I. for S., & Programme, U. N. D. (1995). *Gender mainstreaming: A study of efforts by the UNDP, the World Bank and the ILO to institutionalize gender issues.* United Nations Research Institute for Social Development.

Sharp, D., Burns, A., & Barr, T. (2005). *Smart internet 2010—Social networks.* Swinburne, Australia: Faculty of Life and Social Sciences, Swinburne University of Technology.

Stephen, T. (2000). Concept analysis of gender, feminist, and women's studies research in the communication literature. *Communication Monographs,* (67): 193–214. doi:10.1080/03637750009376504

Stevens, I., & Van Lamoen, I. (2001). *Manual on gender mainstreaming at universities: Equal opportunities at universities: Towards a gender mainstreaming approach.* The Netherlands: Garant Uitgevers NV.

Tizhoosh, H. R., & Michaelis, B. (1999). *Subjectivity, psychology and fuzzy techniques: A new approach to image enhancement.* Paper presented at the 18th International Conference of the North American.

Verloo, M. (2005). Mainstreaming gender equality in Europe. A critical frame analysis approach. *The Greek Review of Social Research, 117,* 11–34.

Wankel, C. (2009). Management education using social media. *Organization Management Journal, 6*(4), 251–262. doi:10.1057/omj.2009.34

KEY TERMS AND DEFINITIONS

Architecture of Equality: We propose the term "equality architecture" as framing the effects of gender mainstreaming within the academic curriculum, namely the convergence of the mainstreaming process towards disciplines and processes, which are perceived as fundamental for our experience and existence, either as students/teachers and/or users/learners.

Architecture of Participation: The term was first used by O'Reilly (O'Reilly, 2006) when referring to the network effects created by "consuming and remixing data from multiple sources". In our case, from the point of view of the pedagogical setting, we propose the following substitutes, namely representational effects created by *consuming and remixing knowledge from multiple users.*

Gender Mainstreaming: Gender mainstreaming is the (re)organization, improvement, development and evaluation of policy processes, so that a gender equality perspective is incorporated in all policies at all levels and at all stages, by the actors normally involved in policy-making. Gender Mainstreaming is a typical example of a strategy that involves multiple levels in governance, but also multiple shifts in governance.[...] Gender Mainstreaming involves individual and institutional actors from inside and outside the state bureaucracy, including fields such as science and economy. The strategy of gender mainstreaming aims at a multiplication of the actors, policy areas and policy levels that are involved in working towards gender equality (Council of Europe, 1998).

Representation of Knowledge: In the context of our study, we consider that the textual, visual and connector elements analyzed form a representation of knowledge on the topic of gender studies, representation specific to each academic institution. We are of opinion that from these representations we can observe the mainstreaming paradigm from a twofold perspective: one with regards to gender mainstreaming in the academic curriculum and the second with regards to participation/collaborative mainstreaming in the learning/teaching setting.

Social Media: We agree to the definition provided by Bruns & Bahnisc (Bruns & Bahnisc, 2009), which encapsulates a three-fold perspective: "We define social media as websites which build on Web 2.0. technologies to provide space for in-depth social interaction, community formation, and the tackling of collaborative projects".

Strategic Teaching: Strategic teaching is a way of making decisions about a course, an individual class, or even an entire curriculum, beginning with an analysis of key variables in the teaching situation. These variables include the characteristics of the learners, the learning objectives, and the instructional preferences of the teacher.(Greenberg & Davila, 2002). In our case, we considered the characteristics of the learners reflected by the words participation (which is tagged with people-centric, conversation, engagement, practice-specific knowledge) and collaborative (which is tagged with networking, community, platform, mashing up, personalization, individualism), the learning objectives, in the case of gender mainstreaming in the academic curriculum, articulate the frequency patterns between gender and concepts, disciplines and processes, and the instructional preferences of the teacher(s) are best visualized in the type of events organized (seminars, lectures, conferences, workshops, book launches) and in the collaborative/participatory fashion these events and the content emerged out of them (user created content - UCC) is embodied as UGC (user generated content).

Web 2.0 Learning/Teaching Setting: As "Web 2.0 is the network as platform, spanning all connected devices"(O'Reilly, 2006), so is the Web 2.0. learning/teaching setting, namely as a pedagogical fabric, *spanning* all knowledge-*connected* users.

ENDNOTES

[1] They were chosen on the basis of web 2.0. tools' integration criterion within the websites and of geographical coverage, namely

belonging to a member-state of the European Union.

2   O'Reilly, T. (2006). Web 2.0. compact definition; Trying again. *COMMUNICATIONS & STRATEGIES, 65*(31), 17-37.

3   By item(s) we refer to a single document containing pieces of information on the university analyzed. Each document receives a number in Word Stat and the words inside the document are indexed accordingly, in order to map the patterns of occurrence/ frequency.

4   The processes were presented by the chromatic circle used for the cover of Halliday's book, *An Introduction to Functional Grammar*, the 2nd edition, printed in 1994.

5   Word Stat uses an average-linkage hierarchical clustering method to create clusters from a similarity matrix. The result is presented in the form of a dendrogram, also known as a tree graph. In such a graph, the vertical axis is made up of the items and the horizontal axis represents the clusters formed at each step of the clustering procedure. Words or categories that tend to appear together are combined at an early stage while those that are independent from one another or those that don't appear together tend to be combined at the end of the agglomeration process.

6   This coefficient is computed from a fourfold table as a/(a+b+c), where a represents cases where both items occur, and b and c represent cases where one item is found but not the other. In this coefficient equal weight is given to matches and non matches.

7   By "grass-root" we understand the basic, first levels of a process.

APPENDIX

Figure 1. Cover of the 2nd edition of M.A.K. Halliday, An Introduction to Functional Grammr, 1994

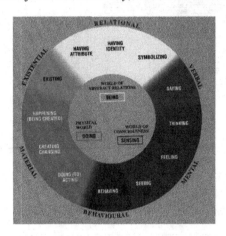

Figure 2. Proximity plot for the key-word gender, in the case of Central European University, Hungary

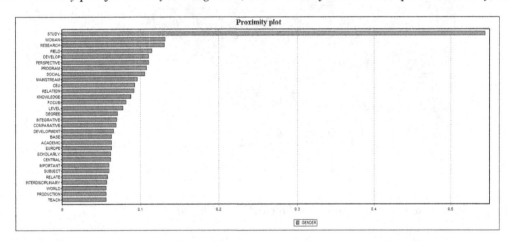

Figure 3. Proximity plot for the key-word gender, in the case of Sweden Universities

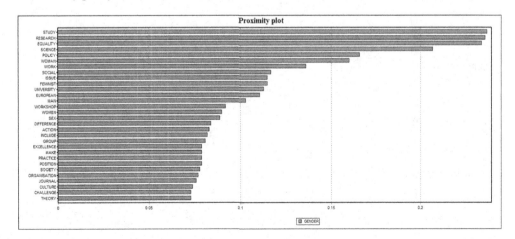

Figure 4. Proximity plot for the key-word gender, in the case of The Netherlands Universities

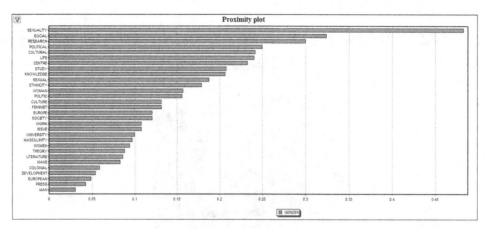

Figure 5. Proximity plot for the key-word gender, in the case of United Kingdom Universities

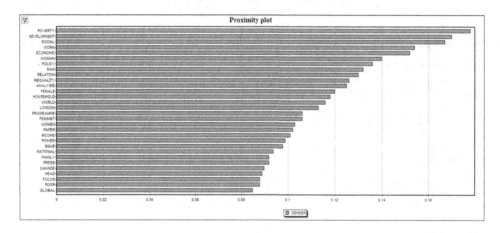

Figure 6. Dendogram segment, exemplifying Jaccard's coefficient

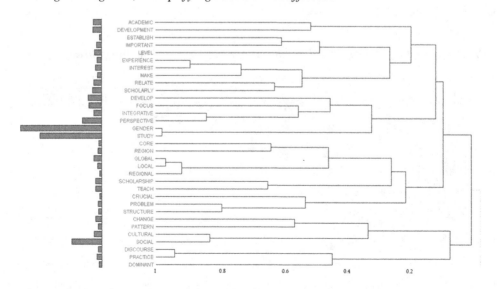

Table 10. Visual elements - logo of the institution

Criterion University/Dept.	Image	Color	Verbs	Process
Central European University Hungary		red	to do, to take action, to create, to change	material
Linköping University in Sweden – The Posthumanities Hub (PH) Sweden 1		blue & white	to see, to feel, to think	mental
Genset Sweden 2		blue & white	to see, to feel, to think	mental
Umeå University - Umeå Centre for Gender Studies (UCGS) Sweden 3		blue	to see, to feel, to think	mental
Utrecht University – Research Institute for History and Culture, Gender Studies The Netherlands 1		policromatic elements of yellow		
University of Amsterdam - Amsterdam Research Centre for Gender And Sexuality The Netherlands 2		black & white		
London School of Economics and Political Science – Gender Institute UK 1		red	to do, to take action, to create, to change	material
The Women's Library, London Metropolitan University UK 2		blue	to see, to feel, to think	mental
University of Cambridge - Centre for Gender Studies UK 3		coat of arms red & white & yellow		

Table 11. Visual elements - logo of the department

Criterion Univ./Department	Image	Color	Verbs	Process
Central European University Hungary	DEPARTMENT OF GENDER STUDIES	red	to do, to take action, to create, to change	
Linköping University in Sweden – The Posthumanities Hub (PH) Sweden 1	The Posthumanities Hub XY	1. yellow 2. orange 3. green 4. violet	1. to have an identity, to symbolize 2. the individual's existence 3. the individual's way of expreesion 4. phsychological moods of the individual	
Genset Sweden 2	genSET	1. blue brown	1. to see, to feel, to think 2. -	
Umeå University - Umeå Centre for Gender Studies (UCGS) Sweden 3		violet	phsychological moods of the individual	
Utrecht University – Research Institute for History and Culture, Gender Studies The Netherlands 1	GENDER STUDIES	1. blue brown	1. to see, to feel, to think 2. -	
University of Amsterdam - Amsterdam Research Centre for Gender And Sexuality The Netherlands 2	Amsterdam Research Centre for Gender and Sexuality (ARC-GS)	1. violet 2. pink 3. red	1. phsychological moods of the individual 2. – 3. to do, to take action, to create, to change	
London School of Economics and Political Science – Gender Institute UK 1	gender institute	violet	phsychological moods of the individual	
The Women's Library, London Metropolitan University UK 2	THE WOMEN'S LIBRARY	violet	phsychological moods of the individual	
University of Cambridge - Centre for Gender Studies UK 3	UNIVERSITY OF CAMBRIDGE Centre for Gender Studies / MPhil in Multi-disciplinary Gender Studies Apply now for October 2012/13	1. coat of arms red & white & yellow 2. yellow 3. green		

Table 12. Visual elements - logo of the significant event(s)/product(s)

Criterion Univ./Department	Image		Color	Verbs	Process
Central European University Hungary		The image is used for the 8th European Feminist Conference: The Politics of Location Revisited: Gender@2012	1. blue 2. yellow 3. green	1. to see, to feel, to think 2. to have an identity, to symbolize 3. the individual's way of expreesion	1. mental 2. relational 3. verbal
Linköping University in Sweden – The Posthumanities Hub (PH) Sweden 1			-	-	-
Genset Sweden 2			-	-	-
Umeå University - Umeå Centre for Gender Studies (UCGS) Sweden 3			1. blue 2. yellow	1. to see, to feel, to think 2. to have an identity, to symbolize	1. mental 2. relational
Utrecht University – Research Institute for History and Culture, Gender Studies The Netherlands 1			-	-	-
University of Amsterdam - Amsterdam Research Centre for Gender And Sexuality The Netherlands 2			1. violet 2. blue	1. phsychological moods of the individual 2. to see, to feel, to think	1.behavioral 2. mental
London School of Economics and Political Science – Gender Institute UK 1			composite visual element	-	-
The Women's Library, London Metropolitan University UK 2			1. red 2. blue 3. yellow 4. orange	1. to do, to take action, to create, to change 2. to see, to feel, to think 3. to have an identity, to symbolize 4. the individual's existence	1.material 2.mental 3.relational 4.existential
University of Cambridge - Centre for Gender Studies UK 3			composite visual element	-	-

Table 13. Logo of the visual elements on Facebook

Logo of the significant event(s)/products				
Criterion Univ./Department	Image	Color	Verbs	Process
Central European University Hungary		composite element		
Linköping University in Sweden – The Posthumanities Hub (PH) Sweden 1		1. yellow 2. orange 3. green 4. violet	1. have an identity, to symbolize 1. individual's existence 2. the individual's way of expreesion 3. phsychological moods of the individual	1.relational 2.existential 3.verbal 4.behavioural
Genset Sweden 2		1. blue green	1. to see, to feel, to think 2. the individual's existence	-
Umeå University - Umeå Centre for Gender Studies (UCGS) Sweden 3		-	-	-
Utrecht University – Research Institute for History and Culture, Gender Studies The Netherlands 1		composite element		
University of Amsterdam - Amsterdam Research Centre for Gender And Sexuality The Netherlands 2		1. violet	1. phsychological moods of the individual	1.behavioural
London School of Economics and Political Science – Gender Institute UK 1		1.yellow 2.green	1. to have an identity, to symbolize 2. the individual's way of expreesion	
The Women's Library, London Metropolitan University UK 2		-	-	-
University of Cambridge - Centre for Gender Studies UK 3		-	-	-

Chapter 4
Integrating Social Media and Traditional Media within the Academic Environment

Swati Jaywant Rao Bute
National Institute of Health and Family Welfare, India

ABSTRACT

With the advancement of technology, new modes of communication have emerged and are being used in the field of academics. Traditional media played a pivotal role in spreading knowledge in all sections of societies in the world. Traditional media proved to be a powerful tool in the process of making learning and teaching more effective, interesting, and simple to insure everyone benefits to the maximum. Social media are newly-emerged communication networks which are in use not only for sharing information but also for education, knowledge transfer, and for building a global community of academicians. Different tools of social media are in use in different streams of education. Over the years, it has been realized that both traditional and social media have much potential and use in education at all three levels e.g. primary, secondary, and higher education. But, the integration of traditional and social media still has a long way to go in terms of acceptance. This chapter highlights some major points related to changing academic environment, with the use of technology in classes, students vs. teachers' perspectives on learning and teaching, academics, and use of media – Traditional vs. New media in classes and integrating traditional and social media within the academic environment.

INTRODUCTION

The gradual growth of human civilization has witnessed mammoth changes and communication has been the determining element for each and every leap towards progress. At different developmental stages of the human civilization, we invented and used different modes of communication. However, the goal of inventions remained the same in each era and that was transferring the knowledge. From symbolic transformation of messages to written communication and from print to electronic me-

DOI: 10.4018/978-1-4666-2970-7.ch004

dia, today we are living in a digitalized era. In today's digitalized world, it is easy to share the knowledge and information in a very transparent fashion. Technology has given us wide scope for exploring and sharing our knowledge and talent with the world. People in all parts of the world are using different technologies for different purposes.

Benefits of new technology are being utilized in academics, education through radio and TV programs, web conferencing, satellite telecast, and distance education and now through social media. In recent time, lot of research has been done to find out new methods and techniques for teaching, to understand student's interest, to increase their involvement in learning process, to make teaching and learning more interesting and issues related to changing academic environment. All over the world academicians are involved in developing new methods, new techniques and tools to make teaching learning process easy and interesting. In today's context, a significant amount of work is being done to explore the advantages in academics. Use of new media in education is a new area of research for academicians. But if we can go little back and see, we find that over the years traditional media also played very important role in teaching and learning, and integrating both these two media in contemporary education system can give us tremendous success in academics.

Traditional Media

Traditional media includes contemporary modes of communication such as television, radio, newspapers, magazines, newsletters. In traditional media, usually the sender or the source of the information decides what to publish, broadcast or telecast, while receiver (readers/audiences and viewers) always receives the information. Receivers can respond their views, opinions on the subject and on presentation of the program or news which is published or broadcast from any media organization but normally they do not play any role in the creation of any news story or program. In private and public media organiza-

tions normally owners of the organizations control, hold and are responsible for the content and material published, broadcast or telecast. There are also some authorized agencies which play a very responsible and important role in the overall functioning of public and private media and in providing permission to start and run a media organization and also in deciding certain code of conducts for functioning of a media organization and it's process of information sharing.

Social Media

The term, "Social Network" is defined by the Webster Online Dictionary to be - Forms of electronic communication (as Web sites for social networking and micro blogging) through which users create online communities to share information, ideas, personal messages, and other content (as videos).

Social media is digitalized, computerized and networked form of information sharing which includes different network groups which operates certain social websites e.g. Google plus, Facebook, MySpace etc. Social media gives lot of freedom in the creation of information and in information sharing. Any user can start communication on any topic and anybody can participate. It is always user's choice on what they want to discuss and share. The organizations which hold the network generally do not take any responsibility on the quality and content of the conversation or any uploaded information. These social networks can be used for multiple purposes such as chatting with like minded people, to do online business and also for knowledge and information sharing. Special features give lot of choices to the users.

This chapter will highlight issues related to integrating tradition and social media within the academic environment, such as:

1. Changing academic environment in education system.
    a. Use of advanced technology and changing academic environment.

b.   Changing patterns of teaching; Distance and Blended patterns of teaching.
2.   Teacher VS Student's perspectives on teaching and learning.
3.   Academics and use of media.
    a.   Traditional vs. New Media.
4.   Integrating traditional and social media within the academic environment.

BACKGROUND

Use of traditional media in academics has a long history. In some countries it is very successful and showed very positive results in providing education to the underprivileged people and also in creating a positive atmosphere towards the education. Newspapers, magazines, radio and television are in use in academics since a long time. In digitalized era when everything is digitally connected and gives a lot of opportunities to communicate, traditional media still has more acceptability as the main mode of communication in the field of academics.

Radio Technology was first developed during the late nineteenth century and came into popular usage during the early twentieth century. Though sometimes overshadowed by television, radio represents a medium capable of reaching a wide geographic audience at a low production cost with proven educational results (Couch, 1997). Studies by the U.K. Open University have demonstrated that radio has a greater value for weak students who benefit from radio as a supplementary learning tool (Tripp & Roby, 1996). The Agency for International Development has shown that radio is more cost-effective and results in a greater learning effect size than textbooks or teacher education (Tripp & Roby, 1996). Radio has the advantage of teaching subjects in which classroom teachers are deficient or untrained. An added benefit for multi-grade classrooms is that it provides instruction for one group of students while the teacher works with another group. Radio can also bring new or unavailable resources into the classroom (Muller 1985) (R.V. Vyas, Dr. R.C. Sharma, Ashwini Kumar).

Radio, in reality, has been used extensively as an educational medium both in developed and developing countries since beginning. Its educational programs supported in a wide range of subject areas in different countries. Educational radio has also been employed within a wide variety of instructional design contexts. In some cases it is supported by the use of printed material, by local discussion group, and by regional study centers. It is sometimes so designed to permit and encourage listeners' reaction and comments. Evaluations are also carried out with the feedbacks received. (J. K. Das).

Jaminson and McAnany (1978) reported three main advantages of usage of radio in academics - to improve educational quality and relevance, to reduce educational costs and to improve access to educational inputs particularly to disadvantaged groups (McIsaac & Gunawardena, 1996).

The popularity, availability, and low cost of radio made it a convenient and practical medium for use in programs for learning at a distance and is mostly used in combination with other media, such as with print medium followed by face-to-face teaching etc. Although, educational use of radio started around 1930, but perhaps U.K.O.U. was first make its utilization effective.

Satyanarayana and Sesharatnam (2000) found that radio is useful in providing remedial tutorials, or some other forms of tutorial based feedback; providing corrections, alterations or updating of material, where print re-make budgets are limited, or where print cannot reach students quickly enough; recordings of naturally occurring events, e.g. political speech, children talking, concerts or performances, talks previously recorded for other than Open University proposes eyewitness interviews at historical events; presenting material in a dramatized form, enabling students to identify with the emotions and viewpoints of the main participants; providing an alternative view to that presented in the correspondence text and/or television programs; and enabling students to perceive the different points of view that exist, and observe ideas being challenged, through discussion and interviews (R.V. Vyas, Dr. R.C. Sharma, Ashwini Kumar, 2002).

In last few years it has been observed that usage of internet and computers has increased very rapidly. It has become a global phenomena, people are using internet not only in urban areas but also in small villages all over the world. Governments of developed and developing nations are trying to make it accessible to everyone so that everybody can be a part of mainstream development and education. Use of internet for the growth in areas such as education, health, agriculture, business, governance and information sharing is being promoted.

Over the past years, the use of social media for academic purposes has continued to grow rapidly. A study carried out in year 2011 shows rapid growth in the use of social media in dissemination of research results. Academicians' use of new media services such as Twitter continues to spur a sharply divided debate. It shows a continuous growth in the number of academics utilizing Twitter to discuss literature, for teaching and to enrich conferences. Many PhD students are turning to blogs and social media for tips on writing a thesis. Social media is inherently a system of peer evaluation and is changing the way scholars disseminate their research, raising questions. Social media is, at its core, a system of peer evaluation where participation and engagement are recognized and rewarded through dynamic social interactions. The tools used in continual publishing across blogs and social media provide accessible quantitative metrics which can be easily legitimized to measure impact (Danielle Moran and Amy Mollett, 2011).

Social media, from blogs to wikis to tweets, have become academic media, new means by which scholars communicate, collaborate, and teach. Many young adults have incorporated social media into their daily practices, both academically and personally. They use these tools to connect, collaborate, communicate and create (John Palfrey, Henry N.).

Debates about digital technology and its place in academia continue. Understanding the benefits and costs of using digital technology is crucial when deciding what a particular tool; site or package may be used for. Digital technologies can enhance three core areas of academic practice: accessing, searching and sifting information; communicating with others; and building peer-to-peer networks. The benefits of social media to help them search for information learn to communicate effectively and works collaboratively are documented across the disciplines (Dr Ruth Page).

Interactive, synchronous web conferencing software such as WebEx, Blackboard Collaborate and even Skype are innovative tools that can be implemented by faculty teaching both hybrid and fully online courses. There are certain advantages of interactive web conferencing as it increases the accessibility, it increases student-to-student and student-to-teacher interaction and promotes active learning as well as adds variety (Linda Macaulay, EdD and La Tonya Dyer).

A. CHANGING ACADEMIC ENVIRONMENT IN EDUCATION SYSTEM

The traditional method of teaching and use of traditional media in classrooms is considered as a one way process of teaching, where students are passive listeners and are not involved in the overall discussion and critical analysis of the subject. This method is less effective and do not help in nurturing students creativity and thought process. At the end of the class, teachers generally give assignments to the students but that also do not help in getting students original thoughts as mostly student search the material on the internet, copy it and present. In the semester pattern of examination, generally exams held after three months (on completion of trimester) or after six month for which students take help from class notes and again download material from net and write their exam. Their answers do not show any extra self-effort but come as a set and established facts and formulas. To increase student's involvement in analyzing the subject and problem, it is necessary to continuously involve them in finding the solutions and discussions.

Sometimes it is a contemporary setup of the classroom in which students do not feel informal and discuss openly with the teachers and go for counter arguments with the teachers and classmates. Sometimes it is also a fear of failure or wrong reasoning and analysis, which makes students less active in the live class. But it is being observed that if given a chance and appropriate atmosphere, where students feel less pressurized and more open to come forward with their own thoughts. Social media is a place, where they hang out with friends and discuss and share their thoughts more openly. The sharing of their own thoughts may not be accurate but it provides them a platform to express their own ideas and views and definitely paves way for improvement. Integrating social media with tradition media in academic environment can definitely help in nurturing students' creativity and analytical thought process.

Use of Advanced Technology and Changing Academic Environment

Different tools for learning, knowledge and information sharing are in practice and after the invention of web 2.0, the use of all these tools has increased leaps and bounds. This has changed the overall teaching – learning process. Students and teachers are using multimedia software's as well as video and audio technology in classrooms. Research studies show that there are certain positive results of using technology in the classrooms; it helps tremendously in improving students' attitude, enthusiasm and engagement in the studies.

Over the years, significant amount of changes has been observed in the teacher – student relationship in classrooms; students now take more responsibility for their own learning and doing things by themselves by putting different ideas, while teachers now work more as a facilitator and motivator. The Web is facilitating the future of learning. It has revolutionized the traditional methods which teachers use. The advent of electronic and digital communication as an integral part of academic discourse has profoundly changed the ways in which universities and their faculties pursue teaching. Students' bringing their cell phones and computers to class makes students collaborators in the learning process digital devices can also make them more engaged in the material (Mary Bart).

Changing Patterns of Teaching: Distance and Blended Patterns of Teaching

To fulfill the educational requirement of people and to make it more easy and approachable with limited resources and manpower new methods of teaching were adopted and implemented. Distance and blended learning are two methods which have revolutionized the entire education pattern and system which not only opened up new ways to provide education to the people of all sectors in a more liberalized way but also opened up several new opportunities of experimentation to improve teaching learning process. Blended learning refers to a mixing of different learning environments. It combines traditional face-to-face classroom methods with computer-mediated activities. Blended learning is a mix of delivery methods that have been selected and fashioned to accommodate the various learning needs of a diverse audience in a variety of subjects. (McSporran & King 2002). We can make it more innovative by adding blended learning with social media, such as Twitter/Facebook and blogs which provides the social aspect that we need when it comes to learning so that it does not become a lone-learning environment.

While distance education or distance learning is a field of education that focuses on teaching methods and technology with the aim of delivering teaching, often on an individual basis, to students who are not physically present in a traditional educational setting such as a classroom. It has been described as "a process to create and provide access to learning when the source of information and the learners are separated by time and distance, or both (Wikipedia). Use of traditional media is common in both the teaching methods. Universities and colleges generally use traditional media during the contact programs in the distance learning courses. This somewhere changed the set definitions of contemporary teaching learning process and helped in creating an environment of dialogue between teachers and students.

B. TEACHER VS. STUDENT'S PERSPECTIVES IN TEACHING AND LEARNING

Economic development not only helped in improving and boosting the financial condition globally but directly or indirectly it also helped in changing the contemporary pattern of teaching. Today most of the companies or organizations want to hire ready professionals. Such professionals play very active role in all activities from the first day of their joining. Organizations do not want to spend time and money in grooming them and converting college pass outs in to professionals. In most of the private educational institutes stress is given on building professionals and academic curriculum and teaching pattern is also designed accordingly. Focus is more on making them perfect in skills required by the industry. Generally after first semester of academic calendars students select their specialization and also select companies and organizations where they want to work after completion of course. They demand and prefer skill based education instead of simply following universities and college's contemporary curriculum and teaching pattern and style. Educational institutes also try hard to match with the Industries requirements so that their students can get easy placements. Showing hundred percent placements increase such educational institutes demand and reputation to get more admissions. Such attitude is mostly observed with undergraduate students who do not want to go for higher studies and prefer job experience more than theoretical experience and learning.

In such a changing environment when students' interest is more in completing their degrees and getting high salary jobs, they do not consider quality and in-depth education as a good option, while teachers sometimes find it difficult to compromise with the quality of education.

A new learner in a higher education environment (post-secondary) is in a transition. He is coming from the school system, where the content and the teaching are expected to be taken hook line and sinker. Typically, the student knowledge transfer at this stage is both uncontested and uncontestable and the student depends exclusively on teachers, textbooks and the rote learning of facts. In contrast, learners in a higher education environment are expected to be able to think for themselves, and consequently, process knowledge, make arguments and explanations, form hypotheses, and make conjectures. It is therefore expected that the higher education student would no longer simply be a passive recipient but would assume a more participatory approach as evidenced in more frequent seminar presentations, exchange programs, group tasks and online forums and integration of ICT into his learning environment; where, according to Brown, (2003) "methods are evolving from being high in teacher participation and control (e.g. a formal lecture) to being high in student participation and control (e.g. student presentations)". The 3P model developed by Biggs in 1989 conceptualizes the learning process as an interacting system of three sets of variables (M. Limniou and M. Smith).

- **Presage:** The learning environment and student characteristics.
- **Process:** Students' approach to learning.
- **Product:** Learning outcomes.

Sometimes teachers and students perspectives also differ on method of teaching and learning, which includes assignment pattern, exam pattern, class activities and mode of teaching. Students always prefer innovative methods of teaching including open space teaching, hands on practice, updated knowledge and experimenting with latest and innovative equipment. While sometimes teachers find it difficult to provide all these things because of certain reasons such as overcrowded classes, academic work load and unavailability of latest facilities in most cases. Lack of induction trainings and faculty development programs are also identified reasons for teachers not fulfilling student's acceptations.

C. ACADEMICS AND USE OF TRADITIONAL AND SOCIAL MEDIA

There is long history of use of traditional media in academics, traditional media which is mostly used in academics is - Print, Radio, Television, Video conferencing, Educational Radio, CDs, DVDs, Audio Clippings.

While the Social Media tools which are mostly in use in academics are - Wiki's, Scribd, Word Press, Facebook, Twitter, Academia.edu, LinkedIn, Google+, Mendeley, Researchgate, Dropbox, myExperiment, Elgg, WebCT, GoingOn, Profology, Skype, BibMe, bubbl.us, CiteULike, Confolio, Connotea, Gapminder, Mendeley, Mindmeister, and Zotero.

D. INTEGRATING TRADITIONAL AND SOCIAL MEDIA WITHIN THE ACADEMIC ENVIRONMENT

In recent time social media played very important and effective role in political and economic downfalls and uplifts in some parts of the world. The inception and use of social media affected almost all areas and sectors; even the contemporary global media industry is also facing very tough competition with the use and increasing popularity of social media. Social media gives a freedom to the user to be a part of the event, s/he can instantly register her/his views and thoughts and that is the major advantage of use of social media as well as major reason for its popularity among people of all age groups, all over the world.

Contemporary media industry has realized and identified this particular specialty of social media and they accepted it with their traditional pattern of news and program publishing, broadcasting and telecasting. Now media organizations are using social media as a source for news and parallel using it in their day-to-day news and program production, which can also be done in academics. Integrating social media with traditional media within the academic environment will not increase student's involvement and interest but will also give new opportunities to invent new ways and methods of teaching and learning.

Social Media for Elementary Education

Some of the social media sites such as Skype is playing very important role in providing education to the poor and underprivileged people and children. Skype is involving celebrities of developing countries in this work where education for all is still a major problem and billions of children are still not getting elementary education. Skype also helping students in doing their homework's through its easy to use tutorials.

New Social Media Tools for Higher Education

Use of social media is very much increased in recent time. People involved in higher education and research are finding it very friendly and useful. It is useful for sharing information, taking advice, publishing their work and discussing with diverse people with diverse background which is giving a new perspective to their work. Multiple social media tools are available which can be used for multiple functions such as - For posting transcripts and then embedding them in other sites, Bloggers or blogging platforms, creation and editing of interlinked web pages via a web browser, to discuss a topic, plan a meeting or share ideas for a grant proposal, for academic research and education, search function, to update status with information about current events that may be of interest to others; one can also upload, track and download academic papers, academics asking for peer reviews of drafts of papers, download academic papers for free, one can also pose questions to followers, one can easily invite colleagues to the site, Users can add people as contacts and send them messages, update their personal profiles to notify contacts about their activities, and both recommend and be recommended by contacts for their professional skills. Users can join groups to communicate with others in their field and can ask and answer questions related to their area of work, multiple-person video conversations, email multiple papers, one can publish abstracts from papers and journal articles, create and track conferences, search for conferences, view the speakers and sessions and contact the organizers to request more information, allow access to documents from anywhere and share them easily. One can also create digital versions of scientific workflow, receive reviews of your workflow and review others' workflows. Create wish lists of works internal to documents and distribute among the sites' data packs. Cre-

ate groups with private memberships, discussion groups, view your timeline of interactions to help assess your own development, Browse other users for potential research collaboration opportunities, to embed academic courses in a rich, interactive, collaborative environment. Provides members with individualized, discipline-specific content, and enables collaboration with colleagues across academia, discover new articles and resources, automated article recommendations, share references with your peers, find out who's reading what you're reading, Store and search your PDFs, store files, links, ideas, collaborate with others by sharing info, publish opinions on contributions of others, save and organize links to your references, easily share references with colleagues, access references from any computer, sharing, building online research libraries, collaboration.

SOLUTIONS AND RECOMMENDATIONS

Social media is a new media connecting people and providing platform to share information and ideas. Including and integrating it with traditional media in academic environment will definitely enhance the capacity of both students and teachers. There are certain constraints of use of social media in academics e.g. possibility of misuse of liberty and freedom which can also adversely affect the academic environment in case academic institutes fully permit its uses and integrate it with the academic environment. There are no regulatory bodies to control or scrutinize the content and also no norms are set for self regulations in such case integrating social media in higher education is also not recommendable from security point of view as it can be a threat for information and data related to important projects and research work. Integration can also dilute the academic excellence and standards.

To overcome such problems individual universities or group of universities can set and establish some norms or code of conduct for fair use and proper utilization of new media in academics which can be only for academic purposes. Some monitory bodies can also be set to control the content and material shared and distributed through these network sites.

FUTURE RESEARCH DIRECTIONS

In the past several research studies were done to know use of social media, its uses and different aspects related to virtual world and human behavior and emotions and also to know the relationship between virtual and real world but very few studies have been done to know the academic value of social and new media and its integration with academic environment.

Social media is very much common in youth and teenagers. This group is also different than other groups as it uses it for multiple purposes rather than just using it according to set functions e.g. mail, chatting and for developing business relations. They know the versatility of the media and use it. A future study can be done to know what percentage of youth use social media for academic purposes and on what topics (related to academics) they discuss more while using social media. Researchers all over the world use social media for discussion and to publish their work, a study can be done to know how social media is helping them and what are the constraints of using social media in academics?

CONCLUSION

From the Stone Age to the digitalized era, human civilization has come a long way and is still in the process of improving the ways to connect to each other. We started with using sign language to communicate our thoughts, feelings, expressions and knowledge and then we went on developing verbal language to do the same. But, one thing was always very clear that the knowledge and information needs to be passed because it gives the opportunity to learn from past mistakes and to gain from the previously achieved knowledge. This gave birth to the concept of teaching and learning process. Those who have knowledge would pass it to the next generation, the receiver would adopt the knowledge, analyze it, improve it, would add new changes to it and then pass it on to the next generation and the cycle would go on.

Over the centuries, the methods of pursuance changed in a big way but the basic concept remained the same, which was transfer the knowledge to make the existing ideas better for the future generations.

Today access to information and knowledge is just a click or a slide away for anybody in any corner of the world. It was not the same always. In the very beginning of civilization, when we humans were just emerging from the flock of other animals to become the leaders of a civilized society, the very first thing we learned was to stand tall on our two feet among others, which separated us from the rest. This apparently was not an overnight change. It must have taken a long time to learn and understand that standing on two feet, instead of using all four legs to walk, is something which makes us different from others and has the advantage of using the other two legs as hands to do things which four-legged animals can't do. This simple concept of proper usage of limbs to improve performance was a major milestone for the tremendous growth we achieved in last few years.

This progress was not possible if the ancestors had not passed the knowledge to the successors. Initially, the process of passing the information began as a non-verbal method where the owners of the knowledge would leave the legacy in the form of pictures on cave walls for others to learn. This method of transferring the knowledge definitely had its own advantage but it was the most effective way. So, we figured out that something betters needs to done to convey the right knowledge and so we developed a verbal form of communication which was called language. This proved to be an important tool for the knowledge transfer. Now, it was easy to tell what the existing knowledge meant and what was needed to be changed.

In the beginning, this newly-developed tool was used within a smaller circle of folks and the knowledge stayed confined within a smaller circle. Gradually, with the growing needs for survival, the humans started travelling from one place to another and with them; the knowledge also travelled and started spreading. The process, however, was still shaping up. Then we decided that instead of letting the knowledge float randomly, there should be a better way to secure the information from one generation to the other. And then come the concept of schooling where certain people were authorized to pass the acquired knowledge and gave a proper shape to the process of knowledge transfer. Still, the process was in its preliminary stage and needed to be improved. So we kept going on and came up with better methods and concepts of connecting to each other to gain from experiences.

Development of technology helped us achieve our goals in an effective manner. Radio technology proved to be a major milestone. It didn't require physical presence of the teacher and the learner to exchange the knowledge. But we didn't stop here either. We kept on going and came up with newer modes of communications to make the process easy and fancy. Television was one such method, which was not just audio but it had pictures to show how the things are done.

With advancement of technology we found easier modes of communication. Internet equipped us to share the knowledge on a bigger platform. With every passing moment, we are being introduced to newer modes of communication. It definitely impacted the traditional way of teaching-learning process and today it is just not limited to classrooms but has become widespread. It is a fascinating fact that the development of civilization started with sign language and after travelling a long distance, we are again using non-verbal codes to develop new ways of communication where everything is virtual but the knowledge.

When we compare the traditional methods of learning with the newer ones, there seems to be a significant change not only in methods but also in the approach of acquiring knowledge and information. But, ideally both conventional and innovative ways of teaching-learning process have their own pros and cons.

Going back to the stone age when pictures and signs used to be the main equipment to pass the knowledge, it was definitely the least effective way of teaching, but it had its own advantages and pictures carved on cave walls still help us trace back the era of human civilization. In other words, everything new is just a passing phase to pave the path for newer advancement.

Today social networking and micro-blogging websites provide us the opportunity to keep the whole world informed about every fraction of a second. They are the most powerful tools to keep the whole world connected can prove to be the best way to enhance the teaching-learning process.

It is high time to welcome the newer methods with open arms but at the same time the traditional methods should also be secured because they are the base of all the growth which has brought the civilization to where it is today.

Time is moving fast and so is growth of technology. We have to keep pace with both. It is need of the hour to adopt the blend of traditional and ever changing methods to gain to the maximum.

REFERENCES

Apple. (n.d.). *Technology's impact on learning*. Retrieved from http://www.info.apple.com/education

Bart, M. (2011, August 9). Effective uses of video in the online classroom, teaching with technology. *Faculty Focus.*

Doak, J. (2012). *Using new media tools to promote faculty research. Counsel for Advancement and Support of Education.* CASE.

Electronic Frontier Foundation. (2009). *Definition of media.* Retrieved from www.eff.org/files/filenode/social_network/media_def_resp.pdf

Limniou, M., & Smith, M. (2010). *Teachers' and students' perspectives on teaching and learning through virtual learning environments.* UK: University of Manchester.

Macaulay, L., & Dyer, L. T. (2011, November 14). Teaching with technology: Interactive Web conferencing brings big benefits to the online classroom. *Faculty Focus.*

Moran, D., & Mollett, A. (2011). *Altmetrics, a guide to Twitter for academics and increasing your academic footprint.* Round-Up of Social Media Blogs.

Orlando, J. (2011, October 11). Wikis in the classroom: Three ways to increase student collaboration. *Faculty Focus.*

Page, R. (2011, March 14). Social media savvy - The universities and academics leading the way. *The Guardian.*

Palfrey, J., & Ess, H. N. (2011, May 3). *Academic uses of social media: Exploring 21st century communications.* Webcast Event: Faculty Development & Diversity at Harvard and the Harvard Office of News and Public Affairs.

Visser, J. (1994). *Distance education for the nine high-population countries: A concept paper based on the informal planning meeting on distance education of the nine high-population countries, Manila.* Learning Technologies and Educational Communication for Basic Education, UNESCO Basic Education Division.

Vyas, R. V., Sharma, R. C., & Kumar, A. (2002). Educational radio in India. *Turkish Online Journal of Distance Education, 3*(3). ISSN 1302-6488

Webopedia. (n.d.). *New media.* Retrieved from www.webopedia.com/TERM/N/new_media.html

KEY TERMS AND DEFINITIONS

Academic Environment: Overall atmosphere in an education setting which influence, force and generate intrest in teaching and learning.

Digital Technology: Use of digital software and hardware.

Integration: The act of combining.

Social Media: Social media is digitalized, computerized and networked form of information sharing which includes different network groups which operates certain social websites e.g. Google plus, Facebook, MySpace etc.

Students Perspective: Students vision for learning.

Teachers Perspective: Set goal, objective, vision, method and technique for teaching.

Traditional Media: Traditional media includes contemporary modes of communication such as television, radio, newspapers, magazines, newsletters.

Chapter 5
Using Facebook in Teaching

Ioana Boghian
"Vasile Alecsandri" University of Bacău, Romania

ABSTRACT

Educators have started to turn to social networking sites as they began to recognize the assistance that such sites may provide in information dissemination, creation and cooperation activities, and also in receiving feedback. As promoter of personality, individuality, self-expression, self-assertion, and communication, Facebook responds well to the particularities and requirements of the student-centered approach to teaching and learning. By critically analyzing certain pedagogic approaches to Facebook and by highlighting the common denominator of Facebook and student-centered strategies in terms of didactic benefits, this paper intends to answer the following questions: Can Facebook be regarded and used as an effective and efficient educational tool? If yes, in what way(s)?

INTRODUCTION

Social networking sites such as MySpace, Facebook or Bebo have been increasing in popularity ever since they were invented. The number of people using social networking sites has grown to such an extent that their power of communication, of establishing and maintaining connections has drawn the attention of academics and industry researchers.

With an alleged – credible and increasing – number of over 900 million users (it seems that about 100 million users joined Facebook in the course of the last nine or ten months since at the moment that I started working on this article the number of Facebook users reported by various Internet sources was 800 million users), we consider that Facebook deserves particular attention in terms of the educational opportunities it may provide for both students and teachers. Studies

DOI: 10.4018/978-1-4666-2970-7.ch005

on pedagogic approaches to Facebook and social networking sites have already been carried out and their results have already been published and disseminated (Matthews, 2006; Hewitt and Forte, 2006; Mazer, Murphy and Simonds, 2007; Charnigo and Barnett-Ellis, 2007; Selwyn, 2009; Towner and VanHorn, 2007). A concern for training educators on how to use social networking sites in their didactic activities has also been increasingly visible in recent years (Rego, 2009; Munoz and Towner, 2009; Ragupathi, 2011).

The student-centered approach to education focuses on the needs of the students rather than on the needs of the other actors involved in the educational process. Classroom activities involve students particularly in group-work, also encouraging initiative and decision-taking from the part of the student. In the student-centered class, teacher talk has diminished drastically to give way to student talk, student-student interaction and student assertion. In this way students are encouraged to create and develop their own learning style. The teacher's role has shifted from that of main source of information to that of mediator and guide. Besides promoting peer communication, collaboration and active learning or learning through discovery, student-centeredness also aims at turning students into independent, autonomous learners by creating and developing self-motivation and self-regulation skills. Such skills may serve them in future self-educating initiatives (McCombs and Whistler, 1997; O'Neil and MacMahon, 2010; Cojocariu, 2012; Arends, 2012).

As promoter of personality, individuality, self-expression, self-assertion and communication, Facebook responds well to the particularities and requirements of the student-centered approach to teaching and learning. On Facebook, students have been found to take pieces of information and repeat or "share" them to their groups of friends, thus performing mentoring and advising activities. Educational cooperative activities are also carried out on Facebook as, for example, when groups of students move their teamwork projects on the level of the virtual 'chat room'. Moreover, Facebook also complies with each learner's unique style of learning, which constitutes another basic principle of student-centered education. Instant feedback is also provided through Facebook so that one piece of information posted by some student gets several responses almost instantaneously.

Taking into consideration the ideas presented above, the main objectives of our paper are: a theoretical approach to using Facebook in teaching and to student-centered educational strategies, with the specification of the pros and cons for using Facebook in the didactic process and also the identification of the common points between Facebook and student-centered strategies in terms of students' learning benefits and advantages; the identification and formulation of best practice recommendations for teachers on how to use Facebook in teaching of the type dos and don'ts; providing illustrative examples on how to use Facebook in teaching for various educational subjects and educational levels; our attempt to propose an experimental future project of using Facebook in teaching with the purpose of identifying the impact of using Facebook in learning and particularly in distance learning. Thus, one section of the paper will focus on defining the key concepts underpinning our paper, the following section will constitute an attempt at approaching Facebook as an educational tool from the perspective of student-centeredness and the last section will be concerned with providing some concrete examples on how to combine the use of Facebook and student-centered strategies for educational purposes.

DEFINITION OF KEY TERMS

Facebook is a social networking site, the most popular online social networking site among university students (Cheung et al., 2011, p. 1337) that was originally designed for college students but is now open to anyone 13 years of age or older. A social networking site may be defined generally as a web-based service that allows individuals to build a public or semi-public profile within a confined environment, to connect with other users that occur in a so-called list of friends and to view the friends' lists of connections (Boyd and Ellison, 2007). One of the debates that we regard as relevant for our paper concerns the question of whether what we generally know as social networks should be referred to by the phrase "social network sites" or "social networking sites". We believe that this debate is relevant for us because the conflict between these two terms – 'network' and 'networking' – concerns, in fact, the identification of the main purpose of such sites and because we shall later attempt to find common key words and features between Facebook as a social network(ing) site and student-centering. We chose to begin with the definition given to social networking sites by Boyd and Ellison because we agree with the main points that these authors highlighted in their definition of social 'network' sites. Nevertheless, we consider that these points refer to the concrete actions that users perform on such sites, the main effect of such actions being, in fact, communication and interaction: behind the actions of building an online profile, of connecting with others online, of making an online list of friends, we believe that there stands the human need for communication, self-assertion, self-expression and interaction, the need of social acceptance, inclusion and appreciation. Boyd and Ellison (2007) explain their preference for the word 'network' because, they claim, the term 'networking' "emphasizes relationship initiation, often between strangers", adding the idea that networking, though possible and present on such sites, "is not the primary practice on many of them nor is it what differentiates them from other forms of computer-mediated communication" (p. 2). But, we may argue, no dictionary definition of the term 'networking' supports the idea of networking as relationship initiation often between strangers: according to various dictionaries, the noun 'net-

working' basically means the activity of meeting and talking to people to exchange information and advise about work or interests;[1] the exchange of information or services among individuals, groups or institutions; specifically: the cultivation of productive relationships for employment or business;[2] creating a group of acquaintances and associates and keeping it active through regular communication for mutual benefit; 'networking' is based on the question 'How can I help?' and not on 'What can I get?'[3] Since the paradigm of student-centering focuses on the students' needs, our approach to Facebook as an educational tool implies the use of this social networking site as a way of improving student performance, of promoting the students' professional and personal development. If we also take into consideration Beer's argument that 'social network sites' is a term implying a broader field of study that may bring about confusion rather than illumination, whereas the term 'social networking site' is "more differentiated and descriptive of the processes" (Beer, 2008, p. 520) characteristic of such sites (Facebook, Twitter, MySpace, hi5, Bebo as different from Youtube, Linkedin or Slideshare, to name just a few[4]) we consider ourselves to be in favor of the 'social networking site' terminology.

Our choice of Facebook to the detriment of other social networking sites may be motivated, from the perspective of the topic of our paper, first of all, by its popularity: the idea of using Facebook in teaching is a time-saver as most of my students already have a Facebook account (the fact that most students already have a Facebook account is a reality also supported by Matthews, 2006); moreover, due to its highly user-friendly interface, any explanations that might be needed would involve little effort from the part of the teacher. The second most important reason for choosing Facebook is the feature called Create Group: this feature allows the Facebook user – the teacher, in our case – to create a group – a group that includes all the students in one class, for example – and to share information under various forms with all the members of that group simultaneously and in real time. Group norms, together with subjective norm and social identity, constitutes one of the modes of social influence with an impact upon the We-Intention, defined as "the joint intention made by a group of people that everyone will perform his/her own part (individual intention of joining and using online social networks continually) to perform a joint action together with others (continue to use online social networks together)" (Cheung et al., 2011, 1338). The influence of the group norm upon the We-Intention relies upon the idea of adopting a decision based on the similarity of one's values with the values of other group members, whereas the influence of the subjective norm translates as compliance with the expectations of relevant others and social identity refers to the "self-awareness of one's membership to a group" (idem, 1339). Thus, the Create Group Facebook feature is also a time-saver and an assurance that all the students included in the respective group receive all the information the teacher sends.

Communication and interaction on Facebook is a continuation of real-life communication and interaction – interaction briefly defined as mutual action or influence. The main reasons for which students use Facebook are: to maintain existing relationships; to meet new people; using Facebook is fun and cool; to make oneself more popular; to pass time; to present or express oneself; for learning purposes; as a task management tool; for student activism (Hew, 2011, 664-665). By creating a profile, which may be done by answering a series of questions, Facebook users create an identity. According to the privacy settings selected, the profile, the identity we may say, becomes more or less visible. Communication, interaction, identity and visibility are key paradigms for activities conducted on Facebook. But communication, interaction, identity, visibility translated as self-assertion and self-expression are also key paradigms in the student-centered approach to teaching and learning.

The student-centered approach to teaching and learning differs from the teacher-centered approach in terms of theoretical foundations, the teacher's and the students' role, planning tasks, learning environment and assessment procedures: this approach to the didactic process, often referred to as the constructivist approach to teaching and learning, "holds that knowledge, instead of being objective and fixed, is somewhat personal, social and cultural. Meaning is constructed by the learner" (Arends, 2012, p. 355). The basic idea of student-centeredness is that students should be provided with learning skills during the didactic process so that they may develop their own learning style. Whereas some authors believe that student-centered strategies should mainly promote the students' responsibility for such activities as planning learning, interacting with teachers and with other students, researching and assessing learning[5], others consider that learning centered on the beneficiary of learning should mainly focus on supporting and encouraging students in finding their own learning style, in understanding the motivation of learning and in building some learning skills that may enhance life-long learning (Hall, 2006, p. 1). The main principles of student-centered learning are (McCombs & Whisler, 1997, p. 5):

- The learning process is "active, volitional and internally mediated"; meaning is discovered and constructed from information and experience, "filtered through the learner's unique perceptions, thoughts and feelings".
- The goal of the learning process is to create "meaningful and coherent representations of knowledge regardless of the quantity and quality of data available".
- The learner constructs new knowledge based on "existing and future guided knowledge", past experience and present applications and practice in a unique and meaningful way.

- Students should acquire higher order thinking skills that may allow them to display creative and critical thinking, and also flexibility in responding to new situations, as the bases for lifetime learning.
- The student-centered approach to teaching and learning takes into consideration the learner's system of beliefs, values, interests, goals, expectations and emotional states as motivational influences – that may be positive or negative – on the learning process.
- Learning is influenced by the learner's intrinsic motivation which manifests itself by involvement, curiosity, enthusiasm for understanding what they have to learn.
- Student-centered learning tasks should appeal to and stimulate the learner's curiosity, creativity and higher order thinking.
- The student-centered approach to teaching and learning takes into consideration the fact that each learner is unique in terms of physical, intellectual, emotional and social development that determines the way they learn, remember, understand and do things.
- Social and cultural diversity are regarded as factors that should support interaction among students with a view to developing interpersonal skills.
- The learning environment should promote social acceptance and self-esteem: learning is enhanced when students feel appreciated and socially accepted.
- Learners have and develop different and unique learning styles as an effect of their different biological, cultural and social backgrounds.
- The learner's prior learning acts as a cognitive filter, that is, as a basis for constructing reality and interpreting life experiences.

The ideas of active involvement, social integration, self-reflection and personal validation as pillars of the student-centered paradigm are also supported by other authors, such as O'Neill and MacMahon (2005) or Cojocariu (2012). We chose here to refer to the principles of student-centered learning in the view of McCombs and Whisler for the fact that they relate to all the learner-related aspects that we regard as having a significant part in the students' professional and personal development.

From these principles, we may draw the conclusion that a student-centered classroom environment should promote individualization, interaction and integration (Moffet & Wagner, 1992, p. 21).

Among the most common types of student-centered learning, also referred to as the constructivist perspective on teaching and learning, we may mention:

- **Collaborative Learning:** Through cooperation, the members of a group build consensus, the most efficient way of working being that in which the skills and contributions of each of the members of the group are highlighted, acknowledged, respected and turned to advantage; collaboration is opposed to competition as the way of highlighting only the best individuals in a group (Panitz, 1997, p. 2).
- **Experiential Learning:** Learning through experience means learning by doing or learning through reflection on doing (Kolb, 1984).
- **Mediated Learning:** The specificity of mediated learning consists in the way in which the learner is helped, guided and supported in structuring his activity of learning (Cojocariu, 2012, p. 103).

These three types of learning, together with other types of learning such as simulation-based learning, problem-based learning, interactive learning, are called student-centered because they all imply a process of learning focused on the beneficiary of learning, i.e., the student. The teacher's role in student-centeredness is that of mediator and guide, of "coach, facilitator and co-learner" (Vighnarajah & al., 2008, p. 38). Thus, the teacher should be able to convey and digest information from one situation to another, should adapt his instruction to the developmental level of his students, should pay attention to individual differences in learning as each student is unique, should pay attention to the students' expectations concerning the outcome of their learning as compared to the objectives stated for the course. A teacher's skills in student-centered approaches should include the ability to give useful practical suggestions and constructive feedback, to act as a resource, to monitor students' work, to improvise if necessary, to cope with unexpected situations in class, to cope with students that have different learning styles, to create their own materials, to help students in planning their learning, to approach the community for help.

The fact that each learner is unique takes us to another significant defining feature of student-centeredness, the students' needs, that basically refers to the fact that each learner is unique in terms of personality, socio-economic background, creativity, (intrinsic, extrinsic) motivation, past experiences, previous acquisitions, learning style, learning rhythm, response to new information and all these parameters affect their process of learning. In student-centeredness, the student's role is an active one, the student being encouraged to interact with others and get involved in investigation and problem-solving activities (Arends, 2012, p. 356). By taking into consideration the students' needs, student-centeredness promotes a more equal relationship between learners, thus enhancing growth and development, and also an advantageous interlacing of the student's cognitive and affective dimensions (O'Neill & MacMahnon, 2005, p. 3).

FACEBOOK AS AN EDUCATIONAL TOOL

Facebook and Student-Centered Strategies: Commonalities

It is a known fact that Facebook has generated many contradictory discussions and still does. Fears concerning Facebook users relate to potential risks such as alienation, identity theft or offline stalking. Authorities try to educate people concerning what should or should not be posted on Facebook. Special attention is paid to the use of Facebook by children. On the other hand, the opportunities Facebook provides in transmitting information are undeniable, the speed of information and almost instant feedback being two of its major strong points, not to forget about the large number of people that one may send information to simultaneously and in real time.

When it comes to using Facebook in education, opinions differ particularly concerning the time involved in preparing and conducting educational activities on Facebook, the attitude of teachers and students towards the use of Facebook as an academic tool, limitations of using Facebook for teaching and learning purposes (for example, can assessment rely upon educational activities conducted on Facebook? or, to what extent could teachers impose the use of Facebook for educational purposes upon their students?), the material and human resources involved (students belonging to poorer social backgrounds may not always own an Internet connection at home or in an environment that may be suitable for learning activities; how can problems such as Internet connection failures be dealt with especially when assessment of educational activities conducted via Facebook is involved).

As far as the pros of using Facebook in education are concerned, the literature covered and our own perspective on this issue led us to formulating the following conclusions:

- Facebook displays a significant potential to become a learning network defined mainly by structure and flexibility (Couillard, 2010, p. 5), a "necessity" (Towner & al., 2007, p. 1), particularly by such features as the possibility to create an online community and the possibility to interact and share knowledge. Facebook can help teachers connect with students about assignments, upcoming events, post useful links and samples of work, and all these outside the classroom. Facebook also automatically displays the links to the user's favorite books, authors or links on the profile information page.

- Facebook is a cost-effective teaching resource and a lot of students are already using it, and for those who are not using it yet there are plenty of resources providing guidelines and advice concerning this matter.

- Teacher self-disclosure is an efficient way to connect with students, provide them with richer experiences and increase students' motivation (a view supported by such authors as Couillard, 2010. Mazer, Murphy and Simonds, 2007. Towner and VanHorn, 2007) though contact on Facebook has been found to have no influence on students' ratings of professors (Hewitt and Forte, 2006). We understand the concept of teacher self-disclosure not necessarily by the very private information that the teacher may include in his Facebook profile (which is not even indicated when using Facebook for educational purposes) but, for example, by the favorite quotations, educational- or art-related events, favorite books, favorite philosophers, scientists, painters, sculptors that the teacher may chose to display on his profile information page.

- Though often labeled as belonging to informal communication and recommended to be avoided in professional, formal communication, we agree with the fact that the use of some happy faced emoticon now and then may support shy students in overcoming their inferiority complex and become more self-assertive and open[6].

- As an Internet based learning tool, Facebook involves students actively in learning as they are stimulated, encouraged and lured into navigating to various information sites, posting comments and getting engaged in online discussions (Couillard, 2010, p. 6).

- Facebook allows students to contact other students about questions regarding assignments or exams and work together in an online group.

- Uploading videos and photos is very easy on Facebook and "the generous 1024 MB limit on videos and the compatibility with a wide variety of web browsers are superior to some courseware options" (Munoz & Towner, 2009, p. 2626).

- Facebook allows for the creation of groups that may share common interests: from this perspective, a classroom of students may constitute a Facebook Group with the teacher as coordinator of activities, mediator of communication, facilitator of information for that group.

The cons of using Facebook as an educational tool do not necessarily reject the idea of using Facebook for teaching and learning completely but rather lead us to conclude that, at least for the moment and without the support of some officially recognized, standard and certified procedure for turning Facebook into an approach to the teaching-learning process, Facebook educational activities remain in the area of the optional and the experimental. Such barriers for turning Facebook into an efficient and effective educational tool are basically related to the following aspects:

- The need for all learners involved in Facebook educational activities to adopt proper language and behavior, to constantly display a self-monitoring attitude when engaging in Facebook interaction and communication as the use of Facebook as an educational tool may be regarded as a prolongation of the activities conducted in the classroom, requiring thus compliance with a certain moral and ethical etiquette; educational discussions on Facebook should maintain a certain level of professionalism both in teacher-students and in student-student interaction and personal (Ragupathi, 2011, p. 2).

- The time involved in preparing and conducting educational activities may be regarded as a limitation since some teachers may not be willing to spend part of their free time in online interaction and communication with their students via Facebook.

- Lack of officially and nationally or internationally recognized standards concerning the use of Facebook as a teaching method and lack of certified, institutionalized ways of assessing educational activities conducted on Facebook or of evaluating the results of activities conducted on Facebook.

- The concerns about privacy of Facebook users regards students and teachers as well, that is why, in the following section of our paper, we shall highlight the types of information that should be displayed on the profile information page; it has been found that a significant amount of Facebook users do not restrict accessibility to their Facebook profiles (Hew, 2011), hence students and teachers alike should be encouraged to use privacy settings to protect their accounts; we mentioned here the fact that teachers also, adults that are – presumably – aware of the potential risks of leaving a Facebook profile open for everyone to view, should use privacy settings to protect the identity of children in their friends' list if not their own identity, too.

- The efforts that may be required for engaging students in Facebook educational activities: a study by Madge, Meek, Wellens and Hooley (2009) showed that the main reason for which students use Facebook is social purposes; the second reason students use Facebook is for informal (student-to-student) learning whereas most students responded that they never used Facebook for formal teaching, that is, teaching that would involve staff and part of formal assessment (Madge et al., 2009, p. 143); Hew (2011) also concludes that at least so far, Facebook has seen very little educational use.

- Social networking could result in such effects as alienation, disengagement and disconnection with the real world, distraction of students from their studies (Selwyn, 2009, p. 165).

We shall here try to identify the commonalities of Facebook and student-centered strategies from the perspective of the learner's benefits or, in other words, in terms of advantages and disadvantages. For this, we shall take into consideration some of the pros and cons for using Facebook as an educational tool and the principles of the student-centered approach to teaching and learning that we have previously enumerated. Thus, the common denominator of Facebook and student-centered strategies may be regarded as promoting all the following aspects:

- The learner's active participation and involvement in the process of learning.

- Student-student interaction prevails whereas teacher-student interaction is secondary.

- Facebook and the student-centered approach promote the learner's individuality and self-assertion.

- Motivation and affect: Facebook and the student-centered approach enhance the learner's motivation for learning by encouraging students to get involved in interesting, creative activities, by encouraging them to express themselves, by the chances that students have to assert that which makes them unique, their personality and individuality.

- Variation in types of learning and, therefore, a constant high level of interest in activities: students are thus encouraged to create their own learning style, they learn from others and 'teach' others on a daily basis.
- Learning may be done at all times and in all places.
- Group activities as a good way of learning in which collaboration and cooperation among the members of the group play relevant parts.
- **Assessment and Feedback:** Facebook provides an ideal environment for peer assessment and feedback, and even for self-assessment if we think of the fact that a student may see the comments of his classmates to a certain topic, a thing that was impossible in the case of traditional, individual tests.

In terms of disadvantages, one of the drawbacks that we have identified mentioned most often in the literature, and also that we may think of, is the time spent in preparing both educational activities conducted on Facebook and in student-centered activities: we have already mentioned the fact that in the absence of official, legal standards and norms for conducting educational activities on Facebook, these remain marginal, optional and experimental in nature. One can force neither teachers nor students to spend their free time at home, interacting on Facebook for educational purposes unless, of course, they want to. Teachers have been found to prefer the traditional approach to teaching because it is what they already know to do best and because the reflection, assessment and implementation of new student-centered approaches in class would require even more of

their free time. This viewpoint is supported by Hall (2006) who also adds the idea that students themselves may find student-centered learning activities, tasks and assignments as more time consuming, for example a group project, than, let's say, the traditional homework consisting of several exercises from the handbook to be solved individually at home. O'Neil and MacMahon (2005) draw attention to the fact that students may not be familiar with the term of student-centered learning and may feel disoriented when faced with such an approach. These facts also translate into additional time for the teacher to inform the students regarding the student-centered approach, its implications and to persuade them of the advantages of such an approach. The same authors also stress the risks of an approach that centers too much upon the individual learner which, they claim, may lead to the learner's physical isolation as the importance of the social context and social interaction are minimized, together with the pedagogic impossibility of having a student-centered approach with all the students in larger classes and the disregard for the needs of the whole class. If we think of educational activities conducted on Facebook, there may occur the risk that some students may become too self-assertive, whereas others may feel left aside.

As a conclusion to this section of our paper, we may say that the use of Facebook and student-centered strategies may significantly enhance student performance and student growth and development, particularly by encouraging the sharing of knowledge and of ideas, of opinions, by stimulating collaboration defined as cooperation among the members of a group that may lead to the shared creation of meaning and understanding, and even of new knowledge.

How Can Facebook Befriend Teachers?

The recommendations for teachers concerning the use of Facebook for educational purposes refer to the following aspects: what information a teacher should display on his/her Facebook profile and whether the teacher should display any personal information at all; the types of files that may be used on Facebook for educational purposes; how to create groups on Facebook (for example, how to include all the students from one real classroom into one Facebook group); how to share files to a Facebook group; educational content that may be shared on Facebook (for example, exercises for further practice, homework items, lists of words, formulas, links to various educational materials, additional explanation of a topic that one or more students may not have understood during class); how to avoid ethics related problems (for example, a teacher should pay attention to the language used on Facebook as much as when in class or, a teacher should keep relations strictly professional on Facebook, too, just like in real life).

Here are the recommendations to be taken into consideration by a teacher when deciding to use Facebook to get in touch with students[7]:

- The first thing that a teacher should take into consideration is the Facebook policy concerning the age of the users; to avoid any problems related to this issue, teachers should ask for signed parental consent concerning their children's use of Facebook.
- Teachers may feel uncomfortable with sharing their personal social and family life with their students or, to keep matters strictly professionally, they should indeed not share such parts of their life with students: to this effect, a teacher may create two Facebook accounts, one for the teacher as an individual irrespective of his profession and one for the individual whose profession is that of teacher; there may even be a third account for the teacher's former students that may not be interested in all the interaction the teacher may be involved in with his current students[8].

- Students should not show the teacher photos, videos, status updates, friends, posts or notes and Mini-feed and Photo Albums should also be turned off.
- The teacher's profile picture should reflect the teacher's professional image and this image should be as closest as possible to how the students see the teacher in school.
- The teacher should maintain a professional tone in all the comments posted, all the e-mails sent, all the photos and all the materials shared on Facebook; the photos that show students should also comply with the Facebook policy.
- The teacher may create a group for each class of students and give a name to each group or, better, have the students give a name to their Facebook group.
- Applications should be filtered: the recommendation is that as a teacher, one should only add applications that support the teacher's professional image.
- Joining groups as a teacher should also be restricted so as to comply with one's professional image; one should keep in mind that the teachers Facebook image is not shared only with the students but with the students' parents, with colleagues, administrators, colleagues from other schools, faculties, universities, educational centers.
- The photos posted either by the teacher or the students are an important way of increasing the sense of belonging; nevertheless, photos should focus on educational activities and should comply with the Facebook policy in terms of tagging and displaying somebody else's face on a social networking site.
- The teacher should establish professional boundaries with students: students should keep a respectful tone online just like in class; if the teacher allows students to e-mail him or if the teacher is going to

chat with the students online, the teacher should inform the students with regard to the virtual office hours within the limits of which these activities could take place; if the teacher chooses to chat to students individually, there should be a time limit for this as well and the students should be informed about it, also.

- Teacher may tag students in notes, anecdotes that happened in class or thoughts about class content but without embarrassing students and without displaying any preference for some student or another.
- Teachers are advised not to invite students as their friends on Facebook unless, we may add, this is done for educational purposes that were clearly stated to the student in advance, as this may be perceived as an invasion of privacy (Munoz & Towner, 2009, p. 8).
- Build a personal learning network on Facebook: this means that the teacher may join professional groups, may friend colleagues, Teachers' Associations, follow education-related blogs.

Studies related to the use of Facebook by students aim at identifying the reasons for which students use Facebook in relation to education (Towner, VanHorn and Parker, 2007; Munoz and Towner, 2009; Selwyn, 2009), the type of personal information that students display on their profile and the way in which this information may have upon their professionalism (Ferdig et al., 2008; Ellison, Steinfeld and Lampe, 2007); recommendations for teachers based on Facebook features that both teachers and students may use in their online interaction for educational purposes (all the studies mentioned so far), the impact of Facebook on university libraries (Charnigo and Barnett-Ellis, 2007); the implications for social networking sites use for the development of identity and peer relationship (Pempek et al., 2009) the relationship between Facebook use and academic performance (Kirschner & Karpinski, 2010; Junco, 2012).

A study on the possible relationship between Facebook and academic performance approaches two widely-spread, modern day "truths", that is, children do no possess multitasking skills that may support them in learning and, respectively, the daily accessing of the multiple channels of information available in the modern era affects the processing of information in a negative way (Kirschner & Karpinski, 2010, 1237). Also referring to other studies, Kirschner and Karpinski argue that using modern information technology on a daily basis does not mean that the respective users know how to access and acquire information via these channels: technology that was found to have a positive impact on academic achievement was not popular and was used less frequently; moreover, studies have documented no link between computer use and academic performance. Kirschener's and Karpinski's study highlighted an obvious connection between Facebook use and academic performance: for example, Facebook users were found to have lower mean GPAs, a conclusion reached by Junco (2012) as well. Also, the authors concluded that multitasking may be possible in terms of quantity but not in terms of quality: in other words, students may indeed combine learning and Facebook use but the impact is a negative effect upon both to these actions (idem, 1244).

We came across difficulties in finding concrete examples of courses or educational activities related to conducting teaching-learning activities on Facebook. To this effect and based on the useful recommendations that we found in the studies mentioned above and in the literature, we shall attempt to provide some examples on how to use Facebook in teaching.

We shall here present our perspective upon the use of Facebook as an educational tool in relation to the teaching of the subject of Romanian Language and Literature for the level of the 9th grade with activities spanning throughout the entire school year. We shall not take into consideration the use of Facebook as an educational tool for students younger than 13 of age due to Facebook policy:

students in the 9th grade are usually 13 or 14 of age. The teacher of Romanian Language and Literature may take into consideration the following ideas that we have tried to outline by keeping in mind the defining characteristics of a student-centered approach to teaching and learning, ideas that may be adapted to other subjects as well:

- At the start of the school year, during the first class which is also, usually, introductory by nature, the teacher may allot 5-10 minutes to introduce the students to his Facebook profile, he may briefly present the features of Facebook that may be used with regard to educational activities and invite students to create their own Facebook profiles and add the teacher as a friend; subsequently, the teacher may create a group for the respective class of students; the teacher should also establish a set of rules concerning the language used and behavior on Facebook and should inform his students of these from the very beginning; by such a brief introductory part, the teacher will raise the students' awareness and interest in using Facebook in school-related activities.

- The teacher may initiate activities on Facebook similar to those conducted in the classroom, such as: invite the students to comment upon a quotation, express opinions concerning a certain literary fragment, get involved in providing their own explanations for newly introduced words, notions and concepts; such activities conducted on Facebook continue the activities conducted in the classroom and also have the advantage that they provide all the students in the respective class with the occasion of forming and expressing opinions on various issues, an opportunity that may be hindered during classroom activity due to the time that is usually limited to 50 min-

utes per class; such activities may bring out the best in students, enhancing their self-assertion and self-expression potential.

- The teacher may post links to additional studying material or to learning resources on his Facebook profile and distribute it to the group; the links may lead students to, for example: online dictionaries and encyclopedias, official pages of the authors studied, pages of museums, work of the authors studied that is available online, critical approaches to the authors studied; such activities encourage the students to search for new knowledge, to select information, to start creating their own learning style.

- The teacher may challenge students to undertake online projects such as, for example, creating a Facebook account for their favorite literary character: each student will have to sign in to Facebook by using the name of his/her favorite character and fill in the profile information, post status updates, comments and even pictures or photos that the student may regard as defining for the respective character; the finality of such a project may consist in the students' voting for the best character Facebook account.

- The teacher may encourage students to share their book reviews online with the rest of the group; students may also be encouraged to share their favorite fragments from a literary work or their favorite books, or just keep their classmates informed on the latest book they have read; such activities may help students in finding common interests and common points of view or may stimulate discussions related to the literary fragments or books mentioned; such activities increase the sense of equality among students as everybody in the group/class is invited and expected to get involved in sharing and in the discussions triggered by the shared materials.

- The teacher may involve students in brainstorming on topics related to an upcoming lesson or on assignments; Facebook may also constitute a perfect environment for collaboration in group assignments or tasks.
- The teacher should stay constantly active as a Facebook user as an example for his students and to motivate the students to keep interacting and sharing knowledge in the online environment.
- The teacher may use the Calendar application to keep the class informed on upcoming school and national contests, assignments, due dates, tests, school or community events, artistic, sporting events.
- The teacher may encourage students to discuss upon grammar issues on Facebook: if students have difficulties in solving a certain grammar exercise at home or in finding, for example, the correct use of a certain word, they may ask for help from their colleagues and answers and explanations may be received in response.
- By means of the application Book Tag the teacher may create reading lists for the class/group and even quizzes related to the books included on the compulsory reading list for the subject of Romanian Language and Literature; the supplemental reading material, assignments or class syllabus may also be uploaded via the Files application.

The ideas above may be adapted for different subjects and grades, for higher education, too, as Facebook provides instructors with the Mathematical Formulas application by means of which teachers and students may share mathematical information and formulas, the Courses application that allows one to post lecture notes or additional study material, Webinaria that allows the teacher to record classes and then post them on Facebook so that students may review them or the Make a Quizz! application, and the list continues[9]. When used as an educational tool in higher education and as there is a growing trend for the use of electronic books or electronically distributed books and research material, generally, we may argue that Facebook may turn into the teacher's right hand when it comes to distributing study materials to students. Students will be left without the excuse of not having found a certain book or study material in the library since they will be "faced" with the respective text on their Facebook account. Some may argue that Facebook may be more suitable for certain educational subjects whereas for others it may not constitute such a great support. Nevertheless, we believe that the potential of Facebook to provide a proper environment for interaction is the key in counteracting such an opinion: there may not be as much research material to share via Facebook in Mathematics or Chemistry as compared to, for example, the English or American Literature, but in all cases Facebook acts as a facilitator of interaction and exchange of ideas: used in relation to all subjects and for all levels of education, from high-school, to university and post-academic studies, Facebook supports students in asking for and giving advice or explanations, searching for and offering ideas or comments, initiating discussions on various topics and getting engaged in online discussions, asking for and providing links to research materials. The possibilities of Facebook educational use are endless and customizable, able to be adjusted to any subjects of study: for example, besides the possibility of sharing books and materials on the form of documents, for Geography there will be links to all types of maps to share and access; for Biology, Chemistry or Physics there will be links to research centers, to the latest discoveries in the field, to collections of images and to the pages of various scientists; for students studying journalism there will be links to the pages of politicians, to various famous blogs on controversial topics, to the latest news all over the world; for Engineering students there will be links to various architectural, industrial projects; for all students there is the quick possibility to find lists of reference literature on topics they are interested in and to share those lists with their peers; for all students there is the possibility to join Facebook groups with similar (educational) interests; for all students there is the chance to find out about contests and competitions in their field of interest, of projects they may get involved in as students or as future professionals.

As we have shown so far, the Facebook-student-centered approach constitutes a perfect pair for the future of education and for future educational trends and models. We shall support our viewpoint with yet another attempt to propose an experimental project of using Facebook in teaching with the purpose of clearly identifying the impact of using Facebook in learning and particularly in distance learning. Because there is no legal support yet to implement a course conducted entirely or even partially on Facebook, we believe that an experiment that would involve volunteer students would be the best option for now. We also believe that distance learning is the best choice for such an experiment because we consider that the results obtained by applying such an experiment to students involved in distance learning will be even more relevant. Thus, the experiment would involve three groups of students involved in distance learning: one group would consist of students attending the course traditionally, that is, by periodical modular classes with the teacher; another group will consist of students attending the course both traditionally and on Facebook and, another group would consist of students attending the course only on Facebook. Based on what we now know regarding the impact of Facebook in education, we assume that the students attending the course both traditionally and on Facebook would have the best educational outcomes in terms of understanding of the notions taught, correct realization of assignments and tasks, interaction and relationships with the other students in the group; this group will be closely followed in terms of results by the students attending the course on

Facebook, and only after that by those attending the course in the traditional way, that is, attending the few lectures conducted by the teacher in class. We believe that such an experiment would be able to prove the relevance that the teacher-student and the student-student offline and online interaction may have on school performance and success. In other words, we believe that the more interaction there is the better. Our expectations concerning such an experiment are based on the ideas expressed in this paper, ideas that were supported with the arguments and conclusions of other authors preoccupied with the educational potential of Facebook.

CONCLUSION

Our chapter constituted an attempt to give an answer to the question 'Can Facebook be regarded as an effective and efficient educational tool? And if yes, in what way(s)?'. We have approached the idea of using Facebook as an educational tool from the perspective of the student-centered approach to teaching and learning and we have tried to identify some best practice recommendations for teachers in this respect. The basic conclusion is that Facebook may indeed be used as an educational tool but there remains the problem of assessing the educational results and school performance related to the teaching and learning activities conducted on Facebook. Due to lack of legal support for implementing courses and lessons conducted on Facebook, using Facebook for educational purposes stays in the area of the optional and the experimental. Moreover, as many and as relevant as the advantages of using Facebook in education may be, certain limitations are still hindering a decisive application of Facebook with a view to educational ends. Such limitations are related to the time invested both by teachers and students in Facebook activities, the resources involved, be they educational, human or material resources (for example, the human resources involved in maintaining computers in a proper working state or the risk of Internet connection failures). Nevertheless, our belief is that teachers should do their best to turn Facebook into an educational tool and an educational "friend", and to engage students in online interaction and online sharing of knowledge. Combined with and supportive of student-centered strategies, Facebook is able to contribute significantly to the students' personal and professional development, to the enhancement of their creativity, emotional intelligence, to the creation and development of students' personal and customized learning style that may respond best to their needs as individual learners that are defined by their learning motivation, their learning rhythm and pace, their ideals and interests, their affectivity. We appreciate that the students' intelligent and emotional potential may best be valorized, augmented, improved and developed by means of student-centered strategies and we strongly believe that the future belongs to uninhibited, self-assertive and self-educating individuals that are open to and embrace the idea of life-long learning.

REFERENCES

Arends, R. I. (2012). *Learning to teach*. New York, NY: McGraw-Hill.

Beer, D. (2008). Social network(ing) sites…revisiting the story so far: A response to danah boyd and Nicole Ellison. *Journal of Computer-Mediated Communication, 13*(2), 516-529. Retrieved February 15, 2012, from http://onlinelibrary.wiley.com/doi/10.1111/j.1083-6101.2008.00408.x/full

Boyd, D. M., & Ellison, N. B. (2007). Social network sites: Definition, history and scholarship. *Journal of Computer-Mediated Communication, 13*(1), 210-230. Retrieved February 15, 2012, from http://jcmc.indiana.edu/vol13/issue1/boyd.ellison.html

Cannon, R. (2000). *Guide to support the implementation of the learning and teaching plan year 2000. ACUE*. The University of Adelaide.

Charnigo, L., & Barnett-Ellis, P. (2007). Checking out Facebook.com: The impact of a digital trend on academic libraries. *Information Technology and Libraries, 1*(1), 23-34, Retrieved January 14, 2012, from http://www.ala.org/lita/ital/sites/ala.org.lita.ital/files/content/26/1/charnigo.pdf

Cheung, C. M. K., Chiu, P. Y., & Lee, M. K. O. (2011). Online social networks: Why do students use Facebook? *Computers in Human Behaviour, 27*(4), 1337-1343. Retrieved June 6, 2012, from http://linkinghub.elsevier.com/retrieve/pii/S0747

Cojocariu, V. (2012). *Educational strategies centered on the beneficiary of learning. Constructivism and efficient practices*. Saarbrücken, Germany: Lambert Academic Publishing.

Couillard, C. (2010). *Facebook: The pros and cons of use in education*. A Research Paper Submitted in Partial Fulfillment of the Requirements for the Master of Science Degree in Information and Communication Technologies. University of Wisconsin-Stout. Retrieved February 5, 2012, from http://clairecouillard.weebly.com/uploads/5/1/9/8/5198042/research_paper_tcs_701.pdf

Ellison, N., Steinfeld, C., & Lampe, C. (2007). The benefits of Facebook friends, social capital and college students' use of online social network sites. *Journal of Computer-Mediated Communication, 12*(3). Retrieved January 17, 2012, from http://jcmc.indiana.edu/vol12/issue4/ellison.html

Ferdig, R. E., Dawson, K., Black, E. W., & Thomson, L. A. (2008). Medical students' and residents' use of online social networking tools: Implications for teaching professionalism in medical education. *First Monday, 13*(9). Retrieved January 17, 2012, from http://www.uic.edu/htbin/cgiwrap/bin/ojs/index.php/fm/article/view/2161/2026

Hall, B. (2006). *Student-centered learning*. A blog on writing and learning. Retrieved October 26, 2011, from http://secondlanguagewriting.com/explorations/Archives/2006/Jul/StudentcenteredLearning.html

Hew, K. F. (2011). Students' and teachers' use of Facebook. *Computers in Human Behavior, 27*(2), 662-676. Retrieved June 6, 2012, from http://www.sciencedirect.com/science/article/pii/S0747563210003651

Hewitt, A., & Forte, A. (2006). *Crossing boundaries: Identity management and student/faculty relationships on the Facebook*. Conference Paper presented at the CSCW, Canada. Retrieved January 16, 2012, from http://www-static.cc.gatech.edu/~aforte/HewittForteCSCWPoster2006.pdf

Junco, R. (2012). Too much face and not enough books: The relationship between multiple indices of Facebook use and academic performance. *Computers in Human Behavior, 28*(1), 187-198, Retrieved June 6, 2012, from http://www.sciencedirect.com/science/article/pii/S0747563211001932

Kirschner, P. A., & Karpinski, A. C. (2010). Facebook(R) and academic performance. *Computers in Human Behaviour, 26*(6), 1237-1245, Retrieved June 6, 2012, from http://www.sciencedirect.com/science/article/pii/S0747563210000646

Kolb, D. A. (1984). *The experiential learning: Experience as the source of learning and development*. Prentice-Hall.

Madge, C., Meek, J., Wellens, J., & Hooley, T. (2009). Facebook, social integration and informal learning at university: 'It is more for socialising and talking to friends about work than for actually doing work'. *Learning, Media and Technology, 34*(2), 141–155. doi:10.1080/17439880902923606

Matthews, B. S. (2006). Do you Facebook! Networking with students online. *College and Research Libraries News, 67*, 306-307. Retrieved January 28, 2012, from http://crln.acrl.org/content/67/5/306.full.pdf

Mazer, J. P., Murphy, R. E., & Simonds, C. J. (2007). I'll see you on "Facebook":The effects of computer-mediated teacher self-disclosure on student motivation, affecctive learning, and classroom climate. *Communication Education, 56*(1), 1–17. doi:10.1080/03634520601009710

McCombs, B., & Whistler, J. S. (1997). *The learner-centered classroom and school*. San Francisco, CA: Jossey-Bass.

Moffet, J., & Wagner, B. J. (1992). *Student-centered language arts, K-12*. Portsmouth, NH: Boynton/Cook Publishers Heinemann.

Munoz, C., & Towner, T. (2009). Opening Facebook: How to use Facebook in the college classroom. In I. Gibson et al., (Eds.), *Proceedings of Society for Information Technology & Teacher Education International Conference 2009* (pp. 2623-2627). Chesapeake, VA: AACE. Retrieved from http://www.editlib.org/p/31031

O'Neill, G., & McMahon, T. (2005). Student-centered learning: What does it mean for students and lecturers? In G. O'Neill, S. Moore, & B. McMullen (Eds.), *Emerging issues in the practice of university learning and teaching*. Dublin, Ireland: AISHE. Retrieved February 14, 2012, from http://www.aishe.org/readings/2005-1/index.html

Panitz, T. (1997). *Collaborative versus cooperative learning – A comparison of the two concepts which will help us understand the underlying nature of interactive learning*. Retrieved December 14, 2011, from http://www.slideshare.net/tmvcr/collaborative-versus-cooperative-learning-3314777

Pempek, T. A., Yermoloyeva, Y. A., & Calvert, S. I. (2009). College students' social networking experiences on Facebook. *Journal of Applied Developmental Psychology, 30*(3), 227-238. Retrieved June 6, 2012, from http://www.sciencedirect.com/science/article/pii/S0193397308001408

Ragupathi, K. (2011). Facebook for teaching and learning: By Dr. Erik Mobrand. *Technology in Pedagogy, 1*, 1-4. Retrieved January 26, 2012, from http://www.cdtl.nus.edu.sg/technology-in-pedagogy/articles/Technology-in-Pedagogy-1.pdf

Rego, B. (2009). *A teacher's guide to using Facebook*. Retrieved January 16, 2012, from http://www.scribd.com/doc/16957158/Teachers-Guide-to-Using-Facebook-Read-Fullscreen

Selwyn, N. (2009). Faceworking: Exploring students' education-related use of Facebook. *Learning, Media and Technology, 34*(2), 157–174. doi:10.1080/17439880902923622

Towner, L. T., VanHorn, A., & Parker, L. S. (2007). *Facebook: Classroom tool for a classroom community?* (pp. 1-18). Midwestern Political Science Association. Retrieved December 16, 2011, from http://citation.allacademic.com//meta/p_mla_apa_research_citation/1/9/7/1/3/pages197133/p197133-1.php

Vighnarajah, L. W. S., & Kamarish, A. B. (2008). The shift in the role of teachers in the learning process. *European Journal of Social Sciences, 7*(2), 33-41. Retrieved February 19, 2012, from http://www.eurojournals.com/ejss_7_2_03.pdf

KEY TERMS AND DEFINITIONS

Distance Learning: Also known as distance education, it focuses on teaching methods and means with the purpose of delivering teaching to individuals who are not physically present in a classroom or other traditional educational setting.

Facebook: A social networking site with an alleged number of 900 million users; it provides users with such features as: building a more or less public profile, creating lists of friends, creating groups of persons including people from work, family or very close friends, sharing online information such as photos, videos, texts, and receiving feedback to the information that one shares in the form of comments, votes, messaging other users, playing online games.

Peer Communication: Coomnunication and interaction between and among students; the result of peer communication is increased motivation with regard to learning and hence improved school results.

Social Networking Site: A web-based service that allows users to build an online more or less public profile and to interact with other users; communication among users of such networking sites involves the online sharing of interests, ideas, activtities, uploading of photos, videos, and receiving feedback for the information that one shares.

Student-Centered Learning: An approach to education that focuses on the students' needs, abilities, interests and learning styles; the teacher's role is mainly that of guide and facilitator of learning; students are active participants, responsible of their own learning.

Student Talk: The overall amount of time when the student is speaking during a class.

Teacher Talk: The overall amount of time when the teacher is speaking during a class.

ENDNOTES

1. *Macmillan English Dictionary for Advanced Learners*, 2006, p. 951.
2. *Merriam-Webster's Dictionary*, Retrieved February 15, 2012, from http://www.merriam-webster.com/dictionary/networking
3. *Business Dictionary*, Retrieved February 15, 2012, from http://www.businessdictionary.com/definition/networking.html

4   See Plate 1 The Conversation Prism in Grau, O., Veigl, T. (2011). *Imagery in the 21ˢᵗ Century*. Cambridge, MA: MIT Press, p. 187, also on http://www.theconversationprism.com/, Retrieved February 15, 2012, for a whole view of the media universe categorized and organized according to how people use each network.

5   Cannon, R. (2000). *Guide to support the implementation of the Learning and Teaching Plan Year 2000*. ACUE, The University of Adelaide, p. 3.

6   Waldey, Kearney and Plax (2001), cited in Mazer, J., P., Murphy, R., E., Simmonds, C., J. (2007). I'll See You On "Facebook": The Effects of Computer-Mediated Teacher Self-Disclosure on Student Motivation, Affective Learning and Classroom Climate. *Communication Education, 56 (1)*, 1-17. Retrieved December 5, 2011, from http://onlinesocialnetworks.blogspot.com/2007/06/ill-see-you-on-facebook.html

7   Rego, B. (2009). *A Teacher's Guide to Using Facebook*. Retrieved January 16, 2012, from http://www.scribd.com/doc/16957158/Teachers-Guide-to-Using-Facebook-Read-Fullscreen

8   Drive Belonging and Engagement in the Classroom. Retrieved January 14, 2012, from http://org.elon.edu/catl/conference/documents/FacebookEducation.pdf

9   See also http://www.onlinecollege.org/2009/10/20/100-ways-you-should-be-using-facebook-in-your-classroom/ and http://blog.facebook.com/, both Retrieved January 15, 2012.

Section 2
Student 2.0

Chapter 6
Personalization of Learning Environments in a Post–Industrial Class

Ilya Levin
Tel Aviv University, Israel

Andrei Kojukhov
Tel Aviv University, Israel

ABSTRACT

The chapter deals with trends of educational processes and learning environments in post-industrial society. A historicist approach is used for this purpose. This approach is based on two theoretical recourses: analysis of historical forms of acquiring knowledge and analysis of historical forms of educational processes. The authors show that the contemporary educational process is greatly affected by two innovative phenomena: social media and personal identity online (PIO). They consider socialization and personalization as two unique entities having opposite characteristics of the post-industrial educational process. Based on such a dialectic approach to the educational process, they define the concept "Personal Ubiquitous Educational Environment". The authors report the preliminary results of research on a teachers' training course conducted on the basis of such an environment. The research focuses on clarifying both innovative components of contemporary educational processes: social media and PIO.

1. INTRODUCTION

One of the main goals of any society is to provide an educational system that includes a set of tools that can be utilized to ameliorate problems encountered in the social and economic world. The corresponding educational process and curriculum usually aim at targeting the knowledge and skills needed for dealing with problems throughout the world.

The transition of our society to the post-industrial epoch (Masuda, 1981; Huber, 1984) serves as a background and an initial point of our study. Post-industrial society has become

DOI: 10.4018/978-1-4666-2970-7.ch006

more a society of services rather than a society of production. It creates new ways of human interaction with society, where artificial interfaces separate individuals from the real world social environment. One of the trends of the previous industrial society, namely, the globalization and formalization of social institutions, and as a consequence, the decreasing role of the individual, has recently been replaced by personalization, placing the individual at the center of the world (Every, Garcia & Young, 2010).

Accordingly, recently the main objectives of education have changed to reflect these tendencies. The newly conceived educational process requires changing the role of the teacher to the learner (Carolyn & Foster, 2010; Fazal, DeSimone, & Lieman, 2010). Thus, the teacher is not a single content provider any more. The learner becomes increasingly freer to collect knowledge as needed and has the power to decide. Owing to the latest achievements in information and communication technology, e.g., wireless broadband, IP, and cloud computing, the learning has become increasingly more ubiquitous, meaning that the world is adapting to the learner's mobility with no formal class distinction (Dede, 2011).

Obviously, it is senseless for the educational system to compete with the Internet and other innovative sources of educational content. On the contrary, it is much more promising to utilize this means for enhancing students' personal skills and abilities to improve the effectiveness of leaning.

Western society, in general, and education, in particular, is evolving toward personalization. This personalization is strongly connected with the new phenomenon of Personal Identity Online (PIO) that has been intensively studied in recent years (Bowman, 2009; Rodogno, 2011). The concept of PIO personifies a specific characteristic of an individual's behavior in a network environment, which manifests itself in a unique opportunity to form the individual's identity differently from that in reality. The world network opens up new opportunities for self-expression and for forming

identity. The PIO is the form of personalization that typifies post-industrial learning environments (Floridi, 2011).

Another remarkable factor characterizing the coming epoch is the phenomenon of social media. Social media are traditionally defined as the use of Web applications supporting the creation and exchange of user-generated content. Here, we give to the concept of social media a more general and culturological interpretation, rather than the technological one. We consider the social media as a cultural phenomenon, substantially intensifying and enhancing interpersonal communication and significantly altering the nature of the relationship between an individual and a society "personality-society". Note that the relationships "personality-personality" and "personality-society" are immediately perceived as simple and are unprecedentedly multifaceted. The simplicity of relationships/mutual connections is clearly seen in the availability of new communication tools (from mobile devices to social networking sites) for any level of the society, regardless of education, age, and economic status. Diversity of communication connections is a new phenomenon related, for example, to the above-mentioned phenomenon of PIO, and to the fact that an identity (a personality) in cyberspace can be perceived not only as a real person, but also as an "infosphere" directly associated with the person (Floridi, 2011). The infosphere of an individual consists of the memory of the discussed personality/individual, the memory about the personality and multiple media documents related to the personality, lifestyle, etc. Infosphere of an individual somehow exists and functions in the cyberspace, independently of the corresponding personality. It is clear that this has created a new media reality that, in our opinion, is the most important tool for understanding the phenomenon of social media. In the era of social media, social consciousness is formed in accordance with new, previously unknown principles, thus establishing new goals in all public institutions. It is obvious that education is not an exception. In Web 2.0, the possible forms of network activity of modern students are extremely diverse. These forms include blogs and forums, social networks, wikis, etc.

Thus, the above two phenomena: the social media and the personal identity online determine new forms of an educational process and new learning environments.

In this way, the increased personalization is strongly connected with the increased importance of "soft" skills, such as creativity, motivation, meta-cognition, etc. (Cohen, 2009; Shute et al., 2009). In order to achieve soft skills, the development of learning environments of the new type must become a reality. The study of such learning environments, called Personalized Ubiquitous Educational (PUE) environments, is the subject of this chapter. One of the best examples of the PUE is a cloud educational environment (Sultan, 2010; Geth, 2010).

An important point in our study is in understanding that the concept of personalization in recent educational situations greatly differs from the conventional concept. This new understanding is based on considering the PUE as a social environment and not just a technological one.

We hypothesize that the socially oriented PUE environment will provide teachers with the means to prepare a student for "multi-dimensional abilities required from them in the 21st century" (Kojukhov & Levin, 2010; Johnson, 2010), which refers to such soft skills as creativity, motivation, meta-cognition (Cohen, 2009; Shute et al., 2009). We study teachers' training programs oriented toward the extensive use of the personalized ubiquitous educational environment tools as a key for success. We hypothesized that integrating such tools enhances the students' acquisition of soft skills. The results of our study indicated that the main principles of the Personalized Ubiquitous Educational Environment are indeed justified.

Our chapter is organized as follows. Section 2 discusses the theoretical sources of the study. The two main sources are considered: section 2.1 - historical forms of acquiring knowledge, and section 2.2 - historical forms of educational processes. Section 3 presents the concepts of personal identity online (PIO) and social media in an educational context. The study of the teachers' training, based on the Personalized Ubiquitous Educational Environment, is presented in section 4. Conclusions are given in section 5.

2. SOURCES OF STUDY

2.1. Historical Forms of Acquiring Knowledge

Historically, a number of forms of acquiring knowledge were developed. These forms correspond to different types of observations of the surrounding world.

Chronologically, the first form of acquiring knowledge was the period of direct observation. At this stage of human development, a person observed the surrounding world, analyzed it, and tried to draw conclusions. An observation is based on the direct impact of the object on the senses of the observer. Obviously, direct observation is determined by the observer's five senses, which, in turn, are biologically limited.

The above limitation of human senses was overcome by applying instruments, thus forming the next form of acquiring knowledge, namely, indirect observation, which, in turn, includes two forms. If a device placed between an object and the sensory organs of the subject amplifies the quantitative impact of the object on the subject, then this kind of observation is called an indirect observation of the first type. Devices of this type are mechanical or optical devices that enhance or improve human perception of reality (examples: a magnifier, an optical telescope, a microscope, etc.). Such devices of the first type appeared earlier than tools of the second type. The tools of the second type are tools used for indirect observation, which ensure that observation takes place. Such a tool, when placed between an object and the sensory organs of the subject, changes qualitatively the effect of the object such that it becomes observable. Instruments of the second type include devices that ensure human observation of such physical phenomena and processes, which are not observable with the available human senses. Examples of such devices are a compass, a Geiger counter, and a manometer.

Note that both of these types of observations are based on converting energy from one form to another.

Until quite recently, the above-mentioned types of observation were considered the only possible ways of learning about the world. However, the advent and wide dissemination of computer tools and devices whose operation is based not on energy conversion, but on transforming information, has suggested a fundamentally new way of observing reality.

At the beginning, the information technology was not perceived as a new form of acquiring knowledge. This is due to a number of reasons. We will mention two of the most important reasons.

The first reason is that historically, computers were seen as a technological tool designed to compete with the human brain. The obvious future of the computer was considered to be the creation of artificial intelligence. Moreover, it was thought that artificial intelligence (AI) would replace the currently used instruments to better understand reality, but that AI would not replace learning tools. The second reason is that since computer environments, by definition, were understood to replace reality to some extent and therefore, they could not be considered to be tools for studying reality.

That is why today, when proclaiming that information technology is a cognitive paradigm, we interpret the place of computers in society in a new way – as a mediator between humans and the social reality. As a result, our society has become virtualized (Ivanov, 2006). The new virtualized society corresponds to a new acquiring

knowledge form in which reality is mediated by devices whose operation is based not on energy transformation, but on transformation of information. The virtualization process is obviously related to the intensive introduction/embedding of various computer tools (from microchips up to complex computer networks) for use in various household appliances. However, virtualization takes place only if these tools create artificial micro-worlds where human beings may exist and where their personality is formed/affected. Virtual perception and the corresponding acquiring knowledge are based on the construction of such artificial micro-worlds. In fact, people study reality by observing its simulation. Belief in the epistemological omnipotence of virtual environments characterized the period when personal computers appeared and the contemporary feeling of progress into an information society.

A modern person, when studying the world and its culture, enjoys all of the above acquiring knowledge forms - direct, indirect, and virtual. Such acquiring knowledge can be defined as an integral, scientific cognitive process, in which physical reality is complemented by technological means of learning. Note that combining the real world and artificial micro-worlds was accepted as a reasonable compromise, as a balanced habitat. Such a combined environment, as well as the acquiring knowledge based on this type of environment, will be termed the physical-technological environment and the physical-technological acquiring knowledge, correspondingly.

All of the above forms of acquiring knowledge could be classified as science-technological. Such an acquiring knowledge was formed during the industrial era, and dominated then. In our new, post-industrial society, a new acquiring knowledge was formed, which can be characterized as a socio-technological. The virtual cognitive process, based on constructing computer micro-worlds, gives way to such cognitive processes in which the social component complements the physical component, and sometimes even dominates it.

According to constructionist epistemology, artificial micro-worlds in cognitive processes are strongly linked to the era of computer simulations. It even created the impression that the world, where technology dominates, becomes synthetic and virtual, and formed the belief in the all-conquering power of technology in any society.

In our post-industrial society, the social component plays the dominant role in acquiring knowledge – and this is due to several reasons:

1. A society of services is socially oriented. (Industrial society was oriented toward science and technology. Recall that medieval society was religiously, spiritually oriented).
2. The success of communication technologies. Certain devaluations of the value of knowledge favor the media. For the first time in the history of modern civilization, people may intelligently communicate, regardless of the distance and, in some sense, even regardless of time.
3. Forms of social consciousness change, as well as the ways of forming them. Modern means of communication raise the social component of reality to an unprecedented height.
4. Personality and identity is being formed in a new way. Personality increasingly expresses itself in virtual space, which is a new international social reality.

Thus, nowadays, it is appropriate to speak about a new, socio-technological acquiring knowledge. This new type of cognitive study underlies educational processes and learning environments of post-industrial society, which is the focus of this chapter.

2.2. Historical Forms of an Educational Process

In this section, we consider and analyze the evolution of an educational process during and related to various historical epochs. Three epochs

are considered: pre-industrial, industrial, and post-industrial. We discuss both a representative educational process and a learning environment for each of the epochs.

In pre-industrial society, the dominance of individual education was quite suitable for the structure of medieval social production. There are two types of the pre-industrial education: (1) skills-oriented practical education, meaning education of the type "do-as-I do"; (2) advanced theoretical education comprising a number of subjects, where the teacher was a highly qualified expert who taught the subject according to his/her individual plans. Consequently, education in pre-industrial society as well as the corresponding educational environment can be characterized as personal, with direct teacher-student contact.

The bright ideas brought forth by John Amos Comenius served as the basis for education in industrial society. A class-oriented educational system was created that perfectly matched that of society, with its orientation toward the production of goods and industrial progress. One of the main peculiarities characterizing industrial society education is its social orientation toward formalization/standardization. The meanings and terms of a formal curriculum, a formal class, and a formal lesson were established in the Age of Enlightenment. The classroom-lesson environment unifies and standardizes relations between teachers and students, thus, defining the social role of the teacher in society. In contrast to pre-industrial society education, which is personalized education, industrial society can be characterized as having socialized education.

In contrast, post-industrial society is considered as a society of services rather than a society of production. In our opinion, post-industrial education has undergone a new process of fulfilling the role of a teacher (the teacher's authority). This is manifested by the self-educational activity of today's students having ubiquitous access to information, in which the teacher is no longer the unique content provider. In the post-industrial school, the classic classroom-lesson system loses its usual significance. The ubiquitous manner of acquiring knowledge changes the conventional meaning and the essence of the traditional classroom. We refer to this new type of classroom as a ubiquitous classroom.

The idea of personalizing the educational process was first proposed by Seymour Papert (Papert, 1980). It is clear that the idea of personalization conflicts with the conventional classroom-based educational process. Papert and his followers perceived the classroom-based system as an obstacle to social progress and as contradicting the fundamental principles of cognition (Papert, 1991). Naturally, this brings to mind a dichotomy view in which society is divided into two portions: (1) conservative, based on a classroom-oriented system, the centralized curriculum, the authoritarian teacher, the omnipotence of the Ministry of Education, and (2) progressive, having students at the center and symbolizing the rejection of centralism and based on the principle of individualism.

Papert and his followers consider the new liberal school as based on the principles of constructionism (Harel and Papert, 1991; Cakir, 2008). According to these principles, the student builds his own micro-world, in which he implements his own cognitive abilities. In this way, the idea of decentralization and individualization has merged with the ideas of progress, freedom, and creativity. In contrast, the old, classroom-oriented system was associated with a centralized authoritarian education that does not take into account the individual student. At the same time, the idea of constructionism was fundamentally related to the use of computers in the classroom. The computer has played a revolutionary role in the constructionist approach, radically changing classroom-based education.

As seen from the above, an idea proclaimed 30 years ago returns to the forefront of educational processes and learning environments, and in fact, it serve as their principal component. Obviously, nobody speaks about returning to the Middle Ages, with their "do-as-I do" education. The personal

micro-worlds mentioned in the preceding section are of major importance, since a student studies the surrounding world when operating in his personal micro-world. Nevertheless, one may obviously notice that the growth of the personalization component in the educational process proceeds concomitantly with a significant reduction in the role of the social component of education.

One of the important points of our paper lies in understanding the fact that such a highly individualized educational process does not correspond enough to our increasingly complex urban post-industrial society. Neglecting the social component in favor of personal component, while constituting the core idea, poses a serious problem. Developing a modern society is linked to rapid growth of communications and as a result, with unprecedented socialization of society. Under these circumstances, obviously, private individual micro-worlds that generated such an impressive breakthrough in the 1980s will soon be transformed into so-called social micro-worlds, though the remaining personal component. Such social micro-worlds can now be seen in the form of various social networks, blogs, Web 2.0 means, etc., which has changed the live styles of millions of people and has become increasingly more popular in our daily life. The relationships of our personal and social lives are rapidly changing. This, in turn, has affected education both at the level of the educational process and at the level of learning environments.

It is important to emphasize that both historical forms of acquiring knowledge considered in the previous chapter, and the historical forms of educational processes discussed in the present chapter indicate the great importance and inevitability of the socialization of education and the learning environments. Note that this does not occur by accident: awareness of the fact that the information technology is a social phenomenon and is not a technological phenomenon constitutes one of the most important achievements in the development of our modern society at this stage.

3. PERSONALIZATION OF THE CONTEMPORARY LEARNING ENVIRONMENT

3.1. Personal Identity Online in a Post-Industrial Class Society

Pure virtual micro-worlds, when representing a highly personal learning environment, are often devoid of the most important component of education - the social component. This highly significant component has successfully fulfilled learning environments in the post-industrial era. But does a student's connection to a global network deprive the learning environments from their individual, private components? (The private component has always been an essential component of learning environments). The answer is unequivocally negative. The fact is that "a network-based student" implements a so-called cyberspace Personal Identity Online (PIO) (Floridi, 2011).

The concept of PIO is relatively new. It personifies a specific characteristic of an individual's behavior in a network environment, which manifests itself in the form of a unique opportunity to form and exhibit the individual's identity differently than is done in reality. The world network of unsurpassed access to data opens up new opportunities for self-expression and the formation of identity. We consider the PIO to be a form of personalization that typifies modern learning environments.

3.2. Personal Identity Online as an Extension of Papert's Ideas

The last 30 years ushered in years of intensive computerization of society and of incredible achievements in information technology. Perhaps the idea that micro-worlds will replace classroom-based education was just an illusion. Our goal is to show that this was not the case. Here, we will show that the constructionist approach successfully describes the coming post-industrial educational system, but that it needs some clarifications.

The first clarification concerns individualization of the educational system and its resources. Modern ideas about a new educational system are based mainly on the opposite opinion. Personalization is not considered to be related to individualization of computerized resources. On the contrary, the distribution of our resources turned out to be more intensive and that is why distribution increased personalization. This is especially evident in the phenomenon of "cloud" computing in education (Sultan, 2010; Geth, 2010).

The second clarification concerns the intimacy of the educational process. This position is worthy of our support. Papert noted that 30 years ago and we also see that personalization of the learning process is strongly connected with expressing and forming the learner's personal identity. Moreover, today we extend the concept by introducing Personal Identity Online (PIO) (Floridi, 2011) - an identity that a user establishes in online communications – the concept that constitutes the essence of post-industrial digital life. As is well known, the task of forming a learner's personality is one of the main pedagogical tasks that concern today's educators. In former societies, this task was carried out by the education system in reality. However, personality is something multi-dimensional and goes beyond its "linear" incarnation. The PIO removes personality from its default state, enabling it to appear in a new dimension.

The recent learning environments are not just customized microworlds but instead are individual micro-worlds constructed in virtual space and are interconnected with one another.

On the one hand, Papert's ideas for reforming education, such as a virtualized environment for learning, are, without a doubt, much appreciated in our study. On the other hand, over the past 30 years, many changes have occurred in an ever-developing society that could not be accounted for by Papert. Among them is the rapid development of mobile technologies and ubiquitous communication in the background of a complete virtualization of society. These changes led us to conclude that ubiquitous communication with virtual reality is not just a technology but is also a way of life. Taking into account the examined trends, as well as the fact that educational technology is increasingly becoming a part of our daily lives; it seems reasonable to expand the instrumentalist approach of Papert. To this end, we propose to review and study a virtual learning environment as an alternative system, including the ends and means and human-controlled technology; in other words, implementing a virtual adaptive training system for the virtual community.

All together, with the latest development in broadband wireless communications, a growing number of virtual communities are being created where a user (a student or teacher) actively behaves behind his personal identity in creating the Personal Identity Online (Ke et al., 2011; Rodogno, 2011). Personal Identity Online is a social identity platform that a user establishes in online communities and websites. Although some people prefer to use their real names online, some internet users prefer to be anonymous, identifying themselves by means of pseudonyms that reveal varying degrees of personally identifiable information (Bowman, 2011; Rodogno, 2011).

In a modern world, in which the division between online and offline is being erased (Floridi, 2011), and where the online world does not respect geographical boundaries, "the self uses the digital imaginary concerning itself to construct a virtual identity through which it seeks to grasp its own personal identity (the question ''who am I for you?'' becomes ''who am I online?''), in a potentially feedback loop of adjustments and modifications leading to an equilibrium between the off-line and the online selves" (Floridi, 2011).

We propose developing Seymour Paper's Personalization and Virtualization approach, which one may call a Personal Identity Off-line by adding a Ubiquitous trend to the new Personal Identity Online that we study in the context of the Personalized Ubiquitous Educational Environment. Specifically, we study (1) the role of the Personal Identity Online in creating the soft skills

used by the students and (2) how the teachers may help students to apply these skills (Cohen, 2009; Shute, 2009).

In this context we study both the identity a user constructs by him and the identity the user constructs through others (Amelung, 2007). In the Personalized Ubiquitous Educational Environment, the identity that a user constructs through another person comes from the information that is currently available. The forms of information, including online availability, quality of work contributed, and replies in discussion forums, significantly contribute to shaping and transforming his identity.

Another important point related to identity is that the online identity is always present and accessible to others (Amelung, 2007). For any objects uploaded to the environment, or, for example, communications in collaborative tools, the information remains readily available and continues to influence the actions of others, even if the user is not currently on-line in the system. Users construct identities of others by knowing about and interacting with the continuously changing information provided through ongoing learning activities. Therefore, a user constructs his identity by first knowing what information he has contributed to the social context and more importantly, by knowing how others act on that information. This activity has an impact on the shared social context of a learning social community because the artifacts that personalize each user are always available and accessible (e.g. ubiquitous).

3.3. Personal Identity in On-Line Discussion Forums

The increased personalization in education is also realized by the increased importance of soft skills, such as discussion ability and meta-cognition (Cohen, 2009; Shute et al, 2009), compared with professional skills. We also believe that in order for students to master soft skills, modern teachers should apply these skills on a regular basis.

Teachers' meta-cognition is one of the most important personal variables that affect their engagement in modern educational environments, which include the information-seeking behaviors, the processing of information gathered in online environments, discussion forums, etc. Activities such as planning how to approach a given task, monitoring comprehension, evaluating progress toward the completion of a task, and knowledge of these activities are meta-cognitive in nature, so an important step in enhancing the education environment outcomes is to obtain clarity with regard to the influence of meta-cognition on how and how often teachers and learners bring themselves into the learning process in online forum discussions.

As part of our main hypothesis described in the Introduction we propose investigating the relationship between different components of the Personalized Ubiquitous Educational environment and participation in online discussions as well as analyzing strategy variables or factors that can influence cognition and knowledge building. One such component is Personal Identity Online, which as discussed in (Ke et al., 2011). This is correlated with the content of students and teachers' participation in online discussion and hence, facilitates building collective knowledge. It is critical to design online interaction contexts to support identity presence in a manner that promotes students' meta-cognition and development of soft-skills for constructing a community collective knowledge rather than simply sharing experiences and individual insights.

Teachers' meta-cognition affects their effective participation in online discussions and in comprehending the main ideas in online discussions, in constructing links between previous and new knowledge in multiple message sequences, and in evaluating the available resources. Teachers who effectively use meta-cognitive knowledge are largely strategically inclined and may utilize a cognitive platform to identify relevant content and applicable services in the right place and at the right time, depending on their context. Mutual message exchange between participants can take place at any time. Participants must read the messages and ask questions, make comments; provide answers, and other useful feedback.

In the developed Personalized Ubiquitous Educational environment, each teacher is obligated to participate at least twice a week in the educational discussion forum, thus increasing the interactivity. Each teacher's message in the forum discussions is assessed in terms of the interaction types of the coding technique developed by McKinnon (2000). A grading rubric developed by Topku&Ubiz (2008) is used to score the teachers' messages, thereby determining the quality of their participation in covering all the components of meta-cognition: meta-cognitive knowledge, meta-cognitive judgments and monitoring, and self-regulation and control of cognition.

In order to investigate how discussion forums influence students' soft skills, teachers should encourage students to participate in discussion forums as well. Teachers help their students to use search tools such as Google, Yahoo, and other education cloud searching tools and to follow useful links in an educational Web site such as Moodle. They should even provide some keywords, depending on the context and new information or experiences, and set up checkpoints for knowledge of self as well as deepen the discussions.

The online discussions in general also serve to provide teachers with a tool to support their students with one of the most important soft skills, namely, the ability to effectively communicate. The results will help teachers adjust the topics of the online discussion forums.

Personal Identity On-line, as part of the social presence of the participants, directly affects variance in the quality of the participation, which refers to the degree of engagement in meaningful discussions and collective knowledge building (Ke et al, 2011). PIO promotes the creation of new features in a system of education that would induce scaffolding of students' thinking, which consequently can increase students' "knowledge of self", stimulate interactive, rich messages, and stimulate effective use of the educational cloud computing tools. Instructing and guiding tools may force students to assess their learning needs, and enhance the use of meta-cognition strategies.

3.4. Personal Identity On-Line in Digital Curation

Digital curation (Higgins, 2011) is one of the most innovative and widespread kinds of network behavior. Curation a special form of blogging, in which students receive an input stream of data generated in accordance with a predefined set of keywords (tags), and then carry out their own filtering (with supervision) by selecting the messages (data), which in the student's opinion, are of interest and are "worthy" of being included in their personal "curation blog".

The result of "individual curation" is a comprehensive curation stream. This stream, in turn, has quite a personal character, because an element of the infosphere has been introduced. The curation corresponds perfectly to the present stage of social media. The streams, whose authors are both students and teachers, may freely interact, thus forming meaningful networks. The role of these networks and their dynamics in education is great. The curated streams are able to interact with each other. Meta-curation should be understood as management of the curated streams. In post-industrial classes, meta-curation may become one of the main activities used by the teacher. Hence, the new conditions greatly change the previous role of the teacher. The Meta-curator (teacher) directs the streams in a productive direction, in accordance with the curriculum. Actually, in a classroom, the teacher can be considered as the curator, who is the first among equals.

One can imagine a variety of learning activities associated with the curated content.

In the above context, one should note that the learning activities have evolved in the classroom as follows.

- In a traditional classroom, the process goes from observation - to forming the content, then to an oral and written statement of the content. Alternatively, the process may start by remembering something, or from reading some content, and it may be followed by remembering the content and introducing it as a restatement; this process may consist of a presentation or a composition.

- In the post-industrial class, the process may be much shorter: from learning the material, web surfing, and searching, the process may comprise analysis and preservation of the content and, ultimately will lead to the curation.

It is important to emphasize that the apparent superficiality of the modern educational process, in comparison with the traditional process, may be just an illusion. Perhaps we are simply not accustomed to the new reality of information that, in turn (and of course), needs to be investigated.

3.5. The Concept of Personalized Ubiquitous Educational Environment

We consider a post-industrial society as virtualized (Ivanov, 2006), where man-machine interfaces increasingly alienate an individual from social reality. The epistemological basis of our study lies in using the constructionist approach, which claims that human learning is achieved within socialized personal micro-worlds created by humans (Papert, 1980). Virtual society is a complex global micro-world created by individuals from their micro-worlds, which replaces the social reality of the industrial society.

We define the following three principles, which are applicable for education:

- Virtualization of reality involves transforming reality into a new context - a form of simulated reality, a new form of manifesting universal human activity by creating new knowledge, thus expanding the boundaries of objective reality. One of the major new examples of virtualized reality is that of the cloud (Satyanarayanan et al., 2009), where the educational content forms a new educational cloud paradigm (Sultan, 2010; Geth, 2010).

- Ubiquitous reality is a virtual reality (including educational content), with which the student and teachers maintains permanent communication in time and space. This permanent communication with the educational content by also adding learners' location and social context is called Ubiquitous Learning (Dede, 2011; Graf & Kinshuk, 2008).
- Personalization is concerned with forming a personalized learning environment. This process is based on adapting to the learner's profile by using various technologies for investigating the specific learning history of past training activities, i.e. personal identity by using educational data mining.
- The above three phenomena are graphically presented in Figure 1.

Ubiquitous reality, as shown in Figure 1, is a personalized projection of virtual reality, available for the student with the help of a mobile terminal (laptop, cell phone, iPhone, iPad, etc.).

In a Post-Industrial society, in which the division between online and offline is being erased, "the self uses the digital imaginary concerning itself to construct a virtual identity through which it seeks to grasp its own personal identity in a potentially feedback loop of adjustments and modifications leading to an equilibrium between the off-line and the online selves" (Floridi, 2011). From the other hand, Seymour Papert's Personalization and Virtualization approach, which one may call a personal identity off-line by adding a Ubiquitous trend transforms to the new Personal

Figure 1. Scheme of a personal ubiquitous educational environment based on three principles: Virtualization, ubiquitous reality, and personalization

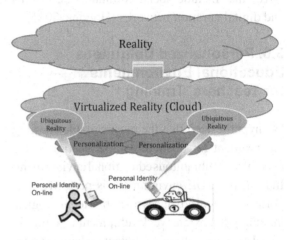

Identity On-line (PIO) that we study in the context of the Personalized Ubiquitous Educational (PUE) environment.

Activities such as planning how to approach a given task, monitoring comprehension, evaluating progress toward the completion of a task, and knowledge of these activities are meta-cognitive in nature, so an important step in enhancing the education environment outcomes is to obtain clarity with regard to the influence of meta-cognition on how and how often teachers and learners bring themselves into the learning process in online forum discussions. PIO is correlated with the content of students and teachers' participation in online discussion. It is critical to design online interaction contexts to support PIO presence in a manner that promotes students' meta-cognition and development of soft-skills for constructing a community collective knowledge rather than simply sharing experiences and individual insights.

Teachers' meta-cognition affects their effective participation in online discussions and in comprehending the main ideas in online discussions, in constructing links between previous and new knowledge, and in evaluating the available resources and exploring those tools that will be used in communicating with the teachers' community as well as for creating and customizing their Personalized Learning Networks (PLNs) (Curos, 2010) that include social communities, forums and digital curation networks (Higgins, 2011).

3.6. Personalized Ubiquitous Educational Environments for Teachers' Training

We hypothesized that the most suitable learning environment for postindustrial education is the personalized ubiquitous educational environment. Indeed, the PUE environment is perfectly supported by recent advances in mobile technologies, including the extensive development of multiple social networks, allowing students to be constantly linked to the material being studied, as part of various educational forums (Cohen, 2010, Johnson, 2010, Yang, 2006).

The personalized ubiquitous educational environment can be characterized by the following (See Figure 2):

- It comprises all the necessary components that can be formalized/computerized.
- The environment may take the form of a dialog system adaptable to specific stu-

dents' needs, and it is based on information about the student (educational data mining), which is strictly private and stored in his profile.

- The teacher's position in the environment is radically changed in comparison with the traditional class. The teacher (the mentor) now becomes a counselor and coordinator. The teacher is also one of the developers and users of the environment, including curriculum products and tools used to evaluate the progress (rather than knowledge) of the learner.
- Any educational content can be automatically synthesized and transformed to any form that is most applicable for the student, with extensive use of multimedia.
- An important component of the learning environment is a user's Social Presence status and his location, which can be used to adapt learning materials according to a specific geographical location and a situation within a learning environment. The Social Presence status includes the Personal Identity On-line (Rodogno, 2011; Amelung, 2007), which will constitute one of the main parts of our study.

Figure 2. Personalized ubiquitous educational environment for teachers' training

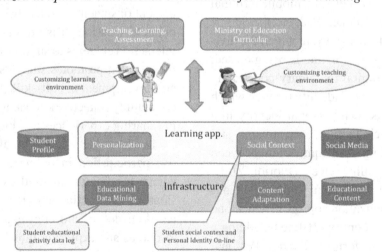

The study of the proposed Personalized Ubiquitous Educational (PUE) environment is done in the context of teachers' communication with the environment, its use in the class and even active participation in its customization. The study includes the development of a curriculum for teachers training in the PUE environment. During the training interviews with the teachers are held with the purpose of understanding how teachers use technology in their classrooms (practices), as well as why they decide to use technology in those ways (values, beliefs, targeting specific needs), as proposed by Lopez & Willis (2004). The results of these interviews are studied in conjunction with the epistemology tests that teachers undergo before, during and after the training – specifically using the environment by teachers in the class (Russel M et al., 2007). The collected data includes evaluations on teachers' traffic pattern during their use of the environment. These evaluations pass meta-cognition analysis in order to assess the level of meta-cognition of their interaction with the environment as proposed in Topku & Ubiz (2008). The correlations among the various aspects of teachers' beliefs and their participation in online discussions in the forums using their Personal Identity On-line are studied by using the methods described by Wang & Chai (2010) and Song & McNary (2011).

4. STUDY OF TEACHERS' TRAINING BASED ON A PERSONALIZED UBIQUITOUS EDUCATIONAL ENVIRONMENT

In this section, we provide a description and some preliminary results of our research, the aim of which is to check the main idea presented in the previous sections. We investigate what occurs in a contemporary teachers' training class with intensive use of the Personal Ubiquitous Educational (PUE) Environment. Specifically, we study two main fundamental phenomena: personalization and socialization.

4.1. Research Methodology

The research includes developing a curriculum for teachers' training in the Personalized Ubiquitous Educational Environment. During the training, we study meta-cognitive aspects of teachers and students' interaction with the environment and the inter-connection between meta-cognitive and epistemological aspects of this interaction.

Population Studied

A group of 10 teachers took part of the course and participated in the study. The course lasted half a year (1 semester). Teachers were required to have only a basic understanding of using technology in their classes, such as the ability to use Power Point software for preparing teaching material and having only basic Internet skills. There were no limitations regarding the professional background of the participants. The participating teachers were requested to adopt a Personalized Ubiquitous Educational environment in their classes.

Research Tools

Interviews

The research included personal interviews with the participants before the intervention and afterwards. The interviews were based on (Lopez & Willis, 2004) and (Russell M et al., 2007). During the interviews, the teachers were asked about their epistemic beliefs regarding using educational technology in their classes. The study uses the life experiences of the teachers in order to better understand how teachers use technology in their classes, as well as why they decide to use technology in specific ways (values, beliefs, targeting specific needs). During and after the course, additional interviews with the teachers were conducted. The interviews were semi-structured and based on correlations among the various aspects of teachers' beliefs and their online interactions in building knowledge using the methods described in (Wang & Chai, 2010).

Personalized Ubiquitous Educational Environment

The Moodle-based environment is used as a tool for collecting the data and as a data-mining tool. This tool collects data about teachers' online interaction with the content as well as during their online discussions in forums. In this context, we studied both parts of the teacher's Personal Identity Online: the identity that a teacher constructs by himself and the identity that the teacher constructs from others (Amelung, 2007). In the Personalized Ubiquitous Educational Environment the identity that a teacher constructs from others comes from the available information. The forms of information, including on-line availability, the quality of the work contributed, and replies in discussion forums, significantly contribute to shaping the identity. The collected data are analyzed in conjunction with the data collected from the interviews.

4.2. Course of Study

The study includes both qualitative and quantitative research and is divided into three parts answering the three research questions as part of main research hypothesis described in the Introduction.

The First Part of Study: Preliminary Interviews

The first part of the study includes interviews with the participating teachers, which focus on their epistemic beliefs about using educational technology in their classes. The study uses the life experiences of the teachers in order to better understand how teachers use educational technology in their classrooms (in practice), as well as why they decide to use this technology in specific ways (values, beliefs, targeting specific needs, etc.), as proposed in (Lopez&Willis, 2004). The collected data include (Russell M et al., 2007) the following factors (or categories) for using teacher technology:

1. Teacher's use of technology for preparation.
2. Teacher's use of technology for delivery.
3. Teacher-directed student's use of technology.
4. Teacher's use of personalized learning networks (social communities, discussion forums, etc.).

The main purpose of the first part of the study is answering the first research question: how teachers' beliefs may potentially affect their success in deploying a new environment and in developing their Personal Identity On-line.

The Second Part of Study: Intervention

A new course for teaching in a Personalized Ubiquitous Educational Environment is being developed in the School of Education at Tel-Aviv University. This course includes a number of essential theoretical topics that allow teachers to better understand the new sociological and technological trends influencing education, as described in the previous chapters. There are a number of practical exercises within the agenda of the course, allowing teachers to explore those tools that will be used in communicating with the teachers' community as well as for creating and customizing their Personalized Learning Networks (PLNs) (Curos, 2010). For instance, the teachers' PLN includes social communities, forums and digital curation networks.

The second part includes evaluations of teachers' traffic patterns during their use of Moodle. These evaluations encompass meta-cognition analysis in order to assess the level of meta-cognition of their interaction with the environment, as proposed in (Topku&Ubiz, 2008).

The discussion forum is an example of a tool used for constructing and managing knowledge collaboratively by posing certain types of engaging activities, such as facilitative/guiding questions and examples of real cases (e.g., videos and episode dialogues). Teachers' meta-cognition is one of the most important personal variables that affect students' engagement in the environment task as well as their creative ability to solve problems. This includes a deeper level of understanding, the development of higher-order thinking, increased information-seeking behaviors, the processing of information gathered in online environments, etc. Activities such as planning how to approach a given task, monitoring comprehension, evaluating progress toward completing a task, and knowledge of these activities are meta-cognitive in nature, so an important step in enhancing education environment outcomes is to obtain improved clarity with regard to the influence of meta-cognition on students' learning and to assess how often teachers and students are engaged in the learning process through online forum discussions.

Therefore, the main purpose of the second stage is answering the second research question: what is the relationship between different components of the environment and teachers' participation in online discussions as well as what are the strategy variables or factors that can substantially influence cognition and knowledge building. One such component is the Personal Identity Online, through which students and teachers participate in online discussions and correlate content, and hence, engage in collective knowledge building. It is critical to design online interaction contexts to support identity presence in a manner that promotes students' meta-cognition and development of soft-skills for constructing community-based collective knowledge rather than simply sharing experiences and individual insights. Teachers' meta-cognition affects their effective participation in online discussions, comprehending the main ideas in online discussions, constructing links between previous and new knowledge in message sequences, and in evaluating the available resources. Teachers who effectively use meta-cognitive knowledge are largely and strategically inclined and might have a cognitive platform to effectively identify the relevant content and applicable services in the right place and at the right time, depending on their context. Mutual

exchange of messages between participants can take place at any time. Participants must read the messages and ask questions, make comments, and provide answers.

Each teacher must participate in the discussions at least twice a week. The discussion forums are based on the learning environment, causing increased interactivity. Each message from teachers in the forum discussions is assessed regarding the interaction types of coding technique developed by McKinnon (2000). A grading rubric developed by Topku&Ubiz (2008) is used to score the teachers' messages, thereby determining the quality of their participation; it covers all components of meta-cognition: meta-cognitive knowledge, meta-cognitive judgments and monitoring, as well as self-regulation and control of cognition.

In order to study how discussion forums affect teachers' soft skills, teachers are encouraged to participate in the discussion forums. It is suggested that they use search tools such as Google, Yahoo, and other education cloud searching tools and that they follow useful links at the Moodle site. The teachers are even provided with some keywords, depending on the context and new information or experiences, to set up checkpoints for knowledge of self and to deepen the discussions.

The correlations between the various aspects of teachers' beliefs and their online interactions are studied by using the method described in (Wang & Chai, 2010).

The Third Part of Study: Interviews after the Intervention

The third part includes interviews with teachers centered on their practical experience in using the Personalized Ubiquitous Educational Environment. The purpose of this part is answering the third research question: how teachers expect to use the new environment in their classes as well as what features they believe are more successful and what factors should be considered for further development. The results may promote the creation of new features that would help the scaffolding of students' thinking and stimulate interactive and rich messages and effective use of education tools. New instructive and guiding tools may force students to assess their learning needs, and enhance the use of meta-cognition strategies.

4.3. Preliminary Results of Study

The results of the teachers' participation in the discussions are scored in terms of meta-cognition (Topku&Ubiz, 2008). The following interaction types are taken into account:

- Acknowledgement
- Questions
- Comparison
- Contrast
- Evaluation
- Idea for an Example
- Clarification/Elaboration
- Cause and Effect

The distribution of the teachers' messages according to interaction type and their meta-cognition level, as well as the number of interactions (initial post, response to the initial post, response to other responses, etc.) is coded accordingly (Topku&Ubiz, 2008).

The preliminary results imply that instructors should encourage teachers to promote their Personal Identity On-line by sending messages explaining or clarifying concepts using examples from their education practices. Using keywords or tags as described above in the context of digital curation is highly appropriate for this purpose. These messages usually contained high levels of interactions, motivating teachers to control and check in their minds their knowledge structure as related to concepts under discussion. This fosters high-level meta-cognition and stimulates students' awareness of knowledge of the task and self. It also relates the course content to prior knowledge and experience, as well as makes inferences.

In measuring the correlation between the presence of Personal Identity On-line in the discussions and the high level of meta-cognition, the following findings were reported:

Online posts and replies in discussion forums with high-quality work and out-of-box thinking significantly contribute to shaping the Personal Identity, gain followers, and promote multiple citations.

On-line discussions with participants who's Personal Identity relies on trustful personal experience, based on educational practice, are usually associated with more follow-up participation in discussions, implying a higher rate of meta-cognition in the overall discussion.

One of the most significant findings of our analysis is that online forum designers should explicitly encourage Personal Identity Online expression within online interactions. This may be achieved by developing the tools and means needed to promote discussions that are both creative and present identity. For instance, educational instructors can reward highly meta-cognitive online discussions that present identity.

Another finding, also suggested in (Ke et al, 2011), is that in order to promote meaningful on-line discussions, it is critical to promote the creation of social community-based identity. This idea links identity presence with collaborative knowledge, where online students not only express their personal identities but also construct a joint social identity in order to achieve collaborative knowledge building.

5. CONCLUSION

Recently society has been undergoing a period of significant changes in all aspects of life. The educational system, as one of the fundamental institutions of modern society, consequently is strongly affected by these changes. The new educational processes that have appeared in our post-industrial society, as well as the corresponding innovative learning environments, were the focus of our paper.

We considered the new education system in a historical perspective by analyzing the evolutions of (1) forms of acquiring knowledge and (2) forms of educational processes.

In analyzing both of the above evolutions, we claim that recently education has evolved under the strong influence of two contradictory tendencies: personalization and socialization. Personalization is manifested as a new phenomenon "Personal Identity On-line", characterizing the recent most popular activity of humans – their life in cyberspace. Socialization is manifested in the form of the phenomenon of Social Media, characterized by new forms of social relations and public awareness of a virtualized post-industrial society.

In view of such a dialectic point of view regarding the personalization and socialization phenomena, we formulated requirements for the educational environment of a new type – the Personalized Ubiquitous Educational (PUE) Environment. We conducted our research on the basis of the PUE.

Our study, conducted in a teachers' training course, and which was based on the extensive use of the PUE, was aimed at addressing a number of questions in order to verify our hypothesis about personalization and socialization.

In particular, we studied the phenomena of the Personal Identity On-line and Social Media by analyzing the behavior of teachers participating in the teachers' training course in our "post-industrial class". As was reported in the paper, the preliminary results of our study strongly support our initial beliefs.

The main result of our paper is justification of our working hypothesis that a) personalization, which is manifested as a new form of Personal Identity Online and b) socialization, which is manifested as various forms of social media, are correct and useful concepts for studying and better understanding the educational environments of our post-industrial society.

We believe that the presented approach opens up the way for future studies concerning various issues involving our post-industrial educational systems.

REFERENCES

Amelung, C. (2007). Using social context and e-learner identity as a framework for an e-learning notification system. *International Journal on E-Learning*, 6(4), 501–517.

Bell, D. (1973). *The coming of post-industrial society*. New York, NY: Basic Books.

Bowman S. (2009). Presence, identity, and the cloud of knowing. E-learning, politics and society. *Journal of Moray House School of Education*, 1-7.

Cakir, M. (2008). Constructivist approaches to learning in science and their implications for science pedagogy: A literature review. *International Journal of Environmental and Science Education*, 3(4), 193–206.

Carolyn, B., & Foster, C. (2010). Alternative certification: An effective model of online supported teacher education. In D. Gibson & B. Dodge (Eds.), *Society for Information Technology & Teacher Education International Conference 2010*, (pp. 17-32). Chesapeake, VA: AACE.

Cohen, P., et al. (2010). *Roadmap for education technology*. Global Resources for Online Education, a project sponsored by the National Science Foundation and the Computing Community Consortium. Tempe, Arizona.

Curos, A. (2010). Developing personal learning networks for open and social learning. In Veletsianos, G. (Ed.), *Emerging technologies in distance education, part 2: Learning designs for emerging technologies* (pp. 109–128).

Dede, C. (2011). Emerging technologies, ubiquitous learning, and educational transformation. towards ubiquitous learning. *Proceedings of 6th European Conference of Technology Enhanced Learning, EC-TEL 2011*, Palermo, Italy, September 20-23, 2011.

Every, V., Garcia, G., & Young, M. (2010). A qualitative study of public wiki use in a teacher education program. In D. Gibson & B. Dodge (Eds.), *Society for Information Technology & Teacher Education International Conference 2010*, (pp. 55-62). Chesapeake, VA: AACE.

Fazal, M., DeSimone, J., & Lieman, L. (2010). Involving pre-service school leaders and teachers in assessing pilot electronic portfolio implementation. In D. Gibson & B. Dodge (Eds.), *Proceedings of Society for Information Technology & Teacher Education International Conference 2010*, (pp. 63-65). Chesapeake, VA: AACE.

Floridi, L. (2011). The informational nature of personal identity. *Minds and Machines, 21*(4), 549–566. doi:10.1007/s11023-011-9259-6

Graf, S., & Kinshuk. (2008). Adaptivity and personalization in ubiquitous learning systems. In A. Holzinger (Ed.), *USAB, LNCS 5298*, (pp. 331–338). Berlin, Germany: Springer-Verlag.

Harel, I., & Papert, S. (1991). *Constructionism*. Ablex Publishing.

Higgins, S. (2011). Digital curation: The emergence of a new discipline. *International Journal of Digital Curation, 6*(2), 78–88. doi:10.2218/ijdc.v6i2.191

Huber, G. P. (1984). The nature and design of post-industrial organizations. *Management Science, 30*, 928–951. doi:10.1287/mnsc.30.8.928

Hwang, G.-J., Tsai, C.-C., & Yang, S. J. H. (2008). Criteria, strategies and research issues of context-aware ubiquitous learning. *Journal of Educational Technology & Society, 11*(2), 81–91.

Ivanov, D. (2006). The past, present and future in the perspective of dialectical theory. *Proceedings of 16th ISA World Congress of Sociology*, (pp. 1-25). Durban, South African Republic.

Johnson, L., Smith, R., Levine, A., & Haywood, K. (2010). *2010 horizon report: K-12 edition*. Austin, TX: The New Media Consortium.

Ke, F., Chávez, A. F., Causarano, P.-N. L., & Causarano, A. (2011). Identity presence and knowledge building: Joint emergence in online learning environments? *International Journal of Computer-Supported Collaborative Learning, 6*(3), 349–370. doi:10.1007/s11412-011-9114-z

Kojukhov, A., & Levin, I. (2010). *Ubiquitous personalized learning environment in post-industrial society*. London, UK: International Conference on Information Society (i-Society 2010).

Masuda, Y. (1981). *The information society as post-industrial society*. USA: World Future Society.

McKinnon, G. R. (2000). The dilemma of evaluating electronic discussion groups. *Journal of Research on Computing in Education, 33*(2), 125–132.

Papert, S. (1980). *Mindstorms: Children, computers, and powerful ideas*. New York, NY: Basic Books.

Papert, S. (1991). Perestroika and epistemological politics. In *Constructionism*. Ablex Publishing.

Rodogno, R. (2011). *Personal identity online. Special Issue in Journal of Philosophy & Technology, 24*. Netherlands: Springer.

Russell, M., Bebell, D., O'Dwyer, L., & O'Connor, K. (2003). Examining teacher technology use: Implications for preservice and inservice teacher preparation. *Journal of Teacher Education, 54*(4), 297–310. doi:10.1177/0022487103255985

Satyanarayanan, M., Bahl, P., Caceres, R., & Davies, N. (2009). The case for VM-based cloudlets in mobile computing. *Pervasive Computing*, *8*(4), 14–22. doi:10.1109/MPRV.2009.82

Shute, V. J., Zapata, D., Kuntz, D., Levy, R., Baker, R., Beck, J., & Christopher, R. (2009). *Assessment: A vision*. Global Resources for Online Education, a project sponsored by the National Science Foundation and the Computing Community Consortium, Tempe, Arizona.

Sultan, N. (2010). Cloud computing for education: A new dawn? *International Journal of Information Management*, *30*, 109–116. doi:10.1016/j.ijinfomgt.2009.09.004

Topcu, A., & Ubuz, B. (2008). The effects of metacognitive knowledge on the pre-service teachers' participation in the asynchronous online forum. *Journal of Educational Technology & Society*, *11*(3), 1–12.

Wang, B., & Chai, C. S. (2010). *Preservice teachers' epistemic beliefs and their online interactions in a knowledge building community*. Knowledge Building Summer Institute. New Assessments and Environments for Knowledge Building, Toronto, Canada, August 3-6.

Yang, S. J. H. (2006). Context aware ubiquitous learning environments for peer-to-peer collaborative learning. *Journal of Educational Technology & Society*, *9*(1), 188–201.

KEY TERMS AND DEFINITIONS

Personal Identity Online (PIO): Identity that a user establishes in online activities and experienced in a variety of ways depending on what activity is undertaken: e-mail exchange, participating in web forums, exploring virtual worlds, or simply surfing around the Internet. One's online activities through one's PIO can affect, expand and alter the way in which one view him-self.

Personalization: A process concerned with forming a personalized learning environment. This process is based on adapting to the learner's profile by using various technologies for investigating the specific learning history of past training activities, i.e. personal identity by using educational data mining.

Personalized Ubiquitous Educational (PUE) Environment: An educational environment leveraging virtualization of social reality, personalization processes in education and ubiquitous access to the learned content. PUE comprises all the necessary components that can be computerized and be adaptable to specific users' needs where students and teachers are both the developers and the users of the environment. An important component of the environment is users' personal identity online that can be used to adapt learning materials.

Social Media: A cultural phenomenon, substantially intensifying and enhancing interpersonal communication and significantly altering the nature of the relationship between an individual and a society.

Ubiquitous Reality: Virtual reality (including educational content), with which the student and teachers maintains permanent communication in time and space.

Virtualization of Reality: A process that involves transforming reality into a new context - a form of simulated reality, a new form of manifesting universal human activity by creating new knowledge, thus expanding the boundaries of objective reality.

Chapter 7
Personal Knowledge Management and Social Media:
What Students Need to Learn for Business Life

Marie-Luise Groß
University of Vienna, Austria

ABSTRACT

Today's students are tomorrow's knowledge workers. They will be paid to find innovative solutions to organizations' most pressing problems. In times of decreasing training budgets and a dynamic job market, employees have to take over responsibility for their own personal development. Social Media and Social Software both on the WWW and organizations intranets offer a myriad of possibilities to employees and managers to be successful knowledge workers in increasingly virtual organizations and to ensure continuous learning. However, social media also puts new challenges on employees. Particularly young people, who – as the Generation Y'ers – are expected to possess extensive social media skills, need to know how they can use social media in a business context to ensure their personal development and be successful in their jobs. In this chapter, the Personal Knowledge Management model is used to discuss influential factors of successful knowledge work and personal development and to outline what students need to learn to be prepared for Enterprise 2.0.

INTRODUCTION

Post-industrialism puts many challenges on knowledge workers. The fast generation and dissemination of new knowledge, the emergence of new technologies, and the trend towards networked

teams instead of hierarchical structures in organizations facilitate constantly changing working environments (David & Foray, 2002).

Knowledge workers have to find timely solutions to often inexpected challenges. Managers do not give orders or supervise the completion of

DOI: 10.4018/978-1-4666-2970-7.ch007

tasks. They manage people instead of processes (Romhardt, 1998) and are there to support their teams. Employees manage their own workload by themselves: "It is the knowledge worker's decision what he or she should be held accountable for in terms of quality and quantity regarding time and regarding cost" (Drucker, 1999). Although knowledge is considered a forth resource in the postindustrial economy (Bullinger, 1998), training budgets and education timeframes become tighter and we can see the trend going against traditional classroom training during which participants sit in a room for days, listening to an instructor who tells them what to learn and how. Instead, there is a clear trend towards collaborative, ad-hoc, and on-the-job learning approaches. There is also a shift from employer-initiated training towards employees themselves ensuring self-managed and lifelong learning in collaboration with others. Prerequisite for the success of these new approaches is the awareness of how important knowledge sharing is both on the employer and the employee side (Klamma et al., 2007). However, individuals have to know how they can enhance their skills, solve problems, and make timely decisions in highly networked, increasingly virtual work environments. Social Media provide an extensive tool set for these purposes and companies expect employees to know how to make best use of them.

Many organizations have already adopted Social Media tools both for internal and external usage. To the external world, Social Media serve as channels for engaging with customers and partner companies or for promoting products and services to prospects. Youtube videos and Facebook activities are used for brand-building purposes and for presenting a more social side of the enterprise. Inside organizations, Social Media are used in many more ways than for communications and marketing purposes only. Particularly multinational companies and institutions use Social Media to support collaboration among their employees who are spread across the globe. Employees are expected to work together and to coordinate their activities using discussion forums, virtual 'rooms' or micro-blogging tools which they can find on the corporate intranet. Instead of writing meeting minutes and documentations and distributing them through e-mail or storing them on a server, employees can share relevant information through team blogs or even record short videos with webcams integrated in their laptops which they can upload and use for knowledge sharing and asynchronous communication with their colleagues. Although companies still struggle with the implementation of such changed working behaviors and some firms still have to jump on the Social Media bandwagon, they all expect their employees to go with the shift towards the so-called "Enterprise 2.0" (McAfee, 2006).

Todays' college and university students will become knowledge workers in the near future. They will be employed and paid to support accelerated innovation cycles and ensure their organizations' success in fast-paced environments. Project-based work and virtual teams put an emphasis on self-efficacy and self-managed work effort. Employees need to collaborate with their peers across time zones and regions, dealing with diverse cultures and language barriers. These challenges they will have to approach with the support of social, web-based technology. The ability to use Social Media effectively for fostering their personal careers is becoming increasingly important. When first-time employees enter a corporate environment after graduating from college or university, they find themselves in a new situation where they quickly have to take on responsibility for their personal careers. The majority of students may have gained working experience already during their studies, and may therefore already know that and how Social Media are used in companies. They are also aware of the fact that, although employed, they might never really leave the job market again: "A changed employment has resulted in a new generation of first-time employees who realise that they need to be more self-sufficient than their predecessors as that they cannot rely on the same position throughout their employment lifetime" (Smedley, 2009, p.222). However, this might be the first time they realize that continuous learning, the ability to make informed decisions, and to find creative solutions to problems are vital to their personal development and their professional careers. This is where knowledge management (KM) activities come into play. Sharing knowledge with colleagues, learning from previous experiences of others, knowing how to consult experts – all these things are important for knowledge workers' success.

In the past, these activities were initiated and supported by organizational knowledge management. The objectives of most organizational KM initiatives of the past were to identify, store and disseminate knowledge within the organization. The main goal was to create a universal organizational memory which preserved all the knowledge of any individual in the company, so turnover, retirement or employees' illness would not have a bad impact on the company's competitiveness. However, in today's changed working environment and the shift from a We- to a Me-mentality (Richter & Koch, 2009), which we experience on the Social Web and, due to the usage of Social Media, within organizations, Personal Knowledge Management (PKM) activities become increasingly important.

In this chapter, I approach the need for Social Media in higher education from a Personal Knowledge Management perspective. The objective is to highlight the areas where Social Media tools gain importance in organizations and the challenges students need to be prepared for when they enter the job market. As a theoretical framework, I use Smedley's (2009) personal knowledge management (PKM) model, which relates individual learning and personal development to overall organizational knowledge management activities. I will extend her model by Social Media activities and argue that new hires' engagement in both, personal and organizational knowledge management benefits their own as well as their organizations' success. The suggestions and recommendations

made in this chapter reflect experiences and findings from a knowledge management perspective. It describes how first-time employees should embrace the bandwidth of tools and opportunities Social Media and Social Software offers and concludes with recommendations and ideas for anyone engaged in higher education teaching on how to integrate Social Media in teaching activities. This chapter is not about Social Media usage of teachers. It tackles students' Social Media usage instead. University teachers can use this information for developing ideas of new teaching approaches, including collaborative work in distributed teams as well as sharing and creating knowledge by using Social Media.

KNOWLEDGE WORK IN THE 21ST CENTURY

Knowledge work is a creative endeavor. It is unpredictable, often conducted in an unstructured way, and it is difficult to plan in advance (Fuchs-Kittowski, 2007). Knowledge work is always problem-centered (Dörner, 1979), as it differs from a mere fulfillment of assigned tasks in that it originates from knowledge gaps. If individuals experience a knowledge gap and their existing knowledge is sufficient to determine the occurring problem, but not to resolve it, then new knowledge needs to be generated (in an individual or group effort) or accessed from other knowledge resources. Resulting from the differences between the challenges of the work process and the individual's knowledge, a knowledge gap is highly subjective. Hence, the complexity of knowledge gaps and the challenges in knowledge work will be perceived differently from person to person (Pfiffner & Stadelmann, 1998).

The creation of new knowledge, either in an individual or in a collaborative effort together with others, is a creative process. The majority of knowledge workers are therefore accepted to belong to Florida's Creative Class, which includes people in science and engineering, architecture and design, education, arts, music and entertainment, whose economic function is to create new ideas, new technology and/or new creative content. Around the core, the Creative Class also includes a broader group of creative professionals in business and finance, law, health care and related fields. These people engage in complex problem solving that involves a great deal of independent judgment and requires high levels of education and human capital (Florida, 2002, p.8).

It is also safe to assume that the majority of students in higher education will become such creative knowledge workers who will be paid by their employers to provide solutions to companies' complex future challenges. Moreover, many of them strive for a management position. For this challenge, personal knowledge management skills and acknowledgment of the importance of hierarchical and peer support is vital (Smedley, 2009).

Communities of Practice, Then and Now

Organizations do well to support their knowledge workers by fostering an open-minded, knowledge sharing culture (McAfee, 2006; Guenther, 2010), by providing powerful information and communication technology (ICT) and by constantly adapting organizational routines and processes to new knowledge (Davenport & Prusak, 1998). Many corporations have established a designated knowledge management (KM) role or team for this purpose. The objective is to govern "a process that 'organizationally' amplifies the knowledge created by individuals and crystallizes it as a part of the knowledge network of the organization" (Nonaka & Takeuchi, 1995, p.59). While in the 1990ies, the prevalent knowledge management paradigm aimed at fully IT-supported organizational memories – databases in which the comprehensive knowledge of the organization could be stored and would be accessible whenever needed – some organizations also realized that knowledge creation and dissemination takes place through employees'

social interaction. To foster this effect, they established Communities of Practice (CoP) in which employees could participate in knowledge sharing activities and learn from experience.

The concept of CoP is not a new one. Similar to the education of apprentices by experienced masters and fellows in ancient guilds (Lave & Wenger, 1991; Wenger & Snyder, 2000), a CoP is an affiliation of individuals in which processes of social learning and collaborative problem solving take effect. Communities of Practice "consist of three components: people, places and things. They are composed of people who interact on a regular basis around a common set of issues, interests or needs." (Lesser et al., 2000, p.vii) Hereafter, CoP will be understood as informal groups of individuals, who team up on a voluntary basis in order to accomplish a common goal in a joint effort based on knowledge sharing, social learning and mutual support (Lehner, 2008) in organizations and across.

The CoP approach has become even more important nowadays, as globalization, multinational companies and strategic cooperation among partners and competitors across the globe require virtual collaboration and asynchronous communication, independent of hierarchical structures. Innovation and efficient collaboration with different parties require flexible platforms which support social interaction and community building. Social Media tools or social software applications act as enablers of human work in such global, increasingly virtual corporate environments.

Social Media and Social Software

Social Media is a term predominantly used in a business, marketing or media context. In scientific discourse, the term Social Software is widely used. Both terms are used as labels for the same software applications which are web-based and facilitate human interaction, identity management, social networking and information sharing. Coates (2005, n.p.) defines social software as "software which supports, extends, or derives added value from, human social behaviour." Different models and approaches for the classification of social media and social software applications exist. Koch and Richter (2009) created an adapted version of Schmidt's social software triangle (2006), exchanging "connection management" for "communication" and adding "networking" to the category "identity management" (See Figure 1) (Nehm 2009).

In this model, the different social software applications are assigned to the category they belong to. Richter and Koch also discuss Andrew McAfee's SLATES approach (McAfee, 2006) as a possible classification scheme for social software, which draws on possible use cases for the various tools in the Enterprise 2.0. The acronym SLATES stands for Search, Links, Authoring, Tagging, Extensions, and Signals. In their view, Authoring relates to the possibility to easily create, publish and edit contents. Through Tagging, users can easily add metadata and structure content, so it will be findable and re-findable. Authors can also add Links to the content they create and thus add valuable information from other (external) resources, even in the form of various media. For example, a user can create a written blog post, link to blog posts or online-articles from other users and embed a Youtube video into the post and significantly enrich their own content, but also embed it into a given structure or thematic framework of other information. Signals refers to

information services, such as RSS-feeds. Users can subscribe to websites and will receive either notification messages whenever the content on the website changes or new information (e.g. a new blog post) will be forwarded to them directly. This enables them to keep track of topics or the latest news in a certain field. Powerful Search engines and tools make it easier for users to find required or interesting information. Tagging, Linking and structuring activities of users support search engines' algorithms in understanding users' information needs. Extensions refers to the modular, service-oriented, and data-centered architecture of web-based social applications (Koch & Richter, 2009). All these features and functionalities of social software and social media which can be found and used online, on the WWW, are also used by companies for internal purposes and collaboration with their ecosystems. The term Enterprise 2.0 for the adoption of social software by organizations has been coined by Andrew McAfee, who also created the following definition: "Enterprise 2.0 is the use of emergent social software platforms within companies, or between companies and their partners and customers" (McAfee, 2006, cited in Koch & Richter, 2009, p.15)

Generation Y

Today's students and young employees, who were born in the 1980s or after, are often said to belong to "Generation Y" or are referred to as "Digital Natives." It is anticipated that these young people "possess sophisticated knowledge of and skills with information technologies," and that "digital natives have particular learning preferences or styles that differ from earlier generations of students." (Bennett et al., 2008, p.777) As a consequence, companies look into how they can change working models and adopt new technology in order to be more attractive to Generation Y new hires. They worry about how they can close the so-called "digital divide," a term which is used to point out

Figure 1. Social software triangle (Adapted from Koch & Richter, 2009)

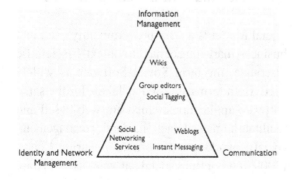

the differences in usage and knowledge about ICT in younger and senior employees. Higher education organizations also discuss new learning curricula so they will meet the new generations' needs. Critics, however, claim that there is not enough empirical evidence of these assumptions being true. As discussed further by Bennett et al. (2008), a common perception of digital natives is that they are active experiential learners and very good at multitasking. They depend on information and communication technologies (ICT), so they can access the information they need and maintain personal interrelations with their peers. A survey conducted with US students about ten years ago showed that almost all students (99.5%) used e-mail programs and word processing software and surfed on the internet in their leisure time. Anyhow, only 21% of the students created their own content or media and shared it online. The authors point out that "a significant proportion of students had lower level skills than might be expected of digital natives." (Kvavik, Caruso & Morgan, 2004; cited in: Bennett et al., 2008, p.778) Another study (Lenhart, Madden & Hitlin, 2005; Livingstone & Bober, 2004; all cited in Bennett et al., 2008) on the internet use of children and teenagers showed that school children spend a lot of time online, mainly for social interaction with their friends and for helping with homework. However, schools and family backgrounds have a strong impact on computer and internet use, online experience and context of online activities. "These findings suggest that technology skills and experience are far from universal among young people" (Bennett et al., 2008, p.778).

Personal and Professional Skills for the Knowledge Society

Students and first-time employees need to develop a broad set of competencies in order to be successful in the knowledge society. As argued above, these skills include, but are not limited to:

- Perseverance and Motivation:
  - Self-Directed Learning
  - Self-Directed Personal Development
  - Self-Efficacy
  - Self-Management
  - Leadership and Organization:
  - Decision Making
  - Efficient Self-Coordination
  - Leading a Team
  - Mentoring
  - Problem Solving

- Teamwork:
  - Working in Highly Networked, Increasingly Virtual Work Environments
  - Cooperative and Collaborative Work
  - Building Relationships with Others
  - Learning from Others
  - Sharing Knowledge and Experiences with Others
  - Intercultural Competencies
  - Communication Skills

Social Media and Social Software Competencies

As you can see, these skills are mostly soft skills. Social Media and Social Software usage is about social interaction, coordination and how teams work together. Thus, Social Media skills are more social skills than the knowledge of functions and functionalities. In projects and group work, students can practice and enhance their social skills. The challenge for teachers will be to teach their students social skills and professional soft skills which are to be used while using Social Media. If teachers combine group work and student projects with Social Media usage, students will acquire the Social Media and soft skills required for business life.

PERSONAL KNOWLEDGE MANAGEMENT WITH SOCIAL MEDIA

Employee productivity and sustainability are key to the success of an organization in a highly competitive and constantly changing business world. Organizations need to ensure that they provide an environment and a culture where employees can learn together, free collective aspiration (Senge, 1990) and support the enhancement of employee competences. In the past, employee upskilling was seen mainly as an organizational effort. Companies centrally planned, monitored and regulated a training portfolio and employees had to attend the training courses which were envisaged for their roles. Additionally, organization knowledge management was in charge of documenting and storing employee knowledge, so it would be available for ad-hoc upskilling purposes.

In today's business world, this has changed significantly. Most knowledge-intensive companies provide their employees with free access to the internet and an increasing number of organizations use groupware or social software platforms so their employees can collaborate with each other across time zones and country boarders. In this environment, a myriad of information and knowledge resources are available to the individual, either on the intranet or externally, on the World Wide Web. At the same time, they can also create information for others, share knowledge online and gain more visibility or even the role of an expert through this. With this changed situation, there comes also a shift in personal development and learning from organizational responsibility to employee responsibility. Training budgets are subject to cost-cuttings, project time frames become tighter and innovation cycles shorter. Accordingly, employees and managers have to know how they can leverage their own knowledge and skills, make informed decisions in uncertain situations and assure performance and competitiveness of their organizations.

The combination of Personal Knowledge Management skills and Social Media competences are vital for employees' careers and particularly younger people are expected to have such skills. This is exasperated by the fact that first-time employees "need to be more self-sufficient than their predecessors as that they cannot rely on the same position throughout their employment lifetime. […] PKM is becoming the next major area of management development and a basic competence that every executive will need to possess" (Smedley, 2009, p. 222).

There are different objectives which can be found in the scholarly discussion about PKM. One puts its focus on "managing and supporting personal knowledge and information so that it is accessible, meaningful and valuable to the individual" (Higgison, 2004, n.p.). Another one states that its aim is to "empower each individual to easily apply their own personal knowledge in dealing with new and old problems, to learn from new experience and to create new knowledge" (Cheong & Tsui, 2010). Skyrme also highlights the social factor of PKM, which he sees in "maintaining networks, contacts and communities and making life easier and more enjoyable and exploiting social capital" (Skyrme, 1999). Whichever the focus, most PKM researchers and practitioners agree on one thing: "individuals themselves reap significant long-term benefits. Once they have understood their own value, they can make shrewd choices regarding their own personal development programme." (Higgison, 2004, n.p.) And Higgison cites researcher Lilia Efimova with the words: "It's about being aware of your competencies, strengths and weaknesses, working style, and habits," […] "This allows you to select or shape the working environment that fits your preferences." (ibid.)

In the following section, I will discuss some typical challenges and issues first-time employees experience to raise awareness which competences and skills students need to develop during higher education. I will discuss these from a Knowledge Management practitioner's perspective so experts from the field of Higher Education and Adult Learning, as well as university lecturers and professors can get insights from which they can derive necessary measures or further ideas.

CHALLENGES OF BUSINESS LIFE FOR FIRST-TIME EMPLOYEES

When first-time employees join a company, tasks and responsibilities will be handed over to them after a certain (and, most of the times, quite short) period of on-boarding and introduction to key processes and products. They will have to demonstrate their abilities to complete tasks, manage projects and use optimization potential for their organization. However, in most companies, simply being good at their job will not lead to employees' career advancement. Employees also have to promote their professional successes so their colleagues will recognize their proficiency and management will consider them for higher positions with more responsibilities or (in case of expert careers) for tasks which require higher levels of expertise. Through the implementation of Social Media tools in organizations, the presentation of one's expertise and the visibility in communities of practice are influential factors of individual career opportunities. To achieve recognition in a CoP, soft skills are equally important as is expert knowledge. Proficiency in collaboration and teamwork are skills that are needed to function effectively in the twenty-first century work environment (AAC&U, 2007).

As discussed above, some research findings suggest that today's first-time employees are often not more knowledgeable about the usage of social media and content creation with those applications, particularly for business purposes, than are their colleagues of Generation X or older:

While technology is embedded in their lives, young people's use and skills are not uniform. There is no evidence of widespread and universal

disaffection, or of a distinctly different learning style the like of which has never been seen before. We may live in a highly technologised world, but it is conceivable that it has become so through evolution, rather than revolution (Bennctt et al., 2008, p.783).

Of course, young people use Facebook and other Social Networking Services on a daily basis, they may also write their own weblogs about street fashion or computer games. However, using social software tools in a business context to manage projects, engage with important stakeholders, or gain visibility to upper management are usage scenarios which differ significantly from private social web activities.

Besides technology skills, the usage of social software also puts an emphasis on competences considered as "soft" skills, e.g. collaboration and teamwork skills, which are needed to function effectively in the twenty-first century work environment (Kuh, 2009, p.694). Teamwork and communicating effectively with social software is quite different from collaboration with others who sit together in a room and can interact with each other face-to-face. "From an employer's perspective, college students appeared to be well-prepared in their academic and content areas but fell short in areas that were related to the context of work (for example interpersonal skills, setting principles) and applying their knowledge in work environments" (Pascarella/Terenzini, 2005, p. 534).

Ad-Hoc Learning and Personal Development

In rapidly changing corporate environments, new hires will most likely receive on-boarding training and one or the other professional training, but overall, employees are responsible for their own personal development. Regular up-skilling is very important, because employees cannot rely on keeping their job until retirement. Even if they stay in the same organization, they will probably do a different job from time to time, because changing markets, reorganizations and project-based work will frequently result into new challenges and expose them to new topics.

Ad-hoc learning refers to a timely acquisition of new competencies or knowledge, often from other individuals: "People as self-directed learners will learn by way of informal knowledge sharing in ad hoc learning communities and Learning Networks." (Brouns et al., 2007) Therefore, besides possessing internet-efficacy, first-time employees need to understand how Communities of Practice function, how they can establish relationships with experts and more experienced colleagues, and they need to have the awareness that sharing their own knowledge and information material with their colleagues and peers is important. The lack of willingness to actively participate in learning communities or communities of practice within an organization are among the most common reasons for the failure of Communities of Practice and, as a consequence, personal and organizational failure due to a lack of learning and weak network structures.

Students have been found to first turn to an online search engine when they look for information. Many online sources are very accurate, but students need to learn how they can verify the accuracy of information resources. They need to develop a healthy skepticism regarding the information they obtain from websites. Another influential factor is time: "Indeed, [students] rated most information seeking experiences based on how much time they took, and often will accept inappropriate information or information of lower quality if finding it takes less time. They referred to information seeking as taking time away from other things" (Weiler, 2004, p.50). Also in business life, time – or the lack of it – is the killer argument for any task or extra activity someone does not want to do for any reason. However, the lack of time should not lead to inferior knowledgeability and result in bad decisions. Weiler also points out that most students "expressed the preference to discuss information needs with a ''real person''

rather than find all the needed information on their own" and that "'infoglut' and questionable validity were cited as the most common current obstacles to finding information." (Weiler, 2004, p.50) With regard to creative knowledge work, the challenge of closing knowledge gaps is even greater: Knowledge workers need to come up with new, innovative ideas. In their business lives, they will face new challenges every day and have to find solutions to problems. This often does not only involve research and getting helpful information from others. Knowledge workers need to develop new knowledge. Internet research can be a basis for inspiration or deliver helpful information. However, if the solution to the problem has not been found yet, they will hardly find the answer online.

Another issue is that first-time employees might not exactly know how to use social media for personal development and lifelong learning. They need to understand that they learn for their own benefit and that they need to identify areas for development themselves. Only those employees, who have innovative ideas, solve the organization's problems, and who communicate effectively with stakeholders to make the implementation of the new solution or process easier, gain visibility and will be successful. Furthermore, "cooperative or group learning experiences appear to have a positive influence on self-reported growth in career-related skills such as leadership abilities, public speaking ability, ability to influence others, and ability to work effectively in groups" (Pascarella/Terenzini, 2005: 542).

Collaborative Work

Working collaboratively gains importance particularly in highly networked organizations with flat, permeable hierarchies. Knowledge workers are encouraged to self-responsibly, thus collaboratively elaborate optimized processes, work on new products or deliver services to customers. In virtual, distributed teams, collaborative work is usually supported by software that supports the assignment of workflows, asynchronous and synchronous communication and social networking. As in learning, social media also gains influence when it comes to collaborative team work and knowledge dissemination in organizations (Koch, 2008). In multinational corporations that rely on Social Software tools, the ability to work effectively in groups is not anymore decoupled from the working environment. Working groups can be located all over the world in different time zones, speaking various languages and bringing diverse socio-cultural backgrounds into the project work. Thus, the highly demanded "ability to work effectively in groups" has become the "ability to work effectively in groups with the support of social software".

In a social media influenced corporate environment, leadership abilities are not only required for managers or project leads. Employees also need to demonstrate leadership when they want to develop their own ideas and implement changes. Social Media can be used in different and creative ways to communicate ideas, convince others and promote new products or processes internally and externally.

Effective Communication

The maturing and implementation of ideas and successful project management involves interaction and communication with colleagues and stakeholders. Here, emotional, cultural, and political influence factors need to be considered; and so does the organization's strategic direction. Social media can be used to communicate strategic directions and to discuss ideas and collaborate on them. In a social media working environment, the public speaking ability and the ability to influence others also are extended. Speaking in public now also means speaking in telephone and video conferences, but also goes beyond these things by including writing blogs, sharing ideas and information through micro-blogging, leading

discussions in online forums, and speaking in front of a camera for ad-hoc produced corporate education or presentation videos.

Job Satisfaction

Factors for job satisfaction are: job prestige and earnings, job autonomy, non-routine work (Pascarella/Terenzini, 2005: 535). Social media tools support autonomy and non-routine work in corporate environments. However, social media usage may also lead to an increase in anxiety in employees as studies of Facebook users suggest who have been found to experience high levels of anxiety, due to the pressure to being inventive and entertaining or feelings of exclusion (Charles, 2011). There are no studies that cover this aspect among professionals which I am aware of. However, from my own experience, I know that even Generation Y employees feel insecure about how to use Facebook-like social networking applications in a corporate environment, because they cannot fully assess the impact of their activities and rely very much on other users' (i.e. their colleagues') feedback and opinions. Just as an example, in a private environment on Facebook, not to receive feedback (as comments or likes) on activities (status messages or uploaded images) might not have an impact on an individual's feelings. In a corporate environment, however, this could have a stronger negative impact, because visibility in CoPs and to management is regarded vital to professional success and no feedback may be translated to "not interesting," "not knowledgeable," or "not important to the company".

SOLUTIONS AND RECOMMENDATIONS

To overcome the issues and problems discussed above, I propose that students internalize personal knowledge management strategies and understand how they can use social media to translate their individual PKM strategy into success. I draw on Smedley's Personal Knowledge Management model both for faculty to use as a framework for the development and implementation of curricula in higher education, and for students to understand the key influential factors of their personal development in business life and how to make best use of them. In today's multinational and increasingly virtual organizations, personal knowledge management is closely linked to the use of social media and students should already develop technology and PKM skills during higher education to establish a basis for their personal success: "with increased pace and the use of more informal approaches in workplace communication through modern technologies, success is often determined by the individual knowledge management [...] of the employees themselves indirectly providing organizational benefits." Smedley (2009: 221)

The Personal Knowledge Management Model

To illustrate the different factors of PKM, I use the PKM model developed and introduced by Jo Smedley (2009). With her PKM model, Smedley connects traditional organizational KM with individual learning. It is based on the SECI model of Nonaka and Konno (1998), which is widely used in organizational knowledge management discussions to visualize the process of knowledge creation in four phases: Socialization, Externalization, Combination, and Internalisation (See Figure 2). In the Socialization phase, individuals share tacit knowledge with each other through social interaction which can be face-to-face communication or shared experiences. In the subsequent Externalization phase, individuals develop concepts based on their combined tacit knowledge. Just as concepts, tacit knowledge becomes communicable and, thus, explicit. The Combination of various elements of explicit knowledge leads

Figure 2. The SECI model (Adapted from Nonaka & Konno, 1998)

to the generation of new knowledge, which can be used by individuals, becomes part of their personal knowledge through experience and is transformed into tacit knowledge in the Internalization phase. In this process, individual knowledge becomes an organizational asset, which can be communicated to and used by others. As the spiral proceeds, new knowledge is created and tested, and existing knowledge is being refreshed continually.

The original SECI model and also Smedley's PKM model also use the concept of Ba, which has its origins in Japanese philosophy and is translated as a space or "a platform for advancing individual or collective knowledge and a shared space that serves as a foundation for knowledge creation." (Smedley 2009, p.223) It can exist as a physical (office, university), virtual (WWW, social media), or a mental space, or even as a combination of the three. The concept of Ba will not be discussed in detail hereafter, but it is important to keep in mind that the physical, virtual and intellectual environment is an important influential factor of knowledge creation and learning. Smedley combines the SECI model with Kolb's Learning Style Inventory (Kolb 1984), which highlights the importance of experiential learning. In Kolb's model, learning also takes place in a circular process, with the four phases Reflective Observation, Abstraction Generalization, Active Experimentation, and Concrete Experience. Putting it into simpler words, Kolb assumes that learning happens through watching, thinking, doing and feeling (Smedley 2009). In a business context, emotional and political aspects are also influential factors of experiential learning (Vince 1998).

Smedley sees a close connection between the individual employee, experts, and Communities of Practice in PKM (See Figure 3). Her model relates individual theoretical knowledge to its application in every day work and consequent reflection of experiences. In the Socialization phase, the individual employee establishes personal interrelations with other employees. Through social interaction, the individual becomes aware of accepted norms, desired behavior, communication styles and work practices in the organization. Through reflective thinking, the individual can adapt to the new environment and can identify knowledge gaps and areas of personal development. Using an example of corporate social media usage, this could be the communication of project progress through a weblog on the firm's intranet.

A new Project Manager who takes over the lead of a project will have to identify blogging as an accepted communication channel that she needs to use for communicating with her team and important stakeholders. She will have to learn how

Figure 3. The PKM octohedron (Adapted from Smedley, 2009)

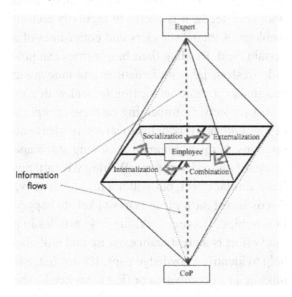

to use the blogging software and develop a concise writing style which fits the medium and the purpose of project communication and stakeholder management. The step of applying the group's practices to her own way of working leads to the Externalization phase of the PKM model. According to Smedley, this phase "represents a challenge to some employees depending on personality, willingness, ability to accept and adjust. Again, the individual reflective aspect is important to encourage the employee to think about the new scenario and to recognise possible aspects for development and challenges that need to be overcome." (Smedley, 2009, p. 229) As the new Project Manager familiarizes herself with blogging as a new communication practice, she starts to recognize her own style of writing, compares her posts with those of other bloggers within and outside the organization and adopts good practices from them. She might also try to further develop the common practice and other social media, e.g. micro-blogging or video-blogging to her communication and thereby propose new methods to the organization. These activities take place in the Combination phase, which can "involve considerable frustration (in the Employee), requires careful supervision (by the Expert) and support (by the Community of Practice) to assure the development of effective PKM skills and approaches to implement the proposed changes." (ibid.) In the Internalization phase, individuals realize how they can use their new skills and knowledge for their own success and, at the same time, provide value to their organization. Smedley describes this discovery as the "most exciting phase from an employability point of view, providing employees with valuable insights into how their newly acquired experiences can be used as their enhanced PKM skills are used in various applications. The reflective skills provide a platform for continuing professional development, encouraging the employee to think, plan approaches and reflect on lessons learned" (ibid.).

The Expert role and the Community of Practice constitute "a supportive network of both individual and community in the overall knowledge enhancement cycle." (Smedley, 2009, p. 230) Social interaction and soft skills are very important for establishing interrelations with experts and members of the CoP. These skills should be acquired as early in education as possible. With regard to their application in business life, students in higher education should have these abilities developed until their graduation. In the following section, I will discuss the various skills that underly successful PKM.

Personal Knowledge Management with Social Media

Various skills are associated with Personal Knowledge Management: "PKM is contextual with the capacity to apply cognitive, information, social and learning competencies through a series of individual, social and organisational competencies." (Smedley, 2009, p.225) These competencies come into play on three levels, according to the PKM model. The first is the individual level, the second level is the Community of Practice in which individuals have to develop and apply skills which positively contribute to the informal group concept. The third level is the mentor role. The skills and competencies specified by Smedley need to be brought together with Social Media use cases in order to derive teaching scenarios for higher education.

Ability to Handle Information

Information can be handled in two different ways, actively as a creator or author and passively as a consumer. Authors of information (e.g. of presentations, documents, wiki-articles or a microblogpost) or simply by actively structuring, rating, or commenting on content of others, have to ask themselves several questions, such as: What information would I like to share with whom? Which

media is appropriate for this purpose? Do I share my knowledge inside the organization only or also outside? How can I connect multiple channels (e.g. blog, micro-blog, video sharing platform, discussion thread in an online community) How can I establish myself as an expert in this field? How do I gain visibility both internally and externally?

In a more passive way, as a consumer of information, employees have to find answers to the questions: Where can I find the information I need? Where can I pose questions to experienced colleagues or experts in a certain field? Where (i.e. on which platform) do these people discuss and engage? Which websites, wikis, social online communities, online discussion forums are relevant for my area of expertise?

It is very important to acknowledge the power of information (Smedley, 2009, p. 224). The saying "knowledge is power" is often translated into "better keep your knowledge to yourself so you won't lose your unique selling proposition." However, information and knowledge need to be shared and discussed in order to create new knowledge and ideas. Students should therefore learn to think about which knowledge and information they can share with whom and through which channel.

Basically all Social Media can be used for information handling and knowledge sharing. Besides keeping up-to-date on the latest news with RSS-feeds, it is useful to regularly consult weblogs of thought leaders and enthusiasts of a certain field. Reading their blog entries can provide fresh insights into changes and innovation and makes it more interesting to deal with specialist subjects. Commenting on these blogposts or blogging actively helps to structure ideas and opinions, helps to improve reasoning skills and to identify knowledge gaps. Writing wiki articles has a similar effect, but will not lead to an active discussion of the topic as is most likely to happen in a weblog. However, writing wiki articles in a joint effort is a great team exercise and will also help to identify knowledge gaps. If knowledge is missing in a certain area or first ideas need to be verified, starting a discussion thread in an online community can generate further ideas or provide useful tips for the course of action.

Mentoring

Informal learning from more experienced colleagues and the informal transfer of knowledge and practices are key in PKM. The mentor, being an experienced, often senior individual supervises the acquisition of skills and methods by newcomers. If an organization does not offer mentoring programs, first-time employees should look out for colleagues who could and would like to informally take on the role of a mentor. This involves the reflective dealing with their own knowledge gaps and the identification of areas of personal development. Young people also have to learn how to build network relations beyond their direct peer groups and to maintain these. In some cases, it might also be applicable to have more than one mentor, e.g. one for technical skills and the other one to learn about organizational politics and norms.

If mentoring is not possible within the organization, young employees can also find a mentor for personal development outside of the organization, e.g. through their participation in online topic groups and CoPs. Professional social networking platforms, such as LinkedIn.com offer a myriad of online groups and discussion forums where thought leaders and enthusiasts come together and discuss. Some professionals also share their knowledge and experiences through personal weblogs. Following a blogger over a certain time can also be a great resource of proven knowledge and tacit knowledge which is made explicit so others can learn from it.

When young employees gain more experience and become increasingly proficient in their positions, they can also act as mentors to new hires or other colleagues and share their personal experiences with them. Just as the mentors discussed in the section above would do it, they can start to act as thought leaders in CoPs, they can start blogging

or help others. Students can already practice the roles of the mentor and the mentee in higher education, by finding themselves a mentor or helping younger students with their studies. Social Media can help to make such initiatives more scalable, e.g. if advanced students blog about a certain topic and elementary students read and comment on those blog posts on a regular basis and use the contents as an additional source for learning. In group work, students could also contact a thought leader through an online community and use their feedback and tips for developing a solution. Through these exercises, students become aware of the benefits of self-directed learning in the context of mentors and a Community of Practice.

Communities of Practice

Virtual teams and changing organizational structures in dynamic business environments leads to an increasing importance of powerful social network structures, as can be found in Communities of Practice. In these loosely bound, informal groups of practitioners and experts, new knowledge is created through social interaction and learning from shared experiences. Social competencies required for effective participation in such communities are "team building and maintenance activities, including communication and conflict resolution skills working in a collaborative environment." (Smedley, 2009, p.226) In higher education, students themselves can establish CoPs. With the support of Social Media, they can open their community up to other individuals who do not belong to their university or institute. These individuals could be students from other learning institutions or practitioners. Students can also individually join online communities, but they should be encouraged to share the insights they gained from discussions and information shared online with their fellow students. They can use these information resources to complete projects and, to give something back to the community, also share their findings and results with the CoP, e.g. through a blog post. Another advantage of such activities is their collaborative and international character. Participating in online communities, students will need to use English as lingua franca and they have to deal with socio-cultural differences, which they might not find to such extent in their classes. Through these experiences, they will be able to develop the "ability to function effectively in complex internal and external social systems, particularly in work teams," which Smedley highlights as a "particularly important skill" for PKM (Smedley, 2009, p.226).

Learning Activities with Social Media Tools

Understanding and exercising Personal Knowledge Management while using Social Media provides students with key competencies for business life. Many universities already have Groupware or Social Media tools in place. Some use collaborative learning platforms or e-learning platforms, which also provide similar functionalities like Social Media. The following scenarios are presented as examples for university and college teachers to exercise personal knowledge management activities and Social Media usage with students. These scenarios are only recommendations from a practitioners perspective. Experienced teaching staff will still know best how to translate these examples into real teaching and which tools to use, universities' e-learning applications or free Social Media on the WWW.

Collaboration in Distributed Teams

Establish an academic partnership with a class in another country (i.e. in a different time zone and using English as lingua franca) and have students work on a project in smaller groups. Students should use Social Media to coordinate activities, share resources and hand-over completed work packages.

With this scenario, students exercise collaboration in virtual teams.

Collaboration with Professionals of a Company

Establish a partnership with professionals of one or more companies, maybe in another country (i.e. in a different time zone and using English as lingua franca). In this scenario, students would work on a project for the company. Collaboration and coordination with the professionals should take place through Social Media. Students can blog on their project's progress, and communicate with the professionals through the comments function. With this scenario, students exercise collaboration in virtual teams in a business context.

Recruit professionals and experts from companies or research institutions to assist students in projects and give advice to them. Social Media should be used for the discussions and consulting activities. Students should engage with the experts frequently, so the latter ones can either fill the expert's role or become mentors in the Community of Practice (CoP) built in this scenario. Here, students will experience how important the different roles in a CoP are.

Advanced students can assist new or intermediate students with their projects by e.g. recording videos or blogging about relevant topics, by giving advice and sharing relevant information and knowledge. Advanced students will be experts in this scenario, whereas the new and intermediate students will have to take care of their personal knowledge management and learning while at the same time they are forming a CoP together with the expert students who also function as mentors.

Expert Collaboration and Community of Practice

In this scenario, students are also assigned to work on projects in small groups. The project is revolved around professional online communities and groups, as can be found on professional networking platforms like LinkedIn.com. Students should follow conversations in one or more groups carefully and gather the information and knowledge. In a second step, they can start their own discussion thread asking for input from the community for the projects. In the meantime, students can blog about the project's progress or share status messages on Twitter. As a final step, students could create a whitepaper which can be made available as an ebook, promoted through their blogs and on Twitter.

Knowledge Sharing through Social Media

Try an experiment: Teach students the very basic definitions and theories of your subject. Then assign a project to them, which would have originally been a writing assignment and a final presentation of the results. Instead, ask them to present intermediate goals through blog posts, and promote their project through Facebook, Twitter and other channels. The final presentation of the results could take place with a video. Require your students to use Social Media (re)sources only to complete their assignment. Despite the common teaching approach of trying to inflict on students the usage of "trustworthy" sources such as books and academic papers and maybe allowing them to have a look at Wikipedia.org, this scenario aims at supporting students to figure out which online resources are trustworthy and how they can find out whether they are in the first place.

These scenarios are only ideas on how to incorporate PKM and Social Media in traditional learning. Again, I would like to emphasize that it is quite difficult to design detailed teaching scenarios without knowing the topics covered, the IT infrastructure and your teaching approach. As with most Social Media activities, I recommend to be open-minded and creative. Therefore, I suggest you follow the Social Media activities of others (companies, professionals, academics, artists) and feel free to try out with your students what you and they like best.

FUTURE RESEARCH DIRECTIONS

Social Media in the workplace is not a new topic anymore, but at the same time it still subject to development and learning. Many organizations still struggle with a clear Social Media strategy for internal usage and wonder how they can measure the effects of social software supported work. At the same time, a new generation of employees enter the job market and are said to change the way of how organizations work. Although research in this field suggests that 'Generation Y' is not that different from Generation X and the Baby Boomers in technology skills and working or learning habits, the perception of changed working behavior in younger employees already has an impact. To determine the effects of social media in organizations and on (Personal) Knowledge Management, further research is required. Important questions to be clarified are, e.g. how do motivational triggers change when knowledge management activities become a natural part of project and team work? How does intrinsic motivation take effect if Personal Knowledge Management is translated from theoretical suggestions into individual attitude and behavior?

Another topic which should be strongly considered for Social Media in higher education is the emerging trend of Gamification. Serious games are also the next big thing in adult education and professional training. Small learning units, Apps for mobile devices and increasingly social learning games draw on social networking effects and on community concepts.

CONCLUSION

In this chapter, I discussed the implications and challenges of post-industrialism and knowledge work for (first-time) employees. Knowledge workers are paid to find solutions to their organizations challenges and create new products or optimize processes in accelerated production and innovation cycles. Managers have changed from supervisors into people managers and mentors (Romhardt, 1998) and employees manage themselves. At the same time, they experience a shift from employer-responsibility to personal responsibility for their own professional development, training, and careers. Prerequisite for employees' professional success is the awareness of how important knowledge sharing and collaboration is. Social Media offers an extensive tool set for these purposes and companies expect employees to know how to make best use of them. Therefore, students should develop Social Media skills in higher education in order to be well-prepared when they join the job market. However, it is vital to acknowledge that technology skills are not enough. Social Media usage will only be sufficient if individuals possess social skills and a professional attitude towards learning and working. Personal Knowledge Management offers a structured approach for the development of these competencies. In combination with Social Media usage, Personal Knowledge Management provides a powerful set of approaches and strategies for knowledge workers' personal development and success.

In order to make the most of Social Media in higher education, students should be encouraged to discover tools and information resources beyond Wikipedia.org and other established resources. University lecturers and professors should offer students a certain freedom to find out what they want to learn, based on what they think will foster their personal development and on emerging topics. They should be able to learn what is possible with different Social Media tools, e.g. use a blog for documentation of learning or project progress. Students will have to adopt a critical attitude towards the reliability and and quality of websites. Furthermore, data security and data privacy is an important issue and young people should know which information can be shared online and how they can actively control their digital footprints. Another vital aspect is the one

of learning from a social network. Mentors and mentees, fellow members of Communities of Practice and thought leaders or enthusiasts who can be approached online can contribute a lot to individual competence development. The extra effort in such teaching approaches and personal activities is beneficial: "[Students] gained more from their studies and other aspects of the college experience when they devoted more time and energy to certain tasks that required more effort than others—studying, interacting with their peers and teachers about substantive matters, applying their learning to concrete situations and tasks in different contexts, and so forth" (Kuh 2009).

Students and future employees experience more job satisfaction from increased creativity through the free use of different social media. Andrew McAfee, principal researcher at MIT Sloan cites his colleague David Weinberger in his blog post on Enterprise 2.0: "The real change here is that people now have a much greater voice inside the enterprise. They don't have to work only within the confines of their cubicle, or their work group, or their job description." (McAfee, 2011) and he concludes: "Enterprise 2.0 is a welcome development. When it's working well, it makes people more central and leaves organizations better off." Higher education does well to prepare students for these modern work scenarios.

REFERENCES

Association of American Colleges and Universities (AAC&U). (2007). *College learning for the new global century: A report from the National Leadership Council for Liberal Education and America's Promise*. Washington, DC: AAC&U.

Bennett, S., Maton, K., & Kervin, L. (2008). The 'digital natives' debate: A critical review of the evidence. *British Journal of Educational Technology*, *39*(5), 775–786. doi:10.1111/j.1467-8535.2007.00793.x

Charles, K. (2011). Facebook stress linked to number of 'friends'. Edinburgh Napier University - News, Media and Events. Retrieved March 11, 2012, from http://www.napier.ac.uk/media/Pages/NewsDetails.aspx?NewsID=187

Cheong, R. K. F., & Tsui, E. (2010). The roles and values of personal knowledge management: An exploratory study. *Vine*, *40*(2), 204–227. doi:10.1108/03055721011050686

Choo, C. W. (2003). Perspectives on managing knowledge in organizations. In Williamson, N. J., & Beghtol, C. (Eds.), *Knowledge organization and classification in international information retrieval* (pp. 205–220). Binghamton, NY: Haworth Press.

Davenport, T. H., & Prusak, L. (1998). *Working knowledge: How organizations manage what they know*. Cambridge, MA: Harvard Business School Press.

Dörner, D. (1979). *Problemlösen als Informationsverarbeitung*. Stuttgart, Germany: Kohlhammer.

Florida, R. (2006). *The rise of the creative class*. New York, NY: Basic books.

Fuchs-Kittowski, F. (2007). Integrierte IT-Unterstützung der Wissensarbeit. Köln, Germany: Eul.

Herring, S. D. (2001). Faculty acceptance of the World Wide Web for student research. *College & Research Libraries*, *62*(5), 251–258.

Higgison, S. (2004). Your say: Personal knowledge management. *Knowledge Management Magazine*, *7*(7), 11–12.

Koch, M. (2008). *CSCW and enterprise 2.0 - Towards an integrated perspective. 21st Bled eConference eCollaboration: Overcoming Boundaries through Multi-Channel Interaction* (pp. 416–427). Slovenia: Bled.

Koch, M., & Richter, A. (2009). *Enterprise 2.0: Planung, Einführung und erfolgreicher Einsatz von Social Software in Unternehmen*. Munich, Germany: Oldenbourg. doi:10.1524/9783486593648

Kuh, G. D. (2009). What student affairs professionals need to know about student engagement. *Journal of College Student Development*, *50*(6), 683–706. doi:10.1353/csd.0.0099

Kvavik, R. B., Caruso, J. B., & Morgan, G. (2004). *ECAR study of students and information technology 2004: convenience, connection, and control*. EDUCAUSE Center for Applied Research. Retrieved March 11, 2012, from http://net.educause.edu/ir/library/pdf/ERS0405/ekf0405.pdf

McAfee, A. (2006). Enterprise 2.0: The dawn of emergent collaboration. *MIT Sloan Management Review*, *47*(3), 21–28.

McAfee, A. (2011). Enterprise 2 at 5. *Andrew McAfee's blog: The business impact of IT*. Retrieved February 28, 2012, from http://andrewmcafee.org/2011/06/enterprise-2-at-5/

Nehm, K. (2009). Social software categories. Enterprise 2.0 blog: Discussing the collaborative enterprise. Retrieved March 11, 2012, from http://enterprise20blog.com/all/2009/08/19/social-software-categories/

Nonaka, I., & Konno, N. (1998). The concept of 'Ba': Building a foundation for knowledge creation. *California Management Review*, *40*(3), 40–54. doi:10.2307/41165942

Pfiffner, M., & Stadelmann, P. (1998). *Wissen wirksam machen – Wie Kopfarbeiter produktiv werden*. Bern, Germany: Haupt.

Reich, J., Murnane, R., & Willett, J. (2012). The state of wiki usage in U.S. K–12 schools. Leveraging Web 2.0 data warehouses to assess quality and equity in online learning environments. *Educational Researcher*, *41*(1), 7–15. doi:10.3102/0013189X11427083

Skyrme, D. (1999). *Knowledge networking: Creating the collaborative enterprise*. Boston, MA: Butterworth Heinemann.

Smedley, J. K. (2009). Modelling personal knowledge management. *OR Insight, 22*(4), 221–233. doi:10.1057/ori.2009.11

Vince, R. (1998). Behind and beyond Kolb's learning cycle. *Journal of Management Education, 22*(3), 304–319. doi:10.1177/105256299802200304

Weiler, A. (2004). Information-seeking behavior in Generation Y students: Motivation, critical thinking, and learning theory. *Journal of Academic Librarianship, 31*(1), 46–53. doi:10.1016/j. acalib.2004.09.009

ADDITIONAL READING

Florida, R. (2006). *The rise of the creative class*. New York, NY: Basic Books.

Garvin, D. A. (2002). *Building a learning organization. Harvard Business Review on Knowledge Management* (pp. 47–80). Boston, MA: Harvard Business School Press.

Head, A. J. (2012). Alison J. Head on modeling the information-seeking process of college students in the digital age [AUDIO]. MediaBerkman: Berkman Center for Internet & Society Podcast. Retrieved March 10, 2012, from blogs.law.harvard. edu/mediaberkman/2012/01/10/alison-j-head-on-modeling-the-information-seeking-process-of-college-students-in-the-digital-age-audio

Higgison, S. (2012). Your say: Personal knowledge management. InsideKnowledge, 7(7). Retrieved March 10, 2012, from http://www.ikmagazine. com/xq/asp/sid.0/articleid.DDDD6EE3-47C6-49CD-9070-F1B1547FD29F/eTitle.Your_say_Personal_knowledge_management/qx/display. htm

Mazer, J. P., Murphy, R. E., & Simonds, C. J. (2007). I'll see you on "Facebook": The effects of computer-mediated teacher self-disclosure on student motivation, affective learning, and classroom climate. *Communication Education, 56*(1), 1–17. doi:10.1080/03634520601009710

Nonaka, I. (2002). *The knowledge-creating company. Harvard Business Review on Knowledge Management* (pp. 21–46). Boston, MA: Harvard Business School Press.

Reich, J. (2012). RB 192: Wikis, teaching, and the digital divide. MediaBerkman: Berkman Center for Internet & Society Podcast, 192. Retrieved March 10, 2012, from http://blogs.law.harvard. edu/mediaberkman/2012/03/01/rb-192-wikis-teaching-and-the-digital-divide/

Weinberger, D. (2012). *Too big to know*. New York, NY: Basic Books.

KEY TERMS AND DEFINITIONS

Community of Practice: Loosely bound group of people in which learning from shared experience, mutual guidance and practical support takes place. CoPs are not a new phenomenon, however, in dynamic and virtual organizations, they constitute a reflective sounding board and a reliable network for employees.

Enterprise 2.0: Organizations that use social software internally and externally, accordingly change their structures and develop new market strategies based on Web 2.0 approaches are called Enterprise 2.0.

Generation Y: Cohort of people born in the late seventies or early eighties until the early 2000s. These people have grown up with the Internet and modern technology and are said to be changing how organizations work with a different attitude towards working and learning.

Organizational Knowledge Management: A dynamic framework of processes, strategy and software to manage information and knowledge within an organization with the objective of bringing the right people together and to support them in their work.

Personal Development: Personal development focusses on individual learning and competence development, employability, social skills and finding a role in society.

Personal Knowledge Management: Strategies and approaches for managing personal information and knowledge with (software) tools and through social network relations.

Social Media/Social Software: Web-based and mobile technologies which allow the creation and exchange of user-generated content and support building and maintaining personal relationships.

Chapter 8

Usage of Social Media by Children and Teenagers:
Results of EU KIDS Online II

Anca Velicu
Institute of Sociology, Romanian Academy, Romania

Valentina Marinescu
University of Bucharest, Romania

ABSTRACT

This chapter presents the results of EU Kids Online II project about the children's and adolescent's uses of the social network sites. The results showed both the main differences and similarities regarding this issue both at the European and at the country (i.e. Romania) level. Although at the European level one can notice the emergence of different groups of users, in Romania, the use of the Internet is only at the beginning and has no clear pattern. The individual characteristics in the self-efficacy variant positively vary with the using of SNS and, at the same time, none of the negative individual characteristics predicts the possessing of a profile on a social network. The strongest connection exists between having competences regarding the use of the Internet and owning a profile on a social network. Moreover, the results agree with previous researches that highlight a complex influence of the parental mediation on the social behaviors.

INTRODUCTION

Perfectly reproducing the structure of the Internet (the multiple-knot one), the social networks have become a sine qua non element of the everyday life for many of the Internet users almost all over the world. Recent results suggest that 73% of the teens and children who use the Internet also use SNS (Pew Research, 2010). In this situation, no wonder the research regarding this phenomenon is so diverse, dealing, one at a time, with issues such as: the time allocated to this activity, the new civic activism the social networks are launching, the issue of creating an identity, network analysis

DOI: 10.4018/978-1-4666-2970-7.ch008

with the purpose of learning how many people can be truly managed in a "friends list" and the distortions of the concept of friendship (Livingstone, 2008), the growth of sociability as a result of this use (or, in reverse, social isolation from the real world the "addiction" to these networks leads to), the new marketing and P.R. opportunities (Solis & Breakenridge, 2009) etc.

However, when these networks are used by children and teenagers, there are certain differences in both the usage patterns and the new issues that appear. For example, regarding the patterns, the studies show that while adults use SNS rather to meet new people, teenagers do it in order to consolidate their existing relations (boyd, 2007, 122). On the other hand, as soon as children and teenagers enter the arena of relating to media (Barker & Petley, 2001), the discussions, of any kind, are especially centered around the issue and from the perspective of protection, the new emerging issues being those regarding the risks and, also, the opportunities. Just as we will show hereinafter in greater detail, risks are usually associated with: the time consuming aspect of using the Internet, and, implicitly, the SNS, which takes the issue of addiction to the extreme (Young, 1998; Young, 2004), the issue of coming into contact with strangers ('meeting stranger') with different implications, cyberbullying, sexting, individual health issues that can turn into public health issues (infantile obesity) etc. On the other hand, as far as opportunities are concerned, researchers talk about the development, in children, of the ability to socialize from the safety of the physical and symbolic distance (and, sometimes, that of anonymity) that computer mediated communication imposes (Tynes, 2007; Rosen, 2006; Diaconescu, Barbovschi, Baciu, 2008). Also, some authors talk about the opportunities of initiating and experiencing certain behavior and age specific emotions, in a relatively safe way, the Internet brings.

The data that was analyzed in this chapter were taken from a European study realized in 2010, that is EU Kids Online, the first study, to our knowledge, ever to use the same methodology for researching the issue of Internet using by 9-16 year old children from 25 states.

REVIEWING THE SPECIALTY LITERATURE

Just as many authors point out, (boyd, 2007, Valkenburg & Peter, 2011, Baker & White, 2010, Holmes, 2009), the research regarding the use of SNS by the youth (from the frequency and motivation of the usage to the opportunities and risks involved) have different and, sometimes, even conflicting results. For example, the motivation of the popularity of SNS among youth has changed in time (boyd, 2007) due to two main reasons: (1) Due to the short history of SNS (Lampe, Ellison, & Steinfield, 2008) and (2) Due to the fast changes at the level of the Internet in general, that accompanied the history of SNSs. As far as the first observation is concerned, even though boyd does not give us an explanatory model for these differences as far as the motivations of usage are concerned, they can be found in the model of the social formation of using a new technology offered by Breton and Proulx (2002). This model, which proposes the understanding of a new technology as a co-operation, a hybrid between the manufacturers and the users, stipulates the existence of three distinct moments, characterized by distinct types of usage, when a new technology appears: (1) The issuing and adoption by the first users; (2) The innovation or the articulation phase of the technical object concept as a result of usage, the phase in which different types of usage can appear, that are not in accordance with the initial concept, such as 'le deplacement' (the transfer), 'l'adaptation' (the adjustment), l'extension (the extension) and le detournement (the rerouting); and 3. The individual appropriation, but at the weight scale of the new technology, phase that is rather seen as individual and subjective as opposed to the first phases, considered to be rather political and collective (Breton & Proulx, 2002, 260-273). Based on this model we can understand that, if in the initial phase, 'By early 2006, many considered participation on the key social network site, MySpace, essential to being seen as cool at school' (boyd, 2007, 119) this was true because the SNS were in the incipient phase of issuing and adjusting. In the same way, we can understand the penetration of the 'copy/ paste culture in using MySpace' as boyd calls it (2007, 128) borrowing the term from Penkel (2006), as being the type of usage in which one no longer stays within the editing functions offered by the program for creating a profile and, with the help of certain programming and coding elements, one personalizes their profile outside the site's 'offer' by default; we would be dealing with, according to the above mentioned model, the innovation phase in which the orientation or the applications are re-routed. And, finally, we can thus understand the third type of usage, studied in the last years (see also Lampe, Ellison, & Steinfield, 2008), together with the generalization of the SNS usage among youth, the usage motivation of which must be researched at an individual level, especially in the perspective of building an identity (boyd, 2007; Valkenburg & Peter, 2011; Valkenburg, Schouten & Peter, 2005).

Regarding the second reason for dealing with unequal and sometimes conflicting studies regarding the use of SNSs, namely the changes undergone by the Internet, we can mention as essential element the democratization of Internet access, together with transferring the research emphasis from discussions on digital divide in terms of access (Wilson, Wallin, & Reiser, 2003), to discussions on digital divide in terms of competences (van Deursen, van Dijk, & Peters, 2011; van Deursen & van Dijk, 2011; van Dijk, 2009) and participation (boyd, 2007, Sharples et al., 2009). These new types of digital divide must be differentiated, as improving them requires different politics. If for the generalization of digital skills and digital knowledge a digital literacy supported policy is sufficient, the issue of the division at a participative

level requires an ideological assuming of a position. Thus, boyd (2007) shows that 'participation divide' can be structured in two components: 1. Teenagers that have unlimited internet access and those that have occasional internet and implicitly SNS access; but this inequality is about to become extinct and 2. The divide regarding the participation in the public life/sphere of teenagers and adults. The latter is more problematic because its improvement requires political will, as it is not due to a factual status but to an ideological concept about childhood and adolescence (Buckingham, 2000, boyd, 2007, Sharples et al., 2009). Also, the stake of this 'participation divide' is a major one and it refers to the civic education of children and teenagers in order to participate in the life of the city (Lim & Nekmat, 2008; Sharples et al., 2009; Valkenburg & Peter, 2009, Livingstone, 2004).

For a better positioning in front of the challenges set before the researchers by the use of SNS by children and teenagers, we will focus first on the more general issue of Internet and children and then on the use of SNS by this specific public group.

A FEW GENERAL DATA REGARDING THE USE OF INTERNET BY CHILDREN AND TEENAGERS

According to the academic research (Livingstone, 2003), the typical use of Internet by children and teenagers takes p lace along three dimensions: (1) fun, (2) education, and (3) what is actually called "edutainment". A fourth category is introduced in the analysis by the approach from a marketing perspective (Tufte, 2006) – the one of "active consumership", children being seen as on-line commerce customers and members of an audience of virtual commercials. This *typology of internet users* is confirmed by geographically dispersed studies (OIVO, 2008; Valcke, Decraene, 2007; Vandebosch, Van Cleemput, Mortelmans, Walrave, 2006).

In addition, the characteristics of children's and teenagers' on-line behavior can be summarized as follows:

1. The place where children and teenagers most frequently use the Internet from is their home (Huang, 2002; Ye, 2003; Valcke, Bonte, De Wever, Rots, 2010). However, Li (2004) promotes the idea that there is a difference between the children and teenagers categories at the different levels of the educational system, as far as the variety of the locations from where they use the Internet is concerned.

2. As far as the purposes for which children and teenagers use the Internet, the on-line games and collecting information rank first (Huang, 2002; Liu, 2003). In addition, the survey done by Li (2004) also shows a residential segmentation between girls and boys regarding the purpose for which they use the Internet. However, this data is contradicted by other research, such as Chang's study (2003) according to which the gender and residential zone have no impact whatsoever on the on-line behavior of children and teenagers.

3. As far as the time allocated to Internet is concerned, children and teenagers spend between one and three hours on-line daily (Liu, 2003) and the significant differences between various sub-groups do not show in the case of the children and teenagers who spend less than an hour a day on the Internet (Huang, 2003).

IMPLICATIONS

From the perspective of children's and teenagers' health, the research showed that spending time in front of the computer is a sedentary activity, practiced on a large scale by children and teenagers. As a result, longer periods of time spent in front of the computer and especially on the Internet are associated with a higher level of body weight (Mutz, Roberts, van Vuuren, 1993) which leads to an increased risk of obesity for this age group (Barnett, O'Loughlin, Sabiston et al, 2010). A research realized in Finland shows that the frequent computer activities have been a risk factor for neck and shoulder pain and for back pain in the case of the teenagers involved in the research (Hakala, Rimpela, Saarni, Salminen, 2006). According to a different set of data, the more time children spend watching TV and playing computer games, the less they sleep (Heins, Seitz, Schuz et al., 2007; Knutson, Lauderdale, 2009).

As far as the learning process is concerned, the studies under the "theory of replacing" reach relatively conflicting results. Some research say that even though medium or reduced Internet using can promote performance and positive behavior by social learning, "heavy using" can replace the time spent studying, reading, playing and socially interacting and can lead to poor school results and a higher level of isolation, a lower self-esteem and the incapacity to relate to others (Calvert, 2002; Lee, Peng, 2006; Subrahmanyam et al., 2001). It is thus considered that the use of Internet by children and teenagers for school purposes has, for elementary and middle school children, certain positive aspects (Padilla-Walker, Nelson, Carroll, Jensen, 2010), such as a longer time dedicated to reading and, indirectly, higher grades at reading and Math tests (Attewell et al., 2003). On the other hand, other studies show that computer gaming is associated to lower school performance (Willoughby, 2008; Jaruratanasirikul, Wongwaitaweewong, Sangsupawanich, 2009).

THE USE OF SNS BY YOUTH

1. About Users and Non-Users of SNS

An interesting study orientation regarding the virtual social networks is the analysis users vs. non-users. According to the analysis dedicated to this topic, Hargittai (2007) shows that there are small significant demographic differences between these two categories. According to this research, (Hargittai, 2007) gender seems to be an important predictor, with a 1.6 higher probability for girls to use social network sites compared to boys. Also, Internet access through friends or family has a significant predictive power on the probability for a child or teenager to use social network sites. However, Hargittai shows (2007), that other traditional indicators, such as race or the parents' level of education do not have significant correlations with the use of social network sites. The same study (Hargittai, 2007) points out the tendency for these virtual social networks to be adopted by masses of people, given the existence of a minimum number of systemic inequalities regarding the access to social network sites among the children and teenagers involved in the research. Even though the majority of such sites claim to be international, the research showed that there are, in fact, preferences at national and even race level, for one or the other SNSs. The results have thus indicated the apparition of some significant correlations between a child's or teenager's race and the distinct community the member of which he was off-line (Hargittai, 2007, boyd, 2007). For example, unlike Caucasian children and teenagers, for the Hispanics the probability to use MySpace was higher and the probability to use Facebook smaller. Similarly, there is a higher probability for Asian children and teenagers to use Xanga and Friendster. Hargittai noticed that the off-line inequalities can persist on-line in the case of the various communities of children and teenagers (Hargittai, 2007). Also, even though SNS are seen as offering an open space, that would do away with the boundaries, many of the SNS willingly narrow their audience thus becoming niche media, either in order to build an identity of intimate community (Facebook at first), either in order to build an elitist identity or due to targeting a certain audience (boyd, 2007). Also, in the cultural spaces where society is very structured on social

classes, such as the caste system in India, these are transferred by the users at the level of the SNS (Orkut, especially), inter-caste socializing being prohibited by the users (boyd, 2007).

In the course of time the question regarding the existence of some distinct groups that have special access to the new communication technologies was part of the research on the "digital divide". But considering "digital divide" as simply opposing and deriving from the access to the respective technology is still not very clear, as long as access in itself can be conceptualized in different ways (Selwyn, 2004, Van Dijk, 2000, Steyaert, 2002). In general four dimensions are mentioned, but in different studies these are different. Van Dijk proposes: psychological access, material access, skills access, usage access while Steyaert starts with the physical access in order to get to the informational one. The majority of the studies suggested though that, even though the spread of technology may have seemed at some point as being the main issue, in the long run the real issues that should be taken into consideration at the level of public policies are the ones regarding the "technology-illiteracy" and "information-illiteracy", the discussion about the digital divide actually going back to the older discussion elaborated in the "knowledge gap theory" (Steyaert, 2002; van Dijk, Hacker, 2000; DiMaggio, Hargitte, 2001). Once technology was generalized, this theoretical context become irrelevant, however a reminiscent of actuality of the issue regarding the differences in the use of the internet still remaining. Thus we move from the concept of "digital divide" to that of "digital inequality" (DiMaggio, Hargitte, 2001; Stiakakis et al., 2009) defined as "inequality among persons with formal access to the Internet" (DiMaggio, Hargitte, 2001). Despite all current interest in the matter, the studies from the perspective of the "digital divide" dedicated to children and teenagers are relatively few. A first axis of differentiating the using of the Internet by children and teenagers is the age variable. Thus, for social network sites there is a high probability that these sites are used by older children (14–17 years old) compared to younger children (12–13 years old) (Steinberg, Albert, Cauffman, 2008). According to the research realized by Centre de Recherche et d'Information des Organisations de Consommateurs (OIVO, 2008), the interest children show in on-line games is dominant for the 10-12 year old age group, the next favored activities being chatting, social networking and the commercial using of the Internet. Starting with the age of 13 social networking dominates in the hierarchy of Internet users (OIVO, 2008). The second axis of differentiating Internet using is the axis of gender. Gros (2004) notices that girls use the Internet more for social networking or chatting while boys tend to focus more on entertainment games and activities (Lenhart, Madden, Macgill, Smith, 2007). Some studies state that boys tend to have more friends on SNS as compared to girls (Raacke, Bonds-Raacke, 2008), while other studies reach opposite results (Pfeil, Arjan, Zaphiris, 2009). Moreover, the results show that boys assume more risks that have to do with the revealing of personal information (Fogel, Nehmad, 2009; Jelicic, Bobek, Phelps, Lerner, Lerner, 2007). Also, a study shows that more girls use MySpace – 55% - compared to boys – 45% (Wilkinson, Thelwall, 2010).

As far as the race variable is concerned, Ahn (2011) examined a representative teenagers group ages 12-17 from a survey done in 2007 by Pew Internet and American Life. If we keep under control other factors, there is a higher probability for Afro-American teenagers to use virtual SNSs compared to their white colleagues.

As we were saying above, the fact that the SNS have a short history can be directly seen in the apparent contradiction in the data offered by the studies. Yet, at structural level, as a typology that is independent from the percentages given at one moment or another or from one cultural space to another, we will say that there are two major types of SNS non-users among teenagers: (1) 'disenfranchised teens' and (2) 'conscientious objector' (boyd, 2007, 121). In the first type, as the name itself tells us, are the ones who do not willingly choose this behavior of non-users, the behavior being the result of a limitation (restricted access to technology or to this kind of sites from some public access places or an interdiction imposed by parents or overseers). The age or the development of technology and the increased access to technology, cost wise, solve, in time, this problem. The second group contains, if we may say so, the "active non-user"; the one who willingly chooses not to use SNS. The motivations are diverse, as boyd shows (2007, 121): 1. In order to protest politically (especially in the North-American space and with direct reference to MySpace which was taken over by a media corporation, the protest being thus against the respective corporation); 2. Based on "obedience" reasons, in the case of those youth who accept and assume the opinions of the adults regarding the risks afferent to SNS[1]; 3. Due to the existence of a contradiction between self-image and the behavior afferent to using SNS (they either have a too low self-esteem and thus don't dare perform the respective behavior ('I am not cool enough for SNS), or they have a too good self-esteem ('I am too cool for SNS).

An interesting issue in the research regarding the use of SNS by youth lays in the conceptualization of 'non-using'. Even though it seems obvious, this varies in the course of time. Thus, especially in the beginning, this was defined as the lack of a personal profile[2] (boyd, 2007). Together with the generalization of this behavior among teenagers, there are studies that consider the "SNS user" to be that person who accesses the network at least two times a day[3] (Baker & White, 2010).

2. On the Motivation of Using SNS

Another way to find the answer to the question "who are the users?" is to find the reason they use SNS. As we argued above, the changes undergone by SNS since their apparition (a little before the beginning of the millennium) until this era of relative stabilization of their use, makes the motivation found by the surveys fluctuate from one period to another, namely in those important aspects, such as that of 'meeting strangers', considered as having a major risk potential for teenagers (Subrahmanyam & Greenfield, 2008; Valkenburg & Peter, 2011). For this reason precisely, beyond the factual data gathered in the course of time by different surveys, another strategy to understand the motivation for using SNSs was, based on the technical characteristics of SNSs, to infer upon the users (Lampe, Ellison, & Steinfield, 2008), spheres that influence the attraction potential, the usage patterns being mentioned also: anonymity, asynchronicity and accessibility (Valkenburg & Peter, 2011, Valkenburg, Schouten, & Peter, 2005) or persistence, searchability, replicability, and invisible audiences.' (boyd, 2007, boyd & Ellison, 2007). Also, for the potential of SNSs in education, the basic characteristics required would be those of 'trust' and 'privacy' (Griffith & Liyanage, 2008). Thus, Valkenburg and his colleagues (2005, 2011) showed how the three characteristics influence directly and positively (in terms of increasing the controllability over them) two of the essential abilities in the process of expressing/communicating namely self-disclosure and self-presentation (Valkenburg & Peter, 2009, Valkenburg & Peter, 2011, Walther, 1996). The possibility for youth to take control over these two aspects fundamentally improves the communication process by giving them the possibility to practice it, from the safety of anonymity, asynchronicity and accessibility (Valkenburg & Peter, 2011).

On the other hand, seeing SNS communication as a type of mediated communication (as opposed to the unmediated one) and, more, a type of networking communication, boyd (2007) talks about its characteristics of replicability, persistence and invisible audience, given by its quality of mediated communication and searchability, as a result of its networking communication characteristic. All these characteristics turn SNS communication into an essential type of public communication that teenagers use (and as a form of exercising for the moment they will enter the public space, generally destined to adults. Thus, hiding behind first instance motivations such as "to maintain

connections with their friends" (boyd, 2007, 126), is in fact a more elaborate process that, through attempt and error, allows public access for the young man under at least three of the aspects of this concept. The popularity of SNS among youth and the profound motivation for access, especially in the American space, is the fact that "they seek access to adult society. Their participation is deeply rooted in their desire to engage publicly" (boyd, 2007, 137). Even though this "publicly" is in fact a type of 'hyperpublic' opened by the star-system, this process is essential for youth in their socializing with the norms and rules of the society and it is greatly prohibited, or at least disapproved, by adults due to a profoundly ideological concept regarding childhood and adolescence on one hand, and the idea of privacy on the other hand (boyd, 2007).

As far as the motivation for using SNS at the level of specific data is concerned, according to the study from 2006 "Parent and Teens" (Lenhart, 2007) the main reason for using SNS for boys was to maintain contact with friends (91%) and start new friendships (49%) (Lenhart, 2007). However, in the same study, girls chose to use these sites rather to maintain their pre-existing friendships than to make new ones (Lenhart, 2007). As far as the age variable is concerned, the main motivation for the 11-15 year olds to use SNSs is not to start new friendships but to maintain the pre-existing ones (Barker, 2009; Ellison, Steinfield & Lampe, 2007; Subrahmanyam, Reich & Waechter, 2008).

The introducing of the "social capital" variables into the analysis shows that some individual psychological characteristics (such as timidity, self-respect and narcissism) are connected to the type of behavior adopted by children and teenagers within SNSs (Barker, 2009; Buffardi & Campbell, 2008; Zywica & Danowski, 2008; Steinfield, Ellison & Lampe, 2008). As far as the relation between social learning and the participation of children and teenagers in SNS is concerned, studies show that SNSs develop new abilities regarding technology. For example, Jenkins (2006) notices that different abilities become vital in the spaces within the network, such as the capacity to collaborate with others, to adopt changing identities when someone navigates on different communities or the capacity to explore new fields of knowledge when someone has an important stock of information available. Other research show that children and teenagers find creative ways to gain access to and participate in the life of different online communities, these on-line activities stimulating them in their learning when there are subjects that they are interested in (Ito et al., 2010). Teenagers also use SNSs in order to offer their colleagues social support (Williams & Merten, 2009), to share their creative work with others and to relate with one another (Greenhow & Robelia, 2009).

In a review of the literature on SNS and the young public, Valkenburg and Peter (2011) show that there are three areas where the impact of SNS on children can be studied: 1. The area of identity; 2. The area of intimacy and 3. The area of sexuality. A number of issues were studied for each of these areas and sometimes the solutions were formulated in opposing hypotheses. Thus, in the area of identity, the studied issues were: 1. Self-esteem and 2. Self-concept clarity, the latter generating two opposing hypotheses: a. the hypothesis of fragmentation and b. the hypothesis of self-concept unity. In the area of intimacy, the studies issues were: 1. Forming new friendships, with two explanatory hypotheses: a. The rich get richer hypothesis (Ellison, Steinfield, & Lampe, 2007; Valkenburg & Peter, 2009; Vergeer & Pelzer, 2009) and b. The social compensation hypothesis and 2. The issue of the quality of existing friendships, with the alternative hypotheses: a. Displacement hypothesis (Al-Saggaf, 2011) and b. Stimulation hypothesis (Young, 2011).

Regarding the consequences of youth using SNS, especially those at the level of school activity, the supported positions are divergent, the debated being on the two hypotheses we've already met: the hypothesis of efficiency (a variant of the stimulation hypothesis) – according to which Internet leads to a growth in the efficiency of human activity, the individuals having more

time for socializing and recreation (Robinson, Kestnbaum, Neustadtl & Alvarez, 2000) – and the hypothesis of replacing ("displacement hypothesis"), according to which using the Internet is an activity that isolates the individual, time being a limited resource, so that using the Internet is not complementary with other activities but in competition with them (Nie et al., 2002). The "displacement theory" says that individuals have a limited period of time available and if this time capital is used for realizing a single type of activity, such as media connected activities, then people have a lot less time for other social activities and they end up neglecting them or not do them at all (Neuman, 1991).

Regarding the relation between the use of Internet by children and teenagers and their engaging in other off-line activities, the displacement hypothesis postulates that the more time the child or teenager will spend with the media, the less time they will spend doing other activities considerate to be important for the health and welfare of this age group, including here reading for pleasure, studying, playing outside the house, sleeping and participating in outdoor games (Lee & Eddie, 2002).

In the course of time there have been elaborated certain theoretical interpretations regarding the reasons for the apparition of this "displacement" caused by media. According to the "marginal activities hypothesis" an important explanatory factor is the perception of the social importance associated to an activity, media users being able to sacrifice those activities they perceive as marginal in favor of media (Brown 1974, apud. Endestad et al., 2011: 20). The "functional likeness" hypothesis states, on the other hand, that children and teenagers give up the activities they appreciate as being less satisfying of their needs and choose, instead, the more efficient alternatives (Hornik 1981, apud. Endestad et al., 2011: 20). Another motivation is offered by the hypothesis "the more, the more", a variant of "the rich get richer" hypothesis (Meyersohn 1968, apud. Endestad et al., 2011: 20), according to which the more active and dynamic the children and teenagers are, the higher the tendency to engage in new activities, such as using media. At a general level, the analyses under the "displacement" theory focused mainly on identifying the negative effects of using the Internet and did not emphasize the differences between different categories of users. Moreover, some authors believe that this theory is rather specific to the beginnings of the SNSs or to a compulsive/additive using, and it cannot be proved in the case of the current and moderate using of SNSs (Valkenburg & Peter, 2011).

3. The Using of SNS and School Results

A common question found in the studies dedicated to the relation between the Internet and children and teenagers is whether the new technologies influence the learning process. Research agree on the fact that a media device in itself does not influence learning (Clark, 1983; Clark, 1991), showing that these devices used in the didactic process do not improve nor do they have a negative influence on learning when compared to the human teaching strategies used in the classroom (Bernard et al., 2004; Clark, 1983; Clark, 1991). What matters is not the computer but the learning behaviors that show inside the software or the educational program.

A research realized by Ben-David and Kolikant (2009) shows that today's pupils live inside two value systems regarding the Internet and making it useful and adequate for learning purposes. Outside school pupils are taught to interact with information by means of collaboration and brico-lage (Brown, 2000: 14): "Today's kids get on the Web and link, lurk, and watch how other people are doing things, then try it themselves".

'Produsaging' (Bonk, 2009) or 'prosuming' (Lim & Nekmat, 2008), sharing (Bonk, 2009) and the so-called "culture of sharing" (Passig, 2003; Passig, 2007) are the main attributes valued by the users of the new communication technologies. On the other hand, in school pupils come into

contact with the independent learning, learning that belongs to a single person (Perkins, 1992; Shaffer & Clinton, 2006) and which cannot be shared, in which case the partnership cu others is legitimate but only with the purpose of acquiring more information which will be used individually.

In a complex study on what pupils, teachers and parents think regarding the using of web 2.0 in education, it is shown that using social media in school education can take the form of collective blogs (it increases the capacity of team work and of collaborating for a project), the wiki system allows for bi-directionality between information and pupil (the pupil can become a source of information not only a consumer; the responsibility and self-esteem grow) and sharing of online resources (Sharples et al., 2009). Also, many authors warn against a correct evaluation between the acceptability of certain risks implied by web 2.0 and the benefits it brings to education (Griffith & Liyanage, 2008; Sharples et al., 2009; Tynes, 2007), showing that these exist on two axis: pupil-pupil and pupil-teacher.

However it is considered that the way the digital immersion influences children and teenagers, especially how it influences their education experience (Bennett, Maton & Kervin, 2008) is a relatively little known topic. Livingstone and Bober (2004) suggests that children and teenagers who use the Internet daily have many benefits from the on-line activities, that is why there is a higher probability for them to use different forms of digital media in the future process of learning. The studies regarding the engagement of children and teenagers in digital media tend to focus on risks and benefits.

Another approach found in the studies regarding the relation writing/reading and SNS using warns against: (1) The benefits SNS communication has regarding the improving of the reading abilities for children and (2) The multiple common aspects literature has with SNS, from creating the 'persona' within the SNS, to playing with identities' co-substantial to literature (Williams, 2008). Thus, beside the writing/reading abilities that SNS as interactive technology par excellence develops, Williams (2008) underlines, like boyd as a matter of fact (2007), the necessity of performing attempt and error type of activities in the process of creating the identity of youth and that of developing abilities of expressing themselves in society.

The relation between school results and digital media was first analyzed as far as school activities are concerned, connecting the level of knowledge in the area of digital media and the attitudes to its applications in school work (Arafeh et al., 2002). The results show that pupils with great skill in using the Internet use these abilities to do their homework and know the ways they can use the Internet to get advantages in their school activity. Also, the way students view the idea of using the Internet in schools allows them to transfer the traditional school tasks in activities pertaining to Internet (Arafeh et al., 2002). Other studies have suggested that using computers and Internet would lead to the raising of the learning level in certain specific fields, such as Mathematics or Science (Wenglinsky, 1998). Espinosa, Laffey, Whittaker and Sheng (2006) studied the role of technology in the early development of children using data from "Early Childhood Longitudinal Study". Their results show that the access to the new communication technologies contributes to the learning potential of pupils. Lei and Zhao (2005) studied the particularities of the access, admitting that when it comes to using technology and the school performance of children and teenagers, it's not so much about quantity as about quality. Particularly, when the quality of technology using is not carefully monitored or assured, the using of the computer can have rather negative than positive effects on the school performance of pupils... Also, the studies did not show the existence of a relation between computer use and school performance. For example, the research realized by Hunley, Evans, Delgado-Hachey, Krise, Rich and Schell (2005) show that there is no relation between the time allocate to Internet at home and school grades, in the case of the teenagers included in the studied group (Hunley

et al., 2005). Other research discovered that using the Internet for recreation is strongly correlated with unequal school performance (Kubey, Lavin & Barrows, 2001). Approximately 10-15% of the participants in the study of Kubey, Lavin and Barrows (2001) declared that they don't have complete control over the Internet and that this activity has negative effects on their homework. The pupils who declared Internet related issues spent five times more time on-line than those who did not have this problem and the probability for them to sleep less and miss school due to Inernet use was higher. Even though the studied teenagers did not explicitly name the SNS, Kubey, Lavin and Barrows (2001) concluded that not so much Internet itself led to the apparition of these problems as they were the results of the new social opportunities offered by the Internet, given the fact that pupils who declared having problems rather used the Internet for real time social activities, such as instant messaging and chat rooms.

There are more perspectives of approaching the relation between the using of the Internet by children and teenagers and school results. A first direction for the research is dedicated to the analysis of the existing connection between Internet addiction and learning, a few studies emphasizing the influence exercised by technology on school accomplishments (Morgan, 1993; Fetler, 1984; Hancox, Milne & Poulton, 2005). For example, those who frequently watch non-educational TV programs tend to have worse grades in school than those who watch educational TV programs (Anderson, Huston, Schmitt, Linebarger, Wright, 2001). Moreover, another research suggests that girls' school grades tend to be more influenced by excessive media use than those of boys' (Huston, Wright, Marguis, Green, 1999). Kubey, Lavin and Barrows (2001) show that those teenagers who spend more time on non-educational sites are those who tend to have poorer school results.

Karpinski (2009) shows that high-school students who use Facebook have lower grades than students who do not use this SNS. Karpinski offers a few explanations for the results, believing, for example, that it is possible for children and teenagers who use Facebook to spend too much time on-line and dedicate less time to learning. But, once again, the above mentioned results are contradicted by other research. Thus, Kolek and Saunders (2008) did not discover the existence of any connection between using Facebook and the grades obtained by pupils and teenagers in school, which was also confirmed by the study of Pasek, More and Hargittai (2009). More recently, an exploratory survey shows that there is a negative relation between using Facebook and school results, as the latter was measured according to the grades declared by the subjects and the hours spent learning during the week (Karpinski & Duberstein, 2009).

Going beyond the limitations inherent to the studies centered on the analysis between Internet addiction and school performance, the approach from the "media literacy" perspective highlights other aspects of using the Internet in the learning process. Jenkins (2006) notices that today's teenagers must be alphabetized in a few practices within the social media. For example, he defines performance as being the capacity to adopt different identities for the purpose of discovering. The "media literacy" studies suggest that teenagers who practice these abilities in the on-line environment, using social media for accessing certain communities that help them learn and practice some particular abilities inside a specific knowledge field (Ito et al., 2009). On the other hand, there is a variety of new practices of "literacy" that appear among children and teenagers, for example writing on SNS, on blogs, e-mails (Fishman, Lunsford, McGregor, Otuteye, 2005).

Finally, the third perspective on the relation between the using of the Internet by children and teenagers and school performance emphasizes the influence of the so called "school environment" ecosystem.

The research realized by Seo (2004a) indicates the fact that the negative effect of using the Internet is limited only to the category of the "heavy users" and does not exercise its influence on the pupils who use the Internet in general, that is those with a moderate activity. In schools having a high percentage of parents from the "white-collar" category pupils tended to have higher levels of motivation and self-regulation than in other schools. As a result, the socio-economic attributes of pupils in a certain school tend to influence the amount of time allocated to Internet by children and their abilities to use the Internet. Another one of Seo's research shows that the "model centered on the Internet" in the didactic relation would be associated with relatively lower school grades (Seo, 2004b: 66-68). The Internet is a neutral "value-free" technology and environment, but school, which is an environment variable, or motivation, which is a psychological and individual variable, are the ones that influence the degree of Internet using and the result of this using. In another study, Jeong (2005) analyzed the difference in the school results of elementary school pupils depending on the using of Internet. His empirical research shows that Internet addiction is significantly and negatively correlated with the school performance of pupils and their emotional attributes. He suggested that the negative aspects of Internet using can be avoided by promoting the pupils' self-regulating capacity with the help of their colleagues and teachers.

4. Parental Mediation and the Using of Internet by Children and Teenagers

The using of the Internet by children and teenagers is, therefore, dependant on the type of relations children and teenagers have with their parents. The studies show that, for example, there is a negative association between the quality of the parent-child relation and the high levels of Internet addiction at children and teenagers (Liu, Kuo, 2007). At the same time, other research show that a lower level of satisfaction with the way the family functions (Ko et al., 2007; Yen et al., 2007), on one hand, and the conflict between the parent and the child, on the other, were positively associated with the teenager's Internet addiction. According to a report of the National School Boards Foundation (NSBF, 2000), the majority of the parents believe that the Internet has positive effects, expecting it to be used by children for educational purposes. Most parents support the using of the internet by their children and believe that it brings benefits to their children (Yen, 2002; Jones, 2006). At the same time, the studies also indicate the fact that parents are worried by the passivity and unilateral character of their children's recreating activities on the Internet. They are also worried because of the possible negative consequences on the Internet on the health of their children, obesity for example (Sothern, 2004). Moreover, sometimes parents deal with the fact that their children have become so attached to the Internet that they can no longer control their on-line activities (Young, 1998; Young, 2004). Also, another danger signaled by parents is the exposure to inappropriate adult contact, exposure to inappropriate materials, and visiting unapproved sites and cyberbullying (Sharples et al., 2009).

Regarding the supervision or the "parental mediation" of Internet using (Wang, Bianchi, Raley, 2005), Lwin, Stanaland and Miyazaki (2008) differentiate between two types of strategies: restrictive mediation and active mediation. Restrictive mediation involves defining certain rules regarding the using of the Internet. These rules can be connected to the time allocated to the using of the Internet or the access to various applications on the Internet. On the other hand, active mediation has to do with the specific act of using the Internet, meaning parents adopt an active position and stick around, they talk about using the Internet or check the computer when the child used it. Wang's research et al. (2005) indicates the existence of certain differences between parents and children in regard to the way each perceives the rules for using the Internet. For 30% of the studied families there is an agreement between children and parents, for 30% of the families both children and parents say there is no rule for children when using the Internet and in approximately 40%

of the cases there are conflicts between children and parents regarding the rules set for children when using the Internet. In Livingstone's and Helsper's study (2008), 53% of the parents say that they establish the rules for using the Internet, 67% do not allow their children to give personal information on the Internet; 59% forbid them to buy things on-line 43%; block using the e-mail; 13% externally control the access to chat rooms and 7% cut instant messaging.

Byrne (2011) shows that the communicational styles and the parental styles lead to conflicts between children and parents in regard to the strategies for preventing possible Internet risks. More specifically, when children feel it is difficult to talk to their parents about using the Internet, they tend to disagree more as far as the strategies of preventing on-line risks are concerned. Anyhow, both parents and children agree on the fact that it is desirable for both children and teenagers to develop as many abilities and knowledge regarding the on-line activities as possible. Too many restrictions can lead to psychological reactions from children, being possible for the latter to feel threatened and to adopt a behavior that would avoid the restriction or the conflict with their parents (Brehm, 1981).

However, some authors question the impact of active mediation or that of restrictive mediation (Lee, Chae, 2007). The research realized by Lwin et al. (2008) shows that both forms of mediation reduce the chances to adopt an on-line risk behavior. Valcke et al. (2008) says that both active and restrictive mediation are associated to a more reduced probability of an on-line risk behavior for children.

HYPOTHESES

As we showed when we presented the studies so far, two major paradigms disputed the pre-eminence in regard to the using of the Internet and SNS by young people. In a nutshell, we are talking about the paradigm of stimulation which, regardless of the fact it may refer to the area of intimacy, identity or to the relation of the young person with school, it says that the use of SNS makes the young person stronger, as it leads to their development and the displacement paradigm which, in the same way, regardless of what it refers to – the relation to self, others or school – sees a danger in the using of these networks by young people, as it doesn't do them any good, mainly by replacing the old forms of socializing or other classic activities (non-online) etc with the new activity. At the latter paradigm we add the studies that talk about the external risks associated with the SNS using by the youth.

As the research questions we have the followings:

RQ1: How many Romanian children and teenagers use SNSs and how are they doing that?

RQ2: What are the relations between, on the one hand, the competencies acquired for using the internet and, on the other, the general image of Internet?

RQ3: What is the relation between the parental mediation strategies of using the Internet and the children and parents personal usages of internet?

In this big picture our research hypotheses are rather placed in the first paradigm, that of stimulation, with its variants 'the more, the more' (Endestad, Heim, Kaare, Torgersen, Brandtzæg, 2011) or 'the rich get richer'. At a specific level we developed hypothesis as follows:

1. The using of SNS is rather associated with a positive perception of the self in the offline space.
2. The using of SNS is rather associated with acquiring competences for using the Internet and/or the young person's perception on possessing these competences.
3. The using of SNS is rather associated with a positive image of the Internet.

4. The restrictive parental mediation strategies of using the Internet explain in a significant proportion the lack of trust is their (e.g. of parents') personal usage of the Internet.

ELEMENTS OF METHODOLOGY

The present project makes a comparative analysis between the transversal study called EU Kids Online II both at aggregate level (for the European Union) as well as at country level (for Romania).

EU Kids Online II is an international project coordinated by Sonia Livingstone and Leslie Haddon, from London School of Economics and Political Science. The first phase of the project (2006-2009) included 21 states and it involved a secondary analysis of all the data from previous research regarding the using of the Internet by children (more than 400 studies were analyzed), both regarding the risks generated by this new environment as well as the opportunities it offers (Livingstone, S, Haddon, L., 2009). The map of using the Internet presented after this phase, even though it brought more knowledge for understanding the new environment but also for making right decisions for unitary politics, at the level of the European Union, regarding child protection, had, however a great minus represented by the lack of a unitary methodology of studying the phenomenon in the different spaces of Europe. So that, in a second phase (2009-2011), the project was completed with a major research targeting the gathering of data on the phenomenon, this time at the level of 25 European states (in order to see the participating states visit http://www2. lse.ac.uk/media@lse/research/EUKidsOnline/ EUKidsII%20(2009-11)/ParticipatingCountries/ Home.aspx).

Therefore, 25.142 Internet users ages 9 – 16 were questioned, and as many adults, parents or tutors (approximately 1000 de internet-users at the level of each country). The interviews were takes in the spring – summer of 2010, at the homes of the children and involved a face to face survey applied to each child, a survey filled in by the child (for the delicate questions) and a face to face survey applied to the adult responsible for the child.

The group for Romania had a volume of 1039 children and teenagers, being representative for the population of the country, ages 9-16, with a +/- 2% margin of error.

The comparative analysis between the EU and Romania uses the set of data interpreted both from the perspective of descriptive statistics as well as by means of explicative modality which is specific for the inductive approach at statistic level.

The analysis of the empirical data is based on descriptive statistics (e.g. frequencies and cross-tabulations) and inferential statistics (logistic regressions).

For the analysis we have used both the questions from the questionnaires and the compound varabiles inclused in the SPSS files.

The Results of the Research: How Many, Who and How Do they Use SNSs?

Among the 9-16 year old young people who use the Internet, the activity of visiting SNSs is relatively widespread even though it does not rank among the first three places in the online[4] activities. Therefore, at European level 62% of the respondents declare that visiting a profile on the SNSs was a recent activity (the past month), while, in Romania, 52% declare this. In the top of the activities that young people declare they have on the Internet, visiting SNSs is on the fifth place at the level of the EU and on the eight place at the level of Romania (out of 7.2, respectively 7.3 of the general activities young people have online). This behavior is not uniformly distributed for the entire population, being, on the contrary, greatly influenced by the age variable (at the level of Romania more than at the level of the EU), but almost not at all dependent on gender.

Visiting a profile on a SNS does not automatically imply having a profile on such a network (even though, in general, these two groups overlap). Thus, 59% of the young people in the EU and 46% of the young people in Romania have such a profile. At the level of the 24 states that were analyzed in this research, Romania ranks last, while, in the country that ranks first, Holland, 80% of the 9-16 year old young people have a profile on a SNS. This time also the results significantly vary depending on age: from 20% for the 9-10 year old group to 60% for the 15-16 year old group in the case of the Romanian children and with an even higher variation at the level of the EU: from 26% to 82%. The gender of the respondents seems to have little influence, this time also, this variable (in the case of Romania the difference between boys and girls is 7% in favor of girls, while, at the level of the EU being only 2%), on the other hand an important variable in having a profile on a SNS seems to be, at least at the level of Romania, the socio-economic status, with a 13% difference between those with a low status and those with a high status, in favor of the latter (for the EU this difference becomes less obvious, being only 4%).

As we showed, when we talked about the research realized so far, an important issue under debate is the existence of any connection between the individual characteristics and the using of SNSs[5]. For the individual characteristics the following aspects were takes into consideration, in the research we relate to: (1) Self efficacy, (2) Emotional problems, (3) Conduct problems, (4) Peer problems, (5) Sensation seeking. We also analyzed whether the using of SNS varies depending on the risk behaviors in offline and on possessing certain competences in online (for the 9-10 year old age group) and depending on the preference for computer mediated communication as opposed to face to face communication (for the 11-16 year olds).

As far as self efficacy is concerned, this was operationalized in four items, for each item existing a variation between the growth of self efficacy and having a profile on a SNS. As we can see from Table 1, between those who answered in favor of the four statements that measure self efficacy, sometimes there are higher differences than 7%[6] between those that have a profile on a SNS and those that don't.

None of the two age groups, neither at the level of Romania nor at that of the EU, showed any significant variations between having a profile on a SNS and emotional issues, in none of the five dimensions this aspect was measured in.

As far as the behavior issues are concerned, only one of its operalizations (namely conformism: "I usually do as I am told") varies depending on having or not having a profile on a SNS, as follows: the percentage of those that declare this statement as being highly relevant of themselves is 10% higher among those who do not have a profile compared to those that do have, for the 9-12 year old age group, for Romania and 7.4 for the EU and 6.7%, respectively 6.3% for the 13-16 year old age group.

Of the five items measuring the issues with those of the same age (peer), only one varies with possessing a profile on a SNS. Thus, the perception of the young people in Romania ages 9-12, that they are "liked" and accepted increases the chances to have a profile on such a network by

7.2%. A 'seeking sensation' type of behavior does not seem to influence in any way having such a profile online.

However, at the level of the EU, for the 13-16 year old young people, the manifestation of a risk behavior in offline positively influences owning a profile on a virtual network. Thus, the difference between those who have a profile and those who don't and the declaration of a risk behavior in offline is as follows: a. At alcohol consumption ('Had so much alcohol that I got really drunk'): 10.5%, b. At 'missed school lessons without my parents knowing (playing truant or bunking off school)': 7.7%, c. At had sexual intercourse: 6.3% and d. At 'been in trouble with teachers for bad behavior': 9.2%. On the other hand, 'Been in trouble with the police' does not seem to influence too much owning a profile in a online SNS (only 1.6% difference; this being a behavior declared only by 3.7% of the 13-16 year old young people at the level of Europe.

Specific questions were asked in order to see to what extent do young people feel more comfortable with internet communication than with face to face communication (questions that were referring to the preference for computer mediated communication as opposed to face to face communication in certain specific situations) only for

Table 1. Self – efficacy depending on the age group (Romania vs. the European Union)

Self Efficacy	9-12 years				13-16 years			
	ROMANIA		EU		ROMANIA		EU	
It is very true that:	have a SNS profile	don't have a SNS profile	have a SNS profile	don't have a SNS profile	have a SNS profile	don't have a SNS profile	have a SNS profile	don't have a SNS profile
I am confident that I can deal with unexpected problems (%)	20.5	16.3	25.2	17.5	29.4	22.8	41.4	33.9
It's easy for me to stick to my aims and achieve my goals (%)	30.6	24.9	31.9	27.7	30.2	28.6	35.4	31.9
If I am in trouble I can usually think of something to do (%)	43.6	33.7	35.0	31.0	47.2	44.0	43.7	36.3
I can generally work out how to handle new situations (%)	32.7	23.4	31.0	24.0	41.7	34.8	38.9	31.8

the 11-16 year old age group within the auto-fill in questionnaire. Thus, the theory according to which it is more likely for those who find it easier to express themselves on the Internet than face to face to make a profile on SNSs (in general or on different or sensitive topics) did not verify in the data of our research. The highest variation, 7.6%, was found in the case of the 11-12 year old young people from Romania who have a profile and those who do not have a profile and agree with the statement 'I talk about different things on the internet than I do when speaking to people face to face'. However we do not consider significant the variation of only one of the three items and for a small percentage of the population.

As we showed in the first part, one of the greatest concerns of the researchers regarding the using of the Internet by young people in general and of SNS in particular is that of the possible addiction. Valkenberg and colleagues (2009, 2011) mentioned every time that the positive results they reached in regard to the benefits of using SNSs for young people are under the conditions of a moderate use and not an addicting and compulsive one. That is precisely why we wanted to test and see if there are differences between users and non-users of SNS regarding an addictive behavior toward the internet. The latter was operationalized in five items, but significant variations were found only in four of them, every time bigger in the case of the mean at the level of the EU than in the case of the mean for Romania.

Thus, the greatest difference between the non-users group and the users group was found in regard to the aimless surfing and especially the one with no particular interest (item that is an indicator of the time consuming character of Internet) where, at the level of the EU, with 19% more non-users, said they never had such a behavior in the last 12 months. To put it in another way, it is more probable that we find this behavior at the SNS users. In the same way, though in a smaller percentage, we have the difference between users and non-users

regarding: the displacement of time for different activities pertaining to real life with the time spent online (16% difference between SNS users and non-users at the level of the EU and 11% at the level of Romania), the attempt to limit the time spent online or experiencing a discomfort caused by the impossibility to go online (See Table 2).

Another aspect we tried to test in order to discover the "portrait" of the young SNSs consumer was their competence in using the Internet. Differently said, the question behind this was whether the using of SNSs is associated with a higher competence in using the Internet. The hypothesis was verified, all the items measuring competence associating, to a greater extent, with those who owned a profile in a SNS and vice versa, those who declared not having a profile were in great part those who did not have any knowledge about what they were being asked (See Table 3).

Therefore, even though our data do not show the direction from the influence takes place, if the perception of a higher competence determines the decision of building a profile in a SNS or, on the contrary, if once he/she uses SNS this makes them more competent in using the Internet, the

Table 2. The percentage difference between SNS users and non-users (Romania vs. the European Union)

The percentage difference between SNS users and non-users that declared, at the same time, that the following things never happened to them in the last 12 months	Romania (%)	EU (%)
I have felt bothered when I cannot be on the internet	10.4	13.5
I have caught myself surfing when I'm not really interested	14.7	19
I have spent less time than I should with either family, friends or doing school-work because of the time I spent on the internet	10.9	16
I have felt bothered when I cannot be on the internet	12.3	13.9

Table 3. The association between the level of competence on the Internet and the SNSs users (Romania vs. the European Union)

And which of these things do you know how to do on the internet?		Romania		EU	
		have a SNS's profile	don't have a SNS's profile	have a SNS's profile	don't have a SNS's profile
Delete the record of which sites you have visited (%)	No	40.3	72.4	35.1	63.6
	Yes	59.7	27.6	64.9	36.4
Change privacy settings on a SNS profile (%)	No	41.7	85.8	24.4	78.0
	Yes	58.3	14.2	75.6	22
Block messages from someone you don't want to hear from (%)	No	32.5	62.5	21.0	59.3
	Yes	67.5	37.5	79.0	40.7
Block messages from someone you don't want to hear from (%)	No	28.9	52.0	28.7	50.6
	Yes	71.1	48	71.3	49.4

strong association between the two variables is a significant result for both the EU space and for the Romanian one.

As we were saying in the beginning, one of the starting hypotheses was that according to which a high perception of the possible "dangers" of Internet is associated at the young people with non-using SNSs. However, the data shows that this is not the case. On the contrary, among those who have a profile in a SNS there are more young people who are willing to admit the possible dangers of the Internet. Also, we notice that at the level of Romania there are more such young people than at the level of the EU. Thus, among the SNS users with ages between 9-16, at the level of Romania 76.7% answer affirmatively to the question 'Do you think there are things on the internet that people about your age will be bothered by in any way?', whereas, at the level of the EU, this percentage is 63.8%. At the same time, SNS non-users who admit the existence on the Internet of certain things that could be unpleasant for those their age are 64.7% at the level of Romania and 52.1% at the level of the EU. Once again, the data do not show the direction of influence but they do not favor a hypothesis about the naïve SNS user who is about to fall into the trap of some possible dangers on the Internet but, on the contrary, they present a young

Internet user fully aware of the possible dangers he exposes himself to. As a work hypothesis for a future research, we would be tempted to say – based on the fact that, at the level of the EU, among non-users there is an almost equal division of the awareness and non-awareness of the existence of some dangers on the Internet – that using SNSs leads to an increased awareness of the existence of dangers and not the other way around, that being aware of the dangers increases the probability of creating a profile in an online SNS. As we were saying, we are yet to research this hypothesis, but if it verifies, it would mean admitting the benefits of using SNSs by young people.

More than testing the knowing of certain specific operations that have to do with using the Internet (See Table 3) and important aspect to be studied is the variation of using SNS with the perception young people has on possessing certain Internet related competences. Thus, not only specific knowledge can play an important part but also positive perception of the possessed knowledge that can be associated with a growth of self-esteem (this aspect was not included in the analysis but one can imagine a research that would take these things into consideration). The results confirmed the hypothesis of the variation of the two aspects with an important mentioning.

At the level of the 9-10 year old group we found that there is a higher probability to declare a positive perception on the knowledge of using the Internet in the group of those that have a profile on a SNS compared to those that do not have one. This difference is smaller at this group compared to that of the 11-16 year old and only one of the two investigated aspects. Thus, at the level of the EU, 7.1% of the young ones agree more with the statement 'I know more about the internet than my parents' than those who do not have a profile on such SNS.

On the other hand, as Table 4 shows, for those with ages between 11-16, there are notable percentage differences of those declaring that it is very true they have more knowledge than their parents as far as the Internet is concerned, or that they know many things regarding the using of the Internet among social SNSs users and non-users. Associating the confidence in Internet related knowledge (either in relation to the parents' knowledge or in them) and the using of SNS is stronger at the level of the EU than at the level of Romania (20, respectively 24 percentage difference for the EU and 15, respectively 20% for Romania). Even though it does not appear in the topic of the present work, we cannot not draw the attention on the major difference (of 20%) between the young people in Romania and those in the EU who say that it is very true that they know more things about the Internet than their parents. These

data do not mean to say that Romanian youth have more Internet related abilities than the youth in the EU, and also, they don't necessarily have a better perception of them than the youth in the EU, but we would be tempted to interpret it as expressing the perception of the young people in Romania on the lack of competences their parents have in using the Internet which, most probably, overlaps over a real lacking of their parents' digital competence. This is an observation that brings back in discussion the generational using of the Internet on which there are more studies (Herring, 2008; Montgomery, 2009; Selwyn, 2009). A methodological commentary is necessary for this item and for the following one. These questions (the two discussed above and the next one we will discuss) were placed in different sections of the questionnaires for the 9-10 and 11-16 year old age groups: for the first group in the auto-filling in section while for the second in the face to face interview section. Even though we have no explanation for the way this difference in data gathering could influence results, we feel responsible to mention it as being a possible influence.

Just as we tested the association of using SNS with a negative perception of the Internet (in the way of becoming aware of the existence of the possible Internet related dangers), in the same way we wanted to test the association between the positive perception of the Internet ('There are lots of things on the internet that are good for

Table 4. Having or not having a profile on SNS vs. self-perception regarding the Internet related competences (Romania vs. the European Union)

The ones saying that it is very true that:	Romania		EU	
	Have a SNS's profile	don't have a SNS's profile	have a SNS's profile	don't have a SNS's profile
I know more about the internet than my parents (11+) (%)	70.4	55	50.9	30.6
I know lots of things about using the internet (11+) (%)	43.3	23.5	47.4	23.1
There are lots of things on the internet that are good for children my age (11+) (%)	55	45.3	52.4	41.6

children my age') and the using of SNS. At the level of the EU, among the very young (9-10) Internet users that can identify with this statement the ones who have, at the same time, profile on an online SNS, are 8.7% more numerous than the ones that do not have one, while at the level of Romania the difference on this item is 6.6% in the same way. For the ones older than 11, the association between the positive perception of the Internet and owning a profile on SNS is bigger, being relatively equal at the level of Romania and the EU, by approximately 10 percent points (See Table 4).

In order to answer the question "how do young people use SNS" we chose to analyze the following aspects, in accordance with the interest items in the specialty literature: (1) The number of friends in the network and the nature of the contacts (Livingstone, Haddon, Görzig, & Ólafsson, 2011; Notley, 2008); (2) The settings of the profile (Lewis, Kaufman, & Christakis, 2008; Patchin & Hinduja, 2010) and the self-disclosure elements (Valkenberg &Peter, 2011, 2009) and (3) The existence of the parental mediating elements associated or not to the using of SNSs by youth.

Talking about the 'list of friends' of the young people in the SNS, in the comparative analysis of the two cultural spaces, the results showed that in Romania there is a type of usage which is not very specific at the level of the EU, young people having, in general, significantly less people in their friends list. Therefore, if at the EU level 70% of the young SNSs users have more than 50 friends in their list (with Hungary, Belgium and the United Kingdom where, among the groups taken into consideration, the most are found in the group 101-300 friends, as follows: 33% for the young people in Hungary, 34% for those in Belgium and 26% for the English young people), at the level of Romania, 63% have up to 10 friends in their list, 24% have between 11 and 50 friends only 13% have more than 50 friends. This result in the case of Romania can be interpreted in two ways, a positive one and a negative one. Thus, having this little friends in

the SNS's the chances to have strangers among them reduce tremendously and therefore the often met risk in the specialty literature, the one of 'meeting stragers' (Blais, 2008; boyd & Ellison, 2007; Sharples et al., 2009; Subrahmanyam & Greenfield, 2008) is at a pretty low level. On the other hand though, research show that a major benefit of practicing online socializing for youth is that of visualizing the friends' network (Biegler & boyd, 2010; boyd, 2007; boyd & Ellison, 2007) and that of expressing the attempt and error type of identity as a results of the feedback offered by the friends in the network, reason for which it is desirable that this list be as diverse as possible in order to have a multitude of answers and not only those in the immediate vicinity which, in general, do not develop the pallet of identities but strengthens the existing ones (Valkenburg & Peter, 2009; Valkenburg & Soeters, 2001; Valkenburg, Schouten, & Peter, 2005).

Another element evaluated as risk factor in the specialty literature is the one related to the privacy setting of the profile. Thus the public exposing of data that could lead to the identification of the young person in the real world by someone other than the ones he knows can represent a risk factor threatening his/her safety. The data of our research show that at the level of the EU 43% of the young people has their profile set as "private", 28% partially private and only 26% have their profile opened for everyone with the setting "public". In Romania however, things are exactly the other way around, the majority having their profile set on public (42%), followed by 'private', 36% and 'partially private' 17%. In both cultural spaces a variation of the privacy character of the profile was discovered, with the gender variable, data that verifies other previous research, but age predicts relatively little and only for the Romanian space the concern for privacy (in the sense of increasing the percentage of those having profiles set on privacy, together with age, from 29% for 9-10 year olds to 40% in the case of the 15-16 year olds. Among the data that is generally exposed, there is the address and/or phone number for 14% of the total of children (therefore not only those who use SNS's or those who have their profiles set on 'public') and 21% of the total of children in Romania. Also, another practice considered to be potentially risky if that of offering false information regarding age (usually in the direction of giving an older age). Considering the research we are referring to, results that at the level of the EU 16% of the total of children post an incorrect age, while in Romania in 12% of the cases we meet this practice. For comparison purposes we will remind that in Spain, Denmark and Portugal we meet most often this type of age deforming (with 27% respectively 25%) while in Hungary and Poland it is less frequent, with 2%, respectively 3%.

As we have already mentioned, when we did a review of the research realized so far and within our analysis, the contact with strangers (or partially strangers but from an interest group) is considered as having both positive valences (for enlarging the sphere of acquaintances in a specific area, for adults, etc.) as well as negative ones (the potential danger for the young people because of the 'sexual plunderers watching in online'). Even though SNS's is not the only place where this 'contact' can take place (virtual word, chat-room, online games, instant messaging or email being as many possibilities) still SNSs being communicational and socializing by nature caught the eye of the researchers. Still, the results at the level of the EU do not justify this concern, the majority of 78% of the SNS's users having friends in their list that they first met face to face, 34% having in their list people they met on the Internet but who are relatives or friends of some acquaintances they met in the real world. Only 12% declare having in their list people they've never met face to face. At the level of Romania things are not as good, more youths having this behavior considered being risky; the three groups have, in the order enunciated above, 69%, 36% and 27%.

According to the data from the research done by the European Commission from 2008, 35% of the interviewed parents always ask their children what they do when they navigate on the Internet; 30% always stay near them when they access the Internet; 22% check the history of Internet pages downloads while 13% always check their children's email and instant messenger.

The data of the EU Kids Online II research show that there are differences between the parental mediation styles regarding the using of the Internet at the level of the European Union and Romania. According to the model of logistic regression presented in Table 5, the fourth work hypothesis is verified at aggregate level (EU) but it is invalidated at country level (Romania). More exactly, a parent from the European Union who established a higher level of restrictive mediation when his child uses the Internet is almost two times more probable that he will declare he does not trust in his personal using of the Internet compared to a parent from Romania (a probability at the EU level of 1.16 vs. a 0.69 probability in the case of Romania – according to Table 5). At the same time, compared to a Romanian parent, the lack of trust in the personal using of the Internet of a parent from the European Union is explained in higher percentage (11% vs. 9%) by the existence of a bigger number of monitored activities of using the Internet by their child.

On the other hand, according to the same model of regression presented in Table 5, there is an eight times higher probability for a Romanian parent (compared to a parent from the European Union) that by adopting a behavior of mediating Internet safety for their child to determine the child to declare his/her lack of trust in using the Internet.

CONCLUSION

The data analyzed and presented above offer a pretty exact picture of the way the online SNSs are used by the young people in Romania and the European Union in general. At the level of the big picture we would say, based on the theories regarding the differentiated using of SNSs in the

Table 5. The logistic regression model for the parents' lack of trust in their personal using of the Internet (Romania vs. the European Union)

	Romania			EU		
	Exp(B)	95,0% C.I. for EXP(B)		Exp(B)	95,0% C.I.for EXP(B)	
		Lower	Upper		Lower	Upper
Number of active mediation of child internet use as reported by parent	944	794	1,260	909	885	932
Number of active mediation of child internet safety as reported by parent	779	684	1,463	924	895	953
Number of parental restrictive mediation of child internet use as reported by parent	1,127	1,001	999	1,024	1,003	1,046
Active mediation of child internet use as reported by parent	553	129	7,771	1,307	1,070	1,598
Active mediation of child internet safety as reported by parent	4,663	1,191	840	680	569	813
Parental restrictive mediation of child internet use as reported by parent	695	317	3,154	1,164	1,003	1,351
Number of parental monitoring of child internet use as reported by parent	992	780	1,282	1,031	1,004	1,059
Hosmer and Lemeshow Test	Chi-square	Df.	Sig	Chi-square	df	Sig.
	5,160	8	740	6,894	8	548

course of time (Biegler & boyd, 2010; boyd, 2007) that the two groups have a different type of using SNSs, the ones from Romania seeming to be at the beginning of using the Internet, not having a stabilized usage yet.

As far as the hypotheses we started with, the majority of them verified. Thus, the individual characteristics in the self-efficacy variant positively vary with the using of SNSs. On the contrary, none of the negative individual characteristics (such as emotional, behavior or friend issues) predicts the possessing of a profile on a SNS.

We found the strongest connection between having competences regarding the using of the Internet and owning a profile on a SNS's. Moreover, even the awareness of having these competences is positively associated with having such a profile.

The third hypothesis, the one regarding the existence of a relation between a positive perception of the Internet and the using of SNS's also partially verified, namely for those older than 11, even though there isn't a very strong relation. This does not mean though that SNS users have an idealized image of the Internet, but, on the contrary, they are more numerous than the SNS non-users ready to admit that on the Internet there can be unpleasant things for the young people their age.

The study of the European Committee done in 2008 emphasized the fact that parents establish more rules when they themselves are not active Internet users thus, parents who do not have experience in using the internet establish a minimal number of rules for their children regarding the using of the Internet. The information of the fourth hypothesis lead us to formulating the alternative hypothesis: "The trust in the personal using of the Internet by parents is explained in high percentage by the existence of active parental mediating strategies of Internet using by their children".

The analysis of the regression models for both the group in Romania as well as that at the level of the entire European Union indicates the validation of this alternative hypothesis both at aggregate level (EU) and at country level (that of Romania).

Thus, for the parent within the European Union a greater number of actions of active mediating of using the Internet by their child explains in proportion of 12% the confidence in the way he himself uses the Internet while for the parent in Romania the explicative contribution of the growth of the number of activities in terms of active mediation is 10%. At the same time, parents from Romania that declare a higher level of active involvement of Internet safety for their children are 1.2 times more probable to declare that they have confidence in the way they themselves use the Internet, the probability for a high level of trust in the way they use the Internet being 1.08 times higher for the parents in the European Union who adopt such behavior in report to their children.

Our results agree with the research realized by Liau, Khoo and Ang (2005) and by Mitchell, Finkelhor and Wolak (2001) who highlight a complex influence of the parental mediation on the social behaviors.

REFERENCES

Ahn, J. (2011). The effect of social network sites on adolescents' social and academic development: Current theories and controversies. *Journal of the American Society for Information Science and Technology, 62*(8), 1435–1445. doi:10.1002/asi.21540

Al-Saggaf, Y. (2011). Saudi females on Facebook: An ethnographic study. *International Journal of Emerging Technologies and Society, 9*(1), 1–19.

Anderson, D. R., Huston, A. C., Schmitt, K. L., Linebarger, D. L., & Wright, J. C. (2001). Early childhood television viewing and adolescent behavior: The recontact study. *Monographs of the Society for Research in Child Development, 66,* I-I147.

Arafeh, S., Levin, D., Rainie, L., & Lenhart, A. (2002). *The digital disconnect: The widening gap between Internet-savvy students and their schools.* Washington, DC: Pew Internet & American Life Project. Retrieved February 28, 2012, from http://www.pewinternet.org/Reports/2002/The-Digital-Disconnect-The-widening-gap-between-Internetsavvy-students-and-their-schools.aspx

Attewell, P., Suazo-Garcia, B., & Battle, J. (2003). Computers and young children: Social benefit or social problem. *Social Forces, 82,* 277–296. doi:10.1353/sof.2003.0075

Baker, R. K., & White, K. M. (2010). Predicting adolescents' use of social networking sites from an extended theory of planned behaviour perspective. *Computers in Human Behavior, 26*(6), 1591–1597. doi:10.1016/j.chb.2010.06.006

Barker, M., & Petley, J. (Eds.). (2001). *Ill effects: The media violence debate-communication and society* (2nd ed.). London, UK: Routledge.

Barker, V. (2009). Older adolescents' motivations for social network site use: The influence of gender, group identity, and collective self-esteem. *Cyberpsychology & Behavior, 12,* 209–213. doi:10.1089/cpb.2008.0228

Barnett, T. A., O'Loughlin, J., & Sabiston, C. M. (2010). Teens and screens: The influence of screen time on adiposity in adolescents. *American Journal of Epidemiology, 172*(3), 255–262. doi:10.1093/aje/kwq125

Ben-David Kolikant, Y. (2009). Digital students in a book-oriented school: Students' perceptions of school and the usability of digital technology in schools. *Journal of Educational Technology & Society, 12*(2), 131–143.

Bennett, S., Maton, K., & Kervin, L. (2008). The 'digital natives' debate: A critical review of the evidence. *British Journal of Educational Technology*, *39*(5), 775–786. doi:10.1111/j.1467-8535.2007.00793.x

Bernard, R. M., Abrami, P. C., Lou, Y., Borokhovski, E., Wade, A., & Wozney, L. (2004). How does distance education compare with classroom instruction? A meta-analysis of the empirical literature. *Review of Educational Research*, *74*(3), 379–439. doi:10.3102/00346543074003379

Bonk, C. (2009). *The world is open: how Web technology is revolutionizing education.* San Francisco, CA: Jossey-Bass.

boyd, d. m., & Ellison, N. B. (2007). Social network sites: Definition, history, and scholarship. *Journal of Computer-Mediated Communication*, *13*(1), Retrieved February 28, 2012, from http://jcmc.indiana.edu/vol13/issue1/boyd.ellison.html

boyd, d. m. (2007). Why youth (heart) social network sites: The role of networked publics in teenage social life. In D. Buckingham (Ed.), *MacArthur Foundation Series on Digital Learning - Youth, Identity, and Digital Media Volume* (pp. 119-142). Retrieved February 28, 2012, from www.danah.org/papers/WhyYouthHeart.pdf

Breton, P., & Proulx, S. (2002). L'explosion de la communication: A l'aube du XXI siècle. Paris, France: éditions La Découverte.

Brown, J. S. (2000). Growing up digital: How the Web changes work, education, and the ways people learn. *Change*, (March/April): 10–20.

Buckingham, D. (2000). *After the death of childhood*. Oxford, UK: Polity.

Buffardi, L. E., & Campbell, W. K. (2008). Narcissism and social networking web sites. *Personality and Social Psychology Bulletin*, *34*(10), 1303–1314. doi:10.1177/0146167208320061

Byrne, S., & Lee, T. (2011). Toward predicting youth resistance to internet risk prevention strategies. *Journal of Broadcasting & Electronic Media*, *55*(1). doi:10.1080/08838151.2011.546255

Calvert, S. L. (2002). Identity construction on the Internet. In Calvert, S. L., Jordan, A. B., & Cocking, R. R. (Eds.), *Children in the digital age* (pp. 57–70). Westport, CT: Praeger.

Chang, W. L. (2003). *A study of information-seeking behavior among senior-level elementary school students in the area of I-Lan*. Master thesis, Fo Guang University, Taiwan.

Clark, R. E. (1983). Reconsidering research on learning from media. *Review of Educational Research*, *53*(4), 445–459.

Clark, R. E. (1991). When researchers swim upstream: Reflections on an unpopular argument about learning from media. *Educational Technology*, *31*(2), 34–40.

DiMaggio, P. & Hargittai, E. (2001). *From the 'digital divide' to `digital inequality': Studying internet use as penetration increases*. Working Paper 15, Summer 2001.

Ellison, N. B., Steinfield, C., & Lampe, C. (2007). The benefits of Facebook "friends:" Social capital and college students' use of online social network sites. *Journal of Computer-Mediated Communication*, *12*(4), 1143–1168. doi:10.1111/j.1083-6101.2007.00367.x

Endestad, T., Heim, J., Kaare, B., Torgersen, L., & Brandtzæg, P. B. (2011). Media user types among young children and social displacement. *Nordicom Review*, *32*(1), 17–30.

Espinosa, L. M., Laffey, J. M., Whittaker, T., & Sheng, Y. (2006). Technology in the home and the achievement of young children: Findings from the Early Childhood Longitudinal Study. *Early Education and Development*, *17*, 421–441. doi:10.1207/s15566935eed1703_5

European Commission. (2008). *Towards a safer use of the Internet for children in the EU: A parents' perspective*. Retrieved February 28, 2012, from http://ec.europa.eu/information_society/activities/sip/docs/eurobarometer/analyticalreport_2008.pdf

Fetler, M. (1984). Television viewing and school achievement. *The Journal of Communication, 34*, 104–118. doi:10.1111/j.1460-2466.1984.tb02163.x

Fishman, J., Lunsford, A., McGregor, B., & Otuteye, M. (2005). Performing writing, performing literacy. *College Composition and Communication, 57*(2), 224–252.

Fogel, J., & Nehmad, E. (2009). Internet social network communities: Risk taking, trust, and privacy concerns. *Computers in Human Behavior, 25*, 153–160. doi:10.1016/j.chb.2008.08.006

Greenhow, C., & Robelia, E. (2009). Old communication, new literacies: Social network sites as social learning resources. *Journal of Computer-Mediated Communication, 14*(4), 1130–1161. doi:10.1111/j.1083-6101.2009.01484.x

Griffith, S., & Liyanage, L. (2008). *An introduction to the potential of social networking sites in education*. Emerging Technologies Conference 2008.

Gros, E. (2004). Adolescent internet use: What we expect, what they report. *Journal of Applied Developmental Psychology, 25*(6), 633–649. doi:10.1016/j.appdev.2004.09.005

Hakala, P. T., Rimpela, A. H., Saarni, L. A., & Salminen, J. J. (2006). Frequent computer-related activities increase the risk of neck-shoulder and low back pain in adolescents. *European Journal of Public Health, 16*(5), 536–541. doi:10.1093/eurpub/ckl025

Hancox, R. J., Milne, B. J., & Poulton, R. (2005). Association of television viewing during childhood with poor educational achievement. *Archives of Pediatrics & Adolescent Medicine, 159*, 614–618. doi:10.1001/archpedi.159.7.614

Hargittai, E. (2007). Whose space? Differences among users and non-users of social network sites. *Journal of Computer-Mediated Communication, 13*(1). Retrieved February 28, 2012, from http://jcmc.indiana.edu/vol13/issue1/hargittai.html

Heins, E., Seitz, C., & Schuz, J. (2007). Bedtime, television and computer habits of primary school children in Germany. *Gesundheitswesen (Bundesverband der Arzte des Offentlichen Gesundheitsdienstes (Germany)), 69*(3), 151–157. doi:10.1055/s-2007-971061

Holmes, J. (2009). Myths and missed opportunities: Young people's not so risky use of online communication. *Information Communication and Society, 12*(8), 1174–1196. doi:10.1080/13691180902769873

Huang, Y. P. (2002). *A study on the network literacy and network usage of elementary school students*. Master thesis, University of Tainan, Tainan, Taiwan.

Hunley, S. A., Evans, J. H., Delgado-Hachey, M., Krise, J., Rich, T., & Schell, C. (2005). Adolescent computer use and academic achievement. *Adolescence, 40*, 307–318.

Huston, A. C., Wright, J. C., Marguis, J., & Green, S. B. (1999). How young children spend their time: Television and other activities. *Developmental Psychology, 35*, 43–51. doi:10.1037/0012-1649.35.4.912

Ito, M., Baumer, S., & Bittanti, M. boyd, d. m., Cody, R., Herr-Stephenson, B., Tripp, L. (2010). *Hanging out, messing around, and geeking out: Kids living and learning with new media*. Cambridge, MA: MIT Press.

Jaruratanasirikul, S., Wongwaitaweewong, K., & Sangsupawanich, P. (2009). Electronic game play and school performance of adolescents in southern Thailand. *Cyberpsychology & Behavior, 12*(5), 509–512. doi:10.1089/cpb.2009.0035

Jelicic, H., Bobek, D. L., Phelps, E., Lerner, R. M., & Lerner, J. V. (2007). Using positive youth development to predict contribution and risk behaviors in early adolescence: Findings from the first two waves of the 4-H study of positive youth development. *International Journal of Behavioral Development, 31*, 263–273. doi:10.1177/0165025407076439

Jenkins, H. (2006). *Confronting the challenges of participatory culture: Media education for the 21st century.* Chicago, IL: The JohnD., & Catherine T. MacArthur Foundation.

Jeong, T. G. (2005). The effects of internet addiction and self control on achievement of elementary school children. *The Korea Journal of Yeolin Education, 13*(1), 143–163.

Jones, P. J. (2006). Resources for promoting online citizenship. *Educational Leadership, 6*(4), 41–51.

Karpinski, A. C. (2009). Media sensationalization of social science research: Social-networking insites. *Teachers College Record.* Retrieved February 28, 2012, from http://www.tcrecord.org/Content.asp?ContentID=15642

Karpinski, A. C., & Duberstein, A. (2009). *A description of Facebook use and academic performance among undergraduate and graduate students.* San Diego, CA: American Educational Research Association.

Knutson, K. L., & Lauderdale, D. S. (2009). Sociodemographic and behavioral predictors of bed time and wake time among US adolescents aged 15 to 17 years. *The Journal of Pediatrics, 154*(3), 426–441. doi:10.1016/j.jpeds.2008.08.035

Ko, C. H., Yen, J. Y., Yen, C. F., Lin, H. C., & Yang, M. J. (2007). Factors predictive for incidence and remission of internet addiction in young adolescents: A prospective study. *Cyberpsychology & Behavior, 10*(4), 545–551. doi:10.1089/cpb.2007.9992

Kolek, E. A., & Saunders, D. (2008). Online disclosure: An empirical examination of undergraduate Facebook profiles. *NASPA Journal, 45*(1), 1–25.

Kubey, R. W., Lavin, M. J., & Barrows, J. R. (2001). Internet use and collegiate academic performance decrements: Early findings. *The Journal of Communication, 51*, 366–382. doi:10.1111/j.1460-2466.2001.tb02885.x

Lampe, C., Ellison, N. B., & Steinfield, C. (2008). Changes in use and perception of Facebook. *Proceedings of the 2008 ACM Conference on Computer Supported Cooperative Work*, (pp. 721–730). ACM.

Lee, S. J., & Chae, Y. G. (2007). Children's Internet use in a family context: influence on family relationships and parental mediation. *Cyberpsychology & Behavior, 10*(5), 640–644. doi:10.1089/cpb.2007.9975

Lee, W., & Eddie, C. Y. K. (2002). Internet and displacement effect: Children's media use and activities. *Journal of Computer-Mediated Communication, 7*, 1–18.

Lei, J., & Zhao, Y. (2005). Technology uses and student achievement: A longitudinal study. *Computers & Education, 49*, 284–296. doi:10.1016/j.compedu.2005.06.013

Lenhart, A., Madden, M., Macgill, A. R., & Smith, A. (2007). *Teens and social media.* Washington, DC: Pew Internet & American Life Project.

Lewis, K., Kaufman & J., Christakis, N. (2008). The taste for privacy: An analysis of college student privacy settings in an online social network. *Journal of Computer-Mediated Communication, 14*(1), 79–100. doi:10.1111/j.1083-6101.2008.01432.x

Li, C. C. (2004). *The digital divide among elementary school students in Taipei, Taiwan.* Master thesis, National Taipei University of Education, Taipei, Taiwan.

Liau, A., Khoo, A., & Ang, P. (2005). Factors influencing 'adolescents' engagement in risky Internet behaviour. *Cyberpsychology & Behavior*, *8*(2), 513–520. doi:10.1089/cpb.2005.8.513

Lim, S. S., & Nekmat, E. (2008). Learning through "prosuming": Insights from media literacy programmes in Asia. *Science, Technology & Society*, *13*(2). doi:10.1177/097172180801300205

Liu, C. Y., & Kuo, F. Y. (2007). A study of Internet addiction through the lens of the interpersonal theory. *Cyberpsychology & Behavior*, *10*(6), 799–804. doi:10.1089/cpb.2007.9951

Liu, W. S. (2003). *A study of internet addiction and internet literacy on elementary school students*. Master thesis, University of Tainan, Tainan, Taiwan.

Livingstone, S. (2003). Children's use of the Internet: Reflections on the emerging research agenda. *New Media & Society*, *5*(2), 147–166. doi:10.1177/1461444803005002001

Livingstone, S. (2004). Media literacy and the challenge of new information and communication technologies. *Communication Review*, *7*(1), 3–14. doi:10.1080/10714420490280152

Livingstone, S. (2008). Taking risky opportunities in youthful content creation: teenagers' use of social networking sites for intimacy, privacy and self-expression. *New Media & Society*, *10*(3), 393–411. doi:10.1177/1461444808089415

Livingstone, S., & Bober, M. (2004). Taking up online opportunities? Children's use of the Internet for education, communication and participation. *E-learning*, *1*(3), 395–419. doi:10.2304/elea.2004.1.3.5

Livingstone, S., & Haddon, L. (2009). *EU kids online: Final report*. London, UK: EU Kids Online. (EC Safer Internet Plus Programme Deliverable D6.5).

Livingstone, S., Haddon, L., Gorzig, A., & Ólafsson, K. (2011). *EU kids online*. London, UK: EU Kinds Online (EC Safer Internet Plus Programme Deliverable D6. 5), Final Report.

Livingstone, S., & Helsper, E. (2008). Parental mediation of 'children's Internet use. *Journal of Broadcasting & Electronic Media*, *52*(4), 581–599. doi:10.1080/08838150802437396

Lwin, M. O., Stanaland, A., & Miyazaki, A. (2008). Protecting 'children's privacy online: How parental mediation strategies affect website safeguard effectiveness. *Journal of Retailing*, *84*, 205–217. doi:10.1016/j.jretai.2008.04.004

Mitchell, K., Finkelhor, D., & Wolak, J. (2001). Risk factors for and impact of online sexual solicitation of youth. *Journal of the American Medical Association*, *285*(23), 3011–3014. doi:10.1001/jama.285.23.3011

Morgan, M. (1993). Television and school performance. *Adolescent Medicine (Philadelphia, Pa.)*, *4*, 607–622.

Mutz, D. C., Roberts, D. F., & van Vuuren, D. P. (1993). Reconsidering the displacement hypothesis: Television's influence on children's time use. *Communication Research*, *20*, 51–75. doi:10.1177/009365093020001003

National School Boards Foundation. (2000). *Research and guidelines for children's use of the internet*. National School Boards Foundation.

Neuman, S. B. (1991). *Literacy in the television age: The myth of the TV effect*. Norwood, NJ: Ablex.

Nie, N. H., & Hillygus, D. S. (2002). Where does internet time come from? A reconnaissance. *IT & Society*, *1*, 1–20.

Notley, T. (2008). Online network use in schools. *The Journal of Youth Studies Australia. Social and Educational Opportunities*, *27*(3), 20–29.

OIVO. (2008). *Youngsters and the Internet.* Retrieved January 10, 2012, from http://www.oivo-crioc.org/files/nl/3906nl.pdf

Padilla-Walker, L. M., Nelson, L. J., Carroll, J. S., & Jensen, A. C. (2010). More than a just a game: Video game and internet use during emerging adulthood. *Journal of Youth and Adolescence, 39*(2), 103–113. doi:10.1007/s10964-008-9390-8

Pasek, J., More, E., & Hargittai, E. (2009). Facebook and academic performance: Reconciling a media sensation with data. *First Monday, 14*(5). Retrieved from http://firstmonday.org/htbin/cgi-wrap/bin/ojs/index.php/fm/article/view/2498/218

Passig, D. (2003). A taxonomy of future thinking skills. *Informatics in Education, 2*(1), 79–92.

Passig, D. (2007). Melioration as a higher thinking skill of future intelligence. *Teachers College Record, 109*(1), 24–50.

Patchin, J. W., & Hinduja, S. (2010). Trends in online social networking: adolescent use of MySpace over time. *New Media & Society, 12*(2), 197–216. doi:10.1177/1461444809341857

Perkel, D. (2006). Copy and paste literacy: Literacy practices in the production of a MySpace profile— An overview. In *Proceedings of Informal Learning and Digital Media: Constructions, Contexts, Consequences* (Denmark, September 21–23, 2006).

Perkins, D. N. (1992). *Smart schools: From training memories to educating minds.* New York, NY: Free Press.

Pew Research. (2010). *Social media and mobile internet use among teens and young adults.* Retrieved February 28, 2012, from http://pewinternet.org/Reports/2010/Social-Media-and-Young-Adults.aspx

Pfeil, U., Arjan, R., & Zaphiris, P. (2009). Age differences in online social networking - A study of user profiles and the social capital divide among teenagers and older users in MySpace. *Computers in Human Behavior, 25*, 643–665. doi:10.1016/j.chb.2008.08.015

Raacke, J., & Bonds-Raacke, J. (2008). MySpace and Facebook: Applying the uses and gratifications theory to exploring friend-networking sites. *Cyberpsychology & Behavior, 11*, 169–174. doi:10.1089/cpb.2007.0056

Robinson, J. P., Kestnbaum, M., Neustadtl, A., & Alvarez, A. (2000). Mass media use and social life among Internet users. *Social Science Computer Review, 18*(4), 490–501. doi:10.1177/089443930001800411

Schouten, A. P., Valkenburg, P. M., & Peter, J. (2007). Precursors and underlying processes of adolescents' online self-disclosure: Developing and testing an "Internet-attribute-perception" model. *Media Psychology, 10*, 292–314. doi:10.1080/15213260701375686

Schouten, A. P., Valkenburg, P. M., & Peter, J. (2009). An experimental test of processes underlying self-disclosure in computer-mediated communication. *Cyberpsychology & Behavior, 3*(2), 1–15.

Selwyn, N. (2004). Reconsidering political and popular understandings of the digital divide. *New Media & Society, 6*, 341. doi:10.1177/1461444804042519

Seo, W.-S. (2004a). Internet usage and life satisfaction of the youth. *Informatization Policy, 11*(2), 87–103.

Seo, W.-S. (2004b). The internet use and adolescent's socialization. *The Information Society, 6*, 51–81.

Shaffer, D. W., & Clinton, K. A. (2006). Tool for thoughts: Reexamining thinking in the digital age. *Mind, Culture, and Activity, 13*(4), 283–300. doi:10.1207/s15327884mca1304_2

Sharples, M., Graber, R., Harrison, C., & Logan, K. (2009). E-safety and Web 2.0 for children aged 11-16. *Journal of Computer Assisted Learning, 25*(1), 70–84. doi:10.1111/j.1365-2729.2008.00304.x

Solis, B., & Breakenridge, D. (2009). *Putting the public back in public relations. How social media is reinventing the aging business of PR* (p. 314). FT Press.

Sothern, M. S. (2004). Obesity prevention in children: physical activity and nutrition. *Nutrition (Burbank, Los Angeles County, Calif.), 20*(7-8), 704–708. doi:10.1016/j.nut.2004.04.007

Steinberg, L., Albert, D., & Cauffman, E. (2008). Age differences in sensation seeking and impulsivity as indexed by behavior and self-report: Evidence for a dual systems model. *Developmental Psychology, 44*, 1764–1778. doi:10.1037/a0012955

Steinfield, C., Ellison, N. B., & Lampe, C. (2008). Social capital, self-esteem, and use of online social network sites: A longitudinal analysis. *Journal of Applied Developmental Psychology, 29*, 434–445. doi:10.1016/j.appdev.2008.07.002

Steyaert, J. (2002). Inequality and the digital divide: myths and realities. In Hick, S., & McNutt, J. (Eds.), *Advocacy, activism and the internet* (pp. 199–211). Chicago, IL: Lyceum Press.

Stiakakis, E., Kariotellis, P., & Vlachopoulou, M. (2010). From the digital divide to digital inequality: A Secondary research in the European Union. In Sideridis, A. B., & Patrikakis, C. Z. (Eds.), *E-Democracy 2009, LNICST, 26* (pp. 43–54). doi:10.1007/978-3-642-11631-5_4

Subrahmanyam, K., & Greenfield, P. (2008). Communicating online: Adolescent relationships and the media. *The Future of Children: Children and Media Technology, 18*, 119–146.

Subrahmanyam, K., Greenfield, P., Kraut, R., & Gross, E. (2001). The impact of computer use on children's and adolescents' development. *Applied Developmental Psychology, 22*, 7–30. doi:10.1016/S0193-3973(00)00063-0

Subrahmanyam, K., Reich, S. M., & Waechter, N. (2008). Online and offline social networks: Use of social networking sites by emerging adults. *Journal of Applied Developmental Psychology, 29*, 420–433. doi:10.1016/j.appdev.2008.07.003

Tufte, B. (2006). Tweens as consumers - With focus on 'girls' and 'boys' Internet use. *Child and Teen Consumption, 53*, 1–18.

Tynes, B. M. (2007). Internet safety gone wild? Sacrificing the educational and psychosocial benefits of online social environments. *Journal of Adolescent Research, 22*(6), 575–584. doi:10.1177/0743558407303979

Valcke, M., Bonte, S., De Wever, B., & Rots, I. (2010). Internet parenting styles and the impact on Internet use of primary school children. *Computers & Education, 55*(2), 454–464. doi:10.1016/j.compedu.2010.02.009

Valcke, M., & Decraene, B. (2007). *Children and the Internet: Help kit to tackle Internetusage by children and adolescents*. Tielt, Belgium: Lannoo NV.

Valkenburg, P. M., & Peter, J. (2009). Social consequences of the Internet for adolescents. *Current Directions in Psychological Science, A Decade of Research, 18*(1), 1.

Valkenburg, P. M., & Peter, J. (2011). Online communication among adolescents: An integrated model of its attraction, opportunities, and risks. *The Journal of Adolescent Health, 48*(2), 121–127. doi:10.1016/j.jadohealth.2010.08.020

Valkenburg, P. M., Schouten, A. P., & Peter, J. (2005). Adolescents' identity experiments on the internet. *New Media & Society, 7*(3), 383–402. doi:10.1177/1461444805052282 van Deursen, A., & van Dijk, J. (2011). Internet skills and the digital divide. *New Media & Society*, *13*(6), 893–911. doi:10.1177/1461444810386774

van Deursen, A. J. A. M., van Dijk, J. A. G. M., & Peters, O. (2011). Rethinking Internet skills: The contribution of gender, age, education, Internet experience, and hours online to medium- and content-related Internet skills. *Poetics, 39*(2), 1–20. Elsevier B.V. doi:10.1016/j.poetic.2011.02.001

van Dijk, J. (2000). Widening information gaps and policies of prevention. In Hacker, K., & van Dijk, J. (Eds.), *Digital democracy, issues of theory and practice*. London, UK: Sage.

van Dijk, J. (2009). One Europe, digitally divided. In Chadwick, A., & Howard, P. (Eds.), *Handbook of internet politics*. London, UK: Routledge.

van Dijk, J., & Hacker, K. (2000). *The digital divide as a complex and dynamic phenomenon*. Paper presented at the 50th Annual Conference of the International Communication Association, Acapulco, 1-5 June 2000.

Velicu, A. (2012). Violența mediatică prin ochii copiilor și adolescenților români [Media Violence throu the Eyes of the Romanian Children and Teenagers]. *Revista de Asistență Socială, 11*(1), 135-147.

Vergeer, M., & Pelzer, B. (2009). Consequences of media and Internet use for offline and online network capital and well-being. A causal model approach. *Journal of Computer-Mediated Communication, 15*(1), 189–210. doi:10.1111/j.1083-6101.2009.01499.x

Walther, J. B. (1996). Computer-mediated communication. Impersonal, interpersonal, and hyperpersonal interaction. *Communication Research, 23*, 3–43. doi:10.1177/009365096023001001

Wang, R., Bianchi, S. M., & Raley, S. B. (2005). Teenagers' Internet use and family rules: A research note. *Journal of Marriage and the Family, 67*(5), 1249-1258. doi:10.1111/j.1741-3737.2005.00214.x

Wenglinsky, H. (1998). *Does it compute? The relationship between educational technology and student achievement in mathematics*. Princeton, NJ: Educational Testing Service.

Wilkinson, D., & Thelwall, M. (2010). Social network site changes over time: The case of MySpace. *Journal of the American Society for Information Science and Technology, 61*, 2311–2323. doi:10.1002/asi.21397

Williams, A. L., & Merten, M. J. (2009). Adolescents' online social networking following the death of a peer. *Journal of Adolescent Research, 24*(1), 67–90. doi:10.1177/0743558408328440

Williams, B. T. (2008). "Tomorrow will not be like today": Literacy and identity in a world of multiliteracies. *Journal of Adolescent & Adult Literacy, 51*(8), 682–686. doi:10.1598/JAAL.51.8.7

Willoughby, T. (2008). A short-term longitudinal study of internet and computer game use by adolescent boys and girls: prevalence, frequency of use, and psychosocial predictors. *Developmental Psychology, 44*(1), 195–204. doi:10.1037/0012-1649.44.1.195

Wilson, K. R., Wallin, J. S., & Reiser, C. (2003). Social stratification and the digital divide. *Communication Research, 21*(2), 133–143. doi:doi:10.1177/0894439303021002001

Ye, S. J. (2003). *A study of elementary school student's behavior and cyberethics on the Internet*. Master thesis, National Pingtung University of Education, Pingtung, Taiwan

Yen, J. Y., Yen, C. F., Chen, C. C., Chen, S. H., & Ko, C. H. (2007). Family factors of internet addiction and substance use experience in Taiwanese adolescents. *Cyberpsychology & Behavior, 10*(3), 323–329. doi:10.1089/cpb.2006.9948

Yen, T. H. (2002). *Research on the relationship between background, behavior of using Internet and psychological characteristics for elementary school students*. Master thesis, University of Tainan, Tainan, Taiwan

Young, K. (2011). Social ties, social networks and the Facebook experience. *International Journal of Emerging Technologies and Society, 9*(1), 20–34.

Young, K. S. (1998). Internet addiction: The emergence of a new clinical disorder. *Cyberpsychology & Behavior, 1*(3), 237–244. doi:10.1089/cpb.1998.1.237

Young, K. S. (2004). Internet addiction: A new clinical phenomenon and its consequences. *The American Behavioral Scientist, 48*(4), 402–415. doi:10.1177/0002764204270278

Zywica, J., & Danowski, J. (2008). The faces of Facebookers: Investigating social enhancement and social compensation hypotheses; Predicting Facebook and offline popularity from sociability and self-esteem, and mapping the meanings of popularity with semantic networks. *Journal of Computer-Mediated Communication, 14*(1), 1–34. doi:10.1111/j.1083-6101.2008.01429.x

ADDITIONAL READING

Abramson, L. (February 9, 2011). Can social networking keep students in school? *NPR: Morning edition.* Retrieved January 14, 2010, from http://www.npr.org/2011/02/09/133598049/can-social-networking-keep-students-in-school

Agosto, D. E., & Abbas, J. (2010). High school seniors' social network and other ict use preferences and concerns. *Proceedings of the American Society for Information Science and Technology, 47*(1), 1–10. doi:10.1002/meet.14504701025

Ahn, J. (2011). Digital divides and social network sites: Which students participate in social media? *Journal of Educational Computing Research, 45*(2).

boyd, d. (2008). *Taken out of context: American teen sociality in networked publics.* PhD Diss., UC Berkeley

Brandtzæg, P. B., Heim, J., & Karahasanovi c, A. (2011). Understanding the new digital divide typology of Internet users in Europe. *International Journal of Human-Computer Studies, 69*(3), 123–138.

Burnett, C., & Wilkinson, J. (2005). Holy lemons! Learning from children's uses of the Internet in out-of-school contexts. *Literacy, 39*, 158–164. doi:10.1111/j.1467-9345.2005.00416.x

Cheung, C. M. K., Chiu, P. Y., & Lee, M. K. O. (2010). Online social networks: Why do students use Facebook? *Computers in Human Behavior, 27*, 1337–1343. doi:10.1016/j.chb.2010.07.028

Cotten, S. R. (2008). Students' technology use and the impacts on well-being. In Junco, R., & Timm, D. M. (Eds.), *Using emerging technologies to enhance student engagement. New directions for student services, issue #124* (pp. 55–70). San Francisco, CA: Jossey-Bass.

D'Amico, A., & Cardaci, M. (2003). Relations among perceived self-efficacy, self-esteem, and school achievement. *Psychological Reports, 92*, 745–754. doi:10.2466/pr0.2003.92.3.745

De Moor, S., Dock, M., Gallez, S., Lenaerts, S., Scholler, C., & Vleugels, C. (2008). *Teens and ICT: Risks and opportunities.* Retrieved July 6, 2010, from. http://www.belspo.be/belspo/fedra/TA/synTA08_nl.pdf.

De Souza, Z., & Dick, G. N. (2009). Disclosure of information by children in social networking–Not just a case of you show me yours and I'll show you mine. *International Journal of Information Management, 29*, 255–261. doi:10.1016/j.ijinfomgt.2009.03.006

Donath, J., & boyd, d. (2004). Public displays of connection. *BT Technology Journal, 22*, 71–82. doi:10.1023/B:BTTJ.0000047585.06264.cc

Donath, J. (2007). Signals in social supernets. *Journal of Computer-Mediated Communication, 13*(1). Retrieved from http://jcmc.indiana.edu/vol13/issue1/donath.html doi:10.1111/j.1083-6101.2007.00394.x

Druin, A., Bederson, B. B., & Quinn, A. (2009). Designing intergenerational mobile storytelling. In *Proceedings of IDC 2009*, (pp. 325-328). ACM Press.

Durrant, A., Taylor, A. S., Frohlich, D., Sellen, A., & Uzzell, D. (2009). Photo displays and intergenerational relationships in the family home. *BCS HCI,* (2009), (pp. 10-19).

Hargittai, E. (2008a). The digital reproduction of inequality. In Grusky, D. (Ed.), *Social stratification* (pp. 936–944). Boulder, CO: Westview Press.

Hargittai, E. (2008b). Whose space? Differences among users and non-users of social network sites. *Journal of Computer-Mediated Communication, 13*(1), 276–297. doi:10.1111/j.1083-6101.2007.00396.x

Heim, J., Brandtzæg, P. B., Kaare, B. H., Endestad, T., & Torgersen, L. (2007). Children's Usage of Media Technologies and Psychosocial Factors'. *New Media & Society, 9*, 425–454. doi:10.1177/1461444807076971

Hinduja, S., & Patchin, J. W. (2008). Personal information of adolescents on the internet: A qualitative content analysis of MySpace. *Journal of Adolescence, 31*(1), 125–146. doi:10.1016/j.adolescence.2007.05.004

Ishii, K., & Ogasahara, M. (2007). Links between real and virtual networks: A comparative study of online communities in Japan and Korea. *Cyberpsychology & Behavior, 10*(2), 252–257. doi:10.1089/cpb.2006.9961

Ji, Y. G., Hwangbo, H., Yi, J. S., Rau, P. L. P., Fang, X. W., & Ling, C. (2010). The influence of cultural differences on the use of social network services and the formation of social capital. *International Journal of Human-Computer Interaction, 26*, 1100–1121. doi:10.1080/10447318.2010.516727

Junco, R. (2009). *Teaching teens to Twitter: Supporting engagement in the college classroom.* Presented at Harvard University's Berkman Center for Internet and Society. Retrieved September 15, 2011, from http://cyber.law.harvard.edu/events/luncheon/2009/12/junco

Kim, J. H., Kim, M. S., & Nam, Y. (2010). An analysis of self-construals, motivations, Facebook use, and user satisfaction. *International Journal of Human-Computer Interaction, 26*, 1077–1099. doi:10.1080/10447318.2010.516726

Kim, J.-Y. (2006). The impact of Internet use patterns on political engagement: A focus on online deliberation and virtual social capital. *Information Policy, 11*(1), 35–49. doi:10.1108/09593840610700800

Kirschner, P. A., & Karpinski, A. C. (2010). Facebook and academic performance. *Computers in Human Behavior, 26*, 1237–1245. doi:10.1016/j.chb.2010.03.024

Kuiper, E., Volman, M., & Terwel, J. (2008). Students' use of web literacy skills and strategies: Searching, reading and evaluating web information. *Information Research: An International Electronic Journal, 13*(3). Retrieved from http://informationr.net/ir/13-3/paper351.htm

Kujath, C. L. (2011). Facebook and MySpace: Complement or substitute for face-to-face interaction? *Cyberpsychology Behavior and Social Networks, 14*, 75–78. doi:10.1089/cyber.2009.0311

Lang, A., Potter, R. F., & Bolls, P. D. (2009). Where psychophysiology meets the media: Taking the effects out of mass communication research. In Bryant, J., & Oliver, M. B. (Eds.), *Media effects: Advances in theory and research* (pp. 185–206). New York, NY: Routledge Taylor and Francis Group.

Lee, S. J. (2009). Online communication and adolescent social ties: Who benefits more from Internet use? *Journal of Computer-Mediated Communication, 14*, 509–531. doi:10.1111/j.1083-6101.2009.01451.x

Lenhart, A., & Madden, M. (2007). *Teens, privacy, & online social networks: How teens manage their online identities and personal information in the age of MySpace*. Washington, DC: Pew Internet &American Life Project.

Lenhart, A., Purcell, K., Smith, A., & Zickuhr, K. (2010). *Social media & mobile internet use among teens and young adults*. Washington, DC: Pew Internet & American Life Project.

Pempek, T., Yermolayeva, Y., & Calvert, S. L. (2009). College students social networking experiences on Facebook. *Journal of Applied Developmental Psychology, 30*(3), 227–238. doi:10.1016/j.appdev.2008.12.010

Reich, S. M. (2010). Adolescents' sense of community on MySpace and Facebook: A mixed-methods approach. *Journal of Community Psychology, 38*, 688–705. doi:10.1002/jcop.20389

Rideout, V., Foehr, U., & Roberts, D. (2010). *Generation M2: Media in the lives of 8- to 18-year-olds*. KFF.

Rizzuto, T. E., LeDoux, J., & Hatala, J. P. (2009). It's not just what you know, it's who you know: Testing a model of the relative importance of social networks to academic performance. *Social Psychology of Education, 12*(2), 175–189. doi:10.1007/s11218-008-9080-0

Rosen, L. D., Cheever, N. A., & Carrier, L. M. (2008). The association of parenting style and child age with parental limit setting and adolescent MySpace behavior. *Journal of Applied Developmental Psychology, 29*, 459–471. doi:10.1016/j.appdev.2008.07.005

Shaffer, D. W., & Clinton, K. A. (2006). Tool for thoughts: Reexamining thinking in the digital age. *Mind, Culture, and Activity, 13*(4), 283–300. doi:10.1207/s15327884mca1304_2

Shih, S. R. (2003). Network characteristics of the virtual world and its influence on the young. *Student Counseling Bimonthly, 89*, 80–89.

Shklovski, I., Kraut, R., & Rainie, L. (2004). The Internet and social participation: contrasting cross-sectional and longitudinal analyses. *Journal of Computer-Mediated Communication, 10*.

Subrahmanyam, K., & Greenfield, P. (2008). Online communication and adolescent relationships. *The Future of Children, 18*(1), 119–146. doi:10.1353/foc.0.0006

Subrahmanyam, K., Reich, S. M., & Waechter, N. (2008). Online and offline social networks: Use of social networking sites by emerging adults. *Journal of Applied Developmental Psychology, 29*, 420–433. doi:10.1016/j.appdev.2008.07.003

Tufecki, Z. (2008). Can you see me now? Audience and disclosure regulation in online social network sites. *Bulletin of Science, Technology & Society, 28*(1), 20–36.

Valentine, G., & Holloway, S. L. (2002). Cyberkids? Exploring children's identities and social networks in on-line and off-line worlds. *Annals of the Association of American Geographers. Association of American Geographers*, 92(2), 302–319. doi:10.1111/1467-8306.00292

Valenzuela, S., Park, N., & Kee, K. F. (2009). Is there social capital in a social network site? Facebook use and college students life satisfaction, trust, and participation. *Journal of Computer-Mediated Communication*, 14(4), 875–901. doi:10.1111/j.1083-6101.2009.01474.x

Valkenburg, P. M., & Peter, J. (2007). Pre adolescents' and adolescents' online communication and their closeness to friends. *Developmental Psychology*, 43, 267–277. doi:10.1037/0012-1649.43.2.267

Valkenburg, P. M., & Peter, J. (2009a). Social consequences of the internet for adolescents. *Current Directions in Psychological Science*, 18(1), 1–5. doi:10.1111/j.1467-8721.2009.01595.x

Valkenburg, P. M., & Peter, J. (2009b). The effects of instant messaging on the quality of adolescents' existing friendships: A longitudinal study. *The Journal of Communication*, 59, 79–97. doi:10.1111/j.1460-2466.2008.01405.x

Valkenburg, P. M., Peter, J., & Schouten, A. P. (2006). Friend networking sites and their relationship to adolescents' well-being and social self-esteem. *Cyberpsychology & Behavior*, 9(5), 584–590. doi:10.1089/cpb.2006.9.584

Valkenburg, P. W., & Peter, J. (2007). Online communication and adolescent well-being: Testing the stimulation versus the displacement hypothesis. *Journal of Computer-Mediated Communication*, 12, 1169–1182. doi:10.1111/j.1083-6101.2007.00368.x

Van de Vord, R. (2010). Distance students and online research: Promoting information literacy through media literacy. *The Internet and Higher Education*, 13(3), 170–175. doi:10.1016/j.iheduc.2010.03.001

Walther, J. B., Van Der Heide, B., Hamel, L., & Shulman, H. (2009). Self-generated versus other-generated statements and impressions in computer-mediated communication: A test of warranting theory using Facebook. *Communication Research*, 36(2), 229–253. doi:10.1177/0093650208330251

Willoughby, T. (2008). A short-term longitudinal study of Internet and computer game use by adolescent boys and girls: Prevalence, frequency of use, and, psychosocial predictors. *Developmental Psychology*, 44, 195–204. doi:10.1037/0012-1649.44.1.195

Winsler, A., Madigan, A. L., & Aquilino, S. A. (2005). Correspondence between maternal and paternal parenting styles in early childhood. *Early Childhood Research Quarterly*, 20(1), 1–12. doi:10.1016/j.ecresq.2005.01.007

Wise, K., Alhabash, S., & Park, H. (2010). Emotional responses during social information seeking on Facebook. *Cyberpsychology and Behavioral Social Networking*, 13, 555–562. doi:10.1089/cyber.2009.0365

Ybarra, M. L., & Mitchell, K. J. (2008). How risky are social networking sites? A comparison of places online where youth sexual solicitation and harassment occurs. *Pediatrics*, *121*(2), 350–357. doi:10.1542/peds.2007-0693

KEY TERMS AND DEFINITIONS

Digital Divide: The existence of an inequality in what concerns the Internet use by various larger groups (which can be as large as whole nations) or smaller ones, inequalities which can manifest as differences in physical access to that technology to uses competencies and actual patterns of use.

Digital Literacy: The derived shape of the media literacy concept; it encompasses the ensemble of knowledge (technical, as well as commonsensical, from encyclopaedical knowledge to types of discourses, use of cultural codes or information on search algorithms, the meaning of information digitization, etc.) necessary to a competent use of the Internet, which means the possibility of finding, understanding and assessing the pertinence of the Information thus found on the Internet.

Digital Skills/Competences: The ensemble of knowledge a certain user holds and which are reflected in specific (and, usually, more complex) patterns of using the Internet; beyond measuring the use' intensity (in terms such as frequency and duration), digital skills are used to differentiate between types of users. Also, they are used as an indicator for the existence of a digital divide in terms of use competencies.

Internet Addiction: Is a problematic relation with the Internet, characterized by heavy using, discomfort in situations in which access is not possible, neglect of social (family, professional etc.) obligations and often with a negative results in healthy and/or social life.

Internet Safety: An ensemble of laws and regulation, ethical or juridical (at an European and national level) which aim to sanction online behaviors which can threaten the psychological and physiological development of children and teens and/or those behaviors which can determine online/offine risk and dangers for children/teens.

Online Risks: Activities associated to the Internet which can be harmful (or can have a negative influence over the future psychological and physiological development of the child or which can lead to on or off-line behavior socially rated as negative.

Parental Mediation: The ensemble of activities the parent involves in order to foster a good relationship between his/her child and the media and in order to reduce the negative impact media could have on the child; mediation can be active or passive and can take different shapes, from media-related discussions and the participation of the parent alongside with the child in media-related activities to regulating use and forbidding access to some particular contents, technologies, platforms, etc.

Privacy Settings: A collection of settings which can allow the Internet user to control de disclosure degree he/she wants to associate to his/her image on the Internet; the disclosure elements do not limit to data allowing identification of the user (such as name, age, sex, picture, work place, address, etc.), but also to activities online, areas of interest, etc.

Social Networking Sites (SNS): Sites allowing interaction (socialization) among users, represented by a profile – with a varying degree of disclosure and various presentation perspectives (such as, professional, family, etc.) – interactions taking place by the means of 'comments' or postings of information visible only to some users ('friends' or, narrowly, only a part of them), which can, subsequently, react to them.

ENDNOTES

[1] On the attitude of children and teens to assume and assert the negative assessment adults (parents, educators or media at large) hold towards the media see Barker and Petley (2001) and, for the Romanian case, Velicu (2012).

[2] According to Boyd (2007), some non-users have accounts made by their friends who feel ashamed that their best friends in real life (i.e., offline) would not also be in their online list of friends (on SNS's), thus creating them a profile in order to be able to add them as 'friends'.

[3] Explanation of this choice: 'The target level of twice a day was based on previous research findings used by Microsoft Digital Advertising Solutions (2007), which reported an average of 2.4 visits to SNSs per user per usage day' (Baker & White, 2010).

[4] We should mention that, in Romania and also in EU, the online declared activity declared by most of the children is the use of the Internet for school, with 88% of the Romanians, respectively, 85% of the European kids; for the 13 to 16 years old girls is more often encountered than at any other age group/gender: 94% for Romania and 90% for Europe). On the second and third place, in EU, there are videogames and watching videos – and for Romania, online games and using instant messaging.

[5] From now on, when we'll say 'the use of social network sites' we will mean the users having an active profile on such sites and not only those who declared having used them at some moment.

[6] In the table we stressed the differences bigger than 7%.

Chapter 9
Students' Publishing Projects and their Impact on Teaching and Learning

Sandra Hofhues
Hamburg University of Applied Sciences, Germany

Anna Heudorfer
University of Augsburg, Germany

ABSTRACT

In this chapter it is assumed that students have only limited interest in reading and writing academic texts. After a brief introduction to the problem, the impact of academic reading and writing skills is shown. Furthermore, the authors want to emphasize how these literacies can support students' development, pedagogically speaking, by using action-based projects. The University of Augsburg provides examples for publishing projects in which students can participate. The examples demonstrate the positive effects of students' participation in such projects on the development of media literacies, especially in the areas of text comprehension and writing. Finally, prospects for student-publishing projects at universities are identified as well as the challenges associated with cross-media development, social software and Web 2.0 (Mayrberger, 2012).

ACADEMIC WRITING? UNDERSTANDING THE STUDENT'S PERSPECTIVE

The understanding of text is essential for scientific work. The ability to compose text is a key skill for academics and "knowledge-workers" as they need to make their scientific results accessible to a wider circle of interested people. The main reason for this is the dissemination of results throughout the scientific community but also the communication of science to a broader audience (e.g. von Hentig, 1999). From a scientific perspective the first reason remains the most important one. How can theoretical and conceptual contributions as well as empirical findings be published and how

DOI: 10.4018/978-1-4666-2970-7.ch009

are they discussed with a professional audience? What skills in (reading and) writing do scientists need in order to publish their (research) results at all? Text encourages research, it is the subject of scientific discourse and an essential channel to introduce new findings to an academic community. From the teacher's perspective, text has a similar function; students, however, rarely perceive text as significant (see Kruse, 2010a). Academic writing is rather considered as "dry" and theoretical, burdened with complex issues and associated with unapproachable discussions. In everyday teaching, this often makes it difficult to encourage students to publish their own results (Hofhues, 2011b). Working with (the medium) text becomes easier for students if they can do this in an action-oriented way, especially in regard of text *production*. Students' motivation for writing increases even more if the relevance of text becomes evident - or opens up job opportunities. The latter is particularly likely in the humanities and social sciences and, more specifically, in media studies. In this field, writing will be essential in the workplace, which is why students hope to obtain the necessary tools while still studying (Hofhues, 2011a). The big challenge in university education is to approach the improvement of students' understanding of reading and writing from different angles and to respond to their needs in a more differentiated way than solely taking an academic view on text. This challenge can be met by students' publishing projects. As educational media, they allow students to experiment in analog and digital media while reflecting their work with peers and mentors as well as gaining writing experience. Analyzing media as well as designing media products are vital elements in this process. Developing appropriate knowledge and skills in media design is essential to identify key design principles and codes "behind" media products (e.g. Kruse, 2010a). The latter is fundamental to developing (critical) analytical skills. Critical analysis again

is considered as the central dimension of scientific work. But an even more important requirement than being able to arouse interest is to understand that every publication follows a different intention and that the place where something is published is also relevant. Different types of media co-exist and offer varied options of use which has led to students drawing a line at certain types of text media. This is even accelerated by cross-media communication and experiences. With the above in mind the intentions of this chapter are:

- To analyze the importance of writing in academic contexts.
- To present three media projects which focus on publishing, always considering the above assumptions.
- To examine in conclusion the significance of practical media analysis for academic writing and also for media education in formal educational contexts.
- To discuss cross-media related developments and challenges of Social Software and Web 2.0, which give students more opportunities to participate in media (e.g. Mayrberger, 2012).

ACADEMIC WRITING, LEARNING AND PUBLISHING: GENERAL ASSUMPTIONS

Below, the aims and the context of this contribution will be explained in detail. First of all, we want to clarify the effects of scientific writing on the process of becoming part of a scientific community. Then we will explain the potential that lies in project-based learning and the development of media literacies, in particular for evolving skills in scientific writing. We will describe technological as well as cross-media trends.

Academic Writing: Getting into a Scientific Community

Scientific discourse depends on knowledge being turned into language to enable a debate within the scientific community. Putting knowledge into certain forms of writing thus promotes the communication of knowledge (Hofhues & Schiefner-Rohs, in print; University of Zurich, 2007, p. 5). Students begin to acquire this style of writing already during their studies by writing term papers, essays or thesises. Writing at university is in two ways associated with learning: writing is used as a means of acquiring knowledge *(writing to learn)*. The expertise is, in turn, used as a means of learning academic writing *(learning to write)* (ibid.). At university the focus is clearly on *writing to learn*, while learning the practice of academic writing is often overlooked.

Learning to write academic text mostly takes place in propaedeutic seminars. Students deal with a clearly defined topic in their field, read original sources and reflect on their learning in written form (ibid., pp. 5-6). But students have to "grow into" this environment first. It is a process of socialization for which several stages can be identified:

- First, the transition from school to university which is characterized by an uncertainty as to new demands on written work.
- The second stage: the student slowly develops an understanding of writing as a scientific activity and builds confidence in his or her own writing. The latter is essential for developing own assessments of the scientific discourse. The first thesis leads to the acceptance of writing as a heuristic process; writing is becoming a habit for the first time. A scientific community and instructions within the field can be put in context. At the same time, doubts are arising whether or not the writing process actually makes sense, especially if it seems to conflict with the prospect of a job offer.

- The academic (reading and) writing as part of the research process is fully absorbed with the dissertation. The student's identity and career now depend substantially on writing (ibid., 9-10).

"Writing research" deals with the subject of learning through writing. Modern writing research focuses on the writing process rather than on the product of writing as was previously the case (Hofer, 2006, pp. 78-79; Kruse, 2010). Hofer (2006) notes that particularly at university "mainly product-oriented writing is present" (ibid., 83). Strict rules and criteria are prevalent here. Only few courses offer techniques for developing creativity through writing methods. The importance of scientific literacy can hardly be denied since the writing of scientific texts accompanies students throughout the whole time of their studies. It should be the remit of the university to offer students support and to encourage them to obtain writing skills. Even though, in scientific everyday life the focus is often on acquiring knowledge *while* writing and not on writing as a competence as such.

Learn to Write: The Vision of Project Learning

Looking at the common style of classroom teaching and the learning practice in educational institutions like universities, it is obvious that a shift from teaching to learning is required. This shift involves putting students and their specific needs at the center of learning arrangements and focusing on an active examination of and engagement with the subject (Reinmann & Mandl, 2006). This basic concept of a culture of learning is supported mainly by problem- or project-based scenarios which assess not only the outcome of learning, but also the learning process itself (see Falchikov, 2004; Knight & Yorke, 2003). Duffy and Cunningham (1996, p. 190) define several characteristics which can be attributed to a "problem" and which can act as starting points for problem solving: the problem can serve as a guide to motivate learners. The problem can be used to test a theory in practice. Usually the problem is also an example of patterns or other common principles. At the same time, the problem can be an incentive to learn at all, and a reason to act authentically. Computers and the Internet often work as a "motor" in formal teaching and learning scenarios. They help to reflect not only the outcome of learning, but also to map the whole process virtually. The process of problem solving requires analytical and productive capabilities of the individual (Seel, 2003, p. 327). Good "problem solvers" are able to narrow a problem down and to use multiple perspectives when considering the problem, e.g. when working on a project. Furthermore, they are able to use different techniques and media to solve the problem. They solve the problem systematically and in an organized, well reflected way; they remain calm, conscientious and flexible at all times until the problem is solved (Funke & Zumbach 2005, p. 212).

With increasing technological development, a growing number of digital tools are available and used in teaching (e.g. Ebersbach, Glaser & Heigl, 2011). They enrich teaching and learning scenarios by adding elements of communication and collaboration. Web 2.0 tools are especially used in courses, which follow a socio-constructivistic view of learning (Mayrberger, 2010). The basic idea of the integration of Web 2.0 is often accompanied by the lack of media use as well as the lack of the students' abilities to organize themselves. In teaching and learning, we increasingly notice a "myth of Web 2.0" (Schiefner, 2011, p. 221) concerning participatory, self-organized learners:

The students have a pragmatic attitude towards the use of new media. They are mainly perceived as useful applications for communication and information retrieval, which are used frequently and willingly (Grell & Rau, 2011, p. 4, translation S.H.).

Whether students are willing to participate actively in open learning environments depends on their self-organization skills. As indicated above, students do not bring these skills necessarily into their studies, they must be trained. At the same time, self-organization includes the ability to control one's own learning processes (Sembill, Wuttke, Seifried, Egloffstein & Rausch, 2007, pp. 3-4). Group learning can – because of its dynamic - only work with an open mind on both sides: the learners who are engaged in self-organized learning scenarios, and the teachers who are assisting the learning process.

Challenges in the Process of Publishing: The Perspective of Media Education

Computers and the Internet offer new "experiences and options for action" (Schulmeister, 2009, p. 148), so that individuals can make their own learning experiences. Especially the Internet facilitates, for example, self-organized or collaborative learning via digital tools or environments as well as research for topics or documentations. Hoping for a change in the habits of participating in the network has become increasingly obsolete, if the most recent findings can be trusted (Grell & Rau, 2011). They show that in Germany the Internet is well-established as a new "mass media". While previously newspapers and television were the number one information media, the Internet is on its way to gain a similar status or has gained it already in the media-conscious population. However, the Web 1.0, which is especially built for receiving journalistic information, is more and more replaced by the Web 2.0, which allows participation and collaboration (O'Reilly, 2005). Social networks like Facebook, blogs and Twitter are prominent examples of this development. The user can easily tell the world what he or she is currently doing. In view of the potential that lies in these developments, the thesis of Digital Natives (Prensky, 2001) or the Net Generation (Oblinger

& Oblinger, 2005) is increasingly met with criticism. Consequently, new media and information literacies are required (Gapski & Tekster, 2009; Schulmeister, 2009, p. 149; Schiefner-Rohs, 2012).

The fact that media are subject of an ongoing technology-driven change opens up three perspectives on media education: media as a source of information, media as an instrument to meet challenges and media as an educational ambient (e.g. Marotzki & Jörissen, 2008). Transporting this into formal educational contexts leads us to the conclusion that universities should offer opportunities for working with media and, especially, of cross-media education in project learning environments (for further reference see Jakubetz, 2008; Schneider, 2007; Schuegraf, 2008; Sjurts, 2002).

STUDENTS' PUBLISHING PROJECTS AT THE UNIVERSITY OF AUGSBURG

With these theoretical and conceptual assumptions in mind, three different media projects which have been implemented at the Institute for Media and Educational Technology, University of Augsburg in Germany (imb; see http://www.imb-uni-augsburg.de/), can be described. Since 2001 this university offers an interdisciplinary degree in media studies: media and communication. the course, an interdisciplinary bachelor's and master's degree, emphasizes empirical project work and fosters project- and research-based learning. It is based on the three core subjects of communication studies, educational science, and media technology. It is supplemented by humanities and social science minors. The course is designed to provide basics, to detect and present media and communication problems and to demonstrate the use of scientific methods to analyze problems. To date, the curriculum includes essential knowledge, empirical and analytical methods as well as complex and diverse contexts of media,

communications, information and knowledge society (see http://www.imb-uni-augsburg.de/institut/english/study-program).

The Media and Communication course lecturers promote students' publishing through three different formats:

1. **Academic Publishing in w.e.b.Square:** w.e.b.Square is an Undergraduate Research Journal. In w.e.b.Square students act from the perspective of scientists in compliance with academic standards (see www.websquare. info).

2. **Journalistic Publishing in Presstige:** Presstige is Bavaria's biggest university magazine. Students take the perspective of journalists, i.e. they research and report independently about everyday life issues at university and beyond (see www.presstige. org).

3. **Organizational Publishing in vitamin b:** vitamin b informs about research, teaching and scientific everyday life issues at the imb. Students take the perspective of public relations agents, so that content is put on the agenda and must be coordinated.

Since the "Begleitstudium" (see www.begleitstudium-problemloesekompetenz.de) offers a university-wide, coherent framework for crediting student projects, the number of participants from outside the Media and Communication course is growing. As a result, it can be assumed that students are in principle interested in writing.

In the following, we will use a formal, academic, educational setting as an example how the implementation works in practice.

a. Academic Publishing in *w.e.b.Square*

The first project is the magazine *w.e.b.Square*. w.e.b.Square was established in 2006 at the Department of Media Pedagogy at the Institute of

Media and Educational Technology, University of Augsburg, in order to promote scientific exchange for students. The acronym stands for knowledge management and e-learning from an educational perspective. "Square" stands for a marketplace of outstanding student ideas. The focal point of the project is a web portal. The site is based on the open source content management system Drupal. Other media are used in addition, such as live streaming, blogs and Twitter. The educational concept is in constant change, as usual for media projects in education. E.g. w.e.b.Square offers possibilities of on-site exchange.

Thus annual conferences are organized by students for students. They even offer students the opportunity of immersion in science. They promote the exchange with the scientific community and the local network at Augsburg University and also on the Internet since all meetings are streamed live. Insights into the creative process of students' presentations are available on digital and social media platforms like Twitter. Blogs are posted throughout the semester. In addition, once a year a call for papers is published. Students from every university have the opportunity to submit their learning_products in context of an everyday life related motto. This way, the focus of the magazine of the University of Augsburg has widened to include all German speaking countries. However, the dual access structure at the University of Augsburg proved to enhance the learning process: while the journal is organized by a student editorial team, the students also learn to plan a conference in a seminar on scientific publishing as part of the Media and Communication course mentioned above. This facilitates the formal assessment of large amounts of work. Furthermore, the seminar provides time for interpersonal exchange and critical reflection of the learning process. The individual issues are publicized four to six times a year, so that the release dates can be seen as milestones of the project work. Some editorial

activities precede the actual publication, e.g. the articulation of a motto for the next issue, responses from potential authors, media presentation, and public relations (See Figure 1).

w.e.b.Square has been growing and its components continue to develop. At its core the project represents a scientific journal. The magazine was devised as an undergraduate research journal, a type of publication well known in the Anglo-American culture. Students have the opportunity to publish their learning products at an early stage of their career. The idea and implementation of the project is very simple: "only" a website is required to allow students' contributions to be published. But the Augsburg example also shows that participation without curricular links does not work. The editorial team needs to organize the essential processes and keep the portal updated. Apart from the formal, organizational prerequisites – the website and the editorial team – an open learning culture encourages the publication of students' contributions. Such a culture is fostered by cooperative learning. After all, many students want to share their positive experiences with the project. Through the curricular linkage, the editors' time and effort can be rewarded. Readers and authors, however, benefit in different ways, e.g. they learn about science by reading students' work. Authors get specific advice, which focuses on the entire research process including the dissemination of the core findings or results. The lecturers at the Institute of Media and Educational Technology have a supportive role because they can guarantee personal, technical or financial help if needed.

w.e.b.Square is a publishing project at Augsburg University that amplifies typical academic writing skills and publishing experience (see above). As mentioned above, taking on the roles of authors and editorial team members is a key factor in the students' efforts to improve their writing or publishing skills.

Figure 1. Front pages of two w.e.b.Square issues; © 2012 Dr. Ulrich Fahrner (Used with permission)

b. Journalistic Publishing in *presstige*

The Media and Communication course at Augsburg University not only provides scientific publishing at all stages, it also includes journalistic publishing and publishing for public relations in a variety of project-based learning scenarios. The learning design and proximity to everyday work situations enhance the motivation of students to deal with media production. After all, the three core professions (Scientist, Journalist, PR-Manager) represent important options for the humanities and social science. Considering competence orientation at higher education, this should not be ignored. Particularly in media studies, writing is a core element and one of the most important tasks also in the future profession. Nevertheless, "learning journalism" and also writing for

organizations appear to be rather unusual in the context of university education. Usually, there is a clear focus on academic writing. Journalistic practices or representations, are studied scientifically, such as in Communication Science. In this field, professional journalists are seen e.g. as "mediators" between public and politics. According to a study by Weischenberg, Malik and Scholl (2006), the majority of German journalists don't consider criticism as their remit. The main finding of the survey of journalists' self-image is that almost 90 percent of German journalists want to inform the public accurately and impartially. Only about half of them would like to criticize instances of maladministration. It becomes clear that journalism in Germany is supposed to be impartial and informative (Weischenberg et al., 2006, pp. 102-116). The separation of news from opinion, objectivity and conscientious research in general (Dulisch, 1998, pp. 51-52) are typical quality standards of German journalism.

Objective journalism is an all-important yet unrealistic credo, as we all know. Journalists choose topics that will determine the form of presentation and when deciding on how to actually write the text they will always act according to their own subjective values. They are also guided by the preferences of readers and editorial staff (Dulisch 1998, pp. 56-57). From the viewpoint of journalists, it is important to become aware of both, the ideals and the reality of the actions required. Actual text production is based on typical forms of representation. They serve different purposes. They have internal features which can be learned and which the reader can recognize (ibid.). To which extent ethical issues come into this still remains questionable. The more important it is to be aware of some ethical principles during journalistic training. A framework for experiencing and creating ethical and reflective guidelines for journalism is offered by training media such as presstige, the biggest student magazine at the University of Augsburg (See Figure 2).

presstige has the highest circulation of university magazines in Bavaria, Germany. Interested students are invited to write articles under the guidance of more experienced students. The magazine is organized like a traditional print magazine with an editorial team. Younger but sucessful students may take up responsible positions in various departments. Although it has been implemented for training purposes, the magazine is very authentic and presents real-life conditions. This also includes that each issue is fully self-financed, for instance through advertising. As a result students add economical skills to journalistic skills which reflects the challenges of publishing. Although these skills are typical for journalistic writing and publishing, they are – as described before – often not taught by way of a focused training in academic publishing.

c. Organizational Publishing in *vitamin b*

In contrast to journalism, which aims to inform impartially and objectively, public relations always act on behalf of a client. When producing text for a client, i.e. organization, it is therefore important to know what this organization stands for. (Dulisch, 1998, pp. 75-76). In the context of public relations, to influence the client's image in a particular way.

Figure 2. Homepage of presstige, University Magazine with the Highest Circulation in Bavaria, Germany; © 2012 Dr. Ulrich Fahrner (Used with permission)

Taken into account that public relations for the purpose of indirect, long-term profits ... use public interests and therefore have to accept social responsibility as a matter of fact, one is inclined to think that, within the mass media landscape, public relations is positioned between journalism and advertising. (Dulisch, 1998, p. 77, translation S.H.)

A typical framework for public relations strategies is corporate or organizational publishing. It is aimed at specific target groups, e.g. journalists (see Bentele 2006, p. 428). Corporate publishing will strive to raise the client's profile with the intention that the client will be noticed in positive ways, will enjoy increased acceptance and will gain in social esteem (Hoffman, Muller & Sauer, 2008, p. 201). Consequently, the purpose of organizational publishing is different from the purposes of academic or journalistic publishing. With the specific intentions of organizational publishing in view, a third project to promote specialized organizational publishing skills was put in place. It is called "Corporate Publishing in the Educational Sector" and started in the winter term 2010/2011. It presented students with challenges in the form of goal-oriented questions regarding the university they attended.

The project group cooperated with an advertising and PR agency. The agency had an active role in the project and provided students with insights into corporate publishing. The agency staff agreed to give professional feedback on students' work results. The aim of the seminar was to create an organizational magazine for the Institute of Media and Educational Technology. Due to the nature of a project seminar, students had the opportunity to learn about the various aspects of creating such a corporate magazine in small groups and in an action-oriented way. The production of text was an essential part of this process. First, the students made themselves familiar with the specific requirements of the articles and then discussed the respective target groups. They also explored topics which were researched at the Institute at that time. As a result of the process students were virtually able to hold their learning product in their hands – a print copy of the magazine *vitamin b,* an authentic corporate publishing product. In consideration of the three projects described several types of publishing can be distinguished (See Table 1).

STUDENTS' PUBLISHING PROJECTS: EMPIRICAL EVIDENCES

It has been described in detail how these publishing projects were structured and how they were implemented in Augsburg. The implementation itself and the fact that they are in place now for a considerable period of time indicate a significant

Table 1. Conceptual distinctions in types of publishing

	Stakeholder	(Educational) Goals	(Educational) Dimensions	Structural Anchorage
Academic Publishing	*Scientific Community*	*Academic Discourse*	*Fixed Rules and Criteria, Growing Expertise, Writing Skills*	*Formal Educational Settings, Research-based Learning*
Journalistic Publishing	*Public*	*Critical and Objective Information Mediation*	*Orientation towards the Reader, Striving for Objectivity, Special Ethical Issues*	*Open Educational Initiatives, Problem-based Learning*
Organizational Publishing	*Organizational Public*	*Goal-oriented Information Mediation*	*Objectives of the Organization and Claims*	*Open Educational Initiatives, Problem-based Learning*

project success. Theoretical and conceptual considerations allow for this conclusion. The empirical evidence presented at this point will give insights into the potential effect of the projects on teaching and learning. The duration of the individual projects differ; for this reason empirical data can only be provided for two out of three projects: presstige and w.e.b.Square.

presstige: Fostering Project-Based Media Literacy

The project *presstige* for journalistic publishing provides the most recent empirical results. They are referred to in a Bachelor's thesis from 2012 where they are put into the context of current research at the University of Augsburg (Amenta, 2012). The empirical analysis focused on the following question:

What potential lies in action-based media education at presstige for university students in a media-related degree course?

Special attention is paid to media literacy and its potential for students' personal development through action-based media education. The research questions were translated into a qualitative research design (Yin, 2003) using five narrative interviews with experts. The key findings of the investigation can be grouped as follows:

- **Fostering Critical Media Literacy:** The research question focused on critical media literacy (Schiefner-Rohs, 2012) and the effect of action-based media education in project presstige. In the interviews, main assumptions about the engagement of students in the project can be confirmed. All interviewees told the interviewer that action-based media education helped to change their view on (different) media. This was attributed to the practical approach of the projects and the students' personal role as media producers. Furthermore, producing media themselves had made them re-

alize that media producers have potential access to ways of manipulation through media. This led to a more critical view on the media itself. The participants, taking the perspective of the producers, had the chance to see "through" the media, they were introduced to the underlying processes, structures and design options. As a result, they were able to reflect critically on the media system - in particular the one in Germany - and on typical text types or media products (Amenta, 2012, pp. 36–37). This shows that participation in media work can promote key elements of media education and help students to reflect on media and on ways of using them. This applies in particular to print media, but was also transferred by the interviewees to other types of media (ibid.).

- **Opportunities for Personal Development:** It can be retraced from the interviews that participants in project presstige see personal responsibility as an important factor in their development. Respondents describe several areas for which this assumption is true: for their own work results, for individual work compared to the project group or for working together as a project team in a learning community. As a result they learned to deal with responsibility which had an effect on other areas of their personal development, if the various challenges had been mastered sucessfully. By participating in the project, participants became aware of what they *can* do and what they *are* capable of - an experience with the potential of strengthening confidence. Closely related to stronger confidence is the development of critical skills. They include the ability of being self-critical and the ability of taking criticism from others. In summary it can be said that, in addition to the basic study program and lectures, active media work opens up opportunities for students' personal development. This is demonstrated by the extent to which the project participants seemed to be personally involved in the project. The design of the project allows for experiencing and developing a sense of responsibility and therefore for gaining in personal maturity. However, the implementation of the project is based on self-organized learning processes which vary from subject to subject. The interviewees further pointed out that the project work has had an impact on other areas of their life which shows that they reflect on their project experience in presstige. This leads to the conclusion that projects like presstige foster sustainable learning processes which manifest themselves in skills and behavior (ibid., pp. 37–42).

- **The Role of Project-Learning:** Self-organized project work, mainly "free" work, is consistently perceived as positive and important. All interviewees appreciate project-based learning for their learning process. It gives them the opportunity to develop personally while experimenting with different kinds of media. Additionally, the interviewees emphasized the significance of an authentic product in the form of a printed magazine as the outcome of their work. As a result, they experience a sense of achievement and positive sentiments such as pride and gratification. Another essential aspect of learning is group learning in its various forms. All processes relate back to the project group, and group success can only be achieved through close cooperation and a shared end result. Taking part in the publishing project involves that individual goals have to be brought in line with group goals yet without imposing a too restrictive set of rules for group success. In addition to that,

authentic and real publishing situations are important to obtain the mentioned skills, as well as the self-organized learning process itself (ibid., pp. 39–41).

Regarding the development of project-based media literacy, we can summarize three main results: Firstly, in media projects participants are able to develop critical media literacy. Secondly, the projects help to educate participants as critical media producers and users. Thirdly, the development of skills depends on the way in which learning processes are organized.

w.e.b.Square: Potentials of an Undergraduate Research Journal for Academic Success

So far, the benefits of media production as part of university education have been discussed. By producing media themselves, learners gain a better understanding of media and their inherent concepts and they are better able to reflect on them critically. Similarly, the use of media contributes to the development of media-specific skills. As seen in the case of the student magazine, this can also influence attitudes in a positive way and enhance academic success. This is especially true when scientific skills are addressed; for reference see *w.e.b.Square*. For this reason an investigation was conducted at the University of Augsburg three years to explore perspectives of users and their particular interests. The investigation focused on the question how students relate to open educational resources. At the same time it was recorded, in which way users would utilize the magazine (Hallermayer & Jocher-Wiltschka, 2009). In a probability sample 89 students answered a questionnaire relating to the above points.

- The first concern was to detect students' *experiences* with writing and distributing their collegiate seminar papers or assignments. From this it emerged that nearly all students have already written different kinds of seminar papers. When planning or writing a seminar paper, the students check the internet for help (80 of 89). 77 students use the academic library where they search for relevant literature. Half of the respondents consult through personal contacts and exchange. Advice from other academics is rarely sought, topic-related online platforms or projects to enhance academic work are hardly frequented.

- 59 out of 89 respondents confirm unlimited *interest* in downloading exemplary papers or assignments of other students online. Apart from that, further 27 people attest interest in an online source only if the papers are associated with their own professional focal point. Nearly all informants tend to think that exemplary works of students should be available online for download (open content). Most of the respondents support digital downloads, as way of finding and stimulating ideas regarding a certain topic (63 of 86). 65 interviewees see online downloads as a possibility to find examples for structuring and devising concepts for academic work. 58 respondents would download collegiate publications in order to research literature about a certain subject. Answers like "Papers of other students are useful for me, because they help me to understand what the assessing academics want to see." or "because I can get information about academic subjects outside my professional domain" are less important for students (See Figure 3).

- Nearly all respondents assume that they would publish their own academic work. They fully agree with the basic idea of open educational resources (OECD, 2007) as a means of sharing knowledge, e.g. with

Figure 3. Student's reasons for using open educational offers (n=89; p.a.)

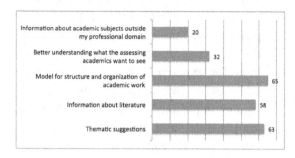

other students. Over half of the students would be prepared to write academic articles in addition to seminar papers etc. 24 interviewees fully agree and 25 students rather agree. The responses to the question whether these academic articles should be available online yielded an even clearer result: 78 of 89 informants support open access to online articles.

Considering this short summary of the most important results on how to make collegiate knowledge products available on the Internet, the findings can be interpreted as follows: they provide clear evidence that there is an apparent demand for online availability of fellow students' publications. Publishing in the Internet is also an important option for a bigger part of the interviewees. Accordingly, widening the study content to include additional topics corresponds with students' demands in relation to the study course and beyond. A coherent and comprehensive accompanying study course would allow for ways of assessment that would recognize students' involvement in projects. Nevertheless, the possibility remains that, in context with the prevailing learning culture, the requirements of some study courses may not be fully compatible with students' preferences for computer, Internet and communication technologies.

LEARNINGS FROM THE CASE STUDY: FOSTERING CROSS-MEDIA LITERACIES?

The above discussion has shown that projects that are based on publishing are generally useful in media education and support the development of media literacies. Through the co-curricular linkage to teaching and learning, they help to deepen the already existing knowledge of media and develop skills in the production of media as well as in their reflection (see below). The special focus on the effects of publishing mainly reflects the project experience. Some students at Augsburg University, however, already take the opportunity to participate in several publishing projects, i.e. they choose not to participate in w.e.b.Square, presstige or vitamin b alone. Instead they try to participate in two or all three projects simultaneously or sequentially. This can be seen in the individual study courses of the project participants. However, is this reason enough to advocate student engagement in publishing projects?

Firstly, it can be stated that the projects do support media literacies. But they differ from context to context. A special focus lies on promoting design-oriented media literacies which Buckingham (2010, p. 62) summarizes as the dimension "production". In addition to language skills, skills in structuring and designing text are promoted and developed.

Secondly, it can be stated that students expand their writing skills considerably. E.g., someone who participates mainly in journalistic projects may become better in journalistic writing, not in scientific writing. This fact indicates that the strategy at Augsburg University has to include new research on media projects.

Thirdly, we must even take the changed media habits into account. Increasingly, different types of media are created in the projects. These do not only require different writing skills. At the same time, a variety of technical skills will be useful. This way, the potential of cross-media education constitutes itself. It should focus on the promotion of cross-media literacies and also enable reflection on the changing media world.

Without having a new *general* model to foster cross-media literacies, a first conceptual reframing with regard to Augsburg University and the mentioned projects already exists (See Figure 4). The diagram shows some additional media projects which focus on other types of media than text production. All of them are part of the co-curricular media educational program at Augsburg University.

Fostering media education is necessary to empower students in active media use in terms of

Figure 4. Fostering crossmedia education at Augsburg University

an apprenticeship, a clearly positioned curricular anchor with self-reflective aims and the use of infrastructure such as ICT-Laboratories with the objective of media production. The focus and accelerator in both theory and practice is on online media with new possibilities for media aggregation and coherence. Enabling further development of this idea would require reflection over a wide area of media phenomena and a flexible focus on media development which is constantly changing. This will need an open attitude towards media both on the side of learners and of the educators, while at the same time having an extensive and permanently changeable media portfolio. On the structural level there is a need of acceptance that cross media education must be part of formal academic education, strongly anchored in curricula (Hofhues & Hoffmann, in print; Reinmann, Sporer & Vohle, 2007; Sporer et al., 2007).

CONCLUSION: PLEADING FOR AN EDUCATIONAL FRAMEWORK

We can resume that fostering cross-media literacies is easy where one accepts that it will add a new layer to the traditional media education as a regular part of formal educational contexts. Even though there is a lack of awareness for the traditional media perspective. But: taking an organizational point of view, constant efforts to encourage the implementation of media-educational courses will have their effects on three levels: stakeholder, process and structure – always reflecting the changes which media undergo and which can or will be adopted (e.g. Seufert & Euler, 2003). It is therefore important that learners themselves are interested in developing their media literacies and especially, their writing skills. Furthermore, there is the need to consider the learning process in addition to the learning outcomes and to reflect both together in project groups within learning communities. Finally, the structures in formal educational con-

texts are important, which automatically create a conflict sometimes between students' and teachers' interests. Open educational initiatives in the sense of Duernberger, Hofhues and Sporer (2011) can compensate here. But without a co-curricular framework the idea of (cross-)media education at universities does not work.

REFERENCES

Amenta, L. (2011). *Die Potenziale der aktiven Medienarbeit für die universitäre Medienbildung: Eine Fallstudie.* [*Potentials of project learning in the concept of action-based media education: A case study.*] (B.A.-Thesis). Augsburg, Germany: University of Augsburg, Institute of Media and Educational Technology.

Bentele, G. (2006). Fach-PR in der Informations- und Kommunikationsgesellschaft – Einige einleitende Bemerkungen. [Public relations in the information and communication society – Some Preliminary remarks.] In Bentele, G. (Ed.), *PR für Fachmedien: Professionell kommunizieren mit Experten* (pp. 11–20). Konstanz, Germany: UVK. [*PR for trade press: Professionally communication with experts.*]

Buckingham, D. (2010). Defining digital literacy. What young people need to know about digital media. In B. Bachmair (Ed.), *Medienbildung in neuen Kulturräumen: Die deutschsprachige und britische Diskussion* [*Media education in new cultural spaces: The German and British discussion*] (pp. 59–71). Wiesbaden, Germany: VS.

Duffy, T. M., & Cunningham, D. J. (1996). Constructivism: Implications for the design and delivery of instruction. In Jonassen, D. H. (Ed.), *Handbook of research on educational communications and technology* (pp. 170–198). New York, NY: Simon & Schuster.

Dulisch, R. (1998). *Schreiben in Werbung, PR und Journalismus. Zum Berufsbild des Texters für Massenmedien* [*Writing in advertising, PR and journalism. Being copywriter for mass media*]. (pp. 45–89). Opladen, Germany: Westdeutscher Verlag.

Dürnberger, H., Hofhues, S., & Sporer, T. (Eds.). (2011). *Offene Bildungsinitiativen* [*Open educational initiatives.*]. Münster, Germany: Waxmann.

Ebersbach, A., Glaser, M., & Heigl, R. (2011). *Social web* (2nd ed.). Konstanz, Germany: UVK.

Falchikov, N. (2004). Involving students in assessment. *Psychology Learning & Teaching, 3*(2), 102–108. doi:10.2304/plat.2003.3.2.102

Funke, J., & Zumbach, J. (2005). Problemlösen. [Problem solving.] In Mandl, H., & Friedrich, H. F. (Eds.), *Handbuch Lernstrategien* [*Handbook learning strategies*]. (pp. 206–220). Göttingen, Germany: Hogrefe.

Gapski, H., & Tekster, T. (2009). *Informationskompetenz in Deutschland: Überblick zum Stand der Fachdiskussion und Zusammenstellung von Literaturangaben, Projekten und Materialien zu einzelnen Zielgruppen* [*Information literacy in Germany: An overview on the current state of the professional discourse and a compilation of references, projects and materials on selected target groups.*]. Düsseldorf, Germany: Landesanstalt für Medien Nordrhein-Westfalen (LfM).

Grell, P., & Rau, F. (2011). Partizipationslücken – Social Software in der Hochschullehre. [Gaps in participation – Social software in higher education.]. *Medienpädagogik, 21*, 1–23.

Hallermayer, M., & Jocher-Wiltschka, C. (2009). *Zentrale Ergebnisse der w.e.b.Square-Bedarfsanalyse* [*Findings of the w.e.b.Square requirements analysis.*]. Augsburg, Germany: Augsburg University, Institute of Media and Educational Technology.

Hofer, C. (2006). *Blicke auf das Schreiben. Schreibprozessorientiertes Lernen: Theorie und Praxis.* [*Views on writing. Writing process-oriented learning: Theory and practice.*] Wien, Austria: Lit.

Hoffmann, B., Müller, C., & Sauer, C. (2008). *Public-Relations kompakt* [*Public relations compact.*]. Konstanz, Germany: UVK.

Hofhues, S. (2011a). From crossmedia publishing to crossmedia education: The Important role of media practice. In ICWE-Secretariat (Eds.), *Online Educa 2011: Book of abstracts* (CON44). Berlin, Germany: ICWE.

Hofhues, S. (2011b). Von studentischer Projektarbeit zum didaktischen Modell: die Augsburger Initiative w.e.b.Square. [From student's project work to a pedagogical model: The open educational initiative "w.e.b.Square" at University of Augsburg.] In Dürnberger, H., Hofhues, S., & Sporer, T. (Eds.), *Offene Bildungsinitiativen* [*Open educational initiatives.*]. (pp. 99–112). Münster, Germany: Waxmann.

Hofhues, S., & Hoffmann, C. (2012). Improving media literacy in universities: Insight into conception and implementation of a media curriculum. In *Proceedings of 2012 IATED Conference.*

Hofhues, S., & Schiefner-Rohs, M. (2012). Doktorandenausbildung zwischen Selbstorganisation und Vernetzung: zur Bedeutung digitaler sozialer Medien. [Graduate programs between self-organizational processes and networked learning: The importance of digital social media.] In *GMW'12* (other data not yet known).

Jakubetz, C. (2008). *Crossmedia*. Konstanz, Germany: UVK.

Knight, P. T., & Yorke, M. (2003). *Assessment, learning and employability*. Buckingham, UK: Open University Press.

Kruse, O. (2010a). Kritisches Denken als Leitziel der Lehre [Critical thinking as key objective of higher education.] *die Hochschule, 1*, 77-86.

Kruse, O. (2010b). *Lesen und Schreiben [Reading and writing*.]. Konstanz, Germany: UVK.

Marotzki, W., & Jörissen, B. (2008). Medienbildung. [Media education.] In U. Sander, F. von Gross, & K.-U. Hugger (Eds.), *Handbuch Medienpädagogik [Handbook media pedagogy]* (pp. 100–109). Wiesbaden, Germany: VS.

Mayrberger, K. (2010). Web 2.0 in der Hochschullehre – Überlegungen zu einer (akademischen) Medienbildung für E-Learning 2.0 [Web 2.0 in higher education - Reflections on (academic) media education for e-learning 2.0.]. In B. Herzig, D. M. Meister, H. Moser, & H. Niesyto (Eds.), *Jahrbuch Medienpädagogik 8. Medienkompetenz und Web 2.0 [Yearbook media pedagogy: Media literacy and Web 2.0]* (pp. 309–328). Wiesbaden, Germany: VS.

Mayrberger, K. (2012). Partizipatives Lernen mit dem Social Web gestalten [Designing participation with the social web.]. *Medienpädagogik, 21*, 1–25.

Oblinger, D., & Oblinger, J. L. (2005). Is it age or IT: First steps toward understanding the net generation. D. Oblinger & J. L. Oblinger (Eds.), *Educating the net generation*. Washington, DC: Educause. Retrieved March 29, 2012, from http://net.educause.edu/ir/library/pdf/pub7101.pdf

OECD. (2007). *Giving knowledge for free: The emergence of open educational resources*. Paris, France: Organization for Economic Co-Operation and Development, Centre for Educational Research and Innovation. Retrieved March 29, 2012, from http://213.253.134.43/oecd/pdfs/browseit/9607041E.pdf

O'Reilly, T. (2005). *What is web 2.0? Design patterns and business models for the next generation of software*. Retrieved March 29, 2012, from http://oreilly.com/web2/archive/what-is-web-20.html

Prensky, M. (2001). Digital natives, digital immigrants. *Horizon, 9*(5). http://www.marcprensky.com/writing/Prensky%20-%20Digital%20Natives,%20Digital%20Immigrants%20-%20Part1.pdf Retrieved March 29, 2012 doi:10.1108/10748120110424816

Reinmann, G., & Mandl, H. (2006). Unterrichten und Lernumgebungen gestalten. [Teaching and learning design.] In Krapp, A., & Weidenmann, B. (Eds.), *Pädagogische Psychologie [Pedagogical psychology]*. (pp. 613–658). Weinheim, Germany: BeltzPVU.

Reinmann, G., Sporer, T., & Vohle, F. (2007). Bologna und Web 2.0: Wie zusammenbringen, was nicht zusammenpasst? [Bologna and Web 2.0: How to bring together what does not fit?] In Kerres, M., & Keil, R. (Eds.), *eUniversity – Update Bologna* (pp. 263–278). Münster, Germany: Waxmann.

Schiefner, M. (2011). Mythos Web 2.0: Medien in Bildungsinstitutionen. [The myth web 2.0: Digital media in educational organizations.] In Weil, M., Schiefner, M., Eugster, B., & Futter, K. (Eds.), *Aktionsfelder der Hochschuldidaktik. Von der Weiterbildung zum Diskurs [Fields of higher education: From further education to discourse]*. (pp. 221–235). Münster, Germany: Waxmann.

Schiefner-Rohs, M. (2012). *Kritische Informations- und Medienkompetenz: Theoretisch-konzeptionelle Herleitung und empirische Betrachtungen am Beispiel der Lehrerausbildung [Critical information and media literacy: Theoretical and conceptual considerations and empirical derivation using the example of teacher training.]*. Münster, Germany: Waxmann.

Schneider, M. (2007). *Crossmedia-Management (PhD-Thesis)*. Wiesbaden, Germany: DUV.

Schuegraf, M. (2008). *Medienkonvergenz und Subjektbildung: Mediale Interaktionen am Beispiel von Musikfernsehen und Internet. [Media convergence and subject development: Media interactions using the example of music television and the internet.]* Wiesbaden, Germany: VS.

Schulmeister, R. (2009). *Gibt es eine Net Generation? Erweiterte Version 3.0. [Does the Net Generation exist? Extended Version 3.0]*. Hamburg, Germany: Universität Hamburg, Zentrum für Hochschul- und Weiterbildung. Retrieved March 29, 2012, from http://www.zhw.uni-hamburg.de/uploads/schulmeister_net-generation_v3.pdf

Seel, N. M. (2003). *Psychologie des Lernens [Psychology of learning.]*. München, Germany: Reinhardt.

Sembill, D., Wuttke, E., Seifried, J., Eggloffstein, M., & Rausch, A. (2007). Selbstorganisiertes Lernen in der beruflichen Bildung – Abgrenzungen, Befunde und Konsequenzen [Self-regulated learning in vocational education – Definitions, findings and conclusions.]. *BWP@*,13. Retrieved March 29, 2012, from http://www.bwpat.de/ausgabe13/sembill_etal_bwpat13.pdf

Seufert, S., & Euler, D. (2003). *Nachhaltigkeit von eLearning-Innovationen [Sustainability of e-learning innovations.]* (SCIL-Arbeitsbericht Nr. 1). St. Gallen, Switzerland: Universität St. Gallen.

Sjurts, I. (2002). Cross-Media Strategien in der deutschen Medienbranche: Eine ökonomische Analyse zu Varianten und Erfolgsaussichten. [Cross-media strategies in the German media industry: An economic analysis of options and chances of success.] In Müller-Kalthoff, B. (Ed.), *Cross-Media Management: Content-Strategien erfolgreich umsetzen [Cross-media management: Implementing content strategies successfully]*. (pp. 3–18). Heidelberg, Germany: Springer.

Sporer, T., Reinmann, G., Jenert, T., & Hofhues, S. (2007). Begleitstudium Problemlösekompetenz (Version 2.0). [The study programme "problem-solving competencies", Version 2.0.] In Merkt, M., Mayrberger, K., Schulmeister, R., Sommer, A., & van den Berk, I. (Eds.), *Studieren neu erfinden – Hochschule neu denken [Reinventing studying - Rethinking higher education]*. (pp. 85–94). Münster, Germany: Waxmann.

University of Zurich. (2007). *Wissenschaftliches Schreiben und studentisches Lernen [Academic writing and student's learning.]*. Zurich, Switzerland: University of Zurich, Arbeitsstelle für Hochschuldidaktik. Retrieved March 29, 2012, from http://www.afh.uzh.ch/instrumente/dossiers/WissSchreiben_01_10.pdf

Von Hentig, H. (1999). Eine nicht lehrbare Kunst. [A not teachable art.] In Narr, W.-D., & Starxy, J. (Eds.), *Lust und Last des wissenschaftlichen Schreibens [Delights and burdens of academic writing]*. (pp. 19–26). Frankfurt, Germany: Suhrkamp.

Weischenberg, S., Malik, M., & Scholl, A. (2006). *Die Souffleure der Mediengesellschaft. Report über die Journalisten in Deutschland [The prompters of the media society. Report on journalists in Germany.]*. Konstanz, Germany: UVK.

Yin, R. (2003). *Case study research* (3rd ed.). Thousand Oaks, CA: Sage.

ADDITIONAL READING

Kerres, M., Stratmann, J., Ojstersek, N., & Preußler, A. (2010). Digitale Lernwelten in der Hochschule. [Digital learning environments in higher education.]. In K.-U. Hugger & M. Walber (Eds.), *Digitale Lernwelten: Konzepte, Beispiele und Perspektiven [Digital learning environments: Concepts, examples and perspectives]* (pp. 141–156). Wiesbaden, Germany: VS.

Kleimann, B. (2007). E-Learning 2.0 an deutschen Hochschulen. [E-learning 2.0 at German universities.] In Merkt, M., Mayrberger, K., Schulmeister, R., Sommer, A., & van den Berk, I. (Eds.), *Studieren neu erfinden – Hochschule neu denken [Reinventing studying – Rethinking higher education]*. (pp. 149–158). Münster, Germany: Waxmann.

Laughey, D. (2011). Media studies 1.0: Back to basics. *Media Education Research Journal, 2*(2). Retrieved March 29, 2012, from http://merj.info/wp-content/uploads/2011/12/MERJ_2-2-p57-64.pdf

Reinmann, G. (2008). *Selbstorganisation im Netz – Anstoß zum Hinterfragen impliziter Annahmen und Prämissen* [Self-regulated learning in the internet – Impulses for implicit assumptions] (Report No. 18). Augsburg, Germany: University of Augsburg, Media Pedagogy.

Wedekind, J. (2004). Medienkompetenz an Hochschulen. [Media literacy at universities.] In Brehmer, C., & Kohl, K. E. (Eds.), *E-Learning-Strategien und E-Learning-Kompetenzen an Hochschulen [E-Learning strategies and media literacies at universities]*. (pp. 267–280). Bielefeld, Germany: Bertelsmann.

KEY TERMS AND DEFINITIONS

Cross-Media Education: Linkage between various media formats and their integration in curricula.

Higher Education: Education at Universities.

Media Literacy: Knowledge, skills and attitudes in the field of media in a context-appropriate way.

Publishing: Process of going online with products of learning.

Publishing Strategies: Planning processes of going online, e.g. with products of learning, having an eye on different publishing goals.

Section 3
Tools and Technological Issues in Web 2.0

Chapter 10

The Potential of Document Sharing for Scaffolding Writing Instruction

Katherine Landau Wright
Texas A&M University, USA

ABSTRACT

As the current focus of education is often on test scores rather than student learning, many public school teachers do not emphasize the development of cross-curricular writing skills in their curriculum. With the inherent pressures of standardized tests and growing class sizes, the burden of assessing writing projects often makes them prohibitive. However, recent research has shown that developing strong cross-curricular writing programs can not only support content knowledge but also raise standardized test scores. Web 2.0 document sharing technology can reduce teacher workload while providing more scaffolding and instruction than traditional writing assignments. Using these programs, instructors can implement collaborative writing projects that will allow students to learn as they write. This chapter uses pedagogical frameworks such as Balanced Literacy, Gradual Release of Responsibility, and Lev Vygotsky's Zone of Proximal Development to support the implementation of cloud software in public schools. It also outlines action research from a middle school classroom using cloud technology and makes practical suggestions for use of free software in secondary curriculum.

INTRODUCTION

At the conclusion of a public school education, students must be competent writers in real life situations. If learners are only completing writing assignments in English/Language Arts classes, they are missing opportunities to apply content knowledge in authentic circumstances. This need for real-world writing instruction is apparent in many corporations. Due to the growing use of technology in the workplace, casual communication frequently happens in writing (such as emails)

DOI: 10.4018/978-1-4666-2970-7.ch010

rather than in conversation. This has been seen in the post-academic world as many professional firms have been forced to hire trainers and consultants to teach their employees proper written language skills (Davies & Birbili, 2000). European nations that provide multiple educational tracks for high school students must bare this fact in mind, as students who traditionally would be successful with minimal literacy skills may now require stronger reading and writing abilities.

Cross-curricular literacy programs in public schools have the potential to address this challenge. Recent studies have proven the correlation between strong literacy skills and standardized test performance. High school students who are able to infer purpose and context while reading exam materials perform better than their peers (O'Reilly & McNamara, 2007; Wiley, et al., 2009). Furthermore, analytical reading and writing skills can compensate for a dearth in content knowledge (Visone, 2010; Gibson & Keyes, 2011). Therefore, literacy development must be every instructor's concern, not just that of the English/Language Arts teacher.

However, in the United States, federal legislation known as the No Child Left Behind Act of 2001 (NCLB) and the Elementary and Secondary Education Act have increased pressures on teachers, administrators, and school districts to "teach to the test" to ensure that student performance meets adequate yearly progress (AYP). While the stated goals of these acts are to provide equal education to all students and prepare them for college and a career, teachers see the immediate threat of state intervention, including the possibility of school closures, should their students not meet performance standards (United States, 2010). Furthermore, NCLB legislation does not define writing as one of the pillars of literacy. In fact, writing is only listed as additional subject matter to be tested if time allows. Many teachers are left feeling that there is little room to integrate cross-curricular literacy instruction into their course,

especially in high-need areas where class sizes and the instructional loads of most educators have increased significantly in recent years.

Instructors in the United States are not alone. After taking control of the government in 1997, the British Labor party began investing in the public education system and demanding concrete results. While celebrated for increasing education spending well beyond the rate of inflation, many have criticized the standardized tests required of public school children. One study done by researchers at Cambridge University found that class time was being spent taking practice tests in order to ensure students were prepared for the exams. One of these researchers openly admitted that the curriculum, especially in elementary schools, had been narrowed to ensure schools have the requisite percent of students pass their English and mathematics exams (Olson, 2004). In both the United States and Great Britain, integrating literacy development into content instruction could broaden curriculum while still preparing students for the state-mandated examinations.

The use of "the cloud," web-based technology services, can provide schools with an opportunity to increase literacy and content writing skills while alleviating some of the pressures on instructors. Through cloud-based document sharing programs, students can work on collaborative writing assignments and the instructor can monitor individual contributions. Not only does this free teachers from the inherent stacks of grading, it also allows students to learn from each other and strengthen their writing skills. However, the indiscriminate adoption of technology contributes little to instruction – pedagogical frameworks are necessary to ensure student growth. As seen by the "educational television" movement, access to technology alone is not effective pedagogy. In the early 1960s, the federal funds to put televisions in classrooms, without any attention to the professional development required, had little effect on day-to-day instruction. While touted as the panacea to all educational woes, televisions did not make great waves in the classroom as they were not integrated into the curriculum (Earle, 2002). The tendency to overspend on materials and underspend on implementation is common in education and leads to wasted money and resources. This chapter explores the uses of cloud-based resources and provides the research-based pedagogy required to support classroom and school-wide implementation of cloud technology.

First, this chapter provides a review of literature regarding cloud technology in the fields of both education and technology. Also included is a description of some of the controversies surrounding the safety and security of these new resources. Balanced Literacy and Writing Across the Curriculum are also outlined because these existing frameworks support the integration of cloud technology into public school curriculums. The second section introduces different cloud-based document sharing programs that are readily available for classroom use. The final section outlines an action research study completed to demonstrate effective implementation of document sharing and cloud technology into existing curriculum. The findings of this action research are discussed in the final section, along with recommendations for further research and implementation.

DOCUMENT SHARING AND PEDAGOGICAL FRAMEWORKS

Since the internet became a common classroom tool, teachers have been searching for ways to integrate it into their curriculum. Early web-based learning encouraged student-teacher interaction but little student-student collaboration. Due to the fact that the internet was first used as a way to receive information, students could log-on to view information from a teacher, but they had few means of becoming actively involved. The new technology available, known collectively as Web 2.0, is changing this paradigm (Dowling, 2011).

Centered on "The Cloud," a series of computers networked through the internet that deliver IT services to multiple users, Web 2.0 is increasing interaction between teachers and students in virtual classrooms (Thomas, 2011). Cloud services are available on any device with an internet connection, allowing students access from anywhere without having to purchase the technology. Even students who do not have computers in their homes can access assignments from school computer labs or at public libraries without having to transfer data. In this manner, all students, even those who traditionally face economic barriers to technology adoption, are able to complete computer-based assignments.

Cloud-Technology

The majority of the literature published on cloud software has been in the fields of science and technology in the form of consumer reviews. Reviews of cloud interfaces have repeatedly appeared in periodicals such as PC Magazine and are generally favorable (see Strohymer, 2011; Bradley, 2011). However, the majority of these reviews focus on the technical specifications of the interface, rather than providing suggestions for its application. There have been some editorial-style publications in the education field, but most are descriptions of implementation trials in singular classrooms rather than research based approaches to the incorporation of cloud technology into curriculum (see Strasma, 2010; Jensen, 2010; McCrea & Well, 2011). Furthermore, these approaches tend to be simply adding, rather than integrating, this technology into their current practices. This makes the student experience less authentic and detracts from the opportunity to develop twenty-first century skills in the content area classroom (Dowling, 2011).

The value of online document sharing in academic settings has not gone unnoticed in the public sector. Simply looking at for-profit companies proves that there is a growing trend to use document sharing and online document editing software when teaching writing skills. Turnitin.com, for example, has expanded from being a plagiarism prevention service to marketing their document editing and sharing software to schools around the country. Using PeerMark, students are able to assess the writing of their peers and, as the company advertises, "learn from their classmates" (iParadigms, n.d.). However, the cost of this and similar programs can make them prohibitive for many school districts.

In order to use cloud-technology in the classroom, there are institutional barriers that educators must overcome. Often, teachers and faculty members do not choose the best cloud software for their course; they choose what they know best (Corn, 2011). Current legislation also requires that any website collecting personal information comply with the Federal Trade Commission's 1998 Children's Online Protection Privacy Act (COPPA). The demands of this act have led many corporations, including Google, to limit access for those less than 13 years of age. For this reason, teachers must educate themselves on the available options and choose the cloud service providers that will be accessible to all their students and best serve the needs of their curriculum.

Cloud Security

Security is also a concern. Traditionally, schools have been able to monitor and control their own network security systems because information resided on an internal server managed by the institution. The use of cloud software requires trust of a third-party over which neither the faculty nor the school have control. Many institutions, especially colleges and universities, have instituted lengthy bureaucratic procedures for instructors to receive permission to use this technology in the classrooms. These are not punitive procedures, but rather they are the institution's attempt to protect itself from liability in the event of a breach in security. In order to overcome these problems,

students and faculty members need to be aware of the risks and accept them as their own, thus removing the responsibility for security from the institution (Corn, 2011).

Despite these risks, cloud computing in education offers an opportunity to revolutionize how we educate our students. Traditional styles of teaching, where the students are passive receptors of information from a well-informed source (the teacher), have been proven ineffective learning strategies for many students. In the move away from this submissive transmission of knowledge, different approaches to teaching have the potential to enhance student engagement and learning.

Teaching Frameworks Consistent with Document Sharing Technology

Lev Vygotsky, educational psychologist and social behaviorist, proposed that children learn best when working within their Zone of Proximal Development (ZPD). In order to ensure students work within their ZPD, teachers must meet students at their level of understanding and provide them with increasingly challenging, but not frustrating, tasks to build academic competence (Chang, Chen & Sung, 2002). Therefore, teachers must scaffold materials and skills until students are able to manage their own learning.

Gradual Release of Responsibility is an approach based on Vygotsky's theories that provides a pedagogical framework for reducing passive classroom instruction. Also described as the "I do, We do, You do" model, the teacher first demonstrates a skill ("I do"), then assists as the student or groups of students complete a similar task ("We do"). Finally, students are asked to demonstrate competency on their own ("You do"). This scaffolding of assistance ensures that students know what is expected from them for each task and how to best accomplish it (Weaver, 2002). While the "I do" and "You do" steps in this model are familiar to most educators (ie: teacher gives information and students are tested about it) it is difficult for many instructors to learn how to integrate the "We do" portion. Using cloud-technology to allow students to work collaboratively can accomplish this goal.

Vygotsky's research is also the foundation of a number of approaches to literacy instruction collectively known as Balanced Literacy, in which instruction takes multiple approaches to teaching literacy skills. The term Balanced Literacy grew out of the debate between phonics and whole language approaches to teaching literacy. In 1996, the whole language approach to teaching literacy was blamed for low standardized test scores in California. In reaction a new reading curriculum, which balanced phonics and whole language instruction, was developed (Asselin, 1999).

The term "Balanced Literacy" has been used to define a plethora of curricula that vary greatly in their implementation, but for this chapter Balanced Literacy is used as defined by Nancy Allison (2009), Nancie Atwell (1998), Katy Wood Ray (2006), and supported by the International Reading Association. Here, the Balanced Literacy approach uses the Gradual Release model to integrate reading and writing instruction and give students real-world experiences for using these skills (International Reading Association, 1998). Using a model outlined by Heather Lattimer (2003), often referred to as consume-critique-produce (CCP), students are first exposed to a number of texts and asked to identify the unique characteristics of that genre. Students then begin to evaluate different examples of the genre, pointing out strengths and weaknesses as well as providing critiques and critical evaluations. It is not until students can identify and analyze pieces in the genre that they are asked to produce original examples. Using this Balanced Literacy approach and the CCP model, teachers are able to not only provide more challenging academic tasks, but also increase the analytical thinking skills required of the students.

Balanced Literacy also focuses on authentic tasks, meaning there is a move away from basal readers and inauthentic writing prompts to reading and writing assignments that mirror what students need and will need in their lives (Frey, Lee, Tollefson, Pass & Massengill, 2005). In self-contained elementary classes, this means that literacy instruction is integrated into every part of the classroom – students not only learn about language during English/Language Arts time, but also read and write about what they are studying in social studies, science, and even math. Ideally, both English/Language Arts and other content teachers would use a Balanced Literacy approach and Vygotsky's Gradual Release of Responsibility model to teach writing across the curriculum.

Benefits of Writing across the Curriculum

Emphasizing writing skills in content-area classes has proven to increase student understanding and standardized test scores. Allowing students to write both formally and informally about what they experience in the classroom helps them better comprehend lessons and naturally leads to a more inquiry-based approach to education (Fordham, Wellman, & Sandmann, 2002). Furthermore, students must be prepared to write for real-world situations after high school. Just as a science teacher would not feel prepared to teach students to write a literature review, an English teacher is not an ideal candidate to teach students how to prepare a laboratory report. This sort of writing needs to occur in the content-area classroom where a knowledgeable instructor can model the skills.

The idea of using writing in content-area classes is by no means new; it was discussed in the works of British educationalist James Britton as early as the 1970s (McLeod, 2000). Writing can give teachers a view into a student's cognitive processes as the students are forced to explain their thoughts in words. With this insight, teachers can do more than simply intervene with struggling students; they can identify what specific aspects of the curriculum students are having difficulty with and provide meaningful intervention.

Writing in content-area classes also supports higher-order thinking. Most science, social studies, and math syllabi will call for students to do more than simply memorize information. Students at all levels of education are being asked to analyze, synthesize, and evaluate content materials. If a student is required to summarize the information in a textbook chapter into just a few sentences, they must think critically to differentiate between primary and ancillary information. It is nearly impossible for a teacher to evaluate whether or not students are engaging in this type of thinking without requiring them to produce written work (Gribbin, 1991).

Opportunities and Challenges of Group Work

Allowing students to work together on writing assignments is one strategy for scaffolding writing instruction both in English and in other content area classes. By collaborating on writing assignments, students can learn from each other's strengths and weaknesses and produce writing that they would not be capable of individually. In the 1980s and 1990s, there was a growth in research in collaborative writing. Much of this research focused on application of collaborative writing when teaching English language learners (for example, see Long & Porter, 1985). However, others examined how collaborative writing can improve practical writing skills for native speakers. Boughey (1997) observed a group of first year occupational therapy students assigned a collaborative writing project. The study focused on their improvement from the first to final drafts of the writing assignment. Achievement varied greatly and Boughey hypothesized that how well the group worked together affected their final product. Regardless of the results, Boughey showed that group work allowed the instructor to provide more feedback during the writing process. Students also reported that they wrote more and felt more confident in their writing due to the peer interaction. Having

multiple authors also allowed for there to be multiple researchers. Thus, each student was able to consult far more resources than they would have been able to access on their own.

While research has shown collaborative projects to be an effective means of instruction, in practice they are often avoided in middle and high schools due to a lack of accountability. As motivations for this age group can vary greatly, one or two students often take on the lion's share of the work. Students frequently express frustrations when they receive the same grade as a classmate who did not contribute as much to the project. Web 2.0 cloud technology can offer an affordable and accessible solution to these problems. Integrated with the Balanced Literacy approach to writing, teachers can have it both ways. Students can work in groups and teachers can monitor individual contributions. In this process, the writing task is a part of the learning process rather than simply a reflection of material learned. Students receive the scaffolding accepted as essential practice and teachers are freed from stacks of papers to grade.

DOCUMENT SHARING PROGRAMS

The variety of available cloud-based software is growing rapidly. All of the named interfaces in the following sections have online document storage and editing capabilities. Where they differ is in their individual options for document collaboration. While there are many cloud-based options for document sharing, Google Docs (www.docs. google.com), SkyDrive (www.skydrive.live.com), Primary Pad (www.primarypad.com), and Zoho (www.zoho.com) are discussed for their ease of use, accessibility, and cost effectiveness. While all four of these programs provide free cloud-based sharing of text documents, that is the limit of their similarities. PrimaryPad is the most simplistic, providing only basic word processing features. Google Docs, Zoho, and SkyDrive all offer word processing, spreadsheet, and presentation programs similar to Microsoft Office but differ in the availability of formatting options and the degree to which previous revisions can be viewed and monitored by an instructor. For a summary of the capabilities and restrictions of each of these programs, See Figure 1.

Accessibility and Capacity

The registration process for these programs is straightforward, generally requiring little more than a username, password, email address, and date of birth. As noted previously, this can be a problem for those who teach younger grades as most services require users to be at least 13 years of age. Microsoft's SkyDrive, however, will allow younger students to register for accounts with parental consent. After registering, students are given the option of sending a request for permission to their parent's email address. While this may result in a logistical challenge for teachers, it does provide an alternative for younger grade students. PrimaryPad offers an even simpler solution. As PrimaryPad does not collect any personal information from users, it does not have to comply with the same legal regulations as other programs. To use PrimaryPad, one person, usually the teacher

or instructor, sets up an administrative account and then creates various "Pads," or simple word processing documents. For someone else to edit the document, they simply need the web address and they will be granted full right of use.

Most of the features of these cloud-based programs can be accessed without downloading anything to the user's device. All allow users to upload documents or create them in the web-browser. Google Docs, SkyDrive, and Zoho also offer spreadsheets, presentations, and other file format options. All four interfaces mimic that of Microsoft Word, however Google Docs and PrimaryPad are not capable of many of the formatting options. While this does lead to many formatting errors when uploading or exporting documents, the simplicity of these interfaces is beneficial when working with less technologically literate students. Zoho offers more options, such as an integrated spell check and thesaurus, and documents are formatted much like Microsoft Word. However, as SkyDrive and Word are both Microsoft products, the transfer of documents is most successful using SkyDrive. SkyDrive does not require the user to have purchased or downloaded Microsoft Office, but this cloud-storage can be easily integrated with its use.

Figure 1. Snapshot comparison of document-sharing software

	Cloud Interface	Free storage capacity	Additional storage available at cost	Age Minimum	Word Processing	Spreadsheets	Presentations	Other Document Formats	Integrated Chat	Collaboration Features	Revision History
Google Docs	None when converted to Google Docs format	Yes	13	Yes	Yes	Yes	Yes	Yes	Collaborators are invited through email and can have permission to edit, only comment, or only view document.	Detailed with authorship highlights
SkyDrive	25 Gigabytes	Yes	None, with parental consent	Yes	Yes	Yes	Yes	No*	Collaborators invited via email and can have editing or only viewing privileges.	Previous versions of document saved
PrimaryPad	None, however only available for 30 days after creation	Documents saved with paid accounts	None	Yes	No	No	No	Yes	Collaborators only need the web address to access documents. Can be password protected.	"Time Slider" creates time-lapse video of all changes with authorship highlights
Zoho	1 Gigabyte	Yes	13	Yes	Yes	Yes	Yes	Yes	Collaborators invited via email and added as viewers, collaborators, or co-owners.	Previous 25 versions of document saved

*Microsoft offers a separate chat application, MSN Messenger, which can be used in conjunction with SkyDrive.

Google Docs is free with some storage and size limits. Documents are limited to just over one-million characters (approximately 1,700 standard single-spaced pages of typing) with similar limits for spreadsheets and presentations. As long as documents are either created in Google Docs or converted to its formatting, there is no storage limit. SkyDrive offers 25 gigabytes of free storage for Word, Excel, PowerPoint, and OneNote files. Zoho provides only one gigabyte of free storage, but as of January, 2012, paid accounts start at three dollars a month per user. PrimaryPad currently does not have any published size limits as documents are all converted to the PrimaryPad format. When using a free account, Pads are saved for thirty days.

Collaboration

Where these interfaces really differ is in their collaboration methods and capabilities. Google Docs facilitates collaboration in many ways. First, users can easily share documents by inviting collaborators through any email address. Once shared, the document's creator can decide how each individual interacts with the document – some may only be able to view the document, others may make comments, while others may have full editing privileges. Once engaged in collaboration, Google Docs saves a revision history. This not only highlights who has made which changes, but also saves previous versions of the document for review. Google Docs also has a separate "comment stream" for each document. This acts like a mini-blog for the document and could allow an instructor to discuss the document with students while it is still a work in progress.

Many math and science teachers have also cited Google Docs as valuable for data collection. While student engagement is generally higher when they collect their own data from experiments, it is often difficult for teachers to require students to collect enough samples to make their numbers statisti-

cally relevant. By using Google Docs, teachers can have students contribute their findings, thus giving each individual student a larger sample with which to work (Bonham, 2011).

When it comes to monitoring individual student contributions, PrimaryPad has some of the best options. Much like Google Docs, all editing is done within the web browser so multiple users can be online making revisions and individuals will see the real-time changes being made. When a student opens the document Pad, there is a place to type in their name, and then any changes made will be highlighted with an assigned authorship color. There is also a chat feature so discussions between collaborators can happen in real time and conversations are saved for the duration of the Pad. One of the greatest resources for an instructor is the "Time Slider" that turns the document into a time-lapse video showing all the edits and changes made over the lifespan of the document.

SkyDrive's document collaboration is not as integrated as Google Docs. It does allow users to view previous versions of the document and identifies which user made the changes to each version, although it does not highlight what changes were made. SkyDrive allows authors to lock sections they are editing, ensuring that another collaborator does not make changes to that section until the revision is submitted. SkyDrive could be used for document sharing and editing in a classroom as long as the instructor did not require detailed data on the changes made by each student. As SkyDrive is so compatible with Microsoft Office products, it would also be a productive way to build an electronic portfolio of student work.

Zoho has been cited as one of the best alternatives to Microsoft Office, which can be cost prohibitive for many students (Noyes, 2011). Zoho allows collaborators to work offline (provided the users have a word processor installed on their device) and the documents can be automatically synced as soon as an internet connection is found. Zoho also saves the previous 25 versions of a document and it is possible to restore an older version if necessary. Each version of the document is clearly labeled to show which collaborator was responsible for that revision.

ACTION RESEARCH METHOD AND PROCEDURES

This action research explored how cloud-based document sharing could be used in heterogeneously grouped middle school classes to promote literacy development. Three questions were investigated:

1. To what extent will using document sharing software allow for peer interaction when working on group projects?
2. To what extent will the teacher be able to effectively use revision histories and comment streams to support, monitor, and grade student participation?
3. How will the use of cloud-based document sharing programs support Balanced Literacy and Gradual Release of Responsibility approaches to literacy instruction?

Two English/Language Arts classes, one seventh grade and one eighth grade, were the subjects for this action research. Google Docs was used as the interface for the eighth graders primarily because the school district already used Gmail as an email platform and Google Docs for a number of administrative tasks. It was trusted for its security and therefore it was easy to obtain permission for its use. In addition, the revision history allowed for close monitoring individual student participation while the project was in progress. PrimaryPad was used for the seventh graders because its simplicity made it more accessible for slightly younger students. Moreover, as it was not necessary to create individual accounts, students who were not yet 13 years of age at the time of this project could participate.

While most students find a means to access the internet when desired for social media, it can be challenging to motivate them to do so when it is required for academics. For this project, the students were brought into the computer lab and led them through the process of acquiring an account, ensuring that all students were properly registered. It was well worth the time required to complete these initial steps as it avoided problems with any technology-related excuses later.

In order to establish heterogeneous groups for the assignment, the students were given individual writing prompts in the genre being studied that marking period. The seventh grade group was asked to write a brief essay explaining how to do something they were knowledgeable about, as they would be studying informational texts. The eighth graders were studying persuasive texts and so wrote a persuasive essay on a school rule they believed should be changed. All students in this school were preparing for the new State of Texas Assessment of Academic Readiness (STAAR), so a modified version of the state provided rubrics was used to evaluate these initial writing attempts.

The STAAR rubrics evaluate writing in three areas: organization/presentation, development of ideas, and use of language/conventions. Essays are given a maximum score of four points based on these categories. For the purposes of this study, the rubrics were modified allowing for a more in-depth examination of the skills being monitored. As provided, the STAAR rubric already disaggregated each category into two to three criteria. These criteria were relabeled and students received a score of one to four for each, allowing students to earn up to 32 points total (See Figure 2).

After evaluating their initial writing assignments, groups of four to five students were created making certain that each group had students with a variety strengths and weaknesses. Each class was given a brief tutorial on how to use the appropriate document sharing program. The initial documents were set up and shared with

Figure 2. STAAR rubric categories and criteria

STAAR provided category	Organization/progression			Development of ideas		Use of Language/ Conventions		
Study identified subcategory	Organization	Controlling Idea	Progression of ideas	Use of details/ examples	Understanding of prompt/ writing genre	Word Choice	Sentence Fluency	Conventions
Points possible	4	4	4	4	4	4	4	4

group members, ensuring that all students had access. The students had one hour in class to plan and break up the assignments, but the remainder of the assignment was completed outside of the classroom. This allowed the teacher to reserve class time for students to consume and critique exemplar writing samples (two thirds of the consume-critique-produce approach) and ensure that students knew how to write in their assigned genre. At the same time, the teacher was able to supervise the students' work to guarantee that progress was being made and to provide feedback while the project was ongoing.

Using the same STAAR rubrics, their projects were evaluated and assigned grades representing 70% of each student's individual grades. Students' individual participation made up the remaining 30% of the project grade. To monitor participation, students were required to log on and contribute to the writing assignment a minimum number of times on different days over the course of the assignment. The seventh graders were required to participate at least four times and the eighth graders at least six times. It was emphasized to the students that they should spread out their participation over the course of the assignment so they would give time for their classmates to contribute and respond to their submissions, however students could decide on which days to do so. Each day they logged in, they could earn up to three points. Students earned one point for simply logging on and making a minor edit to the document or responding to a comment made by a classmate in the discussion thread. Two or three points could be earned when students made lengthy contributions or thoughtful revisions with

comments explaining their thinking. The seventh graders were required to earn 10 points total, while the eighth graders had a minimum of 15 points. This reflected 20% of their final grades for the project. A separate private Google Doc was created to track participation as the project was progressing, allowing the teacher to intervene if students were not participating.

The final 10% of the students' grade was designed to encourage as much participation as possible by allowing students to earn extra credit significant contributions. At the end of the project, the total number of participation points earned by the group as a whole was tallied. If a student contributed a proportional amount or more (ie: 25% or more if there are four members of the group), they earned full credit. For fewer contributions, they earned a relatively lower grade. This also allowed students who contributed more than their proportionally fair share to earn bonus points and receive a higher grade than their classmates.

FINDINGS AND RECOMMENDATIONS

At the conclusion of this assignment, students evaluated the project and experience. They were asked the following open-ended questions:

1. What do you think about Google Docs/ PrimaryPad?
2. How well did Google Docs/PrimaryPad work for you?
3. How well was your group able to communicate while working on the project?

4. What do you think your group's essay will earn for a grade? Explain.

5. What do you think you personally should earn for a grade based upon your effort? Explain.

6. Do you have any other thoughts and reflections you would like to share with me?

The responses to these questions along with the students' project grades and communication logs on both Google Docs and PrimaryPad were examined to answer the questions set out by this action research. The data was analyzed qualitatively and three major themes emerged. The first is the enhanced student metacognition resulting from peer interaction. The benefits of constant scaffolding from the teacher comprise the second theme. The final theme is the success of this project due to its alignment with the Gradual Release of Responsibility approach. Except where indicated, all quotes from students remain unedited, though names have been changed to protect student privacy.

Peer Interaction

Of the students who responded to the third question regarding use of the document interface to communicate, 75% reported that they were able to discuss their projects with their group members. Twenty-one percent of the students wrote about how their group communicated in general, not specifically how the integrated communication programs assisted in their collaboration. Only 4% reported that they did not find the chats and comment streams to be effective modes of communication. However, communicating will only support learning if it pertains to the assignment.

In PrimaryPad, the seventh grade group registered 372 comments using the integrated chat feature. Of those comments, 255 (68%) pertained to the writing assignment. The remaining comments consisted of polite greetings and inquiries as to the whereabouts of a group member (12%)

and those unrelated to the students' projects (20%). The Google Docs participants paint a very different, though possibly misleading, picture. While there were only 75 total messages on the comment streams, nearly 98% were related to the writing project. However, students reported using the integrated chat program along with the comment stream to communicate with one another. These conversations are not saved by Google and therefore their content cannot be accounted for.

Overall, at least 84% of the students were able to use the chat features and comment streams. Groups used the features for different purposes. One group frequently left messages for a student who was sick so he was able to participate from home. Others left messages for each other, asking their peers to review something they had contributed and provide feedback. ELLs (English Language Learners) had the additional benefit of being able to ask their peers for assistance as they wrote. These students contributed more to the group project than their teacher had observed them do in previous class activities. When asked why she was able to contribute so much more, one student expressed that since she knew her group members would be checking her work, she was not afraid that her language difficulties would have a negative effect on the group's grade. This is consistent with previous studies on the use of computer-based classes in ELL classes. These studies from the 1980s and 1990s showed that hesitant writers, including ELL students, were more likely to accept criticisms and make revision based upon written feedback (Sullivan & Pratt, 1996).

The groups were also able to self-monitor their use of sources. As explained in Michael Bugeja's 2004 comparative case study, students with internet access are much more likely to plagiarize than their peers twenty years ago. This is largely due to the access of information granted by the internet and the privacy provided by their own bedrooms; while students twenty years ago would have been required to go to a library during regular hours to acquire sources to copy, students today can copy and paste source writing into their assignments in a matter of seconds. The students in my classes were not exempt from this temptation. However, as the plagiarism was no longer a private matter, students "caught" each other. As is shown in the following conversation, these problems were dealt with quickly without any need for teacher involvement:

Issac: Dude you copied everything you wrote from the internet...
Andrew: No i did not.
Issac: I just found all of it online exactly the same.

Issac then showed Andrew the link to where the information was retrieved. Together, they rewrote the section and added a reference. The remainder of the project was completed without any incident of plagiarism.

Metacognition, one's awareness of the cognitive processes a task requires, has been accepted as a way to judge student learning. If students have to explain how or why they are doing something, they will become more aware of the process and will be more able to apply the skills in other situations (Corno, 1986). When students changed their peers' work, they had to explain why they made those changes. Furthermore, in their discussions of organization and style, students defended their points of view. For example, when a group was debating whether they should write in the first person, one collaborator explained his point of view: "I don't think we want to make it personal lets have it more based on the facts that way its more convin[c]ing". In a traditional assignment, he may never have contemplated why he was making a stylistic decision – it would have been done automatically.

Teacher Interaction and Monitoring

Scaffolding writing instruction can be challenging for a teacher to do outside of the classroom. Even when rough drafts are required, it is difficult to ensure that students do not spend time and energy going the wrong direction with a writing assignment. The teacher in this action research reported frequently feeling she only realized a student is struggling when that student has turned in a paper. Being able to monitor students as they worked alleviated this problem.

As there were only a dozen groups in the two classes, the teacher did not have many projects to monitor. She was therefore able to check in with each group every two to three days. Students would leave comments and ask for assistance. For example, one student wrote "im going to highlight a section that i was editing and i would like to know if it makes since [sic]." The problem with her highlighted section pertained to her choice of words, which she was able to discuss with her teacher in a series of public comments. Eventually she was able to resolve the problem and her group members witnessed the process.

In another instance, an eighth grade group was slightly off-topic. While their focus was the prohibition of smoking in public places, students were researching and discussing various methods for quitting smoking. If this had been a traditional writing assignment, the problem would have gone unnoticed until after the essay had been submitted for a grade. However, as this project was monitored as it was ongoing, the students and their teacher were able to discuss their focus before they had gone too far off topic. Rather than just getting a low grade at the end of the assignment, the students understood how their writing was losing focus and discussed a way to solve the problem.

Both Google Docs and PrimaryPad made documenting student participation simple. The highlighted revision history for Google Docs left no room for author discrepancy. PrimaryPad occasionally led to some confusion as students could change their highlighted authorship colors based upon their preferences. Some students chose similar colors, but this problem was quickly resolved when students realized they may not receive credit for their work.

Monitoring student participation throughout the project also allowed the teacher to intervene when students were not contributing. Teachers at this school frequently report difficulties encouraging students to submit homework assignments and projects on time. In the classrooms used in this action research, the seventh and eighth grade students had only turned in 55% of projects on time in the first half of the school year. However, using Google Docs and PrimaryPad allowed the teacher to support students and teach them how to manage their time. Students who frequently waited until the last minute to begin a project, and subsequently produce mediocre work, were spoken to early in the assignment. They were unable to make claims common when working on long-term projects, such as they had started but left their work at home, and we were able to discuss with their teacher exactly how much time they had to complete the assignment and what was required of them in that time frame. When necessary, parents were contacted and they were grateful for the opportunity to intervene and assist their children. This resulted in over 85% of the students participating in their group's project.

Gradual Release of Responsibility

As previously discussed, effective teachers are able to scaffold instruction so that students are working within their Zone of Proximal Development. One of the greatest benefits of group work is the ability of students to provide that scaffolding for their peers. This is often difficult to observe in collaborative writing projects as students traditionally write by themselves even if they are contributing to a larger piece (Boughey, 1997). The use of cloud-technology in the project allowed students to actively work together and learn from each other's strengths and weaknesses.

Students collaborated on their research topics by sharing their findings on the chat interfaces. They shared resources that they found with one another, allowing them access to more materials than they would have been able or motivated to find on their own. Furthermore, if a student was working on a section and needed more information, they would frequently ask their group mates if anyone knew where relevant materials could be found.

Many of the comments reflect discussion on essay organization. In one group, each student was writing a separate section in the essay. However, the students soon realized that their approach of just putting the sections in order of completion was not a successful way to organize their writing. After a discussion of how to order their paragraphs, they began working as a group to dissect each individual paragraph. Student comments such as "move you[r] sentence to the second paragraph" were common and the group's paper was highly effective.

Students were able to identify each other's strengths and weaknesses and used them to their advantage. In one case, a student who is a reluctant writer but strong speller asked his group mate to begin writing while he watched from his home computer. To contribute, he corrected her spelling as she wrote. This allowed both students to participate at their comfort level and learn from one another.

Most gratifying was the student response to this experience. In their written reflections, many students expressed that their writing had improved because of this project. One student wrote that Google Docs is "a great tool because as you work the teacher can give you advice to improve." Another stated that she liked the project because she could "communicate while working on the group project and [her] friends could help [her] be a better writer." A third discussed how the entire process led to a better end product:

We chatted if we needed help and we deleted some things that we thought were dumb. And then we made them better and we said why we changed it and turned it into something better.

Recommendations and Further Research

A common problem with any action research is that the focus is on one set of students in one school or classroom. It is not a large enough sample to make generalizations about its implementation in all middle school classrooms. However, the significance of this project is not in the method of its implementation but in the opportunities it presents for supporting group work and cross-curricular writing development. This action research was not an attempt to create new theories to support cloud technology but rather used cloud technology to support existing frameworks while allowing students and teacher to participate actively in the writing process. Instructors must examine their existing curriculum to discover ways cloud technology can support their best practices.

Further research is necessary before we can expect to see cloud-technology implemented in classrooms across the country. As this action research focused on a small group of students, it was not possible to create a control group against which to measure student progress. A similar study needs to be completed in a larger school system where some groups can work face-to-face while others can use cloud-technology. Such a study would allow researchers to compare the gains made by the two groups of students and determine how much of a role cloud-technology plays.

An additional way to expand this research would be to incorporate cross-curricular assignments to support Writing Across the Curriculum. Cloud-based document sharing programs may provide a simple solution for content-area teachers who feel ill-equipped to assign and grade writing. Working with an English/Language Arts instructor, both teachers could develop an assignment and then monitor its progress simultaneously. In this way, the English/Language Arts teacher would be modeling literacy instruction for the content area teacher.

While this chapter focuses on the use of cloud-based document sharing programs in U.S. schools, further research could alleviate educational challenges in developing countries. These schools often face large class sizes, limited supplies, and few opportunities for classroom differentiation. Nothing about this action research confines its use to English speaking classrooms. Therefore, the strategies outlined here could have a positive impact on students in the Global South. Given limited access to computers, the free programs outlined above could prove invaluable. Furthermore, this exposure could help close the gap in technology literacy between developing and postindustrial nations.

This action research is a first step in many for using cloud technology to promote cross-curricular literacy development in public school classrooms. It demonstrates that, with proper planning, cloud technology can be used to support and enhance existing curriculum. As cloud technology develops, it can be assumed that the opportunities it provides will grow and expand. However, research-based best practices and pedagogically sound frameworks must support the use of this technology. When appropriately implemented, these tools have the possibility of changing the way we teach our students to write.

REFERENCES

Allison, N. (2009). *Middle school readers: Helping them read widely, helping them read well*. Portsmouth, NH: Heinemann.

Asselin, M. (1999). Balanced literacy. *Teacher Librarian, 27*(1), 69–70.

Atwell, N. (1998). *In the middle: New understandings about writing, reading, and learning*. Portsmouth, NH: Boynton/Cook Publishers, Inc.

Bonham, S. (2011). Whole class laboratories with Google Docs. *The Physics Teacher*, *49*, 22–23. doi:10.1119/1.3527749

Boughey, C. (1997). Learning to write by writing to learn: a group-work approach. *ELT Journal*, *51*(2), 126–134. doi:10.1093/elt/51.2.126

Bradley, T. (2011). Staying in sync. *PC World*, *29*(8), 29–30.

Bugeja, M. (2004). Don't let students "overlook" internet plagiarism. *Education Digest*, *70*(2), 37–43.

Chang, K., Chen, I., & Sung, Y. (2002). The effect of concept mapping to enhance text comprehension and summarization. *Journal of Experimental Education*, *71*(1), 5–23. doi:10.1080/00220970209602054

Corn, M. (2011). Embracing the cloud: Caveat professor. *The Chronicle of Higher Education*, *57*(36), B31–B32.

Corno, L. (1986). The metacognative control components of self-regulated learning. *Contemporary Educational Psychology*, *11*(4), 333–346. doi:10.1016/0361-476X(86)90029-9

Davies, C., & Birbili, M. (2000). What do people need to know about writing in order to write in their jobs? *British Journal of Educational Studies*, *48*(4), 429–445. doi:10.1111/1467-8527.00156

Dowling, S. (September 2011). Web-based learning: Moving from learning islands to learning environments. *TESL-EJ*, *15*(2). Retrieved November 19, 2011, from http://www.teslej.org/wordpress/issues/volume15/ej58/ej58int/.

Earle, R. S. (2002, January-February). The integration of instructional technology into public education: Promises and challenges. *Education Technology Magazine*, *42*(1), 5–13.

Federal Trade Commission. (1998). *Children's online privacy protection act of 1998*. Retrieved January 14, 2012, from http://www.ftc.gov/ogc/coppa1.htm.

Fordham, N. W., Wellman, D., & Sandman, A. (2002). Taming the text: Engaging and supporting students in social studies readings. *Social Studies*, *93*(4), 149–158. doi:10.1080/00377990209599901

Fountas, I. C., & Pinnell, G. S. (1996). *Guided reading; Good first teaching for all children*. Portsmouth, NH: Heinemann.

Frey, B. B., Lee, S. W., Tollefson, N., Pass, L., & Massengill, D. (2005). Balanced literacy in an urban school district. *The Journal of Educational Research*, *98*(5), 272–280. doi:10.3200/JOER.98.5.272-280

Gibson, L., & Keyes, S. E. (2011, December). A preliminary investigation of supplemental computer-assisted reading instruction on the oral reading fluency and comprehension of first-grade African American urban students. *Journal of Behavioral Education*, *20*(4), 260–282. doi:10.1007/s10864-011-9136-7

Gribbin, W. (1991). Writing across the curriculum: Assignments and evaluation. *Clearing House (Menasha, Wis.)*, *64*(6), 365–370.

International Reading Association. (1998). *Phonemic awareness and the teaching of reading: A position statement from the board of directors of the international reading association*. Retrieved February 11, 2012, from http://www.reading.org/General/AboutIRA/PositionStatements/PhonemicAwarenessPosition.aspx.

iParadigms, LLC. (n.d.). *PeerMark*. Retrieved from https://turnitin.com/static/products/peer-mark.php

Jensen, T. (2010, May/June). No student email at school? Google Docs to the rescue! *Library Media Connection*, 52–53.

Lattimer, H. (2003). *Thinking through genre: Units of study in reading and writing workshops grades 4-12*. Portland, ME: Stenhouse Publishers.

Long, M. H., & Porter, P. A. (1985). Group work, interlanguage talk, and second language acquisition. *TESOL Quarterly*, *19*(2), 207–228. doi:10.2307/3586827

McCladdie, K. (2006). *A comparison of the effectiveness of the Montessori method of reading instruction and the balanced literacy method for inner city African American students*. Unpublished doctoral dissertation, Philadelphia, PA: St. Joseph's University.

McCrea, B., & Weil, M. (2011). On cloud nine. *T.H.E. Journal*, *38*(6), 46, 48, 50–51.

McLeod, S. (2000). Writing across the curriculum: An introduction. In S. McLeod & M. Soven (Eds.), *Writing across the curriculum: A guide to developing programs* (pp. 1-8). WAC Clearinghouse Landmark Publications in Writing Studies. Retrieved February 18, 2012, from http://wac.colostate.edu/books/mcleod_soven/chapter1.pdf.

No Child Left Behind Act of 2001 § 6302, Pub. L. No. 107-110, 115 Stat. 1425 (2002).

Noyes, K. (2011, May). Microsoft Office alternatives. *PC World*, 29-30.

O'Reilly, T., & McNaMara, D. S. The impact of science knowledge, reading skill, and reading strategy knowledge on more traditional "high-stakes" measures of high school students' science achievement. *American Educational Research Journal*, *44*(1), 161-196. doi:10.3102/0002831206298171

Olson, L. (2004, May 5). England refines accountability reform. *Education Week*, *23*(4), 1–22.

Strasma, K. (2010). Using Google Documents for composing projects that use primary research in first-year writing courses. *Teaching English in the Two-Year College*, *37*(3), 305–311.

Strohymer, R. (2011). Get the most out of the cloud. *PC World*, *29*(7), 79–84.

Sullivan, N., & Pratt, E. (1996). A comparative study of two ESL writing environments: A computer-assisted classroom and a traditional oral classroom. *System*, *24*(4), 491–501. doi:10.1016/S0346-251X(96)00044-9

Thomas, P. Y. (2011, December 19). Cloud computing: A potential paradigm for practising the scholarship of teaching and learning. *The Electronic Library*, *29*(2), 214–224. doi:10.1108/02640471111125177

United States Department of Education, Office of Planning, Evaluation and Policy Development. (2010). *A blueprint for reform: The reauthorization of the elementary and secondary education act*. Washington, DC: Author.

Visone, J. D. (2010). Science or reading: What is being measured by standardized tests? *American Secondary Education*, *39*(1), 95–112.

Weaver, C. (2002). *Reading process and practice* (3rd ed.). Portsmouth, NH: Heinemann.

Wiley, J., Goldman, S. R., Graesser, A. C., Sanchez, C. A., Ash, I. K., & Hemmerich, J. A. (2009, December). Source evaluation, comprehension, and learning in internet science inquiry tasks. *American Educational Research Journal*, *46*(4), 1060–1106. doi:10.3102/0002831209333183

Wood Ray, K. (2006). *Study driven: A framework for planning units of study in the writing workshop*. Portsmouth, NH: Heinemann.

ADDITIONAL READING

Abram, S. (2007). You can take it with you: Online apps help road warriors. *Information Outlook*, *11*(11), 37–40.

Badger, R., & White, G. (2000). A process genre approach to teaching writing. *ELT Journal*, *54*(2), 153–160. doi:10.1093/elt/54.2.153

Behrend, T. S., Wiebe, E. N., London, J. E., & Johnson, E. C. (2011). Cloud computing adoption and usage in community colleges. *Behaviour & Information Technology, 30*(2), 231–240. doi:10.1080/0144929X.2010.489118

Blue, E., & Tirotta, R. (2011). The benefits & drawbacks of integrating cloud computing and interactive whiteboards in teacher preparation. *TechTrends: Linking Research & Practice to Improve Learning, 55*(3), 31–39.

Cunningham, P., & Wilkins, J. (2009). A walk in the cloud. *Information & Management, 43*(1), 22–33.

Demski, J. (2010). 3 for 3. *T.H.E. Journal, 37*(7), 32–37.

Fredrick, K. (2008). A gaggle of goodies from Google. *School Library Media Activities Monthly, 25*(4), 44–46.

Gallagher, K. (2009). *Readicide: How schools are killing reading and what you can do about it.* Portland, ME: Stehnhouse Publishers.

Keh, C. L. (1990). Feedback in the writing process: A model and methods for implementation. *ELT Journal, 44*(4), 294–304. doi:10.1093/elt/44.4.294

Kim, P., Ng, C., & Lim, G. (2010). When cloud computing meets with semantic web: A new design for e-portfolio systems in the social media era. *British Journal of Educational Technology, 41*(6), 1018–1028. doi:10.1111/j.1467-8535.2010.01055.x

Levitt, C. (2011). Hot tips for putting Google tools to work in your practice. *Law Practice: The Business of Practicing Law, 37*(2), 43–45.

Lingnau, A., Hoppe, H. U., & Mannhaupt, G. (2003). Computer supported collaborative writing in an early learning classroom. *Journal of Computer Assisted Learning, 19*, 186–194. doi:10.1046/j.0266-4909.2003.00019.x

Lowry, P. B., Curtis, A., & Lowry, M. R. (2004). Building a taxonomy and nomenclature of collaborative writing to improve interdisciplinary research and practice. *Journal of Business Communication, 41*(1), 66–99. doi:10.1177/0021943603259363

McPherson, K. (2007). New online technologies for new literacy instruction. *Teacher Librarian, 34*(3), 69–71.

Miller, D. (2009). *The book whisperer: Awakening the inner reader in every child.* San Francisco, CA: Jossey-Bass.

NaOne, E. (2011). Tiny, cloud-powered desktops. *Technology Review, 114*(5), 98.

Noël, S., & Robert, J. (2004). Empirical study on collaborative writing: What do co-authors do, use, and like? *Computer Supported Cooperative Work, 13*, 63–89. doi:10.1023/B:COSU.0000014876.96003.be

Perron, B. E., & Sellers, J. (2011). A review of the collaborative and sharing aspects of Google Docs. *Research on Social Work Practice, 21*(4), 489–490. doi:10.1177/1049731510391676

Roland, C. (2010). Exploring the web with live binders. *School Arts, 109*(9), 28.

Sadoski, M. (2004). *Conceptual foundations of teaching reading: Solving problems in the teaching of literacy.* New York, NY: The Guilford Press.

Sultan, N. (2010). Cloud computing for education: A new dawn? *International Journal of Information Management, 30*(2), 109–116. doi:10.1016/j.ijinfomgt.2009.09.004

Teneyuca, D. (2011). Internet cloud security: The illusion of inclusion. *Information Security Technical Report, 16*(3-4), 102–107. doi:10.1016/j.istr.2011.08.005

Warschauer, M., Arada, K., & Zheng, B. (2010). Laptops and inspired writing. *Journal of Adolescent & Adult Literacy, 54*(3), 221–223. doi:10.1598/JAAL.54.3.8

Wei, C., Maust, B., Barrick, J., Cuddihy, E., & Spyridakis, J. H. (2005). *Wikis for supporting distributed collaborative writing*. Paper presented at the 52nd Annual Conference of the Society for Technical Communication, Seattle, WA.

Wood, M. (2011). Collaborative lab reports with Google Docs. *The Physics Teacher, 49*, 158–159. doi:10.1119/1.3555501

KEY TERMS AND DEFINITIONS

Balanced Literacy: An approach to literacy education that balances whole language and phonics instruction. While definitions vary, most Balanced Literacy approaches integrate critical reading and writing skills while allowing students to read and write for authentic purposes.

Children's Online Protection Privacy Act: (COPPA) Act created by the United States Federal Trade Commission (FTC) to protect children online. Any website or online service that collects personal information from children under 13 years of age must meet the terms of this act. Compliance consists of including specific information in the privacy policy, protecting children's safety online, and obtaining parental consent.

Cloud Computing: Use of internet-based third-party software to create, store, and share files and documents.

Gradual Release of Responsibility: Sometimes described as the "I do, we do, you do" approach to teaching, instructors using a Gradual Release first model skills for students and support their practice in pairs or small groups before students are expected to complete tasks independently.

Web 2.0: Use of the internet as an interactive tool. This is in contrast with Web 1.0 where information is displayed to a viewer with no interaction.

Writing Across the Curriculum: First discussed in the works of British educationalist James Britton during the 1970s, Writing Across the Curriculum describes the integration of writing into all subject areas to promote content understanding and higher-order thinking skills.

Zone of Proximal Development: Level of instruction where children are challenged while not experiencing frustration. Developed by educational psychologist Lev Vygotsky, it is believed that students make the greatest gains in learning when working within this range.

Chapter 11
The Role of the Web Technologies in Connection to the Communication's Streamlining and Diversification between the Actors of a Learning System

Dorin Bocu
Transilvania University of Braşov, România

Răzvan Bocu
Transilvania University of Braşov, România

Bogdan Pătruţ
"Vasile Alecsandri" University of Bacău, România

ABSTRACT

In this chapter, the authors systematically relate to the question: "What are the main ideas that should be considered when elaborating software Systems for the communication's streamlining and diversification (CSD) between the actors of a learning system?" The broader perspective within which these ideas are debated is represented by the context that is created through the inception of what, in the specialized literature, is called social media (as a problematic universe) and Web 2.0 (as a fundamental technological universe). Naturally, the authors will not miss some considerations that highlight the impact of the phenomenon "social media" on the information systems of the near future.

DOI: 10.4018/978-1-4666-2970-7.ch011

1. INTRODUCTION

1.1. The Main Thesis of the Chapter

The quality of the communication in a learning system significantly impacts on its efficiency. The state-of-the-art information technologies offer unlimited resources for the communication's streamlining and diversification in the learning systems.

In this context, a natural problem arises: "How can we realize CSD systems that utilize the state-of-the-art technologies' potential in an optimal manner?"

The peremptory proof that it is not easy to realize such systems is the state of things in the field of the e-learning systems (Bocu & Bocu, 2011). Mainly, the interfaces' rigidity and the theoretical limits of the e-learning systems are two urges that direct the development of the e-learning systems to a superior level. Obviously, we speak about the rigidity of the e-learning systems' interface when comparing them with the performances of the learning systems, in which the role of instructor is assumed by a human actor. In fact, while it is possible for some technical issues to impede on the flexibilization of the e-learning systems' interface, the main obstacle is represented by the theoretical limits of the e-learning systems. Although they are not analyzed in this paper, it is useful to refer to these theoretical limits with the hope that they will constitute a research topic in the academia, and an opportunity for validation in the real world, with the aid of the developers of the IT tools. Therefore, the essential theoretical limitations of the e-learning systems are:

- The utilization of some communication instruments, whose syntactic virtues cannot sustain semantic constructions that are up to the complexity of the real-world communication instruments. We'll discuss again on this matter in the section *Short*

critical analysis of the theoretical challenges that condition the realization of the IT-based learning systems.

- The utilization of some modeling paradigms for the intelligent systems, which approximate the complexity of the human intelligences in an unsatisfactory manner.
- The absolute quantitative and qualitative difficulties that concern the speculative intelligence modeling. This is the only intelligence that is capable to methodically operate structural changes in the case of explanatory or creative demarches.

In Figure 1, we can study a more conclusive image of the challenges that relate to the intelligent systems research. In short, the nowadays e-learning systems are still unconvincing due to these theoretical barriers, whose removal requires the researchers to invent paradigms, models, procedures. Briefly, these can be referred to as next generation technologies.

Nevertheless, the e-learning systems shouldn't be judged in a harsh manner, neither by their producers, nor by their users. Both the academia and the industrial environment make efforts in order to confer a plus of credibility and efficiency, considering all the aspects, to the e-learning systems.

With this belief in mind, in this chapter we present an approach, whose deliberately limited objective is constituted by the description of the Web technologies that are mandatory for the communication's diversification and streamlining between the actors of a learning system.

This approach is motivated by the belief that the enormous impact of the information technologies on the human condition may find an expression *space that is both interesting and useful in the field of learning systems, through the discovery of some efficient formulae for the communication's streamlining and diversification between the actors of learning systems.* What is the direction towards which the man of the future goes, provided

Figure 1. The approximate map of the behavioural invariants, based on which the intelligent systems-related explanation can be commenced

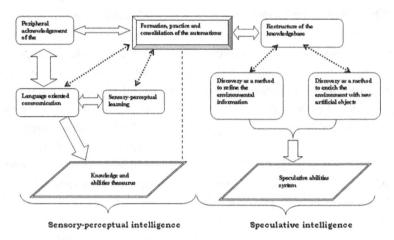

that most of the problems that are symbolically represented in Figure 1 are solved? Only one thing is certain. *The educational technologies that will survive are those that will represent a reliable compromise between pragmatism, traditions and innovations in the educational field.* It is not unlikely for old paradigms to be reactivated in a completely modified technological context. As an example, the classic *workplace apprenticeship* that has been for centuries the foundation of the learning, perpetuation and modernization processes of some jobs, to be reinvented by making appeal to the syntagm *strongly project oriented learning system from the real world.*

A short analysis of the data that is represented in Figure 1 helps us to have an idea regarding the challenges that have to be assumed by researchers, but also on the research subjects that have already produced promising results.

It is certain that learning as a problem is a research topic, in which the notable progresses are not favoured by the paradigms that influence the approach of learning as a problem. The capacity of the human being to describe the learning processes, which he is an active part of, is still limited to the descriptive dimension. The complete understanding of the human learning process, as it can be noticed in Figure 1, depends on the complete understanding of the manner through which the natural human intelligence is organized and functions. Without this complete understanding, the reliable simulation of the learning processes is not possible and, consequently, the digitization of the actors of a learning system is realized at an abstraction level that is unsatisfactory most of the time.

The limits that the human beings exhibit concerning the understanding of their own abilities are doubled by a series of technological limits, on which humans rely in order to realize learning systems that are close to the structural potential of the classic learning systems, but with a consolidated dynamics due to the utilization of the information technologies.

Although they are excellent when taking over routinely activities, the information technologies are still less expressive when taking over creative activities, which are essential in order to ensure the excellence of a modern learning system.

The asymptotic of the knowledge progress will probably reach in the short term a development level, which will contribute to the diminution of the theoretical and technological cloudiness zones that still impede the realization of some efficient learning systems that are based on the information technologies and are comparable to the classic learning systems.

1.2. Statement of Reasons

The main function of the information systems has always been the communication's optimization inside human communities, which are structured towards fulfilling some goals (LeBlanc, 2011). The introduction of computers in the equation of effectively specifying and realizing the information systems has produced essential mutations in the overall activity of the economic organizations, in the early days of the information era. These mutations formed the basis for the communication's streamlining and diversification between the main components of the economic organizations.

The quantitative aspects of the communication (speed, volume), but also its *qualitative aspects* (precision, flexibility, expressiveness) entered into an accumulation phase that determined major structural developments in the field of computer-oriented information technologies.

The emergence of the Internet can be considered an event with complex implications on the structure of the information systems, and also on the laws that govern their evolution. During the age that had favoured the crystallization of the syntagm Web 2.0, the change turned from a threat to the information systems' stability to an ingredient that opens limitless perspectives for the communication's streamlining and diversification in the modern information systems, as it is shown by (Rosen, 2009) and (Agichtein, 2008). *The speed with which people open new pavilions on the land of knowledge* and *restructure the old pavilions*, metaphorically speaking, is the essential outcome of these developments.

The main idea that is valued in this chapter is that a *software system of the type CSD is ideal for the elegant trafficking of some information resources and services*, without being engaged in the methodic monitoring of a knowledgebase development and consultation.

The knowledgebase exists in the teacher's mind. The digitization tools of this knowledgebase constitute a distinct and complex problem. *The student excels through his willingness towards communication*. This native willingness must be efficiently speculated through making use of proper technologies, as it is suggested in (Hawker, 2011) and (Agichtein et al., 2008).

An CSD system unites the two potentials. Thus, a system with a dynamic that is difficult to estimate at this time can be born. We certainly speak about the usefulness of such an approach in the academic and industrial environments. In the daily people's life, one can already notice some mutations, which are primarily behavioural, as a direct consequence of the availability of communication technologies that were unthinkable at the beginning of the information era. The social networks ultimately are, genuine communication tools, in which, although this fact is not readily visible, the preoccupation for streamlining and diversification is constant. This assertion could be better understood if we explored the structural foundations of the "social network" systems.

2. SHORT CRITIQUE PRESENTATION OF THE THEORETICAL CHALLENGES THAT CONDITION THE REALIZATION OF THE IT-BASED LEARNING SYSTEMS

It is correct to specify that particularly the academia shows a distinct preoccupation for the theoretical substantiation of some education paradigms, in which the information technologies tend to play an increasingly important role. Being aware of the fact that an exhaustive inventory is a challenge that goes beyond the scope of this book, we'll briefly present the directions that are followed, both as a theoretical "speech" and also in connection to the efforts to implement these ideas.

The specialized literature in the field of the IT-based learning systems can be appreciated for the diversity of the approaches but, it is still disappointing at least concerning the reliability. In other words, various papers that are presented at the E-learning-themed conferences excels through presenting some very promising learning scenarios, provided they are judged as systemic ambitions promises. These scenarios obviously represent steps forward on the path to the understanding of the manner that is naturally used by human beings in order to learn. Nevertheless, a human being that execises his or her learning abilities should have a proper infrastructure at hand, which offers powerful and reliable capabilities. In the natural systems, except for the particular cases, the human being has to exhibit the following features in order to learn:

- Reliable and powerful hearing.
- Reliable and powerful eyesight.
- Reliable and powerful skills regarding the reading and the writing.
- Reliable and powerful skills regarding the communication by word of mouth, using a natural language.
- Reliable and powerful memory.
- Reliable and powerful speculative skills.
- Reliable and powerful motivation.

How far did the man get regarding the research of these natural human capabilities? It has to be lucidly admitted that not too far. Nevertheless, this should not discourage us. The breaches that the man makes in the unknown that is sourced in himself offer a certain proof for the optimism and pragmatism that define a such highly complex process. The human beings have tried for thousands of years to decipher the universe in order to arrive faster and deeper at themselves, which it is a difficult endeavour. Whether we want to explain, or we target to imitate our own complexity, we will ever face problems. It is not necessary to invent the real axis in order to access part of the infinity's secrets. The man himself is an example of a reality, whose structure is source and expression of the infinity.

Considering that we refer, for example, to the problem of "reliable and powerful hearing", we know what the research directions are:

- The correct recording of an audible message that is emitted by a certain source.
- Noise filtering for the message that is transmitted by a certain source.
- The reliable understanding of an audible message.

The reliable and powerful hearing is not just an ordinary recording tool. It is a complex unidirectional or bidirectional communication tool, as appropriate. This means that when a message is received, a process is triggered that assures the integration of the hearing into a broader system, which could be called the *system for the man's orientation in space and time (SMOST)*. Following, a possible presentation of the process components that allow for the hearing to integrate into SMOST is conducted:

- The syntactic decryption of an audible message (noise filtering, structure identification, structure validation).
- The semantic decryption of an audible message (instantaneous, through the direct link to the current thesaurus of meanings, and speculative, by referencing in a logic and deductive manner the current thesaurus of meanings).
- The structural representation of a message's syntax and semantics. This structural representation should be realized in such a way that the products that are obtained with the aid of the hearing are optimally used by other modules of SMOST.

Does this "story" seem to be simple and largely plausible? Is it feasible to consider the granularity of the above approach? The answer is probably not but, being aware of it, we have an approximate idea regarding the complexity of the challenges that we'll face when confronting with the problem of audible messages traffic-oriented communication.

We ask ourselves this question again: how far did the man get in his temerarious attempt to realize learning systems that intelligently utilize the information technologies? A direct answer to this question could be avoided by saying that it could have been done better. Nevertheless, it is certain that a major qualitative improvement in the field of the learning systems that intelligently use the information technologies depends on the intensification of the resources both on narrow fields of interest and from a broader perspective. The verb "to learn" becomes intelligible from a scientific point of view if we know increasingly more regarding the way the human intelligence acts and about the scenarios that favour the efficient learning. As a consequence, Artificial Intelligence, Psychology and the Pedagogy of Learning, the Didactic Technologies represent some knowledge fields that are expected to offer a plus of knowledge, which is bound to contribute to the realization of the expected major qualitative improvement. Which occupations the human being will still handle, considering that artificial intelligence-enabled machines will become his instructors? Not even teachers will be affected by such a perspective. Thus, considering that artificial intelligence-enabled machines will take over a significant part of the teachers' attributions, the "flesh-and-bones" teacher will have more time to understand and explain himself or herself.

Concerning the technologies that are created as a consequence of the progresses that are obtained in the theoretic research that envisions the understanding of the natural learning systems, it can be stated that there are equally reasons to be optimistic and pessimistic. The reasons to be pessimistic have a direct link to the state of things of the theoretical achievements. The momentary limits of those automatically become limits of the technologies that implement them. Still, there are example of branches that pertain to the artificial intelligence, whose expressiveness and attractiveness maintain the research and implementation effort at an acceptable level. The expert systems, which are build using the languages that offer support for the logic programming constitute an example that

should ne kept in mind. The software systems that solve search problems by making appeal to computational intelligence-specific paradigms (collective intelligence, evolutive systems), also constitute examples that should be kept in mind. Probably, these two main classes of technologies are more than examples to keep in mind. That is a clear proof of the fact that in order to obtain a competitive technology, a reliable theoretical paradigm should be elaborated.

Without such paradigms, what could it be done in order to progress? Some steps can be accomplished, that will be nevertheless necessary when the long-awaited theoretical paradigms will be discovered. Considering the same reasoning path, we can also mention the proposal of this chapter to imply the Web technologies in the communication's streamlining and diversification between the actors of a learning system.

3. TECHNOLOGIES THAT ARE AVAILABLE FOR THE REALIZATION OF THE CSD SYSTEMS

3.1. Short Introduction

It is known the fact that in order to substantiate an idea, one needs access to technologies. The quality of the technologies essentially influences the quality of the ideas' substantiation ((Burstein & Wolska, 2003) and (Asur & Huberman, 2010)). In the IT industry, *the spiral of the technologies development is accelerated and consistent*. It is accelerated as the speed according to which new technologies appear or old technologies are enhanced is significant. It is consistent, as every activity in the IT is accompanied by technologies that contribute to the modernization and faster integration of the development activities. These can be activities that pertain to the proper engineering of the projects, and also activities that express the project management.

In order to realize the CSD systems, we appreciate that there is a rich range of technologies, which represent an important starting point. Among these technologies, we consider that the following have to be mentioned:

- The universe of Web 2.0.
- The plurivalent universe of DBMSs.
- Powerful development environments.
- Pragmatic methods for the project management.
- A large spectrum of complementary technologies.
- Technologies that bear the ambition to reshape the future of the IT.

3.2. The Universe of Web 2.0

This is more a collection of technologies that are difficult to embed together rather than a technology with well defined goals but, it still designates an important stage in the process of maturation of the efforts that enhance the attractiveness, reliability and utility of the Web applications. The Internet still represents a great potential for the currently expanding information society. The exploitation of this potential is accomplished by using both commercial and free technologies (Lenhart et al., 2010). A great "chromatic" variety characterizes the technological landscape that has developed around the promises of the Internet. This state of things can be considered an impediment by those that are passionate by strongly structured systems. These systems do not exhibit the problem of the proper tools choice, but rather their as inspired as possible usage.

The central advantage of the Web infrastructure is given by its practically infinite openness towards communication.

It can be concluded that the Web infrastructure is similar to a massive block of marble out of which each user takes his own slice, in order to immortalize a certain personal vision towards communication. *Starting from here and aiming to put the communication at the service of the socialization initiatives, the path can short and long at the same time.* It is short as the basic human communication needs can be easily fulfilled. It is long as the subtle human communication needs, although they exist in the real life, cannot be easily fulfilled. The subtle forms of communication with the aid of the Web infrastructure have to be discovered, modeled, implemented and tested in the real world. In other words, it is routinely to send to an acquaintance a message that announces the occurrence of a certain event. It relates to the subtlety whether the message is thought and packaged in such a way that the event is perceived only from a calendar point of view or accompanied by a series of defining meanings, which may enrich the poor-in-ideas human world. Thus, we may consider that it is about the difference between drinking a glass of water in one gulp, and savoring the perfume of a glass of red wine.

The tools that different producers added to the primary Web infrastructure essentially feature the goal to optimize the communication between people. The portals, the blogs, the online stores, the institutional sites, the electronic newspapers, the social networks, the virtual libraries, the virtual museums represent only a tiny part of the series of tools that were invented and re-invented with the hope that the optimal solution is found, both from a functional and development-maintenance perspective.

The effort that automates and standardizes the already mentioned applications' realization is particularly remarkable. From the automation perspective, we may mention tools like DotNet-Nuke, which is designed to tremendously automate the management of the Web applications without requiring special technical abilities. While being closely tied to the .NET platform, DotNetNuke remains a powerful tool for the development of the Web applications, in which the content management is essential.

From the standardization perspective, it is worth to signal the effort of the social networks applications producers to define APIs that contribute to the enhancement of the interactivity of these networks. This is a technical trick that is absolutely mandatory in order to imagine social networks that could represent capabilities that come to meet the desire to essentially enhance the subtlety of the communication scenarios.

Such a trend is naturally mapped on the architectural requirements of the CSD systems, which will be discussed in a more detailed manner in Section 4.

3.3. The Plurivalent Universe of the DBMSs

In general, the software systems are inconceivable without the contribution of the databases. In particular, the Web applications essentially rely on the functionalities that are offered by the databases. The approach that the DBMS producers choose in order to represent the data at the three usual layers (logical, virtual, physical), may represent an interesting discussion topic for another paper. It is certain that there is a fairly rich range of DBMS systems, from among which the Web applications developers choose the most appropriate variant, both from a technical and financial perspective. Naturally, the web appications that are centred on communication may substantially benefit from the multiple advantages that are offered by a high-quality DBMS system. Each DBMS features a certain data organization model, which is directly linked to the quality of the realized databases, as this is perceived considering the perspective of a certain user category. The necessity to streamline the communication in various types of Web applications promoted the usage of the XML standard for the data representation. Consequently, the XML databases, in which the fundamental storage unit is the XML document, appeared. The important advantage that is offered by the XML storage technology remains to be completed in real-world Web applications by DBMSs that, apart from offering flexible and complete support for the XML documents trafficking, also offer APIs that sustain the interoperability between XML documents sources, which are fingerprinted by

various producers. It is also important to ensure the interoperability between these databases and various technical categories of frontend clients. MySQL, Oracle and Microsoft SQL Server represent three important names in the DBMS community, which can be used in order to ensure the persistence of the informational flow that pertain to the learning activities, in which the accent that falls on streamlining and diversification is significant. Nevertheless, the field of DBMSs is characterized by a great diversity of approaches that may refer to the data organization model or to the actual implementation model. Considering the data organization model, the central place is occupied by the DBMS that belong to the following categories: relational, object oriented, multidimensional, and distributed. Considering the fact that the information system of an economic or organizational entity is featured by present and history, it is not negligible the contributions that are denoted in the specialized literature as "Data warehouse". The world of DBMS systems is one in which the effort to find more and more efficient solutions in order to store a system's information is strongly sustained by the technical solutions and, also, by the theoretical approaches that generate them. Such a state of things is also beneficial in order to ensure the viability of project that targets the communication's streamlining and diversification in a learning system.

3.4. Powerful Development Environments

The realization of the software systems at the level of the year 2012 is an activity whose complexity remains significant, despite the numerous progresses concerning the theoretical paradigms and the hardware and software technologies that are used. The complexity of the activities that pertain to the development of an IT project can be followed on two essential directions: the solution engineering proper, and the project management. The tight interdependence that exists between the two types of activities is the reason that allows us to speak about a slow but certain integration process of the engineering tools with the management tools, which relate to an IT project. Strictly speaking about the IT projects engineering tools, it is the moment to signal the developers' preoccupation to be able to use two fundamental types of support tools:

- Advanced programming environments (Eclipse, NetBeans, Visual Studio, Delphi, etc.).
- Advanced modeling environments (IBM Rational Rose, MagicDraw, Visual Paradigm, Poseidon, etc.).

The basic idea regarding the realization effort of these tools is the increase of the automation level of the IT projects engineering process. It has to be noted that the indisputable advantages of the IT projects engineering projects are accompanied by a series of potential pitfalls, which may be the germs of some risks with major impact over the quality of these projects. Therefore, the efficient utilization of the advanced programming or modeling environments is a challenge that involves not only routinely skills (training, exercises), but also being accustomed to invest time and skills in order to abstract the solution considering all the perspectives and all the detail levels.

It is also proper to mention that in the world of the development environments appeared the trend to realize tools, which suppose that the modeling and the implementation are integrated, especially in the case of projects that support an agile management. This is also the case with some projects that suppose the realization of Web applications.

3.5. Pragmatic Methods for the Project Management

The problem of the IT projects management is largely debated in the specialized literature and benefits from an enhanced attention in the large family of the Internet, which hosts forums and specialized sites that promote or evaluate the potential of some IT projects management

methods. Following, there are presented several addresses of some websites that illustrate, in part, the undeniable usefulness of such applications in order to promote tools that offer support for the IT projects management (as an example, http://www. easyprojects.net/), or for the general presentation of some support tools that relate to the projects management(http://www.project-management-software.org/):

- http://www.basecamphq.com/
- http://www.aceproject.com/
- http://www.attask.com/
- http://www.axosoft.com/
- http://www.celoxis.com/
- http://www.easyprojects.net/
- http://www.projectinsight.net/
- http://www.minuteman-systems.com/
- http://www.project-management-software.org/

The last link points to a site that fully illustrates the beneficial impact of the technologies that are developed around the concept of social network on an application that essentially promotes the IT project management tools. This represents in an implicit form, at least, an example regarding the communication diversification between the persons that manage the site's content and the persons that are interested by the topics that are discussed on the site.

Obviously, there are numerous other software systems that are dedicated to the IT projects management and not only. Two aspects appear as significant after reviewing some of these software systems. First, it can be stated that the authentic IT industry realized that the projects management is an activity that influences the success of the projects. Furthermore, it is important to note that a higher quality management is costly. Thus, the main dilemma of the IT managers that compete with themselves and with other developers is represented by the specification and implementation of a compromise solution/pragmatic for the management of each separate IT project.

An overall look on the management styles that are practiced in the IT industry shows that the good practices of the success managers may be expressed both in the form of some schemes, in which the preoccupation for formalism prevails, and also in the form of some schemes that promote the actors' freedom of movement as a keyword around which a management philosophy that is open to the novelties on multiples levels develops (note the increasingly consistent impact of the agile experiments for the dynamics of the IT industry).

3.6. A Large Spectrum of Complementary Technologies

The world of the Web applications is so rich in semantic challenges that it became the proving ground of some extremely varied technologies, but having as common denominator the fact that they offer solutions for the numerous problems that appear in the process of the Web applications realization. A few examples of such technologies are:

- The scripting languages (JavaScript, ASP, PHP, Perl, Python, Tcl, VBScript, LotusScript, etc.).
- The ability to create interactive applications (the AJAX style, which combines HTML, XHTML, CSS, JavaScript, XML, XMLHttpRequest).
- The capabilities that are additional to the Web services (XML, SOAP, UDDI, WDSL).
- The ORM technologies (Hibernate, JDO, JPA, EJB, SDO, NHibernate, etc.).
- The Web APIs (RPC, REST, SOA, etc.).
- The modern environments or frameworks for the Web applications development (Adobe Flex, Adobe Dreamweaver, Android SDK, Avaya, etc.).
- The applications of the type CMS (Drupal, Joomla, SilverStripe, XOOPS, etc.).

- The cloud computing technologies (Microsoft Windows Azure, Apaches's Hadoop).
- Etc.

We haven't presented an exhaustive list of the technologies that we called complementary. It is certain the dynamism that characterizes the world of the classic Web applications, and substantially enriched by the world of the wireless communication-based Web applications. This great range of software technologies is accompanied by an at least similar great diversity of equipments, which can sustain or tint the profile of a Web application. This is the climate that can accept the discussion about the communication's streamlining and diversification in a learning system. The problem is not whether we have technologies or not, but the manner through which we integrate these technologies in order to realize increasingly sophisticated Web applications.

3.7. Technologies that Bear the Ambition to Reshape the Future of the IT

It is difficult to predict the future of the IT in general. Substantive spectacular changes are foreseeable provided notable progresses will be obtained in the field of the artificial intelligence. Until these progresses will be achieved, we can count on some changes in shape, which a field that is still capable of providing unexplored resources. Considering the problem that constitutes the object of this chapter, there could be signaled the necessity and, even more important, of some technologies that would have the goal to:

- Documents traffic streamlining between the actors of the Web applications, considering that there are a series of documents representation standards. Probably, this streamlining could be backed by the XML standard, or by a more potent successor. As a consequence, it is necessary to realize some dedicated software systems for the XML format mapping (ADOC2XML-Any DOC to XML), of any document whose representation format has been published. These systems are featured by compatible communication standards in connection to the different types of applications that exist in the world of the Web applications. If these XML mapping software systems of any document are also free, it is even better in order to favour the idea of documents traffic streamlining. In this context, the containerization of such ADOC2XML systems would bring a flexibility and functionality gain, which is much awaited in certain types of social networks.

- The elaboration of some highly abstracted for the communication capabilities of the type "voice over IP", which may contribute to the streamlining of the communication that is based on the "voice over IP" infrastructure in the social networks. Obviously, the abstraction has to be realized by respecting the conceptual and technological framework that is currently elaborated, and that may promote the unification in the world of social networks (Facebook, Twitter, Google Friend Connect, etc.).

- The elaboration of some framework technologies in order to solve some practical problems that appear during the hyperdocuments manipulation activity. As an example, we may wish to perform an API-based cut of some portions of the documents in order to traffic or process them. Practically, if we speak about a multiple choice test with a standard structure and a classic administration pattern, the candidates' assessment can be automated provided that we are able to make use of capabilities that allow for the filled-in tests to be scanned and compared to the correctly filled-in test,

through using the cutting and similarities counting in order to report the achieved score.

- The elaboration of some technologies that open, in a timid but increasingly broader manner, the gates for the semantic analysis of the text oriented messages content.

- Etc.

This kind of technologies will contribute in an obvious manner to the communication's streamlining and diversification in all the software systems that value the communication as an essential ingredient.

4. THE DESCRIPTION OF A NEW APPROACH (CSD) THAT IS CHARACTERIZED BY THE COMMUNICATION'S STREAMLINING AND DIVERSIFICATION BETWEEN THE ACTORS OF A LEARNING SYSTEM, WHICH ARE ACTIVE IN UNCONVENTIONAL PLACES AND SITUATIONS

The conceptual model that is described in this chapter is loosely based on some existing developments. The exhaustive list of all these contributions can be studied in the section that contains the references. Nevertheless, the model that constitutes the object of this chapter is entirely an original contribution that has already been effectively implemented in our routinely academic teaching activities. This allowed for an empirical validation of the method's suitability and appropriateness with very promising results.

4.1. Introduction

The education of a community's members is a very important activity for its existence. Two aspects are essential in order to justify the importance of a community members' education: *the transfer of the collective culture from one generation to another* and *the addition of new and defining elements for the collective culture.* When it is perceived from this perspective, the education can't be regarded just as a chance for the individual's affirmation, but rather as an efficient way for the community to relate to the environment it is a part of. Thus, *the education is the key for a community's culture survival.* Therefore, the urge to optimize the learning systems activity, be them formal or informal, and that exist in a certain cultural space, is a highly serious mission.

We consider that the presence of the man in the third millennium of the Christian calendar is accompanied by a series of progresses regarding the qualitative and quantitative diversification of the learning systems. Without being preoccupied in this paper by the ethic aspects of the education in general, we make the assumption that the education serves some noble goals. In this context, the nowadays technological and scientific level of the human civilization can be considered entirely favourable for some consistent progresses in the field of the education systems. These progresses may be founded on the following essential ideas:

- *The extensive and intensive valorization of the modern information technologies' potential.*
- *The creation of information technologies that may substantially contribute to the communication's streamlining in the case of the IT-based systems.*
- *The creation of information technologies that may substantially contribute to the communication's diversification in the case of the IT-based systems.*
- *The identification and specification of a learning paradigm that optimally values the contribution of the modern information technologies to the communication's streamlining and diversification in the learning systems.*

Although in the real world there are elements that offer a meaning to the syntagm "the communication's streamlining and diversification", we try to define more precisely in the following paragraphs the expectancies that an actor of a learning system has, considering the CSD perspective.

The *communication's streamlining* means the elimination and attenuation of the obstacles that condition the communication in the learning systems (it is preferable to explore the three levels that may contribute to the streamlining: syntactic, semantic and pragmatic).

The *communication's diversification* envisions the elimination and attenuation of the spatial, temporal and other types of constraints that are developed on a cultural basis inside the learning systems.

In Section 3.7, we offered a series of examples for the directions that could be followed in order to substantiate these two natural requirements for any learning system, which values the communication as the main instrument in order to assure the efficiency. In fact, the truth that is verified in practice is that the knowledge and abilities transfer in a certain field of expertise can be accelerated and substantiated, provided that we use the communication in a polyvalent and methodic manner.

4.2. The Extensive and Intensive Valorisation of the Modern Information Technologies' Potential

The idea of this paragraph is to explicitly point out what has already been suggested in Section 3 of this chapter: the logistics for the realization of some flexible and dynamic Web applications exists. The problem that we may focus our attention on in general and in the case of the learning systems in particular is represented by the valorization of this basic logistics. As a consequence, we have two options in order to enhance our IT creations: the *extensive option* and the *intensive option*. The extensive option *supposes the identification of new opportunities to utilize the information technologies. More precisely put, the eye of the expert from the problem domain or from the solution domain is invited to find new semantics that may constitute an opportunity to utilize the information technologies.* From this point of view we may notice, for example, the enthusiasm with which the mobile phones and tablets producers launch applications that are favoured by the capabilities of these equipments. These applications are acclaimed by the users at a sufficient level as for the *intensive valorization efforts of the equipments' potential to be justified. This implies the optimization of the functional and stylistic performances of the applications, from the perspective of some new development paradigms or interests.*

If we insist a little on the intensive option, we highlight the efforts that are made to maintain an ascending trend for the quick acquaintance of the users to the interfaces of the applications that are made available on different types of equipments. *The combination of the proper visual show with the efficacy of the navigation through the functional capabilities of the applications still represents the fundamental list of ingredients in the area of HCI (Human Computer Interface).*

4.3. The Creation of Information Technologies that May Substantially Contribute to the Communication's Streamlining in the IT-Based Systems

The developers of software systems are used to the unpleasant situation that may be encountered when insufficient attention is paid to the problems that may arise when ensuring an optimal streamlining of the IT-based communication exists. The situation that we refer to is that in which an IT system that generously offers capabilities falls short as a consequence of its cumbersome, ambiguous and insipid interface.

Therefore, the first recommendation that we may suggest in a fully knowledgeable manner to the developers of the IT systems is the elaboration of some user-system interfaces, whose structure respects a few minimal requirements:

- The *semantic and syntactic stability of the interfaces.* The compliance to this requirements guarantees a natural streamlining potential of the communication user-system.
- The *removal of the interfaces' ambiguities* up to the limit that is acceptable at the education level of the user.
- The *elimination of the quantitative redundancies* in the demarche to realize the user-system interfaces.
- The *rational usage of the qualitative redundancies* in the demarche that involves the realization the user-system interfaces.
- The *minimization of the syntactic streams* that are associated to the interfaces' usage.
- The *maximization of the semantic streams* that are associated to the interfaces' usage.

Furthermore, in order to support the user-system communication's streamlining, there are necessary technologies that operate in the background of the IT systems, with the goal to facilitate a visible contribution regarding the user's comfort. Among these possible technologies, we enumarte a few that seem to be urgent and validated in practice:

- *The realization of a framework that relieves the user of the possibility/obligation to interact with documents that are represented according to different standards (.doc, .pdf, .rtf, .wp, etc.), which favours focusing the attention on the document's content, in other words there are created favourable conditions for the communication's streamlining. When we say document, we refer to any product in an elec-*

tronic format, which represents according to a certain standard a certain type of semantics. In other words, under the syntagm document we can designate texts, presentations, images, sounds, spreadsheets, models diagrams, projects, etc.

- As we have already mentioned in 3.7, the *elaboration of some highly abstracted APIs for the communication capabilities of the type "voice over IP"* could also contribute to the communication's streamlining.

- We add to the list of the technologies that favour CSD the *elaboration of some framework solutions for solving some practical problems, which may appear during the activity that concerns the documents and hyperdocuments manipulation.*

- Finally, but obviously not the least important, it is significant to mention the elaboration of some technologies that timidly but increasingly wider open the gates for the semantic analysis of the text oriented messages content.

The communication's streamlining in the IT-based systems features inexhaustible reserves that may be highlighted and valued in a more efficient manner through a closer collaboration between computer scientists, niche field experts and communication specialists.

4.4. The Creation of Information Technologies that May Significantly Contribute to the Communication's Diversification in the IT-Based Systems

Considering the problem of the communication's diversification in the IT-based systems and according to the definition that is provided in 4.1, it is considered *the removal or attenuation of the spatial, temporal or other types of constraints, which are developed due to conjunctural reasons.*

The dependence of a system's actor on a single communication interface is, objectively, a drawback. Therefore, we appreciate that it is the time to grant the required attention for communication modalities' diversification in the IT-based systems. There is the necessary infrastructure. There are necessary the proper theoretical and methodological endeavours to convince the developers community of the value that stands behind the idea of communication's diversification.

In connection to the diversification, we appreciate that one can operate extensively and intensively. This suggests the addition of new hardware/software communication tools that have the role to dissolve the spatial-temporal barriers, and also the identification and specification of some new communication techniques with the aid of the existing tools.

4.5. The Identification and Specification of a Learning Paradigm that Optimally Values the Help of the Modern Information Technologies for the Communication's Streamlining and Diversification in the Learning Systems

Speaking about the IT-based learning systems, we believe that the idea of CSD may find a particulare expression paradigm, provided that the researchers will join their efforts in order to identify and specify learning paradigms that optimally value the IT support.

In fact, we refer to the necessity that the developers of the learning systems call for the expertise of the educational problems specialists, in order to realize the optimal junction between the recommendations that pertain to didactic scenarios of the education specialist and the capabilities of the existing information technologies.

Obviously, the promises of the CSD approach induce a series of amendments to the teaching/ learning methods, in which the only actors are the student and the teacher. The proposal that we present in Section 5 is an attempt to value, from the CSD perspective, the projects oriented learning, as it is introduced in (Anderson & Elloumi, 2004).

5. FUNDAMENTAL REMARKS REGARDING THE REALIZATION OF THE LEARNING SYSTEMS ACCORDING TO THE FDC APPROACH

5.1. Preliminaries

We remind the reader the main ideas that we consider in the hypothesis that a learning system is realized according to the CSD approach:

- Projects orientation.
- The usage of the potential of the Web 2.0 universe.
- The development of social media components that pertain to the field in which the learning system operates.
- The utilization of the CSD offer.

Each of the four axes of a CSD system that have just been mentioned, has its roots in the past or more recent history of the learning systems. The formation of the future specialist by making appeal to the pretext of their participation to the complex and real dynamics of the projects is, considering an evolved modality, the re-utilization of the idea of apprenticeship. The apprenticeship has long been the main method to treasure, transmit and enrich the professional and scientific experience of the humanity in a given field. Regardless it was practiced in workshops or in different types of schools, two actors were essential: the master and the apprentice. The project was representing the serious "toy" around which these two actors were spending a lot of their time, by elaborating theories and applying them in practice.

In (Anderson & Elloumi, 2004), it is asserted that: "A learning system is efficient if it organizes its entire activity around some *projects*. Not the learning as a goal in itself will bring the school in the outposts of the knowledge, but the projects, in connection to which the teachers and the students or the pupils, together, naturally solve society's problems". In order to offer some further clarifications regarding the features of a project oriented learning system, we invite the reader to browse through Section 5.2.

5.2. Concepts and Principles in a Projects Oriented Learning System

From the very beginning, the reader is invited to study Figure 2, which presents, with certain intentions, the architecture of a learning system that is heavily oriented towards projects. The changes that are proposed by this architecture are major.

In the case of a learning system that is heavily oriented towards projects, teachers and students put more effort in order to fulfill the specific tasks they have to deal with.

As it can be noticed in Figure 2, the key concepts for a Projects Oriented Learning System are project, communication, lucrative competencies, research competencies and competencies that

Figure 2. The architecture of a learning system that is heavily oriented towards projects

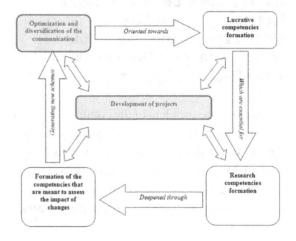

are related to the ability to assess the impact of changes that are generated by the implementation of the projects. Moreover, Figure 2 suggests that the proposed development model relates to the paradigm of the spiral. Thus, it is founded on an organic iterativity, which determines the optimal operation of the whole system.

The Project

Considering the meanings that are promoted through this paper, the concept of project is perceived as a model for the organization of the didactic process, in such a way that learning is not based any more on the assumption that the technologies that are introduced and practiced along the school years are sufficient for the student in order to successfully integrate in production. The new assumption, without bringing anything sensational, suggests that the problem (with all the features of a real-world problem), which needs to be solved, be used as a pretext in order to study with maximum intensity the technologies that are necessary in order to successfully finalize the project. The model is old: the apprentice learns to build walls guided by his craftsman. The tandem student-teacher gains organizational consistence and operates in a natural manner, according to the standards in the industry.

The Communication

The foundations of the communication process in such an approach are superior as compared to the communication style that is usual in the bipolar paradigm. Nevertheless, the optimal efficiency of the learning process in a Projects Oriented Learning System can be obtained if substantial improvements are made, both regarding the shape and the content, to the communication that is established between students and teachers. We refer to the students that are assigned to a certain project, and the teachers that coordinate the dynamics of the project. In a concise manner, it can be stated

that the improvements relate to a permanent effort to dissolve the communicational barriers that may impede the co-operation among the project partners. This involves both the utilization of the classic methods and the various technologies that are based on communicating through an electronic backbone.

The Lucrative Competencies

They relate to the *students' capacity to use the appropriate technologies in order to successfully finalize a project*. This implies a proper choice of technologies, their utilization with a reasonable efficacy and, why not, the optimization of these technologies. The lucrative competencies are effectively and at a large scale built up only by making use of this miraculous concept of project. Let us note another very important aspect of the problem: *along with the competencies that relate to the products' engineering process, the managerial competencies are naturally acquired as well.*

The Research Competencies

We consider the formation of the students' capacity to document in order to find feasible answers for the problems they face during the evolution of a project. As an extension to the idea of gathering relevant information through documenting, we can mention the idea of authentic research, through which the solution of a problem that belongs to a certain field is solved or clarified. The framework that is offered by the concept of project is the optimal solution in this respect, too.

Competencies that Regard the Assessment of the Impact of the Changes that are Generated by the Implementation of the Projects

The intention of this endeavour is to prepare and accustom the student to evaluate the impact of the changes, which the project determines in relation to the real world, considering the short and the long run, from a professional perspective and at a generally human layer. The uncontrolled accumulation of technological changes may provoke the inception or the augmentation of certain undesirable disequilibriums, in the equation of welfare and/or happiness of the human being.

Figure 2 also indicates the fact that the 4+1 architecture of a Projects Oriented Learning System has increased chances to coherently articulate a series of vital demarches for the success of any teaching process. Thus, the optimization and diversification of the communication, which is favoured by the project oriented activity, has to target the formation of the students' lucrative competencies, as a solid premise for triggering the interest for research and documentation, both in a collective setting or independently. Finally, Figure 2 emphasizes the importance of the change impact assessment competencies formation, as a systematic modality to enhance the stability of the products that are realized on the occasion of projects. Moreover, the figure highlights the importance of generating new schemes for the communication optimization and diversification[1]. The assessment of the impact of changes that are generated by the new products, which are realized as a result of the projects, is a problem that is often approached from various angles, but it is solved in an unsatisfactory manner.

5.3. The Architecture of a Learning System that Complies to the Principles of CSD

Figure 3 presents the main components of a learning system that is developed according to CSD, and that may value the valences of the projects orientation. Consequently, considering the items that are represented in Figure 3, we can imagine an operating scenario at a high abstraction level with the following major features:

Figure 3. The architecture of a learning system that is developed according to CSD

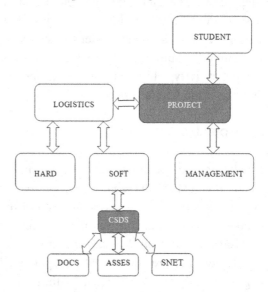

- The *management* of the learning system schedules the contents of the learning process (curricula that are structured according to the projects orientation requirements (Anderson & Elloumi, 2004). As a consequence, there exists a subsystem that assumes the management of all the activities from inside the learning system.

- As a consequence of the strong projects orientation, we have a dedicated system to the management of all the aspects that pertain to the projects that determine the learning activity. This is about the subsystem *Project*, which is essentially interested in the structure of the projects, their dynamics in time, and their connections with the other subsystems.

- The progress of the activities that pertain to the projects is sustained by a proper logistics. The hardware and software information technologies represent an essential part of this logistics. The software component of the logistics is, in fact, synonymous with the *communication's streamlining and diversification subsystem* (CSDS), while realizing a well structured and flexible integration of, at least, three key instruments: the documentation system (DOCS), the assessment system (ASSES), the internal social network (SNET), all of them being fingerprinted by CSD.

- The subsystem *Student* is, obviously, one of the main components of the learning system. Its structuring represents an additional challenge for the system's developers, given the tight connections with the other subsystems, and also the natural availability to the changes of the requirements for the actors that populate this subsystem from an informational perspective.

Considering such an architectural platform, seen from the perspective of what could be called as business logic, a complex endeavour to refine the key subsystems is initiated. This endeavour's main goal should be the assurance of a quality modularization, which favours: modular consistency, the weak coupling between modules and, overall, the assurance of the conditions that are requested by the principle open-closed, which is well known especially in the object oriented modeling.

We highlight once again the fact that a learning system that is structured according to CSD is equally an aggregate of operational tools that the learning system uses in order to optimize its operation that is founded on a given structure, but also a set of capabilities that allow for the cost-efficient integration of some new operational tools to occur, considering the design philosophy of the system.

Generally speaking, the *teacher, as a learning system's actor, has to be informed and also possesses the ability to efficiently transmit the knowledge to the students*. The CSD-based system offers optimal conditions in this respect, at least from a formal perspective.

On the other hand, the practical experience tells us that, making abstraction of the variations, there are numerous syncopes in the learning process. Among these syncopes, we enumerate a few:

1. Real communication difficulties between the teachers and the students due to the fact that they relate to objectives and requirements that are relatively disjunct.
2. The counterproductive stereotypization of the learning process. These stereotypes usually turn the teacher into a dynamic actor and the student into a passive one.
3. The systematic maintenance of some disparities between the real-world demands and the graduates' abilities.
4. The administrative separation of the research activity from the teaching activity, which is approached in different ways in the academic environments.
5. The discreditation of the learning system through its systematic underfunding.
6. The lack of some real link bridges of the academic environments with the local, national and international communities.
7. The creation of some study programmes that are focused on the abilities of the teaching staff.
8. Etc.

We haven't exhausted, not even by far, the list of the syncopes that may be noticed in the universities that pay tribute to the bipolar paradigm. It is true, there are numerous universities in the world that try or have already managed to enrich the bipolar paradigm with practices that contribute to the educational system's performance increase. Nevertheless, nowhere in the world an experiment that is aimed to put the foundations for a new educational paradigm has been initiated. The defining traits of such an experiment, considering the perspective that is offered in this chapter, should relate to the two substantial ideas: the projects orientation and the communication's streamlining and diversification.

What has to be done from a conceptual and technological perspective, in order to assure the success of such an experiment? This is a problem that has to be assumed by the management, and for its resolution it has to allocate the necessary resources, including the research point of view.

CONCLUSION

We can state that in this chapter we attempted to conduct a structured plea for a hypothetical model that concerns the communication's streamlining and diversification in the case of the computer aided learning systems. We drafted the theoretical limits of this initiative and we indicated the available technological resources, eventually together with their limitations.

Finally, we drafted at an architectural level a learning system that is conceived according to the CSD model, with the goal to indicate the place and the utility of the social networks in the effort to realize an e-learning system.

The association of this demarche with the idea of projects oriented learning wished to be an additional argument for the utility of the CSD-based learning systems.

It is obvious the fact that the materialization and the furthering of the ideas that have been presented require consistent analysis, design and implementation efforts, on which computer specialists, the educational problems specialists and other categories of interest holders have to reach an agreement.

REFERENCES

Agichtein, E., et al. (2008). Finding high-quality content in social media. *WSDM '08 Proceedings of the International Conference on Web Search and Web Data Mining*, (pp. 183-194).

Agichtein, E., Brill, E., Dumais, S., & Ragno, R. (2006). Learning user interaction models for predicting web search result preferences. *SIGIR '06 Proceedings of the 29th Annual International ACM SIGIR Conference on Research and Development in Information Retrieval*, (pp. 3-10).

Anderson, T., & Elloumi, F. (Eds.). (2004). *Theory and practice of online learning*. Canada: Athabasca University.

Asur, S., & Huberman, B. A. (2010). *Predicting the future with social media*. arXiv:1003.5699v1

Bocu, D., & Bocu, R. (2011). Strongly project-oriented learning systems: Concepts and fundamental principles. *Scientific Studies and Research Series: Mathematics and Informatics*, *21*(1), 51–60.

Burstein, J., & Wolska, A. (2003). Toward evaluation of writing style: finding overly repetitive word use in student essays. *EACL '03 Proceedings of the Tenth Conference on European Chapter of the Association for Computational Linguistics*, Vol. 1, (pp. 35-42).

Hawker, D. M. (2011). *The developer's guide to social programming*. Pearson Education, Inc.

LeBlanc, J. (2011). *Programming social applications*. O'Reilly.

Lenhart, A., Purcell, K., Smith, A., & Zickuhr, K. (2010). *Social media and mobile internet use among teens and young adults*. Pew Research Center.

Rosen, A. (2009). *E-learning 2.0. Proven practices and emerging technologies to achieve results*. AMACOM.

ADDITIONAL READING

Anderson, T. (2008). *The theory and practice of online learning* (2nd ed.). Athabasca University Press.

Cilesiz, S. (2011). A phenomenological approach to experiences with technology: Current state, promise, and future directions for research. *Educational Technology Research and Development*, *59*(4), 487–510. doi:10.1007/s11423-010-9173-2

Hemmi, A., Bayne, S., & Landt, R. (2009). The appropriation and repurposing of social technologies in higher education. *Journal of Computer Assisted Learning*, *25*, 19–30. doi:10.1111/j.1365-2729.2008.00306.x

Jonassen, D. H., Peck, K. L., & Wilson, B. G. (1999). Learning with technology: A constructivist perspective. *Prentice Hall Special Education*, *16*(1).

Kim, Y. (2005). Pedagogical agents as learning companions: Building social relations with learners. *Proceedings of the 2005 Conference on Artificial Intelligence in Education: Supporting Learning through Intelligent and Socially Informed Technology*, (pp. 362-369).

Laurillard, D. (2001). *Rethinking university teaching: A conversational framework for the effective use of learning technologies*. Routledge.

Limayem, M., & Cheung, C. M. K. (2011). Predicting the continued use of Internet-based learning technologies: The role of habit. *Behaviour & Information Technology*, *30*(1), 91–99. doi:10.1080/0144929X.2010.490956

Maloney, E. J. (2007). What Web 2.0 can teach us about learning. *The Chronicle of Higher Education*, *53*(18), B26.

McLoughlin, C., Lee, M. J. W., (2007), *Social software and participatory learning: Pedagogical choices with technology affordances in the Web 2.0 era*, Proceedings ascilite Singapore 2007, 664-675.

McLoughlin, C., & Lee, M. J. W. (2008). Mapping the digital terrain: New media and social software as catalysts for pedagogical change. *Proceedings ASCILITE*, Melbourne 2008, (pp. 641-652).

Mun, Y. Y., & Hwang, Y. (2003). Predicting the use of web-based information systems: Self-efficacy, enjoyment, learning goal orientation, and the technology acceptance model. *International Journal of Human-Computer Studies*, *59*(4), 431–449. doi:10.1016/S1071-5819(03)00114-9

Salavuo, M. (2008). Social media as an opportunity for pedagogical change in music education. *Journal of Music. Technology and Education*, *1*(2-3), 121–136.

Veletsianos, G. (2007). Cognitive and affective benefits of an animated pedagogical agent: Considering contextual relevance and aesthetics. *Journal of Educational Computing Research*, *36*(4), 373–377. doi:10.2190/T543-742X-033L-9877

Veletsianos, G. (2010). Contextually relevant pedagogical agents: Visual appearance, stereotypes, and first impressions and their impact on learning. *Computers & Education*, *55*(2), 576–585. doi:10.1016/j.compedu.2010.02.019

Wiley, D. A. (2000). Connecting learning objects to instructional design theory: A definition, a metaphor, and a taxonomy. *Learning Technology*, *2830*(435), 1–35.

KEY TERMS AND DEFINITIONS

Communication: Messages exchange between the actors of a learning system.

Communication's Streamlining: Removal or attenuation of the obstacles that condition the communication in the learning systems.

Communication's Diversification: Removal or attenuation of the spatial, temporal or other kind of constraints that pertain to communication.

CSD: Communication's streamlining and diversification.

Lucrative Competencies: The ability of a student to use technologies in order to successfully finalize a project.

Projects Oriented Learning System: Learning system whose activities are structured around the idea of project, which is defined as close as possible to the real world requirements.

Research Competencies: The ability of a student to document and to solve new problems.

ENDNOTES

[1] The communication is approached as a formalism for the representation of the models, based on which products are realized according to the model proposed by a Projects Oriented Learning System.

Chapter 12
@Twitter is Always Wondering what's Happening:
Learning with and through Social Networks in Higher Education

Narelle Lemon
RMIT University, Australia

ABSTRACT

Twitter as a learning tool offers many possibilities; however, what comes with use of this platform for education purposes is a need for awareness around and establishment of consistent pedagogies that support learning communities, learners, and the educators themselves. This chapter aims to establish what qualitative researchers in this field have found in regards to Twitter as an explicit social networking platform for educational purposes in higher education, including a discussion of literature. Interwoven is a case study of one Australian academic who is using Twitter both as a networked learner and networked teacher in the higher education learning environment. Exploration is shared into Twitter and what it can offer for different levels of engagement for the teacher as a learner who wants to engage with new and innovative ways of accessing information and knowledge. From this stance, Twitter is seen as learning centered on the teacher for the student in teaching courses and workshops in higher education thus learning with and through social media.

INTRODUCTION

Twitter as a microblogging platform 'enables a real-time interaction between users, using different devices, technologies and applications' (Grosseck & Holotescu, 2008, p.1). Twitter is seen as one of the most popular microblogging applications (Java, Song, Finin, & Tseng, 2007) with over 572,000 accounts (Twitter, 2011). Allowance is made for users to write up to a 140 character messages via the Internet, short message service (SMS), instant messaging clients, and by third

DOI: 10.4018/978-1-4666-2970-7.ch012

party applications and interfaces. Options of promoting blogs, marketing (Larsen & Everton, 2008), networking, news and media sharing (Palser, 2009) are all options within the Twittersphere (the Twitter community or environment). This diversity in audience creates various options for community and a community of learners.

Tweeps, that is the users of Twitter, can use this platform in a variety of ways with the main attractiveness of these options being to 'communicate, to ask questions, to ask for directions, support, advice, and to validate open-ended interpretations or ideas by discussing with the others' (Grosseck & Holotescu, 2008, p.3). Twitter allows a combination of personal publishing and communication with a new type of real-time publishing, allowing opportunities for immediate and anytime, anywhere feedback.

In the Australian context Twitter offers much potential as a social networking medium for educational interactions. The statistics provide interesting numbers to establish the current position; offering perspective for future growth. Twitter numbers indicate a significant increase in Australian visitors to their site (Cowling, 2011). At the end of June 2011, according to the Australian Bureau of Statistics (2011) there were 10.9 million Internet subscribers in Australia (excluding internet connections through mobile handsets). This represents annual growth of 14.8% and an increase of 4.4% since the end of December 2010. At the end of June 2011, there were 9.7 million mobile handset subscribers in Australia that represents an increase of 18.1% from December 2010. Of the 9.7 million mobile handsets, 3.6 million (37%) were dedicated data subscriptions and 6.1 million all other active standard mobile subscriptions. As far as Twitter usage goes, twitter.com has 1.1 million unique Australia visitors each, with an increase of 100,000 since January 2011 and shows that Twitter is a popular social networking channel, with potential to grow with more users (The digital marketing agency, 2011).

Collaboration, community building, participation, and sharing are key outcomes and drivers of social media use. For higher education the collection of Internet websites, services, and practices that support these outcomes can be achieved through use of social networking. The parallels that can be drawn to Twitter to engage and motivate academics as teacher and their students to be more active learners (Hughes 2009) are just beginning to be reported on and researched. Active users are displaying interesting ways to collaborate and participate in the community that is established through Twitter. But as Junco, Heiberger & Loken (2010) comment, 'despite the widespread use of social media...very little empirical evidence is available concerning the impact of social media use on student learning and engagement' (p.1) and also the pedagogical decisions the educators make. This chapter intends to discuss the considerations of learning *with* and *through* the social network platform Twitter. That is from the perspective of the literature and the case of one academic in higher education who has begun to engage with Twitter personally for learning and teaching in the higher education leaning environment. Interwoven is one higher education teacher's reflections. There is a low uptake in Twitter use in the higher education learning environment (Conole & Alevizou, 2010) and this case is one example that can offer a contribution to the field. The case provides one model of how one academic meaningfully engages with Twitter as a social media platform to extend content, context, community and continuity. In maximizing it's benefits, the interweaving of Twitter into learning for both academics and students, all seen as learners in this chapter, allows for innovative embedding of digital technologies into learning practice and acknowledges the need to consider and plan for the limitations and emerging problems that may often be the blockers for non use or low engagement. No one digital technology, nor learning and teaching strategy, can meet all demands and expectations for all learners; but when considering the why and how of use, framed by mutual respect for individuals, content and context a community is established whereby individual reference points can be acknowledged and built upon. The pedagogical approach of exploration is underpinning in the case study shared throughout this chapter whereby as adult learners in the higher education learning environment the philosophy of explore with guidance allows for all learners to consider potential and meaning making for them, their understandings, needs, and potential engagement.

BACKGROUND

What is Twitter as a possibility for learning and teaching has been considered by Kwak, Lee, Park, & Moon (2010) with a study on the topological characteristics of Twitter and its power as a new medium of information sharing. Twitter as a medium promotes *"wondering what's happening"* as a space for communication, content, connectivity and context.

The conceptualization of a classroom and what constitutes learning and teaching often come into conflict when presented with alternative methods to engage learners. Twitter is one such social media that has ignited possibilities of innovative educators. Pedagogical decisions, availability to information, and connections with learners do however require consideration. Such shifts, as Greenhow, Robelia, & Hughes (2009) have discussed, have affected constructs of learning and instruction and thus paths for future research. There is a significant gap in the literature about productive pedagogies for Twitter in educational contexts (Dunlap & Lowenthal, 2009b; Junco, Heiberger & Loken, 2010; Preigo, 2011). Twitter as an instructional tool or integrated digital technology can add value to online and face-to-face university courses that far outweighs its potential drawbacks (Celik, Abel, & Houben, 2011; Preigo, 2011).

Much of the literature centered around the higher education context mentions that Twitter attracts more interest-driven participation. As Dunlap & Lowenthal (2009b) have noted in their study with higher education learners, Twitter participation engaged the students in reflective dialogue about their subject area compared to other social networking mediums such as Facebook, which continue to be used more often for friendship-driven types of participation. Carini, Kuh & Klein (2006) explored relationships between academic performance measures and self-reported gains associated with attending university in the three areas of general education, personal and social development, and practical competence. Identification was acknowledged around student engagement in university (ranked according to study in highest to lowest) such as:

- Level of academic challenge
- Active and collaborative learning
- Student and staff interaction
- Enriching educational experiences
- Supportive campus environment
- Reading and writing
- Quality of relationships
- Institutional emphases on good practices
- Higher-order thinking
- Student-faculty interaction concerning coursework
- Integration of diversity into coursework. (Carini, Kuh & Klein, 2006, p.20)

In drawing parallels to Twitter, the meaningful engagement to support study can be made here particularly in what is possible in engaging higher education learners in higher order thinking, active collaboration, emphasizing good practice and interaction and diversity with subject content. Twitter is purposefully designed to exchange information and to facilitate reciprocal communication; therefore enabling the creation of communities of individuals interested in common topics (Preigo, 2011). Academics and higher education institutions are participating in social media (such as Twitter), as an important aspect of their research and teaching work (Preigo, 2011) and this acknowledges the rapid changes in the production and dissemination of scholarly work and interaction between academics and those 'outside' academic institutions. These parallels do however highlight mixed pedagogies in seeing how Twitter can contribute to learning.

TWITTER FOR LEARNING: MIXED PEDAGOGIES

Emphasis has been made on the value of creating networks and communities via Twitter. Advantages and experiences have been reported in regards to networking, for popularizing projects, or personal blogs and for finding project partners. Grosseck & Holotescu (2008) have recounted that Twitter as an educational tool has value in establishing a classroom community that can share in class or outside of it about learning. They have also reported the possibilities with exploring collaborative writing; to record student cognitive trails and then use them to reflect on their work; to ignite reader response to questions and observations; to explore the potential of microblogging in formal and informal settings; to discuss different kinds of asynchronous online discourse; and to promote collaboration highlighting students ability to organize ideas, reflect, send notes, manage meet-ups; and to project manage.

In the higher education learning environment, qualitative research has been shared and raises possibilities around benefits for learning, particularly around supporting new ways of inquiring. Some ideas have included:

- The microblogging space offers a means to broaden access to a range of views of topics related to the focus of the review and acted as a conduit for sharing of resources, references and discussions (Conole & Alevizou, 2010; Downes, 2010).

- Connections to reflective diaries or learning journals are often connected to Twitter, as a way to share to a wider audience (Conole & Alevizou, 2010) and can be used as a motivational tool to engage discussions, and to seek and gather feedback from a variety of audiences (Crook et al., 2008).

- A method of collecting resources either within formal courses or as a part of professional development (Downes, 2010).

- Facilitating cooperative learning in a constructive environment for supporting the fostering a community of practice (Anson & Miller-Cochran, 2009; Parker & Chao, 2007; Bruns & Humphreys, 2007) which in turn fosters co-creators of content and social dimensions of trust and cooperation (Conole & Alevizou, 2010).

- Opinion sharing and surveying for insights about a particular topic (McNeill, 2009).

- Sharing, collaborations, brainstorming, problem solving and creating within the content of moment-to moment experiences (Dunlop & Lowenthal, 2009).

- Demonstrating to students how it is possible to use social media for professional interactions and to understand the broader impact of technology (Bradshow, 2008).

- Using social media in classroom activities moves discussions and interactions that were once private, happening in a secure classroom, into a public space where potentially the entire connected world can bear witness (Rodriguez, 2011).

- Creating a sense of classroom community and familiarize students with both disciplinary and professional discourses (Briggs, 2008).

- Use of Twitter in large classes to engage more interaction and discussions amongst the students to take away from more teacher centered pedagogical approaches (Ramsden, 2009).

Twitter remains the most popular microblogging platform, despite several other options having become available, and in the literature, reference is often made directly to the use of Twitter for education rather than to the use of microblogging (e.g. Ling 2007, Dunlap & Lowenthal 2009a, Dunlap & Lowenthal 2009b; Rodens 2011; Sinnappan & Zutshi, 2011). However, in acknowledging this, just because one has a Twitter account does not mean it is active. Users of Twitter, as with many digital technologies on offer, are not always active nor creators or sharers of original information. 'Not everyone who creates a Twitter account uses it often nor in an organized way (Grosseck & Holotescu, 2008, p.3) with mixed interactions depending on the users decision of value and connection to their personal or professional lives (Grosseck & Holotescu, 2008). Krishnamurthy, Gill, & Arlitt (2008) have discussed how they have identify distinct classes of Twitter users and their behaviors, geographic growth patterns and current size of the network, and compare crawl results obtained under rate limiting constraints in their research.

Hashtags (# preceding a key word) allow for the Twitter community to organize and aid in the transferring of information to like-minded or interested audiences, groups or discussion groups. Analysis of Twitter communications in Junco, Heiberger & Loken (2010) research showed that students and academic teaching staff were both highly engaged in the learning process in ways that transcended traditional classroom activities. This study provided experimental evidence that Twitter can be used as an educational tool to help engage students and to mobilize staff into a more active and participatory role. Hashtags took a major role in this being able to be tracked.

Celik, Abel, & Houben (2011) have stated that 'relationships can be exploited to enrich and complement existing ontologies' (p.180) with their analysis of the performance in learning relationships specifically connected to certain time periods. The researchers revealed that Twitter is a suitable source for participatory learning relationships as it allows for discovering trending topics with higher accuracy and with lower delay in time than traditional news media. Twitter activities 'enhanced the variety of the constructed profiles and improved accuracy of news article recommendations significantly' (Abel, Gao, Houben & Tao, 2011, p.11).

Duffy and Bruns (2006) detailed the possibilities for using social software tools such as blogs, wikis, and RSS feeds in educational settings, stating that our new 'social' and 'mobile' reality of delivering educational content to students must match what they will encounter after graduation. Using technology to accommodate students' different learning styles and professional atributes is not novel. The strength of social media applications is that they offer an assortment of tools that learners can mix and match to best suit their individual learning styles and increase their academic success (Grover & Stewart, 2009). Careful construction of use and moderation is required on behalf of a higher education academic when considering Twitter for the learning environment (Conole & Alevizou, 2010). Bruns (2008) and Notari (2006) note that before students gain a sense of ownership of the space, the formation of a collective sense of community as a class assists greatly in being able to problem solve, explore, and begin to gain a sense of control.

'Discussion around the use of social network sites, especially amongst young people, is pervaded by sentiments heralding the decline of privacy' (Robards, 2010, p.19) which does raise questions about ways in which individuals are managing their information and identity profiles online. Twitter is one of many social networking sites that stimulate this discussion. Transparency and privacy have been issues since the emergence of the Internet, but have become more favorable in discussions about to engage or not to engage with social networking and 'are often conflated with arguments about the decline of privacy' (Robards, 2010, p.19). Robards discusses that his study showed significantly that questions around privacy and online profiles are created by users who are not naïve with 'many of the young people in [his] study, with a variety of backgrounds and levels of education, highly strategic in managing their privacy and information online' (p.20). This highlights discretion in the sharing of information and a distinct understanding of whom their audience is; an element that is often questioned and discussed in a way that implies users do not know just how much their profile is being transmitted publically. As with other social networking interfaces, Twitter supports varying levels of content control to be exercised in the establishment of a profile with name, location and profile introduction all controlled by the user him/herself.

Explicit control of profile with Twitter challenges undefined notions that can be assumed as 'different sites also carry with them clear differences in practice' (Robards, 2010, p.20). As Huberman, Romero, & Wu (2008) explain, on Twitter 'following' another user does not always ensure two-way interaction. It is possible to follow, but not be followed in turn, whereas many profile-based social network sites require the articulation to be two way; you cannot be 'Friended' without in turn 'being a Friend'.

Twitter as a social media also brings with it questions about the relationship between roles of teacher and learner, challenging the notion of all are learners. As adoption of social network sites continues 'questions about professional identity and managing relationships with students must be renewed and revisited' (Robards, 2010, p.21). Informed and strategic decisions about how to manage these online spaces are required. Dunlap & Lowenthal (2009b) explored Twitter as an instructional tool to provide an informal

way for students to connect with each other and with their teachers throughout the day. Dunlap & Lowenthal (2009b) invited students to participate in Twitter with them, to explore together. In explaining the goals of student-teacher connection and enhanced student engagement the research presented a choice for higher education students to participate in networking for their learning; acknowledging they might already be involved in social-networking activities and not want to take on more, or because of their concerns about privacy and their online footprints. These ideas raise interesting questions about approach to exploration of Twitter verses a must adopt approach in the higher education learning environment and establishing a philosophy that supports all as learners.

Interesting options around using Twitter as a learning tool have also ventured into assessment. The literature presents ideas such as:

- A *tool for assessing opinion*, examining consensus, looking for outlying ideas and foster of interaction about a given topic.
- A *viable platform for metacognition* that can benefit comprehension and retention.
- *Conference use* or as part of a presentation or workshop as a way to provide immediate feedback.
- *Short quiz* as a way to assess key knowledge and concepts connected to themes and fields of study.
- Microblogging for student assessment tasks that can be back channeled but also time limited (Rodrigues, 2011).
- Fosters communication of what has been learnt, transferring understanding into a different format and under the 140 character constraints.

For Michie (2010) in his exploration into Twitter with high school students', utilization of the social media focused on it as a tool for giving feedback as part of assessment for learning. Immediate feedback was made possible. Advocates of Twitter and its capabilities to facilitate communication, collaboration and learning use Twitter's social networking capacity to support dialogue for assessment for learning (Skiba, 2008; Sinnappan & Zutshi, 2011; Faulty Focus Report, 2011). Anytime, anywhere access to feedback has been reported with Twitter to eliminate waiting to physically cue for help or waiting for when one thinks it is appropriate to ask a question. Students can engage with classmates and lecturer outside of the physical classroom, before a class begins and after it ends (Junco, Heiberger & Loken, 2011). The real-time feedback has also been referred to by Wakefield, Warren, Alsobrook (2011) in connecting with dialogue to spark reflective thinking and communication based on classroom topics.

RETHINKING WHAT IS POSSIBLE IN HIGHER EDUCATION

In a recent survey by Faulty Focus report (2011) indication for how higher education academics use Twitter was demonstrated in that the most common activities included staying current on news/trends and networking with colleagues (even those they've never met in person). There were also educators who 'experimented with different ways to use Twitter in the classroom, or have plans to do so for the first time this coming semester' (p.2). This offers interesting parallels to the concept of networked teacher and networked learner. That is explicitly seeing Twitter as meaningful and purposeful for academic work – both from the perspective of being a learner and a teacher. In both cases these roles require an individual to open him or herself up to learning through and with others in a social networked community. For the purposes of this chapter, in reference to Twitter as being a platform for networking, I define networked learner as an academic in higher education who can access Twitter for research and scholarship purposes – learning through Twitter. Being a networked teacher is referred to as focusing on Twitter for teaching and learning possibilities, whether this be for sharing and gaining knowledge to share in the learning environment or actually using Twitter in the delivery of teaching and learning - learning with Twitter. These terms are broadly referred to in a bigger picture of personal learning networks (PLNs) and the personal learning environment (PLEs) - connections with both electronic resources and people (Steeples, Jones, & Goodyear, 2002) are seen as necessary for efficient and effective learning (Collins & Berge, 1996). Being networked refers to particular social structures (networks) in which relationships are structured by networked logic and the accompanying notions of culture, power relations, production and experience (Castells, 1996). In this chapter specific connections to application and use of Twitter in the higher education and thus the subsequent learning environment are deemed more appropriate. These areas will be unpacked further as the chapter progresses.

But what can Twitter offer? Let's go back to the beginning before these are specifically unpacked in relation to the academic and higher education learning environment. Social media in its very definition refers to the sharing of knowledge, ideas and content with a group who could be friends, peers, colleagues, or even others in your field who you do not know or will never meet in person, etc. The social highlight is that in being a part of a group or a network you have the opportunity to act together to learn from each other. Twitter is one of various different social mediums that have this as an underlying focus. Social media are enabling tools, so it is no longer about controlling or managing what people do with these tools, rather encouraging and supporting a self-sufficient approach to smarter learning. There is a self-awareness around networking with others in order to share and continue to build knowledge and ideas.

Social media is redefining how we relate to each other and how we relate to the organizations that serve us. It is about dialog – two way discussions bringing people together to discover and share information (Solis, 2008). As an academic in higher education Reuben (2011) encourages one 'to join the conversation and embrace social media in some form, create strong and effective policies for their use and assign staff members with specific…contribution tasks' (p.11). The very nature of social media offers much potential in association to being a networked teacher and networked learner. The community that can be established through seeing Twitter as a social media that can support learning with and through social media could be defined as limitless.

CONTENT, CONTEXT, CONNECTIVITY, AND CONTINUITY: A COMMUNITY OF PRACTICE FOR THE ACADEMIC IN THE HIGHER EDUCATION SETTING

David Armano (2008) in his work on social networking discusses community in regards to the 4Cs – content, context, connectivity, and continuity – and this framework resonates well with Twitter as a platform for learning. These four aspects in association to concepts closely connected to Wenger, White & Smith's (2009) work on Community of Practice in digital habitats bridges 'valuable perspective on the communal aspects of technology' and how these 'can contribute to the formation of a community of practice' (p.3). Twitter is seen in the context of this chapter as supportive of the notion of learning together and the possibility of connecting to, and thus forming new communities' of practice to extend perspective in regards to learning with and through social networks in higher education. As Kehrwald (2005) states:

In networked learning communities, these rules and processes guide and support the practice of learning by defining roles of participants and structuring the operation of these communities. (p.11)

The 4Cs framework by Armano (2008) has been extended and adapted accordingly for consideration of Twitter being used for the academic environment and learning in higher education (See Figure 1). Each of these four areas has then been unpacked to explicitly link to Twitter and the elements that are present when considering Twitter for and as a learning platform.

Your Twitter identity, who you are on Twitter and the personality you decide to show in how you contribute and participate, is closely connected to the wants and needs from this form of social networking. Both the perspective as an academic engaging in Twitter personally and applying the social media in the higher education environment for learning must be considered. These are not complete, but rather enable considerations to be made based on Figure 2's unpacking of the term content. It offers an opportunity to critically think about this framework with some specific examples unpacked further in the chapter.

For the higher education learning environment consideration is required to be made of *Content* and its connection to the community being engaged with and where one is becoming a part. The choice of how engagement looks is present, however considerations are required, such as:

Content you want to engage with – is the content relevant to your Twitter profile and focuses (consideration for multiple Twitter profiles according

Figure 1. 4Cs framework by Armano (2008)

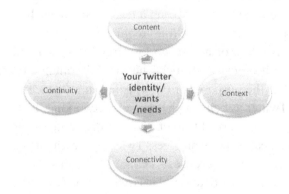

Figure 2. Unpacking of content in relation to Twitter

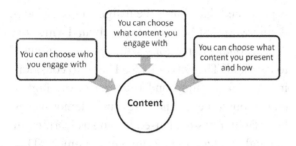

to content and followers in the community)? Is the content valuable? Who is worth connecting with on Twitter in regards to their content? Who is connected with who that can extend the content accessible on your feed? When and how are you going to read your Twitter feed and engage with the content?

Content you present – is content relevant and connectable? Is it valuable? Where does this content come from (your sharing, ideas, connection to blog or other material, or is it a retweet?) How will you present the context to connect to the community? Can you maintain content output? (See Figure 3)

The *Context* of why Twitter is beneficial for the academic and the higher education learning environment is a consideration closely connected to the individual. As with many digital technologies on offer, not all are right for right now. Digital technology, including social media, embedded into practice requires careful considerations in regards to the application, skills required, and outcomes.

Context in regards to one as an academic means investing time in one's Twitter profile that is personalized and appropriate for your interests and areas. As a tool for learning in the higher education context knowing how your users will want to engage with their community is intrinsic. In both cases the community that is attracted, formed, and developed will allow for this context to be either cemented or challenged.

Twitter offers opportunities for multiple connections, and the presentation of these connections to be in multiple forms; often in short bursts of mini interactions or microblogging. That is multiple small tweets and direct messages that are captured in 140 characters each time. The short and concise nature allows for multiple opportunities to make contact with others but also means that the content, inquiry or questions have to be straight to the point. In some ways a conversation is made easy. One's choice to participate is always ones choice. How often you participate, and what you share is also supported by this notion. The Twitter community thrives on these types of interactions and the strength of this platform in connecting immediately with the topic or field. The *connectivity* of Twitter as an academic allows for connections and relationships to be made quickly once engagement begins (See Figure 4). In correlation with Twitter profiles, links to profiles, publications and research, the community does not take long at assess the content and context to allow for connectivity to be quickly made through the mini interactions. The nature of this communication style also allows for the design-

Figure 3. Unpacking the context of Twitter

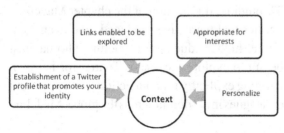

Figure 4. Unpacking the connectivity of Twitter

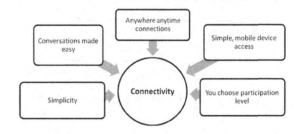

ing of experiences that support the development of connections with fellow Tweeps over time; rather than responding to an immediate demand and commitment that is often associated to face-to-face communities. There is also the benefit as an academic that connectivity can be anytime and anywhere providing opportunities for continued conversation that is not based on contact hours or availability for consultation.

Participation in Twitter can be seen as 'learning opportunities' (Wenger, White & Smith, 2009, p.9) and the richness that can be attained between the distinction of active and passive members are varied. The appeal of Twitter as an academic is the level of participation that can be enacted with the dimensions of the connectivity that supports the work we do in learning and teaching, research, and scholarship. In all these areas, the level, type of, and the how can be varied with no one way to be connected.

The flexibility of the Twitter community for both the academic personally and for the higher education environment advocates that there is no right way to use the interface. Chat, swap, explore, observe, retweet, and so on – are all valid ways of participating. The community thrives on different interactions and again is a strength of being able to build, design, and plan one's Twitter identity to address wants and needs. There are continued connecting points to support *continuity* (See Figure 5), with choice underpinning connectivity, context and content. The flexible nature evolves for each Tweep while still providing a valuable and consistent user experience, which can be sustained over time.

So what do I mean by Twitter for and as learning? In the next section of the chapter a case study is presented that shares the insights into one academic who first began to think about Twitter for professional interactions with resources related to her field. The networks lead her into considering use in teaching and research in the higher education context. The case study demonstrates how Twitter has been used for and as learning in the higher education learning environment. That is, an academic learning to use Twitter for her own learning, and then using it as one of many learning strategies in her teaching. Reflections provide insights into hesitations, questions and possibilities from one perspective.

This next section of the chapter is not about providing and identifying 'distinct classes of Twitter users and their behaviors, geographic growth patterns and current size of the network, and compare crawl results obtained under rate limiting constraints' (Gill & Arlitt, 2008, p. 19), nor is it about a content analysis of Twitter (Humphreys, Gill, & Krishnamurthy, 2010). In validating the benefit of interacting with one case, the reader is offered an opportunity to consider another perspective. This one case is not about right or wrong. It is more about one persons experience, what she has shared and reflected upon, and appreciating this standpoint. From the stance of contributing to the qualitative research around Twitter, the reflective narrative of Madeline is shared.

TWITTER IN THE HIGHER EDUCATION LEARNING ENVIRONMENT: A CASE STUDY

Throughout this section of the chapter Madeline, not her real name, is introduced. She is an Australian higher education academic who has just begun to explore the use of Twitter for her own learning explicitly for connections with peers and colleagues in academia across the globe. Madeline

Figure 5. The continuity of Twitter

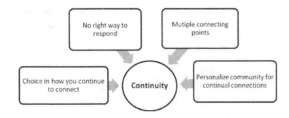

reflects on her movement from networking for her own learning into thinking about and introducing Twitter into her own teaching at the undergraduate degree level. Madeline, shares her first encounters and assumptions around Twitter:

Twitter was originally a social networking site that I viewed like many others from afar. I took the term social literally and assumed the main content shared would be personal updates of what someone was doing or what he or she were thinking about in their personal life. Other ways of working on other social networking platforms influenced these thoughts, but honestly I hadn't connected to Twitter nor had I actually spent time looking at what people do, what they tweet or how it could be useful to me professionally. Not an uncommon assumption but rather shallow and based on presumptions I soon discovered.

What captured my interest in Twitter once I began spending some time with it was the amount of users who shared meaningful content. As I searched and followed different links to people and the information being shared I soon realized its benefit to my own leaning and profile. I began to see the networking capabilities.

The openness for Madeline to explore Twitter on a professional level is demonstrated in her opening reflection. She has allowed for an open mindedness to be formed that supports the establishment of a community where content, context and continuity began to develop. Madeline recognizes that the connection to others is crucial and not based on other social networking sites. There is a shift in seeing how one social media can support professional networking. A challenging of social media that is it often centers around who you know personally, or may have once known, or establishing 'friends' to boast a healthy quota that can be compared to by others. Twitter is not about this. The function of the platform quickly

became apparent to Madeline as she explored and discovered what was possible and how others used Tweets to communicate and share content.

I use Twitter as my personal learning network. To connect with other people around the world who are interested in the areas I am. Organizations, institutions, academics, teachers, artists, or individuals who use Twitter themselves to open their network to access information, ideas, ask questions, and share resources.

The Twitter community does not send invites to become friends rather, recommends Tweeps you may want to follow based on trends in your interests. Those you follow do not have to follow you nor the other way around. The explicit decision to engage with specific connections to profile and content shared is always individual's choice.

Assistance around topics, discussions and resources supports a user to target even further detail related to fields of interest. This is where the hashtag system for tagging key words and discussions allowed Madeline to focus more thoroughly on her field. She could dedicate time to contributing to and participating in discussions centered on her educational needs both as a learner and as a teacher. This is where Madeline begins to become a Networked Learner whereby her Personal Learning Network (PLN) begins to expand. Possibilities for specific connections, sharing of ideas and content as well as continuity of knowledge generation supported access for Madeline to extend her learning. Parallels are possible into various fields of interest within academia –scholarship and research, and learning and teaching.

#edchat is a discussion that has various ideas shared in real time. The opportunity to look back on and mark as favorites, like your own personal list of interesting tweets, is a unique source of information. The sharing of resources and ideas

can easily be directed to what you are focusing on at the time. #phdchat and #myresearch are two threads that for my research have been vital.

Continuing professional development anywhere and anytime is an attractive element of Twitter; a digital communication of networks whereby a PLN emerges for Madeline. PLNs are informal learning networks which consist of the people a learner interacts with and derives knowledge from in a Personal Learning Environment (PLE), and were labeled this way based on the work of George Siemens and Stephen Downes and the theory of connectivisim. A PLE is made up of one or more tools and allows an individual to set their own learning goals, manage their learning (managing both content and process), and communicate with others in the process of learning. An individual learner makes a connection with others in their PLN with the specific intent to learn. They may connect to one or more parts of their interests, fields, or inquiry. In a PLN learners create connections to develop a network that contributes to their professional development, knowledge and meaning making. In PLNs often the learner does not have to know these people personally or will ever meet them in person. Twitter is an example of how Madeline connects, creates, and constructs her learning as a higher education academic moving between the space of being a networked learner and a networked teacher.

As Madeline spent more time exploring Twitter and building up her network it became clear boundaries needed to be established in regards to profile and use. More specifically the need for a personal account was deemed essential to establish prior to introducing Twitter into her higher education learning environment with students, and indeed interests associated to scholarship and research. This inevitably progressed naturally as personal interests in content and connections based on hobbies and personal friendships were remarkably different to areas associated to the academic world Madeline was constructing. Madeline reflects:

I had no problem setting up a second Twitter profile. Actually it became apparent I should do this as my learning field and higher education topics didn't really fit that well with followers who were more interested in coffee, cafes and horse riding, and vice versa. Two different content areas formed based on my own life. These were explicit...so naturally helped me split who I was following and then what content I shared according to the specific profiles. Easy to set up and I made sure I did this before I began using Twitter in the higher education classroom. I didn't want to blur the boundaries. I wanted to set up and model clear expectations of this to my students – the first thing they would check when they had the chance would be who am I am following and what I am sending in my tweets. And honestly no hassle to manage – interfaces allow you to register two profiles and you can simply click between the two feeds.

Madeline commented that her use of Twitter personally became a model in itself for her eventual use in learning and teaching. In thinking critically about the concept of PLNs, it became inevitable that this platform would be beneficial in supporting learners in the higher education context.

I used Twitter for six to seven months before I even thought about using it in my teaching. What stood out to me was the access to content I was using in my teaching. I was finding Twitter useful as a way to access information, resources, ideas and literature. I had been blown away by the links shared and networking possibilities. I just had to share it with my students. Most importantly I wanted to share with them the possibility of social networking for learning and teaching – for their professional connections. I don't think they had ever been actually shown how to connect professionally with social media. Personally, highly likely, but professionally a very low percentage was my guess before I started teaching with Twitter.

Particularly noteworthy was the willingness Madeline displayed as an academic to transfer her learning and engage with students in the higher education learning environment. Madeline's case demonstrates how she could see the potential in utilizing social media for learning; to extend outside her immediate sphere of accessing and teaching with content by introducing Twitter as a social media for the basis of sharing and connecting to content alone. This was an explicit pedagogical decision. A great contribution to this was her willingness to also scaffold students' professional identity using social media.

Madeline demonstrates a bottom heavy pyramid model, whereby the majority of her time has been set in her own use. She has established patterns in her own networking; explored and made connections to content. Her connectivity has been established clearly before even considering transfer into the higher education learning environment. In order to move to the third level of the model presented in Figure 6, Madeline had to make explicit connections to her teaching needs and the relevance for her students. The blended learning approach to curriculum design meant that Madeline had to plan for interweaving the use of Twitter from introduction to explicit connections to curriculum content. In the higher education learning environment relevance and the expected outcomes had to be made transparent in order for the learners to understand the why of embedding, moving into future possibilities of use in the learning context. As Madeline reflected:

When I was thinking about transfer of my Twitter use into the classroom, I really had to think about the 'why'. Why did I begin using Twitter and why would my students use it? It was like the 'so what?' type of moment – so what you are introducing Twitter to us in our university degree, so what you think it is good. I found that by sharing my experience and inviting my student to try Twitter during the duration of their subject study with me I immediately established an openness to explore.

Figure 6. Pyramid model representing Madeline's use of Twitter in the higher education learning environment

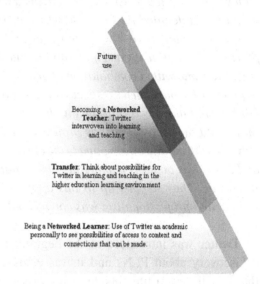

That was the key. I scaffolded their use of Twitter against key learning outcomes for each week of the subject. I guided possibilities but I did not stipulate these were compulsory. Guidance was about their experience and I offered help but opened up possibilities of becoming connected through own inquiries, use and observations. For me it was about blending, interweaving Twitter into our learning experiences. I encouraged use, and if the students didn't like the platform at least they could justify the why by reflecting on their use in my class. It was really all about introducing and seeing where they could take it. I asked them to think, is Twitter for me?

Moving from Networked Learner in to a Networked Teacher is exhilarating for Madeline but also comes with facing fears in allowing for the molding of ideas and future use in the higher education learning environment.

Student interaction for engagement with the subject material and with Twitter itself as a networking tool was embraced by the students. I encouraged them to participate but did not make it compulsory, rather an invite to try and see what is possible and if they didn't like it at least they had engaged with it and had a detailed reason as to why not. The uptake was impressive, I was blown away. The first time explicitly using and integrating it into my teaching came with a combination of nerves and trepidation but the students respected the invite and felt honored that I was introducing them to how they could themselves grow as professionals, to network with me and others outside the classroom and that I was actually making myself available to do this. They stepped up to this approach... respect and professionalism was commendable.

Twitter was introduced at the beginning of a discovery about PLNs and it was envisaged that it will have a life outside of the classroom and beyond the duration of the course. It was designated as an assessment task but the results could either be pass or not satisfactory in order to support participation. The students were invited – again, a key pedagogical decision by Madeline. This approach respected the higher education students as adults training to be professionals. It honors their capabilities and future intentions as professionals who will be required to continue ongoing connections with content relevant to their field. The blended approach of integrating Twitter scaffolded the learners through the exploration of the social medium specifically seeing the learner as a professional. As Madeline reflected, this meant addressing students ideas about being a Networked Learner:

I encouraged the students to explore and think critically about their professional online identity through their engagement with Twitter. I invited them to think about their voice, profile, professional etiquette, making connections, and following people, institutions, company's who were relevant to the subject we were studying … also to think about how this field relates to other subjects within the degree. I wanted the students

to explore, follow, unfollow, tweet, retweet, post new content, ask questions, share photographs, interact with each other and learn how to use hashtags for specific searchers and connecting into the community…and in turn see where this would lead in networking with others. It was about the possibility, the opportunity to professionally connect in my class and beyond.

I scaffolded opportunities to use Twitter during the weekly structure of my class and I did specifically discuss etiquette. I put in writing, in the subjects materials and spoke about my non-negotiable aspects of using Twitter. This wasn't to be a control freak it was about teaching etiquette and stipulating why it is crucial. It was about establishing mutual respect as co-colleagues, peers in our professional field. That really was what I was inviting the students to become a part of. I was inviting them to join me in an online professional space that I had carved out myself. My introduction was helping them gain entry more quickly with care and compassion. But I was also aware this could be a fine line. Upfront talk about this was the best way I thought I could show mutual respect to my student.

Guidelines for etiquette and mutual respect set by Madeline included language such as:

- *Twitter will be what I introduce you to as part of extending your PLN; other options are up to you to explore and Twitter itself and the connections you find will make suggestions – follow what interests you.*
- *We won't be using Twitter as a commentary on class – likes or dislikes, critical comments, put downs – but as a professional voice you may share a strategy, idea, application to teaching, resources, materials, extensions activities.*

- *You can share your reflective practice... which may even lead you to blogging (but again something for you to explore).*
- *We can look at what other professionals, organizations and institutions are sharing content wise, open links into videos, photos and stories. Explore. See where it takes you.*

From upfront mutual respect was established to support the exploration into Twitter; to support content and connections in the higher education learning environment and to support the classroom community, both within class hours and after. Students shared work in progress to their followers, commenting on progress of class and engagement levels, asking peers questions outside of scheduled class hours, and positive reinforcements to each other (Table 1). These examples demonstrated the community forming within the higher education learning environment and how this was explored outside to keep the dialogue of the subject going. In supporting this practice Madeline also made sure she engaged with the students in the Twittersphere:

I made sure that I interacted individually with each student and responded to questions, insights and observations. I modeled Twitter language and short cuts in regards to use of the 140 characters. I also made sure I shared celebrations especially when their networks extended or they were responded to by tweeps who were not involved in the subject and thus demonstrating how connectivity and networking grows through use and interactions.

Remarkably the engagement level was contagious for the students. Their exploration, as Madeline commented, *'was infectious as the more they discovered both in application and content the more they became addicted'*. The guidelines for the subject were easily met with many students

exploring freely within a few weeks and they had completed suggested activities before connections to weekly subject details had been addressed. The ability to find, share, listen to and connect with others in this way challenged the higher education students to engage meaningfully with the social media. Most importantly their engagement levels were in a professional capacity, for many this was the first time this opportunity had been encouraged and introduced in their undergraduate degree. Twitter was utilized by Madeline as a type of formative assessment or assessment as learning whereby the higher education learners engaged with subject topics, shared knowledge and experiences that established theoretical and practical application of their learning. Most importantly the

Table 1. Sample tweets from higher education students using Twitter during a subject

Classification of Tweet	Example Tweet
Sharing work in progress from class experiences with tweets sent during and after class time	S1 (@student one) 2/9/12 4:37 PM The beginnings of my dragon sketch:) I cannot wait to finish it!! #classtag2012 [Tweet had an inserted link to an attached image of artwork]
Commenting on progress of class and engagement levels	S2 (@student two) 2/9/12 11:13 PM Visual arts, what a fun subject:) #classtag2012
Posing questions after hours to peers	S4 (@student 4) 2/9/12 8:31 PM Is applying finishing touches to folio. Inserting an assignment submission sheet inside front cover. Anybody else?? #classtag2012
Positive reinforcements to each other and use of language associated to field of study	S3 (@student three) 2/9/12 5:05 PM @student five I really like your finished piece, the use of tone enhances the colour #classtag2012 S5 (@student five) 2/9/12 5:29 PM @student three Thanks! I love colour, and this was an easy, fun and creative way to use it! #classtag2012

NB: Class hashtag and student handles have been changed to protect the identity of the example tweets. Profile pictures have been removed with the permission of students.

students made connections to Twitter as a social media for their learning and in doing so extended what is possible in critically thinking about their PLN in relation to their higher education and growth as professionals in their specific field.

WHAT TWITTER CAN OFFER HIGHER EDUCATION: SOLUTIONS AND RECOMMENDATIONS

Twitter as a social media does have its advantages and limitations (common issues, controversies and problems are unpacked later in this chapter in Table 3) as well as champions and critics in the higher education environment. The real-time communication provided by Twitter has had profound implications for higher education and if planned with explicit pedagogical decision can support learning and be blended with other learning and teaching tools. The why and how of using Twitter can be explored quickly through critical questions (examples in Table 2).

As touched on previously, Dunlap & Lowenthal (2009b) in their exploration of Twitter as an instructional tool to provide informal connections with curriculum content, invited students to connect with each other and them as educators. They invited students to participate in Twitter with them as a framing around community and the notion of 'us' as learners, explaining their goals clearly as Twitter could offer student-teacher connection and enhance student engagement. Dunlap & Lowenthal did not make the student participation a requirement, rather an invitation, as they wanted to recognize that students might already be involved in social networking activities and possibly would not want to take on more. The invitation also acknowledged student concerns about privacy and their online footprints, however, they did offer through participation, education around what could be possible in supporting an online profile. For the higher education learning environment key solutions and recommenda-

tion came from Dunlap & Lowenthal (2009b) research in the form of guidelines for integrating Twitter for learning and these included:

- Guidelines for instructional use.
- Establish relevance for students.
- Recommend people for students to follow.
- Model effective Twitter use.
- Encourage students' active and ongoing participation.
- Build Twitter-derived results into assessments.
- Continue to actively participate in Twitter.

Madeline's case study reinforces many of the guiding principles for integrating Twitter and considering learning with and through social media as discovered by Dunlap & Lowenthal. Sinnappan & Zutshi (2011) in their research into microblogging in the higher education context, particularly on establishing a community of inquiry, also acknowledged that the 'preliminary studies in the education literature on the use of microblogging in education suggest that it has significant potential, despite some drawbacks' (p.1124). This may be related to findings around

Table 2. A model for embedding Twitter into the learning and teaching of the higher education learning environment needs to consider the why, how, when, and what of pedagogy

Why	Why is Twitter being used?
How	How will the students use twitter? How will Twitter be interwoven into the curriculum and assessment of higher education learning? How will you as teacher make connections to the networking and content relevance? How can Twitter support a community of learners in regards to the 4Cs – content, context, connectivity, and continuity?
When	When will the students access their twitter account? Will students be allowed to access Twitter during class time or outside face-to-face time to capture and share their learning?
What	What connections are being made to learning content?

Table 3. Common issues juxtaposed with solutions and recommendations of Twitter in higher education learning environment

Issues, Controversies, Problems	Solutions and Recommendations
What about the limitations of what's hidden & what's not?	Transparency and privacy (Marshall & Shipman, 201) Issues around ownership of material with social media have been raised by (Marshall & Shipman, 2011) with regards to Twitter and what Tweeps feel they can and can't retweet, comment on or save as a favorite for later reference. The use of Twitter can enhance students' perception of a sense of 'social presence', an important quality that helps promote student involvement, commitment and retention (Dunlap & Lowenthal, 2009a; 2009b)
What about the time commitment?	Find times when you can access Twitter, this could be in the morning, while you are having a coffee, sitting in front of the television. Captures Conversations: The Tweeps in the back of the classroom used to be seen as distractions and disruptions. By using Twitter, many educators are finding ways to capture these "backchannel" conversations, harnessing rather than silencing conversations that occur during lectures and presentations by taking instant polls and asking for feedback through Twitter.
What about access issues and the right technology options?	Accessing Twitter via a mobile device allows the student to be flexible about when they contribute (Lingard, McNeil & Cann, 2010). Free access and easy to set up as Twitter has a wizard to help you through.
I just think Twitter is information overload!	The scanning technique seems to be encouraged when accessing information and in assisting overload. Not everything can be seen or accessed in a Twitter feed and information is always accessible, the decision is how much and when do you want to access it. The # symbol, called a hashtag, is used to mark keywords or topics in a Tweet. It was created organically by Twitter users as a way to categorize messages. This is a great way to target specific areas and interests relevant for an individuals higher education area of research and/or teaching. Twitter, no matter how selectively we curate the sources we follow, require us to become active participants and not merely either information producers or consumers. As academics we are trained in being able to manage information and to make informed appraisals of the sources we find. These skills suit social media perfectly (Preigo, 2011). Hashtags allow for the Twitter community to organize and aid in the transferring of information to like-minded or interested audiences, groups or discussion groups (Grosseck & Holotescu, 2008).
Establishing a community on social networking is just for digital natives I see no use for my higher education learning environment!	Twitter can enhance students' perception of a sense of 'social presence', an important quality that helps promote student involvement, commitment and retention. (Dunlap & Lowenthal, 2009) Twitter is a great way of communicating information to other people. It could be used to send out useful links, recommend reading materials, special lectures, and information from an individual, department or organization (McNeil, 2010). Consider a hashtag for establishing a class or project category and feed that can target specific needs. The more you interact the more you get out of the community. As educators we might learn new ways to reach out and communicate better with a larger segment of students in engaging with social networking platforms such as Twitter (Charnigo, Laurie & Barnett-Ellis, 2007). New technologies have slow adoption cycles, and often the learning curve is steep but totally worth the focus to learn and engage with others (Preigo, 2011). Twitter that allows people to get together and exchange messages does not necessarily make people feel as if they belong to a community (Gruzd, Wellman, & Takhteyev, 2011) Twitter is useful for understanding how people use new communication technologies to form new social connections and maintain existing ones. If you follow me, I do not have to follow you. This means that connections on Twitter depend less on in-person contact, as many users have more followers than they know. Can help with communication outside of the classroom. Although using it for reminders to students could be helpful this platform is designed more for the opportunity to continue engagement in the field of higher education study. Blogging has also been found to reduce students' sense of isolation and increase their feelings of connectedness (Wolf, 2008).

continued on following page

Table 3. Continued

Issues, Controversies, Problems	Solutions and Recommendations
How to introduce to the higher education learning environment	Plan how you are going to use, trial yourself, know the ins and outs so you can trouble shoot and guide the students. Encourage exploration and guidance. Encouraged students to use Twitter in a variety of ways and utilize the different options for engaging with content and connectivity (Dunlap & Lowenthal, 2009) Twitter, a social media, is one technology that educators can use to engage students and encourage higher order thinking (Rockinson-Szapkiw &Tucker, 2011) Twitter and the relationship between roles of teacher and leaner, challenging the notion of all are learners. Twitter allowed us to provide prompt feedback to students, not only for their assignments, but also for a wide variety of questions and issues they faced Sinnappan & Zutshi (2011) Internet resources like Twitter give students access to information — more importantly, perhaps — to people beyond the classroom walls. Supporting the establishment of a PLN and being a networked teacher and networked learner
Why would "I" use it in the higher education learning environment?	Twitter is good for "sharing, collaboration, brainstorming, problem solving, and creating within the context of our moment-to-moment experiences" (Dunlap & Lowenthal, 2009). Using Twitter educators and their students can tap into a global network of others interested in educational topics (Chamberlin & Lehmann, 2011). Instructional uses, such as "to communicate with students" and "as a learning tool in the classroom" are less popular, although both activities saw increases over the previous year (Faculty Focus, 2009). Although the barrier between inside and outside the classroom has been difficult to overcome, new social media forms today are starting to break down that barrier and enable dialogue (Robbins & Bell, 2008). Gives Educators Real-Time Professional Development: Questions posed to Twitter are often answered quickly, and special hashtags provide a forum for where teachers to address specific topics at scheduled times. Thinking through of ideas - reflection on and inaction and assists in developing students into independent lifelong learners (Pang, 2009).
As an academic, I do not want to have my students see my personal interactions and connections?	Consider combining private and professional life and the online community. Solution would be to separate accounts have an 'academic/teacher' & 'private' accounts. Think about the question: Are you there where your students are or do you create a new social learning environment? As academics we still needed is to develop strategies to listen to our peers and audiences better, and to learn how to react publicly (Preigo, 2011).
What about Spam?	Block & report twitter has protocols in place & quick assistance.

Twitter usage generally (i.e. outside the higher education context) such as Java et al. (2007) and Krishnamurthy et al. (2008), which emphasized the social aspects of Twitter usage. However, Sinnappan & Zutshi (2011) reported that Twitter promoted active learning by helping higher education students relate the subject material to their own experiences both inside and outside of the classroom.

A natural not forced pedagogy comes when as an academic who engages with Twitter themself and thus can model and share personal learning and networking experiences. The evidence from practice supports student's interaction with the platform. Establishing a community of learning within the higher education learning environment that transforms into the digital community environment is key to purposeful pedagogy. What Twitter can offer higher education is the opportunity to blend this social media with other strategies, tool, and pedagogical decision to support learning. By challenging the common issues, controversies and problems, solutions and recommendations can be problem solved (Table 3).

Literature is supportive of the benefits and possibilities but what are under developed are the explicit ethical, environmental, emotional and physical considerations (Lemon, 2011) for using such a social media in the learning environment. Ethically new ways of using and integrating Twitter into learning and teaching are inspiring new pedagogical decisions to be made. Integration, the role between teacher and learner, and leaner and learning, require new ways of thinking and construction of learning environments and communities of learners. Twitter participation is by choice – the how, when, where – even when introducing it into the higher education learning environment. However, ethically when participating in an online forum that remembers easily what your name has been associated to, it is a key driver in making sure this content is true, accurate and most of all respectful of others. In observing how others display good practice we did indeed note a small minority that seem to engage in some tweets that perhaps should have been kept to oneself rather than having made them public. Some guidance can be given from the literature available and Madeline's case study in considering ethical, environmental, emotional and physical approaches to Twitter. These guiding principles are not rules, rather suggestions for consideration in networking with Twitter in the higher education learning environment.

- Be careful with assumptions and defaming of others in content shared.
- Content should be accurate and researched.
- Display a professional etiquette and integrity.
- Share and share others material but acknowledge them, even ask for permission.
- You always have as choice to follow, tweet or retweet so use this with discretion.
- Observe what others do and pick up on good etiquette and best practice.
- Consider separate accounts for personal and professional however etiquette still applies.
- Respect underpins the Twitter community – mutual respect goes a long way.
- Trust the students with Twitter.
- Student own handheld devices can be used in class when guidance is provided and don't be surprised at engagement levels in Twitter and don't automatically assume they will multitask with other applications.

- Be careful to not assume learners are all digital natives and using Twitter, and if they are, are they using it for professional networking? High likely they need to be taught and modeled this practice of social networking.
- Consider setting up a hashtag feed for students as an ongoing record of class images, discussions and sharing of links.
- Establish boundaries for when and how you can assist learners via Twitter. The immediacy of communication is attractive but if students are working on learning tasks late at night and Tweet you for advice, consider the immediacy of your response and what you are prepared to do.
- Encourage scrolling back through feed (back channeling) that is connected to hashtag established for class.
- Photos of students in action in the higher education learning environment should display no faces to protect visual identity and mutual respect, unless permission has been granted.

Although not a comprehensive list, it does offer considerations about establishing clear pedagogical decisions in the higher education learning environment that can assist with engaging students with Twitter.

FUTURE RESEARCH DIRECTIONS

Twitter itself is an emerging trend in its use both from the perspective of a networked teacher and a networked learner. The continued growth in PLNs as a way to connect, share ideas, ask questions and collaborate offers much potential for higher education and the subsequent learning environment. The future directions for higher education and Twitter as a digital tool allows for possibilities in engaging in types of use, interactions and the benefits to support both educators and learners. From the higher education learning environment a case study has been shared in this chapter from the perspective of a teacher who sees oneself as a learner and facilitator of learning in the Twittersphere. In connections to sharing research, developing connections for research and use with learners in the learning environment highlighted is the potential of what can be for those looking to engage. It also offers support to those who are currently engaging with Twitter to extend networking capacity and connections with others.

Researching Twitter in higher education and generating data that supports notions of learning, connecting, networking, communication and generation of ideas and information is beginning to emerge. The longer academics engage with this medium the more options emerge to look at and consider questions of interactions for the higher education classroom such as:

- How can Twitter be interwoven into the higher education learning environment through curriculum?
- If students value assessment as a part of their higher education learning experiences, how can Twitter be used to support this belief?
- How can Twitter be meaningfully used in the higher education learning environment to enhance student preparation in their profession?
- How can educators support learners to create a professional identity via Twitter?
- What other platforms can be used and embedded into curriculum to support the development of personal learning networks (PLNs)?
- How can Twitter be used to extend use that situates itself around the platform being used for reminders or literature links in higher education?
- Is meaningful interaction possible with higher education learners inside and outside of the classroom through the use of Twitter?

- How can Twitter support specific field of study in higher education?

As an academic interacting with teaching and research, Twitter offers much consideration of further research into:

- How can Twitter be used to build up networks with fellow academics?
- Can Twitter be a platform to ignite potential research collaborations?
- Are academics open to possibilities of meaningfully engaging with Twitter for professional networking?
- What are the different practices/models of interweaving Twitter into higher education teaching?
- What is the breadth of community in the Twittersphere?

Opening up potential research into the viability of a connectivism paradigm, developing and implementing models, and discussing implementation highlights and issues of interweaving Twitter into the higher education learning environment propose interesting options. Few empirically grounded studies documenting and evaluating use of Twitter are available (McNeill, 2009). Future research opportunities within this domain that produce quality qualitative and mixed methods data would continue to produce tangible data and invite continued connections to what is possible when engaging with Twitter for and as learning.

CONCLUSION

Cooperative and collaborative forms of learning have been influenced by the Internet and digital technology development for a number of years now. The possibilities available for engagement can be considered, as Prensky (2009) recommends, for ways he or she accesses the power of digital enhancements 'to complement innate abilities' and thus 'facilitat[e] wiser decision making' (p.3) in regards to access to information. Twitter as one of these digital technologies generates ones ability to access information, to engage with and learn form this information, and interpret in regards to reference points and needs/wants. The networked element, the connections to new and already established communities, is a characteristic of Twitter that draws attention to the possibilities these types of relationships have between cooperative and collaborative boundaries. Wellman (2001) would concur that in networked communities 'boundaries are permeable, interactions are with diverse others, [and] connections switch between multiple networks' (p.17).

It is clear that Twitter as a social media is one example that an academic can engage with for professional networking and/or for the higher education learning environment. The boundaries of intersections offer multiple options. Consideration, however must be made, into the how and why. From these multiple stance points I have considered the networked academic and the networked learner stance - connecting specifically to the notations of learning thorough and with Twitter – throughout this chapter.

The variety of digital technologies available for the higher education learning environment are vast. Twitter is just one. As with any decision to engage with a technology in the classroom, or outside, the connections to the why, how, associated skills, leaning outcomes, and purpose are crucial. These areas must also be made explicit within the student body (Bennett & Maton, 2011). Generalizations about technology skills and knowledge cannot be made, but are often associated to the higher education student group(s) (Prensky, 2007; Bennett & Maton, 2011). Although this chapter is not about the digital divide discussion associated to who is and isn't a digital native or digital immigrant, acknowledgement is made to this discussion in relation to understanding 'some young people may be confident in using technology, their understandings of how that technology works and how it might help them learn may be extremely limited' (Bennett & Maton, 2011, p. 177).

Recent literature indicates that a significant number of young people in higher education engage with a variety of digital technology, including social media, in their life. Assumptions cannot be made that all use Twitter, nor if they have an account, are active participants. The use and early adaption of this social media is still in its early stages with a variety of different applications being explored, trialed, adapted or even rejected. Introduction to Twitter in the higher education learning environment does not automatically mean participation. Relevance and connection to the why and how are intrinsic. As one student commented from Madeline's class:

'I wouldn't have thought Twitter could be used for learning; hadn't even thought of it.' I have a Twitter account but can't find many other people that I know do, but then again I have to adjust my thinking that Twitter is not like Facebook, it's not about friends and who is friends with who, it's more about making contacts in areas I'm interested in...I'd like to know more about how I could do this'.

This chapter introduces what is possible and through the literature discussions. Madeline's case study provides one perspective, and advocates being transparent about what can be achieved when learning through and with Twitter. Most importantly for the higher education academic in considering using the platform, and thus immersing oneself in the possibilities of being a networked learner and teacher, prior use to introducing it to students is crucial. The why and how must be planned for as too the pedagogical decisions for learning and teaching. The concept that *@twitter is always wondering what's happening* underpins the context, connectivity, continuity and content that is shared, viewed and utilized for learning with and through Twitter in the higher education learning environment.

REFERENCES

Abel, F., Gao, Q., Houben, G.-J., & Tao, K. (2011). Analyzing user modeling on Twitter for personalized news recommendations. In Konstan, J. A. (Eds.), *UMAP 2011, LNCS 6787* (pp. 1–12). Berlin, Germany: Springer-Verlag. doi:10.1007/978-3-642-22362-4_1

Anson, C. M., & Miller-Cochran, S. K. (2009). Contrails of learning: Using new technologies for vertical knowledge-building. *Computers and Composition*, *26*, 38–48. doi:10.1016/j.compcom.2008.11.002

Armano, D. (2008). *Why the four C's of community require the commitment of many: Let content, context, connectivity and continuity guide your efforts*. Digital Next. Retrieved 29 December, 2011, from http://adage.com/article/digitalnext/community-require-commitment/132734/

Australian Bureau of Statistics. (2011). *Internet activity, Australia, June 2011*. Quality Declaration. Retrieved January 22, 2012, from http://www.abs.gov.au/ausstats/abs@.nsf/mf/8153.0

Bennett, S., & Maton, K. (2011). Intellectual field or faith-based religion: Moving on from the idea of digital natives. In Thomas, M. (Ed.), *Deconstructing digital natives: Young people, technology and the new literacies* (pp. 169–185). New York, NY: Routledge.

Bradshow, P. (2008). *Teaching students to twitter: The good, the bad and the ugly*. Blog post 15/02/2008. Retrieved June 2, 2012 from http://onlinejournalismblog.com/2008/02/15/teaching-students-to-twitter- the-good-the-bad-and-the-ugly/

Briggs, L. L. (2008). *Micro blogging with Twitter: A Q and A with David Parry, assistant professor of emerging media at the University of Texas at Dallas' campus technology*. Retrieved June 2, 2012, from http://campustechnolog.com/Articles/2008/03/Micro-Blogging-with-Twitter.aspx?Page=1

Bruns, A. (2008). *Blogs, Wikipedia, Second Life, and beyond: From production to produsage*. New York, NY: Peter Lang.

Bruns, A., & Humphreys, S. (2007). Building collaborative capacities in learners: The M/cyclopedia project revisited. *Proceedings of the 2nd International Symposium of Wikis*, 2007, (pp. 1-10).

Carini, R. M., Kuh, G. D., & Klein, S. P. (2006). Student engagement and student learning: Testing the linkages. *Research in Higher Education*, *47*(1). doi:10.1007/s11162-005-8150-9

Castells, M. (1996). *The information age: Economy, society and culture (Vol. 1)*. Oxford, UK: Blackwell.

Celik, I., Abel, F., & Houben, G.-J. (2011). Learning semantic relationships between entities in Twitter. In Auer, S., Diaz, O., & Papadopoulos, G. A. (Eds.), *ICWE 2011, LNCS 6757* (pp. 167–181). Berlin, Germany: Springer-Verlag. doi:10.1007/978-3-642-22233-7_12

Collins, M., & Berge, Z. (1996). *Facilitating interaction in computer mediated online courses*. Paper presented at the FSU/AECT Distance Education Conference, Tallahasee, Florida.

Conole, G., & Alevizou, P. (2010). *A literature review of the use of Web 20.0 tools in higher education. A report commissioned by the Higher Education Academy. Walton Hall*. Milton Keynes, UK: The Open University.

Cowling, D. (2011). *Social media statistics Australia - October 2011*. Retrieved January 22, 2012, from http://www.socialmedianews.com.au/social-media-statistics-australia-october-2011/

Crook, C., Cummings, J., Fisher, T., Graber, R., Harrison, C., & Lewin, C. Oliver, M. (2008). *Web 2.0 technologies for learning: the current landscape –Opportunities, challenges and tensions. A Becta Report*. Retrieved June 2, 2012, from http://partners.becta.org.uk/uploaddir/downloads/page_documents/research/web2_technologies_learning.pdf

Downes, S. (2010). Blogs in learning. [STRIDE]. *Staff Training and Research Institute of Distance Education, 8*, 88–91.

Duffy, P., & Bruns, A. (2006). The use of blogs, wikis and RSS in education: A conversation of possibilities. In *Proceedings Online Learning and Teaching Conference* (pp. 31-38). Brisbane. Retrieved from http://eprints.qut.edu.au/5398/

Dunlap, J. C., & Lowenthal, P. R. (2009a). Tweeting the night away: Using Twitter to enhance social presence. *Journal of Information Systems Education, 20*(2).

Dunlap, J. C., & Lowenthal, P. R. (2009b). Horton hears a Tweet. *Educause Quarterly, 32*(4). Retrieved January 22, 2012, from http://www.educause.edu/educause+quarterly/educausequarterlymagazinevolum/hortonhearsatweet/192955

Gill, P., & Arlitt, M. (2008). A few chirps about Twitter. *WOSN '08 Proceedings of the First Workshop on Online Social Networks*. New York, NY: Association for Computing Machinery.

Greenhow, C., Robelia, B., & Hughes, J. E. (2009). Learning, teaching, and scholarship in a digital age: Web 2.0 and classroom research: What path should we take now? *Educational Researcher, 38*(4), 246–259. doi:10.3102/0013189X09336671

Grosseck, G., & Holotescu, C. (2008). Can we use Twitter for educational activities? *The Meeting of the 4th International Scientific Conference eLSE: "Elearning and Software for Education* (p. 11). Bucharest.

Grover, A., & Stewart, D. W. (2010). Defining interactive social media in an educational context. In Wankel, C., Marovich, M., & Stanaityte, J. (Eds.), *Cutting edge social media approaches to business education: Teaching with LinkedIN, Facebook, Twitter, Second Life, and blogs* (pp. 7–38). Charlotte, NC: Information Age Publishing.

Huberman, B. A., Romero, D. M., & Wu, F. (2008). Social networks that matter: Twitter under the microscope. *Computing*, 1–9.

Hughes, A. (2009). *Higher education in a Web 2.0 world*. JISC report. Retrieved January 15, 2012, from http://www.jisc.ac.uk/media/documents/publications/heweb20rptv1.pdf

Humphreys, L., Gill, P., & Krishnamurthy, B. (2010). *How much is too much? Privacy issues on Twitter*. Conference of International Communication Association, Singapore, June 2010. Retrieved June 6, 2012, from http://www2.research.att.com/~bala/papers/ica10.pdf

Java, A., Song, X., Finin, T., & Tseng, B. (2007). Why we Twitter: Understanding microblogging. *Network*, 56–65.

Junco, R., Heiberger, G., & Loken, E. (2010). The effect of Twitter on college student engagement and grades. *Journal of Computer Assisted Learning, 27*(2), 119–132. doi:10.1111/j.1365-2729.2010.00387.x

Kehrwald, B. (2005). Learner support in networked learning communities: Opportunities and challenges. In Son, J. B., & O'Neill, S. (Eds.), *Enhancing learning and teaching: Pedagogy, technology and language* (pp. 133–148). Flaxton, Australia: Post Pressed.

Krishnamurthy, B., Gill, P., & Arlitt, M. (2008). A few chirps about Twitter. *Proceedings of the First Workshop on Online Social Networks, WOSP 08* (p. 19). New York, NY: ACM Press.

Kwak, H., Lee, C., Park, H., & Moon, S. (2010). What is Twitter, a social network or a news media? Categories and subject descriptors. *Most*, 591-600.

Larsen, R., & Everton, R. (2008). Making marketing a "Tweet" deal. *Association Meetings*, (June), (pp. 17-19).

Lemon, N. (2011). Arts and technology. In Klopper, C., & Garvis, S. (Eds.), *Tapping into the classroom practice of the arts: From inside out!* (pp. 97–132). Brisbane, Australia: Post Press.

Ling, H. L. (2007). Community of inquiry in an online undergraduate information technology course. *Journal of Information Technology Education, 6*, 153–168.

Marshall, C. C., & Shipman, F. M. (2011). Social media ownership: Using Twitter as a window onto current attitudes and beliefs. *CHI, 2011*, 1081–1090.

McNeill, T. (2009). *Twitter in higher education.* Retrieved June 2, 2012, from http://www.scribd.com/doc/20025500/Twitter-in-Higher-Education

Michie, J. (2010). *Assessment for learning with twitter: Under education, technology.* Retrieved January 22, 2012, from http://jamesmichie.com/blog/2010/02/assessment-for-learning-with-twitter/

Notari, M. (2006). How to use wiki in education: Wiki based effective constructive learning. In *Proceedings of the 2006 International Symposium on Wikis* (WIKISYM), Denmark.

Palser, B. (2009). Hitting the Tweet spot. *American Journalism Review, 31*(2), 54. University of Maryland. Retrieved February 10, 2012 from http://search.ebscohost.com/login.aspx?direct=true&db=ufh&AN=38506878&site=ehost-live

Pang, L. (2009). *Application of blogs to support reflective learning journals.* Retrieved February 10, 2012 from http://.deoracle.org/online-pedagogy/teaching-strategies/application-of-blogs.html37

Parker, K. R., & Chao, J. T. (2007). Wiki as a teaching tool. *Interdisciplinary Journal of Knowledge and Learning Objects, 3*, 57–72.

Prensky, M. (2011, September). *Educational technology, July-August.* Retrieved January 22, 2012 from http://marcprensky.com/writing/Prensky-ChangingParadigms-01-EdTech.pdf

Priego, E. (2011, September 12). How Twitter will revolutionise academic research and teaching. *Guardian Professional.* Retrieved February 10, 2012, from http://www.guardian.co.uk/higher-education-network/blog/2011/sep/12/twitter-revolutionise-academia-research

Pulman, A. (2007). (Manuscript submitted for publication). *Blogging @ BU: IHCS case studies.* Centre for Excellence in Media Practice. *CEMP Work.*

Rodens, M. (2011). What the tweet? Twitter as a useful educational and professional development tool. *Communicating for Learners*, Spring #2.

Sinnappan, S., & Zutshi, S. (2011). *Using microblogging to facilitate community of inquiry: An Australian tertiary experience.* Paper presented at the meeting of the Asclite, Hobart, Tasmania, Australia. Retrieved January 22, 2012, from http://www.leishman-associates.com.au/ascilite2011/downloads/papers/Sinnappan-full.pdf

Sinnappan, S., & Zutshi, S. (2011). *Using microblogging to facilitate community of inquiry: An Australian tertiary experience.* Hobart, Australia: Ascilite. Retrieved January 22, 2012, from http://www.leishman-associates.com.au/ascilite2011/downloads/papers/Sinnappan-full.pdf

Skiba, D. J. (2008). Emerging technologies center: Nursing education 2.0: Twitter & Tweets. Can you post a nugget of knowledge in 140 characters or less? *Nursing Education Perspectives, 29*(2), 110–112.

Solis, B. (2008). *Customer Service: The Art of Listening and Engagement Through Social Media*, 32. Retrieved January 22, 2012 from http://www.briansolis.com/2008/03/new-ebook-customer-service-art-of/

Steeples, C., Jones, C., & Goodyear, P. (2002). Beyond e-learning: A future for networked learning. In *Networked learning: Perspectives and issues* (pp. 323–342). London, UK: Springer. doi:10.1007/978-1-4471-0181-9_19

The Digital Marketing Agency. (2011*). Australian online marketing trends – 2011*. Retrieved January 22, 2012, from http://www.socialmedianews.com.au/social-media-statistics-australia-march-2011/

Twitter. (2011). *#numbers*. Retrieved February 10, 2012, from http://blog.twitter.com/2011/03/numbers.html

Wakefield, S. A., Warren, S. J., & Alsobrook, M. (2011). Learning and teaching as communicative actions: A mixed-methods twitter study. *Knowledge Management & E-Learning: An International Journal, 3*(4). Retrieved February 10, 2012, from http://www.kmel-journal.org/ojs/index.php/online-publication/article/viewArticle/145

Wenger, E., White, N., & Smith, J. D. (2009). *Digital habitats: Stewarding technology for communities*. Portland, OR: CPSquare.

Wolf, K. (2008). A blogging good time: The use of blogs as a reflective learning and feedback tool for final year public relations students. In *Proceedings of World Association for cooperative education-Australian Collaborative Education Network Asia Pacific* (pp. 649–656). Australian Collaborative Education Network.

KEY TERMS AND DEFINITIONS

Higher Education Learning Environment: Considers not just the four walls of the classroom itself but the learning as a holistic environment where inquiry, questioning and investigation can occur for both the teacher/lecturer and the students in face to face, online, workshops, seminars, studios or lecturer formats. All are seen as learners in the higher education learning environment.

Personal Learning Network (PLN): Individuals create connections to develop a network that contributes to their professional development, knowledge and meaning making.

Personal Learning Environment (PLE): Possibilities for specific connections, sharing of ideas and content and continuity of knowledge generation and access that extend your network and are available in your environment.

Networked Learner: Individual who can access online resources and networks for research and scholarship purposes to learn from - for example Twitter.

Networked Teacher: Using online communities such as Twitter for networking about teaching and learning possibilities whether this is for sharing and gaining knowledge to share in the learning environment or actually using Twitter in the delivery of teaching and learning.

Tweeps: The users of Twitter.

Twitosphere: The Twitter community or environment.

Twitter: Twitter is a microblogging interface that enables a real-time interaction between users, using different devices, technologies and applications to communicate content.

Chapter 13

The Universal Appeal of Facebook©:
Providing Access to Tertiary Students from Australian Aboriginal Communities

Maree Gruppetta
University of Newcastle, Australia

Terry Mason
University of Western Sydney, Australia

ABSTRACT

The positive and negative aspects of using Facebook© as a crucial communication tool between Aboriginal academics and their Aboriginal students will be discussed within this chapter. Initially, the authors' use of Facebook© was to provide support for our Australian Aboriginal students within their own communities. The original intention was to supplement existing electronic forums provided by the University to maintain contact with students between study blocks, encourage reluctant technology users to interact online, and build links to the students' own communities and families. In 2009, the authors' students were involved in a research project (Milton, Gruppetta, Vozzo & Mason, 2009) and their use of Facebook© to interact with students was recognised as innovative and the authors were encouraged to investigate the potential within another research project (Vozzo, et al., 2011). From a peripheral practice conducted by two Australian Aboriginal academics, the importance of utilizing Facebook © to build social capital and support an Indigenous Academic community has become crucial to the success and retention of our Aboriginal tertiary students. The authors' most recent research project relies heavily on Facebook© as the main communication tool due to the vast distances between Aboriginal communities in Australia and the variety of technology provided by each state/territory.

DOI: 10.4018/978-1-4666-2970-7.ch013

INTRODUCTION

This Chapter reports on continuing developments in the use of Facebook© as the most effective communication tool between Australian Aboriginal academics and their Australian Aboriginal tertiary students within the Bachelor of Education (AREP) Course at the University of Western Sydney (UWS) in Australia. The authors acknowledge that 'Facebook' is a Trademark and the use of the name is copyrighted as indicated by the initial use of the © symbol. Further reference to Facebook throughout this chapter will omit the symbol to ensure readability, however the authors concede all rights of trademark and copyright remain with the legal owners of Facebook. The positive and negative aspects of using Facebook as a crucial communication tool between Aboriginal academics and their Aboriginal students will be discussed in relation to the available literature on the use of Facebook to support tertiary students and the perceived benefits and detriments involving the use of Facebook in general. Student demographics and the methodologies of two separate research projects conducted over the past three years will be included in order to provide detail of our experiences. Future plans for extending our research in this area will be detailed in the conclusion.

BACKGROUND

Student Demographics

The University of Western Sydney (UWS) has offered the Bachelor of Education (AREP) (Primary) as a block program specifically targeted for Australian Aboriginal students since 1983. The delivery has been via residential blocks of lectures, workshops, tutorials and research, with distance education models employed during the remainder of the semester and between the block residentials. Initially the Aboriginal Rural Education Program (AREP) targeted only rural students but now caters for both rural and metropolitan students and has

an increasingly younger and broader demographic. Many of the accommodations provided to address the circumstances of geographical isolation in the initial program were also found to be of benefit to urban Aboriginal people who were often socially isolated in the wider Australian community. In the early years of the program the majority of students were mature age females but in the last few years we have had an increasing number of younger students and many more male students are enrolling in the course. The course is a four year undergraduate equivalent of a Bachelor of Education (Primary) run over five years.

There are approximately 100 students enrolled across the five years of the AREP Education course with greater numbers in the first two years and fewer in the final three years due to natural attrition and an early exit point. Students with personal circumstances that interfere with their ability to finish the full degree can gain a qualification with a Diploma of Indigenous Studies at eighty credit points, a point which has earned favour from the Australian Aboriginal Communities. Students are aged from 17 years to 65 years with the majority of students aged 17 to 21 years. Students attend their residentials in Sydney, however are drawn from a range of areas across Australia with students residing in Queensland (approximately 1415 km away, almost equivalent to the distance from Luxemburg to Rome), Northern Territory (approximately 4000 km away, a greater distance than the 3,115 km from Lisbon to Copenhagen), Victoria (approximately 877 km, almost equivalent to the distance from Paris to Milan) and Western Australia (approximately 4040 km, almost double the distance from Edinburgh to Naples). In terms of distance travelled by these students, if a map of Australia was overlaid on a map of Europe, the distance from west to east would be greater than the distance between Ireland and Turkey. The distance north to south would be greater than that between Sweden and Spain. In contrast to Europe most of Australia is sparsely populated, arid and very poorly serviced compared to the few large and coastal population centres. This poses immense challenge in maintaining a strong relationship between academics and students. The New South Wales (NSW) based students are technically closer to the campus (between 100 to 1200 km away) yet many are located in remote rural areas with limited Internet access and support, hence the need to find an alternative way to connect with and sustain students between residential blocks. Many students from the Metropolitan Area are parents, hold permanent jobs, engage in multiple Community commitments and are only able to access university education through flexible programs. Although they are closer to the university, they often encounter similar needs to those students living more remotely due to the high demands placed on them. All students are also affected by the varied weather patterns and natural disasters that are common to Australia. With our sweeping plains, ragged mountain ranges, drought and flooding rains, through flood and fire and famine (Mackellar, 1968) and recent cyclones and severe storms, our students must still submit their assignments, complete online tasks and meet the required rigour of university study.

Initial Research Project

In 2009 a large Australian government-funded joint research project between UWS and Charles Darwin University (CDU) in the Northern Territory investigated the Information Communication Technology (ICT) practices currently used by both universities within interactions with their tertiary students (Armitage, et al., 2011). The study used a qualitative design using focus groups and interviews in which the views of first year students who had recently commenced tertiary studies were complemented with third and fourth year students with more experience of tertiary study. Students were asked to complete a brief ICT usage and familiarity survey of a 'tick box' variety seeking information about students' familiarity with, use of, and competence with a range of hardware (e.g. computers, i-phones, i-pads, mobile telephones); the Internet; and University online systems. Within

the larger study a smaller sub group of Aboriginal students were selected to specifically ascertain their experiences of ICT at university. For the next two years a focus group of twenty students from each university were interviewed to ascertain their perspectives, knowledge and uses of ICT resources provided to them (Milton, et al., 2009). The twenty AREP Education students were interviewed individually and then within focus groups annually to provide a range of responses which were fully documented and included in the final publication of the study (Armitage, et al, 2011). While the numbers of Aboriginal students were too small to undertake a comparative analysis between first, third and fourth years, the survey information gave an overall picture of individual and group use of ICTs and a source of verification for the focus group data.

Subsequent Research

In 2011 we, the authors, were asked to participate in another research study, the Assessing Professional Teaching Standards (APTS) Project as a partnership between the University of Western Sydney (UWS); Charles Sturt University (CSU) and Australian Catholic University (ACU) (Vozzo, et al., 2012). The project included Aboriginal and non-Indigenous pre-service teachers and specifically researched how these pre-service teachers could be supported via digital technologies. The main focus of this review is on the use of ePortfolios to evidence and assess teaching standards and to investigate digital technologies to support an online community of teachers and pre-service teachers (Vozzo, et al., 2012). At the time of writing this study is still ongoing and will conclude in December 2012.

Our role, for the purposes of this research study, was to act as 'Key Informants' (Denzin & Lincoln, 2005) to assist the non-Indigenous academics and students in their interactions with Aboriginal students and communities. Within this study 'Digital technologies' was used as a broad term to refer to communication technologies that can be used to build and maintain the virtual network that allows distant participants to interact with each other, demonstrate their engagement in self-study and evidence standards (Vozzo, et al. 2012). The research builds on the findings of other studies: The use of handheld technology in clinical practice within nurse education has been well documented (Wu & Lai, 2009). Videos in web-based computer-mediated communication as supporting tools for self-report, reflection and artefacts for teaching portfolio collections were used by Lee and Wu (2006) within teacher education. Mobile phones were used by Ryan and Walta (2009) to make microteaching videos and podcasts used in online discussion. Hedrick, McGee and Mittag (1999) reported perceptions of pre-service teachers in America, learning through one-on-one tutoring, through e-mail.

The challenge within this study (Vozzo, et al. 2012) was to equip pre-service teachers with the technological means and the curriculum to more readily evidence teaching standards and establish a truly supportive online community which acknowledges that "all (university) students are not created equal" (Fitzgerald & Steele, 2008, p.40). Across the three universities there are a variety of backgrounds represented by these 49 pre-service teachers. Both UWS and ACU have Aboriginal pre-service teachers in block programs, whereas CSU did not. All their students were non-Indigenous but were destined to teach in rural schools with large Aboriginal populations. In terms of technology competency, students varied in their experience, access and ability to use technology depending on their socio-economic circumstances, cultural background and physical location within Australian rural areas. Equally the academics involved in the project varied in their ability to interact with technology.

Facebook Research

Facebook.com is a social-networking Web site, defined by its creators as "a social utility that helps people communicate more efficiently with their friends, family and coworkers." Its popularity is worldwide; with over 350 million active users, Facebook is the second most trafficked social-networking site in the world (Facebook, 2009 cited in Wise, Alhabash & Park, 2010). Due to this popularity, Facebook has become a realm of interest for academics exploring the processes and effects of computer-mediated communication and social networking. Wise, et al. (2010) contend that recent research on Facebook can be loosely divided into three areas: its uses and gratifications at both intrapersonal and interpersonal levels; its socio-political and psychosocial influences, and the privacy implications of its form and function (Wise, et al., 2010). Yet this contention omits specific studies into the differences of gender usage of Facebook (Haferkamp, Eimler, Papadakis, & Kruck, 2012); the degree of narcissism, self-promotional and anti-social behaviour of Facebook users (Carpenter, 2011); the capacity to build social capital (Ellison, Steinfield & Lampe, 2007); and the variety of studies specific to interacting with tertiary students through Facebook (English & Duncan-Howell, 2008; Hewitt & Forte, 2006; Charnigo & Bernett-Ellis, 2007; Orr, Sisic, Simmering, Arseneault & Orr 2009).

Haferkamp, et al., (2012) contend that women's online behavior within Facebook is more interpersonally oriented, while men are more task-and information-oriented. Women, for instance, spend more time writing e-mails, while men use the Web more frequently for information seeking in general. These observations conform to stereotypically assumed offline behavior and illustrate that gender is an important aspect in online research as well (Haferkamp, et al. 2012). Citing Bimber they concluded that around one-half of the 'digital divide' on the Internet is fundamentally gender related (Haferkamp, et al. 2012). The digital divide is often explained by the idea that the Internet is an inherently male technology, which reproduces societal structures and behavioral dispositions and results in gender-specific differences in social networking use (Haferkamp, et al. 2012). In our experience within both research studies there is no apparent gender difference in the behaviour of our students on Facebook. Although we do seem to have some differences in which students choose to be our 'friends' there does not appear to be a gender bias within their choice. The male author has just as many female students as Facebook 'friends' as the female author and vice versa. Nor does there appear to be any major difference in the type of posts by our Aboriginal students; the female students are just as likely to discuss sports and often are more competitive than the male students in supporting their teams; and the male students are just as likely to post cute comments regarding their children, dogs and other pets. Both genders will discuss political issues and current events with us, their fellow students and their other friends. Relationship is one of the key foundations of Aboriginal society and this may be reflected in the content of posts. The exchange of information that builds relationship is more important than filling a perceived role or social expectation based on gender.

Haferkamp, et al. (2012) suggest that their social–psychological findings prove women are more concerned about how they are perceived by others and use their online profiles for self-display. They further contend:

Our findings regarding the motives for the perception of profiles demonstrate that women tend to compare themselves with other users and search for information when they look at other people's online profiles, whereas men follow the initial idea behind social networking, which was to search for friends. (Haferkamp, et al, 2012, p.96)

Neither statement confirms with our experiences of our Aboriginal students on Facebook. Raacke and Bonds-Raacke (2008) also found there was no gender divide in their research and that both men and women of traditional college age are equally engaging in this form of online communication with their result holding true for nearly all ethnic groups.

Many of the Facebook studies completed are not applicable to our experiences with our Aboriginal students. For instance Orr, et al. (2009) investigated the personality trait of shyness and its relation with certain features of an online communication tool (Facebook). Shyness was found to be significantly related to the quantity of time spent on Facebook, the number of contacts added to one's Facebook profile, and having favourable attitudes toward Facebook. In terms of our Aboriginal students' experiences 'shyness' (Orr, et al., 2009) does not even begin to describe the issues they face when starting university. Our students are usually first in family to attend university, they are displaced from their home communities, usually have a lower socio-economic background, and suffer loss of self-esteem as a result of continual racism and low teacher expectation when completing their primary and secondary schooling. Racism is particularly noted in the employment of Aboriginal People in Australia with a resultant lack of belief that education will assist any change in circumstances. Combine this with the high percentage of Aboriginal adults who have had a poor schooling experience (circa 60%) and it is evidenced that there is often little support in many households or even an expectation that one should attend university. Some of our students have used Facebook to defend their choice to study at tertiary level and are then supported by other students and the Aboriginal lecturers, effectively supporting the change in perceptions of tertiary study in the wider community. Facebook can supply some of this support through bolstering knowledge of process, build esteem as the student is not alone in a shared environment and allow those in the wider Facebook community to be involved in the experience. Further investigation is required to determine if this use of Facebook may begin a flow of 'subtle' Bridging Capital between Community/Family and students/university. 'Shyness' (Orr, et al., 2009) is the least of the issues for many.

Lin and Lu (2011) have investigated building Social Capital via social networks such as Facebook. Because Social networking provides users with more opportunities to interact, communicate, and share with others, users are able to develop and maintain relationships. A Social Network, therefore, enables users to maintain online relationships and also helps them to reserve this capital for future use (Lin & Lu, 2011). Social capital is essentially a two-way street such that all involved parties are entitled to access resources provided by their peers (Lin & Lu, 2011). Bridging Capital is defined by Putnam (2000) as making friends with people who are not like you, bridging the differences in beliefs and cultural values. Bridging Capital builds bridges beyond your own cultural social capital. As stated above, whether this Social Capital translates into Bridging Capital requires further investigation. Nevertheless social network sites enable users to express themselves, establish ties, and develop and maintain social relationships (Lin & Lu, 2011) and the importance of relationships within Aboriginal communities cannot be understated. Doherty and Mayer (2003) and Craven (2011) contend the key to any kind of successful education of Aboriginal students, is a strong relationship between teacher and students. The importance of relationship building within tertiary education for Aboriginal students is key to their retention and success (Gruppetta & Mason, 2011).

A variety of studies have been completed on the use of Facebook with tertiary students that are pertinent to our research. Charnigo and Bernett-Ellis (2007) surveyed academic librarians concerning their perspectives toward using Facebook as an online network for students. Many librarians were enthusiastic about the potential of Facebook to promote events and services yet concerned about the distraction Facebook posed when accessed within the library (Charnigo & Bernett-Elles, 2007). Many of these librarians found that strict regulation of access to the site was unfavourable and ultimately the majority concluded that Facebook was external to the purview of professional librarianship (Charnigo & Bernett-Ellis, 2007) and therefore desisted in their efforts to utilise the site to communicate with

tertiary students. In our experience this type of attitude to Facebook by academics in particular is common, many can see no purpose to interacting with students via this forum beyond using it to advertise courses, send announcements, sell books or other goods and promote activities. Many do not see the possibilities presented by this forum or consider it a mere distraction. Others try to impose strict regulation such as restricting personal posts or restricting the use of colloquial abbreviations common to this forum. Therefore students often feel that lecturers are old fashioned and unable to interact with their understanding of the modern world as 'digital natives' (Prensky, 2001). We have found that students tend to react negatively to criticism of their posts on Facebook unless a clear reason is provided. Our students are provided with the explanation that it is a public forum and, despite privacy settings, Facebook could feasibly be accessed by anyone. We then explain that as they are going to be teachers with an expectation of being a role model and exhibiting professional behaviour that they should be aware of the ramifications of posts that include inappropriate language or concepts. In practice all we then have to do is post something like "maybe not?" or "Did we discuss this type of language?" and the student will immediately remove the inappropriate comment or post. The students do not seem to take any offence and none thus far have declined our friendship status on Facebook as a result of this type of gentle regulation. Our use of Facebook in this manner is as an extended tool toward teaching our students about the behaviour and language expected of teachers, any criticism is used as a "teachable moment" (Havighurst, 1953, p.7) and students also recognise that we are functional in the abbreviations commonly used on Facebook and therefore our comments are accepted within that forum.

The abbreviated language used by our students on Facebook is becoming increasingly common these days. The increased use of technology and our fast paced lifestyle has induced the development of an abbreviated language to save both time and money. Changes to language and vocabulary involve common abbreviations used in mobile telephone text 'Short Message Service' (SMS), emails, and discussion forums like Hotmail's Micro Soft Network (MSN) chat rooms. Commonly referred to as HAXXOR (Urban Dictionary, 2006), the "language of juveniles in chat rooms" (Straub, 2004, p. 103), these abbreviations are becoming common slang and are even used within spoken conversations between young people as part of popular culture (Gruppetta & Hall, 2006). Walker (1999) refers to such changes to literacy due to technology as the 'gates to hell', and argues vehemently against the trend, warning of the destruction of communication in the future. Lines will become blurred between the formal mode of writing and the softer mode of speech. Grammar, spelling and punctuation will change, shifting from the formal written standards currently acceptable to academia to the easy abbreviated standards of email (Baron, 2000). Dobson (2002) is again concerned with the implications for the evolution of language, but refers to email as "a medium of impatience" and contends that ardent users "continue to develop an ease and speed of written language that hovers somewhere between speech and shorthand" (p.103). Our students vary in their use of such abbreviations. The younger students are quite versatile in their use of this terminology whereas more mature students struggle to understand meaning. Although both authors are mature age the younger students accept our presence on their Facebook pages and interact in both formal and abbreviated language styles. In Aboriginal society, there is an expectation that older people will share their knowledge and experience in a respectful manner. The terms 'Aunt' and 'Uncle' are used in a familial way and the trust that is implicit in such a relationship facilitates the "teachable moment" (Havighurst, 1953, p.7).

In contrast to our experience Hewitt and Forte (2006) found that tertiary students feel that interactions with their College professors on Facebook is crossing boundaries and that academics should not be on Facebook at all. Many students indicated

that the student/faculty relationship should remain professional and should not be familiar or sociable (Hewitt & Forte, 2006). This contrasts sharply with the expectations of Aboriginal culture. Aboriginal society was structured around the need to have decisions made on a basis of the need of the Community and involving consultation and consensus. Coming from a cultural continuum based on this platform, Elders are seen as the repository of knowledge and experience. They are seen as a resource to be accessed with wisdom to be imparted and any form of communication is welcome, therefore our students often seek our advice.

In our experience the issue of 'privacy' is often discussed, particularly in terms of academics revealing their personal opinions, home lives, family and other areas that are considered 'private' within mainstream academic areas. As Aboriginal people we are less concerned about these issues. We accept that our communities will know our families; that our students come from those communities and therefore will know background information about us, just as we know background information about the students. In our experience Facebook is simply a faster way to get to know each other and really establish the required relationships. As new students learn of our family activities and observe the interactions of our Facebook family, our interest, or lack of interest, in sports, political and social support sites, means they 'know' more of us and appreciate the fairness of our professional relationships with them. It is evident that they are marked on merit and not judged against our own personal beliefs as they are open to all to see. Their differing views are discussed within an open Community forum but respected in assessment under rigour.

The different expectations of privacy could be cultural. Hsu, Wang and Tai (2011) examined whether close relationships impacted on the type and frequency of interaction between Facebook users in Taiwan. Their findings were interesting as they noted that users were less likely to invoke privacy concerned tools with newly acquired friends, contrasting with privacy concerns raised in other studies. They did find that behaviors invoked less time and effort with newly acquired Facebook friends than close long term friends, yet found overall that Facebook is a mechanism for new friends, rather than close friends, to become more acquainted (Hsu, et al. 2011). Although this study is specific to Taiwan it does highlight the differences that can occur in behaviours specific to cultural backgrounds. The issue of 'privacy' did impact on our students although not in the context presented by Hewitt and Forte (2006) nor in relation to the lack of concern reported by Hsu, et al. (2011) as will be explained in the issues, controversies and solutions section of this chapter.

Several studies specifically examined the building of online communities among teachers, (Abbitt, 2007; Roper, 2008; McElraith & Mcdowell, 2008; Reil, 2000 in English & Duncan-Howell, 2008, p. 597). English and Duncan-Howell, (2008), researched the use of social networking tools, such as Facebook to support Business Education students undertaking teaching practicum. These 28 pre-service teachers were invited to post one or more messages on Facebook, using the Web 2.0 platform, while undertaking a four week practicum in Queensland. The site was closed to all except the participants of the study. The opening page of Facebook was "seeded" by the site administrator/academic with statements and questions that provoked or scaffolded student responses, (p.598). These responses fell into five broad themes:

Other (n=54) – related to generalised, affective communication about the practicum; Excitement (n=37) – positive, anticipatory posts written at the start of the practicum and supportive, encouraging comments at the end of the practicum; Problem (n=20) - associated with problems such as nerves, lack of resources, subject, supervisors and student issues; Joke (n=19) – humorous, self deprecating comments; Solution (n=18) – collaborative responses to problems and issues raised by others. (English & Duncan-Howell, 2008, pp.599-600)

The results indicated that digital habits may be used to develop supportive online tools that assist the practicum (English & Duncan-Howell, 2008) and their results are consistent with our experiences. Although we do not have enough students participating to obtain significant quantitative results we have noted that our students were sympathetic and supportive to each other during practicums via online forums.

Other studies reported on the use of Web 2.0 using Skype ©, SMS messaging and applications other than Facebook to support students (Cochrane & Bateman, 2008), to continue relationships with overseas students once they had returned to their own countries (Li, 2011) or to link with overseas students in order to support their learning via flexible delivery (Thomson, Tan & Brook, 2009). Again the Trademark and copyright of these applications are acknowledged by the authors with the use of the © symbol in first reference to each application and thereafter omitted to ensure readability. Thomson, et al, (2009) reported on the use of Skype to support overseas students studying via flexible delivery and results of the survey indicated that the students found this interaction very supportive. Cochrane and Bateman (2008) provided a comparison of the various communications types available and found that students and academics varied in their usage, ability and perceived need to interact in these ways, which was consistent with our experience. Nearly one third of their participants thought it was difficult to control information and that it did not have enough functions for academic use, they preferred to use the site recreationally (Cochrane & Bateman, 2008). Skype was briefly mentioned although apparently not used by many as a tool to support students or interactions between students and/or academics.

Traditionally web-based e-learning systems, for example Blackboard ©, usually support basic academic activities such as delivering teaching materials, online communications and simple online assessments. However, these systems are usually more passive rather than active, less creative, reflective, collaborative and personalised (Li, 2011). Li's (2011) study found that current web 2.0 applications do have the value of potential education but are under-utilized. Although Web 2.0 (Blog, Facebook) applications are popular with students, few use them in their learning (Li, 2011) despite their growing familiarity with this type of technology. Many of the participants report an expectation that any e-learning system should have 'an ease of use' (Li, 2011) and this is consistent with feedback from our students. Students have an expectation that any system should be fairly user friendly and not require hours of training or specialised software or computer settings in order to access it. This expectation is crucial to engaging learners, students must be able to access systems easily or the entire concept of university learning becomes too difficult.

McGrath, Butcher and Stock (2011) did use Skype to continue relationships with Asian students after they had completed their studies in New Zealand. They found the technology useful as it permitted face-to-face conversations with students and maintained the relationship more successfully than Facebook conversations. Broadley, Boyd and Terry, (2009), used video conferencing rather than Skype to connect disparate, remote communities of teachers in Western Australia. Survey results from the 110 teachers involved in professional learning seminars via videoconference produced understanding of the challenges and the successes that outweighed them. Challenges included the technology and venue problems of logistics, skill with tools, synchronous file sharing, the need for technology back up plans and the time expenditure by the voluntary co-ordinators. The successes included initiation of teacher networks at the local level, collaboration and commitment from partner organisations and the delivery of successful professional learning seminars to teachers who would otherwise have no access to them (Broadley, et al, 2009, pp.80-81). The specifics of this study do not include any mention of Aboriginal students or teachers, nor do they discuss specific difficulties with engaging in the technology across distances

which is a major problem we encountered so it is difficult to ascertain whether their success can be replicated within our current study. We used both Skype and video-conferencing within our study and found Skype to be easier for students to access as most of the video-conferencing equipment is controlled by either the schools or the universities and therefore not accessible to most of our students unless used within one of those locations.

Supporting Aboriginal Students

Research into supporting Aboriginal students, particularly Australian Aboriginal students in tertiary situations relates to strategies to support their learning styles (Barnes, 2000; Craven, 2011; Partington, 2003; Stewart, 2002) and more specific research into Information Communication Technology (ICT) to support Aboriginal students (Doherty, 2002; Christie, 2001; McLoughlin & Oliver, 2000) and/or those from lower socio-economic backgrounds in rural areas (Australian Institute for Social Research, 2006; Barraket & Scott, 2001; Kilpatrick & Bound, 2003; Wallace, 2008) which includes the demographic background of the majority of our students in addition to their Aboriginal identity.

Understanding issues of identity and the past history of Aboriginal people in Australia are paramount when teaching Aboriginal students (Craven, 2011). Since colonization the Aboriginal people in Australia have been subject to a variety of policies and the accompanying issues of being treated as less than citizens in their own country. Even though assimilation was 'official' policy, there were many barriers between Aboriginal and non-Indigenous Australians. Many Aboriginal people were legally wards of the State, like children who needed care (Craven, 2011). Many were contained on reserves and missions, their lives at every level controlled by those in charge (Craven, 2011). Aboriginals in rural areas were often discriminated against as to where and how they could marry, work, live and mix with others, and their movements were restricted (Craven, 2011). Although Aboriginal activists had struggled for citizenship rights in the 1930s and 1940s, and there had been some changes, Aboriginals generally were still not able to exercise political rights like voting, civil rights like freedom of movement, or social rights to education and a decent standard of living until the referendum in 1967 (Craven, 2011).

Prior to the referendum in 1967, due to the legal fiction of *Terra Nullius*, Aboriginal people had the same status as the 'flora and fauna' of the country (Irving, 2003). By every measure, Aboriginal people in Australia continue to be disadvantaged (ANTA, 2000) and there are indications across the past decade that the situation is deteriorating (Jonas, 2003). The *Royal Commission into Aboriginal Deaths in Custody* (Johnston, 1991) emphasised the importance of education and employment to self-determination, and the need for the wider community to understand Aboriginal culture and heritage. These recommendations were echoed in *Bringing them Home* report on the separation of Aboriginal and Torres Strait Islander children from their families (HREOC, 1997). History since invasion has left Aboriginal Communities with a cultural continuum that has been influenced by policies of exclusion, persecution, neglect, assimilation, 'self-determination' and currently an attitude that is an amalgam of all the above. The Race Discrimination Policy (1975) has only been withdrawn three times in Australia. All three times the withdrawal of 'racial discrimination' legislation has only concerned Aboriginal People and Land Rights. The legislation was withdrawn to prevent Aboriginal people claiming discrimination under the Racial Discrimination Policy (1975) whilst various Government interventions were implemented. There is currently a bi-partisan Intervention of Aboriginal Communities, particularly in the Northern Territory, by Australian Governments with punitive legislation affecting most areas of Aboriginal life and choice.

The Northern Territory intervention spelt the end to the progress made in generations of struggle for acknowledgement and recognition of Aboriginal people's right to have some control over the future of their families and communities (Brown & Brown, 2007). The very foundational principles on which Aboriginal existence are built — community, culture and collective rights — have been shaken, demonised and exposed to a level of scrutiny unparalleled in recent times (Brown & Brown, 2007). Although the intervention was announced in response to concerns over the health of Aboriginal children, there remains enormous confusion and concern over other elements of the intervention that seem unconnected to child health, such as compulsory land acquisition by the federal government; the abolition of entry permits for Indigenous communities and of Community Development Employment Projects programs; the appointment of government business administrators to "run" Indigenous communities; and the potential threat of community asset-stripping (Brown & Brown, 2007). Further, the legislation covering the Northern Territory intervention places unparalleled control of Indigenous affairs in the hands of the Minister (or his designated delegate), and is largely discretionary and, in critical elements, poorly defined (Brown & Brown, 2007). The current interventions will not empower communities and support them appropriately, in a spirit of collaboration and respect, to adequately deal with the causes, triggers and consequences of abuse. Marginalisation, poverty, disempowerment, colonisation and trauma are the upstream contributors to psychological, physical and sexual abuse in the present (Brown & Brown, 2007; Craven, 2011). Yet the current policy is likely to deliver the very same things, and, as a consequence, risks perpetuating dysfunction and abuse (Brown & Brown, 2007). The government has yet to explain how the removal of Aboriginal people's right to control or participate in decision making and implementation will promote their survival and protection (Brown & Brown, 2007). Current circumstances leave Aboriginal People with great challenges in making headway in such a system. For example, the first Aboriginal

University graduates were Margaret Valadian and Charles Perkins in 1965, fairly recent compared to representatives from non-Indigenous cultural backgrounds.

The implications of such ongoing legislative changes and restrictions for Aboriginal people have left our Aboriginal students with an all pervading mistrust of authorities, particularly relating to education systems, due to past experience of the deficit viewpoint that has restricted their educational opportunities and permitted intervention into every aspect of their lives. Unfortunately there is no way to explain the impact of this history and current experiences of racism to our non-Indigenous colleagues, hence the need for 'Key Informants' (Denzin &Lincoln, 2005) who are not only familiar with the community and culture but are also empathetic to the long term affects of our shared history. The struggle to survive and now achieve, relies on the strength of a culture of kinship bonds and extended family and social relationships. People were always mobile and maintaining 'large' conversations and now, with greater migrations, often for socio-economic reasons, Facebook fits well into this connective process and has therefore become a popular medium for Aboriginal people.

Aboriginal society has always been based on a complex and evolving set of relationships both spiritual and social, between land and people. Aboriginal people saw land and people as kin with interwoven obligations and responsibilities. There is a connection to land and people that underlies Aboriginal relationships. Gibb (2006, p. 23) also found that found that 'connectedness (to others) supports learning' and that broad rather than narrow communication patterns between teachers and students contributed to successful learning experiences. Aboriginal students in particular prefer group work, and there is a cultural reason for achieving as a shared entity rather than individual achievement (Gruppetta, 2010). Harris and Malin's (1994) research supports group learning and peer support as a result of Aboriginal child rearing practice where children are encouraged

to learn co-operatively. Again this highlights the need to establish good relationships and co-operatively learning to facilitate achievement by Aboriginal students.

Issues Relating to Cultural Aspects

Several issues arose during the course of the recent study (Vozzo, et al., 2012) that required attention. Underpinning our education courses is the priority of creating effective teachers. The ability to develop and sustain good relationships with Aboriginal students and their families is a major element in the profile of effective teachers. Such relationships require building rapport, trust, getting to know students as individuals, and taking a personal interest in school and out of school activities (Doherty and Mayer 2003). For Aboriginal students 'who the teacher is' is paramount to building the necessary reciprocal relationships within the classroom. It is difficult to separate the idea of Identity and practice for Aboriginal teachers. So much of the required relationships are based on who you are as well as what you do. Within the project (Vozzo, et. al, 2011) many of the Aboriginal students were conflicted between assisting others with these cultural understandings and openly sharing aspects of Aboriginal culture with non-Indigenous beginning teachers. As noted by O'Riley (2003) discusses the "right to know" (p.154) is a western assumption. The researcher, student, academic world in general believes they have a 'right to know' all facets of the culture or individual being presented. Yet she also speaks of the "right of those who know not to share what they know" (O'Riley, 2003, p.154). She contends that there are intimate knowledges within most cultures that are understood by the members of that culture. From habits to secrets, they are not easily explained to an outsider, and many are not intended to be shared beyond the circle of that specific culture. A participant's right to withhold such information must be respected. The "professionalism of knowledge within western culture has made it a commodity" (O'Riley, 2003, p.154), yet that does not give researchers permission to lack sensitivity when dealing with intimate cultural knowledge. Many of our non-Indigenous researchers have difficulty with these ideas and find it difficult to understand the notion that some cultural information is not considered suitable for non-Indigenous people to share. Equally many of our Aboriginal students felt uncomfortable trying to explain what they felt they could or could not share and this was an issue that needed to be addressed with much cultural sensitivity.

Issues Relating to Communication

Another issue related to our previous discussion on the use of HAXXOR (Urban Dictionary, 2006) which has been an ongoing problem for us in relation to the other academics involved in the project. The official University forum used by UWS, ACU and CSU is Blackboard © and in all three universities the use of such language is forbidden as it is not considered 'academic'. Our students have had to learn that what is acceptable in one forum is not acceptable in another and for some this has been a long journey. We have provided our academic colleagues with a basic dictionary of such terminology in order to allow them to translate some terms and encourage interaction with the students at their level. For instance abbreviations such as LOL which means 'Laugh Out Loud'; BRB which means 'Be Right Back'; Cul8 meaning 'See you later' and the use of the number 2 to represent 'too/as well/to/two' (Gruppetta & Hall, 2006) are commonly used and apparently quite irritating to some of our non-Indigenous academic colleagues. The interaction between two distinctly culturally different groups, Aboriginal and non-Indigenous, has also been tense due to this difficulty in accepting the use of these abbreviations within non university forums. This tension was further exacerbated by the use of Aboriginal English on Facebook forums. Aboriginal English has not been respected in the past by school teachers and many academic staff have tended to dismiss its use as inferior communication. Aboriginal English is a recognised dialect of English and this aspect of communication has required mediation between students and staff at times.

Issues Relating to Tokenism

There have been other difficulties related to the intercultural differences rather than simply a difference in viewpoint. As the 'key informants' (Denzin & Lincoln, 2005) within the study the authors have often felt left out of discussions and are quite often unable to attend meetings that are deliberately scheduled when we have community commitments. The expectation of other academics that we can simply cancel a community engagement because the research meeting should take precedence is in conflict with the expectations of Aboriginal community. We often feel that we are viewed as deficit, not really academics despite having earned degrees and established research careers. We also often feel that our inclusion in the project is tokenism rather than being fully accepted as academic peers. Not all of the researchers perceive us in this way. Many of the academics we work with are culturally sensitive, or at least willing to learn about cultural issues, although some are unable to see the Aboriginal cultural perspective. The most difficulty we have encountered in relation to this lack of intercultural understanding is from those academics who are first generation immigrants to Australia. The assumption is that because they are immigrants, and have therefore felt the perspective of the 'other' when dealing with mainstream Australian society pressures, that they are able to share a common experience with Australian Aboriginal people. Unfortunately this is simply not the case. None of these academics have a history that includes their people being classified as less than citizens. None were ever classified as 'Flora and Fauna' (Irving, 2003; Craven, 1999) rather than actual people and nor did they have to wait until 1967 for a referendum to count them as citizens in their own country (Irving, 2003).

Issues Related to Technology

In regard to the use of various technology trialled within this study (Vozzo, et al, 2012) an issue arose when many of our Aboriginal university students were reluctant to engage in Skype conversations from their own homes. They did not feel comfortable inviting other students or lecturers into their homes and just said 'Shame'. Whether they were concerned they would appear inferior or feel that by participating in the project and completing the portfolio they would appear too 'flash' (a colloquial Aboriginal term for appearing too good) in front of their friends and colleagues is not clear. Many assume the Aboriginal concept of 'Shame' is only to not be 'shamed' in front of another, particularly within community by being seen as deficit in some way (Gibson & Vialle, 2007). It also involves the idea of not standing out in any way, including achieving too highly. As with many Indigenous cultures there are expectations that prevent individuals from striving for personal accomplishment and glory (Gibson & Vialle, 2007). Almost all teachers of Aboriginal children come up against the problem of children not wanting to stand up or do anything by themselves in front of others. They feel real 'shame' when required to do such things. Also they are often unhappy if it is pointed out that they have scored higher or performed better than their friends and relations (Baarda, 1990, p.169, cited in Gibson & Vialle, 2007, p. 207). Equally the thought of shaming themselves or their communities can cause great distress. It is in this context that the use of Skype in the family home may be a problem. Academic language and Western style 'confrontational' debate displayed in front of family may inhibit active participation by tertiary students. Students have expressed strong support for the use of Facebook because it allows the open forum to run concurrent with the closed chat room between those they wish to engage in a more involved discussion of the topic. The issue with using Skype was a major problem within the more recent study. The non-Aboriginal lecturers could not conceive of any problem with using Skype. They were unable to understand that they were asking our Aboriginal students to effectively invite non-Indigenous strangers into their homes.

In relation to the problem of using Skype and other technology there was also the issue of the cost involved. As previously stated many of our students live in quite 'rural' areas which means their connection to the Internet could be via satellite or still be a 'dial-up' type of connection rather than cabled. As well many of our students are classified as low socio-economic and have limited incomes. Some are on connections that require them to pay by the Megabyte or Gigabyte they use. Although technically Skype itself was free it does require considerable cost when paying via data use. Additionally the researchers wanted to have three or more people on Skype at the same time to facilitate discussion which required paid membership to 'Skype Premium' again at a cost prohibitive to most students. The various other types of connective software trialled included Eluminate © which is very similar to Blackboard but allows face-to-face video chat as well as views of each other's desktop. Although we could provide the software to students via the university website we could not restrict the amount of data used when interacting with the software, again causing much cost to students who could ill afford it. One of the academics then contacted a company to see if we could construct our own interactive website to be specifically designed for use within this study (Vozzo, et al., 2012), the quote was $30,000.00AUD and would still not address the problems of remote connections nor data consumption. The other issue with introducing various types of technology was the need for training for both staff and students in order for their use to be effective, yet some of the academics still wanted to persist with experimenting with ever newer and more complicated technology because they felt it was justified within the parameters of the project. Many of the tertiary students and some of the academics did not agree, however we were all continually forced to try new things which only irritated those involved.

Issues Relating to Cyber-Bullying

The final issue that arose was the problem of cyber-bullying. Fortunately this was a mild problem and readily dealt with as the Aboriginal academics were able to quickly intervene. Although we did not directly 'see' the incidents we did see the comments by distressed tertiary students on Facebook © referring to problems with other tertiary students. Some of these issues were between Aboriginal students rather than between Aboriginal and Non-Indigenous students and related to the concept of 'shame' (Gibson & Vialle, 2007). Students who were considered to be self-promoting themselves, thereby being too 'flash', encountered reactions from their peers and there were sometimes issues between the various age groups. The younger students would criticize those who could not use technology easily and the more mature students would criticize the younger students for their youthful behaviour or language. These issues are usually mild when encountered in a face-to-face situation and swiftly dealt with, however given opportunity to interact via online forums the issue became more critical to address. Bullying via online forums can be quite invasive and take place at any time and needed to be addressed swiftly.

SOLUTIONS AND RECOMMENDATIONS

Many of the issues noted in the previous section were dealt with effectively although some remain as ongoing issues. In order to address the initial problem felt by Aboriginal students in regard to sharing cultural understandings, one of the authors, Terry Mason, shared his cultural knowledge with all participants in the study via 'Indigenous cultural competency' (Vozzo, et al., 2012) workshops.

After this type of role modelling the Aboriginal tertiary students felt more able to build on these areas and support the non-Indigenous pre-service teachers with their interactions with Aboriginal school students. By example the Aboriginal lecturer was able to clearly define what is acceptable to share and what to say when asked a question regarding 'secret' knowledge. This type of practical example provided a model for both Aboriginal pre-service teachers and the non-Indigenous pre-service teachers to facilitate Aboriginal students in their classrooms, thereby assisting them to establish their own relationships with their students. Overall these pre-service teachers will be more effective with all students, not just Aboriginal students, as they now not only understand the need to establish a relationship, they also understand the boundaries permissible within that relationship. It is not necessary to share everything with your students to establish a relationship nor do you need to answer every question that they ask, you simply need to share enough of yourself that they can see you as a real person. Nor do you need to know every detail of a student's life in order to establish a relationship of trust. This open approach to establishing a relationship with students has benefitted all involved in the project and enabled communication that would otherwise have been restricted due to concerns on both sides regarding what is and is not appropriate when working with Aboriginal communities and students.

To address the issue of communication on forums via HAXXOR abbreviations (Urban Dictionary, 2006), as noted above academics were supplied with a dictionary of terms to aid their interactions, despite this many still struggle with the idea that students will use this type of language when interacting with academic staff. We have yet to find an effective solution to changing the attitudes of either staff or students in regard to the use of these abbreviations as both sides seem to think they are correct in their attitude. Despite this we have found that many staff members now understand an impressive number of these acronyms and quite often reply to them without realising they have been responding to this type of language. Staff have also overall benefitted from an induction to the grammar of Aboriginal English and the meaning of many words. Some are Aboriginal, some are English words pronounced from an Aboriginal phonetic base and some may have a different meaning from the English word used by staff. Correcting the pronunciation of these words is not culturally acceptable as it changes the meaning and shames the student rather than accepting the language as culturally appropriate. Thus far we have found these issues to be ongoing although we have made some progress toward academics and other tertiary students accepting the use of Aboriginal English and understanding that it is a recognised dialect. We are still working toward academics accepting the use of abbreviations when communicating on Facebook.

The issues of omitting the concerns or ignoring the advice of the authors as Key Informants (Denzin & Lincoln, 2005) to the study were somewhat resolved due to the need to seek our assistance when dealing with various issues that arose. For instance, it was only after intervention by the authors that a compromise to the issue of using Skype was able to be reached. Rather than expect the Aboriginal pre-service teachers to invite non-Indigenous lecturers and students into their homes they would only use Skype when in a school situation or other public area. In this way they could share aspects of their classroom and their teaching without ever having to intrude on their own personal private spaces. This issue was ultimately resolved by the Aboriginal academics using private chat and email facilities within the Facebook forum to resolve these issues without having to involve non-Indigenous academics and students in the discussion. We then explained in depth their concerns to the non-Indigenous academics and participants on behalf of the Aboriginal university students and were firm in the need to find an effective compromise. Equally the issue that arose regarding the cost of some of the technology was initially raised by one of the authors when they found their own Internet bill

excessive after interaction on Skype. When we then raised the issue of excessive cost that could be incurred by participants many of the academics were sympathetic and agreed that students should not have to pay additional cost to be participants in the project. Tertiary students were contacted and asked to check their Internet bills and request reimbursement if the bill was excessive, effectively addressing the issue proactively.

The difficulties encountered with the ever 'newer' trials of technology were again addressed by the authors in response to Aboriginal students complaining about the excessive time involved in learning and interacting with new systems when they had families to care for and work and community commitments in addition to their studies and involvement with the project. Unfortunately we were only heard when other academics complained about the constantly changing systems and after the Reference Group for the project (Vozzo, et al., 2012) was convened. Professor Toni Downes, a well known Australian expert in Information Technology systems with considerable experience in Aboriginal Education, was quite blunt in her assessment of the systems used. She said "I don't understand why you are trialling all these systems given the difficulties of contact in remote areas and adding additional costs to the project, if Facebook works then just use Facebook!" Subsequently no further systems were introduced and our use of Facebook was expanded to include sending files as attachments via the email system, the 'chat' facility on Facebook was used for live contact when required and a private Facebook group was organised for the researchers and participants to discuss matters relating to the project (Vozzo, et al, 2012) without having to reveal their private Facebook pages to those who were not their Facebook friends. The use of Facebook to contact those even in remote areas proved very effective as they could use the system from their homes, laptops, mobile phones and/or log into Facebook from libraries and public Internet access points, ensuring a continual ability to establish contact between all researchers and participants.

Ultimately the increased effectiveness of contact enabled the opportunity for cyberbullying as students were in constant contact. As mentioned above the Aboriginal academics were the first to notice there was a problem in this regard and we immediately privately 'in-boxed' the students and asked for more details and then gave advice on how to deal with the problem rather than immediately intervene ourselves. If the problem had not been resolved we could have then intervened in an official capacity. The students involved expressed gratitude and positive feedback and learned much in the process. They now have strategies to deal with any future encounters with similar incidents of cyber-bullying. As part of our interactions with all the tertiary students involved we then conducted a workshop on bullying and what types of behaviour and commentary were acceptable and not acceptable, specifically highlighting what we perceived as bullying behaviour. These tertiary students will not only have strategies to cope with any future bullying, they will also be able to assist their future students cope with similar experiences. Again this fits with Aboriginal learning practices, it is not enough to fix the immediate problem, the issue becomes a 'teachable moment' (Havinghurst, 1953) and ensures that future generations can learn the skill that is passed along.

Despite the positive solutions discussed here there are areas that still need to be addressed. As Gibb (2006) noted many Aboriginal students do not commence their studies with a cultural orientation that equips them to intuitively understand the discursive practice of universities. There is a need for scaffolding and support from culturally competent academics that we have demonstrated in relation to each of the issues presented above. This type of intervention can only be successful where Aboriginal academics are employed to support Aboriginal students. The lack of cultural competency amongst some of our non-Indigenous colleagues needs to be addressed and the solution must be to require academics external to the culture to undertake cultural training prior to interacting with the students. Additionally the necessity for

culturally appropriate content and language, with scaffolding of the presentation of non-Indigenous ideas and theories (Milton, et al. 2010) is strongly recommended. Aboriginal students should not be required to immediately assimilate into the discourse of universities as a condition of entry. Their cultural backgrounds and past histories must be taken into account as an integral part of their cultural experience and identity. To do otherwise is to ask these students to check their identities at the door in order to gain an education. There must be an enhanced understanding and trust between Community/Family and students/university in a country only very recently removed from an exclusionist White Australia Policy. Without this, Australia will continue with non-pluralistic and non-engaging curriculum that does not cater for the needs of all its citizens. Many Aboriginal students have now taken up the debate over political and social attitudes using Facebook in a way they have not felt comfortable within tutorials, knowing they will have support and reach a wider audience.

FUTURE RESEARCH DIRECTIONS

In our presentation of Facebook research we are not concerned with the ramifications of timewasting, game playing or how much time a person spends Internet surfing, as our viewpoint is purely that of understanding the potential of Facebook to build an online community of learners. Our perspective is more concerned with the need to establish a supportive community environment for Aboriginal students taken from their home communities and learning to survive in an alternative environment. The need to build real relationships with our students and their communities takes priority over the concerns expressed by other academics. In order to support our Aboriginal students, encourage them to access tertiary education and retain their interest and trust such relationships are paramount. An important outcome from using Facebook in this manner that requires further research is the link to establishing Bridging Capital from the already growing Social Capital. Facebook is being used extensively by our alumni. They inform each other of jobs and promotion opportunities, encourage other Community members to apply for jobs and university courses and support them through the intricacies of the process. They share resources and strategies for coping in the workplace and interact with non-indigenous colleagues in a public forum, sharing knowledge of how such relationships can be established and maintained. These are examples of Bridging Capital that can be further researched in future projects.

The issue of cyber-bullying is another area that should be investigated within future studies. The Department of Education in Australia has forbidden all teachers to have their school students as Facebook friends. The reasons are to reduce the risk of students seeing less than perfect role models if the teachers post something deemed inappropriate for students to see or know; reduce the risk of paedophiles grooming students; and prevent perceived invasion of privacy on both sides. Yet, the potential for intervention in cyber-bullying could outweigh these risks, particularly if teachers act responsibly. Many school students in Australia have committed suicide due to cyber-bullying, often because no-one knew about it or the student felt they had no-where to turn. If their teachers had been Facebook friends would they have been able to intervene and deal with the issue earlier? This is a critical area that requires more investigation in the future.

Our current research project (Vozzo, et al, 2012) as previously stated will continue until the end of 2012 and will involve the pre-service teachers from last year becoming part of the online learning community as beginning teachers assisting the next set of pre-service teachers as they take part in the project. As the study is ongoing more issues may arise and solutions will evolve throughout participant and researcher interaction. One of the authors is now at another university and will use what has been learned from these two studies to set up another Facebook learning community, this time for Aboriginal post

graduate research students to support each other through their doctoral experiences. Again this will generate more issues and solutions as time goes on. These projects are ever evolving and provide opportunities to anyone interested in exploring new ways of interacting with tertiary students. We have also recently been approached to assist Maori academics in New Zealand to begin similar Facebook networks to support their Indigenous students. Extending our research to incorporate another Indigenous group will provide immense opportunities to refine what we have learned and build a framework that can be used by other academics to provide similar support.

CONCLUSION

This Chapter reported on the continuing developments in the use of Facebook as the most effective communication tool between Australian Aboriginal academics and their Australian Aboriginal tertiary students within two universities in Australia. The interaction established between these tertiary students and their Aboriginal lecturers was then extended to include non-Indigenous academics, researchers and participants in another research project and again the use of Facebook as a crucial communication tool across the majority of Australia was evident. Although our experiences are supported by some of the literature presented on the use of Facebook with tertiary students, there are some aspects that are unique to our experience. The interaction between Aboriginal staff and students is completely different to the interaction typical between academics and tertiary students as we are already part of their cultural community and have a duality of role when supporting these students. We are both advisors and teachers and can provide a support role unlike that of other lecturers in ensuring these Aboriginal tertiary students can access education in a system that has been historically weighted against Aboriginal people. The additional challenges of distance, rural and urban situations, family and community commitments, lower socio-economic circumstance and the harsh climate within Australia make any type of communication difficult. Accessing technology as a requirement of tertiary study can prohibit access to education for many Aboriginal students. Facebook has proven to be an effective and reliable means of communicating. It can be accessed by all despite distance, varied Internet systems and providers and/or environmental challenges. Overall the positive aspects of using Facebook far outweighed the few negative aspects encountered and have provided several potential research avenues to explore in extending this concept. Our peripheral practice of utilizing Facebook to contact students has become vital to the success and retention of our Aboriginal tertiary students and we recommend others should explore the potential of Facebook as a crucial tool for tertiary student interaction.

REFERENCES

Abbitt, J. T. (2007). Exploring the educational possibilities for a user-drive social content system in an undergraduate course. *Journal of Online Learning and Teaching, 3*(4), 437–447.

ABS. (2012). *Map of remote areas as defined by Australian Bureau of Statistics.* Retrieved from http://www.abs.gov.au/websitedbs/D3310114.nsf/home/remoteness+structure

ANTA. (2000). *Partners in a learning culture national strategy and blueprint for implementation.* Brisbane, Australian National Training Authority. Australian Natural Therapist Association (ANTA).

Armitage, L., Brackenreg, E., Campbell, S., Catterall, J., DeSilva, S., & Davis, J. (2011). *ICT enabled learning and widening participation at the University of Western Sydney: The kindling of a flame: A report forming part of the Charles Darwin University's Diversity and Structural Adjustment Fund project "Achieving Best Practice Flexible Provision at CDU".* Kingswood, Australia. Yang, D.F.: University of Western Sydney.

Australian Institute for Social Research. (2006). *The digital divide: Barriers to e-learning: Final report.* Adelaide, Australia: University of Adelaide.

Barnes, A. (2000). Learning preferences of some Aboriginal and Torres Strait Islander students in the veterinary program. *Australian Journal of Indigenous Education, 28*(1), 8–16.

Baron, N. S. (2000). *Alphabet to email: How written English evolved and where it's heading.* London, UK: Routledge. doi:10.4324/9780203194317

Barraket, J., & Scott, G. (2001). Virtual equality? Equity and the use of information technology in higher education. *Australian Academic and Research Libraries Journal, 32*(2).

Broadley, T., Boyd, D., & Terry, E. (2009). The hot topic community: Videoconferencing to reduce the professional isolation of teachers in rural Western Australia. *ISFIRE Symposium Proceedings,* (pp. 76-83). Armidale, Australia: University of New England.

Brown, A., & Brown, N. J. (2007). The Northern Territory intervention: Voices from the fringe. *The Medical Journal of Australia, 187*(11), 621–623.

Carpenter, J. (2011). Narcissism on Facebook: Self-promotional and anti-social behavior. *Personality and Individual Differences, 52*(4), 482–486. doi:10.1016/j.paid.2011.11.011

Charnigo, L., & Bernett-Ellis, P. (2007). Checking out Facebook.com: The impact of a digital trend on academic libraries. *American Libraries Association, 26*(1), 23–34.

Christie, M. (2001). Aboriginal knowledge on the internet. *A Journal of Australian Indigenous Issues, June,* 33-50.

Cochrane, T., & Bateman, R. (2008, October). *Engaging students with Mobile Web 2.0.* Paper presented at the Teaching & Learning Conference, Eastern Institute of Technology, Hawkes Bay.

Craven, R. (Ed.). (2011). *Teaching Aboriginal studies* (2nd ed.). Sydney, Australia: Allen & Unwin.

Denzin, N. K., & Lincoln, Y. S. (Eds.). (2005). *The Sage handbook of qualitative research* (3rd ed.). Thousand Oaks, CA: Sage.

Dobson, T. (2002). Keeping in touch by electronic mail. In *M. van Manen (2002). Writing in the dark: Phenomenological studies in interpretive inquiry* (pp. 98–116). Canada: Althouse Press.

Doherty, C., & Mayer, D. (2003). E-mail as a "contact zone" for teacher-student relationships. *Journal of Adolescent & Adult Literacy, 46*(7), 592–600.

Ellison, N. B., Steinfield, C., & Lampe, C. (2007). The benefits of Facebook "friends:' Social capital and college students use of online social network sites. *Journal of Computer-Mediated Communication, 12*(4), 1143–1168. doi:10.1111/j.1083-6101.2007.00367.x

English, R., & Duncan-Howell, J. (2008). Facebook goes to college: Using social networking tools to support students undertaking teaching practicum. *Merlot Journal of Online Learning and Teaching, 4*(4), 596–601.

Fitzgerald, R., & Steele, J. (2008). *Digital learning communities: Investigating the application of social software to support networked learning* (CG6-36). Australian Learning and Teaching Council. Retrieved September 1, 2009, from www.mashedlc.edu.au

Gibb, H. (2006). Distance education and the issue of equity online: exploring the perspectives of rural Aboriginal students. *Australian Journal of Indigenous Education, 35*, 21–29.

Gibson, K., & Vialle, W. (2007). The Australian Aboriginal view of giftedness. In Phillipson, S. N., & McCann, M. (Eds.), *Conceptions of giftedness: Sociocultural perspectives.* London, UK: Lawrence Erlbaum.

Gruppetta, M. (2010). *The life journey of gifted adults: a narrative exploration of developmental differences.* Unpublished Doctoral Dissertation. Sydney: The University of Western Sydney.

Gruppetta, M., & Hall, J. (2006, June). Email as communicative data: The tyranny of distance. *International Conference on Technology, Knowledge and Society: Technology & Citizenship,* Montreal, Canada. Retrieved March 30, 2012, from http://ts6.cgpublisher.com/proposals/103/index_html

Gruppetta, M., & Mason, T. (2011). Embracing the Facebook © phenomenon. In Kahn, R., McDermott, J., & Akimjak, A. (Eds.), *Democratic access to education.* Los Angeles, CA: Antioch University.

Gruppetta, M., Mason, T., & Santora, N. Bennet, M. (2011). *Developing inter-cultural relationships through digital technology.* Paper presented at the Australian Association for Research in Education Conference, Hobart, Australia.

Haferkamp, N., Eimler, S. C., Papadakis, A. M., & Kruck, J. V. (2012). Men are from Mars, women are from Venus? Examining gender differences in self-presentation on social networking sites. *Cyberpsychology. Behaviour and Social Networking, 15*(2), 91–98. doi:10.1089/cyber.2011.0151

Harris, S., & Malin, M. A. (1994). *Aboriginal kids in urban classrooms.* Wentworth Falls, Australia: Aboriginal Studies Press.

Havighurst, R. (1953). *Human development and education.* Ann Arbor, MI: University of Michigan.

Hedrick, W., McGee, P., & Mittag, P. (1999). Pre-service teacher learning through one-on-one tutoring: Reporting perceptions through e-mail. *Teaching and Teacher Education, 16*(1), 47–63. doi:10.1016/S0742-051X(99)00033-5

Hewitt, A., & Forte, A. (2006). *Crossing boundaries: Identity management and student/faculty relationships on the Facebook.* Paper presented at the Computer Supported Cooperative Work (CSCW) conference. Alberta.

HREOC. (1997). *Bringing them home: The stolen generation report.* Australian Human Rights Commission. Retrieved March 2, 2012, from http://www.humanrights.gov.au/social_justice/bth_report/index.html

Hsu, C.W., Wang, C.C., & Tai, Y.T. (2011). The closer the relationship, the more interaction on Facebook? Investigating the case of Taiwan users. *CyberPsychology, Behavior and Social Networking, 14*(7-8)

Irving, F. (2003). *Learning to listen to indigenous voice: Dialogue and dilemmas.* Paper presented at the Australian Association for Research in Education Conference, Auckland, NZ

Johnston, E. (1991). *Review of Royal Commission into Aboriginal Deaths in Custody.* Retrieved February 12, 2012 from http://www.austlii.edu.au/au/other/IndigLRes/rciadic/

Jonas, W. (2003). *Native title report.* Human Rights and Equal Opportunity Commission. Indigenous Studies Program, The University of Melbourne. Retrieved March 12, 2012 from http://www.atns.net.au/page.asp?PageID=2#what

Kilpatrick, S., & Bound, H. (2003). *Learning online: Benefits and barriers in regional Australia.* Adelaide, Australia: NCVER.

Lee, G., & Wu, C. (2006). Enhancing the teaching experience of pre-service teachers through the use of videos in web-based computer-mediated communication. *Innovations in Education and Teaching International, 43*(4), 369–380. doi:10.1080/14703290600973836

Li, X. (2011). *Students and some teachers' views of using Web 2.0 technologies in e-learning: Findings from a survey and interviews.* Paper presented at the International Conference on E-Learning Futures 2011: Unitec Institute of Technology 30 Nov-Dec 1 Auckland NZ.

Lin, K. Y., & Lu, H. P. (2011). Intention to continue using Facebook fan pages from the perspective of social capital theory. *Cyberpsychology. Behaviour and Social Networking, 14*(10), 565–570. doi:10.1089/cyber.2010.0472

MacKellar, D. (1968). *I love a sunburnt country.* Poets Australia. Retrieved February 12, 2012, from http://www.imagesaustralia.com/mycountry.htm

McGrath, T., Butcher, A., & Stock, P. (2011). *The impact of returning Asian students of NZ-Asia relationships.* Paper presented at the ISANA International Education Association 22nd Annual Conference: Innovations working with diverse students, 22nd Nov -2nd Dec 2011, Hobart.

McLoughlin, C., & Oliver, R. (2000). Designing learning environments for cultural inclusivity: A case study of indigenous online learning at tertiary level. *Australian Journal of Educational Technology, 16*(1), 58–72.

Milton, M., Gruppetta, M., Vozzo, L., & Mason, T. (2009). *Ideals and retention: Perspectives of students in a BEd (AREP) course.* Paper presented at the AIATSIS Conference: Canberra.

O'Riley, P. A. (2003). *Technology, culture, and socioeconomics: A rihizoanalysis of educational discourses.* New York, NY: Peter Lang.

Orr, E. S., Sisic, M., Ross, C., Simmering, M. G., Arseneault, J. M., & Orr, R. R. (2009). Rapid communication: The influence of shyness on the use of Facebook in an undergraduate sample. *Cyberpsychology & Behavior, 12*(3), 337–340. doi:10.1089/cpb.2008.0214

Partington, G. (2003). Why indigenous issues are an essential component of teacher education programs. *Australian Journal of Teacher Education, 27*, 39–48.

Prensky, M. (2001). Digital natives, digital immigrants. *Horizon, 9*(5), 1–6. doi:10.1108/10748120110424816

Putnam, R. (2000). *Bowling alone: The collapse and revival of American community.* New York, NY: Simon & Schuster. doi:10.1145/358916.361990

Raacke, J., & Bonds-Raacke, J. (2008). MySpace and Facebook: Applying the uses and gratifications theory to exploring friend-networking sites. *CyberPsycology & Behaviour, 11*(2), 169–174. doi:10.1089/cpb.2007.0056

Racial Discrimination Act. (1975). Human Rights Commission. Retrieved March 12, 2012 from http://www.hreoc.gov.au/racial_discrimination/index.html

Roper, C. (2008). Teaching people to bargain online: The impossible task becomes the preferred method. *MERLOT Journal of Online Learning and Teaching, 4*(2), 254-260. Retrieved August 18, 2008, from http://jolt.merlot.org/vol4no2/roper0608.pdf

Ryan, J., & Walta, C. (2009). *Pre-service teacher education partnerships: Creating an effective practicum model for rural and regional pre-service teachers.* ALTC Priority Programs.

seeking on Facebook. *Cyberpsychology, Behaviour and Social Networking, 13*(5) 555-562

Stewart, J. (2002). The relevance of the 'learning styles debate' for Australian indigenous students in mainstream education. *The Australian Journal of Indigenous Education, 30*(2).

Straub, P. (2004). *In the night room.* London, UK: Harpercollins.

Thomson, K., Tan, B. K., & Brook, C. (2009). *Computer mediated communication and the learning experience of those studying via flexible delivery mode.* EDUCAUSE Australiasia Conference: Innovate, Educate and Sustain. Perth, 3-6 May, 2009. CAUDIT: Council of Australian University Directors of Information Technology.

Urban Dictionary. (2006). *Haxxor.* Retrieved September 18, 2007 from http://www.urbandictionary.com/define.php?term=haxxor

Vozzo, L., Santoro, N., Labone, E., Bennett, M., Nanlohy, P., & Pietsch, M. Reid, J. (2012). *Assessing professional teaching standards, for indigenous and non-indigenous pre-service teachers in urban, rural and remote practicum and for accomplished teachers, using digital technology.* Australian Learning and Teaching Council (ALTC). Retrieved from http://www.deewr.gov.au/highereducation/programs/quality/pages/altc.aspx

Walker, J. R. (1999). *Literacy, technology, and change: The gates of hell.* Unpublished doctoral dissertation, University of South Florida.

Wallace, R. (2008). *Engaging remote and very remote Indigenous students with education using information and communication technologies (ICTs): Final report.* Darwin, Australia: Charles Darwin University.

Wise, K., Alhabash, S., & Park, H. (2010). Emotional responses during social information

Wu, C., & Lai, C. (2009). Wireless handhelds to support clinical nursing practicum. *Journal of Educational Technology & Society, 12*(2), 190–204.

ADDITIONAL READING

ABS. (2012). *Map of remote areas as defined by Australian Bureau of Statistics.* Retrieved from http://www.abs.gov.au/websitedbs/D3310114. nsf/home/remoteness+structure

Bonk, C. J., & King, K. S. (1998). *Electronic collaborators: Learner centered technologies for literacy, apprenticeship and discourse.* Mahwah, NJ: Lawrence Erlbaum Associates.

Elison-Bowers, P. (2008). Health science students and their learning environment: A comparison of perceptions of on-site, remote-site, and traditional classroom students. *Perspectives in Health Information Management, 5*(2).

Halse, C., & Robinson, M. (1999). Towards an appropriate pedagogy for Aboriginal children. In Craven, R. (Ed.), *Teaching Aboriginal studies.* St. Leonards, Australia: Allen & Unwin.

Harris, S. (1990). *Two way Aboriginal schooling: Education and cultural survival.* Canberra, Australia: Aboriginal Studies Press.

Howard, C., Schenk, K., & Discenza, R. (Eds.). (2003). *Distance learning and university effectiveness: Changing educational paradigms for online learning.* London, UK: Information Science Publishing. doi:10.4018/978-1-59140-178-0

Hughes, P. (1997). *A compact of Aboriginal education.* Adelaide, Australia: Aboriginal Education unit, Department of Education.

Kember, D. (2007). *Reconsidering open and distance learning in the developing world-Meeting students' learning needs.* New York, NY: Routledge.

Open University. (2012). *Academic credits in Europe and ECTS points.* Retrieved from http://www8.open.ac.uk/study/explained/study-explained/building-your-qualification/what-are-credits

Pearce, S. (2008). Critical reflections on the central role of Indigenous program facilitators in education for social change. *The Australian Journal of Indigenous Education, 37,* 131–136.

Shih, T. K., & Hung, J. C. (Eds.). (2007). *Future directions in distance learning and communication technologies.* London, UK: Information Science Publishing.

Taylor, J. C. (2000). New millennium distance education. In Reddy, V., & Manjulika, S. (Eds.), *The world of open and distance learning* (pp. 475–480). Viva Books Private Ltd.

Valenzuela, S., Kim, Y., & Gil de Zuniga, H. (2011). Social networks that matter: Exploring the role of political discussion for online political participation. *International Journal of Public Opinion Research,* 2011.

Wallace, R. (2008). *Engaging remote and very remote Indigenous students with education using information and communication technologies (ICTs): Final report.* Darwin, Australia: Charles Darwin University.

Wheaton, C. (2000). An Aboriginal pedagogical model: Recovering an Aboriginal pedagogy from the Woodlands Creek. In Neil, R. (Ed.), *Voice of the drum: Indigenous education and culture.* Brandon, Canada: Kingfisher Publications.

Williams, S. (2010). *Being culturally aware: Becoming culturally inclusive: A pathway to cultural competence. An Aboriginal community cultural teaching programme.* Sydney, Australia: Aboriginal Education Consultative Group Incorporated.

Yunkaporta, T., & McGinty, S. (2009). Reclaiming Aboriginal knowledge at the cultural interface. *Australian Educational Researcher, 36*(2), 55–72. doi:10.1007/BF03216899

Zepke, N. (2005). *Improving tertiary student outcomes in the first year of study*. Wellington, NZ: Teaching and Learning Research Initiative.

KEY TERMS AND DEFINITIONS

Aboriginal: The term 'Aboriginal' is preferred by Australian Aboriginal people. 'Aborigine' or 'Indigenous' could mean any people indigenous to a country. Aboriginal is specifically used by Australian Aboriginals to describe themselves.

Credit Points: In Australian Universities 'Credits' measure the student workload required for the successful completion of a study programme or qualification – although universities vary usually one unit (or subject of study) is worth 10 credit points (some universities count 8 credit points per unit, some use 12). For example, if you study an 80-credit module and successfully pass it, you have completed 8 units (subjects) of study over eighteen months. The system used in Europe, the European Credit Transfer System (ECTS) does not provide a direct comparison with the Australian credit point system as the ECTS does not take account of academic level, therefore direct comparisons are difficult to make. However, broadly, at any given level, 60 Australian credit points would be worth 30 ECTS points, and 30 Australian credits would be worth 15 ECTS points (Open University, 2012).

Cultural Competency: A term to describe those that are able to understand and empathise with other cultures. It implies some understanding of customs and protocols when dealing with a culture other than their own.

Indigenous: Indigenous refers to any people native to their country. However in Australia the Government departments use the term Indigenous to describe Aboriginal and Torres Strait Islander peoples. This groups them together consistently, even when only one group is discussed. The term was adopted several years ago as it was thought to save paper by using only the single word instead of six words. Few Australian Aboriginals refer to themselves in this manner.

Metropolitan: A term used to discuss urban residency in cities or larger towns within Australia. A 'metropolitan' area is also defined as a 'major urban' area with a population of over 100,000 residents as defined by the Australian Bureau of Statistics (ABS, 2012).

Remote: The concept of remoteness is an important dimension of policy development in Australia. The provision of many government services are influenced by the typically long distances that people are required to travel outside the major metropolitan areas in order to access government services (ABS, 2012). Remote areas are typically those with small populations (also classified as 'rural) and requiring long travel distances to obtain education, health or other essential services.

Residential: A 'residential' for the purposes of study at an Australian University refers to a period of block study time where students are required to be in 'residence' on campus. Typically students are required to attend University for a period of at least a fortnight to attend face-to-face classes and are permitted to study online between these face-to-face residentials.

Rural: The Australian Bureau of Statistics (ABS, 2012) defines rural as including those areas with a bounded locality, such as small towns with a population of 200 to 999 and any other 'rural balance' where the population of the area is less than 200 and/or the remoteness of the location requires long distance travel to access basic services.

Urban: The Australian Bureau of Statistics (ABS, 2012) defines an urban area as either a 'Major Urban: urban areas with a population of 100,000 and over' of as 'Other Urban: urban areas with a population of 1,000 to 99,999'.

Section 4
Educational and Ethical Issues in Web 2.0 Age

Chapter 14
Risky Media:
Using Subversive Technologies in Education to Question Assumptions about Power, Teaching, and Assessment

Matthew J. Kruger-Ross
Simon Fraser University, Canada

Tricia M. Farwell
Middle Tennessee State University, USA

ABSTRACT

This chapter seeks to critically examine and question common assumptions underpinning educators' use and incorporation of technology in the classroom. Drawing upon transformative learning theory, the authors argue that incorporating technology in education cannot and should not be done without first questioning assumptions regarding power, teaching, and assessment. Technology is transforming education in expected ways, but can also transform education in unexpected, unexplored ways. Educators need to move beyond the quick fix of bulleted lists to explore the implications of technology in the classroom more fully.

INTRODUCTION

Web-based technologies are dramatically redefining the boundaries of higher education. Existing conversations and debates in educational research literature surrounding technology in education have been fruitful and generated an enormous body of literature. Yet considerable theoretical and philosophical blind spots that presuppose the almighty and omniscient power of technology continue to permeate educational circles. These blind spots, preconceived notions or assumptions each educator brings with him or her to their approach to integrating technology into the classroom, often go unexamined. These assumptions provide the context and foundation to the educator's approach to technology in the classroom. Examining the everyday, taken-for-granted, uncritically

DOI: 10.4018/978-1-4666-2970-7.ch014

analyzed assumptions and habits of mind of the education and technology metanarrative will be challenging; but exploring these assumptions also creates a context for increased empowerment and more authentic conversations about the value of education.

Deep philosophical, epistemological, pedagogical, and even metaphysical questions accompany the cacophony of information that surrounds the average college instructor but to date no one has unearthed, named, and extrapolated on these concerns. These include, but are not limited to: When information is everywhere, who authenticates it? When students can watch lectures from professors at MIT and UC Berkeley on YouTube, are they learning? How would we verify such learning? What counts as education? Indeed, what's worth knowing? Instructors in higher education must acknowledge and utilize the availability of multiple perspectives and sources of information.

This chapter focuses on questions, rather than answers. Technology in education, and thus social and new media in education, is subversive. Technology is subversive in the same way that Postman & Weingartner (1969, pp. 34-37) argue for a subversive, inquiry-based education. To accomplish this, the educator must be simultaneously a part of the technological movement and also a spectator. Rather than offer a bulleted list of best practices, we aim to do the opposite. We will avoid telling the reader what he or she "ought to know"; we will avoid offering quick-fix answers to questions. Therefore we will convey our message through asking open, divergent questions in order to foster, support, and encourage critical dialogue. As we do this, we will most likely leave more topics unresolved than resolved, but in doing so we hope to spur the reader to focus on and value the questions rather than trite conclusions.

Our push away from the bulleted, oversimplified lists of what can and should be done with technology can only skim the surface of questions educators face. Questions abound: How exactly can technology be used to transform learning? How

does learning transform technology? What impact does technology have on the "traditional" practices and procedures? What does it all matter? So what? In fact, the number of questions an educator can face may make incorporating technology into the educational process seem to be a daunting, if not impossible, task. Add to these questions, the need to actually show up to class, either online or offline, with a prepared plan of attack creates the scene where often even the simplest question of "Where do I begin?" becomes overwhelming. Yet, despite being overwhelmed, educators are often asked to bet their skills and their students' education on technology. By adding technology to the learning experience, some educators may feel like they are sitting down at a gambling table, being expected to place a bet without knowing the rules and name of the game. Do we really want to bet our students' learning?

The goal of this chapter is to name this game and attempt to draw some tentative boundaries in hopes of providing faculty and instructors with a framework that will urge them to action. Rather than technology-as-enemy, educators will see just how much say they have in the matter of technology integration. Drawing on transformative learning theory and philosophy of technology, common assumptions underpinning the intersection of education and technology are distinguished and critically analyzed.

DISTINGUISHING THE BACKGROUND NOISE: ASSUMPTIONS AND HABITS OF MIND

Before examining the assumptions present in educational technologies, it is necessary to examine the concept of assumptions and why they are critical to our ability to make meaning. We move through life with basic assumptions contextualizing our daily processes. In a way, they are a shorthand version for people to negotiate settings and situations that they have encountered before, either through personal interactions or through second-hand interactions. Where assumptions become dangerous is allowing them to fully govern situations without questioning the outcome. Although acting on assumptions may make us feel safer, it also blinds us to opportunities and potential pitfalls. While we have moved away from some traditional assumptions regarding teaching, such as learning must take place in a face-to-face classroom setting, we are encountering a completely new set of assumptions with the addition of Web 2.0 and social media technologies into the learning process.

In order to fully contextualize the assumptions regarding technology and learning that will be discussed later, we first begin with a discussion of transformative learning, followed by using metaphor to create meaning and contextual technology, and finally an exploration of philosophy of technology.

Transformative Learning

Most educators would agree that the ultimate goal of education is for students to take what they learn and apply it outside of a classroom setting. In other words, we encourage our students to take facts and concepts and create meaning. In order to do that, students must find a way to make information relevant. One theory that argues that the ability to make meaning must be considered within any educational context is transformative learning. This theory, originally applied to adult learning, is based on learners creating an overarching meaning structure called a *frame of reference* (Mezirow, 2000). Frames of reference are best understood as cultural paradigms, large interconnected beliefs, assumptions, and values that, quite literally, structure how people view and engage with reality. Taylor writes: "Frames of reference are structures of assumptions and expectations that frame an individual's tacit points of view and influence their thinking, beliefs, and

actions" (2008, p. 5.). A frame of reference can be broken down into two components: *habits of mind* and *points of view*. A habit of mind is characterized as the individual assumptions that make up a learner's frame of reference. Types of assumptions associated with Mezirow's iteration of transformative learning theory include socio-linguistic, moral-ethical, epistemic, philosophical, psychological, and aesthetic perspectives (2000). A habit of mind is then experienced in action as a point of view.

Although transformative learning theory is conceived as primarily an adult learning theory that is grounded in the ways adults communicate and interpret meaning (Taylor, 2008), it can also be applied to a larger context of learning. When a frame of reference or perspective is transformed the result is "a more fully developed (more functional) frame of reference ... one that is more (1) inclusive, (2) differentiating, (3) permeable, (4) critically reflective, and (5) integrative of experience" (Mezirow, 1996, p. 163). In other words, the learner has created a deeper-meaning and critically-informed system on which to build their knowledge. This process is often painful and can challenge learners to examine their deepest held beliefs and assumptions (Taylor, 2008).

Habits of Mind

As mentioned above, one component of *frames of reference* are habits of mind. These habits, or assumptions, consist of categories or domains of human knowledge that are framed by philosophical assumptions and justifications or habits of mind (Jackson, 2008). For example, there exist philosophies of science that are guided by particular assumptions made about reality and the world. Also, there are philosophies of education that are often referenced to ground research questions or methodologies (e.g. Dewey, Kolb, Friere). As such, these habits of mind become the foundation for how we frame and understand reality and our world.

Cranton, an influential scholar and author in transformative learning theory, writes in her book *Understanding and Promoting Transformative Learning* (2005) about the interconnection between her own habits of mind, or assumptions, and how they influence her frame of reference:

My way of seeing myself (psychological habit of mind) is influenced by my cultural background (sociolinguistic habit of mind). By growing up in an isolated and poor community that did not value education (sociolinguistic), I ended up with great gaps in my knowledge (epistemic habit of mind). Moral-ethical and aesthetic habits of mind are obviously deeply influenced by sociolinguistic, psychological, and epistemic factors. If, for example, I know little about classical music or art (epistemic perspective), my tastes and standards about beauty (aesthetic perspective) will be very different from those of a person well-informed in the arts. Philosophical habits of mind may provide an umbrella for many other of our perspectives (p. 28, 2005).

However, not all assumptions or habits of mind are viewed as positive, or even neutral, foundations. Bowers, throughout his work on cultural assumptions, argues that uncritically accepted assumptions can be detrimental to the natural world (1988; 2000; 2005). Among the assumptions he identifies as uncritically examined are language as a transmission device, the computer and other technologies are neutral and value-free, individualism is preferable to community, and technology can save mankind from the same problems it helped to create (Bowers, 2000).

Often, educators have found reflective devices useful for questioning and examining assumptions. Stephen Brookfield, an adult educator and professor, has written and researched extensively into the intersection of adult education and critical theory. His work includes a number of texts specifically devoted to assisting adult educators and teacher educators to become more critically reflective within the context of their practice. In his text *Becoming a Critically Reflective Teacher*, Brookfield suggests that there are three types of assumptions that are important to examine in order to be a critically reflective educator:

1. Paradigmatic assumptions: Basic axioms that construct our world, paradigmatic assumptions are the most basic scripts we create from the messages we get from significant figures in our lives.
2. Prescriptive assumptions: Based on and widening paradigmatic assumptions, prescriptive assumptions reflect what we think should happen in a certain situation.
3. Causal assumptions: Based on the other two assumptions, causal assumptions deal with "If... then" issues. Included in what we think should happen in any situation is our knowledge about what will happen if we take one path or another (Brookfield, 1995, p. 2-3).

Beliefs and assumptions that are made about reality are directly informed and created within existing and mostly unexamined worldviews (Jackson, 2008). Worldviews are culturally-situated constructions meant to assist in the social harmony and day-to-day functionality of human life (Jackson, 2008; Mezirow & Taylor, 2009). Unfortunately, the unexamined status of most worldviews results in conceptualizations, beliefs and assumptions that are inherently limiting.

For example, the belief "Educational technologies can support student learning" is informed by multiple assumptions beginning with understanding the meaning of the words educational, technologies, support, and student learning. For instance, technologies may be assumed to represent laptops or it might be assumed to mean cell phones and other mobile devices. Depending on the primary assumption, some teachers may need to revise their agreement or disagreement with the stated belief. Another assumption surrounds the use of the word support as well as student learning. Engaging with these overly vague phrases without context surely results in poor communication.

While these may seem like language games, they are, in fact, very serious issues underlying basic assumptions. We turn to some of the key scholars of the linguistic/social science world:

"… our world – the concrete world in which we live – does not come to us as something independent of language; we do not construct our world independently and then add it on to our experience; our world transpires within language" (Barrett, 1978, p. 76). In fact, some might argue that "Language already hides within itself a developed way of conceiving" (Heidegger, 1962; p. 199).

Clifford Geertz (1973) defines an ideology as a cultural phenomenon that structures and frames human experience. Language, the capacity to communicate with shared meaning and understanding, is a cultural and social phenomenon. As Heidegger notes, language comes predetermined with a way of thinking and being. While there are real processes and substances in the external and internal world, Fairclough (2003) argues that discourse, a subset of language, has the power to create, frame, mediate, and help us imagine possibilities for the future. Searle (2010) notes that it is via language that corporations are made and marriages are pronounced. Surely these are not simple language games.

Contextualizing Technology

If transformative learning theory urges us to critically examine our frames of reference and the assumptions (or habits of mind) that support them, we must begin to distinguish the types of assumptions we have about technology. In this endeavor we draw on the work of Feenberg (1991; 1999; 2003) in the philosophy of technology.

As a field, the philosophical study of technology is devoted to the study of the nature of technology. As a subdomain of philosophy, it is a more recent development (Mitcham, 1994), and has grown into two separate branches: engineering and humanities. Peters (2006) argues that philosophy of technology "was seen as the handmaiden of science, a kind of applied knowledge that put into practice the pure theory of science" (p. 97). For this reason, the field of study known as philosophy of technology emerged later rather than sooner. Emerging from science, critical examinations of technology did not develop until the 20th century (Brooks, 2011).

The engineering approach to philosophy of technology aims to examine human experiences and ways of being via technological terms. The humanities approach, including for example, Heidegger and Ellul, means to situate the study of technology as one of many components of human experience (Brooks, 2011). It is the humanities approach that frames and guides the questioning of assumptions and beliefs regarding technology. Therefore, the humanities trajectory informs our inquiry.

Feenberg classifies four philosophical perspectives pertaining to the study and analysis of technology: determinism, instrumentalism, substantivism, and critical theory (1999). Table 1 summarizes the key elements of each philosophies. In the sections that follow each of the philosophical perspectives will be described and expanded. The summary of the perspective will include authors and scholars associated with that perspective.

Determinism

Technological determinism casts humans in the role of spectator. Technology is an autonomous entity that evolves through progress and is simply a tool that is not influenced by cultural or social factors. Brooks (2011) identifies the two underlying assumptions associated with determinism: "(1) technology develops according to a fixed, direct and inevitable course and (2) society must respond and be organized around technological

Table 1. Feenberg's (1999) original chart with key authors assumptions proposed by Brooks (2011)

Technology is...	Autonomous	Humanly Controlled
Neutral (complete separation of means and ends)	Determinism (traditional Marxism) Authors: Darwin, Marx (1) technology develops according to a fixed, direct and inevitable course (2) society must respond and be organized around technological developments	Instrumentalism (liberal faith in progress) Authors: Papert, Negroponte, Noble (1) technology is non-mediating (2) humans control ends
Value-laden (means forms a way of life that include ends)	Substantivism (means and ends linked in systems) Authors: Weber, Heidegger, Ellul, Habermas (1) technology shapes society more than society shapes it (2) technology holds some inherent values	Critical Theory (choice of alternative means-ends systems) Authors: Feenburg, Marcuse, Foucault (1) values embodied in technology are socially specific and not narrowly limited to efficiency or control technology (2) technologies offer frameworks for ways of life (3) the design and configuration of technology does not only meet our ends; it also organizes society and subordinates members into a technocratic order

Feenburg, 1999, p. 9

developments" (p. 39). Darwin (1958) is often classified as a determinist due to his beliefs in the progressive development of technology via natural laws. Technology also helps us increase our knowledge and understanding of the natural world. Brooks (2011) draws on the work of Winner (1986) to demonstrate an anti-technology determinist perspective: "(T)echnologies are not merely aids to human activity, but also powerful forces acting to reshape that activity and its meaning" (1986, p. 6). Winner also notes that technology often comes with unforeseen consequences that are powerful influences in political life.

Instrumentalism

Feenberg argues that instrumentalism is the "standard modern view" inherited from the 18th Century Enlightenment (1999, p. 6). The instrumental perspective maintains that technology is neutral. People are separate from the tools that they use, and the tools have no influence on human nature or value considerations. Pacey (1983) provides an applied example of the instrumental theory by explaining that for those who have negative implications of a particular technology will be blamed on the social actors (e.g., politicians, businesses) rather than the technology. Chen (2011) summarizes the instrumental perspective: "people subscribing to [this theory] separate themselves from the tools they are using. Technology has no bearing on human nature; it does not have any ethical meaning in itself" (p. 57). Within education, an example of positive instrumentalism is given in the work of Seymour Papert (1980). By using computers and technology, Papert argues, children are able to reach new levels of thinking and understanding that would not have been possible without the computer.

Two assumptions provide the foundation for instrumentalism: "(1) technology is non-mediating and (2) humans control ends" (Brooks, 2011, p. 37). The value-neutral instrumentalist perspective has dominated Western understandings of technology with a liberal faith in progress (Feenberg, 2003). Instrumentalism is also the commonly held perspective of natural scientists and positivist researchers. Within this framework, technology seems to operate by the same principles and virtues as scientific rationality (Feenberg, 2005). Bowers (1988; 2000) problematizes the instrumentalist perspective and argues that its effects on language and technology have disastrous consequences for the natural world. While differing in the question of technology and control, the determinist and instrumentalist philosophies are fairly straightforward. We now turn our attention to substantivism and critical theory, which are significantly more complex.

Substantivism

Substantivism frames technology as value-laden because it redefines culture and society into objects of control. The substantivist argues that "technology and society are dialectically intertwined; technology [is] an environment and a way of life." (Chen, 2011, p. 58). The good and bad qualities of technology are overshadowed by rationality and efficiency. This theoretical perspective is supported by German sociologist and political economist Max Weber (1958), French sociologist Jacques Ellul (1964), and German philosopher Martin Heidegger (1977). Substantivism is grounded in two assumptions: "(1) technology shapes society more than society shapes it and (2) technology holds some inherent values" (Brooks, 2011, p. 46).

Substantivist understandings can be traced from Weber's theory of rationality (1958) through other key scholars including Ellul, Habermas and Heidegger (Brooks, 2011).

Chen (2011) notes that Ellul and Heidegger

Share the notion that human civilization is becoming more and more aligned with a standard of efficiency intrinsic to modernity and, in this regard, becomes alien to the tradition of social humanism. Technology has been transforming our society to a more technically oriented system where values and questions are re-defined and solutions are directed to technical ones (p. 58).

Ellul (1964) describes a technological society by way of *technique*:

The term technique, as I use it, does not mean machines, technology, or this or that procedure for attaining an end. In our technological society, technique is the totality of methods rationally arrived at and having absolute efficiency (for a given stage of development) in every field of human activity (p. xxv).

Ellul continues to explore how this technique exists in all areas of society from politics to education. The substantivist view argues that society is positioned towards efficiency, no matter what the cost. Technique "integrates the machine into society. It constructs the kind of world the machine needs and ...clarifies, arranges, and rationalizes...it is efficient and brings efficiency to everything" (Ellul, 1964, p. 5). Feenburg (2003) notes that Martin Heidegger is considered the most prominent, anti-technology substantivist (Brooks, 2011). According to Heidegger (1977), the modern society encourages humans to view the nature world as raw materials under their command. "Thus, in the technology-saturated society, a fixation on progress and the endless pursuit of efficiency motivates all aspects of human endeavour" (Brooks, 2011, p. 44).

Feenberg continues to suggest that the substantivist view is best considered and approached as a way of life or even a religion due to the technology possessing the value rather than a human agent (2003).

When you choose to use technology you do not simply render your existing way of life more efficient, you choose a different way of life. Technology is thus not simply instrumental to whatever values you hold. It carries with it certain values that have the same exclusive character as religious belief. But technology is even more persuasive than religion since it requires no belief to recognize its existence and to follow its commands. Once a society goes down the path of technological development it will be inexorably transformed into a technological society, a specific type of society dedicated to values such as efficiency and power. Traditional values cannot survive the challenge of technology (Feenberg, 2003).

Critical Theory

Feenberg (1999) introduces the technological perspectives of determinism, instrumentalism, and substantivism prior to situating his own version, a critical philosophy of technology. "Technology is not a thing in the ordinary sense of the term, but an ambivalent process of development suspended between different possibilities" (Feenburg, 1991, p. 14). Feenburg argues that any understanding of technology must begin with the social world. "Technological design has historically proven to be political as design choices often reflect the control of privileged actors and not an essential essence of technology" (Brown, 2011, p. 49). Thus, whereas substantivism frames technology as inevitable, critical theory leaves open the possibility for human agency. Three assumptions underlay Feenburg's critical theory of technology (2003): "(1) Values embodied in technology are socially specific and not narrowly limited to efficiency or control technology, (2) Technologies offer frameworks for ways of life; and (3) The design and configuration of technology does not only meet our ends; it also organizes society and subordinates members into a technocratic order" (Brooks, 2011, p. 50).

A history of the critical theory philosophy of technology begins with Marcuse and Foucault's concern with "emancipation from instrumental rationality as an ideology" and continues to Feenberg's interest in "problems of technoscience not separate from, but as part of social life" (Hickman, 2006, p. 72)". The influence of Foucault (1980) on Feenberg's perspective is evident in Feenberg's analysis of technologies within the realm of power and oppression (e.g. Panopticon prison). Foucault's work uncovers the political nature of technology by showing how the "masters of technical systems, corporate and military leaders, physicians and engineers, have far more control over (the organization of society) than all the electoral institutions of our society put together" (Feenberg, 1999, p. 131).

A critical philosophy of technology, Feenberg argues, is one that supports and encourages democratic discussions and deliberations about technology and its integration into social life. In this way, Feenberg "reflects Habermas' notion of a democratic speech community but includes technological design and development to promote the need for a 'democratic rationality' (Brooks, 2011, p. 48). Feenberg (1999) states that technology is ambivalent as it embraces two differing principles: 1. Conservation of hierarchy: social hierarchy can generally be preserved and reproduced as new technology is introduced. 2. Democratic rationalization: new technology can also be used to undermine the existing social hierarchy or to force it to meet needs it has ignored (p. 76). Brooks (2011) summarizes: "As one of these two principles is enacted, technology frames a way of life or predisposes us to a particular way of being and interacting. Feenberg sees the critical theory of technology as a political project intersecting the functional and the social dimensions of technology" (p. 49).

Where substantivism leaves humans destined to whims of technological development, Feenburg's critical theory asserts that social constructivism gives human agency the final say in the way technologies are adopted and practiced. Technology is not determined to evolve in a particular direction; "the illusion of neutrality and autonomy of the technical professions arises from the way in which they construct their history" (Brooks, 2011, p. 50; Feenberg, 1996). Feenberg's philosophy suggests that as members of a democratic society it is our duty to engage with technological understanding and the social world.

"We need to understand ourselves today in the midst of technology and technical knowledge itself cannot help us. Philosophy of technology belongs to the self-awareness of a society like ours. It teaches us to reflect on what we take for granted, specifically, rational modernity. The importance of this perspective cannot be overestimated" (Feenberg, 2003, para. 4). Technology in education, in this view, needs to be examined not as purely instrumental, neutral or natural but rather as a part of the framework for a way of life in teaching and learning (Brooks, 2011; Feenberg, 2003).

If our understanding of reality and technology is situated within language, then we must examine the assumptions that are transparently structuring what we can see, know, and question regarding the use of technology in education. For example, while examining a technological challenge with a colleague we sense the perspective of a determinist, there may not be much productive dialogue given the assumption that technology will evolve neutrally and is beyond our control. In uncovering and examining the assumptions guiding the way we speak and think about technologies, a space opens up in the conversation that allows us to look at challenges anew and from a differing perspective. The next section presents three key questions that demonstrate some of the assumptions made about technology in an effort to examine how they frame, hide, and showcase certain components of the educational experience.

QUESTIONS

Who Authenticates Ubiquitous Information?

Web 2.0 is known for allowing anyone with the inclination to do so to create and publish materials. In doing so, the power for creating, sharing and discussing information has moved from being institutionalized to being free for all. This freedom, while one of the hallmarks of the web, also brings along a question of motivation. One of the primary assumptions regarding people publishing on the web is that they are truly sharing their information with others motivated by passion, expertise or a desire to educate others. In other words, the motive is to share personal experiences, personal interests and personal passions. We assume benevolent motives. This is especially true with students, who when starting a project turn to the web and, most often, take the first piece of information that is closely related to the task at hand.

In the quest to find the quickest answer possible, students may end up at the ever-popular Wikipedia. Originally conceived as "the free encyclopedia that everyone can edit," Wikipedia works under a set of assumptions that counter a top-down educational approach. In fact, Wikipedia plays with the assumption that knowledge or 'truth' comes from traditional educators to the masses. The overarching power structure has shifted, but the habits of mind for many educators have not changed. The assumption is still that those with degrees are the ones most capable to impart the most truthful information. The question of authenticity becomes, as the site points out, an issue when some abuse that power. As the site warns, "Allowing *anyone to edit* Wikipedia means that it is more easily vandalized or susceptible to unchecked information, which requires removal" (Wikipedia: About). While seasoned web citizens may be aware of this, those new to researching on the web may assume that, just because it is published, the information is accurate and factual. This could speak to the larger issue of a need for greater media literacy in general and, more specifically, digital literacy.

Surprisingly, while educators may take issue with the site passing the power of determining authenticity and accuracy to anyone, a 2005 study found that Wikipedia was nearly as accurate as the encyclopedia Britannica (Terdiman, 2005). In fact, the study found that when comparing articles from both encyclopedias, there were on average "2.92 mistakes per article for Britannica and 3.86 for Wikipedia" (Terdiman, 2005). One of the benefits touted by the site is that errors can be corrected quickly with multiple people being able to view, edit and modify the encyclopedia entries. It could be argued that, this is an improvement over the old-fashioned print version of Britannica. While some of the mistakes in the online site entries may be made out of genuine error, others may be intentional. Those with the power to intentionally enter false or misleading information may be motivated not so much by the notion of sharing personal passions, but stroking the ego of the poster. Their motivations are not for the greater good of society, but for the greater good of themselves. In doing this, these posters are not so much concerned about the content they are sharing online, but about how important they are. The groups, as mentioned here, are just a few examples of possible user motivations. In reality, users are not so easily classified or confined into clearly delineated groupings. As Bosker writes so much of Facebook, Twitter and a variety of other technological platforms do not point towards looking at content, but become a platform for the users to show/say how great they are wrapped up in the shroud of sharing key content (2012). Immediately, from an educator's perspective, the reaction is to 'correct' the mistaken fact, not necessarily the mistaken assumption that students may be operating under. At this point students are told to validate their sources and double-check the 'truth' of the facts found. The concern is understandable. No one checks the authenticity of posts before they go live. The transfer of power appears to be complete.

Yet, would it not be more empowering for the student to teach him/her to investigate the assumption he/she was operating under? One of the tenets of technology in education is that it can provide for "engaging and empowered personalized learning experiences" (Transforming, 2010). The concept of empowering personalized learning experiences may be called into question as we look at motivations for creating online courses or those courses mediated with technology. For some educators, the push to incorporate technology in the classroom is a top-down decision. As universities strive to be the most up-to-date as a means of enticing students to attend, the actual implementation of the technology in the classroom becomes the problem of the educator. With the underlying assumption that technology is good, after all, offering online courses can increase the number of courses offered, help the budget, and allow for students to work asynchronously, schools are pushing for more

offerings. Some K-12 schools are even requiring students to take at least one online course before they graduate (Gabriel, 2011). The argument for this move being that students must develop the skills to exist with technology (Gabriel, 2011).

The questioning of this assumption has already begun. Numerous critics have claimed that the move to online courses is a way to reduce spending and compensate for class sizes (Gabriel, 2011). Cynics even point to the fact that the highest rise in online students comes from those who have failed the courses in a face-to-face setting (Gabriel, 2011). Students are turning to online courses in order to pass and schools might be pushing students toward online learning in order to increase graduation rates. Universities may feel the same pressure to develop online courses to increase enrollment and graduation rates. In order to facilitate online course creation, many higher education institutions offer development grants. While there is a cadre of educators who are excited about the potential that technology brings, these grants may also encourage or facilitate those out to pad their wallets to create new courses. Therefore, the quality of the online courses, which in many cases the university owns the rights to, might be questionable. However, it should be noted that online courses are not the only ones which may suffer from quality issues.

How Do Social Media and Web-Based Technologies Transform Learning?

A 2011 *New York Times* article profiled a student who was unsuccessful in the face-to-face version of the online class the student was taking. As the article described the student's completing his homework, the student was described as pasting the homework question into a Google search, finding the answer on Wikipedia, and "cop[ying] the language, spell-check[ing] it and e-mail[ing] it to his teacher" (Gabriel, 2011). Albeit not the only inquiry, this begs the question: what has the student learned. Do we begin to value knowing how to find information, knowing that Google or its equivalent will always be available, or do we conform to a mode of thought which values rote memorization?

The argument could be made that giving the student the ability to search out information will be more valuable to the student's future than being able to randomly define social Darwinism. However, as with all information available online, how do we, as educators, determine the quality of information found or cited? What about plagiarism? As the New York Times article continued, the student's teacher "had not immediately recognized" the answer was copied and pasted from another source (Gabriel, 2011). This brings in question another assumption regarding technology in the classroom, that students are motivated to do well online because they must pass the course.

Granted, part of the brilliance of incorporating technology is the fact that students can learn at their own pace, with their own style and on their own time. They have the power to develop a rich, personalized learning experience. But, underlying this belief is the notion that students are actually motivated to learn for the sake of learning and self-betterment. Opponents to the move towards technology can point to numerous cases where students have cheated, taken the short route or even removed themselves from participating because of technology. For those students, the power is not in the ability to have personalized learning experiences, but in the freedom to find the quickest way imaginable to get the grade. This focus on the grade, we would argue, is a throwback to traditional learning where the educator has the power to determine if learning has happened. Ultimately, one would have to ask if the fact that the student was able to get the grade he/she wanted pursuing the means above, have they learned? While they may not have learned the intended information, they may have learned something that, perhaps, could be more useful to their personal life experiences.

How Do Social Media and Web-Based Technologies Transform Assessment?

In many ways, the question of assessment becomes the primary focus for students and educators. While students see the question being "what grade am I getting in this class," the question for educators is a bit more complex. At the heart of it, however is the basic concept of how do educators know that students are learning what the educators are wanting them to learn? In other words, how does one verify that learning has taken place and that if learning has taken place, was it the intended learning or something unintended.

Often times, either born out of the need for expediency or an assumption that learning can be reduced to a number or letter, assessment of students is translated into a quantifiable measure such as the score on an objective test. Questioning this basic assumption regarding assessment in the form of grades is not new. In fact, as Kohn (2011) has pointed out, the discussion surrounding grades has been around for decades (see Crooks, 1933; De Zouche, 1945; Kirschenbaum, Simon, & Napier, 1971; Linder, 1940; Marshall, 1968). The traditional method of assessing students happens in two parts: gathering student work and then reporting the results (Kohn, 2011). However, the impact of part of this process, reporting, has been questioned by scholars (Kohn, 2011, 1999a, 1999b, 1999c). These studies, Kohn writes, found that grading student work changes the way students see education. Learning is neither fun nor done for its own sake. Instead, knowing that grades will be the final outcome of student work dilutes student interest, promotes students taking the safe route with assignments and focuses students on the end result, not the process (Kohn, 2011). Basically, faking the fun, and perhaps even thought, out of learning. Instead of being inquisitive about the material, this traditional method of assessment seems to be teaching students how to earn grades, not earn knowledge.

So, if educators approach grading and assessment as ineffective in traditional classrooms, how does technology impact the overall assessment of student learning. When educators discuss assessing students when technology is brought into a learning situation, one of the first issues to confront is authenticity of work. Said another way, educators are concerned about cheating. While educators are not blind to the fact that cheating can occur in a traditional classroom setting, the assumption for many is that it is much easier for students to cheat without an educator present. Perhaps this is true. Definitely the opportunity is there for students to capitalize upon. There is the ease of having someone else taking an exam using the graded student's log-on credentials or having a partner look-up the test answers while taking an exam. In many cases, at this point the educator asks the question, "How do I stop cheating with technology".

Once the question is asked in terms of stopping cheating, the educator tends to use technology as a policing tool as an answer. Time limits are set for tests and/or each individual question. Students are asked to go to a location to take the exam in a room where there is a facilitator. Plagiarism checks are added to drop box submissions to rate the likelihood that the work is not original. Instead of using technology to help transform the learning experience, educators fall back into common assumptions of how their teaching would be in a classroom. In a way, this also creates an adversarial relationship between educator and student. It is a throwback to the traditional power structures found in classrooms where the educator is an all-powerful transmitter of information and the student is the receptacle of knowledge (see for example McCroskey and Richmond, 1983; Richmond and McCroskey, 1984; Teven and Herring, 2005; Teven 2007). Learning has taken place because the educator has said so.

However, what if the wrong question is being asked. What if the question should be "What is a more effective way to assess student learning given that technology is a tool to assist learning."

What if the assumption is not that the student is doing something wrong, but that the traditional methods of assessment cannot be made to conform to what technology offers educators. The United States Department of Education points to this in its recommendation for more embedded assessment when using technology. This could translate into educational games that encourage critical thinking skills with assessment incorporated into the final "score" of the game. Or perhaps this could translate into having students complete a series of tasks in a virtual world that are linked to the assessment and outcome goals for a class. In other words, by asking a different question, educators may transform the way they look at incorporating technology into their teaching.

While the goal of assessment has always been to determine if learning has occurred, determining effective methods of assessment becomes complicated with technology. One can imagine the laughter in a college classroom as the professor tells his/her students that the homework for the week is to play a game or travel to a series of islands in Second life. Yet, at the same time, this statement assumes that fun and laughter should be removed from learning. Perhaps what technology is pushing educators to do is rethink how they evaluate learning. Perhaps using technology is not just showing educators what is not working with the traditional system, but amplifying the problems. Perhaps using technology is pushing educators to think beyond their assumptions regarding assessment.

Does this mean educators need to give up assessment? Definitely not. However, it does mean that educators need to confront their assumptions regarding how students are assessed and what exactly learning, and perhaps, teaching looks like. In confronting these assumptions, it becomes clear that a new and better way of assessing learning with technology is needed. This new method of assessment must focus more on the process of learning than the end result. It must take into account the shift from learning as the transfer of knowledge to the construction of knowledge.

CONCLUSION

It would seem that the U.S. Department of Education's Office of Educational Technology had recognized a shift occurring in education with the release of its plan for "Transforming American Education" using technology (2010). Addressed to the members of Congress, the plan provides a number of goals for using technology to improve education (2010, p. 3). While the sentiment is situated as a call to action, the push to integrate technologies into all areas of teaching and learning is driven by the notion that technology is an integral part of daily life. While it is true that technology is part of daily life, what is questionable is the assumption that technology is a source for good and should be incorporated unwittingly into education. Unfortunately, the calls for greater integration of educational technologies do not address critical assumptions made about the intersection of society and technology. While there are any number of assumptions that are made which support these positive claims, in remaining unquestioned and unexplored, they become troublesome.

To be sure, the process of integrating technologies is complex and requires challenging conversations related to funding and human resources. In the current climate of social media gurus and new media consultants, many claim to possess *the* answers. But do they? These answers are stated in top ten lists and bulleted best practices, reducing the complex and challenging conversation to a series of nugget sized points of practice. PowerPoint presentations, webinars, and conference calls have become the hallmark of online and distance gatherings where eager participants await the simplified answers provided by the presenter. These answers are quickly applied within differing environments without consideration for the deeper questions. Eager to devour the quick fix solution, this approach can hinder knowledge of and pursuit towards long-term solutions

In *The End of Education*, Neil Postman reframes an argument made decades before on the subversive qualities of education. In particular,

he continues the theme from *Technopoly* of addressing our complacency with technological development. Postman notes ten core ideas he thinks should be addressed in teaching about the story of technology:

1. All technological change is a Faustian bargain. For every advantage a new technology offers, there is always a corresponding disadvantage.
2. The advantages and disadvantages of new technologies are never distributed evenly among the population. This means that every new technology benefits some and harms others.
3. Embedded in every technology there is a powerful idea, sometimes two or three powerful ideas. Like language itself, a technology predisposes use to favor and value certain perspective and accomplishments and to subordinate others. Every technology has a philosophy, which is given expression in how the technology makes people use their minds, in what it makes us do with our bodies, in how it codifies the world, in which of our senses it amplifies, in which of our emotional and intellectual tendencies it disregards.
4. A new technology usually makes war against an old technology. It competes with it for time, attention, money, prestige, and a "worldview".
5. Technological change is not additive; it is ecological. A new technology does not merely add something; it changes everything.
6. Because of the symbolic forms in which information is encoded, different technologies have different intellectual and emotion biases.
7. Because of the accessibility and speed of their information, different technologies have different political biases.
8. Because of their physical form, different technologies have different sensory biases.

9. Because of the conditions in which we attend to them, different technologies have different social biases.
10. Because of their technical and economic structure, different technologies have different content biases (pp. 192-193).

It is crucial that we address Postman's suggestions in mind as we look to the future of incorporating technology into educational experiences. Just because we *can* embrace technology, does not mean we should... at least not without being aware of the assumptions that we bring along with us.

NOTE

Portions of this chapter were drawn from research reported in Kruger-Ross, M. J. (2012). *Toward a preliminary understanding of educators' assumptions about technology: A case study* (Unpublished Master's thesis). North Carolina State University, Raleigh, North Carolina. Available at http://www2.lib.ncsu.edu/catalog/record/NCSU2671285.

REFERENCES

Barrett, W. (1978). *The illusion of technique: A search for meaning in a technological civilization*. New York, NY: Anchor Books.

Bosker, B. (14 February 2012). The secret to Pinterest's success: We're sick of each other. *The Huffington Post*. http://www.huffingtonpost.com/2012/02/14/pinterest-success_n_1274797.html

Bowers, C. A. (1988). *The cultural dimensions of educational computing: Understanding the non-neutrality of technology*. New York, NY: Teachers College Press.

Bowers, C. A. (2000). *Let them eat data: How computers affect education, cultural diversity, and the prospects of ecological sustainability*. Athens, GA: University of Georgia Press.

Bowers, C. A. (2005). Is transformative learning the Trojan Horse of western globalization? *Journal of Transformative Education, 3*(2), 116–125. doi:10.1177/1541344604273622

Brookfield, S. (1995). *Becoming a critically reflective teacher*. San Francisco, CA: Jossey-Bass.

Brooks, C. D. (2011). *Education and technology policy discourse in Alberta: A critical analysis*. Unpublished doctoral dissertation, University of Alberta, Alberta, Canada.

Chen, R.-J. (2011). Preservice mathematics teachers' ambiguous views of technology. *School Science and Mathematics, 111*(2), 56–67. doi:10.1111/j.1949-8594.2010.00061.x

Cranton, P. (2005). *Understanding and promoting transformative learning*. San Francisco, CA: Jossey-Bass.

Crooks, A. D. (1933). Marks and marking systems: A digest. *The Journal of Educational Research, 27*(4), 259–272.

Darwin, C. (1958). *The origin of species*. New York, NY: Penguin.

De Zouche, D. (1945). "The wound *is* mortal": Marks, honors, unsound activities. *Clearing House (Menasha, Wis.), 19*(6), 339–344.

Ellul, J. (1964). *The technological society*. New York, NY: Alfred A. Knopf.

Fairclough, N. (2003). *Analysing discourse: Textual analysis for social research*. London, UK: Routledge.

Feenberg, A. (1991). *Critical theory of technology*. New York, NY: Oxford University Press.

Feenberg, A. (1999). *Questioning technology.* London, UK: Routledge.

Feenberg, A. (2003). *What is the philosophy of technology?* Retrieved from www.sfu.ca/~andrewf/komaba.htm

Feenberg, A. (2005). Critical theory of technology: An overview. *Journal of Tailoring Biotechnologies, 1*(1), 47–64.

Foucault, M., & Gordon, C. (1980). *Power/knowledge: Selected interviews and other writings, 1972-1977.* New York, NY: Pantheon.

Gabriel, T. (5 April, 2011). More Pupils are learning online, fueling debate on quality. *New York Times.* http://www.nytimes.com/2011/04/06/education/06online.html?pagewanted=all

Geertz, C. (1973). *The interpretation of cultures.* New York, NY: Basic Books.

Heidegger, M. (1962). *Being and time.* London, UK: SCM Press.

Heidegger, M. (1977). *The question concerning technology, and other essays.* New York, NY: Harper & Row.

Hickman, L. A. (2006). Theoretical assumptions of the critical theory of technology. In Veak, T. J. (Ed.), *Democratizing technology: Andrew Feenberg's critical theory of technology* (pp. 71–81). New York, NY: State University of New York Press.

Jackson, M. G. (2008). *Transformative learning for a new worldview: Learning to think differently.* New York, NY: Palgrave Macmillan. doi:10.1057/9780230589940

Kirschenbaum, H., Simon, S. B., & Napier, R. W. (1971). *Wad-ja-get?: The grading game in American education.* New York, NY: Hart.

Kohn, A. (1999a). *Punished by rewards: The trouble with gold stars, incentive plans, A's, praise, and other bribes* (rev. ed.). Boston, MA: Houghton Mifflin.

Kohn, A. (1999b). *The schools our children deserve: Moving beyond traditional classrooms and "tougher standards.".* Boston, MA: Houghton Mifflin.

Kohn, A. (1999c, March). From degrading to de-grading. *High School Magazine,* pp. 38-43. Retrieved on February 27, 2012, from http://www.alfiekohn.org/teaching/fdtd-g.htm

Kohn, A. (2011). The case against grades. *Educational Leadership.* Retrieved on February 27, 2012, from http://www.alfiekohn.org/teaching/tcag.htm

Linder, I. H. (1940, July). Is there a substitute for teachers' grades? *School Board Journal, 25, 26, 79.*

Marshall, M. S. (1968). *Teaching without grades.* Corvallis, OR: Oregon State University Press.

McCroskey, J. C., & Richmond, V. P. (1983). Power in the classroom I: Instructor and student perceptions. *Communication Education, 32,* 175–184. doi:10.1080/03634528309378527

Mezirow, J. (1996). Contemporary paradigms of learning. *Adult Education Quarterly, 46,* 158–172. doi:10.1177/074171369604600303

Mezirow, J. (2000). *Learning as transformation: Critical perspectives on a theory in progress.* San Francisco, CA: Jossey-Bass.

Mezirow, J., & Taylor, E. W. (2009). *Transformative learning in practice: Insights from community, workplace, and higher education.* San Francisco, CA: Jossey-Bass.

Mitcham, C. (1994). *Thinking through technology: The path between engineering and philosophy.* Chicago, IL: University of Chicago Press.

Pacey, A. (1983). *The culture of technology.* Cambridge, MA: MIT Press.

Papert, S. (1980). *Mindstorms: Children, computers, and powerful ideas.* New York, NY: Basic Books.

Peters, M. A. (2006). Towards philosophy of technology in education: Mapping the field. In Weiss, J., Nolan, J., & Hunsinger, J. (Eds.), *The international handbook of virtual learning environments* (pp. 95–116). Springer. doi:10.1007/978-1-4020-3803-7_3

Postman, N. (1993). *Technopoly: The surrender of culture to technology*. New York, NY: Vintage Books.

Postman, N., & Weingartner, C. (1969). *Teaching as a subversive activity*. New York, NY: Dell.

Richmond, V. P., & McCroskey, J. C. (1984). Power in the classroom II: Power and learning. *Communication Education, 33*, 125–136. doi:10.1080/03634528409384729

Searle, J. (2010). *Making the social world: The structure of human civilization*. New York, NY: Oxford University Press.

Taylor, E. W. (2008). Transformative learning theory. *New Directions for Adult and Continuing Education, 119*, 5–15. doi:10.1002/ace.301

Terdiman, D. (2005, December 15). *Study: Wikipedia as accurate as Britannica*. Retrieved on February 27, 2012, from http://news.cnet.com/2100-1038_3-5997332.html

Teven, J. J. (2007). Teacher Machiavellianism and social influence in the college classroom: Implications for measurement. *Communication Research Reports, 24*, 341–352. doi:10.1080/08824090701624247

Teven, J. J., & Herring, J. (2005). Instructor influence in the classroom: A preliminary investigation of perceived instructor power, credibility, and student satisfaction. *Communication Research Reports, 22*, 235–246. doi:10.1080/00036810500230685

Transforming American Education: Learning Powered by Technology. (5 March 2010). Office of Educational Technology, U. S. Department of Education. Retrieved from http://www2.ed.gov/about/offices/list/os/technology/netp.pdf

Weber, M. (1958). *The protestant ethic and the spirit of capitalism* (Parsons, T., Trans.). New York, NY: Scribners.

Wikipedia: About. (12 Feb 2012). Retrieved on February 27, 2012 from http://en.wikipedia.org/wiki/Wikipedia:About

Winner, L. (1986). *The whale and the reactor: A search for limits in an age of high technology*. Chicago, IL: University of Chicago Press.

ADDITIONAL READING

Baumgartner, L. M. (2001). An update on transformational learning. *New Directions for Adult and Continuing Education, 89*, 15–24. doi:10.1002/ace.4

Bitter, G., & Legacy, J. (2007). *Using technology in the classroom*. Boston, MA: Allyn & Bacon.

Bloom, K., & Johnston, K. M. (2010). Digging into YouTube videos: Using media literacy to promote cross-cultural understanding. *Journal of Media Literacy Education, 2*(2), 113–123.

Bowers, C. A. (2007). The Janus machine: Computers, language, and the enclosure of the cultural commons. *Language & Ecology*, 1-17.

Bowers, C. A. (2009). The language of ecological intelligence. *Language & Ecology, 3*(1), 1–24.

Bowers, C. A. (2010). The insights of Gregory Bateson on the connections between language and the ecological crisis. *Language & Ecology, 3*(2).

Brookfield, S. (2003). The praxis of transformative education: African American feminist conceptualizations. *Journal of Transformative Education, 1*(3), 212–226. doi:10.1177/1541344603001003003

Brookfield, S. (2005). *The power of critical theory: Liberating adult learning and teaching*. San Francisco, CA: Jossey-Bass.

Bryson, M., & Castell, S. D. (1998). New technologies and the cultural ecology of primary schooling: Imagining teachers as luddites in/deed. *Educational Policy*, *12*(5), 542–567. doi:10.1177/0895904898012005005

Closs, L., & Antonello, C. S. (2011). Transformative learning: Integrating critical reflection into management education. *Journal of Transformative Education*, *9*(2), 63–88. doi:10.1177/1541344611429129

Cranton, P. (2002). Teaching for transformation. *New Directions for Adult and Continuing Education*, *93*, 63–72. doi:10.1002/ace.50

Cranton, P. (2010). A transformative perspective on the Scholarship of Teaching and Learning. *Higher Education Research & Development*, *30*(1), 75–86. doi:10.1080/07294360.2011.536974

Dirkx, J. M., Mezirow, J., & Cranton, P. (2006). Musings and reflections on the meaning, context, and process of transformative learning: A dialogue between John M. Dirkx and Jack Mezirow. *Journal of Transformative Education*, *4*(2), 123–139. doi:10.1177/1541344606287503

Dyson, M. (2011). What might a person-centred model of teacher education look like in the 21st century? The transformism model of teacher education. *Journal of Transformative Education*, *8*(1), 3–21. doi:10.1177/1541344611406949

Earl, L. M. (2003). *Assessment as learning: Using classroom assessment to maximize student learning*. Thousand Oaks, CA: Corwin.

Elshof, L. (2008). Toward sustainable practices in technology education. *International Journal of Technology and Design Education*, *19*(2), 133–147. doi:10.1007/s10798-008-9074-4

Erichsen, E. A. (2011). Learning for change: Transforming international experience as identity work. *Journal of Transformative Education*, *9*(2), 109–133. doi:10.1177/1541344611428227

Giroux, H. A. (2001). *Theory and resistance in education*. Westport, CT: Praeger.

Herbers, M. S., Antelo, A., Ettling, D., & Buck, M. A. (2011). Improving teaching through a community of practice. *Journal of Transformative Education*, *9*(2), 89–108. doi:10.1177/1541344611430688

Kahn, R., & Kellner, D. (2007). Paulo Freire and Ivan Illich: Technology, politics and the reconstruction of education. *Policy Futures in Education*, *5*(4), 431–448. doi:10.2304/pfie.2007.5.4.431

Kilbourn, B., & Alvarez, I. (2008). Root-metaphors for understanding: A framework for teachers and teacher educators of information and communication technologies. *Computers & Education*, *50*(4), 1354–1369. doi:10.1016/j.compedu.2006.12.004

Kincheloe, J. L. (2003). Critical ontology: Visions of selfhood and curriculum. *Journal of Curriculum Theorizing*, *19*(1), 47–64.

Kincheloe, J. L. (2005). On to the next level: Continuing the conceptualization of the bricolage. *Qualitative Inquiry*, *11*(3), 323–350. doi:10.1177/1077800405275056

Kincheloe, J. L. (2008). Critical pedagogy and the knowledge wars of the twenty-first century. *International Journal of Critical Pedagogy*, *1*(1), 1–22.

Kincheloe, J. L. (2008). Introduction: What we call knowledge is complicated and harbors profound consequences. *Knowledge and critical pedagogy: An introduction* (pp. 3-25).

King, K. P. (2002). Educational technology professional development as transformative learning pportunities. *Computers & Education*, *39*(3), 283–297. doi:10.1016/S0360-1315(02)00073-8

Lange, P. G. (2007). *Commenting on comments: Investigating responses to antagonism on YouTube*. Society for Applied Anthropology Conference.

Lange, P. G. (2008). Publicly private and privately public: Social networking on YouTube. *Journal of Computer-Mediated Communication, 13*(1), 361–380. doi:10.1111/j.1083-6101.2007.00400.x

Lawrence, R. L., & Dirkx, J. M. (2010). Teaching with soul: Toward a spiritually responsive transformative pedagogy. *Conference Proceedings of the 29th Annual Midwest Research-to-Practice Conference in Adult, Continuing, Community and Extension Education,* (pp. 141-146).

Mamgain, V. (2011). Ethical consciousness in the classroom: How Buddhist practices can help develop empathy and compassion. *Journal of Transformative Education, 8*(1), 22–41. doi:10.1177/1541344611403004

Marglin, S. (2010). *The dismal science: How thinking like an economist undermines community.* Cambridge, MA: Harvard University Press.

Mayer, R. E. (2009). *Multimedia learning* (2nd ed.). New York, NY: Cambridge University Press. doi:10.1017/CBO9780511811678

Merriam, S. B. (2007). *Non-western perspectives on learning and knowing: Perspectives from around the world.* Malabar, FL: Krieger Publishing Company.

Mezirow, J. (2003). Transformative learning as discourse. *Journal of Transformative Education, 1*(1), 58–63. doi:10.1177/1541344603252172

Palmer, P. J., Zajonc, A., & Scribner, M. (2010). *The heart of higher education: A call to renewal.* San Francisco, CA: Jossey-Bass.

Petrina, S. (2000). The political ecology of design and technology education: An inquiry into methods. *International Journal of Technology and Design Education, 10*(3), 207–237. doi:10.1023/A:1008955016067

Petrina, S. (2002). Getting a purchase on "The School of Tomorrow" and its constituent commodities: Histories and historiographies of technologies. *History of Education Quarterly, 42*(1), 75–111. doi:10.1111/j.1748-5959.2002.tb00101.x

Petrina, S., Feng, F., & Kim, J. (2008). Researching cognition and technology: How we learn across the lifespan. *International Journal of Technology and Design Education, 18*(4), 375–396. doi:10.1007/s10798-007-9033-5

Pitler, H., Hubbel, E. R., & Kuhn, M. (2007). *Using technology with classroom instruction that works.* Alexandria, VA: Association for Supervision and Curriculum Development.

Solomon, D. L. (2001). *Toward a philosophy of instructional technology: An exploration of perspectives, foundations and elements of postmodernism in theory and practice.* Unpublished doctoral dissertation, Wayne State University, Detroit, Michigan.

Taylor, E. W. (2007). An update of transformative learning theory: A critical review of the empirical research (1999–2005). *International Journal of Lifelong Education, 26*(2), 173–191. doi:10.1080/02601370701219475

Valtonen, T., Dillon, P., Hacklin, S., & Väisänen, P. (2010). Net generation at social software: Challenging assumptions, clarifying relationships and raising implications for learning. *International Journal of Educational Research, 49*(6), 210–219. doi:10.1016/j.ijer.2011.03.001

Voithofer, R. (2007). Web 2.0: What is it and how can it apply to teaching and teacher preparation? *American Educational Research Association Conference* (pp. 1-21).

Wallace, B. A. (2004). *The taboo of subjectivity: Toward a new science of consciousness.* New York, NY: Oxford University Press.

Yang, S.-H. (2009). Using blogs to enhance critical reflection and community of practice. *Journal of Educational Technology & Society, 12*(2), 11–21.

Zajonc, A. (Ed.). (2004). *The new physics and cosmology dialogues with the Dalai Lama.* New York, NY: Oxford University Press.

KEY TERMS AND DEFINITIONS

Critical Theory: A philosophical point of view allowing for the examination and critiques of topics with particular attention paid to power relations.

Determinism: Passive acceptance of the fact that technological change is bound to happen and there is nothing to be done to stop it.

Habits of Mind/Assumptions: A way of thinking, based on experience, ideas, or beliefs that are followed unquestioningly.

Instrumentalism: A way of looking at technology as a neutral tool, the predominant view of Western society.

Philosophy of Technology: A way of thinking about or categorizing the impact of technology on people's lives.

Social Media: Tools such as Facebook and Twitter that capitalize on web-based technologies to foster discussion and interaction.

Substantivism: A way of looking at technology as having good and bad elements, but intertwined and interconnected with life.

Transformative Learning Theory: A theory of learning, often used in reference to adult education, where students are asked to identify limiting assumptions that can be transformed for greater empowerment and choice.

Web 2.0/Web-Based Technologies: Rather than representing an entirely new type of technology, Web 2.0 is used to describe a way of interacting with the Internet and web-based technologies that reposition and challenge the traditional roles of "content producer" and "recipient".

Chapter 15
Online Anxiety:
Implications for Educational Design in a Web 2.0 World

David Mathew
Centre for Learning Excellence, University of Bedfordshire, UK

ABSTRACT

This chapter argues that as educators moving into a Web 2.0 world, we are likely to experience anxiety, which is an important part of the educational process (as it is for our learners). It is also a response to a perception of an older and worn out version of the internet. Anxiety has implications for the design of Web 2.0 educational materials. Web 2.0 is more than a tool for the beginnings of the future of education: it is also, in and of itself, the beginnings of the future of education. Web 2.0 is about learning from the learner, and this chapter asks: What role does the educator play in his/her own developmental learning of the tools of the trade? How does this inform his/her preparations for the learners' experiences? The chapter also argues that in addition to online educational environments owning their own systems of localized logic and systems of internal rules, they are also sentient systems.

INTRODUCTION

In 'Task and Sentient Systems and Their Boundary Controls' (Trist and Murray 1990), Eric J. Miller and A.K. Rice define a *sentient system* or group as "one that demands and receives loyalty from its members." Not only does the environment provide a milieu that is safe for learners who would ordinarily struggle with more orthodox academic vehicles, it might also be instrumental in the building of confidence and the honing of social abilities. These play important roles in the fashioning of personal identities and the shaping of social mores. The chapter also argues that or every learner who becomes enabled and empowered by a contiguous existence in an online milieu,

DOI: 10.4018/978-1-4666-2970-7.ch015

there might evolve a learner who develops anti-social tendencies in the very same environment; furthermore, I propose that these ontological dichotomies are essential (if unpleasant to some), even if they involve bullying and learner anxiety. Brief examples of learners on an online learning programme at Master's degree level are presented. Certain learners who came from geographical areas in the world in which values of prudence and propriety are *traditionally* present, became influenced by the pushing of boundaries while online. The proposition is that some learners use the online environment as a kind of psychic retreat (Steiner 1993) and regard it as the only non-threatening place available.

What are the implications for educators in a Web 2.0 existence? Unless we tack on a caveat that says something like '...in twenty years time', a prediction of the future of online learning is likely to be weighted in a conservative, staid manner. We are realists. Despite the fact that our burgeoning field is more fruitful than ever; despite the fact that many of our occupations did not exist two decades ago – or even one decade ago – and despite the fact that occupations have been made redundant to create our posts, when contemplating the future of online learning we are apt to keep our feet on the ground. We do not lose our heads, with ambition being one thing, dreamy optimism quite another. But when we reflect on the achievements to date, if we have pause for thought, why do we not Think Big or Bigger? Quite possibly any sense of self-restraint (posing as pragmatism) is a conscious or unconscious acknowledgement of our current restrictions. For example, as yet we do not have infinite bandwidth; we do not have instantaneous synchronous facilities for groupwork for learners in every time zone; we do not have cranial receptor accessories; so we tend to predict based on a Web 1 mentality, and err somewhat on the side of caution – for fear of appearing foolish or naive. Furthermore, the unknown can seem scary; but what exactly is there to be scared of? And is anxiety the same as fear anyway?

What is Anxiety?

Anxiety is a condition experienced, to one extent or another, by every man, woman and child, and arguably even by some animals (separation anxiety in pet dogs and horses, for example); it is therefore of little surprise that a considerable amount of literature has formed around the subject. But what is it? For the purposes of this essay we will be clear to distinguish anxiety from stress: they are not the same. Nor is anxiety a synonym for fear, although the terms are often used interchangeably. FreeDictionary (2012) puts it thus: "Fear is a direct, focused response to a specific event or object, and the person is consciously aware of it. Most people will feel fear if someone points a loaded gun at them or if they see a tornado forming on the horizon. They also will recognize that they are afraid. Anxiety, on the other hand, is often unfocused, vague, and hard to pin down to a specific cause."

In short, anxiety is a sensation of unease that is caused by a prediction (often made on an unconscious level) of something bad that is about to happen; and it is plain to see why it has been a subject much covered in the fields of psychology and psychoanalysis. Freud (1926) gave us an early full-length explication of anxiety, which is often cited even to this day. "If a mother is absent or has withdrawn her love from her child," he writes (1926: 87), "it is no longer sure of the satisfaction of its needs and is perhaps exposed to the most distressing feelings of tension." His theory of anxiety having a root in childhood experience has been influential. Klein (1948: 25) writes: "Freud put forward to begin with the hypothesis that anxiety arises out of a direct manifestation of libido"; and expands this opinion by stating that "in young children it is unsatisfied libidinal excitation which turns into anxiety" and that "the earliest content of anxiety is the infant's feeling of danger lest his need should not be satisfied because the mother is 'absent'" *(ibid*: 26). Klein (1946:1) had previously written: "In early infancy anxieties characteristic of psychosis arise which drive the ego to develop specific defence-mechanisms" – which made a link between anxiety and the systems of defence that we use in troublesome situations, or in the predictions of troublesome situations. She makes it clear in the later of these two papers that her belief is that "anxiety is aroused by the danger which threatens the organism from the death instinct" and "anxiety has its origin in the fear of death" (Klein 1948: 28). She adds: "if we assume the existence of a death instinct, we must also assume that in the deepest layers of the mind there is a response to this instinct in the form of fear of annihilation of life… the danger arising from the inner working of the death instinct is the first cause of anxiety" (*ibid*: 29).

Childhood is, of course, the time when we learn many of the lessons that we take with us throughout our lives. Meltzer (1955: 11) informs us that " the anxiety apparatus is a vital tool in the hands of the ego for the achievement of learning and the accomplishment of maturation" and that 6 "the capacity of anxiety is innate in the mental apparatus" (*ibid*: 6). In the child's very early years, when he is unable "to distinguish body from external object, the infant cannot… experience yearning-towards or frustration-by, but only distress" (*ibid*: 6). This distress is closely linked to "two forms of anxiety, persecutory and depressive, [which] are the primitive forms and the prototypes for later objective and instinctual anxieties. The distinction between the primitive and mature forms is founded on the degree of reality underlying them" (*ibid*: 9).

Furthermore, Meltzer tells us that our acquired anxieties are indeed based on expectations and predictions. "When the objects are not performing in the expected way – that is, when they have become bad and persecuting – the infant is unable to form a prospective phantasy of relief" (*ibid:* 7); and "when a prediction that is of importance with regard to plans for relief of tension fails, the phantasy that results is of the current tension extended in time. The content of this phantasy will extend to eternity until a new prediction is formulated"

(*ibid*: 9). Meltzer also points to the link between anxiety as a condition and the illness that it might precede. "But the warding off of anxiety is quite another matter," he writes. "Here the ego… adopts a policy never again to experience some specific anxiety phantasy and its affect. This is quite a serious determination, for such a policy implies the abandonment of maturation within the life-space compartment involved. The result is a functional disease" (*ibid*: 11). Here, "affect" might be defined as an emotional response or expression.

However, anxiety is a useful emotional commodity: it is more than the inappropriate switching on of "flight or fight" response to deal with a threat to one's survival – a threat that might not even exist. In common with the brains of our primitive forefathers, the brain scans one's environment for threats but it cannot always tell the difference between a real threat and a perceived threat, and so both possibilities are treated in the same manner. A region in the brain called the amygdala "connects" the two situations and forms an unconscious memory of the association. When a stimulus occurs later, the amygdala is activated in the same way that it was in the presence of the original threat. Similarly, when one is in a situation somewhat like a situation of threat from the past, the brain notes the similarities and triggers the flight or fight response again, even if such a response is not called for. Anxiety might manifest itself as a sense of mounting physiological arousal, or as bodily and thinking symptoms – a headache, a stomach ache, the inability to recall something that is seemingly important. How, then, can anxiety be considered important in an educational milieu?

Building a relationship between motivation and anxiety, Hebb (1955) opines that one needs an optimal quantity of pressure under which to work and learn. One's performance (linked to one's sense of personal well-being) is achieved at a moderate level of emotional arousal: if the arousal is too little, the result is boredom, and if the arousal is too much, the result is anxiety. Both of these conditions will inhibit effective efficiency. But should this mean that no anxiety is the gold standard? Apter (1989) sets out two modes of experience: one of these describes the polar opposites of excitement and boredom; the other describes the polar opposites of relaxation and anxiety. It would seem unlikely for one to enjoy a fruitful learning experience without the presence of anxiety. In the words of Atherton (2011: n.p.): "learning is best achieved in a state of minimal anxiety and relaxation" – and yet we know that minimal does not mean *none*.

ANXIETY ABOUT GROWTH

Despite the sense of anxiety that might be instigated – 'fear with a definable content', in the words of Juutinen and Saariluoma (2010) – we should probably regard the near future and its implications for educational design in a web 2.0 world. Within the online learning industry, very few practitioners would argue with the consensus view that growth is one of its few certainties. How we understand the concept of growth, on the other hand, is open to any number of interpretations; and when contemplating the likely characteristics of the future of online learning, commentators are likely to fall into one of several camps. Commentators such as Nagel (2010) might emphasise the fiscal and financial spurts that the industry is likely to experience; whereas Bates (2011) is keen to promote the idea that online learning will replace more traditional modes of delivery, irrespective of concerns that technology is often not employed to a high standard. Chiming nicely with Bates's views, Downes (2008) writes: "While technology changes rapidly, people do not. People want to use tools that look and feel like tools they've always used, and will tend to adopt tools only if they see a clear benefit either in productivity or in savings."

Although Milligan (2006) was perhaps slightly ahead of his time with the notion of the PLE – the Personalised Learning Environment – the prescience of his conclusions is obviously bearing fruit as our industry develops and as more emphasis is placed on the learner's ways of communicating

and creating. But if we ask what might facilitate the emergence of Milligan's vision, one simple answer would be: growth. Of course, growth is only as successful as the time and money that are planted as seeds at the beginning of any project. Armstrong and Franklin (2008) write that in organisations and institutions where life-long and distance learning contexts are already prominent, there are more positive institutional drivers extant; they also note that pedagogic and marketing strategies can align neatly with a learner's opportunities for communication and collaboration.

Perhaps the anxiety about growth in a Web 2.0 environment is really an anxiety about quality. A question posed might be: Are the learners really getting more for their time, their money and for their efforts? Are they even getting as much as they got before the Web 2.0 world? Certainly, on an anecdotal level, we might hear quibbles from our colleagues about the efficiency of contemporary and future pedagogy, and more formally than this, there are issues surrounding the perceived quality and efficacy of education based wholly on the Web. Zhang (2009), for example, is positive about the possibilities inherent in online social interactions, sharing and interactivity, but is realistic about the difficulties faced when it comes to transferring the qualities of Web 2.0 into an educational space. As long ago as 2004, Surowiecki argued that an accumulation of information would lead to a better decision than one made by any single person; but Keen (2007) warns that Web 2.0, and the expansion of information that it contains, creates a levelling of knowledge, a milieu in which there is no 'expert', only those who share in a comradely manner. Keen refers to this phenomenon as the 'cult of the amateur' (Keen 2007: 17); and in this vision, it is reasonable enough to ask how we might continue to ensure quality, not only of the material itself, but of the learner's journey and experience.

Or perhaps the anxiety about growth is more connected to the new technology that educators will be obliged (or have already been obliged) to embrace. Among the many hundreds of possibilities, let us list a few of the new ideas. We have digital repositories for content (YouTube, SlideShare, for example) where we used to have libraries, with the danger being that we did not usually deposit our own work in a physical library; we social bookmarking sites (such as Delicious); we have virtual communities (Facebook is probably the most famous example), folksonomies and Open Education Resources. We have tools that encourage peer reflection and communal online growth, such as blogs and e-portfolios. As educators, we are prompted to participate in distributed networks; to write blogs; to co-create knowledge; to critique and share examples of professional practice. For many of our learners, this is the air that they breathe; this is all that they have ever known. The same cannot be said for most educators; and the new (as we have said) can be daunting. It can remind us of experiences of when we tried to learn something in the past, and where we experienced difficulty and trauma. Anxiety is a perfectly ordinary reaction to an acceptance of a working environment changing swiftly.

The fact that we are transitioning from what will be seen as the 'early days' of online learning (and have yet to get it quite right), to a more 'confident' stance as we gaze into the future, is sure to instigate anxieties for both educators and learners. Arguably, we are moving away from a somewhat worn-out opening foray into online learning – along with its implications of internet fatigue (Horrigan 2009) – to a future that seems bright with pedagogic possibilities, so bright that it makes us somewhat uneasy not to be able to see clearly in the dazzle. In other words, we might argue that the movement is from a sense of (comfortable) fatigue with the current tools of our trade, to a desire that is divided in two: a desire to view the future of online learning as being reliant on the next tool (which will resemble the existing tool); and a desire to peek into a future that is only embryonic.

ANXIETY ABOUT THE ONLINE ENVIRONMENT

The online environment is a paradoxical place. Either as an educator or as a learner, we work alone at a computer interface of some description (in an office, on a bus; surely it won't be much longer before we have the development of the 100% waterproof device, so that we can catch up on those emails while taking a shower!). We usually work alone… yet we are connected to a network that is several billion people strong: as of the end of 2011, the world's population was 6,930,055,154 and the number of people who used the internet was 2,267,233,742 (Internet World Stats 2012). We want to feel important in our solitude, and yet at root we are social animals: by entering the online learning environment we are aware of our tiny drop of water in the vastest of oceans. Furthermore, while Second Life (for example) lends itself to constructivist pedagogies, there is also a possibility that the fluidity and complexity of new online spaces is slowly eroding the distinctions between pedagogical approaches (such as behavioural, cognitive, developmental and critical pedagogy).

But for now let us look at the anxiety that is engendered by the dichotomy between isolation and groups. Returning to the grandfather of all anxieties, Freud, De Board (1978: 16) writes: "The basic question which Freud attempted to answer concerns the nature of the social instinct in man. Do human beings form groups and behave in a social manner because of a basic instinct that is 'given' by man's very nature and that is, therefore, not capable of further dissection? Or is the social instinct and group behaviour an expression of other, more primary, instincts?" It is also important to include Freud's *Civilization and its Discontents* (Strachey 2001: 108) in this context. Freud pondered on whether or not it was too simplistic to envisage "a cultural community consisting of double individuals like this, who, libidinally satisfied in themselves, are connected with one another through the bonds of common work and common interests".

We should also acknowledge once more that Web 2.0 pedagogies are an example of organizational change. Hoyle writes (Huffington *et al* 2004): "During any period of organizational change, there is the potential for heightened creativity... The anxiety evoked by the process of change can be a major barrier to implementing successful change and it is, indeed, the central tenet of the psychoanalytic theory of the sources of resistance to change." Ironically, perhaps, educators become part of an organization which attempts to eliminate learner anxiety by embracing online anxiety themselves; an organization in which the educators act as both participants and as caregivers; an organization that might even exhibit the feel of a commune. Much work occurs in silence; if either the educator or the learner has not taken on the full responsibilities of their given role, thoughts may remain unvocalized – or are assumed (often incorrectly) to have been shared telepathically. It is up to both parties in the learning transaction to engage and to participate: without this commitment, a daily repetition of pedagogic chores is the means by which we might endeavour measure educational progress; and the same goes for the collective store of excitation in the group. It will not be long, given these conditions, before the learner leaves the course.

No one is suggesting that the online educational experience is strictly akin to a group therapy situation, but certain factors do overlap, we might say. As Rickman (2003: 133) puts it: "psycho-therapists are not the only people with a professional interest in the relief of mental pain..." He might well be referring to the role of the educator., & doesn't Rickman's definition of group therapy actually ring true of life experienced in a successful educational dynamic: "a number of people are assembled together for purposes of explanation of their condition or for exhortation, or for that 'companionate therapy' which comes when groups are formed mainly for the purpose of

social amenity" (*ibid*: 134). Or most analogously of all, perhaps: "the patient feels that the dignity of his personality and individuality is being respected" (*ibid*: 140). Replace the word *patient* with *learner* and it should be clear that the two worlds are not so very far apart. It is also easy to opine that as a result of computer work making long-distance transactions and interactions easy, effective face-to-face communication has been lost; and this situation is also a cause of anxiety.

Miller and Rice (Trist and Murray 1990) define a "sentient system or group [as] one that demands and receives loyalty from its members". By this definition alone, we might argue that the online education situation is a sentient group – or it can be – but the word *loyalty* is absolutely key., & participants (whether educators or learners) will only be loyal if there is a reciprocal arrangement; if they believe they are getting valuable out of the system into which they are pouring their time, their energy and their money. "An effective sentient system relates members of an enterprise to each other and to the enterprise in ways that are relevant to the skills and experience required for task performance," the authors continue (*ibid.*); before concluding the paragraph with the key clause: "it also provides its members with some defense against anxiety".

ANXIETY ABOUT WHAT THE LEARNERS WANT

Even more so than they ever were, learners are now in a position to insist that their needs are met; to demand, in a sense, the full quality control of their individual Personalised Learning Environments. As practitioners we should be in a position to want to help them to achieve – rather than reacting to edicts from above about the future of education being online distance learning, whether you like it or not – and surely the nettle is ours to grasp. Losing our amnesia would be a good way to begin to do so. Buckling under the weight of deadlines, marking, meetings and tutorials, it has become the simplest choice to 'forget' – to engage in a wilful act of paramnesiac blindness – that learners often march one by one, not group by group. While educators might try to control the online environment, thereby reducing the number of surprises that distract us, and dosing ourselves to a comfortable numbness with the self-medicative qualities of Web 1, many learners will feel differently. For many learners, the unknown quality is a life *before* the Internet: anxiety is boredom itself, and vice versa. Control is theirs: and they want something new and original. An analogous comparison might be between a surface learner and a deep learner: surface learning tends to be experienced as a boring, depressing uphill battle; deep learning is gratifying and even exciting.

However, let us not run away with the impression that all learners are 'Digital Natives' (Prensky 2001) and fully conversant with all manners and modes of our industry. This is simply not the case. Distance learners, by definition, will be found in some of the areas of the world that struggle to maintain an Internet connection, let alone a fully up-to-date awareness of Web novelties and ephemera. "All our experiences in relation to learners using the LMS pointed towards the existence of anxiety that varied in type and in level across the group," write Saadé and Kira (2009) in their groundbreaking study of learner anxieties. They continue: "Motivated to gain insight into the learners' perceptions of the LMS and document those experiences, we decided to study anxiety as it relates to computer self-efficacy and perceptions." And Houle (1984) tells us that education is a cooperative rather than an operative art: voluntary interaction is implicit; and even solitary learners who have embarked on a programme of study ostensibly *without* the assistance of an educator will occasionally ask for help and elicit the encouragement of others.

The learner enters what, to all intents and purposes, is a virtual world – and one that must be partly at least of his own making. By now, of course, many users and inhabitants of virtual worlds have long since grown used to the idea

that the world in question will be *realistic* (in fact, this is nothing less than a demand); this is also true of the learner's case. The environment must be challenging – but it must also be realistic: realistic to their needs and their ambitions. The uses of and necessity for emotion in online learning is often overlooked; however, these are crucial understandings. If participants do not feel the correct emotional response (confusion, anger, intrigue, wonder – at the very least, intellectual engagement), then the easiest thing is to turn the machine off. The online environment is thereby closed. Perhaps it will not be opened again.

It is important to give the customers what they want – a central tenet of business – but it is also important to give the customers what they *think* they want. The desire to be satisfied with one's environment becomes one of the communal users' shared values: values as defined by Friedman (2006) as something important to a person or (equally as relevant here) to a *group of people*. Pereira (2011: 37) writes: "transformations such as the increased dependence on technology; the end of interface stability; the increased hyperconnectivity; the end of the ephemeral and the increase of creative engagement have redefined our relationship with technology. These transformations draw attention to the existence of a broad set of factors that range from sociability and emotional aspects to issues of scalability, security and performance; such factors are related to human values in the computing age and need to be explicitly considered in technology design... conversations and analysis of the values in technologies generally occur after design and launch. Consequently, most users are faced with undecipherable and sometimes weird decisions already made on their behalf, often not to their benefit".

As long ago as 1996, Friedman (1996) would argue that designers should represent/reproduce values through the technology that is being developed. As well as online environments enveloping their own systems of localized logic and systems of internal rules, they are sentient systems that can reduce anxiety, sometimes (paradoxically) by causing anxiety in others. Hurd (2007) also writes of distance language learners sharing aspects of anxiety with face-to-face learners, where the distance factor is connected to marked differences with regard to the nature and extent of language anxiety; but Hurd's research is fundamental in establishing that there exists evidence to suggest that the distance language learning setting might be connected with a *lowering* of anxiety for some learners, which is perhaps more important here.

What else might we surmise about learners in a online environment? If the world is successful, it will be creative; however, the *vice versa* is not the case. Just because an environment has been developed that would seem to excite a participant's creative instincts, if the element of emotion has not been built in, it is unlikely that it will continue long. Through a psychoanalytic lens, we might say that the world allows the learner to act out – ie. to perform an action in contrast to bearing and managing the impulse to perform it – and it also allows (or encourages) the learner to engage with his/her own aggression. If Bartle (2003) defines virtual worlds as "places where the imaginary meets the real", then we should build into the construction of a "world" (or a learning environment) all of the emotions – and aggression and anxiety – that the real world contains and embodies.

There is also the element of an education environment both being and providing a milieu that is safe for learners who would ordinarily struggle with more orthodox academic vehicles. In this group we might include those learners unable to attend face-to-face academic delivery, for one reason or another (for example, exclusion from the establishment or institution; long-term illness; fear of contact); however, we might argue that it would be suitable simply for those pathologically shy. Certainly, online education would seem to be instrumental in the building of confidence and the honing of social abilities – for some but not all learners. Naturally there are some social and academic skills that are non-transferable; but it is not *wrong* that many learners fail to take from the online environment into the physical world

the very qualities that they have managed to build while on the Internet. In fact, much of any such transferral is one way: the learner has Character/Appearance A. He or she enters the online environment and assumes Character/Appearance B... and to a variable extent *develops this character and moral code*. While this development might represent what, to the outside world, constitutes an improvement; it might be a dramatic failure of manners. But if this is what the learner wants (and is willing to pay for), are educators in any position to try to refuse it, especially if it contributes to a reduction of the learner's emotional excitation and anxiety?

On the other hand, of course, for every learner who becomes enabled and empowered by a contiguous existence in an online milieu, there might evolve a learner who develops anti-social tendencies in the very same environment. As unpleasant as these developments seem, one contention would be that these ontological dichotomies are essential, even if they involve bullying and learner anxiety. Not only is a virtual world a fresh source of inspiration for bullying, if the signs are not read correctly by the tutor, it is a fresh source of inspiration for bullying for *those who would not bully in the physical environment*. Therefore, part of the learner's education is ontological and pedagogically deliberately *anti*-social. It is only via learning 'violence' in such a setting that the learner might identify a healthy means of existence in the physical world.

These are, of course, not pleasant considerations; but they must be made, nevertheless.

ANXIETY ABOUT WHAT LEARNERS BECOME

Learners on online courses demand a good deal of attention (Sapsed and Mathew, 2011). They are prepared to wait their turn (in general), but it is not true to assume that a distance learner will necessarily work methodically through the material with which he/she has been presented.

The following examples are from an online learning programme at Master's degree level. (The subject matter of the course has been made anonymous by request of the Course Team Leader.) Certain learners who come from geographical areas in the world in which values of prudence and propriety are traditionally present, might become influenced by the pushing of boundaries while online. For example, if Character A is shy and repressed and hates this description, the Character B that he or she becomes might be gregarious and sexually predatory. This was certainly the way with certain learners on the course referred to. But what had happened? How did one learner change – so dramatically and so *rapidly* – into almost her ontological polar opposite? Did the virtual world change her, or had the change been inevitable anyway? Perhaps the online environment was nothing more than a catalyst; it is impossible to tell. What we *do* know, however, is that this alteration (or reinvention?) led to a disturbing that resulted in scarcely-controllable threats and sexual propositioning, and the subsequent threats of expulsion from the course.

Once more we might view the online educational environment through the lens of psychoanalysis. What I propose is that some learners use the virtual world as a kind of psychic retreat (Steiner 1993) and regard it as the only non-threatening place available. Being inside this retreat entails a constant oscillation between a paranoid-schizoid and depressive position: the overwhelming *status quo* for the learner will be one of pain and possibly damage to the psychic apparatus. Emergence from the retreat causes strain and anxiety, as does the forcing-together of online groups.

The emotional system itself – emotion work, feeling rules, and social exchange, as they come into play in a personal control system – grow in importance as a way through which people are persuaded and controlled both while on task and off.

Elsewhere from this extreme example, we have found so far that learners from India, Pakistan and Africa in particular are driven to be A-grade learners; and there even persists an incorrect no-

tion that if an overall percentage does not exceed 50% then the qualification cannot be considered a Masters. This latter idea would find sympathy with many academics (here and abroad), but the fact of the matter remains that what might be regarded in some circles as an admirable trait – a drive to succeed – is not in and of itself a universally positive thing. A learner who passed with 46% has taken the matter to the Board of Governors and an Ombudsman, irrespective of the fact that she averaged Cs and Ds throughout the course: one example of the relentless cultural pressures under which some of our learners toil.

Given the prevalence of HIV and Aids in some of the countries where we have learners on the Public Health Masters, we might have imagined these conditions to be important considerations. Not so: a total of eight learners admitted upfront that they were HIV Positive, but did not ask for any concessions or changes or anything: the information was a courtesy only. Far harder to 'confess', on the other hand (or so it would seem), has been the issue of dyslexia. A failure to divulge such an issue (or in fact any issue that might directly impede the learning process) can raise problems. To compare two case studies with similar origins: Learner A (a European female) had dyslexia, which she revealed in advance of the course starting. She was offered the appropriate support. Learner B (a European female) had dyslexia, which she did *not* reveal in advance of the course starting. It was some distance into the course before the troubles began, and the very best that might come out of such a scenario is the imposition of a £400 test for dyslexia, which the learner has to pay for. The lesson to be learned is to be aware of the possibility of learning impediments; to know as much background as possible.

Bipolar disorder, if untreated, would fall into this category. A female learner with bipolar disorder proved problematic in the sense that she refused to have the condition treated. The symptomatology was such that this learner suffered an all-but total erosion to her inhibitions. Her emails were sexually frank and unambiguous; she made inappropriate comments to staff and to her peers, sometimes sending in excess of twenty emails in one day. The behaviour led to two learners being driven away from the course with depression, and several group activities had to be abandoned and reconvened at a later date... It surely qualifies as irony, the fact that in her country this very same learner practiced as a medical General Practitioner!

Of course, the most unpredictable component of any dynamic is the human being. A piece of technology might well let us down, but in general it will work or it will not work. A human being on a distance learning course is infinitely more unpredictable. The very term 'distance learner' could be seen as a gross oversimplification, based on ideals...but perhaps this is a topic for a separate paper. In short, we might say that human beings will not be predicted; and understanding the culture of learners – how they have been educated to date, what constitutes their learning preferences – will only get us so far, and no further. When technology works – and the online environment is all-embracing – the human being might find ways immemorial to change him/herself; to alter the past via a false memory that he/she can *half* believe is true; or by distilling or perfecting a future within the environment that seems applicable and acceptable... even if it is applicable and acceptable because it pushes at superlatives. It is too good/too bad; you are too clever/too stupid. If something exists as a superlative, it cannot last forever. If a place is too cold, life dies. The dynamic is altered.

The learner wants – paradoxically, perhaps – both a system of change and a system to stay precisely the same and controllable. So does the user of the educational environment. Sellen *et al.* (2007) suggest that the biggest challenge confronting the interaction between humans and computers is that a recognition of one's values should be built into the design of the virtual world. Only by doing so, arguably, is the participant able to work/play/live, able to endure pain and distraction in a positive manner. In earlier times, in the opinion of Miller and Rice (*ibid,* above): 'The sentient groups to which professional men and women commit themselves and from which they draw their support are the professional associations and their related learned societies.' Perhaps a more contemporary addition to the possibility of an equivalent to a professional membership would be an online educational environment – or a virtual reality system. 'Societies, in effect, not only defines the boundaries of the task system and of the sentient system, and separates them, but also, through the sentient system, controls professional conduct in the task system'.

By allocating significant resources in order to design strong, engaging distance learning services to meet both the collective and individual needs of our learners in different parts of the world, the online environment grasps the nettle of providing quality education, with the barrier of geographical distance on its way to being overridden once and for all. What educators need to do is build a sense of the participant's mastery. Perfectly arguably, one way of creating a sense of knowledge/potency is through experiences involving mastery. A comprehensive success, or a failure from which an experience of learning derives, is a means to a personal strengthening.

Learner anxiety might also be a gauge of quality of performance (albeit not always a wholly reliable one). A learner who goes into an exam with no worries at all will frequently feel that he or she has under-performed afterwards; and it would appear that a small amount of short term anxiety as one enters a situation might improve one's performance and even be evolutionarily advantageous (Myers 2007). With Web 2.0 we have the opportunity of providing, in a totally positive manner, a fully functioning anxiety-inspiring experience for our learners. Perhaps this will be achieved by acknowledging that anxiety is an addiction or condition best shared: in this case, perhaps, shared among their peers but also shared with their educators. Web 2.0 is more than a tool for the beginnings of the future of education. It is also, *in and of itself*, the beginnings of the future of education: its opportunities, as we rethink our way away from a model of 'text + assessment +

consolidation + text... *ad nauseum* (which we should not have been doing in this industry anyway for the past decade) we might allow ourselves the luxury of *embracing* the new technologies and the pedagogic potentials therein. Web 2.0 is not just the Next Thing, nor is it merely the tool to use, it is something which needs to be understood better itself. Or in other words, it needs to be understood better by the educators. It is the very least that our learners will demand.

CONCLUDING REMARKS

Taking into consideration the money that circulates around the arteries of this industry, it is foolish to assume anything other than a rude future for online education. As we gratefully retire Web 1, and thank it for its years of dedicated (if sporadically reliable) service, we welcome in the new. This is one of the ways that a dynamic evolves, after all: the disuse of one model is replaced by the (temporary) overuse of the next model; and we are likely to see our educators 'trying too hard' with all of the new tools at their disposal., & yet this is one of the ways that we will all learn. Perhaps the educational protocols of Web 2.0 will require more balance and pedagogic poise than was shown throughout some of the early days of online education, when the tools seemed sometimes more important than the educational activities to which they referred.

Let us hope that we have learned from our own past as educators too. Web 2.0 should not involve using every tool in the box as flashily and gaudily as possible, or all at once. We must listen to our learners and take in the knowledge of what they are telling us – even if we have to intuit some of the less spoken messages! We do not want to lead our learners to another iteration of internet fatigue (and learner boredom) in a few years' time. A good model might be to use our wikis and discussion boards (for example) with

enthusiasm but not to place all of our faith in these tools alone. Assume nothing, or at least little; and be prepared to alter our strategies, in precisely the same way that we would in a classroom setting. If X is not working, try Y.

The new generation of web tools will give educators this kind of pioneering freedom, not to mention the chance to learn – really learn – from the learner. Accompanying our course evaluations about what part of the new structure was appreciated by the learner and what part was ignored, about why these things happen and what we do about it later, we have been given the opportunity to play a part in *our own* developmental learning of the tools of our trade. Will this inform our preparations for the learners' experiences? It is a chance to, at the very least. In the words of Maynard Keynes (1935), "The difficulty lies, not in the new ideas, but in escaping from the old ones".

REFERENCES

Apter, M. J. (1989). *Reversal theory: Motivation, emotion and personality.* London, UK: Routledge.

Armstrong, J., & Franklin, T. (2008). *A review of current and developing international practice in the use of social networking (Web 2.0) in higher education.* A report commissioned by the Committee of Enquiry into the Changing Learner Experience. Retrieved February 18, 2012, from http://www.franklin-consulting.co.uk/

Atherton, J. S. (2011). *Teaching and learning.* Retrieved January 14, 2012, from http://www.learningandteaching.info/teaching/course.htm

Bartle, R. A. (2003). *Designing virtual worlds.* New Riders Publishing.

Bates, T. (2011, February 22). *Lecture given at Digital Future of Higher Education.* Thompson Rivers University, Kamloops, BC. Retrieved July 26, 2011, from http://www.tru.ca/digifuture.html

Boud, D. (2000). Sustainable assessment: Rethinking assessment for the learning society. *Studies in Continuing Education, 22*(2), 151–167. doi:10.1080/713695728

De Board. R. (1978). *The psychoanalysis of organizations*. London, UK: Tavistock Publications.

Downes, S. (2008). *The future of online learning: Ten years on*. Half an Hour. Retrieved July 26, 2011, from http://halfanhour.blogspot.com/2008/11/future-of-online-learning-ten-years-on_16.html

FreeDictionary.com. (2012). *Anxiety*. Retrieved February 20, 2012, from http://medical-dictionary.thefreedictionary.com/anxiety

Freud, S. (1926). Inhibitions, symptoms and anxiety. In Strachey, J. (Ed.), *The complete works of Sigmund Freud* (pp. 77–174). London, UK: Hogarth.

Friedman, B. (1996). Value-sensitive design. *Interaction, 3*(6), 16–23. doi:10.1145/242485.242493

Friedman, B. (2006). Value sensitive design and information systems. In Zhang, P., & Galletta, D. (Eds.), *Human-computer interaction and management information systems: Foundations* (pp. 348–372).

Hebb, D. O. (1955). Drives and the CNS (conceptual nervous system). *Psychological Review, 62*, 243–254. doi:10.1037/h0041823

Horrigan, J. (2009). The mobile difference. Pew Internet. Retrieved July 26, 2011, from http://www.pewinternet.org/~/media//Files/Reports/2009/The_Mobile_Difference.pdf

Houle, C. O. (1984). The design of education. In Merriam, S. B. (Ed.), *Selected writings on philosophy and adult education* (pp. 41–50). Malabar, FL: Robert E. Krieger Publishing Company.

Huffington, C. (2004). *Working below the surface*. London, UK: Karnac.

Hurd, S. (2007). Anxiety and non-anxiety in a distance language learning environment: The distance factor as a modifying influence. *System, 35*(4), 487–508. doi:10.1016/j.system.2007.05.001

Internet World Stats. (2012). World internet usage and population statistics. Retrieved February 26, 2012, from http://www.internetworldstats.com/stats.htm

Keen, A. (2007). *The cult of the amateur: How today's internet is killing our culture*. New York, NY: Doubleday.

Klein, M. (1975). *Envy and gratitude*. London, UK: The Hogarth Press.

Maynard Keynes, J. (1935) *The general theory of employment, interest and money*. Retrieved December 15, 2011, from http://www.marxists.org/reference/subject/economics/keynes/general-theory/preface.htm

Meltzer, D. (1994). *Sincerity and other works*. London, UK: Karnac.

Miller, E. J., & Rice, A. K. (1990). Task and sentient systems and their boundary controls. In Trist, E., & Murray, H. (Eds.), *Social engagement of social science* (*Vol. 1*, pp. 259–271). London, UK: Free Association.

Milligan, C. (2006). What is a PLE? The future or just another buzz word? *JISC E-Learning Focus*. Retrieved November 25, 2011, from http://www.elearning.ac.uk/news_folder/ple%20event

Myers, D. G. (2007). *Psychology*. New York, NY: Worth.

Nagel, D. (2010). The future of e-learning is more growth. *Campus Technology*. Retrieved July 26, 2011, from http://campustechnology.com/articles/2010/03/03/the-future-of-e-learning-is-more-growth.aspx

Pereira, R. M., Baranauskas, C. C., & Almeida, L. D. A. (2011). The value of value identifications in web applications. *Proceedings of the WWW/Internet IADIS International Conference,* Rio de Janeiro, Brazil 2011.

Prensky, M. (2001). Digital natives, digital immigrants. *The Horizon Report, 9*(5). Retrieved December 20, 2012, from http://pre2005.flexible-learning.net.au/

Ramsden, P., Beswick, D., & Bowden, J. (1989). Effects of learning skills intervention on first year learners' learning. *Human Learning, 5*, 151–164.

Rickman, J. (1957). *Selected contributions to psycho-analysis*. London, UK: Karnac.

Saadé, R. G., & Kira, D. (2009). Computer anxiety in e-learning: The effect of computer self-efficacy. *Journal of Information Technology Education, 8*. Retrieved July 27, 2011, from http://jite.org/documents/Vol8/JITEv8p177-191Saade724.pdf

Sapsed, S., & Mathew, D. (2011). *The growth of the Public Health Masters at the University of Bedfordshire*. Refereed Program of the E-Leader Conference at Zagreb, Croatia. Retrieved from http://www.g-asa.com/conferences/zagreb/ppt/sapsed%20[Compatibility%20Mode].pdf

Sellen, A. (2009). Reflecting human values in the digital age. *Communications of the ACM, 52*(3), 58–66. doi:10.1145/1467247.1467265

Steiner, J. (1993). *Psychic retreats: Pathological organisations in psychotic, neurotic and borderline patients*. London, UK: Routledge. doi:10.4324/9780203359839

Strachey, J. (2001). *The standard edition of the complete psychological works of Sigmund Freud* (*Vol. 21*, pp. 1927–1931). London, UK: Vintage.

Surowiecki, J. (2004). *The wisdom of crowds: Why the many are smarter than the few and how collective wisdom shapes business, economies, societies and nations*. New York, NY: Little Brown.

Trist, E., & Murray, H. (1990). *the social engagement of social science,* Vol 1. London, UK: Free Association.

Zhang, J. (2009). Toward a creative social Web for learners and teachers. *Educational Researcher, 38*(4), 274–279. doi:10.3102/0013189X09336674

KEY TERMS AND DEFINITIONS

Anxiety: Uncomfortable/displeasing feeling of dread, fear or concern; the sensation that something unpleasant will happen, although often there is no specific obvious threat.

Future: Unspecific period of time following the present time; what is 'next' rather than what is 'now'.

Online Learning: Electronically supported learning and teaching, delivered via the Internet; often an out-of-classroom educational experience.

Web 2.0: Platform for user-centered design, interoperability, information sharing and collaboration on the Internet.

Chapter 16
Cyberbullying:
The Bad and the Ugly Side
of Information Age

Osman Tolga Arıcak
Fatih University, Turkey

Sinem Siyahhan
Arizona State University, USA

Taşkın Tanrıkulu
Fatih University, Turkey

Hüseyin Kınay
Fatih University, Turkey

ABSTRACT

Twenty years ago, who would have thought that children as young as twelve would own a cell phone, or people would check their e-mails and Facebook several times in a given day? Things have changed a lot over the last several years. The information and communication technologies made access to information easier and allowed people to communicate with long-distant family and friends instantly. Despite these positive changes, the advances in information and communication technologies also introduced problems that are unique to information age. In this paper, the authors review one of these problems, namely cyberbullying, which affects school age children. Many studies reported significant number of children late elementary through high school experiencing cyberbullying—the use of electronic means to harass others—through cell phones and the Internet. The authors discuss the nature of cyberbullying and why it became a problem among youth. They conclude this chapter with suggestions for parents and future research.

INTRODUCTION

For the last five to ten years, digital media technologies have dramatically changed the way people connect, socialize, collaborate, learn, and work (Yu, Tian, Vogel, & Kwok, 2010). The unprecedented levels of connectivity and sharing information in the form of text, images, and videos through personal computers and cell phones have become a daily routine. A recent Pew Internet and American Life Project report found that 83% of Americans use cell phones to call, text messages, take and send photos, and play games (Smith, 2011). As of August 2011, 78% of adults in the

DOI: 10.4018/978-1-4666-2970-7.ch016

United States use the Internet to send and read e-mails, use a search engine (e.g. google), research a product or service, check the weather, buy products, get news, make a travel reservation, watch a video, look for information, download music, and play online games (Pew Internet and American Life Project Report, 2011). Additionally, 65% of online adults use social networking sites such as MySpace, Facebook, or LinkedIn (Madden, & Zickuhr, 2011). Similar patterns are observed in European countries as well. For instance, in the United Kingdom 99% of adults own a cell phone, 74% of adults use the Internet, and 48% of adults have a social networking profile (Ofcom, 2011). Other countries, both in and outside of Europe, are also witnessing a rapid increase in the use of cell phones and the Internet (The World Bank, 2011).

Adults are not the only ones who use digital media technologies regularly. According to recent Kiaser Foundation report, 66% of children (ages between 8 and 18) in the United States own cell phones, and send an average of 118 messages a day. Additionally, children spend almost 1.5 hours everyday using computer and playing video games. Children spend most of their time on the computer visiting social networking sites, watching videos, and sending e-mails and messages (Rideout, Foehr, & Roberts, 2010). Similarly, in the United Kingdom, 41% of children (ages 9-19) use the Internet for school work, to look for information, play games, send e-mails, and chat with others. Additionally, 50% of children use cell phones and send, and receive text messages daily (Livingstone, & Bober, 2005). According to the recent European Union Kids Online report, children use the Internet daily more frequently than their parents, and 38% of children (ages 9-12) and 77% of children (ages 13-16) have a profile on a social networking site (Livingstone, & Haddon, 2009).

The increase in the access and use of technology has both positive and negative impact on society. Technology provided people new opportunities to connect and communicate. On the other hand, it introduced new problems like harassment through electronic means, commonly termed cyberbullying. According to NCES report, 6% of children (ages 12-18) experienced cyberbullying in the form of receiving hurtful information on the Internet and being excluded from an online community (NCES, 2011). In a study conducted with Canadian and Chinese seven grade children, Li (2007) found that 28.9% of children were cyberbullied and 17.8% of children were cyberbullies themselves. Similarly, Arıcak et al. (2008) found that 35.7% of children (grade 6 through 10) in Turkey were cyberbullies and 5.9% of children were cybervictims. In the Netherlands, Dehue, Bolman, and Völlink (2008) found that 23% of secondary school children were victims of cyberbullying. An Anti-Bullying Alliance (ANA) report found that one in five children had experiences with cyberbullying in the United Kingdom (BBC News, 2009). Research findings like these, and many more from other countries all around the world, suggest that cyberbullying among youth is an important problem that needs to be addressed as digital media technologies become ubiquitous.

BACKGROUND

Definition of Cyberbullying

Researchers have identified a wide range of behaviors as cyberbullying and suggested different ways to categorize these behaviors. Broadly speaking, cyberbullying behaviors include flaming (sending or posting hostile messages), exclusion (preventing someone from participating in an online group), denigration (sending messages to others about someone), impersonation (pretending to be someone), sexting (sending pornographic images to someone) and cyberstalking (prolonged harassment that involves intimidation and threats) (Siegle, 2010; Walker, 2009; Willard, 2007). According to Arıcak (2011, p.10), "cyberbullying is technical-oriented or relational-oriented harmful behaviors toward a real person or a corporation by using information and communication technologies." Nocentini and collegues (2010) suggest that these behaviors can be categorized as written, verbal, and visual cyberbullying depending on the content of the harming behaviors. From their perspective, threating someone by calling them on a cell phone is considered a verbal cyberbullying while texting them or sending an e-mail is considered as a written cyberbullying, and posting a picture of someone on a social networking site is considered as a visual cyberbullying. Using taxonomy similar to traditional forms of bullying, Vandebosch and Cleemput (2009), on the other hand, suggest that cyberbullying can be divided into two groups: direct and indirect cyberbullying. From this perspective, direct cyberbullying involves physical cyberbullying (e.g. sending viruses and spam e-mails), verbal cyberbullying (using cell phone and the Internet to threaten, intimidate, or insult someone), non-verbal or visual cyberbullying (e.g. sending pictures), and social cyberbullying (e.g. excluding someone from an online group). Indirect cyberbullying involves exposing someone's private information and pictures to public, spending rumors through e-mails, social networking sites, and personal websites, and carrying out a campaign to insult and damage someone's relations.

Drawing upon our previous work, we suggest an alternative way to categorize cyberbullying behaviors to address the issue of power dynamics between the cyberbully and the cybervictim. Cyberbullying can be categorized as electronic bullying (e-bullying) and e-communication bullying (Arıcak, 2011). *E-bullying* refers to the kind of cyberbullying that targets debilitating the hardware, the software, or the online service. Hacking e-mail and online accounts and websites, acquiring passwords and retrieving information, and sending spam e-mails are examples of this type of cyberbullying. E-bullying requires a person or a group to have the necessary technical skills to harm the other person. Here, the power relation between the cyberbully and cybervictim is asym-

metric in that the cyberbully has the technical skills to harm the other person while the cybervictim often lacks such skills and is left incapacitated, making retaliation less likely. *E-communication bullying*, on the other hand, refers to the social side of cyberbullying and involves name-calling, insults, spreading rumors, or sharing pictures through communication technologies. This type of cyberbullying involves the cyberbully, cybervictim, and cyber-onlookers. Here, the power relation between the cyberbully and the cybervictim is symmetrical in that both have access and the skills to use the particular electronic medium, making retaliation more likely. Research suggests that the e-communication bullying is more common among youth than e-bullying that require technical skills on the part of the cyberbullying (Arıcak et al., 2008).

In addition, while some researchers suggested that for online harassing behaviors to be considered cyberbullying the perpetuator(s) must intent to harm the other person and engage in these behaviors repeatedly (Li, 2007; Patchin & Hinduja, 2006), we argue that repetition is not a prerequisite for an online behavior to be considered cyberbullying. The impact of an intentionally hostile behavior, such as posting someone's embarrassing pictures online without the person's consent, can have a long lasting effect on the person's psychology whose pictures are posted as the pictures stored on the web indefinitely and can be viewed by many people outside of the person's control. In other words, even if a person is victimized once, the effect of the victimization instance can do permanent damage to the individual. More broadly, cyberbullying can be defined as "a set of behaviors that aim to do a technical or relational damage to an individual, a group, or an entity using information and communication technologies" (Arıcak, 2011, p. 10). We believe that this broad definition encompasses the coordinated cyber attacks of individuals or groups towards governments, companies, and organizations that have become increasingly common.

Common Cyberbullying Behaviors and Coping Strategies

The most common cyberbullying behaviors involve excluding a person from an online group, spreading rumors, name calling, and insulting someone online, making comments about someone on a website, and hacking someone's e-mail address and private information (Calvete et al., 2010; Dehue, Bolman, & Völlink, 2008). The most common mediums for cyberbullying are e-mail, listserv, cell phones, web cameras, instant messaging, social networking sites, and MMOs (Shariff & Gouin, 2005). According to a recent study with Australian children (ages 10-18) by Price and Dalgleish (2010) found that 27% of children did nothing when they were bullied, 16.1% of children retaliated, 44.2% confronted the cyberbully, 39.4% told a friend, and 29.4% of children told their parents and 24.6% told a teacher. They also found that 68.2% of children did not find confronting the bully, 64.2% of children did not find doing nothing, and 38.1% of children did not find telling a teacher helpful. Similarly, Topçu, Erdur-Baker, and Çapa-Aydin (2008) found that 23.8% of children did not tell anyone that they were being cyberbullied, 28.6% of children told their friends, and only 13.3% of children told their parents and 5.7% told their teachers in Turkey.

Comparing School Bullying and Cyberbullying

Bullying is often defined as repeated aggressive behaviors that are intended to harm another person or a group of people (Carney & Merrell, 2001; Olweus, 1993). Some have argued that bullying also involves the asymmetric power relations between the bully and the victim in that victims are often physically weaker, psychologically more vulnerable and socially peripheral (Olweus, 1993, Pepler, Craig, & O'Connell, 1999). Research suggests that children engage in different forms of bullying depending on the covert or overt acts

of aggressive behaviors. Direct bullying involves physical and verbal attacks such as pushing, hitting, teasing, and insulting (Olweus, 1991, 1993). Indirect bullying, also known as relational bullying, is defined as the harassment through social means, and involves gossiping, spreading rumors, and excluding someone from a peer group (Olweus, 1991, 1993).

Research suggests that children who are bullied in school are also cyberbullied outside of school (Erdur & Baker, 2009; Schneider, O'Donnell, Stueve, & Coulter, 2012; Twyman, Saylor, Taylor & Comeaux, 2010). Both bullying and cyberbullying involves intentional hostile behaviors and have negative effects on children's mental health such as depression and withdrawal. In both bullying and cyberbullying, the lack of parent-child communication or interaction is a risk factor. However, Ayas and Horzum (2010) suggest that cyberbullying have the following qualities that separate cyberbullying from school bullying: (1) cyberbullying involves using technological devices to harm others, (2) perpetuators can hide their identity in the case of cyberbullying, (3) in traditional bullying the spectators are limited to school grounds, however, in the case of cyberbullying spectators could be anyone on the Internet, (4) while victims can escape from their bullies once they leave school, the cybervictims are vulnerable every hour of every day of the year, and (5) the damage of traditional bullying is limited to school while the damage caused by the cyberbullying can be permanent.

The Negative Effects of Cyberbullying on Children

Because the act of cyberbullying is often public and effects the cyber victims' relation to a larger number of people, cyberbullying can have more significant negative effects on children's mental health than traditional forms of bullying (Dooley, Pyżalski, & Cross, 2009). For example, Hinduja and Patchin (2010) found that children who were cyberbullied considered suicide more often than those who were bullied in school. Victims of cyberbullying experience a wide range of emotions such as low self-esteem, sadness, anger, helplessness, fear, shame, and stress (Mason, 2008; Morales, 2011; Schneider, O'Donnell, Stueve, & Coulter, 2012; Price & Dalgleish, 2010). Goebert, Else, Matsu, Chung-Do, and Chang (2011) found that cyber-victims are two and a half times more likely to abuse drugs, two times more likely to be depressed, and female cyber-victims are three and a half times more likely, while male cyber-victims are four and a half times more likely to attempt suicide than the traditionally bullied victims. These negative effects of cyberbullying exacerbated when children are cyber bullied by adults (Anderson, 2010). Additionally, children may have problems with peers, experience insomnia, headaches, and abdomen pain, engage in self-harming behaviors, and withdraw from school and other regular activities (Mason, 2008; Sourander et al., 2010; Wong-Lo, Bullock, & Gable, 2011).

Risk Factors

Research suggests that there are several factors that increase the likelihood of becoming a cyberbully or a cybervictim. Those children who have low social competence and skills, and have interpersonal problems with peers and family members are at the risk of being cyberbullied (Navarro, Yubero, Larrañaga, Martínez, 2012; Vandebosch & Van Cleemput, 2009). Studies also found that frequent Internet use predicts cyber victimization (König, Gollwitzer, & Steffgen, 2010; Smith et al., 2008; Twyman, Saylor, Taylor, & Comeaux, 2010). The risk of cyber-victimization especially increases when children visit web sites that involve sexual content, share their private information with others online, and download and share files online (Dowell, Burgess, Cavanaugh, 2009). Similarly, children who are less knowledgable about cyberbullying and do not share their experiences with adults more frequently experience cybervictimiza-

tion (Yilmaz, 2011). On the other hand, research studies show that those who were victimized both online and offline are more likely to engage in cyberbullying (Katzer et al., 2009; König et al., 2010; Schneider et al., 2112; Vandebosch & Van Cleenput, 2009; Yilmaz, 2011). Additionally, Dilmac and Aydogan (2010) found that authotarian parenting predicts children's engagement with cyberbullying. Children who feel lonely, have low self-esteem, and have low ability to make friends are more likely to cyberbully others (Schoffstall & Cohen, 2011). Finally, Didden et al. (2009) found a relation between high IQ and engagement in cyberbully behaviors.

Researchers have found some factors that increase the risk of being both a cybervictim and a cyberbully. For example, both cyberbullies and victims have lower levels of empathy than non-bullies and non-victims (Ang & Goh, 2010; Schultze-Krumbholz & Scheithauer, 2009). According to Mason (2008), there are three factors that puts children at risk of cyberbullying both as a bully and as a victim: (1) the disinhibition effect, (2) identity transition from private to social self, and (3) poor relationships between parents and children. The lack of physical connection with others and anonymity in online environments creates a sense of invulnerability. This results in people engaging in behaviors that they would not normally engage in when interacting face-to-face. This increases the likelihood of someone engaging cyberbully behaviors in online environments as well as someone sharing information and becoming a victim. Adolescents who are in the process of forming their identities perceive online environments as a space for self-expression and free speech, therefore, are more likely to share information, express their emotions without any filtering, and take action without considering its consequences. Finally, poor parent-child relationships can be a reason for children to engage in cyberbullying and not share their negative online experiences with their parents.

WHY HAS CYBERBULLYING BECOME A PROBLEM?

Today, computers and cellphones without Internet connections are considered ancient. We often forget that the first modern smart phone came out only five years ago in 2007, and web 2.0 technologies (e.g., social web-applications like facebook) are also fairly new innovations. Our adoption of new technologies is as fast as their development in that instant access to information and connectivity has become the norm in many societies. The changes in our daily lives due to the Internet and technology are inevitable, however, it is still unclear how these changes will affect the way people socialize. Is social interaction in online spaces different than face-to-face interaction? Do people replicate face-to-face social interaction patterns in online spaces? Does the nature of social interaction patterns in online spaces look different? These are some of the questions that are facing researchers and educators in the information age.

Cyberbullying is situated within these broader questions. Some studies on cyberbullying suggest that harassment through electronic means is an extension of traditional forms of bullying. Those who harass others in person (offline) use electronic means to continue to harass their victims online. For example, in a representative sample of American children (ages 12-17), Juvonen and Gross (2008) found that repeated school-based bullying experiences increased the likelihood of repeated cyberbullying, and about two thirds of cyberbullying victims reported knowing their perpetrators, and half of them knew the bully from school. Bullies in schools use cell phones and the Internet to threaten, insult, spread rumors, and share photos of their victims with others. This suggests that while cyberbullying occurs beyond the physical boundaries of a school, it is still a problem in the school. In recent years, there has been an increase in the adoption of bullying prevention and intervention programs in U.S. and in European countries, and bullying has received significant attention from media, educators, and parents. If cyberbullying is, indeed, an extension of school bullying, then why are we still facing this problem despite the efforts put into bullying prevention and intervention programs?

We believe that one of the reasons is that educators failed to foresee the impact of the digital media technologies on education and were caught off guard when children rapidly adopted these technologies. Consequently, they integrated technology into the classroom without the pedagogical support and education that is necessary for its proper use. For instance, many schools purchased computers and provided Internet access to their students and staff, however, very few, if any, adopted a program to educate teachers, students, school personnel, and parents about cyberbullying which has its own unique set of characteristics that are not addressed in a traditional bullying prevention/intervention programs. The only strategy that schools universally adopt to prevent cyberbullying is to block student form accessing inappropriate content and social networking sites (e.g. facebook) on school computers. This is a step in the right direction, however, schools need to understand that children can engage in cyberbullying through their cell phones and home computers, and spreading rumors, sharing pictures, threatening someone through a fake e-mail account does not require technical expertise for children to cyberbully others. Therefore, comprehensive cyberbullying prevention programs need to accompany the efforts to integrate technology into the classroom.

Another reason is the lack of parent education and awareness around cyberbullying. The digital media technologies have significant effects on all aspects of life including family relations. As family members spend more time online around the computer and hand held devices, the face-to-face interaction and sharing between family members significantly reduced and resulted in family members living isolated lives under same roof. Parents often lack the knowledge and skills to educate their children about the potential perils of online spaces and monitor their children's use of digital media technologies and cell phones, and participation in online spaces (Strom & Strom, 2005; Willard, 2005). Raising parental awareness and educating parents about the issues of cyberbullying plays an important role in preventing cyberbullying among children. However, if we want children to use digital media technologies and participate in online spaces responsibly, we also need to provide them with models for healthy relations in the real world. Thus, we also need to support parents in adapting strategies to foster healthy parent-child interaction in real life to prevent cyberbullying.

SOLUTIONS AND RECOMMENDATIONS

Schools need to implement comprehensive cyberbullying prevention programs that address the unique features of cyberbullying, in addition to the existing bullying prevention programs. The principles of bullying prevention programs such as fostering a positive school environment, developing school and classroom rules around respectful peer relations, encouraging prosocial behaviors among children, and teaching children conflict resolution strategies can be integrated into a cyberbullying prevention programs (Cowie & Colliety, 2010; Grigg, 2010). Studies suggest that cyberbullying prevention programs can implement the following strategies to raise awareness about cyberbullying in schools (Diamanduros et al., 2008; Kowalski, Limber, & Agatson, 2008; Shariff, 2008; Wong-Lo et al., 2011):

1. Developing a common goal and definition of cyberbullying among school personnel.
2. Introducing clear rules and policies about cyberbullying.
3. Encouraging students to report cyberbullying.
4. Providing information to parents about cyberbullying.

5. Allocating class time on cyberbullying and responsible online participation.
6. Building community, parent, and school partnership.

Efforts to develop and implement cyberbullying prevention programs in schools need to be situated within the larger education system. Specifically, the Department of Education has an important role to play in raising awareness around cyberbullying, passing laws and regulations to prevent and intervene cyberbullying, making sure that cyberbullying prevention programs are implemented in schools, and educating school personnel and parents. The Stop Bullying initiative by U.S. government is an example of how governments can play an active role in providing information and raising awareness around all forms of bullying (see www.stopbullying.gov). Governments starting initiatives such as this can have a significant effect on preventing cyberbullying.

Parents need to be aware of the social networking and other websites that are popular among youth and realize that these sites may involve inappropriate content and put children at risk. According to a recent Common Sense Media report (2012), 12% of American children who have an account on a social networking site reported that their parents do not know about their account, and 16% of parents think that their children share the same information that their children have shared with them on the social networking sites. This suggests that there is a significant gap between what children report about their use and participation in online space in research studies and parents' perception of children's online activities. Parents can do the following to protect children from cyberbullying:

Talking to children about responsible use of technology. Parents can talk to their children about the extent to which children should share information online. Specifically, they can remind their children that information shared in online spaces can be viewed by others and is permanent. Parents can also encourage children to share positive as well as negative online experiences with them.

Participating in online spaces. Parents need to gather information about and participate in online sites (e.g. facebook) that their children use, to better understand the affordances of these sites and potential risks for children. Parents are more likely to be proactive about traditional forms of bullying, while unaware of their children's online activities, and consequently, put less effort into preventing cyberbullying (Tangen & Campbell, 2010). Additionally, children perceive adults as ignorant about technology and cyberbullying, and thus are less likely to inform an adult when they are harassed online (Cassidy, Jackson, & Brown, 2009). Therefore, it is important for parents to know about social networking sites, blogs, online games, and other sites first hand and educate themselves about the potential risks of different sites as part of a general effort to become technically literate.

Helping children understand privacy settings. Recently, companies like Google and Facebook that provide social networking services improved their privacy settings to allow users to have control over which information they want to make it public or private. Parents need to understand the privacy settings of online services and sites that children use, and talk to their children about how to change their privacy settings.

Monitoring children's online participation. Parents need to set rules around their children's online participation. Research found that those children whose parents have rules around computer and cell phone use (e.g. blocking children's access to certain websites) have significantly less experiences with cyberbullying (Mesch, 2009). Specifically, children whose parents have access to their accounts are less likely to be cyber victims than those whose parents do not have access to their children's accounts (Twynman et al. 2010). Parents can use "internet use contract" and "cell phone use contract" to set rules about appropriate and respectful use of communication technologies (Siegle, 2010).

Keeping an open communication. It is important for parents to keep an open communication with their children and make them feel safe to share their online experiences so that when children have unpleasant or distressing experiences online, they are willing to inform their parents. Research suggests that children who share online experiences with their parents are less likely to be cyberbullied and more likely to adopt healthy coping strategies in the face of cyberbullying. Parents can also start casual conversations with their children and ask simple questions such as "Has any offline argument or instance carried over to online?", "Has anyone said anything sexually offensive to you over the Internet? If so, how did you deal with it?", "Is anyone bothering you via phone, chat, e-mail, or text message?", etc. that would allow parents gain insights into their children's experiences.

Contacting the service providers. Parents need to be proactive when they suspect that their children are cybervictims or cyberbullies. Parents need to contact with the site administrators and request that their children's account is closed. Additionally, parents need to encourage their children to keep the records of harassment such as text messages and e-mails, and inform the school personnel if someone in their children's school perpetuates the online harassment.

FUTURE RESEARCH DIRECTIONS

For the last decade, there has been a significant increase in the number of studies published on cyberbullying. This is partially because as our awareness and understanding of children's use of information and communication technologies and how we can integrate new technologies into classrooms grew, the bad and the ugly side of information and communication technologies also became an issue and a topic for discussion and research. Today, we have strong evidence that (a) children are experiencing cyberbullying, and yet, they rarely share their negative online experiences with teachers and parents, and (b) there is a relationship between bullying in school and cyberbullying. At the same time, researchers have barely scratched the surface of the problem and much work needs to be done to address cyberbullying.

One area that needs the most attention is clarification of definition and conceptualization of cyberbullying. As discussed earlier, many researchers, drawing upon the definition of traditional forms of bullying, defined cyberbullying as having the characteristics of being repeated and having power asymmetry. We argued in this chapter that this narrow definition of cyberbullying fails to capture the nature of cyberbullying and its effects on children as well as the features that differentiate cyberbullying from traditional bullying. For example, one student teasing another or calling the other person a name once is less likely to cause the victim of that one instance to be depressed or commit suicide, however, one student sharing an embarrassing or inappropriate picture of another person online with the entire school and public only once has a potential to cause a severe psychological damage to the person as one act of sharing a picture can have long lasting consequences for the victim.

Today, many schools in the U.S. and European countries implement some form of bullying prevention and intervention program, and many researchers are studying the process of developing such programs and the effect of these programs on child outcomes. While there are examples of cyberbullying prevention and intervention programs, more research is needed to understand how to develop cyberbullying prevention and intervention programs, integrate efforts to prevent cyberbullying to ongoing bullying prevention and intervention programs, and the effectiveness of cyberbullying prevention and intervention programs on reducing cyberbullying. Additionally, considering that children rarely share their experiences with their parents and that parents hold misconceptions about the extent to which children are engaged in and exposed to cyberbullying, it is important to investigate how to support school-home connection in fighting against cyberbullying.

Finally, future research on cyberbullying needs to focus on how to raise teacher awareness and improve teacher education about cyberbullying (Shariff, 2008). We believe that teacher education around cyberbullying should be situated within the larger initiatives that target integrating technology into the classroom. Additionally, teacher education need to start in college before teachers enter the classrooms, and should involve not only improving teachers' pedagogical knowledge but also legal standards and responsibilities around cyberbullying.

CONCLUSION

Information and communication technologies have drastically changed people's lives. Today, we cannot imagine a world without the Internet or cell phones. It is this new world, so called the information age, that children today are born into and need to navigate. Research on children's digital media use suggests that children are quick to adapt to new information and communication technologies and use them differently than adults (Lenhart, & Madden, 2005). For example, parents and children engage in different activities with technology. Parents use cell phones and the Internet to facilitate communication with their children and to coordinate activities and daily life routines (Kennedy, Smith, Wells, & Wellman, 2008). Children, on the other hand, spend extensive time online, multitasking (e.g. chatting, downloading music, internet surfing), and connecting with their friends (Ito et al., 2010). While information and communication technologies provide opportunities for children to learn, they also introduce problems like cyberbullying that needs the attention of researchers, educators, and parents.

Many educators, parents, and in some respect, researchers were unprepared and failed to predict how fast children would adopt digital media technologies and the impact of these technologies on education more broadly. The drastic increase in the number of online degree programs, opportunities for professional training and development, and online services for academic learning are few examples of the impact of technology on education. Today, we are at a point where, using Ivan Illich's thesis for deschooling education as a theoretical lens, several educators argue that the Internet will put an end to traditional physical school structure and permanently change education (see Eales & Byrd, 1997; Firat, 2010). The integration of technology in education and into classrooms provides new opportunities for learning. However, in this paper, we also argued that the integration of technology into the classroom without the pedagogical support that is necessary for preventing the misuse of these technologies is at the core of the cyberbullying problem among youth. As noted earlier, research suggests that children who are bullied in school are also cyberbullied outside of school (Erdur & Baker, 2009; Schneider, O'Donnell, Stueve, & Coulter, 2012; Twyman, Saylor, Taylor & Comeaux, 2010). This suggests that cyberbullying prevention and intervention programs can play a significant role in reducing cyberbullying among children.

Future research needs to focus on the development and the effectiveness of cyberbullying prevention and intervention programs as well as how these programs can be integrated into or implemented with existing bullying programs in schools. Research suggests that parents play an important role in children's engagement in and exposure to cyberbullying. Therefore, one of the priorities of the cyberbullying prevention

and intervention programs needs to be building school-home connection. The pedagogical challenge in the case of preventing cyberbullying is threefold: (a) educating children, (b) educating teachers, and (c) educating parents. As mentioned earlier, both cyberbullies and victims have lower levels of empathy than non-bullies and non-victims (Ang & Goh, 2010; Schultze-Krumbholz & Scheithauer, 2009). This suggests that a key to educating children about cyberbullying is to find ways to improve children's abilities to perspective take and feel for others. What are some of the ways to help children develop the skills that are necessary for them to understand the issues of cyberbullying and its consequences? We have some evidence that teachers and parents are less aware of cyberbullying than traditional bullying. What kinds of learning opportunities would allow teachers and parents to recognize and appropriately support children in dealing with cyberbullying? These questions are yet to be answered.

REFERENCES

Anderson, W. L. (2010). Cyber stalking (Cyber bullying): Proof and punishment. *Insights to a Changing World Journal, 4*, 18–23.

Ang, R. P., & Goh, D. H. (2010). Cyberbullying among adolescents: The role of affective and cognitive empathy, and gender. *Child Psychiatry and Human Development, 41*(4), 387–397. doi:10.1007/s10578-010-0176-3

Arıcak, O. T. (2011). Cyberbullying: The new danger waiting for adolescents. [Siber zorbalık: gençlerimizi bekleyen yeni tehlike.] [Career Window]. *Kariyer Penceresi, 2*(6), 10–12.

Arıcak, O. T., Siyahhan, S., Uzunhasanoğlu, A., Sarıbeyoğlu, S., Çıplak, S., Yılmaz, N., & Memmedov, C. (2008). Cyberbullying among Turkish adolescents. *Cyberpsychology & Behavior, 11*(3), 253–261. doi:10.1089/cpb.2007.0016

Ayas, T., & Horzum, M. B. (2010). Sanal zorba/kurban ölçek geliştirme çalışması. *Akademik Bakış Dergisi, 19*, 1.

Calvete, E., Orue, I., Estévez, A., Villardón, L., & Padilla, P. (2010). Cyberbullying in adolescents: Modalities and aggressors' profile. *Computers in Human Behavior, 26*(5), 1128–1135. doi:10.1016/j.chb.2010.03.017

Carney, A. G., & Merrell, K. W. (2001). Bullying in schools: Perspectives on understanding and preventing an international problem. *School Psychology International, 22*(3), 364–382. doi:10.1177/0143034301223011

Cassidy, W., Jackson, M., & Brown, K. N. (2009). Students' experiences with cyberbullying: Sticks and stones can break my bones, but how can pixels hurt me? *School Psychology International, 30*, 383–402. doi:10.1177/0143034309106948

Common, S. M. R. (2012). *Teen social media*. Retrieved January, 25, 2012, from http://www.commonsensemedia.org/teen-social-media

Cowie, H., & Colliety, P. (2010). Cyberbullying: Sanctions or sensitivity? *Pastoral Care in Education, 28*(4), 261–268. doi:10.1080/026439 44.2010.528017

Dehue, F., Bolman, C., & Völlink, T. (2008). Cyberbullying: Youngsters' experiences and parental perception. *Cyberpsychology & Behavior, 11*(2), 217–223. doi:10.1089/cpb.2007.0008

Diamanduros, T., Downs, E., & Jenkins, S. J. (2008). The role of school psychologists in the assessment, prevention, and intervention of cyberbullying. *Psychology in the Schools, 45*(8), 693–704. doi:10.1002/pits.20335

Didden, R., Scholte, R. H. J., Korzilius, H., de Moor, J. M. H., Vermeulen, A., & O'Reilly, M. (2009). Cyberbullying among students with intellectual and developmental disability in special education settings. *Developmental Neurorehabilitation, 12*(3), 146–151. doi:10.1080/17518420902971356

Dilmaç, B., & Aydogan, D. (2010). Parental attitudes as a predictor of cyber bullying among primary school children. *World Academy of Science. Engineering & Technology, 67*, 167–171.

Dooley, J. J., Pyżalski, J., & Cross, D. (2009). Cyberbullying versus face-to-face bullying. *Zeitschrift für Psychologie. The Journal of Psychology, 217*(4), 182–188.

Dowell, E. B., Burgess, A. W., & Cavanaugh, D. J. (2009). Clustering of Internet risk behaviors in a middle school student population. *The Journal of School Health, 79*(1), 547–553. doi:10.1111/j.1746-1561.2009.00447.x

Eales, R. T. J., & Byrd, L. M. (1997). Virtually deschooling society: Authentic collaborative learning via the Internet. *Webnet 97 World Conference of the WWW, Internet & Intranet Proceedings.* Toronto, Canada.

Erdur-Baker, Ö., & Tanrıkulu, İ. (2010). Psychological consequences of cyberbullying experiences among Turkish secondary school children. *Procedia-Social and Behavioral Sciences, 2*, 2771–2776. doi:10.1016/j.sbspro.2010.03.413

Firat, M. (2010). *Bilgi Toplumunda Eğitimin Sürekliliği ve Okulların Geleceği.* International Conference on New Trends in Education and their Implications. Antalya, Turkey.

Goebert, D., Else, I., Matsu, C., Chung-Do, J., & Chang, J. (2011). The impact of cyberbullying on substance use and mental health in a multiethnic sample. *Maternal and Child Health Journal, 15*(8), 1282–1286. doi:10.1007/s10995-010-0672-x

Grigg, D. W. (2010). Cyber-aggression: Definition and concept of cyberbullying. *Australian Journal of Guidance & Counselling, 20*(2), 143–156. doi:10.1375/ajgc.20.2.143

Hinduja, S., & Patchin, J. W. (2010). Bullying, cyberbullying, and suicide. *Archives of Suicide Research, 14*(3), 206–221. doi:10.1080/138111 18.2010.494133

Illich, I. (1973). *Deschooling society*. Harmondsworth, UK: Penguin.

Ito, M., Baumer, S., & Bittanti, M. boyd, d., Cody, R., Herr-Stephenson, B., et al. (2010). *Hanging out, messing around, and geeking out: Kids living and learning with new media*. The John D. and Catherine T. MacArthur Foundation Series on Digital Media and Learning. Cambridge, MA: MIT Press.

Juvonen, J., & Gross, E. (2008). Extending the school grounds? – Bullying experiences in cyberspace. *The Journal of School Health, 78*(9), 496–506. doi:10.1111/j.1746-1561.2008.00335.x

Katzer, C., Fetchenhauer, D., & Belschak, F. (2009). Cyberbullying: Who are the victims? *Journal of Media Psychology: Theories, Methods, and Applications, 21*(1), 25–36. doi:10.1027/1864-1105.21.1.25

Kennedy, T. L. M., Smith, A., Wells, A. T., & Wellman, B. (2008). *Networked families*. Washington, DC: The Pew Internet & American Life Project.

König, A., Gollwitzer, M., & Steffgen, G. (2010). Cyberbullying as an act of revenge? *Australian Journal of Guidance & Counselling, 20*(2), 210–224. doi:10.1375/ajgc.20.2.210

Kowalski, R. M., Limber, P., & Agatston, P. W. (2008). *Bullying in the digital age*. Boston, MA: Blackwell Publishing.

Lenhart, A., & Madden, M. (2005). *Teens and technology*. Washington, DC: The Pew Internet & American Life Project.

Li, Q. (2007). Bullying in the new playground: Research into cyberbullying and cyber victimization. *Australian Journal of Educational Technology, 23*(4), 435–454.

Livingstone, S., & Bober, M. (2005). *UK children go online: Final report of key project findings*. Retrieved from http://www.lse.ac.uk/collections/children-go-online/UKCGO_Final_report.pdf

Livingstone, S., & Haddon, L. (2009). *EU kids online: Final report*. London, UK: EU Kids Online.

Madden, M., & Zickuhr, K. (2011). *65% of online adults use social networking sites*. Washington, DC: Pew Internet & American Life Project. Retrieved from http://pewinternet.org/~/media//Files/Reports/2011/PIP-SNS-Update-2011.pdf

Mason, K. L. (2008). Cyberbullying: A preliminary assessment for school personnel. *Psychology in the Schools, 45*(4), 323–348. doi:10.1002/pits.20301

Mesch, G. S. (2009). Parental mediation, online activities, and cyberbullying. *Cyberpsychology & Behavior, 12*(4), 387–393. doi:10.1089/cpb.2009.0068

Morales, M. (2011). Cyberbullying. *Journal of Consumer Health on the Internet, 15*(4), 406–419. doi:10.1080/15398285.2011.623593

National Center for Education Statistic (NCES). (2011). *Student reports of bullying and cyberbullying: Results from the 2007 school crime supplement to the National Crime Victimization Survey*. Washington, DC: Author. Retrieved http://nces.ed.gov/pubs2011/2011336.pdf

Navarro, R., Yubero, S., Larrañaga, E., & Martínez, V. (2012). Children's cyberbullying victimization: Associations with social anxiety and social competence in a Spanish sample. *Child Indicators Research, 5*(2).

News, B. B. C. (November, 16, 2009). *Cyberbullies hit primary schools*. Retrieved from http://news.bbc.co.uk/2/hi/uk_news/education/8359780.stm

Nocentini, A., Calmaestra, J., Schultze-Krumbholz, A., Scheithauer, H., Ortega, R., & Menesini, E. (2010). Cyberbullying: Labels, behaviours and definition in three European countries. *Australian Journal of Guidance & Counselling, 20*(2), 129–142. doi:10.1375/ajgc.20.2.129

Ofcom. (2011). *A nation addicted to smartphones.* Retrieved from http://consumers.ofcom.org.uk/2011/08/a-nation-addicted-to-smartphones/

Olweus, D. (1991). Bully/victim problems among school children: Some basic facts and effects of a school based intervention program. In Pepler, D., & Rubin, K. (Eds.), *The development and treatment of childhood aggression* (pp. 411–448). Hillsdale, NJ: Erlbaum.

Olweus, D. (1993). Bullies on the playground: The role of victimization. In Hart, C. (Ed.), *Children on the playground: Research perspectives and applications* (pp. 85–128). New York, NY: SUNY Press.

Patchin, J. W., & Hinduja, S. (2006). Bullies move beyond the schoolyard: A preliminary look at cyberbullying. *Youth Violence and Juvenile Justice, 4*(2), 148–169. doi:10.1177/1541204006286288

Pepler, D., Craig, W. M., & O'Connell, P. (1999). Understanding bullying from a dynamic systems perspective. In Slater, A., & Muir, D. (Eds.), *The Blackwell reader in developmental psychology* (pp. 440–451). Oxford, UK: Blackwell Publishing.

Pew Internet & American Life Project. (2012). *Trend data.* Retrieved: http://pewinternet.org/Static-Pages/Trend-Data/Whos-Online.aspx

Price, M., & Dalgleish, J. (2010). Cyberbullying experiences, impacts and coping strategies as described by Australian young people. *Youth Studies Australia, 29*(2), 51–59.

Rideout, V. J., Foehr, U. G., & Roberts, D. F. (2010). *Generation M2: Media in the lives of 8-to-18-year-olds.* Menlo Park, CA: KFF. Retrieved: http://www.kff.org/entmedia/upload/8010.pdf

Schneider, S. K., O'Donnell, L., Stueve, A., & Coulter, R. W. S. (2012). Cyberbullying, school bullying, and psychological distress: A regional census of high school students. *American Journal of Public Health, 102*(1), 171–177. doi:10.2105/AJPH.2011.300308

Schoffstall, C. L., & Cohen, R. (2011). Cyber aggression: The relation between online offenders and offline social competence. *Social Development, 20*(3), 587–604. doi:10.1111/j.1467-9507.2011.00609.x

Schultze-Krumbholz, A., & Scheithauer, H. (2009). Social-behavioral correlates of cyberbullying in a German student sample. *Zeitschrift für Psychologie. The Journal of Psychology, 217*(4), 224–226.

Shariff, S. (2008). *Cyberbullying.* New York, NY: Routledge.

Shariff, S., & Gouin, R. (2005). *Cyberdilemmas: Gendered hierarchies, free expression and cyber-safety in schools.* Retrieved January 30, 2012, from http://www.oii.ox.ac.uk/microsites/cybersafety/?view=papers

Siegle, D. (2010). Cyberbullying and sexting: Technology abuses of the 21st century. *Gifted Child Today, 33*(2), 14–16.

Smith, A. (2011). *Americans and their cell phones.* Washington, DC: Pew Internet & American Life Project. Retrieved from http://pewinternet.org/~/media//Files/Reports/2011/Cell%20Phones%202011.pdf

Smith, P. K., Mahdavi, J., Carvalho, M., Fisher, S., Russell, S., & Tippett, N. (2008). Cyberbullying: Its nature and impact in secondary school pupils. *Journal of Child Psychology and Psychiatry, and Allied Disciplines, 49*(4), 376–385. doi:10.1111/j.1469-7610.2007.01846.x

Sourander, A., Brunstein Klomek, A., Ikonen, M., Lindroos, J., Luntamo, T., & Koskelainen, M. (2010). Psychosocial risk factors associated with cyberbullying among adolescents: A population-based study. *Archives of General Psychiatry, 67*(7), 720–728. doi:10.1001/archgenpsychiatry.2010.79

Strom, P. S., & Strom, R. D. (2005). When teens turn cyberbullies. *Education Digest,* (December): 35–41.

Tangen, D., & Campbell, M. (2010). Cyberbullying prevention: One primary school's approach. *Australian Journal of Guidance & Counselling, 20*(2), 225–234. doi:10.1375/ajgc.20.2.225

The World Bank. (2011). *Internet users.* Retrieved from http://data.worldbank.org/indicator/it.net.user.p2

Topçu, Ç., Erdur-Baker, Ö., & Çapa-Aydin, Y. (2008). Examination of cyberbullying experiences among Turkish students from different school types. *Cyberpsychology & Behavior, 11*(6), 643–648. doi:10.1089/cpb.2007.0161

Twyman, K., Saylor, C., Taylor, L. A., & Comeaux, C. (2010). Comparing children and adolescents engaged in cyberbullying to matched peers. *Cyberpsychology, Behavior, and Social Networking, 13*(2), 195–199. doi:10.1089/cyber.2009.0137

Vandebosch, H., & Van Cleemput, K. (2009). Cyberbullying among youngsters: Profiles of bullies and victims. *New Media & Society, 11*(8), 1349–1371. doi:10.1177/1461444809341263

Walker, J. L. (2009). *The contextualized rapid resolution cycle intervention model for cyberbullying,* Unpublished dissertation, Arizona State University, Tempe, Arizona.

Willard, N. (2005). *Educator's guide to cyberbullying and cyberthreats.* Retrieved from February 1, 2012, from http://www.cyberbully.org/cyberbully/docs/cbcteducator.pdf

Willard, N. (2007). *Cyberbullying and cyberthreats: Responding to the challenge of online social aggression, threats, and distress.* Champaign, IL: Research Press.

Wong-Lo, M., Bullock, L. M., & Gable, R. A. (2011). Cyber bullying: Practices to face digital aggression. *Emotional & Behavioural Difficulties, 16*(3), 317–325. doi:10.1080/13632752.2011.595098

Yilmaz, H. (2011). Cyberbullying in Turkish middle schools: An exploratory study. *School Psychology International, 32*(6), 645–654. doi:10.1177/0143034311410262

Yu, A. Y., Tian, S. W., Vogel, D., & Chi-Wai Kwok, R. (2010). Can learning be virtually boosted? An investigation of online social networking impacts. *Computers & Education, 55*(4), 1494–1503. doi:10.1016/j.compedu.2010.06.015

ADDITIONAL READING

Agatston, P. W., Kowalski, R., & Limber, S. (2007). Students' perspectives on cyber bullying. *The Journal of Adolescent Health, 41,* 59–60. doi:10.1016/j.jadohealth.2007.09.003

Amichai-Hamburger, Y., & Ben-Artzi, E. (2003). Loneliness and Internet use. *Computers in Human Behavior, 19,* 71–80. doi:10.1016/S0747-5632(02)00014-6

Arıcak, O. T. (2009). Psychiatric symptomatology as a predictor of cyberbullying among university students. *Eurasian Journal of Educational Research, 34,* 167–184.

Attewell, P., Suazo-Garcia, B., & Battle, J. (2003). Computers and young children: Social benefit or social problem? *Social Forces, 82*(1), 277–296. doi:10.1353/sof.2003.0075

Betz, C. L. (2011). Cyberbullying: The virtual threat. *Journal of Pediatric Nursing, 26*(4), 283–284. doi:10.1016/j.pedn.2011.04.002

Catherine, E. (2010). Social media: Opportunity or risk? *Computer Fraud & Security, 6,* 8–10.

Cheung, C. M. K., Chiu, P. Y., & Lee, M. K. O. (2011). Online social networks: Why do students use Facebook? *Computers in Human Behavior, 27*(4), 1337–1343. doi:10.1016/j.chb.2010.07.028

Civelek, M. E. (2009). *İnternet çağı dinamikleri.* İstanbul, Turkey: Beta Yayınları.

Coget, J. F., Yamauchi, Y., & Suman, M. (2002). The Internet, social networks and loneliness. *IT&Society, 1*(1), 180–201.

Collier, A., & Magid, L. (2010). *A parents' guide to Facebook.* Retrieved from http://www.connectsafely.org/pdfs/fbparents.pdf

Conn, K. (2010). Cyberbullying and other student technology misuses in K-12 American schools: The legal landmines. *Widener Law Review, 16*(1), 89–100.

David-Ferdon, C., & Hertz, M. F. (2007). Electronic media, violence, and adolescents: An emerging health problem. *The Journal of Adolescent Health, 41*, 1–5. doi:10.1016/j.jadohealth.2007.08.020

Erdur-Baker, O. (2009). Cyberbullying and its correlation to traditional bullying, gender and frequent and risky usage of internet-mediated communication tools. *New Media & Society, 12*(1), 109–125. doi:10.1177/1461444809341260

Eroğlu, Y. (2011). *Koşullu öz-değer, riskli internet davranışları ve siber zorbalık/mağduriyet arasındaki ilişkinin incelenmesi.* Unpublished Master Thesis, Sakarya University Institute of Educational Sciences.

Katzer, C. (2009). Cyberbullying in Germany. *Zeitschrift für Psychologie. The Journal of Psychology, 217*(4), 222–223.

Kowalski, R. M., Limber, S. P., & Agatston, P. W. (2012). *Cyberbullying in the digital age.* Malden, MA: Wiley-Blackwell.

Lam, L. T., Peng, Z., Mai, J., & Jing, J. (2009). Factors associated with Internet addiction among adolescents. *Cyberpsychology & Behavior, 12*, 1–5. doi:10.1089/cpb.2009.0036

Liang, W. (2010). Cyberbullying, Let the computer help. *The Journal of Adolescent Health, 47*(2), 209. doi:10.1016/j.jadohealth.2010.04.013

Marczak, M., & Coyne, I. (2010). Cyberbullying at school: Good practice and legal aspects in the United Kingdom. *Australian Journal of Guidance & Counselling, 20*(2), 182–193. doi:10.1375/ajgc.20.2.182

Meerkerk, G. J., Eijden, R. J. J., Vermulst, A. A., & Garretsen, H. F. L. (2009). The compulsive internet use scale (CIUS): Some psychometric properties. *Cyberpsychology & Behavior, 12*(1), 1–6. doi:10.1089/cpb.2008.0181

Morrison, C. M., & Gore, H. (2010). The relationship between excessive Internet use and depression: A questionnaire-based study of 1,319 young people and adults. *Psychopathology, 43*(2), 121–126. doi:10.1159/000277001

Mottram, A. J., & Fleming, M. J. (2009). Extraversion, impulsivity, and online group membership as predictors of problematic Internet use. *Cyberpsychology & Behavior, 12*(3), 319–321. doi:10.1089/cpb.2007.0170

Nicholson, A. (2011). Schools, bullying, and the law. *Legaldate, 23*(2), 2–4.

O'Keeffe, G. S., & Clarke-Pearson, K., & Council on Communications and Media. (2011). The impact of social media on children, adolescents, and families. *Pediatrics, 127*(4), 800–804. doi:10.1542/peds.2011-0054

Patchin, J. W., & Hinduja, S. (2012). *Cyberbullying prevention and response: Expert perspectives.* New York, NY: Routledge.

Paul, S., Smith, P. K., & Blumberg, H. H. (2010). Addressing cyberbullying in school using the quality circle approach. *Australian Journal of Guidance & Counselling, 20*(2), 157–168. doi:10.1375/ajgc.20.2.157

Raskauskas, J., & Stoltz, A. D. (2007). Involvement in traditional and electronic bullying among adolescents. *Developmental Psychology, 43*, 564–575. doi:10.1037/0012-1649.43.3.564

Siegle, D. (2011). Facing Facebook: A guide for nonteens. *Gifted Child Today, 34*(2), 14–19.

Slonje, R., & Smith, P. K. (2008). Cyberbullying: Another main type of bullying? *Scandinavian Journal of Psychology, 49*(2), 147–154. doi:10.1111/j.1467-9450.2007.00611.x

Totan, T. (2007). Okulda zorbalığı önlemede eğitimcilere ve ebeveynlere öneriler. *AİBÜ Eğitim Fakültesi Dergisi, 7*(2), 190–202.

Uçanok, Z., Karasoy, D., & Durmuş, E. (2011). *Yeni Bir Akran Zorbalığı Türü Olarak Sanal Zorbalık: Ergenlerde Yaygınlığı ve Önemi*. Unpublished TUBITAK Project Report, Project No: 108K424.

Willard, N. E. (2007). *Cyberbullying and cyberthreats: Responding to the problem of online agression, threats, and distress*. Research Press.

Wright, V. H., Joy, J. B., Christopher, T. I., & Heather, N. O. (2009). Cyberbullying: Using virtual scenarios to educate and raise awareness. *Journal of Computing in Teacher Education, 26*(1), 35–42.

KEY TERMS AND DEFINITIONS

Bullying: Repeated aggressive behaviors that are intended to harm another person or a group of people.

Cyberbullying: Technical-oriented or relational-oriented harmful behaviors toward a real person or a corporation by using information and communication technologies.

Direct Bullying: Covert acts of aggressive behaviors that involve physical and verbal attacks such as pushing, hitting, teasing, intimidating, and insulting.

Direct Cyberbullying: Acts of aggressive or harassing behaviors through electronic means that exclusively target a person or a group of people. It involves physical (e.g. sending viruses), verbal (e.g. threating on the phone), and non-verbal (or visual) (e.g. sending pictures) cyberbullying depending on the specific medium through which harassing behavior is expressed.

Disinhibition Effect: Positive or negative changes in people's behaviors when intracting online with others.

E-Bullying: The kind of cyberbullying that requires a person or a group to have the necessary technical skills to harm the other person. The power relation between the cyber bully and cyber victim is asymmetric in that the cyber bully have the technical skills to harm the other person while the cyber victim often lacks such skills and is left incapacitated.

E-Communication Bullying: This kind of Cyberbullying refers to the social side of cyberbullying and involves name-calling, insulting, spreading rumors, sharing pictures through communication technologies. This type of cyberbullying involves the cyber bully, cyber victim, and cyber onlookers.

Indirect Bullying: Overt acts of aggressive behaviors that target damaging a person's or a group of people's social relations and involves behaviors like gossiping, spreading rumors, and excluding someone from a group.

Indirect Cyberbullying: Acts of aggressive or harassing behaviors through electronic means towards a person or a group of people that involve displaying about the person or a group of people to other people.

Chapter 17
Barriers to Emerging Technology and Social Media Integration in Higher Education:
Three Case Studies

Ana Adi
Bournemouth University, UK

Christina Gasser Scotte
Lancaster University, UK

ABSTRACT

With technological innovation and social media infiltrating every field of activity, it was only a matter of time until universities and faculty would need to embrace the technological challenge. This chapter offers three case studies of social media training delivery in universities and researcher centres in the UK, USA, and Bahrain. These case studies cover the use of emerging technologies in higher education research, teaching and policy, and associated first- and second-order barriers to their implementation. Results and impact of the training sessions, including questions asked and feedback provided by participants are also discussed. The chapter emphasizes the increasing interest in training in emerging technologies for educators and affiliated university staff, but also highlights the challenges faced when promoting tools and platforms not supported by either the IT infrastructure of the universities or the policies in place.

INTRODUCTION

Why do we need to integrate emerging technologies and social media in higher education? The first reason is that universities are knowledge-producing and knowledge-sharing systems, and the world is undergoing a fundamental transformation in how it views, utilizes, and shares knowledge. Knowledge is changing due to newer technologies, as well as the ability of the 'net generation' to utilize those technologies to communicate and learn in ways that have heretofore been impossible (Tapscott, 1988). Gibbons et al. (1994) dif-

DOI: 10.4018/978-1-4666-2970-7.ch017

ferentiated between the two types of knowledge, the knowledge of the industrial age and new knowledge. The knowledge of the industrial age has been termed Mode 1 knowledge; which was individually and academically created, and easily disseminated by the traditional university system utilizing books and lectures. The knowledge of the Information Age, Mode 2 knowledge, which is team created; interdisciplinary in its generation having applications in the real world that far surpass mode 1 types of knowledge. Universities of the future will need to make the transition from specializing in mode 1 knowledge to mode 2 knowledge to enjoy continued success in the knowledge economy. Technology implementation will be vital to the success of universities in making this transition, allowing interdisciplinary communication and knowledge generation in ways that have never been seen before.

The second reason for technology integration in higher education institutions is that the world has shifted from an industrialized economy to a knowledge economy (c.f. Hargreaves, 2000), and this change must be reflected in university classrooms. While in an industrial age, universities could function as sources of knowledge which prepared individuals for lifetime employment in a set career. However, society is now thirty years into the Information Age (Knight, Knight, and Teghe, 2006), and today's students need technologies to be fully integrated into the higher educational system, as they are in industry at large.

The evolution to a knowledge economy implies that knowledge will be the new capital of the future, which should be an occasion to rejoice for universities around the globe. Indeed, it means that universities should be revving into high gear, producing newer, better knowledge faster than ever. However, the bureaucracy and institutionalization incumbent in most places of higher education makes them resistant to change (Crow, 2012); although many scholars recognize the need for a fundamental alteration of the current system.

According to Wheeler (2004), "there is...growing opinion that the very fabric of traditional education must change, purely because it is a system originally set up to meet the needs of the industrial revolution, and is now hopelessly outmoded."

These sentiments were echoed by President Crow of Arizona State University in his 2012 presentation: *The Future of the New American University*. He argued that universities need to change from agencies to enterprises, committed to 'knowledge entrepreneurship' and creating graduates who have "knowledge in multiple areas to multiple depths" and "the ability to learn anything" so that they can work for many different employers in a wide range of occupations in the future. Crow's comments highlight the fact that knowledge itself is changing, along with the needs of graduates and the needs of industry. In order to discuss the changes to technological and social media integration as well as their associated barriers, it is first necessary to discuss the concept of change itself.

CHANGE

In their book, *Change: Principles of Problem Formation and Problem Resolution*, Watzlawick, Weakland and Fisch (1974) pioneered two differentiated concepts of change: first-order change and second-order change. First-order changes are fairly linear in nature and would be those which make small, incremental changes to current practices. Second-order changes, however, are non-linear, and involve a transformation from one state to another. For example, making a change where the problem is viewed from a different perspective, causing large changes to practice or a transformation of the system in which the problem resides. Maier (1987) used an excellent example with water, stating that a first order change would be water become warmer or colder, but a second-order change would be water changing to ice or steam.

Maier also stated that second-order changes take greater creativity and time investment, and that one should know if he or she is trying to create first-order or second-order change before attempting the process.

Applying these concepts to technological implementation, an example of a first-order change would be simply utilizing technology for test-taking rather than a paper method. Second-order changes are much larger in scope, and overcoming them requires changing fundamental beliefs about the situation, which leads to an evolution of practice. A relevant example would be utilizing technology so that students from the marketing department can communicate with students from the engineering department to complete a joint project on designing and marketing a new product. Second-order changes tend to lead to structural changes in overall systems due to their fundamental nature.

BARRIERS TO CHANGE

Brickner (1995) advanced these two concepts of change into first-order and second-order barriers to change, which are particularly relevant to the implementation of technology in an educational setting. He described first-order barriers as being those which prohibited linear steps forward and second-order barriers as those which prohibited fundamental or transformational changes in the system or the manner in which technology is implemented. First-order barriers have subsequently been described as extrinsic to teachers: such as equipment, time, training, support; and administrative and policy barriers (Ertmer, 1999; Means and Olson, 1997). Conversely, second-order barriers have been described as being intrinsic to teachers, such as technology-related beliefs, fears, and resistance to change. Kerr (1996) mentioned that teachers may not even know these second-order barriers exist, as they are deeply-rooted in teachers' underlying belief systems. This chapter will

use the idea of first-order barriers as external and second-order barriers as internal in its literature review and case studies.

First-Order Barriers

Research on first-order, or external barriers, can be roughly divided into two categories: resource barriers such as hardware and software, and policy barriers such as time, training, administrative and support policies. A study by Johnston and Mc-Cormack (1996) found that university lecturers complained of inadequate equipment or poorly equipped teaching spaces. Such results might have been expected in 1996, when universities were still upgrading basic resources, a more recent study by Brinkerhoff (2006) found resources to still be the one of the most ubiquitous barriers, including lack of computers, peripherals, software, or solid Internet access. Although access to technological resources is still an abiding obstacle, there are first-order policy barriers which must be considered in addition to resources such as time, expertise, access, and support for the new technologies (Antonacci, 2002), as well as university policies to overcome these barriers.

Brinkerhoff (2006) found several first-order administrative policy barriers to technology integration; including policies that restrict teachers from using outside software on district computers, lack of time allocated to prepare lessons, curriculum focus on test preparation, separation of IT staff and faculty, and teachers who were afraid to ask IT coordinators for help due to the overworked nature of the IT department. Other scholars have also found administrative or institutional policy barriers to technology integration, particularly surrounding insufficient professional development. Loveless (2003) found teacher development too focused on basic technological competence rather than the use of technology in the classroom. Jensen and Lewis (2001) and Mouza (2002) both cited lack of continued support after professional development, with Mousa finding that this lack of follow-up renders the impact of professional development ineffective in actually integrating technology in the classroom. In addition, Brush, Glazewski, Rutnowski, and Berg (2003) reported that teachers themselves felt they were not provided with adequate support to successfully integrate technology into their classrooms.

A study of technology adoption by medical faculty by Zayim, Yildirim and Saka (2006) asked participants what university policies could be put in place to encourage the adoption of new technologies. They found that over 90% of all participants responded that university policy and plans for the diffusion of IT were very important incentives for IT adoption, especially investments in infrastructure, professional training and ongoing support, and financial support. In addition, over 60% of the participants rated reward structures and reduced teaching loads as important incentives to integrate technology.

Much of the research around implementation of technology has focused upon first-order barriers such as those above, especially resources. Fisher, Dwyer, and Yocam (1996) postulate this is due to the fact that first-order barriers are relatively easy to overcome assuming that there is enough money allocated to overcome them. Ertmer (1999) also mentions that this focus could be due to the fact that earlier models of technology integration indicated that if equipment and training were provided, classroom integration would follow. An argument has emerged rather recently that perhaps educational institutions have had too much focus on tangible barriers to the detriment of intangible barriers (Kagima and Hausafus, 2000). Although the presence of technology allows for the capability of using technology to drive learning, technology does not cause learning or knowledge transference in and of itself, enhanced learning, or substantial change in schools (Jasinsky, 1998; Johnston and McCormack, 1996; EDC, 1996). Furthermore, simply offering the latest technological devices or applications with the required resources does not mean that a university is offering a program which utilizes the power of technology to drive the knowledge economy, or that it provides a learning environment which is conducive to the creation of mode 2 knowledge. The question to be asked now is the following: if the focus has been on overcoming these tangible resource barriers, have we overcome them?

Table 1 shows a review of the literature from 12 of the authors in this area from 1999-2011. The top five first-order barriers to technological integration which have been found most often in higher education are the following: (1) lack of time, (2) poor administrative policy and lack of support, (3) lack of access to labs and resources, (4) professional development, and (5) infrastructure. Interestingly, of the top five, three are focused on policy barriers such as time, administrative policy and support, and professional development which show up as factors 23 times in the studies. Resource barriers such as access to resources and infrastructure only show up 9 times in those same studies, so it would appear that these barriers are becoming less important at the higher education level.

Second-Order Barriers

The same review of the literature for first-order barriers provided a list of the most found second-order, or internal barriers, as well. Of the internal barriers, only three are mentioned more than three times. The top five internal barriers to technological integration in the classroom are the following: (1) technical skills and knowledge, (2) integration knowledge, (3) a vision of the benefits or purpose of using technology in the classroom, (4) pedagogical knowledge, and (5) professional attitude. Overall, there are far fewer internal barriers than external barriers which appear in the studies, and most the barriers mentioned seem to focus on direct application and integration of technology in the classroom.

Table 1. Barriers found in higher education studies 1999-2011

Authors	Year	External Barriers														Internal Barriers					
		Teacher Time	Admin Policy and Support	Access / Labs / Resources	Professional Development	Tech Support	Incentives	Culture / Social Support	Infrastructure	Hardware/Software	Funding	Internet Access	Leadership	Curr / Assessment / Standards	Training time	Tech Skills / Knowledge	Integration Knowledge	Vision of Benefits / Purpose	Pedagogical Knowledge	Professional Attitude	Motivation
Spotts	1999	X	X	X				X										X		X	
Beggs	2000	X		X	X											X	X				
Chizmar and Williams	2001	X	X				X	X		X								X		X	
Butler and Sellbom	2002	X	X	X		X			X	X		X					X				
City College of San Francisco	2003			X		X										X					
Wilson	2003	X	X				X				X					X			X		
Brzycki and Dudt	2005	X	X	X	X			X	X				X					X			X
Schoepp	2005		X		X	X	X							X		X	X				
Marwan and Sweeney	2010	X	X		X						X		X						X		
Li and Walsh	2010	X	X		X										X		X				
Mtebe, Dachi, Raphael	2011			X			X		X			X									X
Jensen & Folley	2011	X			X	X										X					
Total:		9	8	6	6	4	4	3	3	2	2	2	2	1	1	5	4	3	2	2	2

Although there are far fewer second-order barriers listed in Table 1, overcoming second order barriers may be much more important to the actual integration of technology into university educational systems. One illustration of this is the fact that several of the studies have shown that most faculty members are integrating only the most basic of technologies. A study by Becker and Riel (2000) showed technology use by faculty: 61% used e-mail, 38% used the internet, and 10% used multimedia packages. A study by Cuban, Kirkpatrick, and Peck (2001) showed that most faculty were using technology for word processing. A study by Wilson (2003) found that when faculty were asked to create e-learning materials or CDs, they were often turned in late.

A very recent study by Jensen and Folley (2011) showed that while 95% of the faculty agreed that they used information and communication technologies (ICTs) to prepare for most of their teaching, only 72% were using slideshow presentations regularly, 55% were using virtual learning environments (VLEs) regularly, and 14% were using e-assessment regularly. Less than 5% of the faculty were regularly using e-portfolios, podcasts, blogs, wikis, or social bookmarks. This is perhaps because faculty survey results showed the technologies they believed would positively impact their teaching were slideshow presentations, VLEs, and e-assessment. However, faculty largely disagreed that podcasts, e-portfolios, blogging, wikis, and social bookmarking would have a positive impact on their classes. The most interesting point here is that the staff who "strongly disagree" with the use of these technologies also indicated that they had never used the technologies, and this lack of familiarity with the material would certainly affect their ability to understand the potential of these technologies to enhance teaching.

Another study by Enyon (2008), comprised of 41 interviews at two UK universities, reported several more curriculum-specific attitudinal barriers to the adoption of IT in the minds of the faculty and staff: the web would only be useful in teaching certain areas, could not be used for more vocational needs, and could not be used to develop critical thinking or other higher-level skills. In other words, the interviewees felt that new technologies would be inappropriate for use in many areas of teaching.

Interactions between First- and Second-Order Barriers

Several studies on barriers at other levels have found interesting results which show the interaction between first-order and second-order barriers. For example, a study by Ertmer, Addison, Lane, Ross and Woods in 1999 found that negative beliefs (a second-order barrier), could interact with first-order barriers such as classroom organization. They also found that beliefs could affect how teachers used technology in the classroom, whether it was seen as a tool for busywork or reward, or whether it was integrated into the curriculum as a learning tool. A third study found that first-order barriers tend to hide the existence of second-order barriers (Marwan and Sweeney, 2010). A study undertaken in Turkey on a group of 155 medical faculty members revealed that mainstream faculty, more than the early adopters, considered first-order barriers, such as the lack of computers, reward structure, and training opportunities among the biggest barriers in adopting technology (Zayim, Yildirim and Saka, 2006). Finally, four studies found that less teaching experience correlates with more barriers (Meskill, Mossop, DiAngelo & Pasquale, 2002; O'Mahony, 2003; Spotts, 1999; Staples, Pugach and Hines, 2005).

The studies above highlight an interesting feature found in the data from Table 1. Since 2005, the need for professional development has been recognized more often among external barriers, and the need for knowledge regarding how to integrate new technologies into the curriculum has also been recognized more often as a barrier. In many places, first-order resource barriers have been largely overcome, allowing other barriers to emerge in regards to the use and integration of these technologies in the curriculum. It would seem that the focus now needs to be on training teachers with technical skills and knowledge, as well as the pedagogical knowledge to properly integrate these technologies in the classroom. Jasinski (1998, p. 1) argued this over a decade ago; "the key to changing conditions for improving learning is how these [technological] options and opportunities are utilized by teachers and learners."

Emphasis should be placed upon the teachers in Jasinski's statement, as they are the designers of the curriculum and the individuals who will ultimately integrate new technologies into their classes. The importance of faculty in the implementation of institutional change has been acknowledged by many scholars. Bates (2000, p. 95) argued that "because of the central role that faculty members play in the work of the universities and colleges, any change, especially in core activities such as teaching and research, is completely dependent on their support." Surry and Land (2000) applied this to technology adoption, arguing that one of the major reasons why universities have not adopted new technologies is that the key role of the faculty in creating change is ignored by university-wide administrative policies. Unfortunately, or perhaps fortunately, this is one instance in which faculty attitudes and motivations cannot be ignored. Faculty must be trained, motivated and provided with the appropriate pedagogical knowledge and understanding of how to incorporate these new technologies into the curriculum to drive universities back to the forefront of education.

One of the most important things to note is that in the last twelve years, not much has changed, and changes which have occurred have been largely incremental rather than transformational. This echoes the sentiment of Al-Batainein and Brooks (2003) who mentioned that although technological innovations and opportunities are advancing at an almost logarithmic pace, the issues around technological integration in education remain disturbingly constant.

Due to the research of the scholars mentioned thus far, these barriers are becoming well-known and are continuing to be studied in a variety of methods. The case studies presented in this chapter are another means of demonstrating these barriers, albeit by a different means. The forums for these case studies were seminars and workshops; the purpose of the first two cases being to teach faculty and staff new technological tools which they can integrate into their research and teaching practices. The last case being a workshop intended to design social media policy for university library use. These cases present insight into the barriers encountered even in situations intended to overcome those very barriers.

CASE STUDIES

The first-order and second-order barriers discussed in this chapter function as the foundation for three case studies of new media training and workshops offered to educators, researchers, and academic staff in the United Kingdom, United States, and Bahrain, and provide a platform for which to discuss their reception and challenges faced from an early-adopter's perspective. The first case study seminars were presented by Adi in 2009 and 2010 at various universities in the UK and USA including Caledonian University in Glasgow and the University of Kansas in Lawrence, Kansas, USA. The second case study workshops were presented by Adi in 2011 at Bahrain Polytechnic in the Kingdom of Bahrain. The third case study workshop on social media policy was presented by Adi in 2010 at the University of the West of Scotland. Taken together, the three case studies exemplify the combination of first- and second-order barriers facing university systems today and some of the efforts being undertaken to combat these barriers.

METHOD

A review of the literature to date indicates the following methods have been used to study barriers to technology integration in higher education: small, qualitative studies; studies with one school or multiple schools; and large, quantitative studies which are nationwide or include multiple nations (See Table 2).

Table 2. Type of study and study scale

Authors	Year	Scale	Type	Data Collection Method
Spotts	1999	one university	qualitative	semi-structured interviews
Beggs	2000	multiple universities	quantitative	questionnaires
Chizmar and Williams	2001	one university	quantitative	questionnaires
Butler and Sellbom	2002	one university	quantitative	questionnaires
City College of San Francisco	2003	one university	quantitative	questionnaires
Wilson	2003	multiple universities	quantitative	questionnaires
Brzycki and Dudt	2005	multiple universities	report	several sources
Schoepp	2005	one university	quantitative	questionnaires
Marwan and Sweeney	2010	small qualitative	qualitative	semi-structured interviews
Li and Walsh	2010	multiple universities	quantitative	questionnaires and focus group
Mtebe, Dachi, Raphael	2011	one university	report	several sources
Jensen & Folley	2011	one university	quantitative	questionnaires

The case studies presented in this chapter contribute to the number of small, qualitative studies. The case study method is used for all three of the studies, as Yin (2003) argued that case studies should be used in three types of situations: when asking how or why, when researchers have little control over events, and when the focus is on mechanisms occurring within a real-life context. In addition, these case studies were exploratory in nature as these technologies are so new many participants had never heard of them. Due to the pattern of results discussed in the literature review regarding the similarity of different case studies spanning time and space over the past 30 years, the results of these case studies might be applicable to a number of university settings around the globe today.

Each university was chosen based upon the fact that they were interested in integrating new technologies. Participants and data collection methods were slightly different in each case, therefore they will be discussed within each individual study.

CASE STUDY 1: NEW MEDIA FOR RESEARCH: RESEARCHING WITH NEW MEDIA

Overview

During November 2009-2010, seminars were given to various universities in the USA and UK which focused on researching new media and were presented into two themes: researching new media and using new media tools for research. The premise of the seminar was that online tools could be used for research and presented them based on the function or data they could perform. Participants were researchers, lecturers and postgraduate students. After the presentations, a question-and-answer discussion session was conducted. The researcher noted main discussion themes after the sessions. Technological tools showcased were chosen based on the following criteria: free, easily accessible, either platform-dedicated or cross-platform or could be used for visualization purposes. Tools presented included Twitter, Trendistic, Trendsmap, Facebook, Backtype, WhosTalking, Wordle, and Many Eyes.

Twitter is a micro-blogging platform where users can communicate using a maximum of 140 characters per message. Twitter researchers benefit from a number of tools that provide data and insight due to users sharing their information into the public domain and due to Twitter's data access specifications. This has enabled the emergence of a variety of tools which have made possible the identification and observation of trends, user patterns, online sentiment or data archival.

Unlike Twitter, Facebook provides more challenges for use in research. There are only a few Facebook tools available enabling network visualizations which can be used to assess network affiliations, study network dynamics or observe age, gender and relationship distributions. In addition, Facebook tools not only required user login for use but also user approval in the sense that every network visualization is unique to the user who generated it. Therefore, for contextual searches and analysis, cross-platform tools are recommended. These included Backtype and WhosTalking, both social media research tools enabling conversation searches.

The seminar offered examples and illustration of how some tools were used for research while also providing a list of alternative tools performing similar functions. For example, tools like Trendistic and Trendsmap enabling researchers to compare volume of certain keywords used within Twitter either in comparison with other words or in relation to a geographical area were indicated to be useful in anticipating or observing interest in a topic, whereas tools like Twopular, Whatthetrend and TweetLabs were just mentioned.

The seminar also presented visualization tools, most of which required researchers to import or upload their datasets, unlike the Twitter, Facebook or cross-platform tools showcased earlier which retrieved data from the Internet. These visualization tools included Wordle, a website generating word clouds based on the frequency of the words within a given text; and ManyEyes, a collaborative platform developed by IBM for data visualization, requested researchers to bring their own data.

Results

Review of the questions asked in the seminars revealed three main themes: access, informed consent, and reliability, validity, and legitimacy.

- **Access:** Participants asked questions regarding whether the tools and platforms were browser-based or needed downloading. This reflected the participants concern that un-licensed software or pre-approved by the IT department will not be acceptable to be installed on university machines. Other inquiries were made about access to data – both of the participants themselves, as well as of other web users that might become subject of research studies.
- **Informed Consent:** Questions about informed consent were asked about conducting research on Facebook communities to which access is gained only after registration and login as well as about collecting data from micro-blogging site Twitter.
- **Reliability, Validity, and Legitimacy:** Concerns were also raised about the validity and reliability of the tools, their data retrieval algorithms and their value for research. As exemplified by a web site comment left after one of the seminars, a participant mentioned that his issue with the tools was "that there are so many of them, some are commercial, some are free and the research community remains sceptical [sic] about their merit as part of 'real' research" (McGillivray - as cited in Adi, 2010). A question regarding 'real' research

was asked as well, which was related to the established methods of data collection and analysis both for qualitative and quantitative research as presented in academic and scholarly literature and which represents the fundament of current research activities.

Discussion

Reflecting on the experience of delivering these seminars, there are several characteristics that all groups, irrespective of country and institution, share in common. The groups to which these seminars were presented included supporters of technology, as well as critics and skeptics. However, instead of dismissing technology and the tools presented, the groups raised many pertinent questions related to access and retrieval of data, ethics of researching online environments and communities and research policies and guidelines. This adds support to Bigum and Kenway's (1998) idea that individuals within these institutions are not opposed to the idea of technology itself, but that they question its use and relevance.

The most important finding from this research was that faculty have beliefs and fears which prohibit them from using newer technologies in their research methodologies. As the seminar presented alternative ways of conducting research and therefore of interpreting research methodologies, it lead to questions related to the researchers' understanding and fears towards using technology as part of their work, reinforcing some of the first- and second-order barriers discussed earlier in the chapter. For example, questions regarding access and approval of software, research policy and guidelines, ethics of researching in online communities, and informed consent illustrate definite first-order barriers, upholding Brinkeroff's (2006) finding that administrative policy barriers inhibit teachers from successfully integrating technology into their practices.

Second-order barriers such as educators' fears and perceptions of technology adoption can be seen in the questions about the validity and reliability of these tools and their value in 'real' research. These hint that educators are not only concerned about their ability to use the tools themselves, but also about the reception of the work by their peers. This partially reinforces Johnston and Mc-Cormack's (1996) findings in which teachers were worried that their colleagues were too entrenched in traditional methods of teaching to value newer methods, and that teachers have fears of implementing technology innovations in teaching. In this case it is applied to research methods rather than classroom methods. This also hints at the research policy behind tools which are allowed and accepted for use in higher education.

The after-seminar discussions reinforced many of the earlier findings on first- and second-order barriers, and raised some new questions about perceptions of the usefulness and validity of new technologies in higher education research. However, there is a wide gap between seminars of this nature and technology integration in the classroom. For technological adoption to happen, enthusiasm and demonstrations are not enough, especially for members of staff skeptical about technology. As previously evidenced by Bullock (2004), successful integration also requires time to practice, peer support and a forum of discussion. Due to the nature of the seminars, they were unable to provide time to practice the new technologies or ongoing peer support. However, the seminars covering new media tools for research have been instrumental in helping to overcome the last of these; creating a dialogue about the efficient uses of technology by researchers and educators.

CASE STUDY 2: TECHIE BREAK – 5 WEEKS, 5 DAYS, 5 SESSIONS OF TECHNOLOGY FOR EDUCATION

Overview

This case study is based on a series of technology workshops organized at Bahrain Polytechnic with the help of the institution's Professional Development Department in an attempt to overcome one of the major shortfalls of the first case study: the need to provide time for the staff to practice using the technology and understand how to integrate it into their pedagogy. Participation in the workshops was completely voluntary and limited due to the fact that workshops were offered during class time, and participants included faculty and staff from the entire Polytechnic.

To test interest in a potential series, one workshop was initially offered about using the alternative presentation software Prezi, which moves classroom and conference presentations away from the linear and static model of Microsoft's Office PowerPoint (Adi, 2011a). The workshop not only presented the software and its advantages and disadvantages, but also contextualized its use to the Polytechnic staff. Participants were provided with a step-by-step sign-up and set-up guide and were given an opportunity to create their own Prezi during the session benefiting from the feedback and support of a trained member of staff, already using the software. Follow-up and feedback opportunities were extended beyond the seminar, encouraging staff to try the software themselves. This model was adopted for all future workshops.

The workshop series that followed focused on cloud technologies, and presented tools and platforms that each performed specific functions that had potential to aid the teaching/learning process. Functions included online collaboration, data portability and cloud archiving. Other criteria used for selecting the platforms included "previous uses in academia, multiple data access options (such as browser-based, smartphone app and desktop application), automated synchronization, (…) and no or low cost" (Adi, 2011b).

The platforms chosen were: Mendeley, the reference manager and academic social network; Audioboo, the mobile and web platform for recording and sharing audio files; Evernote, the storing, sharing, organizing tool; Colaab, the real-time collaboration platform; and WebEx, the platform offering collaboration solutions for online meetings, remote support, webinars and online events. Mendeley was suggested to be used for building up a literature and academic references list or for research projects, Audioboo was presented as a potential solution for language lecturers. Finally, Colaab, Evernote and WebEx were presented as remote teaching and file sharing alternatives supporting and promoting blended learning.

Each workshop introduced the participants to the platform and provided a rationale for its integration in the classroom followed by potential examples of use. After discussing the features of the platforms, privacy settings and data protection, participants were given a series of exercises to perform, thus providing them with repeated opportunities to use the platforms while adding complexity to their activity. At the end of each seminar participants were also shown other tools and platforms performing similar functions giving them a choice to test and experiment with technology on their own.

Results

At the beginning of each seminar participants were invited to complete a questionnaire assessing their perception of technology use in the classroom, their experience with technology in general and web 2.0 tools in particular. At the end of the sessions, participants were asked to complete a second part of the questionnaire asking whether they believed that they would use technology more in their classes as a result of the course. Pre-workshop questionnaires included 17 items with Likert scales ranging from 1 to 7. Post-workshop questionnaires

had four additional items with Likert scales ranging from 1 to 7. Some participants wrote additional feedback in extra space provided. 67 participants in all attended one or more of the workshops, of which twenty-two returned usable questionnaires and five gave follow-up interviews three months after the workshops were complete (See Table 3).

It must be noted that this is perhaps not a normal sample of the entire staff, due to the fact that workshops were voluntary, so those who attended were attending specifically to increase their use of technology. However, several interesting results did emerge from the questionnaire data. Results show that faculty know that technology can enhance their work and are interested in increasing their technological capabilities, but they are less confident in using a variety of technologies and do not feel particularly tech-savvy. Second, although the workshops were voluntary, not all people who attended rated themselves as having a high level of interest in technology, a result similar to the first case study in this chapter. The mean interest was 5.45 out of 7, with five participants rating their general interest in technology as a 4 and one rating his or her level of interest as a 3..

The third, and perhaps most important, result was that participants actually thought that they would use the technology less after they completed the workshop (M=4.89) than they had anticipated upon entering the workshop (M=5.20). After the initial workshop on Prezi, one of the participants wrote in, "need much more practice on tech presentations...[I] usually make PowerPoint or Word files or borrowed ActivBoard (presentations)." ActivBoard was the latest technological innovation at the Polytechnic, and although faculty were required to attend two two-hour training sessions, many of the faculty were still unable to use ActivBoard in their lessons.

A second participant wrote that he would only use Prezi "if we can have correctly branded Prezis," indicating the need for the Polytechnic to purchase a proper license for the software, which was being

Table 3. Questionnaire results

Pre-Workshop Questionnaire	
Item	**Average**
Interest in increasing technological capabilities	6.00
Can use technology to enhance research and admin work	5.86
Level of interest in educational technology	5.85
Open to learning new technologies, even if difficult	5.77
Technology can be used to enhance teaching in a classroom	5.57
Technology is a necessity for today's students	5.54
Like using technology in for work	5.54
Integrating technology will help student's learning	5.47
Level of interest in technology	5.45
Exposure to new technologies is helpful for students	5.40
Using technology enhances student's education	5.36
Learning more about this technology will influence me to use it more in the classroom	5.20
Can confidently use various technologies	4.36
I am a technology person	4.09
Current level of online platforms knowledge	3.40
Current level of offline platforms knowledge	3.80
Worry about using new technologies due to breakdowns	2.81
Using technology in the classroom distracts students	2.27
Post-Workshop Questionnaire	
I will utilize this technology more in the classroom in the future after this course	4.89
I will utilize technology in general more in the future after this course	5.31

used on a trial basis with all of the faculty signing up for free licenses. Upon being asked what the greatest barrier was to using the new technologies from the workshop in the classroom, one of the follow-up interviewees stated, "Lack of time and resources, as there are time restraints...Adding to that, constant changes with class autonomy at times and changes to core courses."

One of the follow-up interviewees brought up another factor which has rarely been discussed; that of the political or external environment which might make teachers less likely to take risks:

I did actually do a lot of follow-up I made some Prezis to use...in the classroom and thought they were quite meaningful and tried to relate them to the students' needs. Then there were the political issues last year, and I was a little bit less willing to take a risk on something that I wasn't sure of.

The last question in the follow-up interviews: 'Do you believe that the benefits of using new technologies justify the effort expended to learn and implement new technologies in the classroom?' allowed participants to comment upon their general beliefs about the usefulness of new technologies in relation to the barriers of implementation. One of the participants stated: "I just have to say broadly, yes, or else we would still be talking blackboards. You've always got to try to move on and for different people, different things take more effort. I have a huge sense of achievement, it's empowering."

Another was not as positive, and mentioned that it all comes down to the platform and its uses, and the tutor's ability to choose the right platform for the learning objectives of the lesson. In addition to the questionnaire and interview results, there was an unanticipated result due to a policy issue regarding one of the proposed platforms, Dropbox, a web-based storage site with mobile and desktop applications that synchronize backed-up data which was on the seminar proposal list due to its portability, sharing and collaboration options.

However, weeks before the seminar series was due to start, a security glitch enabled users to log into any Dropbox account (McCullagh, 2011) without having a password. Taking into account that the recommendation to use Dropbox would have been for sharing working files, lecture notes or students' work for cross-marking, the threat to security had to be taken into account. Moreover, with paid collaboration software SharePoint already in use on campus, presenting Dropbox would have promoted a free and, in this case, less secure alternative. Therefore, days before the seminar series started it had to be withdrawn at the request of the ICT director of the Polytechnic and his concerns to data security and Internet traffic.

Discussion

The positive correlation between those teachers who believed that they could use technology to enhance teaching and the number of technological tools they were currently using in the classroom supports the idea that if teachers feel technology will enhance their teaching, they will be more apt to utilize new technological tools in the classroom.

The idea that teachers felt they were less likely to use the new technology after they had attended the workshop might be linked to a lack of continued professional development, as they knew they would not be receiving continued courses on that specific technology. This supports first-order policy barriers around professional development found by Jensen and Lewis (2001), Mouza (2002), and Brush, Glazewki, Rutnowski, and Berg (2003) who assert that teachers need continued development focusing on integrating new technologies into the classroom. Perhaps faculty members realized that planning courses and integrating the new technologies into their curricula would take more time than they had anticipated before arriving. In addition, using new technologies always raises more questions, and faculty members realized that there would not be continued support on-hand to answer questions during use, as the IT department was overloaded with its regular workload and could not provide

support for newer technologies not utilized by the whole institution. With financial and human resources being invested into implementing particular software on campuses, and with ICT departments still functioning on a "infrastructure control" mind-set, it not unusual for educators promoting the use of digital tools and platforms not to receive support from ICT, as in this case.

The case of Dropbox supports another type of first-order barrier, that of administrative and institutional policy barriers around implementing new technologies. This result supports Brinkeroff's (2006) finding that many institutions restrict teachers from using outside software on institutional computer equipment. Although in this case dropping Dropbox from the workshop list was necessary due to its security features, the reaction from the ICT administration of questioning the need for - and sometimes denying - new platforms is not unusual. Reactions like these should continue to raise questions about the cooperation between administrative and teaching personnel and about the need for more dialogue and integration of each other in the decision making process. While educators might enjoy some freedom in organizing their courses, both with regards to the content and the form in which they present them, they should not try to work around the IT department but rather with it. This brings up new questions regarding policy and technology acquisition as well as training, but this time the training goes beyond the classroom and into the IT room.

The feedback received from the Techie Break series was positive, however there are other workshop conditions which would have been more conducive to a significant change in practice. For example, a higher number of staff should have participated which could have been achieved if the workshop would have offered to specific departments rather than institution wide. Alternatively, the series should have been offered for another term, ensuring that past-participants continued to receive support and refresher-courses while also becoming advocates and supported for those who haven't yet attended the seminars.

Although the applied exercises and platform focused sessions were appreciated, only few platforms were adopted. In recent e-mail exchanges with past participants, Prezi, Evernote and Wordle are the favorite platforms. Prezi was on the past participants list "because it's easy, practical and attracts students" while Evernote and Wordle were indicated to mirror the participants' personality and interests as well as be relevant to the courses they cover. Personal preference and relevance of the platform to the teaching subject/activity are therefore key factors that influence adoption. This is partly linked to perceived second-order barriers where confidence of the tutor in using technology and belief that technology can assist the teaching and learning process influenced adoption.

In fact, when asked about the reasons behind not adopting platforms from those presented during the seminar series, participants indicated that lack of time to practice was among the inhibitors to technology adoption. The lack of computer maintenance and lack of compatibility between existing technologies and new media platforms and tools covered during the seminar added to the barriers participants felt they faced after the seminar series was over. While time factors could be overcome through individual work and practice in the teachers' free time until they gained confidence, this shows that participants believed first-order barriers to be pivotal in adopting technology into their own practices.

Although peer support was readily available and place for safe experimentation was provided during the semester in which the seminar series was offered, this shows once more, that regardless of institution and geographical area, technology adoption patterns remain consistent. While opting in to technology is still a matter a personal choice, higher, more relevant and more efficient integration of digital technologies in education could be obtained if perhaps centrally enforced through policy. However, for policy to change

and adoption to happen the process needs to be bottom-up rather than top-down, and it needs a group of people working together as advocates. The next case study is a good example.

CASE STUDY 3: SOCIAL MEDIA POLICY WORKSHOP – RAISING AWARENESS AND LEADING TO CHANGE

Overview

At the end of 2010, the Library of the University of the West of Scotland was already using a wide range of social media platforms to communicate with students and academic staff. These included a Facebook group, several blogs and a twitter account. However, they felt that their efforts although successful individually could have a higher impact if better coordinated.

A workshop with library staff already involved with social media was organized in early December 2010, its purpose being to help staff identify their strengths and opportunities within social media as well as define their comfort zone by discovering their concerns and worries related to use of technology. The workshop featured 4 parts: social media and current practice; a social media audit of the UWS Library activities; setting up a draft social media policy and social media usage guidelines; and drafting a strategy for social media use.

Results

Unlike the prior workshops, where the focus was on how to set up and use social media platforms, this workshop addressed a strategic need of a specialized group with an interest in social media that had already experimented with digital communications. Another difference from the previous groups was the intended audience; as this was not an educator's group, but was part of an educational institution and their social media efforts had the potential to both support educators as well influence adoption of technology by others. The questions that emerged from the workshop were more focused on functionality; intent on preserving what has been done already and integrating it better both at library level and at a wider university level. Discussions about the role of social media within higher education institutions and the role of organizations and groups within higher education institutions in changing policy and encouraging technological integration took place.

In an email exchange with Gordon Hunt, University Librarian at UWS, following up on the results and impact of the workshop, he indicated that the session has helped raise general awareness among library staff and "has been useful in shaping internal service development". This is supported by a comment left by library staff using the UWS Library username on Adi's blog post about the session, indicating that a few of the lessons learned during the workshop were implemented shortly afterwards:

I think UWS has really learned the value of social networking tools in these last few days while we've tried to communicate with students and staff during the severe weather (UWS Library on anaadi.net, 2010).

Embedding social media in the library's delivery will be a long process but, in his opinion, the workshop was a significant catalyst in generating momentum. He also suggested that the workshop has helped him:

...to gain traction at senior level in the university on the need to engage with social media at institutional level. Having successful staff engagement in the library supports my advocacy of the need to engage more generally. This is now happening through the new learning, teaching and assessment strategy implementation where wider social media policy is an integral element and the library is seen as key to staff and student development in this area.

So in general terms we have tried to position the library as the natural location for support in new technology areas like social media and this is resulting in greater engagement of our staff in wider policy and practical developments. While I wouldn't want to put too much weight on a single event, however successful, workshops such as the one you ran play a key role in setting tone and context for wider developments" (Hunt in e-mail, January 29, 2012).

Discussion

The workshop is a good example of what can be accomplished when many of the barriers to technological integration disappear. If compared to Bigum and Kenway (1998) profiles, the workshop participants would be both Boosters and Critics. While they are positive about technology and its role in education, they were also questioning its usage, efficiency and effectiveness. In this sense, they did not exhibit traditional second-order barriers, as they were already convinced of the value of technological integration. Instead, they focused on finding solutions to overcome the remaining first-order barriers and addressing second-order barriers within faculty and staff at an institutional level.

Moreover, during the workshop, they demonstrated awareness of barriers that other faculty and staff members would encounter and exhibit to using new technologies in the classroom. This shows not only that they understood very well how the system within which they were embedded operated, but also that they have already identified routes through which those barriers could be challenged and overcome.

In the end, Gordon Hunt is right. A single event, workshop or seminar series cannot bring change but can raise awareness, challenge current policies, question current uses and enhance dialogue about how technology can and should be used in academia. The workshop at UWS was part of that wider discussion about technology in higher education. What makes this interesting is that, unlike previous cases which were either discussed in this chapter or completed by others researcher, this discussion was not initiated by teaching/academic staff but rather what could be perceived as support staff. Their endeavor therefore shows how important collaboration between departments is and how innovation does not necessarily have to take place within the classroom but can end up being reflected there. Similarly, their effort to discuss digital media and come up with a strategic use suggests that the existence of digital media usage policy and guidelines can be even more important than ongoing training and support. This is in line with Zayim, Yildrim and Saka's (2006) study whose results showed a similar pattern.

This raises further questions not only about how technology can be adopted in academia but also about who should promote it and in what way. Implications for training as well as future research will be presented in the conclusions below.

CONCLUSION

The literature review and three case studies presented in this chapter give insight into the complexity and different types of barriers encountered when trying to teach faculty and staff new technologies or trying to design policy to integrate new technologies. The results of the first case study brought to light additional first- and second-order barriers which have not been studied before; those of the reliability and validity of using online tools for research, and their legitimacy in the eyes of colleagues and administration. The results of the second case study introduced an added factor of the external environment. Perhaps even major political, social, or even natural events external to the university could cause educators to feel more or less inclined to take risks in their teaching.

The third case study results showed that for those that had used digital and media already – such as the UWS librarians or some of the researchers joining the Caledonian University and Kansas University seminars – the questions raised were mostly related to overcoming first-order barriers such as university or research policies, administrative support or integration of technologies. This finding upholds the findings from the literature review and shows how important faculty and staff members are in the process of change and how the attitudes and motivations of a group can help train, inspire and motivate others.

The case studies confirm the results of Jensen and Lewis (2001), Mousa (2002) and Brush, Glazewski, Rutnowski, and Berg's (2003) when it comes to the need of continued support for professional development as well as for implementation and integration of technology in the classroom. They also illustrate the fact that for those with little experience with technology, second-order barriers may be the most important barriers to conquer. The workshop organizer needs to explain not only how the platforms function, but also why they are relevant to the educators, how they can enhance their work and how they would integrate successfully into the curriculum.

While Fisher, Dwyer, and Yocam (1996) suggest that allocating enough money to technology would be enough to overcome first-order barriers, the reality is that money is not enough. With digital and social media usage and penetration growing at a rapid pace and with platforms being developed and made available at no cost, it is not an issue of funding anymore but rather one of understanding technology, its benefits, risks, opportunities and potentials. Overcoming first-order barriers continues to require an investment, but not in hardware or software as one might expect, but in training in media literacies which in turn would be reflected in an investment in regular assessments of an institution's uses of technology. In this sense time is of essence: time dedicated to test new and emerging technologies, time to discuss the relevance of those platforms, as well as time to assess the most efficient and effective platforms and tools for teaching, learning and research together and evaluate how they can be integrated with current systems, practices and policies. To overcome second-order barriers, Watzlawick, Weakland and Fisch (1974) suggest that change needs to be made in small but incremental steps, adding to current practice rather than radically changing it. However, it would seem that true integration of technology in education requires a transformation of current practices and these small but incremental steps are not enough.

What these case studies show is that personal motivation, perceived relevance of technology and confidence are important factors to technology adoption. Peer support, professional development, integration with current practices can facilitate adoption. However, it is institution-wide openness and support for new and emerging technologies that sees them efficiently and consistently adopted in the classroom. This raises questions not only about the mechanisms that need to be put into place to make technology more appealing to institutions in general but also about the processes and motivations that could trigger this adoption. If successful cases indicate that a small but enthusiastic minority can instill change and adoption, it is university-wide support that is suggested as the favorite route to having technology integrated in the classroom.

There are a few implications for future trainers which can be gleaned from this research. First, and possibly most important, training on new technologies should be done in a workshop format; with examples of integration presented and time allotted for all participants to practice with the new technology and ask questions. Thereafter, ongoing support should be provided on the new technologies, with IT personnel available to help

faculty who are trying to integrate the technology into their courses for specific purposes.

Second, before designing training programs for faculty on implementing new technologies, care should be taken to choose technologies that are user-friendly and educationally effective. Johnston and McCormack (1996) called upon designers to create programs with those qualities, but with such a wide array of tools and applications to choose from, it should also be incumbent upon the trainer to choose platforms which can be more easily integrated into the curriculum to accomplish the teaching tasks required. Choosing the correct types of tools to begin with will go a long way in overcoming many of the first-order barriers by limiting the time, effort, resources, and professional development required to integrate the new technology.

Third, trainers should do pre-workshop surveys to discover what second-order barriers are most prevalent within the participants. If possible, participants could be divided into groups, with workshops focusing either on overcoming resistance to using new technologies by providing clear examples of effectiveness, or overcoming efficacy and confidence issues by allowing more time for practice.

There are also several areas for future research that have emerged from these case studies. Peer support and ongoing professional development are areas which need to be more closely examined for future technological integration. Methods should be examined which can effectively further both of these ends. In addition, as university policy was rated so highly by participants in Zayim, Yildrim and Saka's (2006) study, it seems natural that future studies would examine the outcomes of changes in policy. Is it a foregone conclusion that technological innovation would actually happen if university policy allowed for it? Or does it take more than university policies and procedures to affect the second-order barriers within the minds of the educators?

It seems that this chapter should finish with a larger question: what changes to current university systems will have to occur to overcome these barriers and make them more conducive to transformational innovation? This discussion began with definitive statements on the current transition underway from an Industrial Economy to a Knowledge Economy for many societies in the world, and of the evolution of knowledge itself. These two major shifts leave universities struggling to adapt and graduate students who will be able to function within the new paradigm. Future research should focus on what types of changes need to be made to the overall structure of higher education systems to allow them to innovate, experiment, and adapt so that they can contribute in an effective, meaningful manner to further academia, the growth and transition of knowledge, and society as a whole.

REFERENCES

Adi, A. (2010, April 29). *New media for research. Researching new media.* Retrieved January 25, 2012, from http://www.anaadi.net/2010/04/29/new-media-for-research-researching-new-media/

Adi, A. (2010, December 2). *Social media for university libraries.* Retrieved January 27, 2012, from http://www.anaadi.net/2010/12/02/social-media-for-university-libraries

Adi, A. (2011a, March 31). *Prezi pow wow.* Retrieved January 27, 2012, from http://www.anaadi.net/2011/03/31/prezi-pow-wow/

Adi, A. (2011b, July). *5 weeks, 5 days, 5 sessions of technology for education.* Retrieved February 15, 2012, from http://www.anaadi.net/2011/07/11/5-weeks-5-days-5-sessions-of-technology-for-education/

Al-Bataineh, A., & Brooks, L. (2003). Challenges, advantages, and disadvantages or instructional technology in the community college classroom. *Community College Journal of Research and Practice, 27,* 473–484. doi:10.1080/713838180

Antonnaci, D. S. (2002). *Integrating technology into instruction in higher education.* Kansas City, MO: University of Missouri.

Bates, A. W. (2000). *Managing technological change: Strategies for college and university leaders.* San Francisco, CA: Jossey-Bass.

Becker, H. J., & Riel, M. M. (2000). Teacher professional engagement and constructivist-compatible computer use. Center for Research on Information Technology and Organizations. Irvine, CA: University of Califormia. Retrieved June 10, 2012, from http://www.crito.uci.edu/tlc/findings/report_7/start page.html

Bigum, C., & Kenway, J. (1998). New information technologies and the ambiguous future of schooling - Some possible scenarios . In Hargreaves, A., Lieberman, A., Fullan, M., & Hopkins, D. (Eds.), *International handbook of educational change.* Toronto, Canada: OISE.

Brickner, D. (1995). *The effects of first- and second-order barriers to change on the degree and nature of computer usage of secondary mathematics teachers: A case study.* Unpublished doctoral dissertation, West Lafayette, IN: Purdue University.

Brinkerhoff, J. (2006). Effects of a long-duration, professional development academy on technology skills, computer self-efficacy, and technology integration beliefs and practices. *Journal of Research on Technology in Education, 39*(1), 22–43.

Brush, T., Glazewski, K., Rutowski, K., & Berg, K. (2003). Integrating technology in a field-based teacher training program. *Educational Technology Research and Development*, *51*(1). doi:10.1007/BF02504518

Brzycki, D., & Dudt, K. P. (2005). Overcoming barriers to technology use in teacher preparation programs. *Journal of Technology and Teacher Education*, *13*(4), 619–641.

Bullock, D. (2004). Moving from theory to practice: An examination of the factors that preservice teachers encounter as they attempt to gain experience teaching with technology during field placement experiences. *Journal of Technology and Teacher Education*, *12*(2), 211–237.

Butler, D., & Sellbom, M. (2002). Barriers to adopting technology for teaching and learning. *EDUCAUSE Quarterly*, *25*(2), 22–28.

Chizmar, J. F., & Williams, D. B. (2001). What do faculty want? *Educause Quarterly*, *1*, Spring. Retrieved June 12, 2012, from http://net.educause.edu/ir/ library/pdf/eqm0112.pdf

Crow, M. (2012, January). *The future of the new American university*. Speech presented at Tempe Center for the Arts, Arizona. Retrieved from http://vimeo.com/35585254

Cuban, L., Kirkpatrick, H., & Peck, C. (2001). High access and low use of technology in high school classrooms: Explaining an apparent paradox. *American Educational Research Journal*, *38*(4), 813–834. doi:10.3102/00028312038004813

Education Development Center [EDC]. (1996). *National study tour of district technology integration summary report (CCT Reports, No. 14)*. New York, NY: Center for Children and Technology.

Ertmer, P. A. (1999). Addressing first- and second-order barriers to change: Strategies for technology integration. *Educational Technology Research and Development*, *47*(4), 47–61. doi:10.1007/BF02299597

Ertmer, P. A., Addison, P., Lane, M., Ross, E., & Woods, D. (1999). Examining teachers' beliefs about the role of technology in the elementary classroom. *Journal of Research on Computing in Education*, *32*(1), 54–72.

Eynon, R. (2008). The use of the world wide web in learning and teaching in higher education: Reality and rhetoric. *Innovations in Education and Teaching International*, *45*(1), 15–23. doi:10.1080/14703290701757401

Fisher, C., Dwyer, D., & Yocam, K. (1996). *Education and technology: Reflections on computing in classrooms*. San Francisco, CA: Apple Press.

Gibbons, M., Limoges, C., Nowotny, H., Schwartzman, S., Scott, P., & Trow, M. (1994). *The new production of knowledge: The dynamics of science and research in contemporary societies*. London, UK: Sage.

Hargreaves, D. (2000, March). *Knowledge management in the learning society*. Paper presented at the Forum of OECD Education Ministers, Copenhagen.

Jasinski, M. (1998). *Teaching and learning styles that facilitate online learning: Documentation project: Project report*. Adelaide, Australia: Douglas Mawson Institute of TAFE.

Jensen, J., & Lewis, B. (2001). Beyond the workshop educational policy in situated practice. *Education Canada*, *41*(3), 28–31.

Jensen, K., & Folley, S. (2011). *Teaching with technology in higher education: Exploring how lecturers at the University of Huddersfield use technology in teaching.* Teaching and Learning Institute Working Paper No. 1, University of Huddersfield, UK.

Johnston, S., & McCormack, C. (1996). Integrating information technology into university teaching: Identifying the needs and providing the support. *International Journal of Educational Management, 10*(5), 36–42. doi:10.1108/09513549610146123

Kagima, L. K., & Hausafus, C. O. (2000). Integration of electronic communication in higher education: Contributions of faculty computer self-efficacy. *The Internet and Higher Education, 2*(4), 1–15. doi:10.1016/S1096-7516(00)00027-0

Kerr, S. T. (1996). Visions of sugarplums: The future of technology, education, and the schools . In Kerr, S. T. (Ed.), *Technology and the future of schooling: Ninety-fifty yearbook of the National Society for the Study of Education (Vol. II).* Chicago, IL: University of Chicago Press.

Knight, C., Knight, B. A., & Teghe, D. (2006) Releasing the pedagogical power of information and communication technology for learners: A case study. International *Journal of Education and Development using Information and Communication Technology, 2*(2), 27-34.

Li, L., & Walsh, S. (2010). Technology uptake in Chinese EFL classes. *Language Teaching Research, 15*(1), 99–125. doi:10.1177/1362168810383347

Loveless, A. (2003). The interaction between primary teachers' perceptions of ICT and their pedagogy. *Education and Information Technologies, 8*(4), 313–326. doi:10.1023/B:EAIT.0000008674.76243.8f

Maier, H. W. (1987). *Developmental group care of children and youth: Concepts and practice.* New York, NY: Haworth.

Marwan, A., & Sweeney, T. (2010). Teachers' perceptions of educational technology integration in an Indonesian polytechnic. *Asia Pacific Journal of Education, 30*(4), 463–476. doi:10.1080/02188791.2010.519554

McCullagh, D. (2011, June 20). *Dropbox confirms security glitch--No password required.* Retrieved on January 27, 2012, from http://news.cnet.com/8301-31921_3-20072755-281/DropBox-confirms-security-glitch-no-password-required/

Means, B., & Olson, K. (1997). *Technology's role in education reform: Findings from a national study of innovating schools.* Washington, DC: US Department of Education, Office of Educational Research and Improvement.

Meskill, C., Mossop, J., DiAngelo, S., & Pasquale, R. (2002). Expert and novice teachers talking technology: Precepts, concepts, and misconcepts. *Language Learning & Technology, 6*(3), 46–57. Retrieved from http://llt.msu.edu/vol6num3 /pdf/meskill.pdf

Mouza, C. (2002). Learning to teach with new technology: Implications for professional development. *Journal of Research on Technology in Education, 35*(2), 272–289.

Mtebe, J. S., Dachi, H., & Raphael, C. (2011). Integrating ICT into teaching and learning at the University of Dar es Salaam. *Distance Education, 32*(2), 289–294. doi:10.1080/01587919.2011.584854

O'Mahony, C. (2003). Getting the information and communication technology formular right: access + ability = confident use. *Technology, Pedagogy and Education, 12*(2), 295–314. doi:10.1080/14759390300200159

Oates, K. D. (2001). *University faculty who use computer technology.* Doctoral Dissertation, Georgia State University, USA.

Spotts, T. H. (1999). Discriminating factors in faculty use of instructional technology in higher edcuation. *Educational Technology & Society, 2*(4). Retrieved June 12, 2012, from http://www.ifets.info/journals/2_4/spotts.html

Staples, A., Pugach, M. C., & Himes, D. (2005). Rethinking the technology integration challenge: Cases from three urban elementary schools. *Journal of Research on Technology in Education, 37*(3), 285–311.

Surry, D. W., & Land, S. M. (2000). Strategies for motivating higher education faculty to use technology. *Innovations in Education and Training International, 37*(2), 145–15. doi:10.1080/13558000050034501

Tapscott, D. (1998). *Growing up digital: The rise of the net generation*. New York, NY: McGraw-Hill.

Watzlawick, P., Weakland, J., & Fisch, R. (1974). *Change*. New York, NY: W. W. Norton and Co.

Wheeler, S. (2004). Five smooth stones: Fighting for the survival of higher education. *Distance Learning, 1*(3).

Wilson, W. (2003, January 1). Faculty perceptions and uses of instructional technology. *EDUCAUSE Quarterly*.

Yin, R. K. (2003). *Case study research: Design and methods* (3rd ed.). Thousand Oaks, CA: Sage.

Zayim, N., Yildirim, S., & Saka, O. (2006). Technology adoption of medical faculty in teaching: Differentiating factors in adopter categories. *Journal of Educational Technology & Society, 9*(2), 213–222.

KEY TERMS AND DEFINITIONS

First-Order Barriers: Those barriers which prohibit linear change. The term has been used synonymously with external barriers by Ertmer (1999) for the purposes of technology integration.

First-Order Change: Change which occurs in an incremental, linear fashion.

Knowledge Entrepreneurship: A type of entrepreneurship focused on utilizing knowledge outputs of universities and research bodies by developing associated knowledge practices or products.

Mode 1 Knowledge: Knowledge that was produced before access to higher technologies; mainly individually produced in an academic setting and taught from lecturer to students.

Mode 2 Knowledge: Knowledge that is produced using the capabilities of higher technologies; interdisciplinary, team created, and formed using a wide range of participants such as teachers, students, scientists, and other industry professionals who are able to work together. Mode 2 knowledge is generally created in the process of applied research, and it is typically much more applicable to the 'real world' than Mode 1 knowledge.

Second-Order Barriers: Those barriers which prohibit transformational change. The term has been used synonymously with internal (belief) barriers by Ertmer (1999) for the purposes of technology integration.

Second-Order Change: Change which occurs in a radical, transformational fashion; usually due to some type of radical innovation or change in beliefs.

Technology Integration: The utilization of new technological tools in education.

Chapter 18
Making the Most of Informal and Situated Learning Opportunities through Mobile Learning

Mar Camacho
Universitat Rovira i Virgili, Spain

ABSTRACT

Mobility and networking are two important emerging issues that affect educational practices nowadays. Learners and teachers are continuously involved in ubiquitous relationships with other people on the Internet, swapping information and sharing knowledge and skills. However, in the Mobile Learning area, a great deal of emphasis has been placed on mobile technologies and the transfer of content, whereas the potential to support community building processes and collaboration through their integration within social networks has tended to be underemphasized. With the advent of Mobile Learning, a certain growth in its practice and research has been activated by technological innovation and progress. Mobile technologies offer potentiality for the exploitation of contextual learning and have unbound learners and technologies out of the limitation of classrooms at the time that enhance collaborative processes in informal contexts. The emergence of mobile gadgets has democratized the access to technology, changed the concept of user-generated content, and allowed learners and technologies to experiment with technologies outside the classroom, although it has posed challenges to educational stakeholders on how to match the nature of their practice for both life and learning with those traits that educators would like to heighten.

DOI: 10.4018/978-1-4666-2970-7.ch018

1. BACKGROUND

1.1. Towards a Distinct Mobile Culture: Informing the Nature of 21st Century Learners

The aim of this chapter is to provide a revision through the most relevant theoretical frameworks in the field of Mobile Learning, especially when linked to social learning and the nature of 21st century learners. An overview is offered of the most outstanding features concerning the pedagogical challenges that it may suppose for Higher Education stakeholders, and poses some questions on the challenges that educational institutions have to face, especially concerning the blurring between formal and informal learning. A final part is devoted to account for those issues which could promote successful learning practices through mobile devices in informal situations and to account for a distinctive mobile literacy. The chapter concludes that mobile learning can make valuable contributions to linking different learning environments at the time that it provides many opportunities for exploring ways in which students own mobile devices might be integrated into teaching and learning in higher education. Amongst other benefits, mobile learning is seen as providing considerable opportunities to link formal and informal learning across a range of educational contexts.

The pervasiveness of mobile technology is absolutely changing the way we teach and learn. Mobility is understood as a great catalyst of change, and together with digital media offer learners the tools to develop knowledge, and the skills and social practices required to entirely participate in contemporary society. This continuously changing social landscape evidently affects the ways in which participation is assumed, and whereas young people hold the different practices of mediated social interaction, educators endeavor to discover ways to connect these expressions in order to stimulate learning.

The impact that Mobile Technologies have had upon the learners' lives has led them to become involved through a situation which permits them to be involved in educational undertakings basically driven by personal needs and circumstances. Kukulska-Hume (2010) and Luckin (2010) provide the definition of 'Context-awareness' as the awareness of one's surroundings and their potential to provide information and rich learning experiences, which essentially becomes in this context, a starting point for learning. As the authors state: "Context-aware learning, therefore, is about enabling learners to use personal and social technologies to draw on aspects of their environment, including people who can join in or help, approaching the environment as a dynamic learning resource."

Thus, at the time that a distinct mobile culture emerges, in which learners take mobility and context-awareness as departing point and become more visible as innovators, creators and producers (Kukulska-Hume, 2010) they develop new skills and literacies empowered by mobile technologies that provide them additional opportunities to extend their learning and tie the use of social media to their own context and interests. The omnipresence of mobile technologies appears to be causing these developments and there is evidence that educational institutions and stakeholders need to provide new insights into these emergent practices. Thus, this cultural shift towards a more learner-centered education also poses implications for the adoption of mobile technologies and directly challenges practitioners and researchers to provide appropriate answers. At the same time, and following with Kukulska-Hulme (2010), "the combination of mobile technology and mobility generates a mobile culture where learners' specific needs in relation to their current location and context become important stimuli for learning designs."

Texting, microblogging, video creation or mobile storytelling are instances of educational possibilities that mobile technologies offer, and evidence the value for including them into teaching and learning processes (McFarlane, Triggs and Yee, 2008, p.7) The quick production of mobile technologies offer new opportunities for exploring ways in which students own mobile devices may be included into teaching and learning processes in all educational levels. Although mobile technologies extend learning beyond traditional teacher-led classroom, it is hard to grasp the essence of Mobile Learning, as it will be seen later on in this chapter, to show the way in which it contributes to the theory of educational practices. There is a clear need to provide new insights into emergent practices with mobile technologies that have implications for practitioners, researchers and educational stakeholders.

Regarding the expectations exerted upon 2st century learners and their learning profiles, there emerge from an educators' perspective, a number of learner skills, attributes and competences, which need to be taken into account (See Figure 1). Kukulska-Hulme (2010) addresses the change of key competences in the lifelong learning culture and lists how mobile technologies can be helpful to satisfy the calls for these new competences.

The aim of many educators is to use new technologies in ways that will enable such competences and skills to be reinforced or to occur. Although there is a prevalent opinion that the school as a social institution still has central roles to accomplish, and that in the future it will still be the central building piece where to build educational groundings, there is also solid consciousness of the necessity to adapt its objectives, organization and functioning to the needs and requests of the knowledge society (Drucker, 1994; Kozma & Anderson, 2002).

The internationally recognized NMC Horizon Reports identify and describe emerging technologies likely to have a large impact over the coming five years in education around the globe. Each report is intended to surface significant trends and challenges and to identify a wide array of potential technologies or practices that are likely to enter mainstream use with their focus sectors within three adoption horizons over the next five years.

Figure 1. 21st century learners' skills

- Active, inquiring, analytical
- Engaged citizens
- Equipped with research and inquiry skills
- Exercise independent critical judgment
- Co-creators and producers of knowledge
- Able to function effectively in the real world
- Able to communicate and cross language boundaries or cultural boundaries
- Motivated and equipped to continue learning over a Lifetime

Kukuslku-Hulme, 2010

The 2012 Higher Education Edition, recently published, reports on the following key trends:

1. People expect to be able to work, learn, and study whenever and wherever they want to.
2. The technologies we use are increasingly cloud-based, and our notions of IT support are decentralized.
3. The world of work is increasingly collaborative, driving changes in the way student projects are structured.
4. The abundance of resources and relationships made easily accessible via the Internet is increasingly challenging us to revisit our roles as educators.
5. Education paradigms are shifting to include online learning, hybrid learning and collaborative models.
6. There is a new emphasis in the classroom on more challenge-based and active learning.

Regarding the areas of emerging technology to watch it should be said that both the mobile apps and tablet computing are among the technologies which have one year or less time of adoption, whereas Game-based Learning and Learning Analytics will take from two to four years of adoption.

Considering the expectations that educators have of 21st century learners, as outlined in the previous section, and the importance that Mobile Learning is gaining through the years it is necessary to see how the personal use of mobile technologies may address these challenges.

1.2. Mobile and Contextual Learning in Informal Situations

Mobility and connectedness are altering many features of societies round the world. The developing union between Mobile Learning and informal learning is deeply entangled. Furthermore, the mobile Web and location consciousness of handheld devices are technologies that are estimated to go forward meaningfully in the near future (Gartner 2010). Contexts are fluid and continuously changing, and this has significant consequences for both formal and informal learning experiences. According to Brown (2010) context can be defined as "the formal or informal setting in which a situation occurs; it can include many aspects or dimensions, such as environment, social activity, goals or tasks of groups and individuals...)." Regarding the relationship between context and Mobile Learning, it could be agreed on the fact that it is of vital importance to take context into account. As Wingkvist and Ericsson (2010) argue, "if the context is not understood well enough, the mobile learning system will not survive beyond the scope of the initiative and the project's end date."

The means by which we receive or create content anytime and anywhere through mobile technologies is becoming widely widespread. This fact, obviously causes a myriad of opportunities for informal learning 'on the go', where users can exploit their status of being always connected in their informal circles. Deeply agreeing with Fitzgerald (2012) "If we can embody an effective pedagogy within user-generated content, we can provide learning any time and at any place." In this sense, Hwang et al. (2008) provide different criteria and strategies which relate to context-aware ubiquitous learning which may include the contexts that may prove most for ubiquitous learning and also examples of learning activity design. Authors such as Helmstedt & Ehlers (2011) have also attempted to refer to the issue of user-generated content in higher education and have accounted for a comprehensive framework for how such content could be presented effectively.

A common assumption of mobile learning is the idea that learners are continually on the move, nevertheless, the implications are not only how to be focused on their mobility, in the physical space, rather on the reasons by which they are active in different contexts and how constantly they may change. According to Sharples et al. (2009) "Context is created by interactions among people, their surrounding environment, and the tools or resources available to them."

There are different contextual aspects that are present and are hugely dictated by the learners themselves: "their objectives, their strategies, the resources and the nature of the interaction itself (with a device and/or other people) are all governed by the user" (Fitzgerald, 2012). Thus learning which occurs in these situations is informal, and learners engage with content in a self-directed way, which will probably lead them to achieve successful learning outcomes. Livingstone defines informal learning as 'any activity involving the pursuit of understanding, knowledge or skill which occurs without the presence of externally imposed curricular criteria' (Livingstone 2001). Beckett and Hager (2002), on the other hand, define informal learning as an holistic, activity/experience-based, dependent upon other activities, activated by individual learners, and it is often collaborative (Beckett&Hager 2002, cited in Colley et al. 2003).

Different visions account for the knowledge construction concept which is underlying as well the notion of Mobile Learning, according to Vygotsky (1978) "social interactions between users, in the form of browsing content produced by others, or producing content for others to view (either new content, or in response to existing media) are an important part of learning and knowledge construction." When creating content the user is engaging in experiential thinking (a learning process relating to personal experiences), while the activity of browsing content created by others would result in reflective thinking and metacognition (Norman 1993). Sharples (2010) defines context as "a continually unfolding interaction between people, settings, technologies and other artifacts" and builds up a theory directly linked to Mobile Learning based upon the hierarchy which is established among these thee elements: context, context state and context substate.

As it is stated in the Mobile Learning Infokit (2011), the wider context is the "interaction over time between people, settings, technologies and artifacts, the context state comprises "elements from the learning and setting at one particular point in time, space or goal sequence." And finally, the context substate is configured of "elements from the learner and setting that are relevant to the current focus of learning and desired level of context awareness."

Having said that, the intertwining of the mobile and social web challenges us with specific issues and innovative mechanisms for learning. When accounting for the design of user-generated content for teaching and learning, it is important to ensure that we provide information in an appropriate way (Fitzgerald, 2012). According to the author, "it is likely that the active creation – or co-creation – of content will engender a deep engagement with the learning process through participatory and socio-constructivist learning principles." Nevertheless, although there is research which deals with the design of content for use on mobile devices most of it has mainly centered on human–computer interaction (Hayhoe 2001; Grasso&Roselli 2005; Savio&Braiterman 2007), but little on content creation. The amount of content-generated media which is produced every day, both formal and informal, will -with no doubt- increase the way in which educational stakeholders cope with it in an successful way, this question remains of vital importance for education.

2. BASIC ISSUES UNDERLYING THE DISCUSSION ON MOBILE LEARNING

2.1 Pedagogical Affordances of Mobile Learning

The first studies around Mobile Learning date from 2000, approximately, when Sharples (2000) accounted for the potential for new designs in personal mobile technologies that could promote lifelong learning programs and continuing adult educational opportunities. Agreeing with Mcconatha et al. (2008) many of the ideas which appeared in Sharples' article are still under discussion and are of relevance to Mobile Learning at present.

However, many attempts have been made in order to define Mobile Learning not only considering the devices or technologies, but also in relation to the mobility of learners and learning and the learner's experience of learning with mobile devices. Different schools of thought have tried to account for a definition of Mobile Learning along the years, these definitions –evidently- have been influenced by the technological advances and depict a developing Mobile Learning ecosystem. Thus, in 2004, Mike Sharples defined Mobile Learning as "learning away from one's learning environment or learning involving the use of Mobile devices." Traxler (2009) evidenced that the increasing development of communities of practice in m-learning was different from the established communities of tethered e-learning, whereas Glahn, et al. (2010) pointed out that mobile learning allows "both a high degree of personalisation as well as enabling a much more social method of learning. It therefore, rather uniquely, allows for learning within and across contexts."

In conclusion, Mobile learning assets include the use of mobile devices to perform any of the following achievements:

- Catalyze the process and organization for teaching and learning on the go.
- Foster instant communication and collaboration.
- Conduct assessment and evaluation.
- Provide access to knowledge.

Agreeing with the research around Mobile Learning carried out in the work by Buchem and Camacho, (2011) "the benefit of mobile learning is given by the flexibility and context-awareness of mobile technologies, enabling spontaneous, personalized and situated learning, promoting collaboration and encouraging autonomous, life-long learning" (Naismith et al., 2004; Dyson et al., 2008; Traxler, 2009). The growing potential of Mobile Learning for the improvement of skills essential for successful education and career (Litchfield, Nettleton & Taylor, 2008) and the need to embed Mobile Learning into conventional higher education processes have been highlighted by authors such as (Traxler, 2005; Dyson, Raban, Litchfield & Lawrence, 2008). On the other hand, and as it is going to de described later on in this chapter, when Mobile Learning is based on social constructivism, it highlights the role of social interaction for co-construction of knowledge and meaning. Following with Buchem and Camacho (2011), learners are encouraged to take control of their learning (by shaping learning goals and processes), to collaborate with peers to produce content (instead of consuming content delivered by instructors) and to use mobile tools for investigation and exploration (Loke et al., 2010). Instructors as facilitators design the learning environment and structure learning processes (Jonassen, 1991).

The framework provided by Frohberg et al. (2009), which accounts for a social constructivist approach to mobile learning, highlights the following issues as its main affordances, thus, Mobile Learning:

- Allows embedding learning in socializing contexts for cooperation in learner communities.
- Provides opportunities for co-construction of content leading to deeper understanding, knowledge application, reflection and evaluation.
- Optimizes the level of control by scaffolding activities to enhance orientation and coordination.
- Facilitates the cooperation between learner teams to fulfill a common learning goal (Buchem and Camacho, 2011).

Mobile technologies can sustain social constructivist approaches to learning. Learners live in a determined social, cultural environment in which their learning is seen – according to Sharples (2000) as a "constructive process of acting within an environment and reflecting upon it, where knowledge is constructed and shared as a part of a social process" (Cobcroft et al. 2006, Johnson and Smith, 1991). Thus, this social constructivist view of learning largely supported by academic research and literature (Brown, Collins, & Duguid, 1989; Resnick, 1987; Soloway, Grant, Tinker, Roschelle, Mills, Resnick et al., 1999) considers that students learn best when given the opportunity to learn skills and theories in the contexts in which they are used. Students –thus- construct their interpretations of a subject and communicate those understandings to others (Gay, Stefanone, Grace-Martin, & Hembrooke, 2001). In this sense, Bryant (2006) sees mobile technological tools as an opportunity to "expand discussion beyond the classroom which provides new ways to collaborate and communicate within their class or around the world."

Finally, the JISC Mobile Learning Infokit (2011), in an effort to move from theorization towards an operational and significative use of Mobile Learning, claims for the establishment of

Figure 2. Frameworks for mobile learning (Mobile Learning Infokit, 2011)

•**Behaviourist** - activities that promote learning as a change in learners' observable actions
•**Constructivist** - activities in which learners actively construct new ideas or concepts based on both their previous and current knowledge
•**Situated** - activities that promote learning within an authentic context and culture
•**Collaborative** - activities that promote learning through social interaction
•**Informal and lifelong** - activities that support learning outside a dedicated learning environment
and formal curriculum
•**Learning and teaching support** - activities that assist in the coordination of learners and resources for learning activities

frameworks (See Figure 2) in which educational institutions can focus their practices and provides six broad theory-based categories concerning Mobile Learning:

Although there is a lot of scholarly revision around Mobile Learning, the relevance and need for Mobile Learning practice founded upon learning theories, focused on pedagogically meaningful approaches to Mobile Learning and systematically evaluated with appropriate data collection and analysis tools, remains paramount (Somobnet, 2011).

2.2 Collaborative Practices in Informal Contexts

Mobile technologies suggest substantial affordances to build and grow creative, collaborative and critical relationships into learning practices. According to the work by Cochrane et al. (2011) several authors have referred to the capacity of mobile learning to enhance collaborative interactions and communities of practice (Stead, 2005; Cortez et al., 2004, Colley et al. 2004). These theories have been revisited more recently by the studies of Kukulska-Hulme, 2010; Pachler, Bachmair, & Cook, 2010; Belshaw, 2010, Traxler & Wishart, 2011).

Agreeing with Cochrane et al (2011), communities of practice as a social learning theory (Lave & Wenger, 1991; Wenger, 1998; Wenger et al., 2009) enhance the process of membership

in a community from initial peripheral participation to full participation as core members of the learning community. Learner-generated-contexts, thus, provide a framework that bridges the gap between teacher-directed pedagogy and student-directed learning (Luckin et al., 2010; Pachler et al., 2010). Although there is general coincidence on the collaborative affordances of mobile web 2.0 based upon social constructivist learning theory (Vygotsky, 1978) experts recommend that pedagogical practices be informed by two key teaching and learning frameworks: Communities of Practice (Langelier, 2005; Lave & Wenger, 1991; Wenger, 1998; Wenger et al., 2009), and Learner-Generated Contexts (Luckin et al., 2010). In this sense, agreeing with Cochrane et al. heutagogy should be the framework for students to experience authentic collaboration, being the establishment of student-negotiated groups with clearly determined learning outcomes and assessment mechanisms with the help of mobile-based tools key to success.

Moreover, we firmly believe that Mobile Learning can support the social construction of knowledge amongst learners by enhancing their critical, creative, collaborative engagement within the sites of application of knowledge. By challenging learners to engage collaboratively in the creation of content or game-playing, it can also contribute to building distributed learning networks of diverse participants who are actively participating in creative activities, as well as critically reflecting on their own and others' practice. According to Cochrane et al. (2011) research has shown that functioning in a community can enhance the learning that occurs. Optimal learning outcomes are directly tied to the establishment of social networks among participants engaged a collaborative learning enterprise. Such collaboration has been shown to be very important in the development of a learning community and in achieving the desired learning outcomes.

3. CHALLENGES FOR A SUCCESSFUL IMPLEMENTATION OF MOBILE INFORMAL LEARNING

As mobile technologies become more omnipresent, questions come up as to whether it can make possible for learners to demonstrate or develop these traits. One way to approach this issue is to stare at how learners use their mobile devices for both life and learning in order to see if there is any equivalency between the nature of mobile device uses and the traits that educators would wish to promote. An awareness of these developments can shift perceptions of what can be done with mobile tools, draw attention to the possibility of connecting informal and formal learning, and of course it raises questions about what this means for teachers, curricula, institutions, and for education systems more broadly – how these practices may impact on teaching and learning. After having considered the previous issues, we would like to draw the attention to some key points to make the most of informal and situated learning opportunities provided by mobile technologies.

3.1. The Conflict between Mobile Informal Learning and Traditional Classroom Education

One of the most outstanding affordances of Mobile Learning lies in its capability to tie formal and informal learning along a wide variety of educational contexts, however, researchers are looking for ways to bring the vitality of Mobile 2.0 (Kukulska-Hume, 2010) into formal teaching and learning. In this sense, agreeing with the author, nowadays they are confronted with a "complex and even paradoxical challenge: how can they harness that vitality without stifling its most distinctive feature: the fact that it is user-led?" Furthermore, the power of mobile learning to blur formal and informal activity in people's lives goes without doubt. Mobile technologies suggest new chances for learning that go beyond traditional classrooms. However, it is really difficult to grasp the real essence of Mobile Learning in the sense that there exists nowadays a myriad of theories and practices which is so diverse that it even impedes to see how they contribute to the theory and practice of education. It is important to notice and consider the distinctive power of mobile technologies in blurring formal and informal activity in people's lives.

As mobile technologies for learning become more widespread, studies are beginning to shed light on the value of incorporating them in teaching and learning (McFarlane, Triggs and Yee 2008). These studies also include significant issues, such as the conflict between informal learning with mobile technologies and traditional classroom education (Sharples 2007). Learners are developing new literacies enabled by mobile devices, such as SMS texting, microblogging (writing diaries and weblogs on mobile devices) and mobile video creation. As it will be seen afterwards in this chapter, the integration of the new generations of location-aware mobile phones will offer possibilities, of education services and educational media matched to the learner's context and interests through Mobile Learning.

3.2. The Shift towards a New Mobile Literacy

According to David Parry, "we are already at the moment in which the ability to use social media, and particularly social media as amplified through the power of the mobile web, has become a key literacy" The unwired learning space is about to significantly modify the landscape of teaching with and through technology. The future our students will inherit is one that will be mediated and stitched together by the mobile web, and learners have to see the need to learn how to use these technologies effectively, so that that they end up on the right side of the digital divide: the side that knows how to use social media to band together. Teaching mobile web literacy seems to me as crucial as teaching basic literacy. Since the mobile web opens up a host of pedagogical possibilities, Parry (2011) sketches out a few literacies that we ought to be striving to teach our students and that we also need to undesrtand:

1. **Information Access:** There are situations in which information is quickly needed. The access to it is related to the skill of navigating the web capably. The skill of quick information access and credibility detection, will be, according to this author useful throughout their lives.

2. **Hyperconnectivity:** Encouraging students to Twitter during class can be used as both a collaborative note-taking exercise and an example of how conversation can be extended beyond the classroom boundaries, according to Parry (2011).

3. **The New Sense of Space:** Parry defines this literacy as the most important one. Geolocation and the mobile web will change our daily practices. Web services like Gowalla (http://gowalla.com/) and FourSquare (http://foursquare.com/) will substantially alter how we can intermingle with space. Even augmented reality applications such as Layar (http://www.layar.com/) and Wikitude (http://www.wikitude.org/en) will supply an increasingly complex landscape, full of data. Students need to begin to understand how one "can use a mobile device to both create and access spatial information".

3.3. Developing Specific Frameworks to Support Mobile Learning

While broad frameworks for e-learning provide some guidance for learning designers, the literature review indicates that little attention has been paid to developing specific frameworks to support the design of mobile learning. An initial attempt offered by Sharples et al. (2009, p. 4) suggested that a theory of mobile learning should be

assessed against the following criteria: firstly if the theory is significantly different from current learning theories, secondly, if it accounts for the mobility of learner, thirdly if it covers both formal and informal learning, and finally if it theorizes learning as a constructive and social process considering it as a personal and situated activity mediated by technology. We strongly believe that all these issues remain unanswered.

Studies of mobile and informal learning are often based on the learners' own records and metacognitive analysis of their learning, it is usual to find studies which have gathered data via instruments such as semi-structured interviews, surveys, and diary reflections. These accounts of learning –however- come with restrictions, in terms of precision and of the objectivity needed to account for such retrospective accounts. Moreover, younger learners may not hold the meta-cognitive skills needed for producing sufficient reflective recalls of their learning processes. Mobile and informal learning research methods need to allow us to examine not only the learning that occurs during the learning experience, but also how it develops afterwards, and learning is not to be understood as a consequence from single, individual experiences, but rather as an evolving experience. The experiences children and adults have in these various situations, dynamically interact to influence the ways individuals construct scientific knowledge, attitudes, behaviors, and understanding" (Dierking et al. 2003: 109). The cumulative nature of learning makes it difficult to isolate a distinct learning event for inspection. The inherent inconsistency of the learning practice in mobile contexts in terms of activity structure and learning outcomes (Taylor 2006) makes assessment even more complex.

In our opinion there's the need to focus on mobile and informal learning research methods in order to address whether existing methods are adequate in providing researchers with the data we need, and the proper methodological, practical and ethical concerns with existing methods.

It is also paramount to state and homogeneize which should be the requirements for mobile and informal learning research methods which could inform future work in this area.

3.4. Learning Practices through Mobile Devices in Informal Situations

The NMC Horizon Report 2012 Higher Education Edition is a collaborative effort between the NMC and the EDUCAUSE Learning Initiative (ELI), an EDUCAUSE Program. This ninth edition describes annual findings from the NMC Horizon Project, a decade-long research project designed to identify and describe emerging technologies likely to have an impact on learning, teaching, and creative inquiry in higher education. Six emerging technologies are identified across three adoption horizons over the next one to five years, as well as key trends and challenges expected to continue over the same period, giving campus leaders and practitioners a valuable guide for strategic technology planning.

This year's NMC Horizon Report identifies mobile apps and tablet computing as technologies expected to enter mainstream use in the first horizon of one year or less. Game-based learning and learning analytics are seen in the second horizon of two to three years; gesture-based computing and the Internet of Things are seen emerging in the third horizon of four to five years.

The Mobile Apps have been signaled by the Horizon Report as "the fastest growing dimension of the mobile space in higher education right now, with impacts on virtually every aspect of informal life, and increasingly, every discipline in the university." Apps that take advantage of recent developments with advances in electronic publishing and the convergence of search technology and location awareness, make this category appalling in a higher education context in which there is a lack of apps especially tailored to educational and research needs across the curriculum.

- **Tablet Computing:** Seen by higher education institutions are seeing them not just as an affordable solution for one-to-one learning, but also as a feature-rich tool for field and lab work, often times replacing far more expensive and cumbersome devices and equipment.
- **Educational Gaming:** Educational gaming brings an increasingly credible promise to make learning experiences more engaging for students, while at the same time improving important skills, such as collaboration, creativity, and critical thinking.
- Over the past year, learning analytics has garnered a lot of attention. The ability to synthesize data in real-time is exciting because it changes the structure of the learning dynamic - educators can use the data to make adjustments to their teaching style that better caters to student needs.
- Gesture-based technology has enabled students to learn by doing. Interfaces that react to touch, movement, voice, and facial expression allow more freedom in how we interact with our devices.

The Internet of Things, a notion first outlined by Vint Cerf as one of the many reasons to move to expand the address space of the Internet, is converging with smart objects, and fueling considerable innovation in how these devices communicate with each other and with us.

A significant inclusion into traditional teaching and learning processes of Mobile Apps, geolocation services, augmented reality and other mobile emerging technologies that will clearly have an impact into Higher Education in the oncoming 2-5 years will be key. Furthermore, the relevance of Mobile Apps for teaching, learning and creative inquiry in Higher Education becomes evident when designing project-based workshops, geo-location activities or using storytelling techniques to explore place and community. Successful practices which allow the development of a distinctive mobile literacy, as it was stated previously, together with the power of Mobile Learning to blur formal and informal boundaries account for a new teaching and learning scenario and the reshaping of old traditional patterns.

There are examples of best practices with Mobile Learning which could provide an overview on the potential of mobile technologies and what impact these might have on learning and teaching practices (See Figure 3).

Some of these examples include the use of SMS-enabled treasure hunts led to enhanced peer learning as students need to quickly interpret cues and to exchange ideas to finding correct answers to questions... The exploration of mobile devices to support social work students and mentors when students undertake their placements. (REMORA) http://www.jisc.ac.uk/whatwedo/programmes/ elearningcapital/xinstit2/remora.aspx. The use of pocket PCs to support portfolio development by teaching assistants on foundation degree courses. (WoLF), the use of Augmented reality to enhance teaching and learning (SCARLET) http://www. jisc.ac.uk/whatwedo/programmes/elearning/ltig/ scarlet.aspx, to simultaneously allow students to experience the magic of original materials, whilst enhancing the learning experience. The FAVOR project http://www.jisc.ac.uk/whatwedo/pro-

Figure 3. New teaching and learning scenarios

grammes/ukoer3/favor.aspx (Finding a Voice through Open Resources) which showcases the work of language teachers in universities, by engaging them in activities which will enhance the student experience and contribute to the academic life of their institutions.

And finally, as an example of international and multicultural collaboration we would like to signal The iCollaborate (http://icollab12.wordpress.com/) project constituted by an international community of practice of students and lecturers started in 2011 which aims to explore and evaluate which *mobile web tools*, pedagogic strategies and learning scenarios can be effective to support international student and lecturer *collaboration, participation* in decision-making as part of curriculum development and the development of *21st century skills*. iCollaborate educational activities and research interests include:

Exploring mobile tools for international collaboration of teams of students, engaging students in participatory curriculum development by means of social and mobile media, exploring the creation of digital identities in social and mobile media, using mobile media for situated co-creation of student-generated content and modelling heutagogical approaches to education, the use of mobile web 2.0 as catalyst for pedagogical change/innovation and the fostering of collaborative research in mobile social media integration in higher education

4. DISCUSSION

Against the described background, the significance and need for mobile learning research and practice based upon learning theories, focused on pedagogically eloquent approaches to mobile learning remains vital. At the same time, it becomes extremely central to underline the communication and collaboration affordances of smartphones as they favor teamwork and contribute to facilitate students to negotiate learning outcomes. Institutions have to see how to engage these affordances and integrate them into their educational processes. Agreeing with Kukuslka-Hume (2010) "we need to draw on the findings from recent major projects to show how people artfully engage with their surroundings, peers and technology to create impromptu sites of learning and to carry their conversations from place to place, from time to time, from topic to topic."

Existing related literature shows that while Mobile Learning is proving to be innovative, other factors such ad the balance between pedagogical issues and technological ideals will be determining its ultimate success. It is difficult to predict whether Mobile Learning will become a new paradigm of higher education or will remain a trendy fashion. Notwithstanding this, our society is being increasingly affected by mobility and it is the responsibility of researchers and other education-related stakeholders to provide and design to meet the needs of this changing audiences.

Mobile learning is inherent to the learner's lifestyle, in which s/he shifts from one context to another, swapping locations, social groups and technologies. Although this view of learning is wide-ranging of formal education contexts, it is intensely applicable to informal learning outside academia. Moreover, this vision accounts for the intricacy of Mobile Learning and the associated complexity associated to Mobile Learning research. As it could be derived from the examples provided, perhaps one of the greatest impacts of Mobile Learning into Higher Education will be in changing the main foregrounds of the relationship between institution and classroom-based learning. Since the concepts of time and space are changing as mobile and connected communities do, there emerges the need to further deepen upon the nature of context and to develop policies that facilitate processes of social learning. In the process of interacting with the wider environment, learners construct their knowledge within the community and co-design their learning process.

Mobile and wireless technologies can provide flexible and timely access to learning resources, instantaneous communication, portability, active learning experiences and the empowerment and engagement of learners, particularly those in dispersed communities. However, despite the almost ubiquitous ownership of mobile phones, there is a lack of research that informs its real impact upon educational practices.

A deep understanding of the mobile culture defined in terms of context-awareness, mobility and of learners' specific needs happens to be genuinely important for a successful implementation of mobile technologies and groundbreaking design for learning. New competencies and skills that may developed through the use of mobile technologies demand a very specific mapping between what is expected of learners and how theses technologies may be of help to achieve those objectives. Although generic competences are still legitimate, they also should be connected to ways in which they can be attained, and mobile technologies constitute, in this sense, an integral part of this process. Proactive learners in their use of mobile technologies can point the way to the future, whereas the majority of learners will have to be aware of the opportunities they may face by making a good use of them. In this sense, both educators and learners need to realize that mobile technology is substantially different from desktop computing and they will make use of mobility and context-awareness as departing points for keeping social contact, accessing content and becoming content creators. Thus, they will develop essential skills and competences as 21st century learners. Educational institutions and related stakeholders need to take ownership of change and be able to reshape their landscape as it is being challenged by the mobile revolution.

Regarding future directions, eventually it could be envisioned that mobile technologies will be used in both formal and informal learning contexts.

REFERENCES

Barzaiq, O., & Loke, S. (2010). Adapting the mobile phone for task efficiency. *The International Journal of Pervasive Computing and Communications, 6*(1), 47–87.

Beckett, D., & Hager, P. J. (2002). *Life, work and learning: Practice in postmodernity*. London, UK: Routledge.

Brown, E. (2010). Introduction to location-based mobile learning. In Brown, E. (Ed.), *Education in the wild: contextual and location-based mobile learning in action*. University of Nottingham: Learning Sciences Research Institute.

Bryant, T. (2006). Social software in academia. *EDUCAUSE Quarterly, 2*.

Buchem, I., & Camacho, M. (2011). M-project: First steps to applying action research in designing a mobile learning course in higher education. In K. Rummler, J. Seipold, E. Lübcke, N. Pachler, & G. Attwell (Eds.), *Mobile learning: Crossing boundaries in convergent environments* (pp. 123-132). London Mobile Learning Group. ISSN 1753-3385

Cobcroft, R., Towers, S., Smith, J., & Bruns, A. (2006). Mobile learning in review: Opportunities and challenges for learners, teachers, and institutions. In *Proceedings Online Learning and Teaching (OLT) Conference 2006*, (pp. 21-30). Brisbane, Australia: Queensland University of Technology.

Cochrane, T. (2010). *Twitter tales: Facilitating international collaboration with mobile web 2.0*. Paper presented at the 27th ASCILITE Conference, ASCILITE 2010.

Cochrane, T., & Bateman, R. (2011). Transforming pedagogy using mobile web 2.0. In Parsons, D. (Ed.), *Combining e-learning and m-learning: New applications of blended educational resources* (pp. 281–307). Hershey, PA: IGI Global. doi:10.4018/978-1-60960-481-3.ch018

Cochrane, T., & Rhodes, D. (2011). *iArchi[tech]ture: Heutagogical approaches to education facilitated by mlearning integration*. Paper presented at the International Conference on Information and Communication Technologies in Education ICICTE 2011. Retrieved from http://www.icicte.org/index.htm

Colley, H., Hodkinson, P., & Malcom, J. (2003). *Informality and formality in learning: A report for the learning and skills research centre*. London, UK: Learning and Skills Research Centre.

Colley, J., & Stead, G. (2004). *Mobile learning = collaboration. Proceedings of mLearn 2004 Mobile learning anytime everywhere* (pp. 57–58). London, UK: Learning and Skills Development Agency.

Cortez, C., Nussbaum, M., Santelices, R., Rodríguez, P., Zurita, G., Correa, M., et al. (2004). Teaching science with mobile computer supported collaborative learning (MCSCL). *Proceedings of the 2nd IEEE workshop on wireless and mobile technologies in education* (WMTE '04) (pp. 67–74). JungLi, Taiwan: IEEE Computer Society.

December 10, 2011, from http://www.mlearn.org.za/CD/papers/Stead.pdf

Drucker, P. F. (1994). The age of social transformation. *Atlantic Monthly, 274*(5), 53–80.

FitzGerald, E. (2012). Creating user-generated content for location-based learning: An authoring framework. *Journal of Computer Assisted Learning, 28*(3). doi:10.1111/j.1365-2729.2012.00481.x

Garnett, F. (2010). *Heutagogy and the craft of teaching*. The Heutagogic Archives. Retrieved 19th December, 2011, from http://heutagogicarchive. wordpress.com/2010/11/18/heutagogy-the-craft-of-teaching/#more-340

Gay, G., Stefanone, M., Grace-Martin, M., & Hembrooke, H. (2001). The effects of wireless computing in collaborative learning environments. *International Journal of Human-Computer Interaction, 13*(2), 257–276. doi:10.1207/S15327590I-JHC1302_10

Glahn, C., Börner, D., & Specht, M. (2010). Mobile informal learning. In Brown, E. (Ed.), *Education in the wild: Contextual and location-based mobile learning in action*. University of Nottingham: Learning Sciences Research Institute.

Grasso, A., & Roselli, T. (2005). Guidelines for designing and developing contents for mobile learning. In H. Ogata, M. Sharples, Kinshuk, & Y. Yano (Eds.), *Proceedings of the Third IEEE International Workshop on Wireless and Mobile Technologies in Education* (WMTE '05) (pp. 123–127). Washington, DC: IEEE Computer Society.

Hayhoe, G. F. (2001). From desktop to palmtop: creating usable online documents for wireless and handheld devices. In T.J. Malkinson (Ed.), *Proceedings of the IEEE International Professional Communication Conference* (pp. 1–11). Piscataway, NJ: IEEE.

Hwang, G., Shi, Y., & Chu, H. (2010). A concept map approach to developing collaborative Mindtools for context-aware ubiquitous learning. *British Journal of Educational Technology, 42*, 778–789. doi:10.1111/j.1467-8535.2010.01102.x

Johnson, L., Adams, S., & Haywood, K. (2011). *The NMC horizon report: 2011 K-12 edition*. Austin, TX: The New Media Consortium.

Jonassen, D. H. (1991). Evaluating constructivist learning. *Educational Technology, 31*(9), 28–33.

Keegan, H. (2010). *Immersed in the digital: Networked creativity through mobile content production*. Paper presented at the Association for Learning Technology: ALTC2010. Retrieved from http://altc2010.alt.ac.uk/talks/15004.

Kozma, R., & Anderson, R. (2002). Qualitative case studies of innovative pedagogical practices using ICT. *Journal of Computer Assisted Learning, 18*, 387–394. doi:10.1046/j.0266-4909.2002.00250.doc.x

Kukulska-Hulme, A. (2010). Learning cultures on the move: where are we heading? *Journal of Educational Technology & Society, 13*(4), 4–14.

Lave, J., & Wenger, E. (1991). *Situated learning: Legitimate peripheral participation*. Cambridge, UK: Cambridge University Press. doi:10.1017/CBO9780511815355

Litchfield, A., Nettleton, S., & Taylor, T. (2008). *Integrating work-ready learning into the university curriculum contextualised by profession. World Association of Cooperative Education (WACE)*. Sydney: Asia Pacific Conference.

Livingstone, D. W. (2001). *Adults' informal learning: Definitions, findings, gaps and future research*. NALL (New Approaches to Lifelong Learning), Working Paper #21, Toronto. Retrieved January 30, 2011, from https://tspace.library. utoronto.ca/bitstream/1807/2735/2/21adultsinfo rmallearning.pdf

Lonsdale, P., Baber, C., Sharples, M., & Arvantis, T. N. (2004). A context-awareness architecture for facilitating mobile learning. In Attewell, J., & Savill-Smith, C. (Eds.), *Learning with mobile devices: Research and development*. London, UK: Learning and Skills Development Agency.

Luckin, R., Clark, W., Garnett, F., Whitworth, A., Akass, J., & Cook, J. (2010). Learner-generated contexts: A framework to support the effective use of technology for learning. In Lee, M., & McLoughlin, C. (Eds.), *Web 2.0-based e-learning: Applying social informatics for tertiary teaching* (pp. 70–84). Hershey, PA: IGI Global. doi:10.4018/978-1-60566-294-7.ch004

McConatha, D., Praul, M., & Lynch, M. J. (2008). Mobile learning in higher education: An empirical assessment of a new educational tool. *Turkish Online Journal of Educational Technology, 7*(3).

McFarlane, A., Triggs, P., & Yee, W. (2008). *Researching mobile learning*. Retrieved September 9, 2008, from http://partners.becta.org.uk/upload-dir/downloads/page_documents/research/mobile_learning.doc

Mioduser, D., Nachmias, R., & Forkosh-Baruch, A. (2008). New literacies for the knowledge society. In Voogt, J., & Knezek, G. (Eds.), *International handbook of information technology in education*. Springer.

Naismith, L., Lonsdale, P., Vavoula, G., & Sharples, M. (2005). *Report 11: Literature review in mobile technologies and learning*. Bristol, UK: Futurelab Series. doi: http://www2.futurelab.org.uk/resources/documents/lit_reviews/Mobile_Review.pdf

Norman, D. (1993). *Things that make us smart: Defending human attributes in the age of the machine*. Reading, MA: Addison- Wesley.

Pachler, N., Cook, J., & Bachmair, B. (2010). Appropriation of mobile cultural resources for learning. *International Journal of Mobile and Blended Learning, 2*(1), 1–21. doi:10.4018/jmbl.2010010101

Parry, D. (2011). Mobile perspectives: On teaching mobile literacy. *EDUCAUSE Review, 46*(2). Retrieved from http://www.educause.edu/er

Pettit, J., & Kukulska-Hulme, A. (2011). Mobile 2.0: Crossing the border into formal learning? In Lee, M. J. W., & McLoughlin, C. (Eds.), *Web 2.0-based e-learning: Applying social informatics for tertiary teaching* (pp. 192–208). Hershey, PA: IGI Global.

Resnick, L. (1987). *Education and learning to think*. Washington, DC: National Academy Press.

Savio, N., & Braiterman, J. (2007). Design sketch: The context of mobile interaction. In A. D. Cheok & L. Chittaro (Eds.), *Proceedings of the 9th Conference on Human-Computer Interaction with Mobile Devices and Services* (Mobile HCI 2007) (pp. 284–286). New York, NY: ACM.

Sharples, M. (2000). The design of personal mobile technologies for lifelong learning. *Computers & Education, 34*, 177–193. doi:10.1016/S0360-1315(99)00044-5

Sharples, M. (2010). Foreword. In Brown, E. (Ed.), *Education in the wild: Contextual and location-based mobile learning in action*. University of Nottingham: Learning Sciences Research Institute.

Sharples, M., Milrad, M., Arnedillo Sánchez, I., & Vavoula, G. (2009). Mobile learning: Small devices, big issues. In Balacheff, N., Ludvigsen, S., Jong, T., Lazonder, A., & Barnes, S. (Eds.), *Technology enhanced learning: Principles and products* (pp. 233–249). Heidelberg, Germany: Springer.

Soloway, E., Grant, W., Tinker, R., Roschelle, J., Mills, M., & Resnick, M. (1999). Science in the palm of their hands. *Communications of the ACM, 42*(8), 21–26. doi:10.1145/310930.310953

Stead, G. (2005). *Moving mobile into the mainstream. Proceedings of mLearn 2005*. Retrieved.

Traxler, J. (2009). Learning in a mobile age. *International Journal of Mobile and Blended Learning, 1*(1), 1–12. doi:10.4018/jmbl.2009010101

Vesely, P., Bloom, L., & Sherlock, J. (2007). Key elements of building online community: Comparing faculty and student perceptions. *Journal of Online Learning and Teaching, 3*(3).

Wenger, E. (1998). *Communities of practice: Learning, meaning, and identity.* Cambridge, UK: Cambridge University Press.

Wenger, E., White, N., & Smith, J. (2009). *Digital habitats: Stewarding technology for communities.* Portland, OR: CPsquare.

Wingkvist, A., & Ericsson, M. (2010). A framework to guide and structure the development process of mobile learning initiatives. In M. Montebello, et al., (Eds.), *mLearn 2010: Conference Proceedings,* University of Malta.

KEY TERMS AND DEFINITIONS

Education: The means through which the aims and habits of a group of people sustain from one generation to the next.

Emergent Technologies: Contemporary advances and innovation in various fields of technology which, in the educational field can provide a new paradigm and opportunities to transform learning.

Informal Learning: Form of learning which occurs in a variety of places through daily interactions and shared relationships among members of society independently from instructor-led programs.

Mobile Culture: A shared set of practices, meanings, relationships, norms, exchanges and rituals related to the growing importance of mobile technologies in contemporary society.

Mobile Learning: Learning that happens when the learner takes advantage of the learning opportunities offered by mobile technologies.

Mobile Literacy: Skills that include being aware of the mobile technology landscape and the major current tools, understanding the implications of mobile technologies as trends and tools for information engagement.

Situated Learning: Learning that takes place in the same context in which it is applied.

Chapter 19
Media and Communication Research Facing Social Media

Georgeta Drulă
University of Bucharest, Romania

ABSTRACT

It is already a fact that social media are engaged in research activities. Social media may make the object of research studies or an important data source. This chapter addresses issues related to social media research in media and communication studies. The pursued objective is to capture how researchers consider and analyze social media through scientific methods, in their work with academic purposes, in order to present the discussed theories. The ideas addressed by this chapter are case studies arising from the articles in the academic publications, topics related to social media and media and communication fields, outputs of researches, and appropriate methods for studying social media. The conclusions of this chapter show that social media research in media and communication studies, theories, and methods must be transformed or must be used more appropriate to social media. New and social media are faced with other practices and types of communication related to users' participation and social actions and are based on network studies.

INTRODUCTION

All over-used concept of "social media" is very often differently or partially understood and in many situations addressed inappropriately. There are a lot of definitions that fit to social media. For instance, Cohen (2011) collected 30 definitions for social media from professionals in marketing and public relations field. But in a very simple way, social media is "the term commonly referring to blogs and social network sites online" (Lariscy et al. 2009). Social media are also defined as "forms

DOI: 10.4018/978-1-4666-2970-7.ch019

of electronic communication through which users create online communities to share information, ideas, personal messages, and other content" (Merriam-Webster dictionary).

But, the definition for "social media" continually evolves and develops. Thus, Kaplan and Haenlein (2010) tried to give a more clear and comprehensive understanding of the concept of social media. Their definition of "social media" is related to Web 2.0 and user-generated content (UGC), two concepts that are frequently named in conjunction with it. Their definition says that *"social media is a group of Internet-based applications that build on the ideological and technological foundations of Web 2.0, and that allow the creation and exchange of user generated content"* (Kaplan and Haenlein, 2010, p. 61). The same authors provide various types of social media that are discovered in a classification made on two dimensions: social presence and media richness – with the first dimension being the self-presentation and self-disclosure of the second dimension. Following these dimensions, Kaplan and Haenlein (2010, p. 62) identified six types of social media applications, such as: "collaborative projects (e.g. wikis or social bookmarking applications - Delicious), blogs, content communities (e.g. Youtube, Flickr, or Slideshare), social network sites - SNS (e.g. Facebook, Myspace, or LinkedIn), virtual games (e.g. World of WarCraft) and virtual social worlds (e.g. Second Life)". The same groups and exemplifications of social media are also provided by Rheingold (2008). These six types of social media applications are frequently analyzed in academic research and are also used in the academic environment for learning process. The stress of this paper is devoted to aspects found in the academic research.

Considering this as a start point, the study is developed in the next directions:

1.   One regarding the researching *types of social media* applications (e.g. Twitter, Facebook, blogs, SNS in media and communication) as

well as the specific *activities in social media* (engagement, participation, bookmarking, aggregation, etc.) for media and communication interest.

2.   One regarding the *methodologies, and methods* used for social media research in media and communication studies.

3.   One regarding the *theories and models* used for social media research in media and communication studies.

Researches related to interpersonal and organizational communication, or related to impact of new technologies in communication are permanent interest for companies who search new ways to engage with the customers. Political and intercultural communication, economics of communication have more interest for research in academic or professional environment. Thus, researchers present the challenges released by Web 2.0 and analyze different forms of convergence and new types of products, more attractive for users which are both media consumers and media producers.

In this context, social media have an important role in media and communication research. The purpose of this paper is to create a synthesis of the ongoing work of media scholars and professionals about theories and frameworks of social media research used in communication and media studies.

The questions that we must answer in this paper are: "What subjects are related to social media and communication studies?" and "How are they researched (theories, and methods)?".

This chapter considers the theories and research methods of social media for media and communication studies and presents the research market interested in social media.

Trends in Media and Communication Research

Seminal analyses of professional and academic literature in Europe and the United States based on different aspects of media – journalism, are made by many scientists in last ten years (Deuze, 2004; Mitchelstein and Boczkowski, 2009; Herkman, 2008). These analyses are current studies regarding media and communication research from a digital perspective, taking into account the Internet and the Web as important factors of changing.

Social media applications have provoked important changes of media and communication phenomena. Thus, Bartholomew (2010) considers that we have a new model of communication in social media and the research must be according to this model. This model of communication in social media is based on user-generated content, is characterized especially by "peer-to-peer evaluation" and "bidirectional relationships", and it is also characterized by users' engagement, influence, reach and adequacy.

Regarding the numerous media and journalism studies, there are two approaches in analyzing media and communication phenomena and social media. An approach aimed to *traditional media in digital environments, especially in social media applications*. Other approach is devoted to *specific phenomena of Web 2.0 and social media*, such as user-generated content in media production and strategies of communication. According to first approach, Mitchelstein and Boczkowski (2009) review the scholarship on *online news production*, published since 2000. Their work takes into consideration specific aspects related to Web 2.0 such as: "historical context and market environment, the process of innovation, alterations in journalistic practices, challenges to established professional dynamics, and the role of user-generated content". Another example of analyzing media and communication phenomena and social media is *multimedia journalism*. Deuze (2004) or Jacobson (2010) analyze multimedia journalism based on traditional aspects of media (e.g. institutional perspective, technological and organizational perspective, producer/user perspective, and educational perspective). You may find that academic research topics into traditional media and related to mass-communication and media effects are

becoming less important than research about online communication or communication and new media technologies (Herkman, 2008, p: 17). The analysis of current trends in media research, driven by Herkman (2008), presents the results of the project "Mapping Media and Communication Research" and concludes that the challenges in media and communication research are related to the term "convergence" and are provoked by the *changes in communication technologies*. All these changes are addressed by academic research. Another conclusion given by Herkman's analysis shows that research approaches in media and communication depend on each researcher, and even on the approaches used in his/her research environment.

A. SOCIAL MEDIA IN MEDIA AND COMMUNICATION RESEARCH STUDIES

In research activity, social media is addressed either as *research object* or as environment from which *to collect data* in other studies.

Social Media as Research Object: Topics Addressed in Media and Communication Studies

Social media applications (classified after Kaplan and Haenlein, 2010, p. 62), *as research objects*, are interesting both from informational and social points of view, and open new perspectives on research into media and communication studies. Moreover, activities in social media such as engagement, participation, sharing, bookmarking, aggregation, etc, provoked by specific actions such as Like, Share, Bookmark, Digg It! or Link give others perspectives and possibilities of research in media and communication field. Users are more implicated in the creation and distribution of information. They also have a specific social behavior, and use new forms of communication in social media applications. It is already known that the media content is created both by the media companies and by the users.

Thus, topics and theories related to crowds and connected with large amounts of content and information have emerged. So, if on the site Web a basic rule is to provide the easiest way to navigate the information, in social media it is impossible to organize the content for effective navigation. Informal rules that could be expressed by tags and clouds of tags, manage navigation. The information organization as *clouds of online content* (applications, media, and users' content) is treated in research studies from multiple perspectives. The online content in social media applications can be posted and found in a very simple way, and can be shared and delivered to crowds. *Activities* done in terms of multimedia content (creation, distribution, promotion, sharing) on social media platforms are also addressed in the research papers. The perspective assumed both for online content and activities with this content is a user's perspective. *User-generated content* and new activities based on user's actions are very important in the media research studies.

Possibility to use more sources of information, different types of information and authors (users) has generated new products in media. Thus, other topic frequently found in digital space is convergence and remixing. Fagerjord (2010) considers that remixing is the next step after convergence. While convergence refers more to similarities between different media characteristics, the remix process is largely based on different aspects. The remix culture or "read/write culture", as was named by Lessig (2008), describes the way to create new genres from other pieces of content. The main importance of this culture of convergence and remixing is that it is a culture that encourages creativity and collaboration offered by the Internet and the Web. For instance, content is made up by blogging, and then is added commentaries; Youtube videos are frequently linked on blogs or on Facebook site; television sites are connected

to social media applications for new audiences. Specific characteristics of media products are coming together for creating new ones, better. New products in media are obtained as a hybrid of other products. Lessig (2008) considers that users must gain from this process of creativity.

Not only the media products are reinvented, but even the audience. The online presence can be transformed in a 3D virtual audience. Now, we have more than new social resources on Web, but we may also have a social life on the Web. Virtual people, avatars, can create information, and even business on Web. All these aspects are reflected by the research papers on virtual worlds and on games in changing media and changing audiences. This virtual world is a well-connected world based on relationships and links between people, who create networks. So, Web 2.0 applications, such as social network sites (especially Facebook or Twitter) or multiple-user virtual environments (MUVEs) facilitate the links analysis (Rosen, Rosen, Barnett and Kim, 2011, p: 35). Concerning these networks, research studies focus on groups' behaviors or communication practices. As we can see, the main approaches of research into social media are oriented towards computer-mediated communication (tools, and practices), user-generated content and user participation (content creation or engagement). Many authors dedicated their studies to these topics. Thus, Lenhart and Madden (2005), also mentioned by Rosen, Barnett and Kim (2011), showed that social network sites such as Facebook and Twitter are very appropriate for content creation and interaction. boyd (2006, 2007, 2008)[1] has also done vast research on social network sites.

Some authors studied the *relationship between different types of social media*. Thus, Cha, Navarro and Haddadi (2011) analyze the video content from Youtube that is shared on blogs and show that news videos spreading in the blogosphere are topical. This study observed that users use more information given by others users, as source of information. In their research method, Cha, Navarro and Haddadi (2011) correlated the *spreading patterns of videos* with the topological structure of blogosphere and determined the diffusion of video information.

The research interest has increased in social media as forms of mediated social networks, or in media consumption studies (Stefanone, Lackaff and Rosen, 2010b), and online social capital, and global communication. The *consumption model* of social media compared with traditional media is also a topic found in the literature. The results of the study conducted by Stefanone, Lackaff and Rosen (2010a), and cited by Rosen, Barnett and Kim (2011), show a strong relationship between reality television consumption and the time spend by the users on social network sites, the size of user's networks, and the number of friends.

As far as blogs are concerned, the most important topic addressed by the scholars is the *relationship between mainstream media and social media*. Skoler (2009) concludes in this regard that "mainstream media see social media as a tool that distribute and market the content" and it is only a part of journalists that use social media for their real values, such as "establish relationships and listen to others". His vision about the future of journalism is related to these two values: listening and action on social media in equal time intervals. Similar concerns have Lariscy et al. (2009) who show the significance of *relationship between size of publications and activities on social media platforms* (such as: blogs, video-sharing sites and social networking sites). The study reveals that social media sites are used more on larger publications and journalists accept the social media concept but they less apply it in practice. Another result of Lariscy et al. (2009) study shows that journalists use more web pages and directories as source of information, and less social media. However, social media can contribute to the *agenda-building process*.

"Social media are not doing journalism", considers Skoler (2009), who says that they are not "models for the new journalism", even if they bring

breaking news. He considers that social media just cover the information from mainstream media and act as indicator of relevancy and value-creating. The conclusion of Skoler's study is related to these two values and supports the idea that social media and their culture can guide media companies to relevancy and value-creating. The author advocates for the right choice of social media, not only Twitter or Facebook, "as a fervent attempt to win followers and increase traffic on sites" (Skoler, 2009: p. 39).

The relationship between mainstream media and social media is also rendered by the concept of *participatory journalism or participatory media* Rheingold (2008) emphasizes the specificity of participatory media and public's engagement. Users create content, comments, discuss, and act in a specific social platform way. The author concludes that these practices can influence the civic behavior throughout people's lives. The subject of public engagement is also addressed by Clark and Aufderheide (2009). In relation to the engaged public, actions such as: remixing, creating, sharing, voting, and commenting content, make current media more "people-centered".

Participatory journalism reveals a relationship between newspapers websites and user-generated content (UGC) offered on social media platforms (Hermida and Thurman, 2009). The authors identified a moderation model to adopt the UGC, taking into consideration the issues of trust, legal liabilities and author's reputation. The conclusions given by Hermida and Thurman (2009) presents a gate-keeping approach of UGC integration with professional news, and an editorial structure is kept with more users as occasional reporters. The *adoption of user-generated content* (UGC) by media companies is largely discussed and analyzed in research papers. Gal-Or, Geylani and Yildirim (2010) show that the moderation of the production process of the UGC influences the company's decision related to the creation of an online media product (newspaper). Companies' decision to use UGC for a media product is also dependent on the platform for the creation and the collection of multimedia content and also, on the quantity of the generated content (Thurman, 2008). Thus, though this content may be found in large quantities, its quality is quite different. Hence the preoccupation of the media companies to find users' valuable content (Agichtein et al., 2008). It is definitely accepted by all authors, that users' participation determines the diversification of information and brings changes in the manner of communication with audience.

Engagement as a form of user's participation in the social media is another topic addressed by social media researchers. Concerns related to belonging to a community, trust, knowledge and information sharing, or online communities, are discussed extensively by different authors (Rheingold, 2008; Rosen, Barnett and Kim, 2011).

Users' participation in social media is not only defined in terms of number of actions done on these sites, but also in terms of the *quality of online discussions,* as well as the *sentiments* aroused by these discussions. Thus, Diakopoulos and Naaman (2011) focus on the *quality of discussions in online communities created around news sites.* The study presents the quality of comments in relation to consumption and production of news information and gives the readers' and writers' motivations for the usage of news comments. The notion of quality is interpreted by these authors in normative terms such as "accuracy, reliability, validity, currency, relevancy, comprehensiveness, and clarity" and as "degree of excellence in communicating knowledge".

Social media are also important for communication and marketing mix; consequently, their measurement and metrics are envisaged. Social media are also seen as environment for personal online presentation of individuals and companies' *reputation.* Paine (2009) shows how the reputation of an organization in social media can be measured and appreciated. She conducted several benchmarks reputation studies and established a common methodology that can be used by any organization to measure its relation to social media.

Social media sites, such as Facebook and Twitter are favorites in studies of media and communication research.

Media and Communication Research and Blogs

Blogs as social media application represent a predominant topic in the media and communication research. Preoccupations related to the influence of blogosphere and the relationship between journalism and blogosphere are very common. Topics found in blogosphere are: finding leaders and influence, knowledge exchange between blogs, understanding power in networks, discovering communities of practice, finding news, or managing prestige.

In a first stage, different researchers identified the *differences between blogging and journalism* (Blood, 2003; Lasica, 2003; Wall, 2004; Lowrey, 2006) from the following perspectives: professional values, gathering of information, format of information, and organization of the production process of information. Journalism on blogs has some vulnerability identified by Lowrey (2006): issues are covered subjectively, especially in the case of new topics, content is not complex and specialized, the audience can not judge if this content has success. At this stage, information on blogs is an alternative to journalistic products and is frequently a topic in blog research. Self-expression and personal opinions offered on different media facts and events are also found in the research studies. News articles are also treated in connection with blogs.

When the blogosphere has become more important, next stage of research was required. The *relationships between journalism and blogging* were studied by a lot of scholars, such are: Domingo et al. (2008); Bruns, (2009); Lowrey and Burleson Mackay (2008); Schmidt, (2007); Gil de Zúñiga et al., (2011); Mitchelstein and Boczkoroski, (2009). It is still not clear whether blogging is a form of journalism but all scholars considered that blogging transformed journalism practices, values and norms in various ways. In a very recent study, Cha, Navarro and Haddadi (2011) studied the *influence of blogs in understanding the new journalistic conventions*. The data considered in this study are web feeds from popular blogs. They present the topological structure of blogosphere and the patterns of media content that are shared through blogs. They found that the network structure of blogs is sparsely connected and also that the type of media content in the blogs is different from that in mainstream media. The content in the blogs is spread virally, and sometimes for a long time, meantime the topics such as news and political commentary spread and disappear quickly. Cha, Navarro and Haddadi (2011) also consider that blogosphere has a special structure, different from the other social networks.

Blogosphere is also studied as *virtual community*. Researches of blogosphere identify virtual communities based on different topics, cultures, users' behavior, discussions, communication models and work practices, finding valuable information in blogosphere.

Many studies are dedicated to motivations for blogging. In these studies blogosphere is a space of conversation, and its role is to generate debate, not just a space for writing. Other topics in blogosphere are the quality of social interactivity and the relationships with bloggers' audiences, starting from the fact that bloggers relate both to the known audience of their personal social networks and to the wider blogosphere of unknown readers.

Rosen, Barnett and Kim (2011) analyze *political blogs* and their hyperlinks, social media and multi-user virtual environments, considering Web as a links network, but also as an emergent social structure and a communication network for researchers. Analyses on political blogosphere are also made by Meraz (2009). He examines the relationship between traditional media and social media regarding the influence of agenda setting. He also shows how traditional media use the blog as a journalistic tool. The author considers

that agenda setting follows an inter-media model shared between traditional newsroom blogs and independent political blogs. Meraz (2009) refers to blog influence and blog importance in the media virtual space, and underline that "blog is a platform which redistributes power between traditional media and citizen media". He concludes that the wisdom of the crowd is very important for the Web audience and also for the reinvented media.

Users need norms and rules for participating in social media applications. Deuze (2006) gives some ideas about digital culture theory and its relationship with blogging. He considers blogging as an expression of digital culture with its components: "participation, bricolage and remediation". These components permits actions of "remixing, reusing, and redistribution of content" done by the other users. Blogs as a form of open participatory storytelling produce specific ways of expression, topics and writing. The values of digital culture are sometimes formulated in opposition to those upheld by mainstream corporate media. Deuze (2006) considers that digital culture is more based on personal experiences and beliefs rather than professional and corporate values. Likewise, "self-production" is a key concept in digital culture. For example, the blogger is equally the producer, content manager and marketing specialist of the online product. As forms of convergence between blogs and news sites there appeared "citizen journalism" and user-generated content platforms linked to the news sites.

Media and Communication Research on Twitter and Facebook

An et al. (2011) presents the first study about media landscape in social media, such as Twitter. The authors discuss the type of micro-journalism on Twitter, analyzing the practices in media publishing and consumption, studying how users interact with media on Twitter. An et al. (2011) examine whether social media especially Twitter is a platform for studying the media landscape. They also present the importance of social contacts for diversity of opinion. A conclusion of their study shows that Twitter users follow multiple news sources. This remark is very valuable for researchers and marketers and can help to understand the navigation ways in social media and how users read media updates and news.

A map of media landscape taking into consideration the key features of social media, such as: "the role played by journalists" and "user participation in disseminating information" and not the important coordinates in traditional media, such as media sources and audience, is provided by An et al. (2011). They offer a comparison of the readership of different types of media and conclude that the journalists' audience is often more important than the media organizations' audience. Their study shows that users prefer to receive information from multiple sources on similar topics, and that social media is a favorite place for this.

Referring to how users read news in social media, An et al. (2011) demonstrate that the users who are followed by a large number of other users; in fact, it is the journalists that they all follow. Another useful conclusion given by An et al. (2011) refers to the very readable stories in social media. These stories are those that "generate sentiments, are emotional, critical, sarcastic or humorous". The authors equally observed changes of journalistic conventions and cultures taking place in social media, such as "active participation of media journalists and audience members" and "diversity of information distributed via social contacts".

The preoccupation for social media, e.g. Twitter, and media landscape is revealed by other authors too. The relationship between social media and news is retrieved as a form of "ambient journalism", a concept mentioned by Hermida (2010a, 2010b). This is a term that describes the ubiquitous nature of news, especially on social media platforms. "Ambient journalism" is related to users/audience that became part of the news

making process. The Twitter site is considered to be a platform of "ambient journalism" because users contribute with multimedia content, disseminate and give comments for the news.

If Hermida (2010a, 2010b) considers Twitter as a platform for news making, boyd, Golder and Lotan (2010) consider conversational practices on Twitter platform. They talk about re-tweeting as a conversational practice and examine the users' authorship, attribution and communicative fidelity. Likewise, Yardi and boyd (2010) describe the implications of sharing information in local communities through Twitter and the role of mainstream news in disseminating local information. They found that central individuals in the Twitter network are also located centrally in the physical world and that the users search for local news sources for information.

Kwak et al. (2010) also wonder whether Twitter is a news media. They study the topological characteristics of Twitter and give conclusions related to information sharing and diffusion on this platform. They determine the influential users on Twitter and the information diffusion via re-tweet. Twitter is considered to be an information spreading platform and re-tweeting is considered to be a process of dissemination. In media research, Twitter may be a platform where users receive information via re-tweets. The conclusion reached by Kwak et al. (2010) is that it does not matter how many followers a user has, but the amount of user's tweets spreading via re-tweets. Their argumentation is based on the fact that re-tweeting creates an audience for the user. Thus, the influential user is that who selects the information and spreads it through re-tweets. Re-tweets deliver information to many other users, thus, the community decides on the importance of original tweets.

Social network site such as Facebook is also studied in a lot of media research papers, although, the focus remains on blogs and journalists' work. The same interest in journalistic activities developed on blogs, appears in Facebook studies, too.

But in these studies, the Facebook platform seems more interesting as *source of information,* as well as *agenda building for journalists.*

According to O'Connor (2009), there are several conditions that favor analysis of social media in terms of journalism activities, such as: "the crisis of trust, the oversaturated market of information and news". Selection and filtering the information is a necessary process in social media. So, information marked by other users (voted, liked, commented, etc) is more valuable and useful. From the journalists' point of view, it is important to be committed with Facebook audiences, in order to market and share content with users. This mechanism is a powerful way to gain the trust of the audience.

In the same way as Twitter, Facebook is a social media application often analyzed in media and communication research studies. The topics related to Facebook research refer to investigation of people relationships within community, people's motivations to be connected into a social network, privacy and trust matters in social networks, online self-presentation focusing on identity and branding construction, corporate strategies for social media, or Facebook implication in political and communication campaigns. The political economy of Facebook draws attention to audiences as well as media companies who try to develop new types of relationships with the public, as number and quality.

B. METHODOLOGIES AND METHODS USED FOR SOCIAL MEDIA RESEARCH

Social Media – Data and their Measurements

Research 2.0 is connected with Web 2.0 and is based especially on social media and online research communities. The Web 2.0 opportunities (tools, applications, and environment) give re-

searchers many possibilities to study social media and also to use them in their work, especially to collect data. Finding information is a key aspect of research.

In social media research studies different data and measurements are used. The social media measurements refer to quantitative and qualitative aspects. The quantitative aspects are related to the number of comments, friends, likes, followers and others, and the qualitative aspects are connected with the "sentiments" provoked by the users' actions. Thus, social media as *environment to collect data* offer several quantitative indicators and also measurements of sentiments that occur after the performance of social actions.

Social media change the ways in which research studies are done, using different tools and measurements. Data from online environments bring important contributions to different sciences (Rosen, Barnett and Kim, 2011). These aspects are also called science 2.0 and research 2.0. The hyperlink network configuration is very important to understand how and from where must be collected data from the Internet. Rosen et al. (2011) indicates several important nodes of Web traffic, appropriate to collect data from.

Data from social media can be collected directly from the social networks sites or through questionnaires applied to users on such sites. Although to study the social media phenomenon, data are collected through questionnaires, this method has several limitations caused by inconsistent answers to questions or false answers. An alternative to data collecting through questionnaires are data directly collected from the social network sites. This possibility also presents some limits too, such as privacy matters.

In the case of social network site Facebook, for instance, we have several possibilities to collect data (Whinston, 2009), from its pages. Thus, we can collect data about users' profile, such as: gender, religion, level of education, geographical location, hobbies, or data about users' interactions, monitoring their comments, posts, opinions, and preferences through Like, and Share actions. So, researchers may have the necessary data to analyze the users' behavior and patterns of communication. Moreover, data directly collected from social media sites can be observed on long periods of time. This situation favors identification of general phenomena, as well as particular/individual ones. The dynamicity of different phenomena can be also analyzed on a long period of time, but dynamic data from social media are sometimes difficult to collect and analyze. New tools and measures were developed to capture the time dimension of these data. Thus, there are animations of network evolution and also dynamic social network representations (Rosen, Barnett and Kim, 2011, p.39-40).

Moreover, Facebook enables organization of surveys for a research study, inviting users with a specific profile to take them. Bhaskara (2010) talks about the recruitment process of Facebook users in a survey and gives as solution the Facebook ads.

Very useful in data collection for research studies are *content aggregation* and also *sentiment aggregation,* named syndication. Aggregated content from different sources from the Web are important databases for research studies. For instance, engagement and collaboration activities on social media sites may be measured by the number of RSS subscribers or the number of links to content. As it can be seen, new metrics, more relevant in social aspects, and related to social media activities are necessary. As Gerlitz and Helmond (2011, p: 4) say, the research of social media is based on "user-focused metric".

All activities on the social media sites, such as engagement, collaboration, aggregation or curation on the Web, syndication, sharing, or booking must be identified with *specific metrics* and used in the research papers. Such platform - specific metrics could be RSS feeds used to identify and collect data from different blogs, numbers of retweets on Twitter or numbers of links to content on Youtube site.

Measuring information and its flow in social media applications is an important issue in media research. An important aspect is the fact that precise measures of social media and social networks activities give more possibilities to the quantitative research of the domain. All measurements and their values are used in the research studies and are analyzed with different research methods.

Research Methods in Social Media

Media and communication research methods and approaches spring from other disciplines, such as sociology, literature, psychology or political science. These methodologies are still in progress (Herkman, 2008). It can be seen that some other methods and approaches are more suitable to social media research. It is the case of the methods applied in computer-mediated communication studies. Some of them follow the communicational aspects, others the users' social behavior.

Herkman (2008) shows that both quantitative and qualitative methods are used in media and communication research, however the *quantitative methods* are more important in empirical analysis. The quantitative methods identified are *surveys* and *content analysis* and the qualitative methods used are based on *interviews*. The *discourse analysis* and *textual analysis*, or *ethnographic techniques* applied in virtual communities are also methods used in media and communication research.

In researching phenomena of social media, traditional methods are used, such as interviews or surveys, but specific methods are also need, such as *networks analysis*. Network analysis is very useful for identifying the links structure between people on a social media site, for information diffusion in a social network, for determining the influence and authority in blogosphere or for building online communities around a media product or media topic. Methods to analyze networks are very important in the research studies of media and communication because content, layout and design of information on social media sites, as well as processes of production, distribution and usage of information are different than on other sites.

Another specific method used in research studies of media and communication and emphasizing the uniqueness of social media sites is *Web content analysis (WebCA)*. This method was already used by media studies (Herring et. al., 2006). Considered as a social science method and largely used in communication studies, the content analysis makes a description of the content of communication. The traditional approach is common to the analysis of social field, but the coding scheme is not always completed or implemented in a traditional way for social media applications. The Web content is not only about text, images as in traditional media; it is also about hyperlinks and interactive discussions generated by a text or image. Moreover, time is another dimension in the Web content analysis that must be considered. Herring (2009) presents how the method of Web content analysis (WebCA) must be understood in research studies. It is a method based on the traditional content analysis method, adapted to Web and who showing the specificity of Web. This means that this method is enriched with more tools that can reflect the specificity of Web and of social media implicitly. The new influences are coming from linguistics, sociology, and computational techniques.

The challenging aspect for social media research is however represented by the methods for avatar-based communication analysis in a tri-dimensional virtual environment. Rosen, Barnett and Kim (2011) indicate that the data found on Internet, computer-mediated communication methods and theories, and also online environments influence the research at this time.

As it can be seen, in media and communication studies for social media research, several methods are preferred in some conditions, in the case of some topics.

For instance, in the study conducted by Hermida and Thurman (2009) a survey is used to investigate the *adoption of user-generated content*

by the mainstream news organizations. Then, this research is completed with in-depth interviews with senior news executives. Although *surveys* are also a preferred approach to study the social media phenomenon, their limitations make it necessary to use other methods, such as in-depth interviews or social network analysis. Moreover, animations of network evolution and dynamic social network representations have been used for longitudinal studies over time.

Another topic frequently debated is related to relationships arising on social media sites. The structure of online relationships on social media sites is often analyzed through *social network analysis*. Scientists also use other methods of research, more suited to the online for analyzing social phenomena. Rosen, Barnett and Kim (2011, p. 32) present several topics of research using social network analysis based on online data, such as: political blogosphere and hyperlinks, or social media and multi-user virtual environments. The method of social network analysis is also used by Meraz (2009) in a study regarding influence in political blogosphere. He studied the structural relations in the blogosphere using the links between blogs. The authors consider this method and the theory of social network to explain the "boundaries of potential source influence and the potential power of agenda setters within specified social networks". The blogosphere is a favorite subject to be analyzed through network methods, too. The analysis of links between blogs and bloggers is often used to determine the influential blogs in journalism, to analyze the communication between audiences or media products. As a method to collect data directly from blogs, are used RSS feeds.

Social media, especially social media sites Facebook and Twitter research were also addressed by structural analysis or visual and representational analysis of elements in social networks (Preece and Maloney-Krichmar, 2005 in Rosen, Barnett and Kim, 2011). The social network analysis method proved effective for media consumption analysis too (Rosen, Barnett and Kim, 2011, p.36). A study by Stefanone, Lackaff and Rosen

(2010b) and quoted by Rosen about relationship between the reality television consumption and users behavior on social network sites are based on the same research method.

Virtual words as multi-user virtual environments (MUVEs) are also studied in terms of their interactions and as environments to deliver information from. In these environments, the individuals appear as avatars and communicate through written texts. Analyzing virtual worlds needs suitable tools, such as *semantic network analysis* (Rosen, Barnett and Kim, 2011).

Specific phenomena studied in the field of social media sites are analyzed with more specific methods. Thus, the *information diffusion theories and algorithms* are used in different studies of media and communication research, such as the study done by Kwak et al. (2010). It was demonstrated that Twitter is news medium in terms of information sharing and diffusion on this site. This method and its algorithms are widely used in research in sociology and marketing, but the topic and the idea of information propagation through social networks are frequently found in the research papers. The information diffusion theories and methods were also present in Cha, Navarro and Haddadi (2011) to analyze the spread of media content, especially of videos through blogs. They studied the network structure of the blogosphere but also analyzed the patterns of content sharing in this structure, based on diffusion theory and noticed that the multimedia content is more shared among bloggers, and they obtained a diffusion model of videos depending on topics. Examples found by the authors show that news information, political commentaries and opinions are spread in hours or days, meantime music and entertainment spread over months.

Statistical methods of analysis, such as correlation techniques one-way ANOVA and *Web content analysis* are specific approaches to see different relationships between social media and mainstream media. Herring (2009) presents the method of *Web content analysis (WebCA)* and

uses it to analyze *blogs as social media site and communication platform*. A blog is considered to be a web document, a HTML site, and also a platform to mediate communication between people through computer. Thus, an expanded Web content analysis paradigm is proposed which is based both on discourse analysis and on social network analysis. The two methods cover two roles of the blog. Herring (2009) considers both a traditional approach of Web content analysis and a non-traditional approach. She considers that research methods must address the characteristics of new technological phenomena, and the very diverse types of sites.

Mining techniques are also used to analyze the blogosphere. Blogs mining techniques have origins in different areas such as web mining, social networks analysis, network theory, economic researches on dissemination of information, graphs theory, and game theory. Through these techniques researchers may analyze the degree of activity of bloggers (how many times they post) or the degree of connection between bloggers (links between blogs). Blog mining underlies the analysis of the process used by search engines in the case of blogs. Mining techniques allow identifying trends within large volumes of data such as posts in the case of blogs, and identifying the key attributes of these data, such as significant characteristics of blogs. Blog mining is already considered a qualitative research technique used for a big number of posts to be analysed (Aschenbrenner and Miksch, 2005).

C. THEORIES AND MODELS USED FOR SOCIAL MEDIA RESEARCH

Social Media Theories

Different concepts rose from Web 2.0 and related to journalism are subjects of research in media and communication studies, such as: user-generated content and media companies, convergence of media products, multimedia news, blogosphere and journalism practices, and so on. The research studies related to Web 2.0, user-generated content and social media, and journalism are important and consistent. These topics take into consideration different assumptions and reflect traditional theories in mass media and communication or adaptive theories from other sciences.

Thus, various theoretical frameworks appear and are used in relation to social media, but the most important theories are those that show the specificity of social media, the activities done on these platforms.

Chan (2009) considers that social media bring a shift of paradigm that is reflected in many theories and is demonstrated by research studies. In media and journalism, this paradigm is reflected by the transition from "individual users to social practices, from editor-provided content to user-generated content, from general news of public interest to news of personal, biographical and everyday interest". These transformations in paradigm are caused by the fact that social media sites, as new channels used to deliver messages, generate new values, new models to address audiences, new models of news production.

Based on this paradigm, theories of participation and collaboration are very frequently used in the research of communication studies by interactions analysis. Theories referring to user-generated content or user-generated culture are also dedicated to this direction. The theories of social production and peer-evaluation, theories of convergence, theories of open source, social influence theory or participatory media theory are all of them starting points in the research papers about social media. All these theories can be grouped as social media theories.

In accordance to main characteristic of social media that is participation, a lot of ideas and theories have risen. Thus, Rheingold (2008) refers to the participatory media platforms and their theories.

Engagement is the most active form of participation. For instance, content creation by blogging is an engagement activity. Actions such as the choice of an article by like or share are other forms of participation which the user manifests. All these specific social media theories can be included in the category of communication and information technology theories. In this category one may find theories such as social presence theory, users and gratifications theory, network theory, computer-mediated communication theories, information theories, diffusion of innovation theory, contextual design and others. On the other hand, many theories already working in traditional media and communication field are now inappropriate for social media (Luoma-aho, 2010). The social media transform and renew traditional theories to completely reinvent them. The author advocates for changing the theories of mass communication in Web 2.0.

Media and communication research must turn to social media specificity. This means that companies are facing not only marketing communication or product building, but also communication of users' engagement, and the monitoring of their behavior, opinions and requests. Theories of social media must be built in this direction. Moreover, in the same respect, Gauntlett (2011) proposed the subject of "Media Studies 2.0", in 2007.

Solutions and Recommendations

Directions opened in social media research through media and communication studies in this chapter lead to several conclusions.

Blogs, Twitter and Facebook are the most frequently found in the specialized literature. Blogs are more important to media studies, while Facebook and Twitter are more appropriate to communication studies. The topics addressed by all of them are the following: sources of information, consumption model, journalistic practices, self-presentation and reputation. On the other hand, it can be noticed that there are specific study topics on each of social medium type, such as influence in blogosphere, political blogosphere, information spreading in blogosphere or on Twitter. Agenda settings or strategies of communication are research topics on Facebook.

Direction regarding *types and activities of social media* in media and communication research shows that blogs are the most interesting social media to researchers. Most researches debate the specificity and the convergence between blogging and journalism. Blogging is studied more as a journalistic practice and blogosphere is studied as a virtual community with issues related to authority and influence.

Blogs and blogging practices are studied in terms of similarities and differences when compared to journalism. Blogs are also interesting for communication studies in terms of audiences, quality of conversations, sharing information, or as virtual communities. The most frequently addressed topics about blogs are: relationship between blogging and journalism (gathering information, reliability of information, subjectivity, audiences, or online news production) blogs influence, political blogosphere, multimedia content creation, agenda setting for journalist and bloggers, actions and activities in social media, consumption model, information spreading in blogosphere, mainstream media and blogs.

In terms of Twitter platform, the most frequently addressed topics are: media practices and consumption, audiences, conversational practices, information diffusion, sharing information in local communities, micro-journalism, and news making process.

Facebook is more studied as source of information, agenda building for journalists, journalistic practice, or in terms of relationships between categories of people, relationships between news and audience, or strategies of communication.

Another direction in this study is dedicated to *methodologies and methods* used in social media research in the fields of media and com-

munication. Social media research is associated both to traditional methods and to specific ones. Interviews and surveys are still important to find and analyze data, but in addition to that, the network methods concern other aspects of social media too. Finding the hyperlinks structure, or the phenomena generated by hyperlinks such as information spreading, finding most important nodes (authority, influence), and creating groups of nodes as communities are also studies in social media through network analysis methods. Web Content analysis is also found as a specific method to social media. The coding scheme takes into consideration determinant items in social media. The frequently used methods in social media analysis in media and communication studies are social network analysis and computer-mediated communication approaches. Researchers find more complete modes to describe social interaction, and other social media practices using complex methodological issues.

As Gerlitz and Helmond (2011) consider, research of social media is focused especially on user-centered metric. The social interaction is the most important value of social media and it is analyzed by most of the researchers. As a general conclusion, the frequently used methods in social media analysis are interviews, surveys based on questionnaires, social networks analysis, Web content analysis, computer-mediated communication methods, diffusion methods, statistical methods or mining techniques.

As far as *theories and models* are concerned, social media also transform traditional approaches and offer other possibilities and research clues in media and communication studies. Social media theories, practices for building communication strategies, research methods, topics, outputs of research studies, and activities in social media are all of them ongoing processes in media and communication studies. The journalism associated to social media, and already characterized as participatory or ambient or grassroots journalism is approached in a number of new theories. Also, communication studies preoccupied more with the qualitative and sentiment aspects, related to users, constitute a very generous environment for all research studies. Social media have already transformed and renewed the theories of media and communication field or they must do that very quickly.

FUTURE RESEARCH DIRECTIONS

Social media practices and users creativity manifested on these sites require rethinking of traditional theories in media and communication studies. Other perspectives must be adopted by the theories, paying more attention to online environment power and its specificity. Personalized messages sent through social media sites are different in comparison with the messages sent to a large public, in a uniform way. Theories in this domain must be reformulated starting from the fact that the user is a consumer of information and a producer in the same time. The specificity of social media, with a network structure, must be reflected by models and methods used to analyze media practices and types of communication. Thus, the phenomena analyzed in social media are closer to network science and computer-mediated communication than traditional approaches.

Future research can follow how traditional media theories, such as agenda setting theory, media richness theory, uses and gratifications or theory of framing will be transformed in keeping with social media.

In terms of communication theories, information technologies persistently transform some aspects of communication. Thus the theories must follow them continuously. Information technologies bring modifications to all types of communication from interpersonal communication to organizational communication or self-promotion.

Network theory and analysis, and mainly social network theories give an important perspective on theories in media and communication science. Researchers must find more complete modes to describe social interactions, and other social media practices with appropriate tools. The convergence between different theories is another possibility to create new frameworks for judging the phenomenon of media and communication.

All theories that enrich the literature and refer to social media are based on new paradigms that reflect new practices, new processes and models of production and consumption of information, new professional values, new communicational relationships, new multimedia content. The social interaction is the key element in this new paradigm found in media and communication studies. The future studies will develop the group of theories that present the specific characteristics of social media. Another direction that can be followed could answer the following question: How deeply are the traditional theories transformed by this new paradigm?

CONCLUSION

This study brings up some tendencies and a view regarding the way in which researchers in media and communication studies deal with social media and their activities. The study is a synthesis of important topics, theories and methods applied in media and communication researches.

Several general conclusions arise for this study. The media landscape research shows that the Web and especially some types of social media are very important in current studies.

Several approaches are taken into consideration by the researchers. Thus, traditional issues of media such as: professional matters, sources of information, audiences are transferred and discussed from digital and social media perspectives.

Other new topics in media and communication research are specific to Web 2.0 and social media, such as: participatory media, ambient journalism, adoption of user-generated content by media companies, influence in blogosphere and others. As research object, social media is a very generous subject. Social media sites are analyzed both as informational platforms and as social interaction platforms. New types of interactions in social media such as engagement, participation, bookmarking, aggregation, etc. are analyzed from the media effects perspective, either to explain or to predict them. Researching online communities around news sites often complete the audience studies.

As environment from which to collect data for various studies, social media is also an important database both in quantitative approaches (demographic data, comments, etc.) and in qualitative ones, such as sentiments mining, or opinions, etc. Moreover, social media are also a tool, a channel used to deliver different questionnaires or research results. Social media provide not only real data for qualitative and quantitative research, but also information and data about hyperlinks and relationships, very little identified in the offline environment. The configuration of hyperlinks is a determining aspect to social media analysis in media and communication studies.

It is also another approach that addresses social media in research studies. In this respect, it compares the traditional perspective to Web 2.0 and social media perspective. In these terms, the most relevant topics that concern researchers are the relationship between journalism and blogging or news making process and Twitter.

At this point, both research topics and methods combine the traditional approaches with the new ones. The research market of social media in media and communication field is considered to be important, both in terms of volume of topics and in terms of research methods used. Media and communication studies are facing social media that are mostly biased on building relationships as well as collaborative strategies with the user.

REFERENCES

Agichtein, E., Castillo, C., Donato, D., Gionis, A., & Mishne, G. (2008). *Finding high-quality content in social media*. ACM International Conference on Web Search and Data Mining - WSDM'08, February Palo Alto, California, Retrieved December 1, 2010, from http://www.mathcs.emory.edu/~eugene/papers/wsdm2008quality.pdf

An, J., Cha, M., Gummadi, K., & Crowcroft, J. (2011). Media landscape in Twitter: A world of new conventions and political diversity. *Proceedings of the Fifth International AAAI Conference on Weblogs and Social Media*. Retrieved December 1, 2011, from http://www.cl.cam.ac.uk/~jac22/out/twitter-diverse.pdf

Aschenbrenner, A., & Miksch, S. (2005). *Blog mining in a corporate environment*. Report SAT (Smart Agent Technologies). Retrieved March 20, 2009, from http://ieg.ifs.tuwien.ac.at/techreports/Asgaard-TR-2005-11.pdf

Bhaskara, V. (June 23, 2010). *Social media research - Using Facebook for survey invitations and market research*. Researchaccess.com. Retrieved May 1, 2010, from http://researchaccess.com/2010/06/social-media-research-using-facebook-for-survey-invitations-and-market-research/

Blood, R. (2003). Weblogs and journalism: Do they connect? *Nieman Reports, 57*(3), 61–62.

boyd, d., Golder, S., & Lotan, G. (2010). Tweet, Tweet, retweet: Conversational aspects of retweeting on Twitter. *Proceedings of the International Hawaiian Conference on Social Sciences,* (p. 43). Kauai, HI: IEEE. Retrieved from http://www.danah.org/papers/TweetTweetRetweet.pdf

boyd, d. m., & Ellison, N. B. (2007). Social network sites: Definition, history, and scholarship. *Journal of Computer-Mediated Communication, 13*(1).

Bruns, A. (2009). News blogs and citizen journalism. In KK.iran Prasad (Ed.), *E-journalism: New directions in electronic news media*. New Delhi, India: BR Publishing. Retrieved June 1, 2011, from http://snurb.info/files/News%20Blogs%20and%20Citizen%20Journalism.pdf

Cha, M., Navarro Pérez, J. A., & Haddadi, H. (2011). The spread of media content through blogs. *Social Network Analysis and Mining, 2*(3), 249-264. ISSN: 18695450

Chan, A. (2009). *Social interaction design*. Retrieved from http://www.gravity7.com/paradigm_shift_1.html

Clark, J., & Aufderheide, P. (February 2009). *Public media 2.0: Dynamic, engaged publics*. Centre for Social Media. Retrieved from http://www.uni.edu/fabos/thc/futureopublicmedia.pdf

Cohen, H. (9 May, 2011). *30 Social media definitions*. Heidi Cohen's blog – Marketing expert. Retrieved from http://heidicohen.com/social-media-definition/

Deuze, M. (2004). What is multimedia journalism? *Journalism Studies, 5*(2), 139–152. doi:10.1080/1461670042000211131

Deuze, M. (2006). Participation, remediation, bricolage: Considering principal components of a digital culture. *Journal: The Information Society, 22*(2), 63–75. doi:10.1080/01972240600567170

Diakopoulos, N., & Naaman, M. (2011). Towards quality discourse in online news comments. *Proceedings of the ACM 2011 Conference on Computer Supported Cooperative Work*, (pp. 133-142). New York, NY: ACM. DOI:10.1145/1958824.1958844

Domingo, D., & Heinonen, A. (2008). Weblogs and journalism: A typology to explore the blurring boundaries. *Nordicom Review, 29*(1), 3–15.

Domingo, D., Quandt, T., Heinonen, A., Paulussen, S., Singer, J. B., & Vujnovic, M. (2008). Participatory journalism practices in the media and beyond - An international comparative study of initiatives in online newspapers. *Journalism Practice, 2*(3). doi:10.1080/17512780802281065

Fagerjord, A. (2010). After convergence: YouTube and remix culture. In Hunsinger, J., Allen, M., & Klastrup, L. (Eds.), *The international handbook of internet research* (pp. 187–201). Springer.

Gal-Or, E., Geylani, T., & Yildirim, T. P. (2010, 21 July). *User-generated content in news media*. Retrieved January 1, 2011, from http://www.pitt.edu/~esther/papers/Gal-Or_Geylani_Yildirim_User-Generated%20Content%20in%20News%20Media_July%2021%202010.pdf

Gauntlett, D. (2011). *Media studies 2.0, and other battles around the future of media research*. Retrieved from http://www.theory.org.uk/mediastudies2.htm

Gerlitz, C., & Helmond, A. (7 February 2011). *Hit, link, like and share. Organizing the social and the fabric of the web in a like economy*. Paper presented at the DMI Mini-Conference, 24-25 January 2011 at the University of Amsterdam. Retrieved from http://www.annehelmond.nl/wordpress/wp-content/uploads/2011/04/GerlitzHelmond-HitLinkLikeShare.pdf

Gil de Zúñiga, H., Lewis, S. C., Willard, A., Valenzuela, S., Lee, J. K., & Baresch, B. (2011). Blogging as a journalistic practice: A model linking perception, motivation, and behavior. *Journalism, 12*, 586–606. doi:10.1177/1464884910388230

Herkman, J. (2008). Current trends in media research. *Nordicom Review, 29*(1), 145–159.

Hermida, A. (2010a). Twittering the news: The emergence of ambient journalism. *Journalism Practice, 4*(3). Retrieved January 1, 2012, from http://www.caerdydd.ac.uk/jomec/resources/foj2009/foj2009-Hermida.pdf

Hermida, A. (2010b). From TV to Twitter: How ambient news became ambient journalism. *Journal of Media and Culture, 13*(2). Retrieved May 1, 2011, from http://www.journal.media-culture.org.au/index.php/mcjournal/article/viewArticle/220

Hermida, A., & Thurman, N. (2009). A clash of cultures: The integration of user-generated content within professional journalistic frameworks at British newspaper websites. *Journalism Practice, 2*, 343–356. doi:10.1080/17512780802054538

Herring, S. C. (2009). Web content analysis: Expanding the paradigm. In Hunsinger, J., Allen, M., & Klastrup, L. (Eds.), *The international handbook of internet research* (pp. 233–249). Springer Verlag. doi:10.1007/978-1-4020-9789-8_14

Herring, S. C., Scheidt, L. A., Kouper, I., & Wright, E. (2006). A longitudinal content analysis of weblogs: 2003-2004. In Tremayne, M. (Ed.), *Blogging, citizenship and the future of media* (pp. 3–20). London, UK: Routledge.

Jacobson, S. (2010). Emerging models of multimedia journalism: A content analysis of multimedia packages published on nytimes.com. *Atlantic Journal of Communication, 18*, 63–78. doi:10.1080/15456870903554882

Kaplan, A. M., & Haenlein, M. (2010). Users of the world, unite! The challenges and opportunities of Social Media. *Business Horizons, 53*, 59–68. doi:10.1016/j.bushor.2009.09.003

Kwak, H., Lee, C., Park, H., & Moon, S. (2010). What is Twitter, a social network or a news media? *Proceedings of the 19th International WWW 2010*, April 26–30, 2010, Raleigh, North Carolina. Retrieved December 1, 2011, from http://cs.wellesley.edu/~cs315/Papers/What%20is%20twitter-a%20social%20net%20or%20news%20media.pdf

Lariscy, R. W., Johnson Avery, E., Sweetser, K. D., & Howes, P. (2009). An examination of the role of online social media in journalists' source mix. *Public Relations Review, 35*, 314–316. doi:10.1016/j.pubrev.2009.05.008

Lasica, J. D. (2003). Blogs and journalism need each other. *Nieman Reports, 57*(3).

Lenhart, A., & Madden, M. (2005). *Teen content creators and consumers*. Pew Research Center. Retrieved October 1, 2011, from http://www.pewinternet.org/~/media//Files/Reports/2005/PIP_Teens_Content_Creation.pdf.pdf

Lessig, L. (2008). *Remix culture: Making art and commerce thrive in the hybrid economy*. Bloomsbury Academic, Creative Commons Attribution CC 2008 Lawrence Lessig. Retrieved October 1, 2011, from http://www.archive.org/details/LawrenceLessigRemix

Lowrey, W. (2006). Mapping the journalism-blogging relationship. *Journalism, 7*(4), 477–500. doi:10.1177/1464884906068363

Lowrey, W., & Burleson Mackay, J. (2008). Journalism and blogging - A test of a model of occupational competition. *Journalism Practice, 2*(1), 64–81. doi:10.1080/17512780701768527

Luoma-aho, V. (2010). *Is social media killing our theories?* Paper presented at Communication Resesarch Days, University of Tampere, Finland, February, 2010. Retrieved December 1, 2011, from http://jyu.academia.edu/VilmaLuomaaho/Papers/142043/Is_social_media_killing_our_theories

Meraz, S. (2009). Is there an elite hold? Traditional media to social media agenda setting influence in blog networks. *Journal of Computer-Mediated Communication, 14*, 682–707. doi:10.1111/j.1083-6101.2009.01458.x

Mitchelstein, E., & Boczkowski, P. J. (2009). Between tradition and change: A review of recent research on online news production. *Journalism, 10*(5), 562–586. doi:10.1177/1464884909106533

O'Connor, R. (January 20, 2009). Facebook and Twitter are reshaping journalism as we know it. *RoryOConnor.org*. Retrieved December 1, 2011, from http://kauri.aut.ac.nz:8080/dspace/bitstream/123456789/1839/1/090120.Facebook%20%26%20Twitter%20Are%20Reshaping%20Journalism.pdf

Paine, K. D. (2009). *How to set benchmarks in social media: Exploratory research for social media*. Paper presented to the 12th Annual International Public Relations Research Conference, Florida. Retrieved October 1, 2011, from http://www.instituteforpr.org/wp-content/uploads/Set-Benchmarks_SocialMedia.pdf

Rheingold, H. (2008). Using participatory media and public voice to encourage civic engagement. In Bennett, W. L. (Ed.), *Civic life online: Learning how digital media can engage youth* (pp. 97–118). Cambridge, MA: The MIT Press.

Rosen, D., Barnett, G. A., & Kim, J. H. (2011). Social networks and online environments: When science and practice co-evolve. *Social Network Analysis and Mining, 1*(1), 27-42. Wien, Austria: Springer. Retrieved from http://www.springerlink.com/index/10.1007/s13278-010-0011-7

Schmidt, J. (2007). Blogging practices: An analytical framework. *Journal of Computer-Mediated Communication, 12*(4), article 13. Retrieved June 1, 2010, from http://jcmc.indiana.edu/vol12/issue4/schmidt.html

Schneider, S. M., & Foot, K. A. (2004). The web as an object of study. *New Media & Society, 6*(1), 114–122. doi:10.1177/1461444804039912

Skoler, M. (2009). Why the news media became irrelevant - And how social media can help. *Nieman Reports, Fall,* 38-40. Retrieved November 1, 2011, from http://jclass.umd.edu/classes/jour698m/skoler_files/ContentServer.pdf

Stefanone, M. A., Lackaff, D., & Rosen, D. (2010a). The relationship between traditional mass media and social media: Reality television as a model for social network site behavior. *Journal of Broadcasting & Electronic Media, 54*(3), 508–525. Retrieved from http://www.communication.buffalo.edu/contrib/people/faculty/documents/stefanone_BEM_2010.pdf doi:10.1080/08838151.2010.498851

Stefanone, M. A., Lackaff, D., & Rosen, D. (2010b). Contingencies of self worth and social networking site behavior. *Cyberpsychology, Behavior, and Social Networking, 14*(1-2). doi:doi:10.1089/cyber.2010.0049

Thurman, N. (2008). Forums for citizen journalists? Adoption of user generated content initiatives by online news media. *New Media & Society, 10*(1), 139–157. doi:10.1177/1461444807085325

Wall, M. (2004). Blogs as black market journalism: A new paradigm for news. *Interface on the Internet, 4*(2).

Whinston, A. B. (2009). Opportunities and challenges in analysis of social networks. *AMCIS 2009 Proceedings: AIS Electronic Library*. Retrieved December 1, 2011, from http://aisel.aisnet.org/amcis2009/288

Yardi, S., & boyd, d. (2010). Tweeting from the town square: Measuring geographic local networks. *Proceedings of the Fourth International AAAI Conference on Weblogs and Social Media*. In *ICWSM*. Retrieved November 2011 from http://www.cc.gatech.edu/~yardi/pubs/Yardi_TownSquare10.pdf

ADDITIONAL READING

Al-Deen, H. S. N., & Hendricks, J. A. (Eds.). (2011). *Social Media: Usage and Impact*. Lexington Books.

Bartholomew, D. (12 May 2010). The digitization of research and measurement. MetricsMan Blog. Retrieved from http://metricsman.wordpress. com/2010/05/12/the-digitization-of-research-and-measurement/

Beddows, E. (2008). The methodological issues associated with internet-based research. *International Journal of Emerging Technologies and Society, 6*(2), 124–139. Retrieved May 1, 2010, from http://www.swinburne.edu.au/hosting/ijets/ journal/V6N2/pdf/Article3Beddows.pdf

Claburn, T. (21 October 2009). Web 2.0 summit: Facebook bets on wisdom of friends. *InformationWeek*. Retrieved 23 January, 2012, from http://www.informationweek.com/news/internet/ web2.0/220900041

Clay, S. (2005). *Clay Shirky on institutions vs. collaboration*. Retrieved from http://www.ted.com/ talks/clay_shirky_on_institutions_versus_collaboration.html

Coles, M. (6 July 2009). *Newspapers on Twitter: How the Guardian, FT and Times are winning*. Retrieved January 1, 2012, from http://www. malcolmcoles.co.uk/blog/newspapers-on-twitter/

Daymon, C., & Holloway, I. (2011). *Qualitative research methods in public relations and marketing communications* (2nd ed.). Routledge.

de Spindler, A., Leone, S., Geel, M., & Norrie, M. C. (2010). Using tag clouds to promote community awareness. In Luo, Y. (Ed.), *Cooperative design, visualization, and engineering* (pp. 3–11). Springer. doi:10.1007/978-3-642-16066-0_1

Deuze, M. (1998). The web communicators: Issues in research into online journalism and journalists. *First Monday, 3*(12). Retrieved December 1, 2010, from http://frodo.lib.uic.edu/ojsjournals/index. php/fm/article/view/634/555

Ferneley, E., Heinze, A., & Child, P. (2009). Research 2.0: Improving participation in online research communities. In S. Newell, E. A. Whitley, N. Pouloudi, J. Wareham, & L. Mathiassen, (Eds.), *17th European Conference on Information Systems*. Retrieved February 1, 2012, from http://usir. salford.ac.uk/14628/3/ECIS-Research-2.0-3.pdf

Gray, C. (2011, February 7). *Social media: A guide for researchers*. Research Information Network. Retrieved January 1, 2012, from http://www.rin. ac.uk/our-work/communicating-and-disseminating-research/social-media-guide-researchers

Guosong, S. (2009). Understanding the appeal of user-generated media: A uses and gratification perspective. *Internet Research, 19*(1), 7–25. doi:10.1108/10662240910927795

Hassan, R. (2000). The space economy of convergence. *Convergence (London), 6*(4), 18–35. doi:10.1177/135485650000600403

Hine, C. (2000). Virtual ethnography. *Sage (Atlanta, Ga.)*.

Huberman, B. A., Romero, D. M., & Wu, F. (2008). *Social networks that matter: Twitter under the microscope*. arXiv:0812.1045v1

Jensen, K. B. (Ed.). (2002). *Handbook of media and communication research: Qualitative and qualitative methodologies*. London, UK: Routledge. doi:10.4324/9780203465103

Knapton, K., & Myers, S. (2005). Demographics and online survey response rates. *QUIRK'S Marketing Research Media*. Retrieved December 1, 2010, from http://www.quirks.com/articles/a2005/20050106. aspx?searchID=158898720&sort=9

Manovich, L. (2001). *The language of new media.* MIT Press.

Manovich, L. (2005, October 26). Understanding meta-media. *CTheory.net International Journal of Theory, Technology and Culture.* Retrieved December 1, 2011, from http://www.ctheory.net/articles.aspx?id=493

Matheson, D. (2004). Weblogs and the epistemology of the news: Some trends in online journalism. *New Media & Society, 6*(4), 443–468. doi:10.1177/146144804044329

Newman, N. (2009). *The rise of social media and its impact on mainstream journalism: A study of how newspapers and broadcasters in the UK and US are responding to a wave of participatory social media, and a historic shift in control towards individual consumers.* Working paper, The Reuters Institute for the Study of Journalism. Retrieved December 1, 2011, from http://reutersinstitute.politics.ox.ac.uk/fileadmin/documents/Publications/The_rise_of_social_media_and_its_impact_on_mainstream_journalism.pdf

Niblock, S. (2007). From "knowing how" to "being able": Negotiating the meanings of reflective practice and reflexive research in journalism studies. *Journalism Practice, 1*(1), 20–32. doi:10.1080/17512780601078829

Niblock, S. (2012). Envisioning journalism practice as research. *Journalism Practice, 6*(4). doi:10.1080/17512786.2011.650922

Oppermann, M. (2010). The World Wide Web and digital culture: New borders, new media, new American studies. In Rowe, J. C. (Ed.), *A concise companion to American studies* (pp. 334–349). Oxford, UK: Blackwell-Wiley. doi:10.1002/9781444319071.ch17

Poynter, R. (2010). *The handbook of online and social media research: Tools and techniques for market researchers.* London, UK: Wiley Publishing House.

Report, C. I. B. E. R. (2010, December 14). *Social media and research workflow.* University College London Emerald Group Publishing Ltd. Retrieved January 1, 2012, from http://www.ucl.ac.uk/infostudies/research/ciber/social-media-report.pdf

Spurgeon, C. (2009, July). Co-creative media: Theorizing digital storytelling as a platform for researching and developing participatory culture. *Proceedings of the Australian and New Zealand Communication Association Conference 2009, Communication, Creativity and Global Citizenship.* Queensland University of Technology, Brisbane. Retrieved October 1, 2011, from http://eprints.qut.edu.au/25811/2/25811.pdf

Ulicny, B., & Baclawski, K. (2007). New metrics for news blog credibility. In *Proceedings of International Conference on Weblogs and Social Media,* Colorado. Retrieved March 19, 2009, from http://vistology.com/papers/VIStologyICWSM-07poster.pdf

Wolfgang, G. S. (2007). Folksonomies and science communication: A mash-up of professional science databases and Web 2.0 services. *Information Services & Use, 27*(3), 97-103. Retrieved November 1, 2011, from http://www.phil-fak.uni-duesseldorf.de/fileadmin/Redaktion/Institute/Informationswissenschaft/1194272247inf_servic.pdf

Zimmer, M. (2010). Web search studies: Multidisciplinary perspectives on Web search engines. In Hunsinger, J., Klastrup, L., & Allen, M. (Eds.), *International handbook of internet research* (pp. 507–521). Springer Netherlands. doi:10.1007/978-1-4020-9789-8_31

KEY TERMS AND DEFINITIONS

Media and Communication 2.0: Refers to media and communication phenomena, and their study considering the opportunities offered by the Web 2.0, especially by the social platforms.

New Trends in Journalism Research: Research studies conducted in profession of journalism and media industry considering online environment, and studying practices and phenomena with the purpose of obtaining advances knowledge.

Social Media and Mainstream Media: Define the practices and cases met in the relationship between social media and mainstream media.

Social Media in Communication Research: Theories and methods discussed to study communication processes in social media.

Social Media Research Methods: Techniques that work with qualitative and qualitative data with the purpose of social media content analysis, analyzing social media structure, sentiment analysis, users' communication patters.

Social Media Research in Media and Communication Studies: Using data from different types of social media, and analyzing them with a methodology in matters of media and communication studies such as social media usage in professional practices, sharing and diffusion of information, attitudinal and communicational behaviors, media market research, users' networks and interactions, connections with influencers in social media, and so.

Social Media Theory: Set of ideas, principles and statements that define and explain social media phenomena, users' actions and activities on different types of social media platforms. These principles are obtained from repetitive tested practices on social media platforms and are the bases for further activities.

ENDNOTES

[1]   http://www.danah.org/papers/

Compilation of References

Abbitt, J. T. (2007). Exploring the educational possibilities for a user-drive social content system in an undergraduate course. *Journal of Online Learning and Teaching, 3*(4), 437–447.

Abel, F., Gao, Q., Houben, G.-J., & Tao, K. (2011). Analyzing user modeling on Twitter for personalized news recommendations. In Konstan, J. A. (Eds.), *UMAP 2011, LNCS 6787* (pp. 1–12). Berlin, Germany: Springer-Verlag. doi:10.1007/978-3-642-22362-4_1

Abram, S. (2006). Web 2.0, library 2.0, and librarian 2.0: Preparing for the 2.0 world. *SirsiDynix OneSource*. Retrieved February 26, 2012, from http://www.imakenews.com/sirsi/e_article000505688.cfm

ABS. (2012). *Map of remote areas as defined by Australian Bureau of Statistics*. Retrieved from http://www.abs.gov.au/websitedbs/D3310114.nsf/home/remoteness+structure

Adi, A. (2010, April 29). *New media for research. Researching new media*. Retrieved January 25, 2012, from http://www.anaadi.net/2010/04/29/new-media-for-research-researching-new-media/

Adi, A. (2010, December 2). *Social media for university libraries*. Retrieved January 27, 2012, from http://www.anaadi.net/2010/12/02/social-media-for-university-libraries

Adi, A. (2011a, March 31). *Prezi pow wow*. Retrieved January 27, 2012, from http://www.anaadi.net/2011/03/31/prezi-pow-wow/

Adi, A. (2011b, July). *5 weeks, 5 days, 5 sessions of technology for education*. Retrieved February 15, 2012, from http://www.anaadi.net/2011/07/11/5-weeks-5-days-5-sessions-of-technology-for-education/

Agichtein, E., Brill, E., Dumais, S., & Ragno, R. (2006). Learning user interaction models for predicting web search result preferences. *SIGIR '06 Proceedings of the 29th Annual International ACM SIGIR Conference on Research and Development in Information Retrieval*, (pp. 3-10).

Agichtein, E., et al. (2008). Finding high-quality content in social media. *WSDM '08 Proceedings of the International Conference on Web Search and Web Data Mining*, (pp. 183-194).

Ahn, J. (2011). The effect of social network sites on adolescents' social and academic development: Current theories and controversies. *Journal of the American Society for Information Science and Technology, 62*(8), 1435–1445. doi:10.1002/asi.21540

Al-Allak, B. (2010). Evaluating the adoption and use of internet-based marketing information systems to improve marketing intelligence (the case of tourism SMEs in Jordan). *International Journal of Marketing Studies, 2*(2), 87–101.

Al-Bataineh, A., & Brooks, L. (2003). Challenges, advantages, and disadvantages or instructional technology in the community college classroom. *Community College Journal of Research and Practice, 27*, 473–484. doi:10.1080/713838180

Alexander, B., & Levine, A. (2008). Web 2.0 storytelling. Emergence of a new genre. *EDUCAUSE Review.* Retrieved February 24, 2012, from http://net.educause.edu/ir/library/pdf/ERM0865.pdf

Allison, N. (2009). *Middle school readers: Helping them read widely, helping them read well.* Portsmouth, NH: Heinemann.

Ally, M. (2004). Foundations of educational theory for online learning. In Anderson, T., & Elloumi, F. (Eds.), *Theory and practice of online learning* (pp. 3–31). Athabasca, Canada: Athabasca University.

Al-Saggaf, Y. (2011). Saudi females on Facebook: An ethnographic study. *International Journal of Emerging Technologies and Society, 9*(1), 1–19.

Amelung, C. (2007). Using social context and e-learner identity as a framework for an e-learning notification system. *International Journal on E-Learning, 6*(4), 501–517.

Amenta, L. (2011). *Die Potenziale der aktiven Medienarbeit für die universitäre Medienbildung: Eine Fallstudie. [Potentials of project learning in the concept of action-based media education: A case study.]* (B.A.-Thesis). Augsburg, Germany: University of Augsburg, Institute of Media and Educational Technology.

American Marketing Association. (2008). *Marketing definition.* Retrieved May 1, 2010, from http://www.marketingpower.com/AboutAMA/Documents/American%20Marketing%20Association%20Releases%20New%20Definition%20for%20Marketing.pdf

An, J., Cha, M., Gummadi, K., & Crowcroft, J. (2011). Media landscape in Twitter: A world of new conventions and political diversity. *Proceedings of the Fifth International AAAI Conference on Weblogs and Social Media.* Retrieved December 1, 2011, from http://www.cl.cam.ac.uk/~jac22/out/twitter-diverse.pdf

Anderson, D. R., Huston, A. C., Schmitt, K. L., Linebarger, D. L., & Wright, J. C. (2001). Early childhood television viewing and adolescent behavior: The recontact study. *Monographs of the Society for Research in Child Development, 66*, I-I147.

Anderson, P. (2007). *What is Web 2.0? Ideas, technologies and implications for education. JISC Technology and Standards Watch, February 2007.* Bristol: JISC.

Anderson, T., & Elloumi, F. (Eds.). (2004). *Theory and practice of online learning.* Canada: Athabasca University.

Anderson, W. L. (2010). Cyber stalking (Cyber bullying): Proof and punishment. *Insights to a Changing World Journal, 4*, 18–23.

Ang, R. P., & Goh, D. H. (2010). Cyberbullying among adolescents: The role of affective and cognitive empathy, and gender. *Child Psychiatry and Human Development, 41*(4), 387–397. doi:10.1007/s10578-010-0176-3

Anil, D. (2002, November 13). Introducing the microcontent client. *A Blog about Making Culture.* Retrieved February 21, 2012, from http://dashes.com/anil/2002/11/introducing-microcontent-client.html

Anson, C. M., & Miller-Cochran, S. K. (2009). Contrails of learning: Using new technologies for vertical knowledge-building. *Computers and Composition, 26,* 38–48. doi:10.1016/j.compcom.2008.11.002

ANTA. (2000). *Partners in a learning culture national strategy and blueprint for implementation.* Brisbane, Australian National Training Authority. Australian Natural Therapist Association (ANTA).

Antonnaci, D. S. (2002). *Integrating technology into instruction in higher education.* Kansas City, MO: University of Missouri.

Apple. (n.d.). *Technology's impact on learning.* Retrieved from http://www.info.apple.com/education

Apter, M. J. (1989). *Reversal theory: Motivation, emotion and personality.* London, UK: Routledge.

Arafeh, S., Levin, D., Rainie, L., & Lenhart, A. (2002). *The digital disconnect: The widening gap between Internet-savvy students and their schools.* Washington, DC: Pew Internet & American Life Project. Retrieved February 28, 2012, from http://www.pewinternet.org/Reports/2002/The-Digital-Disconnect-The-widening-gap-between-Internetsavvy-students-and-their-schools.aspx

Arends, R. I. (2012). *Learning to teach.* New York, NY: McGraw-Hill.

Arıcak, O. T. (2011). Cyberbullying: The new danger waiting for adolescents. [Siber zorbalık: gençlerimizi bekleyen yeni tehlike.] [Career Window]. *Kariyer Penceresi, 2*(6), 10–12.

Arıcak, O. T., Siyahhan, S., Uzunhasanoğlu, A., Sarıbeyoğlu, S., Çıplak, S., Yılmaz, N., & Memmedov, C. (2008). Cyberbullying among Turkish adolescents. *Cyberpsychology & Behavior, 11*(3), 253–261. doi:10.1089/cpb.2007.0016

Armano, D. (2008). *Why the four C's of community require the commitment of many: Let content, context, connectivity and continuity guide your efforts.* Digital Next. Retrieved 29 December, 2011, from http://adage.com/article/digitalnext/community-require-commitment/132734/

Armitage, L., Brackenreg, E., Campbell, S., Catterall, J., DeSilva, S., & Davis, J. (2011). *ICT enabled learning and widening participation at the University of Western Sydney: The kindling of a flame: A report forming part of the Charles Darwin University's Diversity and Structural Adjustment Fund project "Achieving Best Practice Flexible Provision at CDU".* Kingswood, Australia. Yang, D.F.: University of Western Sydney.

Armstrong, J., & Franklin, T. (2008). *A review of current and developing international practice in the use of social networking (Web 2.0) in higher education.* A report commissioned by the Committee of Enquiry into the Changing Learner Experience. Retrieved February 18, 2012, from http://www.franklin-consulting.co.uk/

Aschenbrenner, A., & Miksch, S. (2005). *Blog mining in a corporate environment.* Report SAT (Smart Agent Technologies). Retrieved March 20, 2009, from http://ieg.ifs.tuwien.ac.at/techreports/Asgaard-TR-2005-11.pdf

Asselin, M. (1999). Balanced literacy. *Teacher Librarian, 27*(1), 69–70.

Association of American Colleges and Universities (AAC&U). (2007). *College learning for the new global century: A report from the National Leadership Council for Liberal Education and America's Promise.* Washington, DC: AAC&U.

Asur, S., & Huberman, B. A. (2010). *Predicting the future with social media.* arXiv:1003.5699v1

Atherton, J. S. (2011). *Teaching and learning.* Retrieved January 14, 2012, from http://www.learningandteaching.info/teaching/course.htm

Attewell, P., Suazo-Garcia, B., & Battle, J. (2003). Computers and young children: Social benefit or social problem. *Social Forces, 82,* 277–296. doi:10.1353/sof.2003.0075

Atwell, N. (1998). *In the middle: New understandings about writing, reading, and learning.* Portsmouth, NH: Boynton/Cook Publishers, Inc.

Australian Bureau of Statistics. (2011). *Internet activity, Australia, June 2011.* Quality Declaration. Retrieved January 22, 2012, from http://www.abs.gov.au/ausstats/abs@.nsf/mf/8153.0

Australian Institute for Social Research. (2006). *The digital divide: Barriers to e-learning: Final report.* Adelaide, Australia: University of Adelaide.

Ayas, T., & Horzum, M. B. (2010). Sanal zorba / kurban ölçek geliştirme çalışması. *Akademik Bakış Dergisi, 19,* 1.

Baker, M. J. (1994). Marketing intelligence for intelligent marketing, In J. Chapman & C. Holtham (Eds.), *IT in marketing.* Henley on Thames, UK: Alfred Waller in association with UNICOM.

Baker, R. K., & White, K. M. (2010). Predicting adolescents' use of social networking sites from an extended theory of planned behaviour perspective. *Computers in Human Behavior, 26*(6), 1591–1597. doi:10.1016/j.chb.2010.06.006

Baldwin, C. Y., & Clark, K. M. (2000). *Design rules: The power of modularity.* Cambridge, MA: MIT Press.

Barker, M., & Petley, J. (Eds.). (2001). *Ill effects: The media violence debate-communication and society* (2nd ed.). London, UK: Routledge.

Barker, V. (2009). Older adolescents' motivations for social network site use: The influence of gender, group identity, and collective self-esteem. *Cyberpsychology & Behavior, 12,* 209–213. doi:10.1089/cpb.2008.0228

Barnes, G., & Mattson, E. (2009). *Social media and college admissions: Higher-ed beats business in adoption of new tools for third year.* Report 2009.

Barnes, A. (2000). Learning preferences of some Aboriginal and Torres Strait Islander students in the veterinary program. *Australian Journal of Indigenous Education, 28*(1), 8–16.

Barnett, T. A., O'Loughlin, J., & Sabiston, C. M. (2010). Teens and screens: The influence of screen time on adiposity in adolescents. *American Journal of Epidemiology, 172*(3), 255–262. doi:10.1093/aje/kwq125

Baron, N. S. (2000). *Alphabet to email: How written English evolved and where it's heading*. London, UK: Routledge. doi:10.4324/9780203194317

Barraket, J., & Scott, G. (2001). Virtual equality? Equity and the use of information technology in higher education. *Australian Academic and Research Libraries Journal, 32*(2).

Barrett, W. (1978). *The illusion of technique: A search for meaning in a technological civilization*. New York, NY: Anchor Books.

Bart, M. (2011, August 9). Effective uses of video in the online classroom, teaching with technology. *Faculty Focus*.

Bartle, R. A. (2003). *Designing virtual worlds*. New Riders Publishing.

Barzaiq, O., & Loke, S. (2010). Adapting the mobile phone for task efficiency. *The International Journal of Pervasive Computing and Communications, 6*(1), 47–87.

Bates, T. (2011, February 22). *Lecture given at Digital Future of Higher Education*. Thompson Rivers University, Kamloops, BC. Retrieved July 26, 2011, from http://www.tru.ca/digifuture.html

Bates, A. W. (2000). *Managing technological change: Strategies for college and university leaders*. San Francisco, CA: Jossey-Bass.

Baylor, A. L. (2001). Perceived disorientation and incidental learning in a Web-based environment: internal and external factors. *Journal of Educational Multimedia and Hypermedia, 10*(3), 227–251.

Bazzarin, V., & Lalli, P. (2011). *The medium is the community (?). A pilot laboratorial activity at University of Bologna to tell and promote the city. In 2011 Proceedings of Understanding Media Today* (pp. 323–330). Barcelona.

Beaumont, J. R. (1991). GIS and market analysis. In Maguire, D. J., Goodchild, M. J., & Rhind, D. W. (Eds.), *Geographical information systems: Principles and applications* (pp. 139–151). London, UK: Longman.

Becker, H. J., & Riel, M. M. (2000). Teacher professional engagement and constructivist-compatible computer use. Center for Research on Information Technology and Organizations. Irvine, CA: University of Californmia. Retrieved June 10, 2012, from http://www.crito.uci.edu/tlc/findings/report_7/start page.html

Beckett, D., & Hager, P. J. (2002). *Life, work and learning: Practice in postmodernity*. London, UK: Routledge.

Beer, D. (2008). Social network(ing) sites…revisiting the story so far: A response to danah boyd and Nicole Ellison. *Journal of Computer-Mediated Communication, 13*(2), 516-529. Retrieved February 15, 2012, from http://onlinelibrary.wiley.com/doi/10.1111/j.1083-6101.2008.00408.x/full

Bell, D. (1973). *The coming of post-industrial society*. New York, NY: Basic Books.

Benamati, J., Ozdemir, Z., & Smith, J. (2010). Aligning undergraduate IS curricula with industry needs. *Communications of the ACM, 53*(3), 152–156. doi:10.1145/1666420.1666458

Ben-David Kolikant, Y. (2009). Digital students in a book-oriented school: Students' perceptions of school and the usability of digital technology in schools. *Journal of Educational Technology & Society, 12*(2), 131–143.

Benkler, Y. (2006). *The wealth of networks: How social production transforms markets and freedom*. New Haven, CT: Yale University Press.

Bennett, S., & Maton, K. (2011). Intellectual field or faith-based religion: Moving on from the idea of digital natives. In Thomas, M. (Ed.), *Deconstructing digital natives: Young people, technology and the new literacies* (pp. 169–185). New York, NY: Routledge.

Bennett, S., Maton, K., & Kervin, L. (2008). The 'digital natives' debate: A critical review of the evidence. *British Journal of Educational Technology, 39*(5), 775–786. doi:10.1111/j.1467-8535.2007.00793.x

Bentele, G. (2006). Fach-PR in der Informations- und Kommunikationsgesellschaft – Einige einleitende Bemerkungen. [Public relations in the information and communication society – Some Preliminary remarks.] In Bentele, G. (Ed.), *PR für Fachmedien: Professionell kommunizieren mit Experten* (pp. 11–20). Konstanz, Germany: UVK. [*PR for trade press: Professionally communication with experts.*]

Bernard, R. M., Abrami, P. C., Lou, Y., Borokhovski, E., Wade, A., & Wozney, L. (2004). How does distance education compare with classroom instruction? A meta-analysis of the empirical literature. *Review of Educational Research, 74*(3), 379–439. doi:10.3102/00346543074003379

Bhaskara, V. (June 23, 2010). *Social media research - Using Facebook for survey invitations and market research.* Researchaccess.com. Retrieved May 1, 2010, from http://researchaccess.com/2010/06/social-media-research-using-facebook-for-survey-invitations-and-market-research/

Bigum, C., & Kenway, J. (1998). New information technologies and the ambiguous future of schooling - Some possible scenarios. In Hargreaves, A., Lieberman, A., Fullan, M., & Hopkins, D. (Eds.), *International handbook of educational change.* Toronto, Canada: OISE.

Blood, R. (2003). Weblogs and journalism: Do they connect? *Nieman Reports, 57*(3), 61–62.

Bocu, D., & Bocu, R. (2011). Strongly project-oriented learning systems: Concepts and fundamental principles. *Scientific Studies and Research Series: Mathematics and Informatics, 21*(1), 51–60.

Bonaiuti, G. (Ed.). (2006). *E-learning 2.0.* Trento, Italy: Erickson.

Bonham, S. (2011). Whole class laboratories with Google Docs. *The Physics Teacher, 49,* 22–23. doi:10.1119/1.3527749

Bonk, C. (2009). *The world is open: how Web technology is revolutionizing education.* San Francisco, CA: Jossey-Bass.

Bonsón, E., & Flores, F. (2011). Social media and corporate dialogue: The response of global financial institutions. *Online Information Review, 35*(1), 34–49. doi:10.1108/14684521111113579

Borchorst, A. (2011). *Institutionalizing intersectionality: The Danish board of equal treatment as case.* Presented at The Financial Crisis, Welfare State Challenges and New Forms of Risk Management, Aalborg, Denmark.

Bosker, B. (14 February 2012). The secret to Pinterest's success: We're sick of each other. *The Huffington Post.* http://www.huffingtonpost.com/2012/02/14/pinterest-success_n_1274797.html

Boud, D. (2000). Sustainable assessment: Rethinking assessment for the learning society. *Studies in Continuing Education, 22*(2), 151–167. doi:10.1080/713695728

Boughey, C. (1997). Learning to write by writing to learn: a group-work approach. *ELT Journal, 51*(2), 126–134. doi:10.1093/elt/51.2.126

Bowers, C. A. (1988). *The cultural dimensions of educational computing: Understanding the non-neutrality of technology.* New York, NY: Teachers College Press.

Bowers, C. A. (2000). *Let them eat data: How computers affect education, cultural diversity, and the prospects of ecological sustainability.* Athens, GA: University of Georgia Press.

Bowers, C. A. (2005). Is transformative learning the Trojan Horse of western globalization? *Journal of Transformative Education, 3*(2), 116–125. doi:10.1177/1541344604273622

Bowman S. (2009). Presence, identity, and the cloud of knowing. E-learning, politics and society. *Journal of Moray House School of Education,* 1-7.

boyd, d. m. (2007). Why youth (heart) social network sites: The role of networked publics in teenage social life. In D. Buckingham (Ed.), *MacArthur Foundation Series on Digital Learning - Youth, Identity, and Digital Media Volume* (pp. 119-142). Retrieved February 28, 2012, from www.danah.org/papers/WhyYouthHeart.pdf

boyd, d. m., & Ellison, N. B. (2007). Social network sites: Definition, history, and scholarship. *Journal of Computer-Mediated Communication, 13*(1).

boyd, d., Golder, S., & Lotan, G. (2010). Tweet, Tweet, retweet: Conversational aspects of retweeting on Twitter. *Proceedings of the International Hawaiian Conference on Social Sciences,* (p. 43). Kauai, HI: IEEE. Retrieved from http://www.danah.org/papers/TweetTweetRetweet.pdf

Bradley, T. (2011). Staying in sync. *PC World, 29*(8), 29–30.

Bradshow, P. (2008). *Teaching students to twitter: The good, the bad and the ugly.* Blog post 15/02/2008. Retrieved June 2, 2012 from http://onlinejournalismblog.com/2008/02/15/teaching-students-to-twitter-the-good-the-bad-and-the-ugly/

Brady, K., Holcomb, L., & Smith, B. (2010). The use of alternative social networking sites in higher educational settings: A case study of the e-learning benefits of Ning in education. *Journal of Interactive Online Learning, 9*(2), 151–170.

Brady, M., Saren, M., & Tzokas, N. (1999). The impact of IT on marketing: An evaluation. *Management Decision, 37*(10), 758–767. doi:10.1108/00251749910302854

Brander, P., Gomes, R., Keen, E., Lemineur, M.-L., Oliveira, B., Ondráčková, J., Surian, A., et al. (2002, May). *COMPASS: A manual on human rights education with young people.* Council of Europe Publishing F-67075 Strasbourg Cedex.

Breton, P., & Proulx, S. (2002). L'explosion de la communication: A l'aube du XXI siècle. Paris, France: éditions La Découverte.

Brickner, D. (1995). *The effects of first- and second-order barriers to change on the degree and nature of computer usage of secondary mathematics teachers: A case study.* Unpublished doctoral dissertation, West Lafayette, IN: Purdue University.

Briggs, L. L. (2008). *Micro blogging with Twitter: A Q and A with David Parry, assistant professor of emerging media at the University of Texas at Dallas' campus technology.* Retrieved June 2, 2012, from http://campustechnolog.com/Articles/2008/03/Micro-Blogging-with-Twitter.aspx?Page=1

Brinkerhoff, J. (2006). Effects of a long-duration, professional development academy on technology skills, computer self-efficacy, and technology integration beliefs and practices. *Journal of Research on Technology in Education*, *39*(1), 22–43.

Broadley, T., Boyd, D., & Terry, E. (2009). The hot topic community: Videoconferencing to reduce the professional isolation of teachers in rural Western Australia. *ISFIRE Symposium Proceedings*, (pp. 76-83). Armidale, Australia: University of New England.

Brookfield, S. (1995). *Becoming a critically reflective teacher.* San Francisco, CA: Jossey-Bass.

Brooks, C. D. (2011). *Education and technology policy discourse in Alberta: A critical analysis.* Unpublished doctoral dissertation, University of Alberta, Alberta, Canada.

Brown, A., & Brown, N. J. (2007). The Northern Territory intervention: Voices from the fringe. *The Medical Journal of Australia*, *187*(11), 621–623.

Brown, E. (2010). Introduction to location-based mobile learning. In Brown, E. (Ed.), *Education in the wild: contextual and location-based mobile learning in action.* University of Nottingham: Learning Sciences Research Institute.

Brown, J. S. (2000). Growing up digital: How the Web changes work, education, and the ways people learn. *Change*, (March/April): 10–20.

Brown, J. S., & Adler, R. P. (2008). Minds on fire: Open education, the long tail, and learning 2.0. *EDUCAUSE Review*, *43*(1), 16–32.

Bruner, J. (1991). The narrative construction of reality. *Critical Inquiry*, *18*(1), 1–21. doi:10.1086/448619

Bruns, A. (2009). News blogs and citizen journalism. In KK.iran Prasad (Ed.), *E-journalism: New directions in electronic news media.* New Delhi, India: BR Publishing. Retrieved June 1, 2011, from http://snurb.info/files/News%20Blogs%20and%20Citizen%20Journalism.pdf

Bruns, A., & Bahnisc, M. (2009). *Social media: Tools for user-generated content social drivers behind growing consumer participation in user-led content generation* (State of the Art No. Volume 1) (p. 60). Eveleigh NSW, Australia 201: Smart Services CRC Pty Ltd., Australian Technology Park Locomotive Workshop.

Bruns, A., & Humphreys, S. (2007). Building collaborative capacities in learners: The M/cyclopedia project revisited. *Proceedings of the 2nd International Symposium of Wikis*, 2007, (pp. 1-10).

Bruns, A. (2008). *Blogs, Wikipedia, Second Life, and beyond: From production to produsage.* New York, NY: Peter Lang.

Bruns, A., & Humpreys, S. (2005). Wikis in teaching and assessment: The M/cyclopedia project. [San Diego, CA, USA.]. *WikiSym*, *05*(October), 16–18.

Brush, T., Glazewski, K., Rutowski, K., & Berg, K. (2003). Integrating technology in a field-based teacher training program. *Educational Technology Research and Development*, *51*(1). doi:10.1007/BF02504518

Bryan, A. (2006). Web 2.0: A new wave of innovation for teaching and learning. *EDUCAUSE Review*, *41*(2), 32–44.

Bryant, T. (2006). Social software in academia. *EDUCAUSE Quarterly*, 2.

Brzycki, D., & Dudt, K. P. (2005). Overcoming barriers to technology use in teacher preparation programs. *Journal of Technology and Teacher Education*, *13*(4), 619–641.

Buchem, I., & Camacho, M. (2011). M-project: First steps to applying action research in designing a mobile learning course in higher education. In K. Rummler, J. Seipold, E. Lübcke, N. Pachler, & G. Attwell (Eds.), *Mobile learning: Crossing boundaries in convergent environments* (pp. 123-132). London Mobile Learning Group. ISSN 1753-3385

Buckingham, D. (2010). Defining digital literacy. What young people need to know about digital media. In B. Bachmair (Ed.), *Medienbildung in neuen Kulturräumen: Die deutschsprachige und britische Diskussion [Media education in new cultural spaces: The German and British discussion]* (pp. 59–71). Wiesbaden, Germany: VS.

Buckingham, D. (2000). *After the death of childhood.* Oxford, UK: Polity.

Buffardi, L. E., & Campbell, W. K. (2008). Narcissism and social networking web sites. *Personality and Social Psychology Bulletin, 34*(10), 1303–1314. doi:10.1177/0146167208320061

Bugeja, M. (2004). Don't let students "overlook" internet plagiarism. *Education Digest, 70*(2), 37–43.

Bullock, D. (2004). Moving from theory to practice: An examination of the factors that preservice teachers encounter as they attempt to gain experience teaching with technology during field placement experiences. *Journal of Technology and Teacher Education, 12*(2), 211–237.

Burnett, C. (2011). Medium for empowerment or a centre for everything: Students' experience of control in virtual learning environments within a university context. *Education and Information Technologies, 16*(3), 245–258. doi:10.1007/s10639-010-9122-z

Burns, A. C., & Bush, R. F. (2000). *Marketing research.* Prentice Hall.

Burstein, J., & Wolska, A. (2003). Toward evaluation of writing style: finding overly repetitive word use in student essays. *EACL '03 Proceedings of the Tenth Conference on European Chapter of the Association for Computational Linguistics*, Vol. 1, (pp. 35-42).

Butler, D., & Sellbom, M. (2002). Barriers to adopting technology for teaching and learning. *EDUCAUSE Quarterly, 25*(2), 22–28.

Buttery, A., & Tamaschke, R. (1996). The use and development of marketing information systems in Queensland, Australia. *Marketing Intelligence & Planning, 14*(3), 29–35. doi:10.1108/02634509610117339

Byrne, S., & Lee, T. (2011). Toward predicting youth resistance to internet risk prevention strategies. *Journal of Broadcasting & Electronic Media, 55*(1). doi:10.1080/08838151.2011.546255

Cakir, M. (2008). Constructivist approaches to learning in science and their implications for science pedagogy: A literature review. *International Journal of Environmental and Science Education, 3*(4), 193–206.

Calvert, S. L. (2002). Identity construction on the Internet. In Calvert, S. L., Jordan, A. B., & Cocking, R. R. (Eds.), *Children in the digital age* (pp. 57–70). Westport, CT: Praeger.

Calvete, E., Orue, I., Estévez, A., Villardón, L., & Padilla, P. (2010). Cyberbullying in adolescents: Modalities and aggressors' profile. *Computers in Human Behavior, 26*(5), 1128–1135. doi:10.1016/j.chb.2010.03.017

Cannon, R. (2000). *Guide to support the implementation of the learning and teaching plan year 2000. ACUE.* The University of Adelaide.

Carini, R. M., Kuh, G. D., & Klein, S. P. (2006). Student engagement and student learning: Testing the linkages. *Research in Higher Education, 47*(1). doi:10.1007/s11162-005-8150-9

Carney, A. G., & Merrell, K. W. (2001). Bullying in schools: Perspectives on understanding and preventing an international problem. *School Psychology International, 22*(3), 364–382. doi:10.1177/0143034301223011

Carolyn, B., & Foster, C. (2010). Alternative certification: An effective model of online supported teacher education. In D. Gibson & B. Dodge (Eds.), *Society for Information Technology & Teacher Education International Conference 2010,* (pp. 17-32). Chesapeake, VA: AACE.

Carpenter, J. (2011). Narcissism on Facebook: Self-promotional and anti-social behavior. *Personality and Individual Differences, 52*(4), 482–486. doi:10.1016/j.paid.2011.11.011

Carroll, F., Jenkins, A., Woodward, C., Kop, R., & Jenkins, E. (2011). Exploring how social media can enhance the teaching of action research. *Action Research, 9*(4), 1–19.

Caruso, J., & Kvavik, R. B. (2005). *ECAR study of students and information technology, 2005: Convenience, connection, control, and learning.* EDUCASE Report.

Cassidy, W., Jackson, M., & Brown, K. N. (2009). Students' experiences with cyberbullying: Sticks and stones can break my bones, but how can pixels hurt me? *School Psychology International, 30,* 383–402. doi:10.1177/0143034309106948

Castells, M. (1996). *The information age: Economy, society and culture (Vol. 1).* Oxford, UK: Blackwell.

Celik, I., Abel, F., & Houben, G.-J. (2011). Learning semantic relationships between entities in Twitter. In Auer, S., Diaz, O., & Papadopoulos, G. A. (Eds.), *ICWE 2011, LNCS 6757* (pp. 167–181). Berlin, Germany: Springer-Verlag. doi:10.1007/978-3-642-22233-7_12

Cha, M., Navarro Pérez, J. A., & Haddadi, H. (2011). The spread of media content through blogs. *Social Network Analysis and Mining, 2*(3), 249-264. ISSN: 18695450

Chan, A. (2009). *Social interaction design.* Retrieved from http://www.gravity7.com/paradigm_shift_1.html

Chang, W. L. (2003). *A study of information-seeking behavior among senior-level elementary school students in the area of I -Lan.* Master thesis, Fo Guang University, Taiwan.

Chang, K., Chen, I., & Sung, Y. (2002). The effect of concept mapping to enhance text comprehension and summarization. *Journal of Experimental Education, 71*(1), 5–23. doi:10.1080/00220970209602054

Chapman, M. (1988). *Constructive evolution: Origins and development of Piaget's thought.* Cambridge, UK: Cambridge University Press.

Charles, K. (2011). Facebook stress linked to number of 'friends'. *Edinburgh Napier University - News, Media and Events.* Retrieved March 11, 2012, from http://www.napier.ac.uk/media/Pages/NewsDetails.aspx?NewsID=187

Charnigo, L., & Bernett-Ellis, P. (2007). Checking out Facebook.com: The impact of a digital trend on academic libraries. *American Libraries Association, 26*(1), 23–34.

Cheng, E., Davis, S., Burnett, I., & Ritz, C. (2010). The role of experts in social media - Are the tertiary educated engaged? *IEEE International Symposium on Technology and Society,* (pp. 205-212).

Chen, R.-J. (2011). Preservice mathematics teachers' ambiguous views of technology. *School Science and Mathematics, 111*(2), 56–67. doi:10.1111/j.1949-8594.2010.00061.x

Cheong, R. K. F., & Tsui, E. (2010). The roles and values of personal knowledge management: An exploratory study. *Vine, 40*(2), 204–227. doi:10.1108/03055721011050686

Chesbrough, H. W. (2003). *Open innovation: The New imperative for creating and profiting from technology.* Boston, MA: Harvard Business School Press.

Chesbrough, H. W. (2003). The era of open innovation. *Sloan Management Review, 44*(3), 35–41.

Cheung, C. M. K., Chiu, P. Y., & Lee, M. K. O. (2011). Online social networks: Why do students use Facebook? *Computers in Human Behaviour, 27*(4), 1337-1343. Retrieved June 6, 2012, from http://linkinghub.elsevier.com/retrieve/pii/S0747

Chi-Lun, L. (2011). Contact information management system architecture for social media. In *Proceedings of 20th International Conference on Computer Communications and Networks* (ICCCN), (pp. 1–5).

Chizmar, J. F., & Williams, D. B. (2001). What do faculty want? *Educause Quarterly, 1,* Spring. Retrieved June 12, 2012, from http://net.educause.edu/ir/ library/pdf/eqm0112.pdf

Choo, C. W. (2003). Perspectives on managing knowledge in organizations. In Williamson, N. J., & Beghtol, C. (Eds.), *Knowledge organization and classification in international information retrieval* (pp. 205–220). Binghamton, NY: Haworth Press.

Christie, M. (2001). Aboriginal knowledge on the internet. *A Journal of Australian Indigenous Issues, June,* 33-50.

Clark, J., & Aufderheide, P. (February 2009). *Public media 2.0: Dynamic, engaged publics.* Centre for Social Media. Retrieved from http://www.uni.edu/fabos/thc/futureopublicmedia.pdf

Clark, R. E. (1983). Reconsidering research on learning from media. *Review of Educational Research*, *53*(4), 445–459.

Clark, R. E. (1991). When researchers swim upstream: Reflections on an unpopular argument about learning from media. *Educational Technology*, *31*(2), 34–40.

Clever, N., Kirchner, A., Schray, D., & Schulte, M. (2009). *User-generated content*. 453 Research Compile. Retrieved February 14, 2012, from http://453.stilled.net/wp-content/uploads/2010/06/Eessay-user-generated-content.pdf

Click, A., & Petit, J. (2010). Social networking and Web 2.0 in information literacy. *The International Information & Library Review*, *42*, 137–142. doi:10.1016/j.iilr.2010.04.007

Cobcroft, R., Towers, S., Smith, J., & Bruns, A. (2006). Mobile learning in review: Opportunities and challenges for learners, teachers, and institutions. In *Proceedings Online Learning and Teaching (OLT) Conference 2006*, (pp. 21-30). Brisbane, Australia: Queensland University of Technology.

Cochrane, T. (2010). *Twitter tales: Facilitating international collaboration with mobile web 2.0*. Paper presented at the 27th ASCILITE Conference, ASCILITE 2010.

Cochrane, T., & Bateman, R. (2008, October). *Engaging students with Mobile Web 2.0*. Paper presented at the Teaching & Learning Conference, Eastern Institute of Technology, Hawkes Bay.

Cochrane, T., & Rhodes, D. (2011). *iArchi[tech]ture: Heutagogical approaches to education facilitated by mlearning integration*. Paper presented at the International Conference on Information and Communication Technologies in Education ICICTE 2011. Retrieved from http://www.icicte.org/index.htm

Cochrane, T., & Bateman, R. (2011). Transforming pedagogy using mobile web 2.0. In Parsons, D. (Ed.), *Combining e-learning and m-learning: New applications of blended educational resources* (pp. 281–307). Hershey, PA: IGI Global. doi:10.4018/978-1-60960-481-3.ch018

Cohen, H. (2011, September 5). *30 social media definitions*. HeidiCohen.com. Retrieved February 26, 2012, from http://heidicohen.com/social-media-definition/

Cohen, P., et al. (2010). *Roadmap for education technology*. Global Resources for Online Education, a project sponsored by the National Science Foundation and the Computing Community Consortium. Tempe, Arizona.

Cojocariu, V. (2012). *Educational strategies centered on the beneficiary of learning. Constructivism and efficient practices*. Saarbrücken, Germany: Lambert Academic Publishing.

Cole, K. (2008). *The Bolivarian alternative for the Americas and the regional political architecture of equality*. Presented at the XXVIII International Congress of the Latin American Studies Association, Rio de Janeiro.

Colley, H., Hodkinson, P., & Malcom, J. (2003). *Informality and formality in learning: A report for the learning and skills research centre*. London, UK: Learning and Skills Research Centre.

Colley, J., & Stead, G. (2004). *Mobile learning = collaboration. Proceedings of mLearn 2004 Mobile learning anytime everywhere* (pp. 57–58). London, UK: Learning and Skills Development Agency.

Collins, M., & Berge, Z. (1996). *Facilitating interaction in computer mediated online courses*. Paper presented at the FSU/AECT Distance Education Conference, Tallahasee, Florida.

Common, S. M. R. (2012). *Teen social media*. Retrieved January, 25, 2012, from http://www.commonsensemedia.org/teen-social-media

Conole, G., & Alevizou, P. (2010). *A literature review of the use of Web 20.0 tools in higher education. A report commissioned by the Higher Education Academy. Walton Hall*. Milton Keynes, UK: The Open University.

Corcoran, S. (2009). *Defining owned, earned, and paid media*. Retrieved September 30, 2010, from http://blogs.forrester.com/interactive_marketing/2009/12/defining-earned-owned-and-paid-media.html

Corn, M. (2011). Embracing the cloud: Caveat professor. *The Chronicle of Higher Education*, *57*(36), B31–B32.

Corno, L. (1986). The metacognitive control components of self-regulated learning. *Contemporary Educational Psychology*, *11*(4), 333–346. doi:10.1016/0361-476X(86)90029-9

Cortez, C., Nussbaum, M., Santelices, R., Rodríguez, P., Zurita, G., Correa, M., et al. (2004). Teaching science with mobile computer supported collaborative learning (MCSCL). *Proceedings of the 2nd IEEE workshop on wireless and mobile technologies in education* (WMTE '04) (pp. 67–74). JungLi, Taiwan: IEEE Computer Society.

Couillard, C. (2010). *Facebook: The pros and cons of use in education*. A Research Paper Submitted in Partial Fulfillment of the Requirements for the Master of Science Degree in Information and Communication Technologies. University of Wisconsin-Stout. Retrieved February 5, 2012, from http://clairecouillard.weebly.com/uploads/5/1/9/8/5198042/research_paper_tcs_701.pdf

Council of Europe. (1998). *Conceptual framework, methodology and presentation of good practices: Final report of activities of the group of specialists on mainstreaming* (No. [EG-S-MS (98) 2]). Strasbourg, France.

Cowie, H., & Colliety, P. (2010). Cyberbullying: Sanctions or sensitivity? *Pastoral Care in Education, 28*(4), 261–268. doi:10.1080/02643944.2010.528017

Cowling, D. (2011). *Social media statistics Australia - October 2011*. Retrieved January 22, 2012, from http://www.socialmedianews.com.au/social-media-statistics-australia-october-2011/

Cranton, P. (2005). *Understanding and promoting transformative learning*. San Francisco, CA: Jossey-Bass.

Craven, R. (Ed.). (2011). *Teaching Aboriginal studies* (2nd ed.). Sydney, Australia: Allen & Unwin.

Creagh, S. (2011). Princeton goes open access to stop staff handing all copyright to journals unless waiver granted. In *Conversation*, September 28, 2011.

Crook, C., Cummings, J., Fisher, T., Graber, R., Harrison, C., & Lewin, C. Oliver, M. (2008). *Web 2.0 technologies for learning: the current landscape –Opportunities, challenges and tensions*. A Becta Report. Retrieved June 2, 2012, from http://partners.becta.org.uk/uploaddir/downloads/page_documents/research/web2_tech nologies_learning.pdf

Crooks, A. D. (1933). Marks and marking systems: A digest. *The Journal of Educational Research, 27*(4), 259–272.

Crow, M. (2012, January). *The future of the new American university*. Speech presented at Tempe Center for the Arts, Arizona. Retrieved from http://vimeo.com/35585254

Cuban, L., Kirkpatrick, H., & Peck, C. (2001). High access and low use of technology in high school classrooms: Explaining an apparent paradox. *American Educational Research Journal, 38*(4), 813–834. doi:10.3102/00028312038004813

Cui, X., Wang, H., & Cao, Z. (2008). An Ajax-based terminology system for e-learning 2.0. In Z. Pan, X. Zhang, A. Rhalibi, W. Woo, & Y. Li (Eds.), *Proceedings of the 3rd International Conference on Technologies for E-Learning and Digital Entertainment* (Edutainment '08), (pp. 135-146). Berlin, Germany: Springer-Verlag.

Curos, A. (2010). Developing personal learning networks for open and social learning. In Veletsianos, G. (Ed.), *Emerging technologies in distance education, part 2: Learning designs for emerging technologies* (pp. 109–128).

Curry, R., Kiddle, C., & Simmonds, R. (2009). Social networking and scientific gateways. In *Proceedings of the 5th Grid Computing Environments Workshop* (GCE '09). (p. 10). New York, NY: ACM.

Daniel, E., Wilson, H., & McDonald, M. (2003). Towards a map of marketing information systems: An inductive study. *European Journal of Marketing, 37*(5/6), 821–847. doi:10.1108/03090560310465161

Darwin, C. (1958). *The origin of species*. New York, NY: Penguin.

Davenport, T. H., & Prusak, L. (1998). *Working knowledge: How organizations manage what they know*. Cambridge, MA: Harvard Business School Press.

Davidson, M. A., & Yoran, E. (2007). Enterprise security for Web 2.0. *Computer, 40*(11), 117–119. doi:10.1109/MC.2007.383

Davies, C., & Birbili, M. (2000). What do people need to know about writing in order to write in their jobs? *British Journal of Educational Studies, 48*(4), 429–445. doi:10.1111/1467-8527.00156

De Board. R. (1978). *The psychoanalysis of organizations*. London, UK: Tavistock Publications.

De Choudhury, M., & Sundaram, H. (2011). Why do we converse on social media? An analysis of intrinsic and extrinsic network factors. ACM SIGMM International Workshop on Social Media (WSM '11), (pp. 53-58). New York, NY: ACM.

De Kerchove, D. (1997). *Connected intelligence, the arrival of the web society*. Toronto, Canada: Somerville House.

De Zouche, D. (1945). "The wound *is* mortal": Marks, honors, unsound activities. *Clearing House (Menasha, Wis.)*, *19*(6), 339–344.

DeAndrea, D., Ellison, N., LaRose, R., Steinfield, C., & Fiore, A. (2012). Serious social media: On the use of social media for improving students' adjustment. *The Internet and Higher Education*, *15*(1), 15–23. doi:10.1016/j.iheduc.2011.05.009

December 10, 2011, from http://www.mlearn.org.za/CD/papers/Stead.pdf

Dede, C. (2011). Emerging technologies, ubiquitous learning, and educational transformation. towards ubiquitous learning. *Proceedings of 6th European Conference of Technology Enhanced Learning, EC-TEL 2011*, Palermo, Italy, September 20-23, 2011.

Dehue, F., Bolman, C., & Völlink, T. (2008). Cyberbullying: Youngsters' experiences and parental perception. *Cyberpsychology & Behavior*, *11*(2), 217–223. doi:10.1089/cpb.2007.0008

Denzin, N. K., & Lincoln, Y. S. (Eds.). (2005). *The Sage handbook of qualitative research* (3rd ed.). Thousand Oaks, CA: Sage.

Deuze, M. (2004). What is multimedia journalism? *Journalism Studies*, *5*(2), 139–152. doi:10.1080/1461670042000211131

Deuze, M. (2006). Participation, remediation, bricolage: Considering principal components of a digital culture. *Journal: The Information Society*, *22*(2), 63–75. doi:10.1080/01972240600567170

Dewey, J. (1986). Experience and education. *The Educational Forum*, *50*(3), 241–252. doi:10.1080/00131728609335764

Diakopoulos, N., & Naaman, M. (2011). Towards quality discourse in online news comments. *Proceedings of the ACM 2011 Conference on Computer Supported Cooperative Work*, (pp. 133-142). New York, NY: ACM. DOI:10.1145/1958824.1958844

Diamanduros, T., Downs, E., & Jenkins, S. J. (2008). The role of school psychologists in the assessment, prevention, and intervention of cyberbullying. *Psychology in the Schools*, *45*(8), 693–704. doi:10.1002/pits.20335

Didden, R., Scholte, R. H. J., Korzilius, H., de Moor, J. M. H., Vermeulen, A., & O'Reilly, M. (2009). Cyberbullying among students with intellectual and developmental disability in special education settings. *Developmental Neurorehabilitation*, *12*(3), 146–151. doi:10.1080/17518420902971356

Dilmaç, B., & Aydogan, D. (2010). Parental attitudes as a predictor of cyber bullying among primary school children. *World Academy of Science. Engineering & Technology*, *67*, 167–171.

DiMaggio, P. &Hargittai, E. (2001). *From the 'digital divide' to `digital inequality': Studying internet use as penetration increases*. Working Paper 15, Summer 2001.

Doak, J. (2012). *Using new media tools to promote faculty research. Counsel for Advancement and Support of Education*. CASE.

Dobson, T. (2002). Keeping in touch by electronic mail. In *M. van Manen (2002). Writing in the dark: Phenomenological studies in interpretive inquiry* (pp. 98–116). Canada: Althouse Press.

Doherty, C., & Mayer, D. (2003). E-mail as a "contact zone" for teacher-student relationships. *Journal of Adolescent & Adult Literacy*, *46*(7), 592–600.

Domingo, D., & Heinonen, A. (2008). Weblogs and journalism: A typology to explore the blurring boundaries. *Nordicom Review*, *29*(1), 3–15.

Domingo, D., Quandt, T., Heinonen, A., Paulussen, S., Singer, J. B., & Vujnovic, M. (2008). Participatory journalism practices in the media and beyond - An international comparative study of initiatives in online newspapers. *Journalism Practice*, *2*(3). doi:10.1080/17512780802281065

Dooley, J. J., Pyżalski, J., & Cross, D. (2009). Cyberbullying versus face-to-face bullying. *Zeitschrift für Psychologie. The Journal of Psychology, 217*(4), 182–188.

Dörner, D. (1979). *Problemlösen als Informationsverarbeitung*. Stuttgart, Germany: Kohlhammer.

Dowell, E. B., Burgess, A. W., & Cavanaugh, D. J. (2009). Clustering of Internet risk behaviors in a middle school student population. *The Journal of School Health, 79*(1), 547–553. doi:10.1111/j.1746-1561.2009.00447.x

Dowling, S. (September 2011). Web-based learning: Moving from learning islands to learning environments. *TESL-EJ, 15*(2). Retrieved November 19, 2011, from http://www.teslej.org/wordpress/issues/volume15/ej58/ej58int/.

Downes, S. (2004, February 13). Beyond learning objects. *Australian Flexible Learning Framework*. Retrieved March 3, 2012, from http://community.flexiblelearning.net.au/GlobalPerspectives/content/article_5173.htm

Downes, S. (2005) E-learning 2.0. [Quick Edit] *eLearn Magazine, 2005*(10).

Downes, S. (2008). *The future of online learning: Ten years on*. Half an Hour. Retrieved July 26, 2011, from http://halfanhour.blogspot.com/2008/11/future-of-online-learning-ten-years-on_16.html

Downes, S. (2010). Blogs in learning. [STRIDE]. *Staff Training and Research Institute of Distance Education, 8*, 88–91.

Doyle, C. (2010). A literature review on the topic of social media. Retrieved February 21, 2012, from http://cathaldoyle.com/ph-d/

Drucker, P. F. (1994). The age of social transformation. *Atlantic Monthly, 274*(5), 53–80.

Duffy, P., & Bruns, A. (2006). The use of blogs, wikis and RSS in education: A conversation of possibilities. In *Proceedings Online Learning and Teaching Conference* (pp. 31-38). Brisbane. Retrieved from http://eprints.qut.edu.au/5398/

Duffy, T. M., & Cunningham, D. J. (1996). Constructivism: Implications for the design and delivery of instruction. In Jonassen, D. H. (Ed.), *Handbook of research on educational communications and technology* (pp. 170–198). New York, NY: Simon & Schuster.

Dulisch, R. (1998). *Schreiben in Werbung, PR und Journalismus. Zum Berufsbild des Texters für Massenmedien* [*Writing in advertising, PR and journalism. Being copywriter for mass media*]. (pp. 45–89). Opladen, Germany: Westdeutscher Verlag.

Dunlap, J. C., & Lowenthal, P. R. (2009). Horton hears a Tweet. *Educause Quarterly, 32*(4). Retrieved January 22, 2012, from http://www.educause.edu/educause+quarterly/educausequarterlymagazinevolum/hortonhearsatw eet/192955

Dunlap, J. C., & Lowenthal, P. R. (2009). Tweeting the night away: Using Twitter to enhance social presence. *Journal of Information Systems Education, 20*(2).

Dürnberger, H., Hofhues, S., & Sporer, T. (Eds.). (2011). *Offene Bildungsinitiativen* [*Open educational initiatives.*]. Münster, Germany: Waxmann.

Eales, R. T. J., & Byrd, L. M. (1997). Virtually deschooling society: Authentic collaborative learning via the Internet. *Webnet 97 World Conference of the WWW, Internet & Intranet Proceedings*. Toronto, Canada.

Earle, R. S. (2002, January-February). The integration of instructional technology into public education: Promises and challenges. *Education Technology Magazine, 42*(1), 5–13.

Earley, C., & Ang, S. (2003). *Cultural intelligence: Individual interactions across cultures*. Stanford University Press.

Earley, C., & Mosakowski, E. (2004). Cultural intelligence. *Harvard Business Review*, (October): 1–9.

Ebersbach, A., Glaser, M., & Heigl, R. (2011). *Social web* (2nd ed.). Konstanz, Germany: UVK.

Ebner, M., Holzinger, A., & Maurer, H. (2007). Web 2.0 technology: Future interfaces for technology enhanced learning? In C. Stephanidis (Ed.), *Proceedings of the 4th International Conference on Universal Access in Human-Computer Interaction: Applications and Services* (UAHCI'07), (pp. 559-568). Berlin, Germany: Springer-Verlag.

Education Development Center [EDC]. (1996). *National study tour of district technology integration summary report (CCT Reports, No. 14)*. New York, NY: Center for Children and Technology.

Electronic Frontier Foundation. (2009). *Definition of media*. Retrieved from www.eff.org/files/filenode/social_network/media_def_resp.pdf

Ellison, N., Steinfeld, C., & Lampe, C. (2007). The benefits of Facebook friends, social capital and college students' use of online social network sites. *Journal of Computer-Mediated Communication, 12*(3). Retrieved January 17, 2012, from http://jcmc.indiana.edu/vol12/issue4/ellison.html

Ellison, N. B., Steinfield, C., & Lampe, C. (2007). The benefits of Facebook "friends:' Social capital and college students use of online social network sites. *Journal of Computer-Mediated Communication, 12*(4), 1143–1168. doi:10.1111/j.1083-6101.2007.00367.x

Ellul, J. (1964). *The technological society*. New York, NY: Alfred A. Knopf.

Endestad, T., Heim, J., Kaare, B., Torgersen, L., & Brandtzæg, P. B. (2011). Media user types among young children and social displacement. *Nordicom Review, 32*(1), 17–30.

English, R., & Duncan-Howell, J. (2008). Facebook goes to college: Using social networking tools to support students undertaking teaching practicum. *Merlot Journal of Online Learning and Teaching, 4*(4), 596–601.

Erdur-Baker, Ö., & Tanrıkulu, İ. (2010). Psychological consequences of cyberbullying experiences among Turkish secondary school children. *Procedia-Social and Behavioral Sciences, 2*, 2771–2776. doi:10.1016/j.sbspro.2010.03.413

Ertmer, P. A. (1999). Addressing first- and second-order barriers to change: Strategies for technology integration. *Educational Technology Research and Development, 47*(4), 47–61. doi:10.1007/BF02299597

Ertmer, P. A., Addison, P., Lane, M., Ross, E., & Woods, D. (1999). Examining teachers' beliefs about the role of technology in the elementary classroom. *Journal of Research on Computing in Education, 32*(1), 54–72.

Espinosa, L. M., Laffey, J. M., Whittaker, T., & Sheng, Y. (2006). Technology in the home and the achievement of young children: Findings from the Early Childhood Longitudinal Study. *Early Education and Development, 17*, 421–441. doi:10.1207/s15566935eed1703_5

European Commission. (2008). *Towards a safer use of the Internet for children in the EU: A parents' perspective*. Retrieved February 28, 2012, from http://ec.europa.eu/information_society/activities/sip/docs/eurobarometer/analyticalreport_2008.pdf

European Commission. (2008). *User-created-content: Supporting a participative information society* (No. SMART 2007/2008).

European Commission. (2010). *EUROPE 2020: A strategy for smart, sustainable and inclusive growth*. April 24, 2011.

European Commission. (2011). Document 78. *The lifelong learning programme: Education and training opportunities for all*. Retrieved from http://ec.europa.eu/education/lifelong-learning-programme/doc78_en.htm

European Council. (2000). *The Lisbon Special European Council: Towards a Europe of Innovation and Knowledge*, March 23-24, Lisbon.

Everett, C. (2010). Social media: opportunity or risk? *Computer Fraud & Security, 6*, 8–10. doi:10.1016/S1361-3723(10)70066-X

Every, V., Garcia, G., & Young, M. (2010). A qualitative study of public wiki use in a teacher education program. In D. Gibson & B. Dodge (Eds.), *Society for Information Technology & Teacher Education International Conference 2010*, (pp. 55-62). Chesapeake, VA: AACE.

Eynon, R. (2008). The use of the world wide web in learning and teaching in higher education: Reality and rhetoric. *Innovations in Education and Teaching International, 45*(1), 15–23. doi:10.1080/14703290701757401

Fagerjord, A. (2010). After convergence: YouTube and remix culture. In Hunsinger, J., Allen, M., & Klastrup, L. (Eds.), *The international handbook of internet research* (pp. 187–201). Springer.

Fairclough, N. (2003). *Analysing discourse: Textual analysis for social research*. London, UK: Routledge.

Falchikov, N. (2004). Involving students in assessment. *Psychology Learning & Teaching*, *3*(2), 102–108. doi:10.2304/plat.2003.3.2.102

Fazal, M., DeSimone, J., & Lieman, L. (2010). Involving pre-service school leaders and teachers in assessing pilot electronic portfolio implementation. In D. Gibson & B. Dodge (Eds.), *Proceedings of Society for Information Technology & Teacher Education International Conference 2010*, (pp. 63-65). Chesapeake, VA: AACE.

Federal Trade Commission. (1998). *Children's online privacy protection act of 1998*. Retrieved January 14, 2012, from http://www.ftc.gov/ogc/coppa1.htm.

Feenberg, A. (2003). *What is the philosophy of technology?* Retrieved from www.sfu.ca/~andrewf/komaba.htm

Feenberg, A. (1991). *Critical theory of technology*. New York, NY: Oxford University Press.

Feenberg, A. (1999). *Questioning technology*. London, UK: Routledge.

Feenberg, A. (2005). Critical theory of technology: An overview. *Journal of Tailoring Biotechnologies*, *1*(1), 47–64.

Feng, B., Ma, J., & Fan, Z.-P. (2011). An integrated method for collaborative R and D project selection: Supporting innovative research teams. *Expert Systems with Applications*, *38*(5), 5532–5543. doi:10.1016/j.eswa.2010.10.083

Ferdig, R. E., Dawson, K., Black, E. W., & Thomson, L. A. (2008). Medical students' and residents' use of online social networking tools: Implications for teaching professionalism in medical education. *First Monday*, *13*(9). Retrieved January 17, 2012, from http://www.uic.edu/htbin/cgiwrap/bin/ojs/index.php/fm/article/view/2161/2026

Ferdig, R. E., Roehler, L. R., Boling, E. C., Knezek, S., Pearson, P. D., & Yadav, A. (2004). Teaching with video cases on the Web: Lessons learned from the reading classroom explorer. In Brown, A., & Davis, N. E. (Eds.), *Digital technology, communities and education: World yearbook of education 2004* (pp. 164–175). London, UK: Routledge Falmer. doi:10.4324/9780203416174_chapter_10

Fetler, M. (1984). Television viewing and school achievement. *The Journal of Communication*, *34*, 104–118. doi:10.1111/j.1460-2466.1984.tb02163.x

Firat, M. (2010). *Bilgi Toplumunda Eğitimin Sürekliliği ve Okulların Geleceği*. International Conference on New Trends in Education and their Implications. Antalya, Turkey.

Fisher, C., Dwyer, D., & Yocam, K. (1996). *Education and technology: Reflections on computing in classrooms*. San Francisco, CA: Apple Press.

Fishman, J., Lunsford, A., McGregor, B., & Otuteye, M. (2005). Performing writing, performing literacy. *College Composition and Communication*, *57*(2), 224–252.

Fitzgerald, R., & Steele, J. (2008). *Digital learning communities: Investigating the application of social software to support networked learning* (CG6-36). Australian Learning and Teaching Council. Retrieved September 1, 2009, from www.mashedlc.edu.au

Fitzgerald, S., Hanks, B., & McCauley, R. (2010). Collaborative research in computer science education: A case study. In *Proceedings of the 41st ACM Technical Symposium on Computer Science Education* (SIGCSE '10), (pp. 305-309). New York, NY: ACM.

FitzGerald, E. (2012). Creating user-generated content for location-based learning: An authoring framework. *Journal of Computer Assisted Learning*, *28*(3). doi:10.1111/j.1365-2729.2012.00481.x

Flecha, R. (2000). *Sharing words: Theory and practice of dialogic learning*. US: Rowman and Littlefield Publishers.

Florida, R. (2006). *The rise of the creative class*. New York, NY: Basic books.

Floridi, L. (2011). The informational nature of personal identity. *Minds and Machines*, *21*(4), 549–566. doi:10.1007/s11023-011-9259-6

Fogel, J., & Nehmad, E. (2009). Internet social network communities: Risk taking, trust, and privacy concerns. *Computers in Human Behavior*, *25*, 153–160. doi:10.1016/j.chb.2008.08.006

Foltz, B., O'Hara, M., & Wise, H. (2004). Standardizing the MIS course: Benefits and pitfalls. *Campus-Wide Information Systems*, *21*(4), 163–169. doi:10.1108/10650740410555043

Fordham, N. W., Wellman, D., & Sandman, A. (2002). Taming the text: Engaging and supporting students in social studies readings. *Social Studies*, *93*(4), 149–158. doi:10.1080/00377990209599901

Foucault, M., & Gordon, C. (1980). *Power/knowledge: Selected interviews and other writings, 1972-1977*. New York, NY: Pantheon.

Fountas, I. C., & Pinnell, G. S. (1996). *Guided reading; Good first teaching for all children*. Portsmouth, NH: Heinemann.

Fraser, M., & Dutta, S. (2008). *Throwing sheep in the boardroom*. Cornwall, UK: Wiley.

FreeDictionary.com. (2012). *Anxiety*. Retrieved February 20, 2012, from http://medical-dictionary.thefreedictionary.com/anxiety

Freire, J. (2008). Universities and Web 2.0: Institutional challenges. *eLearning Papers*, *8*.

Freud, S. (1926). Inhibitions, symptoms and anxiety. In Strachey, J. (Ed.), *The complete works of Sigmund Freud* (pp. 77–174). London, UK: Hogarth.

Frey, B. B., Lee, S. W., Tollefson, N., Pass, L., & Massengill, D. (2005). Balanced literacy in an urban school district. *The Journal of Educational Research*, *98*(5), 272–280. doi:10.3200/JOER.98.5.272-280

Friedman, B. (1996). Value-sensitive design. *Interaction*, *3*(6), 16–23. doi:10.1145/242485.242493

Friedman, B. (2006). Value sensitive design and information systems. In Zhang, P., & Galletta, D. (Eds.), *Human-computer interaction and management information systems: Foundations* (pp. 348–372).

Fuchs-Kittowski, F. (2007). Integrierte IT-Unterstützung der Wissensarbeit. Köln, Germany: Eul.

Funke, J., & Zumbach, J. (2005). Problemlösen. [Problem solving.] In Mandl, H., & Friedrich, H. F. (Eds.), *Handbuch Lernstrategien* [*Handbook learning strategies*]. (pp. 206–220). Göttingen, Germany: Hogrefe.

Gabriel, T. (5 April, 2011). More Pupils are learning online, fueling debate on quality. *New York Times*. http://www.nytimes.com/2011/04/06/education/06online.html?pagewanted=all

Gaggioli, A., & Riva, G. (2008). Working the crowd. *Science*, *321*(5895), 1443. doi:10.1126/science.321.5895.1443a

Galliani, L., & De Waal, P. (2009). Learning face to face, in action and on line: integrated model of lifelong learning. In Bernath, U., Szucs, A., Tait, A., & Vidal, M. (Eds.), *Distance and e-learning in transition: Learning innovation, technology and social challenges*. Budapest, Hungary: ISTE-Wiley.

Gal-Or, E., Geylani, T., & Yildirim, T. P. (2010, 21 July). *User-generated content in news media*. Retrieved January 1, 2011, from http://www.pitt.edu/~esther/papers/Gal-Or_Geylani_Yildirim_User-Generated%20Content%20in%20News%20Media_July%2021%202010.pdf

Gapski, H., & Tekster, T. (2009). *Informationskompetenz in Deutschland: Überblick zum Stand der Fachdiskussion und Zusammenstellung von Literaturangaben, Projekten und Materialien zu einzelnen Zielgruppen* [*Information literacy in Germany: An overview on the current state of the professional discourse and a compilation of references, projects and materials on selected target groups.*]. Düsseldorf, Germany: Landesanstalt für Medien Nordrhein-Westfalen (LfM).

Garnett, F. (2010). *Heutagogy and the craft of teaching*. The Heutagogic Archives. Retrieved 19th December, 2011, from http://heutagogicarchive.wordpress.com/2010/11/18/heutagogy-the-craft-of-teaching/#more-340

Gauntlett, D. (2011). *Media studies 2.0, and other battles around the future of media research*. Retrieved from http://www.theory.org.uk/mediastudies2.htm

Gay, G., Stefanone, M., Grace-Martin, M., & Hembrooke, H. (2001). The effects of wireless computing in collaborative learning environments. *International Journal of Human-Computer Interaction*, *13*(2), 257–276. doi:10.1207/S15327590IJHC1302_10

Geertz, C. (1973). *The interpretation of cultures*. New York, NY: Basic Books.

Gerlitz, C., & Helmond, A. (7 February 2011). *Hit, link, like and share. Organizing the social and the fabric of the web in a like economy.* Paper presented at the DMI Mini-Conference, 24-25 January 2011 at the University of Amsterdam. Retrieved from http://www.annehelmond.nl/wordpress/wp-content/uploads/2011/04/GerlitzHelmond-HitLinkLikeShare.pdf

Gibb, H. (2006). Distance education and the issue of equity online: exploring the perspectives of rural Aboriginal students. *Australian Journal of Indigenous Education*, *35*, 21–29.

Gibbons, M., Limoges, C., Nowotny, H., Schwartzman, S., Scott, P., & Trow, M. (1994). *The new production of knowledge: The dynamics of science and research in contemporary societies.* London, UK: Sage.

Gibson, K., & Vialle, W. (2007). The Australian Aboriginal view of giftedness. In Phillipson, S. N., & McCann, M. (Eds.), *Conceptions of giftedness: Sociocultural perspectives.* London, UK: Lawrence Erlbaum.

Gibson, L., & Keyes, S. E. (2011, December). A preliminary investigation of supplemental computer-assisted reading instruction on the oral reading fluency and comprehension of first-grade African American urban students. *Journal of Behavioral Education*, *20*(4), 260–282. doi:10.1007/s10864-011-9136-7

Gil de Zúñiga, H., Lewis, S. C., Willard, A., Valenzuela, S., Lee, J. K., & Baresch, B. (2011). Blogging as a journalistic practice: A model linking perception, motivation, and behavior. *Journalism*, *12*, 586–606. doi:10.1177/1464884910388230

Gilbert, E., & Karahalios, K. (2009). Predicting tie strength with social media. Paper presented at the 27th International Conference on Human Factors in Computing Systems (CHI '09), (pp. 211-220). New York, NY: ACM.

Gill, P., & Arlitt, M. (2008). A few chirps about Twitter. *WOSN '08 Proceedings of the First Workshop on Online Social Networks.* New York, NY: Association for Computing Machinery.

Glahn, C., Börner, D., & Specht, M. (2010). Mobile informal learning. In Brown, E. (Ed.), *Education in the wild: Contextual and location-based mobile learning in action.* University of Nottingham: Learning Sciences Research Institute.

Godwin-Jones, R. (2006). Emerging technologies tag clouds in the blogosphere: Electronic literacy and social networking. *Language Learning & Technology*, *10*(2), 8–15.

Goebert, D., Else, I., Matsu, C., Chung-Do, J., & Chang, J. (2011). The impact of cyberbullying on substance use and mental health in a multiethnic sample. *Maternal and Child Health Journal*, *15*(8), 1282–1286. doi:10.1007/s10995-010-0672-x

Graf, S., & Kinshuk. (2008). Adaptivity and personalization in ubiquitous learning systems. In A. Holzinger (Ed.), *USAB, LNCS 5298*, (pp. 331–338). Berlin, Germany: Springer-Verlag.

Grasso, A., & Roselli, T. (2005). Guidelines for designing and developing contents for mobile learning. In H. Ogata, M. Sharples, Kinshuk, & Y. Yano (Eds.), *Proceedings of the Third IEEE International Workshop on Wireless and Mobile Technologies in Education* (WMTE '05) (pp. 123–127). Washington, DC: IEEE Computer Society.

Green, S., Nacheva-Skopalik, L., & Pearson, E. (2008). An adaptable personal learning environment for e-learning and e-assessment. In B. Rachev & A. Smrikarov (Eds.), *Proceedings of the 9th International Conference on Computer Systems and Technologies and Workshop for PhD Students in Computing* (CompSysTech '08). New York, NY: ACM.

Greenberg, J., & Davila, M. (2002). *Teaching materials - What is strategic teaching?* MIT Teaching and Learning Laboratory. Retrieved February 21, 2012, from http://web.mit.edu/tll/teaching-materials/teaching-strategically/TLL-Strategic-Teaching-Diagram.pdf

Greenhow, C., Robelia, B., & Hughes, J. E. (2009). Learning, teaching, and scholarship in a digital age: Web 2.0 and classroom research: What path should we take now? *Educational Researcher*, *38*(4), 246–259. doi:10.3102/0013189X09336671

Greenhow, C., & Robelia, E. (2009). Old communication, new literacies: Social network sites as social learning resources. *Journal of Computer-Mediated Communication*, *14*(4), 1130–1161. doi:10.1111/j.1083-6101.2009.01484.x

Grell, P., & Rau, F. (2011). Partizipationslücken – Social Software in der Hochschullehre. [Gaps in participation – Social software in higher education.]. *Medienpädagogik, 21*, 1–23.

Gribbin, W. (1991). Writing across the curriculum: Assignments and evaluation. *Clearing House (Menasha, Wis.), 64*(6), 365–370.

Griffith, S., & Liyanage, L. (2008). *An introduction to the potential of social networking sites in education.* Emerging Technologies Conference 2008.

Grigg, D. W. (2010). Cyber-aggression: Definition and concept of cyberbullying. *Australian Journal of Guidance & Counselling, 20*(2), 143–156. doi:10.1375/ajgc.20.2.143

Gros, E. (2004). Adolescent internet use: What we expect, what they report. *Journal of Applied Developmental Psychology, 25*(6), 633–649. doi:10.1016/j.appdev.2004.09.005

Grosseck, G., & Holotescu, C. (2008). Can we use Twitter for educational activities? *The Meeting of the 4th International Scientific Conference eLSE: "Elearning and Software for Education* (p. 11). Bucharest.

Grossman, L. (2006, December 13). Time's person of the year: You. *Time Magazine.* Retrieved from http://www.imli.com/imlog/archivi/001051.html

Grover, A., & Stewart, D. W. (2010). Defining interactive social media in an educational context. In Wankel, C., Marovich, M., & Stanaityte, J. (Eds.), *Cutting edge social media approaches to business education: Teaching with LinkedIN, Facebook, Twitter, Second Life, and blogs* (pp. 7–38). Charlotte, NC: Information Age Publishing.

Gruppetta, M. (2010). *The life journey of gifted adults: a narrative exploration of developmental differences.* Unpublished Doctoral Dissertation. Sydney: The University of Western Sydney.

Gruppetta, M., & Hall, J. (2006, June). Email as communicative data: The tyranny of distance. *International Conference on Technology, Knowledge and Society: Technology & Citizenship,* Montreal, Canada. Retrieved March 30, 2012, from http://ts6.cgpublisher.com/proposals/103/index_html

Gruppetta, M., Mason, T., & Santora, N. Bennet, M. (2011). *Developing inter-cultural relationships through digital technology.* Paper presented at the Australian Association for Research in Education Conference, Hobart, Australia.

Gruppetta, M., & Mason, T. (2011). Embracing the Facebook © phenomenon. In Kahn, R., McDermott, J., & Akimjak, A. (Eds.), *Democratic access to education.* Los Angeles, CA: Antioch University.

Haenlein, M., & Kaplan, A. (2009). Unprofitable customers and their management. *Business Horizons, 52*(1), 89–97. doi:10.1016/j.bushor.2008.09.001

Haferkamp, N., Eimler, S. C., Papadakis, A. M., & Kruck, J. V. (2012). Men are from Mars, women are from Venus? Examining gender differences in self-presentation on social networking sites. *Cyberpsychology. Behaviour and Social Networking, 15*(2), 91–98. doi:10.1089/cyber.2011.0151

Haihe, S. (2011). A practical teaching approach to management information system course. *6th International Conference on Computer Science & Education* (ICCSE), (pp. 631–633).

Haiyan, C. (2010). An impact of social media on online travel information search in China. *3rd International Conference on Information Management, Innovation Management and Industrial Engineering,* (pp. 509-512).

Hakala, P. T., Rimpela, A. H., Saarni, L. A., & Salminen, J. J. (2006). Frequent computer-related activities increase the risk of neck-shoulder and low back pain in adolescents. *European Journal of Public Health, 16*(5), 536–541. doi:10.1093/eurpub/ckl025

Hall, B. (2006). *Student-centered learning.* A blog on writing and learning. Retrieved October 26, 2011, from http://secondlanguagewriting.com/explorations/Archives/2006/Jul/StudentcenteredLearning.html

Hallermayer, M., & Jocher-Wiltschka, C. (2009). *Zentrale Ergebnisse der w.e.b.Square-Bedarfsanalyse [Findings of the w.e.b.Square requirements analysis.].* Augsburg, Germany: Augsburg University, Institute of Media and Educational Technology.

Halliday, M. A. K. (2004). *An introduction to functional grammar* (3rd ed.). London, UK: Arnold.

Hancox, R. J., Milne, B. J., & Poulton, R. (2005). Association of television viewing during childhood with poor educational achievement. *Archives of Pediatrics & Adolescent Medicine, 159,* 614–618. doi:10.1001/archpedi.159.7.614

Hanna, R., Rohm, A., & Crittenden, V. (2011). We're all connected: The power of the social media ecosystem. *Business Horizons, 54*(3), 265–273. doi:10.1016/j.bushor.2011.01.007

Hansen, D. (2011). Exploring social media relationships. *Horizon, 19*(1), 43–51. doi:10.1108/10748121111107726

Harasim, L. (1990). Online education: An environment for collaboration and intellectual amplification. In Harasim, L. (Ed.), *Online education: Perspectives on a new environment* (pp. 39–66). New York, NY: Praeger Publishers.

Harel, I., & Papert, S. (1991). *Constructionism.* Ablex Publishing.

Hargittai, E. (2007).Whose space? Differences among users and non-users of social network sites. *Journal of Computer-Mediated Communication, 13*(1). Retrieved February 28, 2012, from http://jcmc.indiana.edu/vol13/issue1/hargittai.html

Hargreaves, D. (2000, March). *Knowledge management in the learning society.* Paper presented at the Forum of OECD Education Ministers, Copenhagen.

Harmon, R. (2003). Marketing information systems. In Bidgoli, H. (Ed.), *Encyclopedia of information systems* (*Vol. 3*, pp. 137–151). Elsevier Science. doi:10.1016/B0-12-227240-4/00110-6

Harris, S., & Malin, M. A. (1994). *Aboriginal kids in urban classrooms.* Wentworth Falls, Australia: Aboriginal Studies Press.

Havenstein, H. (2007, September 7). IT is a key barrier to corporate Web 2.0 adoption, users say. *Computerworld.*

Havighurst, R. (1953). *Human development and education.* Ann Arbor, MI: University of Michigan.

Hawker, D. M. (2011). *The developer's guide to social programming.* Pearson Education, Inc.

Hayhoe, G. F. (2001). From desktop to palmtop: creating usable online documents for wireless and handheld devices. In T.J. Malkinson (Ed.), *Proceedings of the IEEE International Professional Communication Conference* (pp. 1–11). Piscataway, NJ: IEEE.

Hebb, D. O. (1955). Drives and the CNS (conceptual nervous system). *Psychological Review, 62,* 243–254. doi:10.1037/h0041823

Hedrick, W., McGee, P., & Mittag, P. (1999). Pre-service teacher learning through one-on-one tutoring: Reporting perceptions through e-mail. *Teaching and Teacher Education, 16*(1), 47–63. doi:10.1016/S0742-051X(99)00033-5

Heiberger, G., & Harper, R. (2008). Have you Facebooked Astin lately? Using technology to increase student involvement. *New Directions for Student Services, 124,* 19–35. doi:10.1002/ss.293

Heidegger, M. (1962). *Being and time.* London, UK: SCM Press.

Heidegger, M. (1977). *The question concerning technology, and other essays.* New York, NY: Harper & Row.

Heinrichs, J., Jeen-Su, L., & Kee-Sook, L. (2011). Influence of social networking site and user access method on social media evaluation. *Journal of Consumer Behaviour, 10,* 347–355. doi:10.1002/cb.377

Heins, E., Seitz, C., & Schuz, J. (2007). Bedtime, television and computer habits of primary school children in Germany. *Gesundheitswesen (Bundesverband der Arzte des Offentlichen Gesundheitsdienstes (Germany)), 69*(3), 151–157. doi:10.1055/s-2007-971061

Heinze, N., & Reinhardt, W. (2011). Future social learning networks at universities – An exploratory seminar setting. In Wankel, C. (Ed.), *Educating educators with social media.* Emerald Publishing Group. doi:10.1108/S2044-9968(2011)0000001010

Herkman, J. (2008). Current trends in media research. *Nordicom Review, 29*(1), 145–159.

Hermida, A. (2010). Twittering the news: The emergence of ambient journalism. *Journalism Practice, 4*(3). Retrieved January 1, 2012, from http://www.caerdydd.ac.uk/jomec/resources/foj2009/foj2009-Hermida.pdf

Hermida, A. (2010). From TV to Twitter: How ambient news became ambient journalism. *Journal of Media and Culture, 13*(2). Retrieved May 1, 2011, from http://www.journal.media-culture.org.au/index.php/mcjournal/article/viewArticle/220

Hermida, A., & Thurman, N. (2009). A clash of cultures: The integration of user-generated content within professional journalistic frameworks at British newspaper websites. *Journalism Practice, 2*, 343–356. doi:10.1080/17512780802054538

Herring, S. C. (2009). Web content analysis: Expanding the paradigm. In Hunsinger, J., Allen, M., & Klastrup, L. (Eds.), *The international handbook of internet research* (pp. 233–249). Springer Verlag. doi:10.1007/978-1-4020-9789-8_14

Herring, S. C., Scheidt, L. A., Kouper, I., & Wright, E. (2006). A longitudinal content analysis of weblogs: 2003-2004. In Tremayne, M. (Ed.), *Blogging, citizenship and the future of media* (pp. 3–20). London, UK: Routledge.

Herring, S. D. (2001). Faculty acceptance of the World Wide Web for student research. *College & Research Libraries, 62*(5), 251–258.

Hess, R., Rubin, R., & West, R. Jr. (2004). Geographic information systems as a marketing information system technology. *Decision Support Systems, 38*(2), 197–212. doi:10.1016/S0167-9236(03)00102-7

Hew, K. F. (2011). Students' and teachers' use of Facebook. *Computers in Human Behavior, 27*(2), 662-676. Retrieved June 6, 2012, from http://www.sciencedirect.com/science/article/pii/S0747563210003651

Hewitt, A., & Forte, A. (2006). *Crossing boundaries: Identity management and student/faculty relationships on the Facebook.* Paper presented at the Computer Supported Cooperative Work (CSCW) conference. Alberta.

Hickman, L. A. (2006). Theoretical assumptions of the critical theory of technology. In Veak, T. J. (Ed.), *Democratizing technology: Andrew Feenberg's critical theory of technology* (pp. 71–81). New York, NY: State University of New York Press.

Higgins, S. (2011). Digital curation: The emergence of a new discipline. *International Journal of Digital Curation, 6*(2), 78–88. doi:10.2218/ijdc.v6i2.191

Higgison, S. (2004). Your say: Personal knowledge management. *Knowledge Management Magazine, 7*(7), 11–12.

Hinduja, S., & Patchin, J. W. (2010). Bullying, cyberbullying, and suicide. *Archives of Suicide Research, 14*(3), 206–221. doi:10.1080/13811118.2010.494133

Hofer, C. (2006). *Blicke auf das Schreiben. Schreibprozessorientiertes Lernen: Theorie und Praxis. [Views on writing. Writing process-oriented learning: Theory and practice.]* Wien, Austria: Lit.

Hoffmann, B., Müller, C., & Sauer, C. (2008). *Public-Relations kompakt [Public relations compact.]*. Konstanz, Germany: UVK.

Hofhues, S. (2011). From crossmedia publishing to cross-media education: The Important role of media practice. In ICWE-Secretariat (Eds.), *Online Educa 2011: Book of abstracts* (CON44). Berlin, Germany: ICWE.

Hofhues, S., & Hoffmann, C. (2012). Improving media literacy in universities: Insight into conception and implementation of a media curriculum. In *Proceedings of 2012 IATED Conference.*

Hofhues, S., & Schiefner-Rohs, M. (2012). Doktorandenausbildung zwischen Selbstorganisation und Vernetzung: zur Bedeutung digitaler sozialer Medien. [Graduate programs between self-organizational processes and networked learning: The importance of digital social media.] In *GMW'12* (other data not yet known).

Hofhues, S. (2011). Von studentischer Projektarbeit zum didaktischen Modell: die Augsburger Initiative w.e.b.Square. [From student's project work to a pedagogical model: The open educational initiative "w.e.b.Square" at University of Augsburg.] In Dürnberger, H., Hofhues, S., & Sporer, T. (Eds.), *Offene Bildungsinitiativen [Open educational initiatives.]*. (pp. 99–112). Münster, Germany: Waxmann.

Holmes, J. (2009). Myths and missed opportunities: Young people's not so risky use of online communication. *Information Communication and Society, 12*(8), 1174–1196. doi:10.1080/13691180902769873

Horrigan, J. (2009). The mobile difference. Pew Internet. Retrieved July 26, 2011, from http://www.pewinternet.org/~/media//Files/Reports/2009/The_Mobile_Difference.pdf

Houle, C. O. (1984). The design of education. In Merriam, S. B. (Ed.), *Selected writings on philosophy and adult education* (pp. 41–50). Malabar, FL: Robert E. Krieger Publishing Company.

Howe, J. (2006). The rise of crowdsourcing. *Wired, 14-06.*

HREOC. (1997). *Bringing them home: The stolen generation report.* Australian Human Rights Commission. Retrieved March 2, 2012, from http://www.humanrights.gov.au/social_justice/bth_report/index.html

Hsu, C.W., Wang, C.C., & Tai, Y.T. (2011). The closer the relationship, the more interaction on Facebook? Investigating the case of Taiwan users. *CyberPsychology, Behavior and Social Networking, 14*(7-8)

Huang, Y. P. (2002). *A study on the network literacy and network usage of elementary school students.* Master thesis, University of Tainan, Tainan, Taiwan.

Huber, G. P. (1984). The nature and design of post-industrial organizations. *Management Science, 30,* 928–951. doi:10.1287/mnsc.30.8.928

Huberman, B. A., Romero, D. M., & Wu, F. (2008). Social networks that matter: Twitter under the microscope. *Computing,* 1–9.

Huffington, C. (2004). *Working below the surface.* London, UK: Karnac.

Hughes, A. (2009). *Higher education in a Web 2.0 world.* JISC report. Retrieved January 15, 2012, from http://www.jisc.ac.uk/media/documents/publications/heweb20rptv1.pdf

Humphreys, L., Gill, P., & Krishnamurthy, B. (2010). *How much is too much? Privacy issues on Twitter.* Conference of International Communication Association, Singapore, June 2010. Retrieved June 6, 2012, from http://www2.research.att.com/~bala/papers/ica10.pdf

Hunley, S. A., Evans, J. H., Delgado-Hachey, M., Krise, J., Rich, T., & Schell, C. (2005). Adolescent computer use and academic achievement. *Adolescence, 40,* 307–318.

Hurd, S. (2007). Anxiety and non-anxiety in a distance language learning environment: The distance factor as a modifying influence. *System, 35*(4), 487–508. doi:10.1016/j.system.2007.05.001

Huston, A. C., Wright, J. C., Marguis, J., & Green, S. B. (1999). How young children spend their time: Television and other activities. *Developmental Psychology, 35,* 43–51. doi:10.1037/0012-1649.35.4.912

Hwang, G.-J., Tsai, C.-C., & Yang, S. J. H. (2008). Criteria, strategies and research issues of context-aware ubiquitous learning. *Journal of Educational Technology & Society, 11*(2), 81–91.

Hwang, G., Shi, Y., & Chu, H. (2010). A concept map approach to developing collaborative Mindtools for context-aware ubiquitous learning. *British Journal of Educational Technology, 42,* 778–789. doi:10.1111/j.1467-8535.2010.01102.x

Illich, I. (1973). *Deschooling society.* Harmondsworth, UK: Penguin.

Interactive Advertising Bureau. (2008). *User generated content, social media, and advertising — An overview.* Interactive Advertising Bureau.

International Reading Association. (1998). *Phonemic awareness and the teaching of reading: A position statement from the board of directors of the international reading association.* Retrieved February 11, 2012, from http://www.reading.org/General/AboutIRA/Position-Statements/PhonemicAwarenessPosition.aspx.

Internet World Stats. (2012). World internet usage and population statistics. Retrieved February 26, 2012, from http://www.internetworldstats.com/stats.htm

iParadigms, LLC. (n.d.). *PeerMark.* Retrieved from https://turnitin.com/static/products/peermark.php

Irving, F. (2003). *Learning to listen to indigenous voice: Dialogue and dilemmas.* Paper presented at the Australian Association for Research in Education Conference, Auckland, NZ

Islam, M., & Tsuji, K. (2010). Assessing information literacy competency of information science and library management graduate students of Dhaka University. *IFLA Journal, 36,* 300–316. doi:10.1177/0340035210388243

Ito, M., Baumer, S., & Bittanti, M. boyd, d., Cody, R., Herr-Stephenson, B., et al. (2010). *Hanging out, messing around, and geeking out: Kids living and learning with new media.* The John D. and Catherine T. MacArthur Foundation Series on Digital Media and Learning. Cambridge, MA: MIT Press.

Ivanov, D. (2006). The past, present and future in the perspective of dialectical theory. Proceedings *of 16th ISA World Congress of Sociology*, (pp. 1-25). Durban, South African Republic.

Jackson, M. G. (2008). *Transformative learning for a new worldview: Learning to think differently*. New York, NY: Palgrave Macmillan. doi:10.1057/9780230589940

Jacobs, S., Egert, C., & Barnes, S. (2009). Social media theory and practice: Lessons learned for a pioneering course. *39th IEEE International Conference on Frontiers in Education Conference* (FIE'09), (pp. 1125-1129). Piscataway, NJ: IEEE Press.

Jacobson, S. (2010). Emerging models of multimedia journalism: A content analysis of multimedia packages published on nytimes.com. *Atlantic Journal of Communication, 18*, 63–78. doi:10.1080/15456870903554882

Jakubetz, C. (2008). *Crossmedia*. Konstanz, Germany: UVK.

Jaruratanasirikul, S., Wongwaitaweewong, K., & Sangsupawanich, P. (2009). Electronic game play and school performance of adolescents in southern Thailand. *Cyberpsychology & Behavior, 12*(5), 509–512. doi:10.1089/cpb.2009.0035

Jasinski, M. (1998). *Teaching and learning styles that facilitate online learning: Documentation project: Project report*. Adelaide, Australia: Douglas Mawson Institute of TAFE.

Java, A., Song, X., Finin, T., & Tseng, B. (2007). Why we Twitter: Understanding microblogging. *Network*, 56–65.

Jelicic, H., Bobek, D. L., Phelps, E., Lerner, R. M., & Lerner, J. V. (2007). Using positive youth development to predict contribution and risk behaviors in early adolescence: Findings from the first two waves of the 4-H study of positive youth development. *International Journal of Behavioral Development, 31*, 263–273. doi:10.1177/0165025407076439

Jenkins, H. (2006). *Confronting the challenges of participatory culture: Media education for the 21st century*. Chicago, IL: The JohnD., & Catherine T. MacArthur Foundation.

Jensen, K., & Folley, S. (2011). *Teaching with technology in higher education: Exploring how lecturers at the University of Huddersfield use technology in teaching*. Teaching and Learning Institute Working Paper No. 1, University of Huddersfield, UK.

Jensen, J., & Lewis, B. (2001). Beyond the workshop educational policy in situated practice. *Education Canada, 41*(3), 28–31.

Jensen, T. (2010, May/June). No student email at school? Google Docs to the rescue! *Library Media Connection*, 52–53.

Jeong, T. G. (2005). The effects of internet addiction and self control on achievement of elementary school children. *The Korea Journal of Yeolin Education, 13*(1), 143–163.

Johnson, L., Adams, S., & Haywood, K. (2011). *The NMC horizon report: 2011 K-12 edition*. Austin, TX: The New Media Consortium.

Johnson, L., Smith, R., Levine, A., & Haywood, K. (2010). *2010 horizon report: K-12 edition*. Austin, TX: The New Media Consortium.

Johnston, E. (1991). *Review of Royal Commission into Aboriginal Deaths in Custody*. Retrieved February 12, 2012 from http://www.austlii.edu.au/au/other/IndigLRes/rciadic/

Johnston, S., & McCormack, C. (1996). Integrating information technology into university teaching: Identifying the needs and providing the support. *International Journal of Educational Management, 10*(5), 36–42. doi:10.1108/09513549610146123

Jonas, W. (2003). *Native title report*. Human Rights and Equal Opportunity Commission. Indigenous Studies Program, The University of Melbourne. Retrieved March 12, 2012 from http://www.atns.net.au/page.asp?PageID=2#what

Jonassen, D. (1999). Designing constructivist learning environments. In Reigeluth, C. (Ed.), *Instructional design theories and models: A new paradigm of instructional theory* (Vol. II, pp. 215–239). Mahwah, NJ: Lawrence Erlbaum Associates.

Jonassen, D. H. (1991). Evaluating constructivist learning. *Educational Technology, 31*(9), 28–33.

Jones, P. J. (2006). Resources for promoting online citizenship. *Educational Leadership, 6*(4), 41–51.

Jonghun, P., Yongwook, S., Kwanho, K., & Beom-Suk, C. (2011). Searching social media streams on the Web. *2011 International Conference on Computational Aspects of Social Networks* (CASoN), (pp. 278–283).

Junco, R. (2012). Too much face and not enough books: The relationship between multiple indices of Facebook use and academic performance. *Computers in Human Behavior, 28*(1), 187-198, Retrieved June 6, 2012, from http://www.sciencedirect.com/science/article/pii/S0747563211001932

Junco, R., Heiberger, G., & Loken, E. (2010). The effect of Twitter on college student engagement and grades. *Journal of Computer Assisted Learning, 27*(2), 119–132. doi:10.1111/j.1365-2729.2010.00387.x

Juvonen, J., & Gross, E. (2008). Extending the school grounds? – Bullying experiences in cyberspace. *The Journal of School Health, 78*(9), 496–506. doi:10.1111/j.1746-1561.2008.00335.x

Kagima, L. K., & Hausafus, C. O. (2000). Integration of electronic communication in higher education: Contributions of faculty computer self-efficacy. *The Internet and Higher Education, 2*(4), 1–15. doi:10.1016/S1096-7516(00)00027-0

Kamel Boulos, M. N., & Wheeler, S. (2007). The emerging Web 2.0 social software: An enabling suite of sociable technologies in health and health care education1. *Health Information and Libraries Journal, 24*(1), 2–23. doi:10.1111/j.1471-1842.2007.00701.x

Kaplan, A. M., & Haenlein, M. (2010). Users of the world, unite! The challenges and opportunities of Social Media. *Business Horizons, 53*, 59–68. doi:10.1016/j.bushor.2009.09.003

Karpinski, A. C. (2009). Media sensationalization of social science research: Social-networking in sites. *Teachers College Record*. Retrieved February 28, 2012, from http://www.tcrecord.org/Content.asp?ContentID=15642

Karpinski, A. C., & Duberstein, A. (2009). *A description of Facebook use and academic performance among undergraduate and graduate students.* San Diego, CA: American Educational Research Association.

Katsouyanni, K. (2008). Collaborative research: Accomplishments and potential. *Environmental Health, 7*(3).

Katzer, C., Fetchenhauer, D., & Belschak, F. (2009). Cyberbullying: Who are the victims? *Journal of Media Psychology: Theories, Methods, and Applications, 21*(1), 25–36. doi:10.1027/1864-1105.21.1.25

Keegan, H. (2010). *Immersed in the digital: Networked creativity through mobile content production.* Paper presented at the Association for Learning Technology: ALTC2010. Retrieved from http://altc2010.alt.ac.uk/talks/15004.

Keen, A. (2007). *The cult of the amateur: How today's internet is killing our culture.* New York, NY: Doubleday.

Ke, F., Chávez, A. F., Causarano, P.-N. L., & Causarano, A. (2011). Identity presence and knowledge building: Joint emergence in online learning environments? *International Journal of Computer-Supported Collaborative Learning, 6*(3), 349–370. doi:10.1007/s11412-011-9114-z

Kehrwald, B. (2005). Learner support in networked learning communities: Opportunities and challenges. In Son, J. B., & O'Neill, S. (Eds.), *Enhancing learning and teaching: Pedagogy, technology and language* (pp. 133–148). Flaxton, Australia: Post Pressed.

Kelm, O. (2011). Social media: It's what students do. *Business Communication Quarterly, 74*(4), 505–520. doi:10.1177/1080569911423960

Kennedy, T. L. M., Smith, A., Wells, A. T., & Wellman, B. (2008). *Networked families.* Washington, DC: The Pew Internet & American Life Project.

Kerr, S. T. (1996). Visions of sugarplums: The future of technology, education, and the schools. In Kerr, S. T. (Ed.), *Technology and the future of schooling: Ninety-fifty yearbook of the National Society for the Study of Education* (Vol. II). Chicago, IL: University of Chicago Press.

Khan, B. H. (2004). *Comprehensive approach to program evaluation in open and distributed learning (CAPEODL) model.* George Washington University.

Kietzmann, J., Hermkens, K., McCarthy, I., & Silvestre, B. (2011). Social media? Get serious! Understanding the functional building blocks of social media. *Business Horizons,54*(3), 241–251. doi:10.1016/j.bushor.2011.01.005

Kilpatrick, S., & Bound, H. (2003). *Learning online: Benefits and barriers in regional Australia*. Adelaide, Australia: NCVER.

Kim, A., & Ko, E. (2011). Do social media marketing activities enhance customer equity? An empirical study of luxury fashion brand. *Journal of Business Research, 65*(10).

Kirschenbaum, H., Simon, S. B., & Napier, R. W. (1971). *Wad-ja-get?: The grading game in American education*. New York, NY: Hart.

Kirschner, P. A., & Karpinski, A. C. (2010). Facebook(R) and academic performance. *Computers in Human Behaviour, 26*(6), 1237-1245, Retrieved June 6, 2012, from http://www.sciencedirect.com/science/article/pii/S0747563210000646

Kitchen, P., & Dawes, J. (1995). Marketing information systems in smaller building societies. *International Journal of Bank Marketing, 13*(8), 3–9. doi:10.1108/02652329510098864

Klein, M. (1975). *Envy and gratitude*. London, UK: The Hogarth Press.

Knight, C., Knight, B. A., & Teghe, D. (2006) Releasing the pedagogical power of information and communication technology for learners: A case study. International *Journal of Education and Development using Information and Communication Technology, 2*(2), 27-34.

Knight, P. T., & Yorke, M. (2003). *Assessment, learning and employability*. Buckingham, UK: Open University Press.

Knutson, K. L., & Lauderdale, D. S. (2009). Sociodemographic and behavioral predictors of bed time and wake time among US adolescents aged 15 to 17 years. *The Journal of Pediatrics, 154*(3), 426–441. doi:10.1016/j.jpeds.2008.08.035

Ko, C. H., Yen, J. Y., Yen, C. F., Lin, H. C., & Yang, M. J. (2007). Factors predictive for incidence and remission of internet addiction in young adolescents: A prospective study. *Cyberpsychology & Behavior, 10*(4), 545–551. doi:10.1089/cpb.2007.9992

Koch, M. (2008). *CSCW and enterprise 2.0 - Towards an integrated perspective. 21st Bled eConference eCollaboration: Overcoming Boundaries through Multi-Channel Interaction* (pp. 416–427). Slovenia: Bled.

Koch, M., & Richter, A. (2009). *Enterprise 2.0: Planung, Einführung und erfolgreicher Einsatz von Social Software in Unternehmen*. Munich, Germany: Oldenbourg. doi:10.1524/9783486593648

Kohn, A. (1999c, March). From degrading to de-grading. *High School Magazine*, pp. 38-43. Retrieved on February 27, 2012, from http://www.alfiekohn.org/teaching/fdtd-g.htm

Kohn, A. (2011). The case against grades. *Educational Leadership*. Retrieved on February 27, 2012, from http://www.alfiekohn.org/teaching/tcag.htm

Kohn, A. (1999). *Punished by rewards: The trouble with gold stars, incentive plans, A's, praise, and other bribes* (rev. ed.). Boston, MA: Houghton Mifflin.

Kohn, A. (1999). *The schools our children deserve: Moving beyond traditional classrooms and "tougher standards."*. Boston, MA: Houghton Mifflin.

Kojukhov, A., & Levin, I. (2010). *Ubiquitous personalized learning environment in post-industrial society*. London, UK: International Conference on Information Society (i-Society 2010).

Kolb, D. A. (1984). *The experiential learning: Experience as the source of learning and development*. Prentice-Hall.

Kolek, E. A., & Saunders, D. (2008). Online disclosure: An empirical examination of undergraduate Facebook profiles. *NASPA Journal, 45*(1), 1–25.

König, A., Gollwitzer, M., & Steffgen, G. (2010). Cyberbullying as an act of revenge? *Australian Journal of Guidance & Counselling, 20*(2), 210–224. doi:10.1375/ajgc.20.2.210

Koplowitz, R., & Young, G. O. (2007, September 14). *Web 2.0 social computing dresses up for business*. Forrester Research.

Kotler, P. (1984). *Marketing management: Analysis, planning, and control*. Prentice-Hall.

Kowalski, R. M., Limber, P., & Agatston, P. W. (2008). *Bullying in the digital age*. Boston, MA: Blackwell Publishing.

Kozma, R., & Anderson, R. (2002). Qualitative case studies of innovative pedagogical practices using ICT. *Journal of Computer Assisted Learning, 18,* 387–394. doi:10.1046/j.0266-4909.2002.00250.doc.x

Krishnamurthy, B., Gill, P., & Arlitt, M. (2008). A few chirps about Twitter. *Proceedings of the First Workshop on Online Social Networks, WOSP 08* (p. 19). New York, NY: ACM Press.

Kruse, O. (2010). Kritisches Denken als Leitziel der Lehre [Critical thinking as key objective of higher education.] *die Hochschule, 1,* 77-86.

Kruse, K., & Keil, J. (1999). *Technology-based training.* San Francisco, CA: Jossey-Bass/ Pfeiffer.

Kruse, O. (2010). *Lesen und Schreiben [Reading and writing.].* Konstanz, Germany: UVK.

Kubey, R. W., Lavin, M. J., & Barrows, J. R. (2001). Internet use and collegiate academic performance decrements: Early findings. *The Journal of Communication, 51,* 366–382. doi:10.1111/j.1460-2466.2001.tb02885.x

Kuh, G. D. (2009). What student affairs professionals need to know about student engagement. *Journal of College Student Development, 50*(6), 683–706. doi:10.1353/csd.0.0099

Kukulska-Hulme, A. (2010). Learning cultures on the move: where are we heading? *Journal of Educational Technology & Society, 13*(4), 4–14.

Kvavik, R. B., Caruso, J. B., & Morgan, G. (2004). *ECAR study of students and information technology 2004: convenience, connection, and control.* EDUCAUSE Center for Applied Research. Retrieved March 11, 2012, from http://net.educause.edu/ir/library/pdf/ERS0405/ekf0405.pdf

Kwak, H., Lee, C., Park, H., & Moon, S. (2010). What is Twitter, a social network or a news media? Categories and subject descriptors. *Most,* 591-600.

Kwak, H., Lee, C., Park, H., & Moon, S. (2010). What is Twitter, a social network or a news media? *Proceedings of the 19th International WWW 2010,* April 26–30, 2010, Raleigh, North Carolina. Retrieved December 1, 2011, from http://cs.wellesley.edu/~cs315/Papers/What%20is%20twitter-a%20social%20net%20or%20news%20media.pdf

Lampe, C., Ellison, N. B., & Steinfield, C. (2008). Changes in use and perception of Facebook. *Proceedings of the 2008 ACM Conference on Computer Supported Cooperative Work,* (pp. 721–730). ACM.

Lariscy, R. W., Johnson Avery, E., Sweetser, K. D., & Howes, P. (2009). An examination of the role of online social media in journalists' source mix. *Public Relations Review, 35,* 314–316. doi:10.1016/j.pubrev.2009.05.008

Larsen, R., & Everton, R. (2008). Making marketing a "Tweet" deal. *Association Meetings,* (June), (pp. 17-19).

Lasica, J. D. (2003). Blogs and journalism need each other. *Nieman Reports, 57*(3).

Lattimer, H. (2003). *Thinking through genre: Units of study in reading and writing workshops grades 4-12.* Portland, ME: Stenhouse Publishers.

Lave, J., & Wenger, E. (1991). *Situated learning: Legitimate peripheral participation.* Cambridge, UK: Cambridge University Press. doi:10.1017/CBO9780511815355

LeBlanc, J. (2011). *Programming social applications.* O'Reilly.

Lee, G., & Wu, C. (2006). Enhancing the teaching experience of pre-service teachers through the use of videos in web-based computer-mediated communication. *Innovations in Education and Teaching International, 43*(4), 369–380. doi:10.1080/14703290600973836

Lee, M. J. W., & McLoughlin, C. (2007). Teaching and learning in the Web 2.0 era: Empowering students through learner-generated content. *International Journal of Instructional Technology and Distance Learning, 4*(10), 21–34.

Lee, S. J., & Chae, Y. G. (2007). Children's Internet use in a family context: influence on family relationships and parental mediation. *Cyberpsychology & Behavior, 10*(5), 640–644. doi:10.1089/cpb.2007.9975

Lee, W., & Eddie, C. Y. K. (2002). Internet and displacement effect: Children's media use and activities. *Journal of Computer-Mediated Communication, 7,* 1–18.

Lei, J., & Zhao, Y. (2005). Technology uses and student achievement: A longitudinal study. *Computers & Education, 49,* 284–296. doi:10.1016/j.compedu.2005.06.013

Lemon, N. (2011). Arts and technology. In Klopper, C., & Garvis, S. (Eds.), *Tapping into the classroom practice of the arts: From inside out!* (pp. 97–132). Brisbane, Australia: Post Press.

Lenhart, A., & Madden, M. (2005). *Teen content creators and consumers.* Pew Research Center. Retrieved October 1, 2011, from http://www.pewinternet.org/~/media//Files/Reports/2005/PIP_Teens_Content_Creation.pdf.pdf

Lenhart, A., & Madden, M. (2005). *Teens and technology.* Washington, DC: The Pew Internet & American Life Project.

Lenhart, A., Madden, M., Macgill, A. R., & Smith, A. (2007). *Teens and social media.* Washington, DC: Pew Internet & American Life Project.

Lenhart, A., Purcell, K., Smith, A., & Zickuhr, K. (2010). *Social media and mobile internet use among teens and young adults.* Pew Research Center.

Leskovec, J. (2011). Social media analytics: tracking, modeling and predicting the flow of information through networks. 20th International Conference Companion on World Wide Web *(WWW '11)*, (pp. 277-278). New York, NY: ACM.

Lessig, L. (2008). *Remix culture: Making art and commerce thrive in the hybrid economy.* Bloomsbury Academic, Creative Commons Attribution CC 2008 Lawrence Lessig. Retrieved October 1, 2011, from http://www.archive.org/details/LawrenceLessigRemix

Lessig, L. (2001). *The future of ideas.* Vintage Books.

Lessig, L. (2004). *Free culture: The nature and future of creativity.* New York, NY: Penguin Press.

Leverick, F., Littler, D., Wilson, D., & Bruce, M. (1997). The role of IT in the reshaping of marketing. *Journal of Marketing Practice: Applied Marketing Science, 3*(2), 87–106. doi:10.1108/EUM0000000004324

Levy, P. (1997). *Collective intelligence: Mankind's emerging world in cyberspace.* Cambridge, UK: Perseus.

Lewis, K., Kaufman & J., Christakis, N. (2008). The taste for privacy: An analysis of college student privacy settings in an online social network. *Journal of Computer-Mediated Communication, 14*(1), 79–100. doi:10.1111/j.1083-6101.2008.01432.x

Li, C. C. (2004). *The digital divide among elementary school students in Taipei, Taiwan.* Master thesis, National Taipei University of Education, Taipei, Taiwan.

Li, X. (2011). *Students and some teachers' views of using Web 2.0 technologies in e-learning: Findings from a survey and interviews.* Paper presented at the International Conference on E-Learning Futures 2011: Unitec Institute of Technology 30 Nov-Dec 1 Auckland NZ.

Liau, A., Khoo, A., & Ang, P. (2005). Factors influencing 'adolescents' engagement in risky Internet behaviour. *Cyberpsychology & Behavior, 8*(2), 513–520. doi:10.1089/cpb.2005.8.513

Li, C., & Bernoff, J. (2008). *Groundswell: Winning in a world transformed by social technologies.* Boston, MA: Harvard Business Press.

Li, L., & Walsh, S. (2010). Technology uptake in Chinese EFL classes. *Language Teaching Research, 15*(1), 99–125. doi:10.1177/1362168810383347

Limniou, M., & Smith, M. (2010). *Teachers' and students' perspectives on teaching and learning through virtual learning environments.* UK: University of Manchester.

Lim, S. S., & Nekmat, E. (2008). Learning through "prosuming": Insights from media literacy programmes in Asia. *Science, Technology & Society, 13*(2). doi:10.1177/097172180801300205

Lin, C., & Hong, C. (2009). Development of a marketing information system for supporting sales in a tea-beverage market. *Expert Systems with Applications, 36*(3), 5393–5401. doi:10.1016/j.eswa.2008.06.056

Linder, I. H. (1940, July). Is there a substitute for teachers' grades? *School Board Journal, 25*, 26, 79.

Ling, H. L. (2007). Community of inquiry in an online undergraduate information technology course. *Journal of Information Technology Education, 6*, 153–168.

Lin, K. Y., & Lu, H. P. (2011). Intention to continue using Facebook fan pages from the perspective of social capital theory. *Cyberpsychology. Behaviour and Social Networking, 14*(10), 565–570. doi:10.1089/cyber.2010.0472

Li, Q. (2007). Bullying in the new playground: Research into cyberbullying and cyber victimization. *Australian Journal of Educational Technology, 23*(4), 435–454.

Litchfield, A., Nettleton, S., & Taylor, T. (2008). *Integrating work-ready learning into the university curriculum contextualised by profession. World Association of Cooperative Education (WACE).* Sydney: Asia Pacific Conference.

Liu, W. S. (2003). *A study of internet addiction and internet literacy on elementary school students.* Master thesis, University of Tainan, Tainan, Taiwan.

Liu, C. Y., & Kuo, F. Y. (2007). A study of Internet addiction through the lens of the interpersonal theory. *Cyberpsychology & Behavior, 10*(6), 799–804. doi:10.1089/cpb.2007.9951

Livingstone, D. W. (2001). *Adults' informal learning: Definitions, findings, gaps and future research.* NALL (New Approaches to Lifelong Learning), Working Paper #21, Toronto. Retrieved January 30, 2011, from https://tspace.library.utoronto.ca/bitstream/1807/2735/2/21adultsinformallearning.pdf

Livingstone, S., & Haddon, L. (2009). *EU kids online: Final report.* London, UK: EU Kids Online. (EC Safer Internet Plus Programme Deliverable D6.5).

Livingstone, S., Haddon, L., Gorzig, A., & Ólafsson, K. (2011). *EU kids online.* London, UK: EU Kinds Online (EC Safer Internet Plus Programme Deliverable D6. 5), Final Report.

Livingstone, S. (2003). Children's use of the Internet: Reflections on the emerging research agenda. *New Media & Society, 5*(2), 147–166. doi:10.1177/1461444803005002001

Livingstone, S. (2004). Media literacy and the challenge of new information and communication technologies. *Communication Review, 7*(1), 3–14. doi:10.1080/10714420490280152

Livingstone, S. (2008). Taking risky opportunities in youthful content creation: teenagers' use of social networking sites for intimacy, privacy and self-expression. *New Media & Society, 10*(3), 393–411. doi:10.1177/1461444808089415

Livingstone, S., & Bober, M. (2004). Taking up online opportunities? Children's use of the Internet for education, communication and participation. *E-learning, 1*(3), 395–419. doi:10.2304/elea.2004.1.3.5

Livingstone, S., & Haddon, L. (2009). *EU kids online: Final report.* London, UK: EU Kids Online.

Livingstone, S., & Helsper, E. (2008). Parental mediation of 'children's Internet use. *Journal of Broadcasting & Electronic Media, 52*(4), 581–599. doi:10.1080/08838150802437396

Long, M. H., & Porter, P. A. (1985). Group work, interlanguage talk, and second language acquisition. *TESOL Quarterly, 19*(2), 207–228. doi:10.2307/3586827

Lonsdale, P., Baber, C., Sharples, M., & Arvantis, T. N. (2004). A context-awareness architecture for facilitating mobile learning. In Attewell, J., & Savill-Smith, C. (Eds.), *Learning with mobile devices: Research and development.* London, UK: Learning and Skills Development Agency.

Loveless, A. (2003). The interaction between primary teachers' perceptions of ICT and their pedagogy. *Education and Information Technologies, 8*(4), 313–326. doi:10.1023/B:EAIT.0000008674.76243.8f

Lowrey, W. (2006). Mapping the journalism-blogging relationship. *Journalism, 7*(4), 477–500. doi:10.1177/1464884906068363

Lowrey, W., & Burleson Mackay, J. (2008). Journalism and blogging - A test of a model of occupational competition. *Journalism Practice, 2*(1), 64–81. doi:10.1080/17512780701768527

Luckin, R., Clark, W., Garnett, F., Whitworth, A., Akass, J., & Cook, J. (2010). Learner-generated contexts: A framework to support the effective use of technology for learning. In Lee, M., & McLoughlin, C. (Eds.), *Web 2.0-based e-learning: Applying social informatics for tertiary teaching* (pp. 70–84). Hershey, PA: IGI Global. doi:10.4018/978-1-60566-294-7.ch004

Luoma-aho, V. (2010). *Is social media killing our theories?* Paper presented at Communication Resesarch Days, University of Tampere, Finland, February, 2010. Retrieved December 1, 2011, from http://jyu.academia.edu/VilmaLuomaaho/Papers/142043/Is_social_media_killing_our_theories

Lwin, M. O., Stanaland, A., & Miyazaki, A. (2008). Protecting 'children's privacy online: How parental mediation strategies affect website safeguard effectiveness. *Journal of Retailing, 84*, 205–217. doi:10.1016/j.jretai.2008.04.004

Macaulay, L., & Dyer, L. T. (2011, November 14). Teaching with technology: Interactive Web conferencing brings big benefits to the online classroom. *Faculty Focus*.

MacKellar, D. (1968). *I love a sunburnt country*. Poets Australia. Retrieved February 12, 2012, from http://www.imagesaustralia.com/mycountry.htm

Madden, M., & Zickuhr, K. (2011). *65% of online adults use social networking sites*. Washington, DC: Pew Internet & American Life Project. Retrieved from http://pewinternet.org/~/media//Files/Reports/2011/PIP-SNS-Update-2011.pdf

Madge, C., Meek, J., Wellens, J., & Hooley, T. (2009). Facebook, social integration and informal learning at university: 'It is more for socialising and talking to friends about work than for actually doing work'. *Learning, Media and Technology*, *34*(2), 141–155. doi:10.1080/17439880902923606

Maier, H. W. (1987). *Developmental group care of children and youth: Concepts and practice*. New York, NY: Haworth.

Malesky, A. Jr., & Peters, C. (2012). Defining appropriate professional behavior for faculty and university students on social networking websites. *Higher Education*, *63*, 135–151. doi:10.1007/s10734-011-9451-x

Marotzki, W., & Jörissen, B. (2008). Medienbildung. [Media education.] In U. Sander, F. von Gross, & K.-U. Hugger (Eds.), *Handbuch Medienpädagogik* [*Handbook media pedagogy*] (pp. 100–109). Wiesbaden, Germany: VS.

Marshall, C. C., & Shipman, F. M. (2011). Social media ownership: Using Twitter as a window onto current attitudes and beliefs. *CHI*, *2011*, 1081–1090.

Marshall, M. S. (1968). *Teaching without grades*. Corvallis, OR: Oregon State University Press.

Marwan, A., & Sweeney, T. (2010). Teachers' perceptions of educational technology integration in an Indonesian polytechnic. *Asia Pacific Journal of Education*, *30*(4), 463–476. doi:10.1080/02188791.2010.519554

Mason, K. L. (2008). Cyberbullying: A preliminary assessment for school personnel. *Psychology in the Schools*, *45*(4), 323–348. doi:10.1002/pits.20301

Masuda, Y. (1981). *The information society as post-industrial society*. USA: World Future Society.

Mathioudakis, M., Koudas, N., & Marbach, P. (2010). Early online identification of attention gathering items in social media. *Third ACM International Conference on Web Search and Data Mining* (WSDM '10), (pp. 301-310). New York, NY: ACM.

Matthews, B. S. (2006). Do you Facebook! Networking with students online. *College and Research Libraries News*, *67*, 306-307. Retrieved January 28, 2012, from http://crln.acrl.org/content/67/5/306.full.pdf

Maynard Keynes, J. (1935) *The general theory of employment, interest and money*. Retrieved December 15, 2011, from http://www.marxists.org/reference/subject/economics/keynes/general-theory/preface.htm

Mayrberger, K. (2010). Web 2.0 in der Hochschullehre – Überlegungen zu einer (akademischen) Medienbildung für E-Learning 2.0 [Web 2.0 in higher education - Reflections on (academic) media education for e-learning 2.0.]. In B. Herzig, D. M. Meister, H. Moser, & H. Niesyto (Eds.), *Jahrbuch Medienpädagogik 8. Medienkompetenz und Web 2.0* [*Yearbook media pedagogy: Media literacy and Web 2.0*] (pp. 309–328). Wiesbaden, Germany: VS.

Mayrberger, K. (2012). Partizipatives Lernen mit dem Social Web gestalten [Designing participation with the social web.]. *Medienpädagogik*, *21*, 1–25.

Mazer, J. P., Murphy, R. E., & Simonds, C. J. (2007). I'll see you on "Facebook": The effects of computer-mediated teacher self-disclosure on student motivation, affecctive learning, and classroom climate. *Communication Education*, *56*(1), 1–17. doi:10.1080/03634520601009710

McAfee, A. (2011). Enterprise 2 at 5. *Andrew McAfee's blog: The business impact of IT*. Retrieved February 28, 2012, from http://andrewmcafee.org/2011/06/enterprise-2-at-5/

McAfee, A. (2006). Enterprise 2.0: The dawn of emergent collaboration. *Sloan Management Review*, *47*(3), 21–28.

McCladdie, K. (2006). *A comparison of the effectiveness of the Montessori method of reading instruction and the balanced literacy method for inner city African American students*. Unpublished doctoral dissertation, Philadelphia, PA: St. Joseph's University.

McCombs, B., & Whistler, J. S. (1997). *The learner-centered classroom and school*. San Francisco, CA: Jossey-Bass.

McConatha, D., Praul, M., & Lynch, M. J. (2008). Mobile learning in higher education: An empirical assessment of a new educational tool. *Turkish Online Journal of Educational Technology, 7*(3).

McCrea, B., & Weil, M. (2011). On cloud nine. *T.H.E. Journal, 38*(6), 46, 48, 50–51.

McCroskey, J. C., & Richmond, V. P. (1983). Power in the classroom I: Instructor and student perceptions. *Communication Education, 32*, 175–184. doi:10.1080/03634528309378527

McCullagh, D. (2011, June 20). *Dropbox confirms security glitch--No password required.* Retrieved on January 27, 2012, from http://news.cnet.com/8301-31921_3-20072755-281/DropBox-confirms-security-glitch-no-password-required/

McFarlane, A., Triggs, P., & Yee, W. (2008). *Researching mobile learning.* Retrieved September 9, 2008, from http://partners.becta.org.uk/upload-dir/downloads/page_documents/research/mobile_learning.doc

McGrath, T., Butcher, A., & Stock, P. (2011). *The impact of returning Asian students of NZ-Asia relationships.* Paper presented at the ISANA International Education Association 22nd Annual Conference: Innovations working with diverse students, 22nd Nov -2nd Dec 2011, Hobart.

McKinney, D., Dyck, J. L., & Luber, E. S. (2009). iTunes University and the classroom: Can podcasts replace professors? *Computers & Education, 52*(3), 617–623. doi:10.1016/j.compedu.2008.11.004

McKinnon, G. R. (2000). The dilemma of evaluating electronic discussion groups. *Journal of Research on Computing in Education, 33*(2), 125–132.

McLeod, S. (2000). Writing across the curriculum: An introduction. In S. McLeod & M. Soven (Eds.), *Writing across the curriculum: A guide to developing programs* (pp. 1-8). WAC Clearinghouse Landmark Publications in Writing Studies. Retrieved February 18, 2012, from http://wac.colostate.edu/books/mcleod_soven/chapter1.pdf.

McLoughlin, C., & Oliver, R. (2000). Designing learning environments for cultural inclusivity: A case study of indigenous online learning at tertiary level. *Australian Journal of Educational Technology, 16*(1), 58–72.

McNeill, T. (2009). *Twitter in higher education.* Retrieved June 2, 2012, from http://www.scribd.com/doc/20025500/Twitter-in-Higher-Education

Means, B., & Olson, K. (1997). *Technology's role in education reform: Findings from a national study of innovating schools.* Washington, DC: US Department of Education, Office of Educational Research and Improvement.

Mehlenbacher, B., McKone, S., Grant, C., Bowles, T., Peretti, S., & Martin, P. (2010). Social media for sustainable engineering communication. *28th ACM International Conference on Design of Communication* (SIGDOC '10), (pp. 65-72). New York, NY: ACM.

Meltzer, D. (1994). *Sincerity and other works.* London, UK: Karnac.

Meraz, S. (2009). Is there an elite hold? Traditional media to social media agenda setting influence in blog networks. *Journal of Computer-Mediated Communication, 14*, 682–707. doi:10.1111/j.1083-6101.2009.01458.x

Mesch, G. S. (2009). Parental mediation, online activities, and cyberbullying. *Cyberpsychology & Behavior, 12*(4), 387–393. doi:10.1089/cpb.2009.0068

Meskill, C., Mossop, J., DiAngelo, S., & Pasquale, R. (2002). Expert and novice teachers talking technology: Precepts, concepts, and misconcepts. *Language Learning & Technology, 6*(3), 46–57. Retrieved from http://llt.msu.edu/vol6num3/pdf/meskill.pdf

Mezirow, J. (1996). Contemporary paradigms of learning. *Adult Education Quarterly, 46*, 158–172. doi:10.1177/074171369604600303

Mezirow, J. (2000). *Learning as transformation: Critical perspectives on a theory in progress.* San Francisco, CA: Jossey-Bass.

Mezirow, J., & Taylor, E. W. (2009). *Transformative learning in practice: Insights from community, workplace, and higher education.* San Francisco, CA: Jossey-Bass.

Michaelidou, N., Siamagka, N. T., & Christodoulides, G. (2011). Usage, barriers and measurement of social media marketing: An exploratory investigation of small and medium B2B brands. *Industrial Marketing Management, 40*(7), 1153–1159. doi:10.1016/j.indmarman.2011.09.009

Michie, J. (2010). *Assessment for learning with twitter: Under education, technology.* Retrieved January 22, 2012, from http://jamesmichie.com/blog/2010/02/assessment-for-learning-with-twitter/

Miller, E. J., & Rice, A. K. (1990). Task and sentient systems and their boundary controls. In Trist, E., & Murray, H. (Eds.), *Social engagement of social science (Vol. 1,* pp. 259–271). London, UK: Free Association.

Milligan, C. (2006). What is a PLE? The future or just another buzz word? *JISC E-Learning Focus.* Retrieved November 25, 2011, from http://www.elearning.ac.uk/news_folder/ple%20event

Milton, M., Gruppetta, M., Vozzo, L., & Mason, T. (2009). *Ideals and retention: Perspectives of students in a BEd (AREP) course.* Paper presented at the AIATSIS Conference: Canberra.

Mioduser, D., Nachmias, R., & Forkosh-Baruch, A. (2008). New literacies for the knowledge society. In Voogt, J., & Knezek, G. (Eds.), *International handbook of information technology in education.* Springer.

Mitcham, C. (1994). *Thinking through technology: The path between engineering and philosophy.* Chicago, IL: University of Chicago Press.

Mitchell, J., & Sparks, L. (1988). Marketing information systems in the major UK banks. *International Journal of Bank Marketing, 6*(5), 14–28. doi:10.1108/eb010840

Mitchell, K., Finkelhor, D., & Wolak, J. (2001). Risk factors for and impact of online sexual solicitation of youth. *Journal of the American Medical Association, 285*(23), 3011–3014. doi:10.1001/jama.285.23.3011

Mitchelstein, E., & Boczkowski, P. J. (2009). Between tradition and change: A review of recent research on online news production. *Journalism, 10*(5), 562–586. doi:10.1177/1464884909106533

Moffet, J., & Wagner, B. J. (1992). *Student-centered language arts, K-12.* Portsmouth, NH: Boynton/Cook Publishers Heinemann.

Molka, J., Bryan, D., Carter, W., & Creelman, A. (2009). Empathy in virtual learning environments. *International Journal of Networked Virtual Organizations, 6*(2), 123–139. doi:10.1504/IJNVO.2009.022971

Morales, M. (2011). Cyberbullying. *Journal of Consumer Health on the Internet, 15*(4), 406–419. doi:10.1080/15398285.2011.623593

Moran, D., & Mollett, A. (2011). *Altmetrics, a guide to Twitter for academics and increasing your academic footprint.* Round-Up of Social Media Blogs.

Morgan, M. (1993). Television and school performance. *Adolescent Medicine (Philadelphia, Pa.), 4,* 607–622.

Moser, R. P., Hesse, B. W., Shaikh, A. R., Courtney, P., Morgan, G., & Augustson, E. (2011). Grid-enabled measures: Using Science 2.0 to standardize measures and share data. *American Journal of Preventive Medicine, 40*(5Suppl. 2), 134–143. doi:10.1016/j.amepre.2011.01.004

Mouza, C. (2002). Learning to teach with new technology: Implications for professional development. *Journal of Research on Technology in Education, 35*(2), 272–289.

Mtebe, J. S., Dachi, H., & Raphael, C. (2011). Integrating ICT into teaching and learning at the University of Dar es Salaam. *Distance Education, 32*(2), 289–294. doi:10.1080/01587919.2011.584854

Munoz, C., & Towner, T. (2009). Opening Facebook: How to use Facebook in the college classroom. In I. Gibson et al., (Eds.), *Proceedings of Society for Information Technology & Teacher Education International Conference 2009* (pp. 2623-2627). Chesapeake, VA: AACE. Retrieved from http://www.editlib.org/p/31031

Mutz, D. C., Roberts, D. F., & van Vuuren, D. P. (1993). Reconsidering the displacement hypothesis: Television's influence on children's time use. *Communication Research, 20,* 51–75. doi:10.1177/009365093020001003

Myers, D. G. (2007). *Psychology.* New York, NY: Worth.

Nagel, D. (2010). The future of e-learning is more growth. *Campus Technology.* Retrieved July 26, 2011, from http://campustechnology.com/articles/2010/03/03/the-future-of-e-learning-is-more-growth.aspx

Naismith, L., Lonsdale, P., Vavoula, G., & Sharples, M. (2005). *Report 11: Literature review in mobile technologies and learning.* Bristol, UK: Futurelab Series. doi: http://www2.futurelab.org.uk/resources/documents/lit_reviews/Mobile_Review.pdf

National Center for Education Statistic (NCES). (2011). *Student reports of bullying and cyber-bullying: Results from the 2007 school crime supplement to the National Crime Victimization Survey*. Washington, DC: Author. Retrieved http://nces.ed.gov/pubs2011/2011336.pdf

National School Boards Foundation. (2000). *Research and guidelines for children's use of the internet*. National School Boards Foundation.

Navarro, R., Yubero, S., Larrañaga, E., & Martínez, V. (2012). Children's cyberbullying victimization: Associations with social anxiety and social competence in a Spanish sample. *Child Indicators Research, 5*(2).

Nehm, K. (2009). Social software categories. Enterprise 2.0 blog: Discussing the collaborative enterprise. Retrieved March 11, 2012, from http://enterprise20blog.com/all/2009/08/19/social-software-categories/

Neuman, S. B. (1991). *Literacy in the television age: The myth of the TV effect*. Norwood, NJ: Ablex.

News, B. B. C. (November, 16, 2009). *Cyberbullies hit primary schools*. Retrieved from http://news.bbc.co.uk/2/hi/uk_news/education/8359780.stm

Nicholas, D., Watkinson, A., Rowlands, I., & Jubb, M. (2011). Social media, academic research and the role of university libraries. *Journal of Academic Librarianship, 37*(5), 373–375. doi:10.1016/j.acalib.2011.06.023

Nie, N. H., & Hillygus, D. S. (2002). Where does internet time come from? A reconnaissance. *IT & Society, 1*, 1–20.

No Child Left Behind Act of 2001 § 6302, Pub. L. No. 107-110, 115 Stat. 1425 (2002).

Nocentini, A., Calmaestra, J., Schultze-Krumbholz, A., Scheithauer, H., Ortega, R., & Menesini, E. (2010). Cyberbullying: Labels, behaviours and definition in three European countries. *Australian Journal of Guidance & Counselling, 20*(2), 129–142. doi:10.1375/ajgc.20.2.129

Nonaka, I., & Konno, N. (1998). The concept of 'Ba': Building a foundation for knowledge creation. *California Management Review, 40*(3), 40–54. doi:10.2307/41165942

Norman, D. (1993). *Things that make us smart: Defending human attributes in the age of the machine*. Reading, MA: Addison-Wesley.

Notari, M. (2006). How to use wiki in education: Wiki based effective constructive learning. In *Proceedings of the 2006 International Symposium on Wikis* (WIKISYM), Denmark.

Notley, T. (2008). Online network use in schools. *The Journal of Youth Studies Australia. Social and Educational Opportunities, 27*(3), 20–29.

Noureddine, A. A., & Damodaran, M. (2008). Security in web 2.0 application development. In G. Kotsis, D. Taniar, E. Pardede, & I. Khalil (Eds.), *Proceedings of the 10th International Conference on Information Integration and Web-based Applications and Services* (iiWAS '08), (pp. 681-685). New York, NY: ACM.

Noyes, K. (2011, May). Microsoft Office alternatives. *PC World*, 29-30.

O'Neill, G., & McMahon, T. (2005). Student-centered learning: What does it mean for students and lecturers? In G. O'Neill, S. Moore, & B. McMullen (Eds.), *Emerging issues in the practice of university learning and teaching*. Dublin, Ireland: AISHE. Retrieved February 14, 2012, from http://www.aishe.org/readings/2005-1/index.html

O'Reilly, T. (2005). *What is Web 2.0: Design patterns and business models for the next generation of software*. O'Reilly Media.

O'Reilly, T. (2006). Web 2.0 compact definition: Trying again. *Communications & Strategies, 65*(31), 17–37.

O'Riley, P. A. (2003). *Technology, culture, and socioeconomics: A rihizoanalysis of educational discourses*. New York, NY: Peter Lang.

Oakes, K. (2002). E-learning. *Training & Development, 4*, 68–70.

Oates, K. D. (2001). *University faculty who use computer technology*. Doctoral Dissertation, Georgia State University, USA.

Oblinger, D., & Oblinger, J. L. (2005). Is it age or IT: First steps toward understanding the net generation. D. Oblinger & J. L. Oblinger (Eds.), *Educating the net generation*. Washington, DC: Educause. Retrieved March 29, 2012, from http://net.educause.edu/ir/library/pdf/pub7101.pdf

O'Brien, T., Schoenbachler, D., & Gordon, G. (1995). Marketing information systems for consumer products companies: A management overview. *Journal of Consumer Marketing, 12*(5), 16–36. doi:10.1108/07363769510147777

O'Connor, R. (January 20, 2009). Facebook and Twitter are reshaping journalism as we know it. *RoryOConnor. org*. Retrieved December 1, 2011, from http://kauri.aut. ac.nz:8080/dspace/bitstream/123456789/1839/1/090120. Facebook%20%26%20Twitter%20Are%20Reshaping%20Journalism.pdf

OECD. (2007). *Giving knowledge for free: The emergence of open educational resources*. Paris, France: Organization for Economic Co-Operation and Development, Centre for Educational Research and Innovation. Retrieved March 29, 2012, from http://213.253.134.43/oecd/pdfs/browseit/9607041E.pdf

OECD. (2007). *Participative web and user-created content. Web 2.0, wikis, and social networking*. Paris, France: OECD.

Ofcom. (2011). *A nation addicted to smartphones*. Retrieved from http://consumers.ofcom.org.uk/2011/08/a-nation-addicted-to-smartphones/

OIVO. (2008). *Youngsters and the Internet*. Retrieved January 10, 2012, from http://www.oivo-crioc.org/files/nl/3906nl.pdf

Olson, L. (2004, May 5). England refines accountability reform. *Education Week, 23*(4), 1–22.

Olweus, D. (1991). Bully/victim problems among school children: Some basic facts and effects of a school based intervention program. In Pepler, D., & Rubin, K. (Eds.), *The development and treatment of childhood aggression* (pp. 411–448). Hillsdale, NJ: Erlbaum.

Olweus, D. (1993). Bullies on the playground: The role of victimization. In Hart, C. (Ed.), *Children on the playground: Research perspectives and applications* (pp. 85–128). New York, NY: SUNY Press.

O'Mahony, C. (2003). Getting the information and communication technology formular right: access + ability = confident use. *Technology, Pedagogy and Education, 12*(2), 295–314. doi:10.1080/14759390300200159

O'Reilly, T. (2007). What is Web 2.0: Design patterns and business models for the next generation of software. *International Journal of Digital Economics, 65*, 17–37.

Orlando, J. (2011, October 11). Wikis in the classroom: Three ways to increase student collaboration. *Faculty Focus*.

Orr, E. S., Sisic, M., Ross, C., Simmering, M. G., Arseneault, J. M., & Orr, R. R. (2009). Rapid communication: The influence of shyness on the use of Facebook in an undergraduate sample. *Cyberpsychology & Behavior, 12*(3), 337–340. doi:10.1089/cpb.2008.0214

Pacey, A. (1983). *The culture of technology*. Cambridge, MA: MIT Press.

Pachler, N., Cook, J., & Bachmair, B. (2010). Appropriation of mobile cultural resources for learning. *International Journal of Mobile and Blended Learning, 2*(1), 1–21. doi:10.4018/jmbl.2010010101

Padilla-Walker, L. M., Nelson, L. J., Carroll, J. S., & Jensen, A. C. (2010). More than a just a game: Video game and internet use during emerging adulthood. *Journal of Youth and Adolescence, 39*(2), 103–113. doi:10.1007/s10964-008-9390-8

Page, R. (2011, March 14). Social media savvy - The universities and academics leading the way. *The Guardian*.

Paine, K. D. (2009). *How to set benchmarks in social media: Exploratory research for social media*. Paper presented to the 12th Annual International Public Relations Research Conference, Florida. Retrieved October 1, 2011, from http://www.instituteforpr.org/wp-content/uploads/SetBenchmarks_SocialMedia.pdf

Palfrey, J., & Ess, H. N. (2011, May 3). *Academic uses of social media: Exploring 21st century communications*. Webcast Event: Faculty Development & Diversity at Harvard and the Harvard Office of News and Public Affairs.

Palfrey, J., & Gasser, U. (2008). *Born digital: Understanding the first generation of digital natives*. Basic Books, Perseus Books Group.

Paloff, R. M., & Pratt, K. (1999). *Building learning communities in cyberspace* (p. 206). San Francisco, CA: Jossey-Bass.

Paloff, R. M., & Pratt, K. (2001). *Lessons from the cyberspace classroom: The realities of online teaching* (p. 204). San Francisco: Jossey-Bass.

Paloff, R. M., & Pratt, K. (2003). *The virtual student: A profile and guide to working with online learners*. San Francisco, CA: Jossey-Bass Publishers.

Paloff, R. M., & Pratt, K. (2005). *Collaborating online: Learning together in community* (p. 112). San Francisco, CA: Jossey-Bass.

Palser, B. (2009). Hitting the Tweet spot. *American Journalism Review, 31*(2), 54. University of Maryland. Retrieved February 10, 2012 from http://search.ebscohost.com/login.aspx?direct=true&db=ufh&AN=38506878&site=ehost-live

Pang, L. (2009). *Application of blogs to support reflective learning journals*. Retrieved February 10, 2012 from http://deoracle.org/online-pedagogy/teaching-strategies/application-of-blogs.html37

Panitz, T. (1997). *Collaborative versus cooperative learning – A comparison of the two concepts which will help us understand the underlying nature of interactive learning*. Retrieved December 14, 2011, from http://www.slideshare.net/tmvcr/collaborative-versus-cooperative-learning-3314777

Papert, S. (1980). *Mindstorms: Children, computers, and powerful ideas*. New York, NY: Basic Books.

Papert, S. (1991). Perestroika and epistemological politics. In *Constructionism*. Ablex Publishing.

Parker, K. R., & Chao, J. T. (2007). Wiki as a teaching tool. *Interdisciplinary Journal of Knowledge and Learning Objects, 3*, 57–72.

Parra-López, E., Bulchand-Gidumal, J., Gutiérrez-Taño, D., & Díaz-Armas, R. (2011). Intentions to use social media in organizing and taking vacation trips. *Computers in Human Behavior, 27*(2), 640–654. doi:10.1016/j.chb.2010.05.022

Parry, D. (2011). Mobile perspectives: On teaching mobile literacy. *EDUCAUSE Review, 46*(2). Retrieved from http://www.educause.edu/er

Partington, G. (2003). Why indigenous issues are an essential component of teacher education programs. *Australian Journal of Teacher Education, 27*, 39–48.

Pasek, J., More, E., & Hargittai, E. (2009). Facebook and academic performance: Reconciling a media sensation with data. *First Monday, 14*(5). Retrieved from http://firstmonday.org/htbin/cgiwrap/bin/ojs/index.php/fm/article/view/2498/218

Passig, D. (2003). A taxonomy of future thinking skills. *Informatics in Education, 2*(1), 79–92.

Passig, D. (2007). Melioration as a higher thinking skill of future intelligence. *Teachers College Record, 109*(1), 24–50.

Patchin, J. W., & Hinduja, S. (2006). Bullies move beyond the schoolyard: A preliminary look at cyberbullying. *Youth Violence and Juvenile Justice, 4*(2), 148–169. doi:10.1177/1541204006286288

Patchin, J. W., & Hinduja, S. (2010). Trends in online social networking: adolescent use of MySpace over time. *New Media & Society, 12*(2), 197–216. doi:10.1177/1461444809341857

Paulus, P. B., & Nijstad, B. A. (Eds.). (2003). *Group creativity: Innovation through collaboration*. Oxford, UK: Oxford University Press.

Pempek, T. A., Yermoloyeva, Y. A., & Calvert, S. I. (2009). College students' social networking experiences on Facebook. *Journal of Applied Developmental Psychology, 30*(3), 227-238. Retrieved June 6, 2012, from http://www.sciencedirect.com/science/article/pii/S0193397308001408

Pepler, D., Craig, W. M., & O'Connell, P. (1999). Understanding bullying from a dynamic systems perspective. In Slater, A., & Muir, D. (Eds.), *The Blackwell reader in developmental psychology* (pp. 440–451). Oxford, UK: Blackwell Publishing.

Pereira, R. M., Baranauskas, C. C., & Almeida, L. D. A. (2011). The value of value identifications in web applications. *Proceedings of the WWW/Internet IADIS International Conference*, Rio de Janeiro, Brazil 2011.

Perkel, D. (2006). Copy and paste literacy: Literacy practices in the production of a MySpace profile— An overview. In *Proceedings of Informal Learning and Digital Media: Constructions, Contexts, Consequences* (Denmark, September 21–23, 2006).

Perkins, D. N. (1992). *Smart schools: From training memories to educating minds*. New York, NY: Free Press.

Peters, M. A. (2006). Towards philosophy of technology in education: Mapping the field. In Weiss, J., Nolan, J., & Hunsinger, J. (Eds.), *The international handbook of virtual learning environments* (pp. 95–116). Springer. doi:10.1007/978-1-4020-3803-7_3

Pettit, J., & Kukulska-Hulme, A. (2011). Mobile 2.0: Crossing the border into formal learning? In Lee, M. J. W., & McLoughlin, C. (Eds.), *Web 2.0-based e-learning: Applying social informatics for tertiary teaching* (pp. 192–208). Hershey, PA: IGI Global.

Pew Internet & American Life Project. (2012). *Trend data*. Retrieved: http://pewinternet.org/Static-Pages/Trend-Data/Whos-Online.aspx

Pew Research. (2010). *Social media and mobile internet use among teens and young adults*. Retrieved February 28, 2012, from http://pewinternet.org/Reports/2010/Social-Media-and-Young-Adults.aspx

Pfeil, U., Arjan, R., & Zaphiris, P. (2009). Age differences in online social networking - A study of user profiles and the social capital divide among teenagers and older users in MySpace. *Computers in Human Behavior, 25*(3), 643–654. doi:10.1016/j.chb.2008.08.015

Pfiffner, M., & Stadelmann, P. (1998). *Wissen wirksam machen – Wie Kopfarbeiter produktiv werden*. Bern, Germany: Haupt.

Piccoli, G., Ahmad, R., & Ives, B. (2001). Web-Based virtual learning environments: A research framework and a preliminary assessment of effectiveness in basic IT skills training. *Management Information Systems Quarterly, 25*(4), 401–426. doi:10.2307/3250989

Postman, N. (1993). *Technopoly: The surrender of culture to technology*. New York, NY: Vintage Books.

Postman, N., & Weingartner, C. (1969). *Teaching as a subversive activity*. New York, NY: Dell.

Prandini, M., & Ramilli, M. (2011). Security considerations about the adoption of web 2.0 technologies in sensitive e-government processes. In E. Estevez & M. Janssen (Eds.), *Proceedings of the 5th International Conference on Theory and Practice of Electronic Governance* (ICEGOV '11), (pp. 285-288). New York, NY: ACM.

Prenksy, M. (2001). Digital natives, digital immigrants. *Horizon, 9*(5), 1–6. doi:10.1108/10748120110424816

Prensky, M. (2011, September). *Educational technology, July-August*. Retrieved January 22, 2012 from http://marcprensky.com/writing/Prensky-ChangingParadigms-01-EdTech.pdf

Price, M., & Dalgleish, J. (2010). Cyberbullying experiences, impacts and coping strategies as described by Australian young people. *Youth Studies Australia, 29*(2), 51–59.

Priego, E. (2011, September 12). How Twitter will revolutionise academic research and teaching. *Guardian Professional*. Retrieved February 10, 2012, from http://www.guardian.co.uk/higher-education-network/blog/2011/sep/12/twitter-revolutionise-academia-research

Proctor, R. (1991). Marketing information systems. *Management Decision, 29*(4), 55–60. doi:10.1108/00251749110141824

Prohaska, B. (2011). Social media for the collaborative enterprise. *IT Professional, 13*(4), 64–66. doi:10.1109/MITP.2011.67

Pulman, A. (2007). (Manuscript submitted for publication). *Blogging @ BU: IHCS case studies*. Centre for Excellence in Media Practice. *CEMP Work*.

Putnam, R. (2000). *Bowling alone: The collapse and revival of American community*. New York, NY: Simon & Schuster. doi:10.1145/358916.361990

Raacke, J., & Bonds-Raacke, J. (2008). MySpace and Facebook: Applying the uses and gratifications theory to exploring friend-networking sites. *Cyberpsychology & Behavior, 11*, 169–174. doi:10.1089/cpb.2007.0056

Racial Discrimination Act. (1975). Human Rights Commission. Retrieved March 12, 2012 from http://www.hreoc.gov.au/racial_discrimination/index.html

Ragupathi, K. (2011). Facebook for teaching and learning: By Dr. Erik Mobrand. *Technology in Pedagogy, 1*, 1-4. Retrieved January 26, 2012, from http://www.cdtl.nus.edu.sg/technology-in-pedagogy/articles/Technology-in-Pedagogy-1.pdf

Ramsden, P., Beswick, D., & Bowden, J. (1989). Effects of learning skills intervention on first year learners' learning. *Human Learning, 5*, 151–164.

Rego, B. (2009). *A teacher's guide to using Facebook*. Retrieved January 16, 2012, from http://www.scribd.com/doc/16957158/Teachers-Guide-to-Using-Facebook-Read-Fullscreen

Reich, J., Murnane, R., & Willett, J. (2012). The state of wiki usage in U.S. K–12 schools. Leveraging Web 2.0 data warehouses to assess quality and equity in online learning environments. *Educational Researcher, 41*(1), 7–15. doi:10.3102/0013189X11427083

Reid, B. (2006). *Cognitive strategy instruction, teaching strategy*. Retrieved February 26, 2012, from http://cehs.unl.edu/csi/teachingstrategy.shtml#definition

Reinhardt, W., Moi, M., & Varlemann, T. (2009). Artefact-actor-networks as tie between social networks and artefact networks. In *Proceedings of the 5th International ICST Conference on Collaborative Computing: Networking, Applications and Worksharing*, CollaborateCom 2009.

Reinmann, G., & Mandl, H. (2006). Unterrichten und Lernumgebungen gestalten. [Teaching and learning design.] In Krapp, A., & Weidenmann, B. (Eds.), *Pädagogische Psychologie [Pedagogical psychology]*. (pp. 613–658). Weinheim, Germany: BeltzPVU.

Reinmann, G., Sporer, T., & Vohle, F. (2007). Bologna und Web 2.0: Wie zusammenbringen, was nicht zusammenpasst? [Bologna and Web 2.0: How to bring together what does not fit?] In Kerres, M., & Keil, R. (Eds.), *eUniversity – Update Bologna* (pp. 263–278). Münster, Germany: Waxmann.

Resnick, M. (1996). Distribuited constructionism, In *Proceeding for International Conference on the Learning Science*, AACE, Northwestern University.

Resnick, L. (1987). *Education and learning to think*. Washington, DC: National Academy Press.

Reyneke, M., Pitt, L., & Berthon, P. (2011). Luxury wine brand visibility in social media: An exploratory study. *International Journal of Wine Business Research, 23*(1), 21–35. doi:10.1108/17511061111121380

Rheingold, H. (2008). Using participatory media and public voice to encourage civic engagement. In Bennett, W. L. (Ed.), *Civic life online: Learning how digital media can engage youth* (pp. 97–118). Cambridge, MA: The MIT Press.

Richmond, V. P., & McCroskey, J. C. (1984). Power in the classroom II: Power and learning. *Communication Education, 33*, 125–136. doi:10.1080/03634528409384729

Rickman, J. (1957). *Selected contributions to psycho-analysis*. London, UK: Karnac.

Rideout, V. J., Foehr, U. G., & Roberts, D. F. (2010). *Generation M2: Media in the lives of 8-to-18-year-olds*. Menlo Park, CA: KFF. Retrieved: http://www.kff.org/entmedia/upload/8010.pdf

Robinson, D. K. (in press). Web 2.0? Why should we care? *eweek.com*.

Robinson, J. P., Kestnbaum, M., Neustadtl, A., & Alvarez, A. (2000). Mass media use and social life among Internet users. *Social Science Computer Review, 18*(4), 490–501. doi:10.1177/089443930001800411

Rodens, M. (2011). What the tweet? Twitter as a useful educational and professional development tool. *Communicating for Learners*, Spring #2.

Rodogno, R. (2011). *Personal identity online. Special Issue in Journal of Philosophy & Technology, 24*. Netherlands: Springer.

Romeiro-Serna, J., & Garmendia, F. (2007). Marketing information systems - MIS: More than simple technological boxes. *EsicMarket, 128*, 81–93.

Roper, C. (2008). Teaching people to bargain online: The impossible task becomes the preferred method. *MERLOT Journal of Online Learning and Teaching, 4*(2), 254-260. Retrieved August 18, 2008, from http://jolt.merlot.org/vol4no2/roper0608.pdf

Rosen, D., Barnett, G. A., & Kim, J. H. (2011). Social networks and online environments: When science and practice co-evolve. *Social Network Analysis and Mining, 1*(1), 27-42. Wien, Austria: Springer. Retrieved from http://www.springerlink.com/index/10.1007/s13278-010-0011-7

Rosen, A. (2009). *E-learning 2.0. Proven practices and emerging technologies to achieve results*. AMACOM.

Rowley, J. (1994). Marketing information systems. *Aslib Proceedings, 46*(7/8), 185–187. doi:10.1108/eb051364

Rowley, J. (1999). Loyalty, the Internet and the weather: The changing nature of marketing information systems? *Management Decision, 37*(6), 514–519. doi:10.1108/00251749910278032

Rugg, B. M. (2009). Getting iTunes U at Ithaca College up and running! In *Proceedings of the 37th Annual ACM SIGUCCS Fall Conference* (SIGUCCS '09), (pp. 275-282). New York, NY: ACM.

Russell, M., Bebell, D., O'Dwyer, L., & O'Connor, K. (2003). Examining teacher technology use: Implications for preservice and inservice teacher preparation. *Journal of Teacher Education, 54*(4), 297-310. doi:10.1177/0022487103255985

Ryan, S., Magro, M., & Sharp, J. (2011). Exploring educational and cultural adaptation through social networking sites. *Journal of Information Technology Education: Innovations in Practice, 10.*

Ryan, J., & Walta, C. (2009). *Pre-service teacher education partnerships: Creating an effective practicum model for rural and regional pre-service teachers.* ALTC Priority Programs.

Saadé, R. G., & Kira, D. (2009). Computer anxiety in e-learning: The effect of computer self-efficacy. *Journal of Information Technology Education, 8.* Retrieved July 27, 2011, from http://jite.org/documents/Vol8/JITEv8p177-191Saade724.pdf

Sapsed, S., & Mathew, D. (2011). *The growth of the Public Health Masters at the University of Bedfordshire.* Refereed Program of the E-Leader Conference at Zagreb, Croatia. Retrieved from http://www.g-asa.com/conferences/zagreb/ppt/sapsed%20[Compatibility%20Mode].pdf

Satyanarayanan, M., Bahl, P., Caceres, R., & Davies, N. (2009). The case for VM-based cloudlets in mobile computing. *Pervasive Computing, 8*(4), 14-22. doi:10.1109/MPRV.2009.82

Savio, N., & Braiterman, J. (2007). Design sketch: The context of mobile interaction. In A. D. Cheok & L. Chittaro (Eds.), *Proceedings of the 9th Conference on Human-Computer Interaction with Mobile Devices and Services* (Mobile HCI 2007) (pp. 284-286). New York, NY: ACM.

Scardamalia, M., & Bereiter, C. (1992). An architecture for collaborative knowledge-building. In Dc Corte, E., Linn, M., Mandl, H., & Verschaffel, L. (Eds.), *Computer-based learning environments and problem solving* [NATO-ASI Series F: Computer and Systems Science]. (pp. 41-46). Berlin, Germany: Springer-Verlag. doi:10.1007/978-3-642-77228-3_3

Schiefner, M. (2011). Mythos Web 2.0: Medien in Bildungsinstitutionen. [The myth web 2.0: Digital media in educational organizations.] In Weil, M., Schiefner, M., Eugster, B., & Futter, K. (Eds.), *Aktionsfelder der Hochschuldidaktik. Von der Weiterbildung zum Diskurs* [*Fields of higher education: From further education to discourse*]. (pp. 221-235). Münster, Germany: Waxmann.

Schiefner-Rohs, M. (2012). *Kritische Informations- und Medienkompetenz: Theoretisch-konzeptionelle Herleitung und empirische Betrachtungen am Beispiel der Lehrerausbildung* [*Critical information and media literacy: Theoretical and conceptual considerations and empirical derivation using the example of teacher training.*]. Münster, Germany: Waxmann.

Schmidt, J. (2007). Blogging practices: An analytical framework. *Journal of Computer-Mediated Communication, 12*(4), article 13. Retrieved June 1, 2010, from http://jcmc.indiana.edu/vol12/issue4/schmidt.html

Schneider, M. (2007). *Crossmedia-Management (PhD-Thesis).* Wiesbaden, Germany: DUV.

Schneider, S. K., O'Donnell, L., Stueve, A., & Coulter, R. W. S. (2012). Cyberbullying, school bullying, and psychological distress: A regional census of high school students. *American Journal of Public Health, 102*(1), 171-177. doi:10.2105/AJPH.2011.300308

Schneider, S. M., & Foot, K. A. (2004). The web as an object of study. *New Media & Society, 6*(1), 114-122. doi:10.1177/1461444804039912

Schoffstall, C. L., & Cohen, R. (2011). Cyber aggression: The relation between online offenders and offline social competence. *Social Development, 20*(3), 587-604. doi:10.1111/j.1467-9507.2011.00609.x

Schouten, A. P., Valkenburg, P. M., & Peter, J. (2007). Precursors and underlying processes of adolescents' online self-disclosure: Developing and testing an "Internet-attribute-perception" model. *Media Psychology, 10,* 292-314. doi:10.1080/15213260701375686

Schouten, A. P., Valkenburg, P. M., & Peter, J. (2009). An experimental test of processes underlying self-disclosure in computer-mediated communication. *Cyberpsychology & Behavior, 3*(2), 1-15.

Schuegraf, M. (2008). *Medienkonvergenz und Subjektbildung: Mediale Interaktionen am Beispiel von Musikfernsehen und Internet.* [*Media convergence and subject development: Media interactions using the example of music television and the internet.*] Wiesbaden, Germany: VS.

Schulmeister, R. (2009). *Gibt es eine Net Generation? Erweiterte Version 3.0.* [*Does the Net Generation exist? Extended Version 3.0*]. Hamburg, Germany: Universität Hamburg, Zentrum für Hochschul- und Weiterbildung. Retrieved March 29, 2012, from http://www.zhw.uni-hamburg.de/uploads/schulmeister_net-generation_v3.pdf

Schultze-Krumbholz, A., & Scheithauer, H. (2009). Social-behavioral correlates of cyberbullying in a German student sample. *Zeitschrift für Psychologie. The Journal of Psychology, 217*(4), 224–226.

Searle, J. (2010). *Making the social world: The structure of human civilization.* New York, NY: Oxford University Press.

seeking on Facebook. *Cyberpsychology, Behaviour and Social Networking, 13*(5) 555-562

Seel, N. M. (2003). *Psychologie des Lernens* [*Psychology of learning.*]. München, Germany: Reinhardt.

Sellen, A. (2009). Reflecting human values in the digital age. *Communications of the ACM, 52*(3), 58–66. doi:10.1145/1467247.1467265

Selwyn, N. (2004). Reconsidering political and popular understandings of the digital divide. *New Media & Society, 6*, 341. doi:10.1177/1461444804042519

Selwyn, N. (2009). Faceworking: Exploring students' education-related use of Facebook. *Learning, Media and Technology, 34*(2), 157–174. doi:10.1080/17439880902923622

Sembill, D., Wuttke, E., Seifried, J., Eggloffstein, M., & Rausch, A. (2007). Selbstorganisiertes Lernen in der beruflichen Bildung – Abgrenzungen, Befunde und Konsequenzen [Self-regulated learning in vocational education – Definitions, findings and conclusions.]. *BWP@,* 13. Retrieved March 29, 2012, from http://www.bwpat.de/ausgabe13/sembill_etal_bwpat13.pdf

Seo, W.-S. (2004). Internet usage and life satisfaction of the youth. *Informatization Policy, 11*(2), 87–103.

Seo, W.-S. (2004). The internet use and adolescent's socialization. *The Information Society, 6*, 51–81.

Seufert, S., & Euler, D. (2003). *Nachhaltigkeit von eLearning-Innovationen* [*Sustainability of e-learning innovations.*] (SCIL-Arbeitsbericht Nr. 1). St. Gallen, Switzerland: Universität St. Gallen.

Shaffer, D. W., & Clinton, K. A. (2006). Tool for thoughts: Reexamining thinking in the digital age. *Mind, Culture, and Activity, 13*(4), 283–300. doi:10.1207/s15327884mca1304_2

Shariff, S., & Gouin, R. (2005). *Cyberdilemmas: Gendered hierarchies, free expression and cyber-safety in schools.* Retrieved January 30, 2012, from http://www.oii.ox.ac.uk/microsites/cybersafety/?view=papers

Shariff, S. (2008). *Cyberbullying.* New York, NY: Routledge.

Sharma, M. (2008). *Elgg social networking: Create and manage your own social network site using this free open-source tool.* Packt Publishing.

Sharp, D., Burns, A., & Barr, T. (2005). *Smart internet 2010—Social networks* (No. 2010, p. 170). Swinburne, Australia: Faculty of Life and Social Sciences, Swinburne University of Technology.

Sharples, M. (2000). The design of personal mobile technologies for lifelong learning. *Computers & Education, 34*, 177–193. doi:10.1016/S0360-1315(99)00044-5

Sharples, M. (2010). Foreword. In Brown, E. (Ed.), *Education in the wild: Contextual and location-based mobile learning in action.* University of Nottingham: Learning Sciences Research Institute.

Sharples, M., Graber, R., Harrison, C., & Logan, K. (2009). E-safety and Web 2.0 for children aged 11-16. *Journal of Computer Assisted Learning, 25*(1), 70–84. doi:10.1111/j.1365-2729.2008.00304.x

Sharples, M., Milrad, M., Arnedillo Sánchez, I., & Vavoula, G. (2009). Mobile learning: Small devices, big issues. In Balacheff, N., Ludvigsen, S., Jong, T., Lazonder, A., & Barnes, S. (Eds.), *Technology enhanced learning: Principles and products* (pp. 233–249). Heidelberg, Germany: Springer.

Shepherd, C. (2011). Does social media have a place in workplace learning? *Strategic Direction*, 27(2), 3–4. doi:10.1108/02580541111103882

Shiju, Z. (2007). On the curriculum arrangement & teaching procedures in management information system. *International Conference on Wireless Communications, Networking and Mobile Computing, WiCom 2007* (pp. 6281–6284).

Shipin, C., Yongfeng, D., & Jianpin, Z. (2011). Social media: Communication characteristics and application value in distance education. *The 2011 International Conference on Electrical and Control Engineering* (ICECE), (pp. 6774–6777).

Shirky, C. (2003). *Planning for Web services: Obstacles and opportunities*. O'Reilly.

Shute, V. J., Zapata, D., Kuntz, D., Levy, R., Baker, R., Beck, J., & Christopher, R. (2009). *Assessment: A vision*. Global Resources for Online Education, a project sponsored by the National Science Foundation and the Computing Community Consortium, Tempe, Arizona.

Siegle, D. (2010). Cyberbullying and sexting: Technology abuses of the 21st century. *Gifted Child Today*, 33(2), 14–16.

Silius, K., Kailanto, M., & Tervakari, A.-M. (2011). Evaluating the quality of the social media in an educational context. *2011 IEEE Global Engineering Education Conference* (EDUCON), 04-06 April 2011, Amman, Jordan, (pp. 505–510).

Silius, K., Miilumki, T., Huhtamki, J., Tebest, T., Meriladieinen, J., & Pohjolainen, S. (2010). *Social media enhanced studying and learning in higher education. 2010 IEEE Education Engineering* (pp. 137–143). EDUCON.

Simon, J., & Soliman, K. (2003). An alternative method to measure MIS faculty teaching performance. *International Journal of Educational Management*, 17(5), 195–199. doi:10.1108/09513540310484913

Singh, V., Jain, R., & Kankanhalli, M. (2009). Motivating contributors in social media networks. *Proceedings of the First SIGMM Workshop on Social Media* (WSM '09), (pp. 11-18). New York, NY: ACM.

Sinnappan, S., & Zutshi, S. (2011). *Using microblogging to facilitate community of inquiry: An Australian tertiary experience*. Hobart, Australia: Ascilite. Retrieved January 22, 2012, from http://www.leishman-associates.com.au/ascilitc2011/downloads/papers/Sinnappan-full.pdf

Sjurts, I. (2002). Cross-Media Strategien in der deutschen Medienbranche: Eine ökonomische Analyse zu Varianten und Erfolgsaussichten. [Cross-media strategies in the German media industry: An economic analysis of options and chances of success.] In Müller-Kalthoff, B. (Ed.), *Cross-Media Management: Content-Strategien erfolgreich umsetzen [Cross-media management: Implementing content strategies successfully]*. (pp. 3–18). Heidelberg, Germany: Springer.

Skiba, D. J. (2008). Emerging technologies center: Nursing education 2.0: Twitter & Tweets. Can you post a nugget of knowledge in 140 characters or less? *Nursing Education Perspectives*, 29(2), 110–112.

Skoler, M. (2009). Why the news media became irrelevant - And how social media can help. *Nieman Reports, Fall*, 38-40. Retrieved November 1, 2011, from http://jclass.umd.edu/classes/jour698m/skoler_files/ContentServer.pdf

Skyrme, D. (1999). *Knowledge networking: Creating the collaborative enterprise*. Boston, MA: Butterworth Heinemann.

Smedley, J. K. (2009). Modelling personal knowledge management. *OR Insight*, 22(4), 221–233. doi:10.1057/ori.2009.11

Smith, A. (2011). *Americans and their cell phones*. Washington, DC: Pew Internet & American Life Project. Retrieved from http://pewinternet.org/~/media//Files/Reports/2011/Cell%20Phones%202011.pdf

Smith, M., Barash, V., Getoor, L., & Lauw, H. (2008). Leveraging social context for searching social media. *2008 ACM Workshop on Search in Social Media* (SSM '08), (pp. 91-94). New York, NY: ACM.

Smith, M., Hansen, D., & Gleave, E. (2009). Analyzing enterprise social media networks. *2009 International Conference on Computational Science and Engineering* - Vol. 4 (CSE '09), (pp. 705-710). Washington, DC: IEEE Computer Society.

Smith, P. K., Mahdavi, J., Carvalho, M., Fisher, S., Russell, S., & Tippett, N. (2008). Cyberbullying: Its nature and impact in secondary school pupils. *Journal of Child Psychology and Psychiatry, and Allied Disciplines, 49*(4), 376–385. doi:10.1111/j.1469-7610.2007.01846.x

Solis, B. (2008). *Customer Service: The Art of Listening and Engagement Through Social Media,* 32. Retrieved January 22, 2012 from http://www.briansolis.com/2008/03/new-ebook-customer-service-art-of/

Solis, B., & Breakenridge, D. (2009). *Putting the public back in public relations. How social media is reinventing the aging business of PR* (p. 314). FT Press.

Solomon, B. S., Duce, D., & Harrison, R. (2011). Methodologies for using social media collaborative work systems. *First International Workshop on Requirements Engineering for Social Computing* (RESC), 2011, (pp. 6–9).

Soloway, E., Grant, W., Tinker, R., Roschelle, J., Mills, M., & Resnick, M. (1999). Science in the palm of their hands. *Communications of the ACM, 42*(8), 21–26. doi:10.1145/310930.310953

Sothern, M. S. (2004). Obesity prevention in children: physical activity and nutrition. *Nutrition (Burbank, Los Angeles County, Calif.), 20*(7-8), 704–708. doi:10.1016/j.nut.2004.04.007

Sourander, A., Brunstein Klomek, A., Ikonen, M., Lindroos, J., Luntamo, T., & Koskelainen, M. (2010). Psychosocial risk factors associated with cyberbullying among adolescents: A population-based study. *Archives of General Psychiatry, 67*(7), 720–728. doi:10.1001/archgenpsychiatry.2010.79

Sporer, T., Reinmann, G., Jenert, T., & Hofhues, S. (2007). Begleitstudium Problemlösekompetenz (Version 2.0). [The study programme "problem-solving competencies", Version 2.0.] In Merkt, M., Mayrberger, K., Schulmeister, R., Sommer, A., & van den Berk, I. (Eds.), *Studieren neu erfinden – Hochschule neu denken* [*Reinventing studying - Rethinking higher education*]. (pp. 85–94). Münster, Germany: Waxmann.

Spotts, T. H. (1999). Discriminating factors in faculty use of instructional technology in higher edcuation. *Educational Technology & Society, 2*(4). Retrieved June 12, 2012, from http://www.ifets.info/journals/2_4/spotts.html

Stahlschmidt, T., Ziemer, L., & Kuhn, N. (2011). Social media in the context of academic marketing - Case study: The Umwelt-Campus blog. *International Conference on Computational Aspects of Social Networks* (CASoN) 2011, (pp. 114-119).

Staples, A., Pugach, M. C., & Himes, D. (2005). Rethinking the technology integration challenge: Cases from three urban elementary schools. *Journal of Research on Technology in Education, 37*(3), 285–311.

Stead, G. (2005). *Moving mobile into the mainstream. Proceedings of mLearn 2005.* Retrieved.

Steeples, C., Jones, C., & Goodyear, P. (2002). Beyond e-learning: A future for networked learning. In *Networked learning: Perspectives and issues* (pp. 323–342). London, UK: Springer. doi:10.1007/978-1-4471-0181-9_19

Stefanone, M. A., Lackaff, D., & Rosen, D. (2010). The relationship between traditional mass media and social media: Reality television as a model for social network site behavior. *Journal of Broadcasting & Electronic Media, 54*(3), 508–525. Retrieved from http://www.communication.buffalo.edu/contrib/people/faculty/documents/stefanone_BEM_2010.pdf-doi:10.1080/08838151.2010.498851

Stefanone, M. A., Lackaff, D., & Rosen, D. (2010). Contingencies of self worth and social networking site behavior. *Cyberpsychology, Behavior, and Social Networking, 14*(1-2). doi:doi:10.1089/cyber.2010.0049

Steinberg, L., Albert, D., & Cauffman, E. (2008). Age differences in sensation seeking and impulsivity as indexed by behavior and self-report: Evidence for a dual systems model. *Developmental Psychology, 44,* 1764–1778. doi:10.1037/a0012955

Steiner, J. (1993). *Psychic retreats: Pathological organisations in psychotic, neurotic and borderline patients.* London, UK: Routledge. doi:10.4324/9780203359839

Steinfield, C., Ellison, N. B., & Lampe, C. (2008). Social capital, self-esteem, and use of online social network sites: A longitudinal analysis. *Journal of Applied Developmental Psychology, 29,* 434–445. doi:10.1016/j.appdev.2008.07.002

Stevens, I., & Van Lamoen, I. (2001). *Manual on gender mainstreaming at universities: Equal opportunities at universities: towards a gender mainstreaming approach.* The Netherlands: Garant Uitgevers NV.

Stewart, J. (2002). The relevance of the 'learning styles debate' for Australian indigenous students in mainstream education. *The Australian Journal of Indigenous Education, 30*(2).

Steyaert, J. (2002). Inequality and the digital divide: myths and realities. In Hick, S., & McNutt, J. (Eds.), *Advocacy, activism and the internet* (pp. 199–211). Chicago, IL: Lyceum Press.

Stiakakis, E., Kariotellis, P., & Vlachopoulou, M. (2010). From the digital divide to digital inequality: A Secondary research in the European Union. In Sideridis, A. B., & Patrikakis, C. Z. (Eds.), *E-Democracy 2009, LNICST, 26* (pp. 43–54). doi:10.1007/978-3-642-11631-5_4

Strachey, J. (2001). *The standard edition of the complete psychological works of Sigmund Freud* (Vol. 21, pp. 1927–1931). London, UK: Vintage.

Strasma, K. (2010). Using Google Documents for composing projects that use primary research in first-year writing courses. *Teaching English in the Two-Year College, 37*(3), 305–311.

Straub, P. (2004). *In the night room.* London, UK: Harpercollins.

Strobbe, M., Van Laere, O., Dauwe, S., Dhoedt, B., De Turck, F., & Demeester, P. (2010). Interest based selection of user generated content for rich communication services. *Journal of Network and Computer Applications, 33*(2), 84–97. doi:10.1016/j.jnca.2009.12.008

Strohymer, R. (2011). Get the most out of the cloud. *PC World, 29*(7), 79–84.

Strom, P. S., & Strom, R. D. (2005). When teens turn cyberbullies. *Education Digest,* (December): 35–41.

Subrahmanyam, K., & Greenfield, P. (2008). Communicating online: Adolescent relationships and the media. *The Future of Children: Children and Media Technology, 18*, 119–146.

Subrahmanyam, K., Greenfield, P., Kraut, R., & Gross, E. (2001). The impact of computer use on children's and adolescents' development. *Applied Developmental Psychology, 22*, 7–30. doi:10.1016/S0193-3973(00)00063-0

Subrahmanyam, K., Reich, S. M., & Waechter, N. (2008). Online and offline social networks: Use of social networking sites by emerging adults. *Journal of Applied Developmental Psychology, 29*, 420–433. doi:10.1016/j.appdev.2008.07.003

Sullivan, N., & Pratt, E. (1996). A comparative study of two ESL writing environments: A computer-assisted classroom and a traditional oral classroom. *System, 24*(4), 491–501. doi:10.1016/S0346-251X(96)00044-9

Sultan, N. (2010). Cloud computing for education: A new dawn? *International Journal of Information Management, 30*, 109–116. doi:10.1016/j.ijinfomgt.2009.09.004

Sumi, K. (2008). Anime de Blog: Animation CGM for content distribution. In *2nd International Conference on Advances in Computer Entertainment Technology*, Vol. 352, Yokohama, Japan (pp. 187-190).

Surowiecki, J. (2004). *The wisdom of crowds: Why the many are smarter than the few and how collective wisdom shapes business, economies, societies and nations.* New York, NY: Little Brown.

Surry, D. W., & Land, S. M. (2000). Strategies for motivating higher education faculty to use technology. *Innovations in Education and Training International, 37*(2), 145–15. doi:10.1080/13558000050034501

Sweetser, K., & Kelleher, T. (2011). A survey of social media use, motivation and leadership among public relations practitioners. *Public Relations Review, 37*(4), 425–428. doi:10.1016/j.pubrev.2011.08.010

Syvänen, A., Muukkonen, J., & Sihvonen, M. (2009). Are the open issues of social software-based personal learning environment practices being addressed? In *Proceedings of the 13th International MindTrek Conference: Everyday Life in the Ubiquitous Era* (MindTrek '09) (pp. 142-148). New York, NY: ACM.

Talvinen, J. (1995). Information systems in marketing: Identifying opportunities for new applications. *European Journal of Marketing, 29*(1), 8–26. doi:10.1108/03090569510075307

Tangen, D., & Campbell, M. (2010). Cyberbullying prevention: One primary school's approach. *Australian Journal of Guidance & Counselling, 20*(2), 225–234. doi:10.1375/ajgc.20.2.225

Tapscott, D. (1998). *Growing up digital: The rise of the net generation.* New York, NY: McGraw-Hill.

Tapscott, D., & Williams, A. D. (2006). *Wikinomics: How mass collaboration changes everything.* New York, NY: Penguin.

Taylor, E. W. (2008). Transformative learning theory. *New Directions for Adult and Continuing Education, 119*, 5–15. doi:10.1002/ace.301

Terdiman, D. (2005, December 15). *Study: Wikipedia as accurate as Britannica.* Retrieved on February 27, 2012, from http://news.cnet.com/2100-1038_3-5997332.html

Teven, J. J. (2007). Teacher Machiavellianism and social influence in the college classroom: Implications for measurement. *Communication Research Reports, 24*, 341–352. doi:10.1080/08824090701624247

Teven, J. J., & Herring, J. (2005). Instructor influence in the classroom: A preliminary investigation of perceived instructor power, credibility, and student satisfaction. *Communication Research Reports, 22*, 235–246. doi:10.1080/00036810500230685

The Digital Marketing Agency. (2011*). Australian online marketing trends – 2011.* Retrieved January 22, 2012, from http://www.socialmedianews.com.au/social-media-statistics-australia-march-2011/

The World Bank. (2011). *Internet users.* Retrieved from http://data.worldbank.org/indicator/it.net.user.p2

Thomas, P. Y. (2011, December 19). Cloud computing: A potential paradigm for practising the scholarship of teaching and learning. *The Electronic Library, 29*(2), 214–224. doi:10.1108/02640471111125177

Thomson, K., Tan, B. K., & Brook, C. (2009). *Computer mediated communication and the learning experience of those studying via flexible delivery mode.* EDUCAUSE Australiasia Conference: Innovate, Educate and Sustain. Perth, 3-6 May, 2009. CAUDIT: Council of Australian University Directors of Information Technology.

Thurman, N. (2008). Forums for citizen journalists? Adoption of user generated content initiatives by online news media. *New Media & Society, 10*(1), 139–157. doi:10.1177/1461444807085325

Toffler, A. (1980). *The third wave.* Bantam Books.

Topcu, A., & Ubuz, B. (2008). The effects of metacognitive knowledge on the pre-service teachers' participation in the asynchronous online forum. *Journal of Educational Technology & Society, 11*(3), 1–12.

Topçu, Ç., Erdur-Baker, Ö., & Çapa-Aydin, Y. (2008). Examination of cyberbullying experiences among Turkish students from different school types. *Cyberpsychology & Behavior, 11*(6), 643–648. doi:10.1089/cpb.2007.0161

Towner, L. T., VanHorn, A., & Parker, L. S. (2007). *Facebook: Classroom tool for a classroom community?* (pp. 1-18). Midwestern Political Science Association. Retrieved December 16, 2011, from http://citation.allacademic.com//meta/p_mla_apa_research_citation/1/9/7/1/3/pages197133/p197133-1.php

Transforming American Education: Learning Powered by Technology. (5 March 2010). Office of Educational Technology, U. S. Department of Education. Retrieved from http://www2.ed.gov/about/offices/list/os/technology/netp.pdf

Traxler, J. (2009). Learning in a mobile age. *International Journal of Mobile and Blended Learning, 1*(1), 1–12. doi:10.4018/jmbl.2009010101

Trist, E., & Murray, H. (1990). *the social engagement of social science,* Vol 1. London, UK: Free Association.

Tufte, B. (2006). Tweens as consumers - With focus on 'girls' and 'boys' Internet use. *Child and Teen Consumption, 53*, 1–18.

Twitter. (2011). *#numbers*. Retrieved February 10, 2012, from http://blog.twitter.com/2011/03/numbers.html

Twyman, K., Saylor, C., Taylor, L. A., & Comeaux, C. (2010). Comparing children and adolescents engaged in cyberbullying to matched peers. *Cyberpsychology, Behavior, and Social Networking, 13*(2), 195–199. doi:10.1089/cyber.2009.0137

Tynes, B. M. (2007). Internet safety gone wild? Sacrificing the educational and psychosocial benefits of online social environments. *Journal of Adolescent Research, 22*(6), 575–584. doi:10.1177/0743558407303979

UNAIDS. (1999). *Peer education and HIV/Aids: Concepts, uses and challenges* (UNAIDS Best Practice Material) (p. 39). Geneva, Switzerland: UN.

United States Department of Education, Office of Planning, Evaluation and Policy Development. (2010). *A blueprint for reform: The reauthorization of the elementary and secondary education act*. Washington, DC: Author.

University of Zurich. (2007). *Wissenschaftliches Schreiben und studentisches Lernen [Academic writing and student's learning.]*. Zurich, Switzerland: University of Zurich, Arbeitsstelle für Hochschuldidaktik. Retrieved March 29, 2012, from http://www.afh.uzh.ch/instrumente/dossiers/WissSchreiben_01_10.pdf.

Urban Dictionary. (2006). *Haxxor*. Retrieved September 18, 2007 from http://www.urbandictionary.com/define.php?term=haxxor

Valcke, M., Bonte, S., De Wever, B., & Rots, I. (2010). Internet parenting styles and the impact on Internet use of primary school children. *Computers & Education, 55*(2), 454–464. doi:10.1016/j.compedu.2010.02.009

Valcke, M., & Decraene, B. (2007). *Children and the Internet: Help kit to tackle Internet usage by children and adolescents*. Tielt, Belgium: Lannoo NV.

Valkenburg, P. M., & Peter, J. (2009). Social consequences of the Internet for adolescents. *Current Directions in Psychological Science, A Decade of Research, 18*(1), 1.

Valkenburg, P. M., & Peter, J. (2011). Online communication among adolescents: An integrated model of its attraction, opportunities, and risks. *The Journal of Adolescent Health, 48*(2), 121–127. doi:10.1016/j.jadohealth.2010.08.020

Valkenburg, P. M., Schouten, A. P., & Peter, J. (2005). Adolescents' identity experiments on the internet. *New Media & Society, 7*(3), 383–402. doi:10.1177/1461444805052282

Valtonen, T., Hacklin, S., Dillon, P., Vesisenaho, M., Kukkonen, J., & Hietanen, A. (2012). Perspectives on personal learning environments held by vocational students. *Computers & Education, 58*(2), 732–739. doi:10.1016/j.compedu.2011.09.025

van Deursen, A. J. A. M., van Dijk, J. A. G. M., & Peters, O. (2011). Rethinking Internet skills: The contribution of gender, age, education, Internet experience, and hours online to medium- and content-related Internet skills. *Poetics, 39*(2), 1–20. Elsevier B.V. doi:10.1016/j.poetic.2011.02.001

van Deursen, A., & van Dijk, J. (2011). Internet skills and the digital divide. *New Media & Society, 13*(6), 893–911. doi:10.1177/1461444810386774

van Dijk, J., & Hacker, K. (2000). *The digital divide as a complex and dynamic phenomenon*. Paper presented at the 50th Annual Conference of the International Communication Association, Acapulco, 1-5 June 2000.

van Dijk, J. (2000). Widening information gaps and policies of prevention. In Hacker, K., & van Dijk, J. (Eds.), *Digital democracy, issues of theory and practice*. London, UK: Sage.

van Dijk, J. (2009). One Europe, digitally divided. In Chadwick, A., & Howard, P. (Eds.), *Handbook of internet politics*. London, UK: Routledge.

Vandebosch, H., & Van Cleemput, K. (2009). Cyberbullying among youngsters: Profiles of bullies and victims. *New Media & Society, 11*(8), 1349–1371. doi:10.1177/1461444809341263

Velicu, A. (2012). Violenţa mediatică prin ochii copiilor şi adolescenţilor români [Media Violence throu the Eyes of the Romanian Children and Teenagers]. *Revista de Asistenţă Socială, 11*(1), 135-147.

Vergeer, M., & Pelzer, B. (2009). Consequences of media and Internet use for offline and online network capital and well-being. A causal model approach. *Journal of Computer-Mediated Communication, 15*(1), 189–210. doi:10.1111/j.1083-6101.2009.01499.x

Vesely, P., Bloom, L., & Sherlock, J. (2007). Key elements of building online community: Comparing faculty and student perceptions. *Journal of Online Learning and Teaching, 3*(3).

Vie, S. (2008). Digital divide 2.0: 'Generation M' and online social networking sites in the composition classroom. *Computers and Composition, 25*(1), 9–23. doi:10.1016/j.compcom.2007.09.004

Vighnarajah, L. W. S., & Kamarish, A. B. (2008). The shift in the role of teachers in the learning process. *European Journal of Social Sciences, 7*(2), 33-41. Retrieved February 19, 2012, from http://www.eurojournals.com/ejss_7_2_03.pdf

Vince, R. (1998). Behind and beyond Kolb's learning cycle. *Journal of Management Education, 22*(3), 304–319. doi:10.1177/105256299802200304

Visone, J. D. (2010). Science or reading: What is being measured by standardized tests? *American Secondary Education, 39*(1), 95–112.

Visser, J. (1994). *Distance education for the nine high-population countries: A concept paper based on the informal planning meeting on distance education of the nine high-population countries, Manila.* Learning Technologies and Educational Communication for Basic Education, UNESCO Basic Education Division.

Von Hentig, H. (1999). Eine nicht lehrbare Kunst. [A not teachable art.] In Narr, W.-D., & Starxy, J. (Eds.), *Lust und Last des wissenschaftlichen Schreibens* [*Delights and burdens of academic writing*]. (pp. 19–26). Frankfurt, Germany: Suhrkamp.

Von Hippel, E. (2005). *Democratizing innovation.* MIT Press.

Vozzo, L., Santoro, N., Labone, E., Bennett, M., Nanlohy, P., & Pietsch, M. Reid, J. (2012). *Assessing professional teaching standards, for indigenous and non-indigenous pre-service teachers in urban, rural and remote practicum and for accomplished teachers, using digital technology.* Australian Learning and Teaching Council (ALTC). Retrieved from http://www.deewr.gov.au/highereducation/programs/quality/pages/altc.aspx

Vyas, R. V., Sharma, R. C., & Kumar, A. (2002). Educational radio in India. *Turkish Online Journal of Distance Education, 3*(3). ISSN 1302-6488

Vygotsky, L. S. (1978). *Mind in society: The development of higher psychological processes* (Cole, M., John-Steiner, V., Scribner, S., & Souberman, E., Eds.). Cambridge, MA: Harvard University Press.

Wagner, R. (2011). Social media tools for teaching and learning. *Athletic Training Education Journal, 6*(1), 51–52.

Wakefield, S. A., Warren, S. J., & Alsobrook, M. (2011). Learning and teaching as communicative actions: A mixed-methods twitter study. *Knowledge Management & E-Learning: An International Journal, 3*(4). Retrieved February 10, 2012, from http://www.kmel-journal.org/ojs/index.php/online-publication/article/viewArticle/145

Walker, J. L. (2009). *The contextualized rapid resolution cycle intervention model for cyberbullying,* Unpublished dissertation, Arizona State University, Tempe, Arizona.

Walker, J. R. (1999). *Literacy, technology, and change: The gates of hell.* Unpublished doctoral dissertation, University of South Florida.

Wall, M. (2004). Blogs as black market journalism: A new paradigm for news. *Interface on the Internet, 4*(2).

Wallace, R. (2008). *Engaging remote and very remote Indigenous students with education using information and communication technologies (ICTs): Final report.* Darwin, Australia: Charles Darwin University.

Walther, J. B. (1996). Computer-mediated communication. Impersonal, interpersonal, and hyperpersonal interaction. *Communication Research, 23,* 3–43. doi:10.1177/009365096023001001

Wang, B., & Chai, C. S. (2010). *Preservice teachers' epistemic beliefs and their online interactions in a knowledge building community.* Knowledge Building Summer Institute. New Assessments and Environments for Knowledge Building, Toronto, Canada, August 3-6.

Wang, R., Bianchi, S. M., & Raley, S. B. (2005). Teenagers' Internet use and family rules: A research note. *Journal of Marriage and the Family, 67*(5), 1249–1258. doi:10.1111/j.1741-3737.2005.00214.x

Watzlawick, P., Weakland, J., & Fisch, R. (1974). *Change.* New York, NY: W. W. Norton and Co.

Weaver, C. (2002). *Reading process and practice* (3rd ed.). Portsmouth, NH: Heinemann.

Weber, M. (1958). *The protestant ethic and the spirit of capitalism* (Parsons, T., Trans.). New York, NY: Scribners.

Weber, S. (2005). *The success of open source.* Harvard University Press.

Webopedia. (n.d.). *New media.* Retrieved from www.webopedia.com/TERM/N/new_media.html

Webster, J. (2000). *Gender policy review policy directions report version 1* (No. Version 1). Retrieved February 20, 2012, from ftp://ftp.cordis.europa.eu/pub/citizens/docs/webster_report_en.pdf

Weerkamp, W. (2010). Finding people and their utterances in social media. *33rd International ACM SIGIR Conference on Research and Development in Information Retrieval* (SIGIR '10), (pp. 918-918). New York, NY: ACM.

Weiler, A. (2004). Information-seeking behavior in Generation Y students: Motivation, critical thinking, and learning theory. *Journal of Academic Librarianship, 31*(1), 46–53. doi:10.1016/j.acalib.2004.09.009

Weinberg, B., & Pehlivan, E. (2011). Social spending: Managing the social media mix. *Business Horizons, 54*(3), 275–282. doi:10.1016/j.bushor.2011.01.008

Weinberger, D. (2007). *Everything is miscellaneous: The power of the new digital disorder* (p. 288). Henry Holt.

Weischenberg, S., Malik, M., & Scholl, A. (2006). *Die Souffleure der Mediengesellschaft. Report über die Journalisten in Deutschland* [*The prompters of the media society. Report on journalists in Germany.*]. Konstanz, Germany: UVK.

Wenger, E., White, N., & Smith, J. (2009). *Digital habitats: Stewarding technology for communities.* Portland, OR: CPsquare.

Wenger, E. (1998). *Communities of practice: Learning, meaning and identity.* Oxford, UK: Oxford University Press.

Wenglinsky, H. (1998). *Does it compute? The relationship between educational technology and student achievement in mathematics.* Princeton, NJ: Educational Testing Service.

Wen-Huei, C., Yu-Ting, L., & Kuang-Hsia, L. (2010). Decent digital social media for senior life: A practical design approach. *2010 3rd IEEE International Conference on Computer Science and Information Technology* (IEEE ICCSIT 2010), 9-11, July 2010, Chengdu, China, (pp. 249–253).

Wheeler, S. (2004). Five smooth stones: Fighting for the survival of higher education. *Distance Learning, 1*(3).

Whinston, A. B. (2009). Opportunities and challenges in analysis of social networks. *AMCIS 2009 Proceedings: AIS Electronic Library.* Retrieved December 1, 2011, from http://aisel.aisnet.org/amcis2009/288

Wikipedia: About. (12 Feb 2012). Retrieved on February 27, 2012 from http://en.wikipedia.org/wiki/Wikipedia:About

Wiley, J., Goldman, S. R., Graesser, A. C., Sanchez, C. A., Ash, I. K., & Hemmerich, J. A. (2009, December). Source evaluation, comprehension, and learning in internet science inquiry tasks. *American Educational Research Journal, 46*(4), 1060–1106. doi:10.3102/0002831209333183

Wilkinson, D., & Thelwall, M. (2010). Social network site changes over time: The case of MySpace. *Journal of the American Society for Information Science and Technology, 61*, 2311–2323. doi:10.1002/asi.21397

Willard, N. (2005). *Educator's guide to cyberbullying and cyberthreats.* Retrieved from February 1, 2012, from http://www.cyberbully.org/cyberbully/docs/cbcteducator.pdf

Willard, N. (2007). *Cyberbullying and cyberthreats: Responding to the challenge of online social aggression, threats, and distress.* Champaign, IL: Research Press.

Williams, A. L., & Merten, M. J. (2009). Adolescents' online social networking following the death of a peer. *Journal of Adolescent Research, 24*(1), 67–90. doi:10.1177/0743558408328440

Williams, B. T. (2008). "Tomorrow will not be like today": Literacy and identity in a world of multiliteracies. *Journal of Adolescent & Adult Literacy, 51*(8), 682–686. doi:10.1598/JAAL.51.8.7

Willoughby, T. (2008). A short-term longitudinal study of internet and computer game use by adolescent boys and girls: prevalence, frequency of use, and psychosocial predictors. *Developmental Psychology*, *44*(1), 195–204. doi:10.1037/0012-1649.44.1.195

Wilson, K. R., Wallin, J. S., & Reiser, C. (2003). Social stratification and the digital divide. *Communication Research*, *21*(2), 133–143. doi:doi:10.1177/0894439303021002001

Wilson, W. (2003, January 1). Faculty perceptions and uses of instructional technology. *EDUCAUSE Quarterly*.

Wingkvist, A., & Ericsson, M. (2010). A framework to guide and structure the development process of mobile learning initiatives. In M. Montebello, et al., (Eds.), *mLearn 2010: Conference Proceedings,* University of Malta.

Winner, L. (1986). *The whale and the reactor: A search for limits in an age of high technology.* Chicago, IL: University of Chicago Press.

Wise, K., Alhabash, S., & Park, H. (2010). Emotional responses during social information

Witell, L., Kristensson, P., Gustafsson, A., & Lofgren, M. (2011). Idea generation: Customer co-creation versus traditional market research techniques. *Journal of Service Management*, *22*(2), 140–159. doi:10.1108/09564231111124190

Wolf, K. (2008). A blogging good time: The use of blogs as a reflective learning and feedback tool for final year public relations students. In *Proceedings of World Association for cooperative education-Australian Collaborative Education Network Asia Pacific* (pp. 649–656). Australian Collaborative Education Network.

Wong-Lo, M., Bullock, L. M., & Gable, R. A. (2011). Cyber bullying: Practices to face digital aggression. *Emotional & Behavioural Difficulties*, *16*(3), 317–325. doi:10.1080/13632752.2011.595098

Wood Ray, K. (2006). *Study driven: A framework for planning units of study in the writing workshop.* Portsmouth, NH: Heinemann.

Wood, E. (2001). Marketing information systems in tourism and hospitality small- and medium-sized enterprises: A study of Internet use for market intelligence. *International Journal of Tourism Research*, *3*, 283–299. doi:10.1002/jtr.315

Wright, F. L. (1970). *An organic architecture: The architecture of democracy.* Cambridge, MA: MIT Press Classic.

Wu, C., & Lai, C. (2009). Wireless handhelds to support clinical nursing practicum. *Journal of Educational Technology & Society*, *12*(2), 190–204.

Wunsch-Vincent, S., & Vicker, G. (2006). *Participative Web: User-created content.* Organisation for Economic Co-operation and Development, Directorate for Science, Technology and Industry Committee for Information, Computer and Communications Policy.

Xu, X. (1999). The strategic orientation of marketing information systems – An empirical study. *Marketing Intelligence & Planning*, *17*(6), 262–272. doi:10.1108/02634509910293070

Yan Yu, A., Wen Tian, S., Vogel, D., & Chi-Wai Kwok, R. (2010). Can learning be virtually boosted? An investigation of online social networking impacts. *Computers & Education*, *55*(4), 1494–1503. doi:10.1016/j.compedu.2010.06.015

Yang, S. J. H. (2006). Context aware ubiquitous learning environments for peer-to-peer collaborative learning. *Journal of Educational Technology & Society*, *9*(1), 188–201.

Yardi, S., & boyd, d. (2010). Tweeting from the town square: Measuring geographic local networks. *Proceedings of the Fourth International AAAI Conference on Weblogs and Social Media*. In *ICWSM*. Retrieved November 2011 from http://www.cc.gatech.edu/~yardi/pubs/Yardi_TownSquare10.pdf

Ye, S. J. (2003). *A study of elementary school student's behavior and cyberethics on the Internet.* Master thesis, National Pingtung University of Education, Pingtung, Taiwan

Yen, T. H. (2002). *Research on the relationship between background, behavior of using Internet and psychological characteristics for elementary school students.* Master thesis, University of Tainan, Tainan, Taiwan

Yen, J. Y., Yen, C. F., Chen, C. C., Chen, S. H., & Ko, C. H. (2007). Family factors of internet addiction and substance use experience in Taiwanese adolescents. *Cyberpsychology & Behavior*, *10*(3), 323–329. doi:10.1089/cpb.2006.9948

Yilmaz, H. (2011). Cyberbullying in Turkish middle schools: An exploratory study. *School Psychology International, 32*(6), 645–654. doi:10.1177/0143034311410262

Yin, R. K. (2003). *Case study research: Design and methods* (3rd ed.). Thousand Oaks, CA: Sage.

Young, G. O. (2007, September 7). *Passionate employees: The gateway to enterprise web 2.0 sales.* Forrester Research.

Young, K. (2011). Social ties, social networks and the Facebook experience. *International Journal of Emerging Technologies and Society, 9*(1), 20–34.

Young, K. S. (1998). Internet addiction: The emergence of a new clinical disorder. *Cyberpsychology & Behavior, 1*(3), 237–244. doi:10.1089/cpb.1998.1.237

Young, K. S. (2004). Internet addiction: A new clinical phenomenon and its consequences. *The American Behavioral Scientist, 48*(4), 402–415. doi:10.1177/0002764204270278

Yu, A. Y., Tian, S. W., Vogel, D., & Chi-Wai Kwok, R. (2010). Can learning be virtually boosted? An investigation of online social networking impacts. *Computers & Education, 55*(4), 1494–1503. doi:10.1016/j.compedu.2010.06.015

Zayim, N., Yildirim, S., & Saka, O. (2006). Technology adoption of medical faculty in teaching: Differentiating factors in adopter categories. *Journal of Educational Technology & Society, 9*(2), 213–222.

Zeiller, M., & Schauer, B. (2011). Adoption, motivation and success factors of social media for team collaboration in SMEs. In S. Lindstaedt & M. Granitzer (Eds.), *11th International Conference on Knowledge Management and Knowledge Technologies* (i-KNOW '11). New York, NY: ACM.

Zhang, J. (2009). Toward a creative social Web for learners and teachers. *Educational Researcher, 38*(4), 274–279. doi:10.3102/0013189X09336674

Zhongke, Z. (2010). The study on the application of marketing information system. *The 2nd IEEE International Conference on Information Management and Engineering* (ICIME), (pp. 428–431).

Zittrain, J. (2006). The generative internet. *Harvard Law Review, 119*, 1974–2040.

Zywica, J., & Danowski, J. (2008). The faces of Facebookers: Investigating social enhancement and social compensation hypotheses; Predicting Facebook and offline popularity from sociability and self-esteem, and mapping the meanings of popularity with semantic networks. *Journal of Computer-Mediated Communication, 14*(1), 1–34. doi:10.1111/j.1083-6101.2008.01429.x

About the Contributors

Monica Pătruţ is Senior Lecturer in Political Science. Her domains of research are political communication and computer science applied in social and political sciences. She is member of the editorial advisory board of *BRAND: Broad Research in Accounting, Negotiation, and Distribution*. She published several academic books on applying computer science in educational, social and political topics, and papers in international journals like *Public Relations Review* and *Journal of Media Research*.

Bogdan Pătruţ is Associate Professor in Computer Science at "Vasile Alecsandri" University of Bacău, Romania. His domains of interest/ research are multi-agent systems and computer science applied in social and political sciences. He published more than 25 book on programming, algorithms, artificial intelligence, and interactive education. He also is the editor-in-chief of *BRAIN: Broad Research in Artificial Intelligence and Neuroscience*, and software developer in EduSoft company.

* * *

Ana Adi is a Lecturer in Marketing and Corporate Communications in the Media School of Bournemouth University where she delivers courses related to emerging media and digital communication. Before joining BU, she worked in Romania, Belgium, USA and Bahrain. Ana has a background in public relations, strategic communication, management, and business communication. She obtained her degrees from in Romania, the United States and Scotland. Ana is also a *public relations consultant* specialising in social media strategies and training for small and medium companies. She has served American and European clients, both from the profit and the non-profit sector including Netlog from Belgium, Help Our World from Brazil, Coca-Cola in Romania, and Deloitte in the USA. She is also an Advisory Board member of the Social Media Global Education Connection Project (SMGECP), an education initiative of the Social Media Club (founded by Chris Heuer) focused on improving the quality of Social Media education in universities and empowering its community of Social Media professors.

Osman Tolga Aricak is the chairperson of Psychology at Fatih University. Arıcak received his PhD in Psychological Guidance and Counselling at Marmara University. His research interests are cyberbullying, career self-esteem, and structural equation modeling. He teaches Research Methods in Psychology, Statistics in Behavioral Sciences, Developmental Psychology, and Educational Psychology courses.

Dorin Bocu has been a Professor of Computer Science at Transilvania University of Brasov, Romania since 1990. He is a PhD in Mathematics at the Transilvania University of Brasov, Romania. Currently, he concentrates on topics around software engineering, IT project management, intelligent computational systems, modern software design, and implementation paradigms. He has been Head of the Department of Computer Science, Transilvania University of Brasov. In this context, it can be stated that he created two state-of-the-art BSc and MSc study programmes. Furthermore, he initiated and developed the academic institutional relationship with the IT industry that is active in Brasov.

Răzvan Bocu has been a Lecturer of Computer Science at Transilvania University of Brasov, Romania since 2005. He received his PhD in Computer Science from the National University of Ireland, Cork, in 2010. He currently focuses on the following topics: bioinformatics and large networked structures, object oriented programming, software engineering, computer networks, modern programming techniques for both mobile devices, and desktop computers. He also continuously improves his didactic approaches and values the collaboration with the IT industry. Thus, he is a technical advisor and permanent collaborator of Route 66 R&D in Brasov.

Ioana Boghian is Assistant Professor at the Department of Foreign Languages and Literatures at "Vasile Alecsandri" University of Bacău, Romania. She holds a PhD from "Alexandru Ioan Cuza" University of Iaşi, Romania. Her doctoral thesis was published in 2010 under the title *Houses in Victorian Novels: A Semiotic Approach*. Her topics of interest are English and American literature, semiotics, and cultural studies.

Swati Jaywant Rao Bute is working at National Institute of Health and Family Welfare (New Delhi) as an Assistant Professor – Print Media (*ad hoc*). She is PhD in Mass Communication and Journalism from University of Pune; she did her Master's in Science and Technology Communication, she also did her M.Sc. in Organic Chemistry from Devi Ahilaya Vishwavidyalaya, Indore. She has experience of working with both print and electronic media. Earlier she worked as a Professor at International School of Business and Media, Pune; Subjects - Global Comparative Media, Current Affairs, Introduction to Journalism and Radio Journalism and Production. She worked with Indira School of Communication, Pune as a Professor; Subjects - Radio Journalism and Production; she also worked with Suryadutta School of Communication, Pune as a Visiting Faculty and taught Global Media and Current Affairs. She has six years experience of working with All India Radio (Khandwa, Indore, and Bhopal Radio Stations) as an Assistant Producer and Program Presenter (Casual). She worked as a trainee at Audio-Visual Research Centre (AVRC), Devi Ahilya Vishwavidyalaya, Indore and has written around ten scripts on different health related issues for the documentary films which were telecasted on Doordarshan (Under UGC's Countrywide Classroom Programme).

Mar Camacho is Doctor in Educational Technology, Lecturer and Researcher at the Department of Pedagogy of the School of Education at Universitat Rovira i Virgili (Tarragona - Catalonia), and member since 2001 of the ARGET Research group on Educational Technology of the same university. Author of several publications regarding the use of ICT in teaching and learning processes, her latest research streamlines have been the the use of Web 2.0 tools and resources and the use and implementation of mobile learning and emerging technologies as tools which help transform, enrich, and extend the learning experience. During recent years, she has been working on research projects concerning educational methodologies and ICT, the design and development of teacher training courses addressed to language teachers and the usage of mobile tools aimed at enhancing learning processes, including the use of podcasting as a tool to facilitate the acquisition of communicative competences and to promote diversity in multicultural Europe. Currently, she works on different projects which concern mobile learning, the use of social media to construct digital identity, and simulations and gaming. At the same time, in the last years she has actively participated in seminars, round tables and conferences such as Online Educa Berlin, Edutec, IADIS Mobile Conference, EDEN, ECER, PLE Conference, E-Challenges, and Ed-Media.

Domenico Consoli graduated in Electronic Engineering at University of Padova (1981) and in Economics at University of Urbino (1994), holds the first PhD in Artificial Intelligent Systems (Information Engineering) at Polytechnic University of Marche (2009). Currently he is PhD candidate (to get a second PhD) in Economics and Management at University of Urbino. He is Professor of Computer Science in High Schools and, in the past, was Professor of Information Communication Technology at University of Urbino. He is author of 6 books on information technologies and of more than 55 scientific papers (conference proceedings, journals, book chapters) on ICT and Business. His research area focuses on information communication technology that supports enterprise strategies and mainly on the implementation of the new model of Enterprise 2.0, an enterprise that interact with customer by Web 2.0 tools to improve product/services, in a context of customer satisfaction.

Georgeta Drulă is Associate Professor at the Faculty of Journalism and Communication Studies, University of Bucharest. Her main fields of interest and research are digital media, media and communication studies, and new technologies. She teaches courses in digital media, under the titles: Multimedia, Communication Studies and New Technologies, Online Multimedia Production, and Online Corporate Communication. She gained grants and led four national and international research projects in digital media field and contributed with articles published in peer reviewed journals and conferences proceedings. She is member of Romanian Association of Trainers in Journalism and Mass Communication (AFCOM) and European Communication Research and Education Association (ECREA). She is the director of master programme "Multimedia and Audio-Video Production".

Tricia M. Farwell (Ph.D., Arizona State University) is an Assistant Professor in the School of Journalism in the College of Mass Communication at Middle Tennessee State University. She has served in various leadership roles for divisions of the Association for Education in Journalism and Mass Communication (AEJMC) and the entertainment and sports section for the Public Relations Society of America (PRSA). Her research interests include gender issues in mass communication and applications of social media in advertising and public relations. Her work has appeared in various books and journals. She is the author of *Love and Death in Edith Wharton's Fiction*.

Christina Gasser Scotte is currently a PhD student at Lancaster University, and her thesis is centered around skills that business graduates in Korea need to be successful in industry. She has a special interest in teaching and researching business research methods and her thesis methodology is currently focusing on using a critical realist perspective as the foundation of a mixed methods study. Her research interests are business education, graduate competencies, Korean management, mode 2 knowledge, knowledge entrepreneurship, critical realism, and technology integration in the classroom. Christina has lectured in South Korea, China, and Bahrain for the past seven years and has also consulted and designed curriculum for business schools in Korea and Bahrain. Christina's peer-reviewed publications and conferences include works on tacit and codified knowledge transference, innovation in higher education, technology integration in higher education, problem-based learning in business education, and consumer behavior.

Marie-Luise Groß has over five years working experience in the fields of knowledge management and enterprise social software in various industries, such as the construction and the IT sector. Currently, she is responsible for knowledge management at a mid-size management consulting company in Germany and is finishing her PhD at the University of Vienna. Her research interest is on the influence of social media usage on the knowledge flows in strategic alliances of freelance workers. She also teaches Knowledge Management methods and techniques at the Wilhelm Büchner University of Applied Sciences, keeping a strong focus on social media usage for knowledge sharing and collaboration.

Maree Gruppetta is a Guyinbaraay woman currently working in the Wollotuka Centre at the University of Newcastle. Prior to her current position as Associate Professor Research and Research Engagement, Maree was Senior Lecturer and AREP Education Course Advisor at the Badanami Centre for Indigenous Education at the University of Western Sydney (UWS) for four years after teaching in the School of Education at UWS for eight years and prior to that was teaching in schools. Maree has taught in both Primary and Secondary classrooms, after completing a B.Tch (Primary), and a B. Ed (Hons), followed by a M.Teach in Special Education (Secondary) before returning to complete her PhD. Maree was nominated in the top 10 lecturers of the year at UWS in 2009, and was nominated for a Deadly Award in 2011.

Anna Heudorfer, born in 1988, studied "Media and Communication" at the University Augsburg (B.A.). She worked as Student Assistant at the chair of Media Pedagogy where she, among others, designed and held a project oriented class for other students. Connected to this class with the title "Corporate Publishing in the educational Field" was the participation in the International Conference "Teaching is touching the future: from vision to practice" at the Ruhr University Bochum in June 2011. Within the field of media pedagogics is her Bachelor thesis about Public Relations in schools, which contained a case study and a conceptual part in cooperation with a German high school.

Sandra Hofhues is a Research Fellow in e-learning and blended-learning at the Hamburg University of Applied Sciences. Between 2007 and 2011, she worked in the field of media pedagogy in the Institute of Media and Educational Technology at Augsburg University where she finished her interdisciplinary Bachelor and Master studies "Media and Communication" from 2002 to 2007. In early 2012, she received her PhD on "Learning through cooperation" at the Universitaet der Bundeswehr in Munich, Germany. Her PhD is based on the evaluation of the corporate volunteering project business@school – an initiative of The Boston Consulting Group. In Augsburg, she was responsible for several publishing projects in higher education, e.g., w.e.b.Square and vitamin b.

Hüseyin Kinay is the Research Assistant at Fatih University in the field Computer Education and Instructional Technologies. He is a PhD degree candidate. His research interests are information security, cyber security, computer aided learning, and computer assisted language learning.

Andrei Kojukhov received the MSc degree in Computer Engineering form the Moscow State Technical University in 1986 and made his PhD study in Error Correction algorithms in 1988 - 1991. From 1998, A. Kojukhov worked as a System Architect in leading high-tech companies such as Texas Instruments, Cisco, and AT&T. During the last 11 years he contributed to main Telecom and Datacom standardization committees: IEEE, ETSI, 3GPP, and ITU-T, especially in the domains of wireless, 4G mobile technologies, and IP Multimedia. In 2008 A. Kojukhov started his research and the Ph.D. study in the School of Education in Tel-Aviv University in the area of convergence between new wireless technology and education. His research interests are focused on the newest educational trends in postindustrial society such as ubiquitous learning and personal identity on-line. A. Kojukhov is an author of more than 30 publications and standardization contributions in information technologies and wireless communications.

Matthew J. Kruger-Ross is a Doctoral student in the Curriculum Theory & Implementation: Philosophy of Education program in the Faculty of Education at Simon Fraser University. After completing his BS in Middle Grades Education from NC State University in May 2005, Matthew stepped into the classroom at Carolina Friends School, an independent Quaker school in Durham, North Carolina, where he taught math, music, and technology in the middle school. After four wonderful years, he chose to leave CFS and pursue advanced degrees in Educational Technology, Philosophy, and Critical Studies. In May 2012, Matthew completed his Master's of Science in Instructional Technology at NC State University in Raleigh, North Carolina. His thesis was titled "Toward a Preliminary Understanding of Educators' Assumptions About Technology: A Case Study". Matthew's research interests include educational technology, Web-based tools and learning, educational philosophy, transformative learning, and critical studies.

Narelle Lemon is a Practitioner Researcher with RMIT University, Melbourne, Australia, with a background in image based research methods where young people are seen as co-researchers. Her learning and teaching focus is based around social learning theory, reflective practice, co-operative teaching and learning and establishing a community of learners. Narelle publishes in the areas of the 21st century learner and the utilization of meaningfully embedding digital technologies, including social media. Dr Lemon has published over 40 publications as well as curriculum documentations, commissioned reports, and has been invited nationally and internationally to present on image based research, early years voice, young people as photographers, and communities of practice. Her connections to industry have demonstrated substantial contributions to the fields of teacher professional development, arts education, and image based research.

Ilya Levin received the MSc degree in Computer Engineering form the Petersburg State Transport University in 1976 and Ph.D. degree from the Latvian Academy of Science in 1987. From 1977-79 he worked as a Software Developer in high-tech industry. From 1979, I. Levin is a researcher, and in 1985, Head of the Computer Science Department of Institute of Analytical Instrumentation of the Academy of Science of the USSR. During 1985-1990 he was the Head of the Computer Science Department in the Leningrad Institute of New Technologies (Russia). During 1993-1997 I. Levin was the Head of the Computer Systems Department of the Holon Technological Institute (Israel). In 1996-97, he was a Visiting Researcher in Boston University and Visiting Fellow the University of Massachusetts. During 2003-2006, he was an Associate Professor of the School of Engineering of the Bar Ilan University. Presently he is a Professor and the Head of Department of Math, Science and Technology Education of the Tel Aviv University. During the last decade, he was the principle investigator of a number of international projects in the field of information security, trust, safety, and privacy awareness design. Recent research interests of Prof. Levin are focused on cultorological issues of information and communication technologies in postindustrial society. Prof. Levin is an author of more than 150 research papers both in computer engineering and information technologies.

Mădălina Manolache works as a Communication Consultant at Europe Direct Bacau Information Centre and is a member of ROASS and ECREA associatons. She is 30 years old and currently a PhD student in Marketing, at Transilvania University of Brasov. Her research interests cover topics such as: gender studies, social media, IMC, soft power, the EU, and consumer behaviour. She has published articles on gender policy of the European Union and on the communication instruments used within the public space of EU for topics like; equality, justice, rights, and gender pay gap. Her hobbies are travelling, photography, classical and jazz music, and enjoying a good cup of tea, in the delightful company of a good book.

Valentina Marinescu, Ph. D, Reader at the Faculty of Sociology and Social Work – Bucharest University (Bucharest, Romania). She teaches undergraduate and graduate courses in media and society, and methods of researching mass communication. Her interests lie in gender, media, and communication studies in Eastern Europe, particularly in Romania. She has also published articles and book chapters on those subject matters (Shade of Violence: The Media Role, Women's Studies, International Forum, 32-2009, Elsevier, Media coverage of grassroots violence against women: A comparative analysis for Romania and Canada, in Brazilian Journalism Research, vol. 4, Nr.1, 2008, pp. 140-158, Challenges of the european information market and Romanian investigative journalism, in Alec Charles (ed.) "Media in the Enlarged Europe", Intellect Publishers Inc. 2009, pp.187-191;Communication and Women in Eastern Europe: Challenges in Reshaping the Democratic Sphere – in Leslie Regan Shade and Katharine Sarikakis (eds.), "Feminist International Communication Studies", Rowman and Littlefield Publisers Inc., 2007).

Terry Mason is from the land of the Awabakal language group and works in the Badanami Centre, University Western Sydney as a Senior Lecturer. He is a former Academic Co-ordinator of the BEd. Aboriginal Rural Education Program, involved with alternative entry processes and student learning support, currently deputy chair of National Tertiary Education Union Indigenous Policy Committee and Chair of the Board of the Welfare Rights Centre. Terry has a long involvement with diverse Community groups and was a reader of written submissions to the "2004 NSW Review of Aboriginal Education", a key researcher in the "Successful transition programs from prior-to-school to school for Aboriginal and Torres Strait Islander children" project, contributes to Australian and overseas publications, and presents papers in the area of cultural communication, transition, starting school, and student support.

David Mathew works in the Centre for Learning Excellence at the University of Bedfordshire, UK, and as an independent researcher and writer. His wide areas of interest include psychoanalysis, linguistics, distance learning, prisons and online anxiety. With approximately 600 published pieces to his name, including a novel based on his time working in the education department of a maximum security prison (*O My Days*), he has published widely in academic, journalistic and fiction outlets. In addition to his writing, he co-edits *The Journal of Pedagogic Development*, teaches academic writing, and he particularly enjoys lecturing in foreign countries and learning about wine. He is a member of the Tavistock Society of Psychotherapists and Allied Professionals, Evidence Informed Policy and Practice in Education in Europe (EIPPEE), and the European Association for the Teaching of Academic Writing. He is also a member of The Health Technology Assessment programme (www.hta.ac.uk), as part of the NIHR Evaluation, Trials and Studies Coordinating Centre at the University of Southampton (2009 - Present).

Sinem Siyahhan is an Assistant Research Professor in the School of Social and Family Dynamics at Arizona State University where she designs, develops, and studies video games and online environments to support K-12 education. Siyahhan received her PhD in Learning and Developmental Sciences at Indiana University. Most of her work focuses on intergenerational play, a concept that describes times when the parent and the child share information and strategies, and use physical and conceptual tools to make sense of a problem as equally contributing partners in a game context. Siyahhan also studies traditional and electronic forms of bullying, and is currently developing video games to prevent aggressive behaviors and gender stereotypes among youth.

Taşkın Tanrikulu is the instructor at Fatih University in the field of Psychological Counselling and Guidance. He is a PhD candidate at Sakarya University in the field of Psychological Counselling and Guidance. His research interests are cyberbullying and reality therapy.

Theodosios Tsiakis is a Lecturer in the Department of Marketing, of ATEI of Thessaloniki. He belongs in the Division of Organization and Management, expert in economics and specialized in Management of Information Systems. He graduated from the department of International and European Economic and Political Studies from the University of Macedonia and received his Ph.D. in Information Security Economics from the department of Applied Informatics, of the University of Macedonia. His research interests are security economics, e-business, risk management, trust and Information Systems Management. He has published several articles in international scientific journals and conferences.

Anca Velicu is Senior Researcher at the Institute of Sociology (Sociology of Communication and Public Space Laboratory) within the Romanian Academy. She is also an Associate Researcher with the Media and New Technologies Studies Center, University of Bucharest. In 2009 she got her PhD from the University of Bucharest with a thesis on Children Relationship with Television and NTIC. Her main research interests include sociology of the media, children' uses of NTIC, children and the media, and media violence. She co-authored two volumes, among which Tele-visual Representation of Violence and Child Protection (with Drăgan, Ştefănescu, & Povară, 2009, Vanemonde Publishing, Bucharest). She participated in national and international research projects in this field.

Katherine Landau Wright is a Doctoral student with a focus on Reading and Language Arts Education at Texas A&M University. She received her Bachelor's degree in Humanities from Wheelock College and her Master's in the Art of Teaching (MAT) from Northeastern University. She has taught middle school English/Language Arts and social studies in Massachusetts and Texas, serving as English Department chair for grades six through twelve and mapping curriculum for middle school English, Civics, and World Geography courses. Her research interests include cross-curricular literacy development, reading intervention, and technological innovation in English and Social Studies classrooms.

Index